FreeHand™ 8 Bible

FreeHand™ 8 Bible

Deke McClelland

IDG Books Worldwide, Inc.
An International Data Group Company
Foster City, CA ✦ Chicago, IL ✦ Indianapolis, IN ✦ New York, NY

FreeHand™ 8 Bible
Published by
IDG Books Worldwide, Inc.
An International Data Group Company
919 E. Hillsdale Blvd., Suite 400
Foster City, CA 94404
www.idgbooks.com (IDG Books Worldwide Web site)

Library of Congress Catalog Card No.: 98-071153

ISBN: 0-7645-3234-0

Printed in the United States of America

10 9 8 7 6 5 4 3 2 1

1E/QU/QW/ZY/FC

Distributed in the United States by IDG Books Worldwide, Inc.

Distributed by Macmillan Canada for Canada; by Transworld Publishers Limited in the United Kingdom; by IDG Norge Books for Norway; by IDG Sweden Books for Sweden; by Woodslane Pty. Ltd. for Australia; by Woodslane (NZ) Ltd. for New Zealand; by Addison Wesley Longman Singapore Pte Ltd. for Singapore, Malaysia, Thailand, Indonesia, and Korea; by Norma Comunicaciones S.A. for Colombia; by Intersoft for South Africa; by International Thomson Publishing for Germany, Austria, and Switzerland; by Toppan Company Ltd. for Japan; by Distribuidora Cuspide for Argentina; by Livraria Cultura for Brazil; by Ediciencia S.A. for Ecuador; by Ediciones ZETA S.C.R. Ltda. for Peru; by WS Computer Publishing Corporation, Inc., for the Philippines; by Unalis Corporation for Taiwan; by Contemporanea de Ediciones for Venezuela; by Computer Book & Magazine Store for Puerto Rico; by Express Computer Distributors for the Caribbean and West Indies. Authorized Sales Agent: Anthony Rudkin Associates for the Middle East and North Africa.

For general information on IDG Books Worldwide's books in the U.S., please call our Consumer Customer Service department at 800-762-2974. For reseller information, including discounts and premium sales, please call our Reseller Customer Service department at 800-434-3422.

For information on where to purchase IDG Books Worldwide's books outside the U.S., please contact our International Sales department at 650-655-3200 or fax 650-655-3297.

For information on foreign language translations, please contact our Foreign & Subsidiary Rights department at 650-655-3021 or fax 650-655-3281.

For sales inquiries and special prices for bulk quantities, please contact our Sales department at 650-655-3200 or write to the address above.

For information on using IDG Books Worldwide's books in the classroom or for ordering examination copies, please contact our Educational Sales department at 800-434-2086 or fax 317-596-5499.

For press review copies, author interviews, or other publicity information, please contact our Public Relations department at 650-655-3000 or fax 650-655-3299.

For authorization to photocopy items for corporate, personal, or educational use, please contact Copyright Clearance Center, 222 Rosewood Drive, Danvers, MA 01923, or fax 978-750-4470.

DreamLight Web pages courtesy of Michael Scaramozzino, DreamLight Inc. www.dreamlight.com/dreamlt

is a trademark under exclusive license to IDG Books Worldwide, Inc., from International Data Group, Inc.

ABOUT IDG BOOKS WORLDWIDE

Welcome to the world of IDG Books Worldwide.

IDG Books Worldwide, Inc., is a subsidiary of International Data Group, the world's largest publisher of computer-related information and the leading global provider of information services on information technology. IDG was founded more than 25 years ago and now employs more than 8,500 people worldwide. IDG publishes more than 275 computer publications in over 75 countries (see listing below). More than 90 million people read one or more IDG publications each month.

Launched in 1990, IDG Books Worldwide is today the #1 publisher of best-selling computer books in the United States. We are proud to have received eight awards from the Computer Press Association in recognition of editorial excellence and three from *Computer Currents'* First Annual Readers' Choice Awards. Our best-selling *...For Dummies*® series has more than 50 million copies in print with translations in 38 languages. IDG Books Worldwide, through a joint venture with IDG's Hi-Tech Beijing, became the first U.S. publisher to publish a computer book in the People's Republic of China. In record time, IDG Books Worldwide has become the first choice for millions of readers around the world who want to learn how to better manage their businesses.

Our mission is simple: Every one of our books is designed to bring extra value and skill-building instructions to the reader. Our books are written by experts who understand and care about our readers. The knowledge base of our editorial staff comes from years of experience in publishing, education, and journalism — experience we use to produce books for the '90s. In short, we care about books, so we attract the best people. We devote special attention to details such as audience, interior design, use of icons, and illustrations. And because we use an efficient process of authoring, editing, and desktop publishing our books electronically, we can spend more time ensuring superior content and spend less time on the technicalities of making books.

You can count on our commitment to deliver high-quality books at competitive prices on topics you want to read about. At IDG Books Worldwide, we continue in the IDG tradition of delivering quality for more than 25 years. You'll find no better book on a subject than one from IDG Books Worldwide.

John Kilcullen
CEO
IDG Books Worldwide, Inc.

Steven Berkowitz
President and Publisher
IDG Books Worldwide, Inc.

WINNER
Eighth Annual
Computer Press
Awards ≥1992

WINNER
Ninth Annual
Computer Press
Awards ≥1993

WINNER
Tenth Annual
Computer Press
Awards ≥1994

WINNER
Eleventh Annual
Computer Press
Awards ≥1995

Credits

Acquisitions Editor
Andy Cummings

Development Editors
Susannah Pfalzer
Kathi Duggan

Technical Editor
Susan Glinert-Stevens

Copy Editor
Tracy Brown

Project Coordinator
Ritchie Durdin

Graphics and Production Specialists
Stephanie Hollier
E. A. Pauw
Ed Penslien
Dina F Quan

Graphics Technicians
Linda J. Marousek
Hector Mendosa

Quality Control Specialists
Mick Arellano
Mark Schumann

Cover Design
Murder By Design

Contributing Illustrators
Trevor Johnston
Stephen Issakson

Proofreader
Arielle Carole Mennelle

Indexer
James Minkin

About the Author

Deke McClelland has authored more than 30 books on desktop publishing and the Macintosh computer, and his work has been translated into more than 20 languages. He is author of IDG Books Worldwide's *CorelDRAW! 7 For Dummies*, *PageMaker 6 For Windows For Dummies*, and *Photoshop 4 For Dummies*. Deke is a contributing editor to *Macworld* magazine and also writes for *Publish*. He also hosts "Digital Gurus," a syndicated TV show about personal computing, from his home base in Colorado. Deke started his career as artistic director at the first service bureau in the United States.

Deke won the Ben Franklin award for Best Computer Book in 1989, a Society of Technical Communication Award in 1994, and an American Society for Business Press Editors award in 1995. He also won the prestigious Computer Press Association Award in 1990, 1992, 1994, and 1995.

Foreword

Welcome to the *FreeHand 8 Bible.* And, because we are guessing that you have purchased Macromedia FreeHand 8, we thank you for exploring and using this wonderful tool.

We have applied a heavy dose of software engineering to make Version 8 a compelling tool to add to your digital toolbox. FreeHand continues to be considered the most robust and reliable illustration tool and we've now added a slew of new features and capabilities, including an editable transparency effect, a new freeform drawing tool, and new functions for print and Web publishing. In addition, you can discover how to create dynamic Web graphics and image maps and use them with Flash — the hot, new Web tool. And if that is not enough, you can become more productive by using the new interface that customizes toolbars and toolboxes and creates shortcuts matching those of other commonly used applications.

The program covers a lot of territory, and we can only mention a few of the highlights here. So that's where guru Deke McClelland and IDG Books Worldwide come in.

Thanks to Deke and IDG Books Worldwide, versions of this book have been around as long as FreeHand. Deke was the guy who took a chance to write a book on software from a little startup company in Richardson, Texas, called Altsys. He believed the program would be the best in its category. Altsys also caught the eye of heavy weight Aldus which threw its backing to FreeHand. And now, under the Macromedia fold since Version 5, FreeHand is still going strong.

And so is this book. Now in its seventh incarnation, it's been the best-selling title on FreeHand since its original publication in 1988 and winner of the prestigious Computer Press Association Award. If you've seen or purchased an earlier edition of this book, you should be pleased to know that every new feature of FreeHand is documented here. Plus, Deke provides expert advice and counsel on how to get the most out of Version 8 capabilities and features. Deke's well-known style provides an engaging and insightful look into our program. We often learn things from reading the *FreeHand Bible.*

We believe that this book is an excellent way to dive deep into FreeHand, which we encourage you to do. And then let us know what you think. Enjoy!

Tom Hale
Director of Product Management
Macromedia

Preface

Versions of this book have been around as long as FreeHand. Soon after Adobe Illustrator first hit the shelves in March 1987, my partner — still fulfilling the seemingly slight demands of his senior year of college — informed me that he and I would write a book about a piece of illustration software from a little startup company in Richardson, Texas, called Altsys. He assured me that the program would be every bit the equal of Illustrator, if not better. It was called Masterpiece, so naturally we would call the book *Mastering Masterpiece*. The program wouldn't sell all that well — how could these folks located out in the industry equivalent of Pago Pago hope to compete with Adobe? — so we wouldn't sell that many books, either. But at least we could get our feet in the door of computer publishing.

But things change quickly in the computer industry. By the time we met with the programmers in November of that year, the still unreleased product had become such a hot property that Altsys had signed a licensing agreement with the first name in desktop publishing, Aldus, maker of PageMaker. Altsys hit the jackpot. Now that it had the support of a major software vendor, the product suddenly had a chance of competing with Illustrator. Never mind that Aldus changed the name of the program to FreeHand and ruined our infinitesimally clever title — FreeHand had major backing and so, by default, did we.

Several years later, FreeHand is still going strong. And happily, so is this book. It's been the best-selling title on FreeHand since its original publication in 1988, despite considerable — and in some cases, praiseworthy — competition.

If you've seen or purchased an earlier edition of this book, you should be pleased to know that every new feature of FreeHand is documented here. Take the McClelland challenge: see if you can figure out all the new features using only the Help file and documentation that comes with FreeHand; then see how you do when using this book. Believe me, I've done some legwork for you.

I've also given extensive attention to FreeHand's new Flash capabilities — by my vote, Version 8's hottest advancement. FreeHand's competitors, no doubt, are scurrying to implement these features as you read this.

How This Book Differs from the Rest

Although you can find many solid books on FreeHand in your bookstore, this one is a little different from the rest. Actually, it's a lot different. Here are some of the features that set *FreeHand 8 Bible* apart:

✦ **Fundamental drawing issues:** Regardless of how powerful an illustration package is, it won't do you any good if you can't draw with it. That's why this book devotes more space than competing titles to the fundamental issues of drawing and editing FreeHand's amazingly deft but equally complex Bézier curves. Understanding these concepts is essential to creating successful drawings in FreeHand — or in any drawing program, for that matter. Yet many books don't explain them thoroughly or even adequately, leaving you to flail about on your own or, worse, to give up in frustration.

✦ **Equal footing on a Mac or a PC:** FreeHand is now, essentially, the same program on both a Mac and a PC. A number of us have had the experience of working on one platform at work and a different one at home. For example, there's nothing more frustrating than starting a document on, say, a Macintosh at work, and then trying to finish it at home on a PC, only to find that the two programs bear little resemblance to each other. With FreeHand 8, aside from a handful of keyboard shortcuts, the FreeHand you see on a Macintosh is the FreeHand you see in the Windows environment.

✦ **No stone left unturned:** You'll also find a wealth of information not included in the Macromedia software manual. Granted, the manual includes interesting and useful tips for drawing perspective illustrations, printing gradations without banding, and creating translucent objects. But strangely, its coverage of basic information is either abrupt or nonexistent. By contrast, the *FreeHand 8 Bible* is written so any user, regardless of experience level, can understand not just the basics, but also the advanced techniques covered.

I know, I know — this all sounds like a sales pitch. Forgive me; like any parent, I'm a little too proud of my baby. But I honestly believe that these elements will make it easier for you to exploit FreeHand's capabilities fully.

How This Book Is Organized

Here's a quick look at what topics are covered in each chapter and how the different parts of the book are organized.

✦ **Part I: Taking the Fear Out of FreeHand:** If you've never used FreeHand, or you don't know the first thing about creating computer graphics, here's your chance to get acquainted. In Part I, I walk you through the installation

process, stroll you around the FreeHand milieu, and end with a vigorous
stride around external modules.

✦ **Part II: Drawing in FreeHand:** Bézier curves can be as intimidating as they
are powerful. In Part II, I show you how to approach and execute an
illustration, draw lines and shapes using a variety of tools, and make use of
FreeHand's precision editing capabilities.

✦ **Part III: Adding Text:** Text is FreeHand's claim to fame. The program offers
more text creation and formatting functions than dedicated text wranglers
PageMaker and QuarkXPress. The chapters in Part III show how to get the
most out of these features.

✦ **Part IV: Applying Color and Form:** Without fill and stroke, the shapes and
lines you draw in FreeHand are empty and meaningless skeletons. The
chapters in Part IV show how you can apply colors, gradations, custom
patterns, and other special decorations to the interiors and outlines of
graphic objects and text.

✦ **Part V: Special Effects:** Learning to make manual artistic enhancements to
your drawing is important. But if time and energy are precious to you, you
also need to know how to take advantage of FreeHand's automated features.
Part V shows you ways to manipulate text blocks and graphic objects using
automated operations.

✦ **Part VI: Desktop Publishing:** FreeHand is the best program in all the world
for creating small documents — you can quote me on that. In addition to
supplying the wealth of text-editing functions described in Part III, FreeHand
offers sophisticated import and export features, a unique capability to scale
and orient pages independently within a document, and powerhouse printing
functions. Part VI explains how to get full use from these capabilities.

Conventions Used in This Book

In an effort to avoid as much confusion as possible, I try to write the same way
from one book to the next. I don't always use the exact terms as the FreeHand
manual, subscribing instead to more universal terminology whenever possible.
This way, if you should ever venture beyond FreeHand, you'll be prepared to
address the full gamut of the real world.

This book assumes you have a basic familiarity with a Mac or PC. If you are
unclear with any issues, such as using menus, scroll bars, or the Clipboard, please
refer to your *Macintosh System Software User's Guide* or to your *Introducing
Microsoft Windows 95* guide.

Vocabulary

As soon as the English-first folks get done making us all speak a common language, no doubt they'll get to work making doctors, lawyers, and propeller-heads like me shape up and stop using industry jargon. But, regardless, I can't explain the Mac or FreeHand in graphic and gruesome detail without reverting to the specialized language of the trade. However, to help you keep up, I have italicized vocabulary words (as in preview mode) with which you may not be familiar or which I use in an unusual context. An italicized term is followed by a definition.

Commands and options

To distinguish the literal names of commands, dialog boxes, buttons, and so on, I capitalize the first letter in each word (for example, "click the Cancel button"). The only exceptions are option names, which can be six or seven words long and filled with prepositions such as "to" and "of." Traditionally, prepositions and articles (a, an, the) don't appear in initial caps, and this book follows that time-honored rule, too.

When discussing menus and commands, I use an arrow symbol to indicate hierarchy. For example, Choose File ⇨ Open means to choose the Open command from the File menu. If you have to display a submenu to reach a command, I list the command used to display the submenu between the menu name and the final command. Choose Modify ⇨ Combine ⇨ Blend means to choose the Combine command from the Modify menu and then choose the Blend command from the Combine submenu. (If this doesn't quite make sense to you now, don't worry; future chapters will make it abundantly clear.)

Keys

Much like any other program worth its price tag, FreeHand is full of keyboard shortcuts. Using a keyboard shortcut is an alternative to choosing commands manually from the various menus with the mouse. For example, to start a new document, you can choose File ⇨ New. This works fine, but it's not half as fast as using the shortcut. On a Mac, just press ⌘-N; on a PC, just press Ctrl-N. Throughout this book, I also ask you to press one or more keys while clicking or dragging with your mouse. These are not shortcuts, but necessary steps that you must take to produce specific results.

Because this book is meant to address the needs of Mac and PC users equally, I use a shorthand to denote that you should press a keyboard combination. Instead of asking you as the reader to press ⌘-Option-Shift-T (if you're working on a Macintosh) or press Ctrl-Alt-Shift-T (if you're working on a Windows machine) to execute the View ⇨ Text Rulers command, I've shortened the notation. To denote the Text Rulers shortcut, I say press ⌘/Ctrl-Option/Alt-Shift-T. The ⌘/Ctrl combination means that Mac users should press the ⌘ key and that Windows users should use the Ctrl key. The Option/Alt works similarly: Mac people press the Option key and Windows folk press the Alt key. Because the Shift and the T keys are common to both platforms, I only state them once.

Also, I instruct you to press Return/Enter a number of times in this book. The Return is meant for the Mac users and the Enter is for the Windows people. Mac users may find this a bit confusing because they have both a Return key and an Enter key on their standard keyboard — standard PC keyboards have only Enter keys. Although you Mac users have both these keys, they are not always interchangeable. To be on the safe side, be sure to use your Return key unless otherwise stated.

Icons

Okay, I admit it, icons are overused. But not in this book. Here, I use the icons sparingly, just frequently enough to focus your eyeballs smack dab on important information. The icons make it easy for you to skim through the book and touch on information that's either new to Version 8 or just new to you. They serve as little insurance policies against short attention spans. On the whole, they're pretty self-explanatory, but I'll explain them anyway.

The Caution icon warns you that a step you're about to take may produce disastrous results. Well, perhaps "disastrous" is an exaggeration. Inconvenient, then. Uncomfortable. For heaven's sake, use caution.

The Note icon highlights some little tidbit of information related to the topic at hand.

The FreeHand 8 icon calls your attention to a brand new feature or one that works differently than in previous versions. If you've made the switch to Version 8, the information presented by these icons will help you master this upgrade.

This book is bursting with tips and techniques. If I were to highlight every one of them, whole pages would be gray with little icons popping out all over the place. The Tip icon calls attention to shortcuts and techniques that are specifically applicable to FreeHand. For the bigger, more useful power tips, I'm afraid you actually have to read the text.

The Cross-Reference icon tells you where to go for information related to the current topic.

How to Bug Me

Even with all these great editors and technical reviewers at my disposal, you may still manage to locate a few errors and oversights. If you notice such things and you have a few spare moments, please let me know what you think.

You can contact me at the following addresses:

dekemc@aol.com

dekemc@internetmci.com

http://www.dekemc.com

Don't fret if you don't hear from me for a few days, or months, or ever. I read every letter and try to implement nearly every idea anyone takes time to send me.

Now that I've gotten all of this important introductory information out of the way, on to the good stuff. Turn the page and dive right in, and rest assured that even if FreeHand seems a little intimidating to you at first, with a little time and patience, you'll soon be able to enjoy amazing success. In fact, I think that you'll be just as happy as I am that those folks from Richardson, Texas, put their heads together way back when and came up with this gem of a program.

Contents at a Glance

Contents

Part III: Adding Text — 215

Part IV: Applying Color and Form 339

Taking the Fear out of FreeHand

FreeHand Wants to Be Your Friend

What Is FreeHand?

Every time I start writing a book, I embark down the inevitable road of trashing my office. I've already managed to surround myself with manuals, open software boxes, sticky notes, and other trappings of what is sometimes laughingly called computer journalism. Soon I'll be ignoring my mail, throwing my magazines in unread piles, misplacing cold slices of pizza, and topping it all off with spilled coffee.

No doubt I'll get another reader letter complaining, "Can't you stick to the subject? The first paragraph of Chapter 1 has nothing to do with FreeHand. Must we put up with the author's diatribes? Doesn't anyone edit these books?" Well, you might as well know right now: I get to rambling every once in a while. It can't be helped. Top behavioral scientists and dog breeders have worked on me to no avail.

To quote the sweet potato, "I yam what I yam."

So, What Is FreeHand?

FreeHand is a top-selling drawing application. (*Application*, incidentally, is just another word for a computer program.)

FreeHand enables you to draw pristine line art and smooth-as-silk technical drawings. Tasks that used to be exceedingly nerve-wracking or downright unlikely 10 or 20 years ago—such as getting two thick pen lines to meet and form a perfectly sharp corner—are a breeze in FreeHand. With very little effort and not much more in the way of experience, you'll be churning out stuff in FreeHand that would make you bleed, sweat, and cry were you to approach the task using traditional drawing tools. Better still, there's no mess. Unlike pens (which can clog), ink (which can dry up), brushes (which can harden), paint (which can stain your clothes), and paper (which you can rip and soil), FreeHand has all the advantages of a tool that exists exclusively in your computer's imagination. Until you print your drawing, there's nothing real or physical about it. And if you rip or soil your final artwork, you just print another one.

Is FreeHand the Right Program for You?

Before I venture further into the wonderful world of FreeHand, let's make sure you chose the right application. Perhaps you're making a decision between FreeHand and Adobe Photoshop, one of the most powerful and popular graphics programs ever written. FreeHand and Photoshop are both two-dimensional graphics programs, but that's where the similarities end. FreeHand is categorized as a drawing program, whereas Photoshop is categorized as a painting program.

FreeHand works its magic by looking at artwork in terms of *objects*, which are independent, mathematically defined lines and shapes. For this reason, drawing programs are described as being *object-oriented*. Some folks prefer the term *vector-based*, but I reckon FreeHand is complex enough without making it sound like a science fair experiment.

By contrast, Photoshop is an *image editor*, which means it lets you alter photographs and other scanned artwork. You can retouch a photograph, apply special effects, and swap details between photos—all functions that FreeHand can't match. Image editors fall into the larger software category of *painting programs*. In a painting program, you draw a line and the application converts it, then and there, to tiny square dots called pixels. The painting itself is called a *bitmapped image*, but *bitmap* or *image* on its own is equally acceptable.

Bitmapped image editors work on an arrangement of square pixels much like a mosaic—when the resolution is high, the image is sharp. High resolution creates large computer image files—slow to work with, but necessary for images to print sharply. On the other hand, vector-based drawing applications use the PostScript language to define the shapes, lines, and fills of illustrations. These applications have an easily-understood, flexible interface with a metaphor more like pipe-cleaners and cut-out shapes. Because the PostScript language describes illustration elements, and is the language used by a wide variety of desktop printers, FreeHand files print sharply to PostScript printers.

Note

Other examples of PostScript drawing programs include Adobe Illustrator, Fractal Design "Expression," Canvas, CorelDRAW, and ClarisDraw on the Macintosh, as well as Windows Draw and CorelDRAW on the PC. Painting programs include Fractal Design Painter, PixelPaint Pro, Color It!, and the Mac's first program, MacPaint.

The relative benefits of drawing

Some artists shy away from FreeHand because it features tools without real-world counterparts. The process of drawing might better be called constructing, because you actually build lines and shapes point-by-point and stack them on top of each other to create a finished image. Each object is independently editable — one of the few structural advantages of an object-oriented approach — but you're still faced with the task of building your artwork one chunk at a time.

Nevertheless, because a drawing program defines lines, shapes, and text as mathematical equations, these objects automatically output to the maximum resolution of the *output device*, whether it's a laser printer, imagesetter, or film recorder. The drawing program sends the math to the printer, and the printer *renders* the math to paper or film. In other words, the printer converts the drawing program's equations to printer pixels. And since your printer offers far more pixels than your screen — a 300 dot-per-inch laser printer, for example, offers 300 pixels per inch — the printed drawing appears smooth and sharply focused regardless of the size at which you print it, as shown in Figure 1-1.

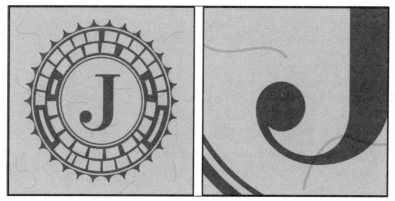

Figure 1-1: No matter how large or small you print your FreeHand drawing, it retains smooth edges and sharp contrast.

Furthermore, FreeHand drawings take up relatively little room on disk. The size of a drawing depends on the quantity and complexity of the mathematical equations or the objects it contains. Thus, drawing size has almost nothing to do with the size of the printed image. A thumbnail drawing of a garden that contains hundreds of leaves and petals consume several times more disk space than a poster-sized drawing that contains three rectangles.

The relative drawbacks of painting

Painting programs are indisputably easier to use than drawing programs. For example, although many of Photoshop's features are complex — exceedingly complex on occasion — its core painting tools are as straightforward as a pencil. You alternately draw and erase until you reach a desired effect, just like you've been doing since grade school.

The drawback of a painting program is that it limits your *resolution* options. Because bitmaps contain a fixed number of pixels, the resolution of an image — the number of pixels per inch — is dependent upon the size at which the image is printed, as demonstrated in Figure 1-2. Print the image small and the pixels become tiny, which increases resolution. Print the image large and the pixels grow, which decreases resolution. An image that fills up a standard 13-inch screen (480×640 pixels) will print with smooth color transitions when reduced to, say, half the size of a postcard. But if you print that same image without reducing it, you may be able to distinguish individual pixels, which means that you can see jagged edges and blocky transitions. The only way to remedy this problem is to increase the number of pixels in the image, which will dramatically increase the size of the file on disk.

Figure 1-2: Paintings appear smooth or jagged in direct relation to the size at which they are printed.

When to use FreeHand

Thanks to their specialized methods, drawing and painting programs fulfill distinct and divergent purposes. FreeHand and other drawing programs are best suited to the following kinds of artwork:

✦ Poster art and other high-contrast graphics that heighten the appearance of reality.

✦ Architectural plans, product designs, or other precise line drawings.

✦ Business graphics, charts, and "infographics" that reflect data or show how things work.

✦ Traditional logos and text effects that require crisp, ultra-smooth edges (draw programs are unique in allowing you to edit character outlines to create custom letters and symbols).

✦ Brochures, flyers, and other single-page documents that mingle artwork, logos, and standard-sized text (such as the text you're reading now).

When to use Photoshop instead

You're better off using Photoshop or some other painting program if you're interested in creating or editing more naturalistic artwork, such as the following:

✦ Scanned photos, including photographic collages and embellishments that originate from scans.

✦ Realistic artwork that relies on the play between naturalistic highlights, midranges, and shadows.

✦ Impressionistic-style artwork and other images created for purely personal or aesthetic purposes.

✦ Logos and other display type that feature soft edges, reflections, or tapering shadows.

✦ Special effects that require the use of filters and color enhancements that you can't achieve in a drawing program.

If you're serious about computer graphics, you should own at least one painting program and one drawing program. FreeHand and Photoshop are ideal candidates for any artist's software library.

What's New in FreeHand 8

If you consider FreeHand a familiar friend, this upgrade to PostScript language Version 8 makes that friendship more meaningful. If you're new to FreeHand, be assured that Macromedia went to great lengths to ensure that FreeHand's features, both existing and new, win your heart.

Perestroika

Remember perestroika and what an essential concept it was during the lifting of the iron curtain? A government, which was once a closed black box, was opened to the people. This enabled the people to interact with the government and determine how to fit their needs to its structure. Switching to open architecture in software is analogous to accepting a policy of perestroika in government.

Open architecture means that FreeHand is not just a black box that you must take "as is." Many features are now contained in external modules. Within FreeHand, external modules are known as Xtras. You can add and delete Xtras within FreeHand, using the Xtra Tools panel. These modules can be FreeHand-specific, ones that you create using newly available information, and even Adobe Illustrator plug-ins.

You look mah-velous, simply mah-velous!

FreeHand 8's user interface has been refined, in an elegant and upscale style. While the application is more visually appealing, old familiar features operate the same as in recent past versions of FreeHand. If you're a FreeHand 7 user, you can sit down to FreeHand 8 and still find everything.

Overall, FreeHand 8 is much more responsive than earlier revisions — it launches much faster than it did in the past and the screen redraws quicker (and quicker still if you use the fast modes); and when you need to, you can easily interrupt FreeHand's redraw of previews for work in progress or, the preview of placed TIFFs.

More power tools, please

A number of new Xtra tools accompany FreeHand 8. These tools combine several steps to let you quickly implement complex effects to your artwork. With a single click of the shadow tool, you can add a drop shadow to you drawing. Click with the emboss tool and one of five different embossing effects provide texture and depth to your paths. The mirror tool lets you duplicate paths numerous times as though you have a portable house-of-mirrors right on your screen. Spray and spew pre-made images willy-nilly throughout your document via the graphic hose tool.

Make my life easier

I categorize the next group of changes as convenience features. The biggest convenience in the FreeHand upgrade is its capability to customize the toolbars and keyboard shortcuts. If you desire that one of FreeHand's five toolbars should include the click-to-use icon of some particular FreeHand command, you merely have to drag the icon onto the toolbar. All of the keyboards shortcuts in FreeHand may be changed to suit your tastes and shortcut templates from other programs are included with FreeHand 8. If you really like Photoshop's shortcuts and you want to use them inside FreeHand, you can implement them easily. The Chart Xtra feature edits existing chart elements, making it easier to add or remove pictographs from finished artwork. The Color List stores and names the colors in your illustration without editing the FreeHand preferences. Easily change a color from process to "spot" or replace colors in a list, or rearrange the order of colors in the color panel. The Fill and Stroke Inspector updates your changes instantly! With the drag and drop interface, you can drag one color on top of another to replace it, and all instances of the color's use in your drawing are updated. Magic! With the Gradient Panel, you create and edit multicolor fills, both Process and Spot. Hi-Fi color provides support for Kodak's Digital Science color space and is able to adjust images created in various ICC color spaces for display with greater accuracy from monitor to printed material. With the new Lens fill capabilities, you can add transparent qualities to your fills without converting your line drawings to their bitmap equivalents. Line Widths are now accessible from a pop-up menu in the Inspector Panel.

And the rest of them

Several nice, miscellaneous items round out FreeHand 8's new feature set. For example, FreeHand has made advancements in the area of guides. You're no longer confined to the old way of using guides, because horizontal or vertical guidelines have a special layer on the Layer's Panel. See Chapter 6 for more on this.

FreeHand 8 has also made impressive improvements in interapplication communication. You can now easily drag and drop elements between applications, and there is support for a wide range of file formats: MIX, PDF, Adobe Photoshop, PNG, Adobe Illustrator, saving as EPS with embedded FreeHand document, xRES LRG files, DXF import, GIF export, JPEG (progressive for Internet use) import and export, Targa import, and BMP export. Individual objects can easily be printed, or exported to separate files, saving you the trouble of creating a new document, cutting and pasting, and saving with a new name.

FreeHand 8 supports Hot Links to Adobe PageMaker, and to QuarkXPress documents. FreeHand 8 supports all Adobe Photoshop 4.0 plug-ins. The Help file is dramatically improved with features searchable by keyword or index, and a What's New section introduces new features of Version 8.

FreeHand 8 opens up a whole new world of fills. The six varieties of Lens options give you the power to create partially transparent fills that allow you to see through the path to the objects below. These fills seem to transform your paths into pieces of glass that add color or even magnify.

FreeHand's documentation is still the bare-bones, but that's why I'm here. This book should give you the information that your need to master FreeHand's old and new features.

✦   ✦   ✦

Touring the FreeHand Neighborhood

Getting Started with FreeHand

Remember when you were a newborn? (Of course you don't — but go ahead and play along with me for a moment.) You do? Well, then you no doubt remember how you weren't exactly sure what to do with your tiny arms and legs, how your uncle's face scared you silly, and how hard it was to keep all that excess saliva in your mouth. Nowadays, your appendages are more familiar (if not always particularly coordinated), you've come to terms with your relatives (perhaps through counseling), and you don't drool nearly so often (only when a pillow is embedded in your face).

This, my friends, is the difference between being a novice at something and having become accustomed to it through experience. If FreeHand is new to you, then you may find it somewhat intimidating. With time, of course, you'll be drawing and creating documents with the best of them; but in the meantime, you may live in abject fear of the program.

This chapter is designed to ease the transition from newness to familiarity. Rather than allowing you to look into the deepest recesses of FreeHand and freeze with terror like a fawn caught in the headlights, I'll walk you through the software one step at a time. By the chapter's end, you'll scoff at your early apprehensions about FreeHand.

Installing FreeHand

This part isn't scary. In fact, it's duller than stale bread. But the sad fact is, you can't use FreeHand until you install it on your computer's hard drive. Luckily, the process of installing FreeHand is well documented (see Chapter 1 of the Using FreeHand guide included with FreeHand 8) and remarkably straightforward to boot. So, rather than insult your intelligence with blow-by-blow descriptions, I'll just move on to bigger and better things.

First, a quick warning: Just like Freehand 7, FreeHand 8 does not open FreeHand 1 documents. I know — it's not fair, but it's true. If you own FreeHand 3 or 3.1, keep that version's application file and FreeHand filters file on your hard disk. You can then open FreeHand 1 documents in FreeHand 3/3.1, save the documents in 3/3.1 format, and open the 3/3.1 formatted documents in Freehand 8.

Taking Your First Look at FreeHand

After you install FreeHand, you can run the program by locating its icon on the Finder desktop and double-clicking it. Shortly thereafter, the FreeHand *splash screen* appears, as shown in Figure 2-1.

Figure 2-1: The FreeHand splash screen appears after you successfully install the program.

The FreeHand desktop

After the launch process completes and the splash screen disappears, the FreeHand *desktop* looms into view. Figure 2-2 shows the desktop as it would appear when a certain dinosaur drawing is opened.

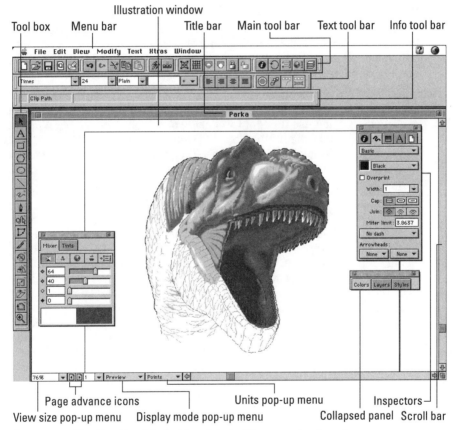

Figure 2-2: The FreeHand 8 desktop, labeled for your viewing pleasure.

Note

Featured in Figure 2-2, and in several other figures, is Portland-based Steve Cowden's T-Rex drawing, called Cowden. It's one of the best examples of object-oriented realism I've seen. Even if you are sick of dinosaurs — personally, I can't get enough of them — it just goes to show: you don't have to live in California or New York to create amazing art.

If you are accustomed to the Macintosh or PCs, many of the elements labeled in Figure 2-2 should be familiar to you. The other elements that appear in Figure 2-2 work as follows:

✦ **Illustration window:** This is where all the action is. Here you create and prefect your masterpieces. You can open as many documents in FreeHand as memory permits — each open document occupies its own independent window.

Tip

If you ever want to see your creation in its most uncluttered glory, just press ⌘/Ctrl-Option/Alt-T followed by ⌘-Shift-H on Macs and Ctrl-Alt-H on PCs. The only thing left on screen will be your work — well, that and the Menu bar, Title bar, and Scroll bars.

✦ **Toolbox:** The toolbox offers 17 *tool icons*, each of which represents a selection, navigation, drawing, text, or transformation tool. To select a tool, click its icon. Then use the tool by clicking or dragging inside the illustration window. By default, the toolbox resides along the left side of the desktop, but you can move it to any location on the screen, as either a *floating palette* or as a *stationary toolbar*. Simply click just below the top of the toolbox and move it to its new locale.

✦ **Floating panels:** FreeHand 8 offers ten standard floating panels and a number of specialized floating panels (including five toolbars and five inspectors). The term *floating* refers to the fact that each panel is independent both of the image window and of other panels. By clicking the collapse box in the upper right corner of the panel, you can collapse the panel so only the title bar remains visible, thus saving limited screen space. FreeHand 8 enables you to dock panels so they move together. Hold down the ⌘/Ctrl key and drag one panel towards another. When one panel is within 12 pixels of another panel they dock together. To undock the panels click the gray dock between the panels or hold the ⌘/Ctrl key while dragging the header bar of a docked panel away from its adjacent panel. Dock several panels together and you end up with a FreeHand barge — not very useful, but fun to play with. (Toot! Toot!) You can also drag any of the toolbars around to suit your needs. They can be attached to the top, bottom or the sides or appear hanging about in a portion of the illustration window. For more on floating panels, see the upcoming "Floating Panels" section.

Tools

Figure 2-3 shows the FreeHand 8 toolbox complete with labels. Press any of the tool's keyboard shortcuts to switch to that tool.

The *preference indicators* mean that you can double-click these tools icons to access tool-dependent dialog boxes where you can adjust tool behavior.

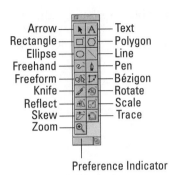

Figure 2-3: The FreeHand 8 toolbox, with all the points of interest well labeled.

Arrow — Text
Rectangle — Polygon
Ellipse — Line
Freehand — Pen
Freeform — Bézigon
Knife — Rotate
Reflect — Scale
Skew — Trace
Zoom —

Preference Indicator

The following list explains how to use each tool. Unless I specify otherwise, you use the tool inside the illustration window. So if I say *click on*, you click on with the tool in the illustration window; if I say *click on the tool icon*, you click on the specified icon in the toolbox.

 Arrow: Click an object with this tool to select the object. Shift-click to select multiple objects. Option/Alt-click to select an object inside a group. Click and drag a marquee around multiple objects to select the surrounded objects. Click and drag one or more selected objects to move them.

 Text: Click with the text tool to create a new text block. Drag with the tool to define the size of the new text block. Drag inside an existing text block to select characters you want to format or edit.

 Rectangle: Drag to create a rectangle. Shift-drag to draw a square. Option/Alt-drag to draw a rectangle from a center point. Double-click the tool icon to set the corner radius for drawing a rectangle with rounded corners.

 Polygon: Drag to create a regular polygon or star. Double-click the tool icon to specify the number of sides or points in the shape and to select whether the shape is a polygon or star.

 Ellipse: Drag with this tool to draw an oval. Shift-drag to draw a circle. Option/Alt-drag to draw a rectangle from a center point.

 Line: Drag with the line tool to draw a straight line. Shift-drag to draw a line at a 45-degree angle or multiples thereof. Option/Alt-drag to draw a straight line from the center outward.

 Freehand: Drag with the freehand tool to draw a free-form line. Press the ⌘/Ctrl key while drawing to erase a portion of the line. Double-click the tool icon to create calligraphic shapes and to make the tool compatible with a pressure-sensitive tablet.

 Pen: Use the pen tool to create a line or shape one point at a time. Click to add a corner to the line or shape in progress; drag to add a curve. The pen tool is more precise than the bézigon tool because you can specify both the locations of points and the curvature of connecting segments.

Freeform: New to Freehand 8, this tool allows you to reshape paths on the fly. Just click anywhere on a path and drag to change the shape of the effected segment. Click-drag just inside or outside a path to push or pull it into more curvaceous versions of its former self.

Knife: Simply drag with the knife to slice through any selected line or shape that lies in your path. Double-click the tool icon to choose between cutting straight or freehand lines, to specify how closely to track your mouse movements, and to specify the width of the cut.

Note

Observant FreeHand 4 users may notice that the knife tool icon now includes a preference indicator. The difference between the FreeHand 4 knife tool and the FreeHand 8 knife tool is equivalent to the difference between an ordinary kitchen knife and a Swiss army knife. Don't leave home without it!

Bézigon: Like the pen tool, the bézigon tool creates a line or shape one point at a time. Click to add a corner; Option/Alt-click to add an arc. Unlike the pen tool, the bézigon tool lets you specify the locations of the points only; FreeHand determines the curvature of the segments automatically.

Rotate: Drag with this tool to rotate one or more selected objects. The point at which you start dragging acts as the center of the rotation. Shift-drag to rotate the objects in 45-degree increments. Double-click the tool icon to display the Rotate panel in the Transform panel.

Reflect: Drag with the reflect tool to flip selected objects. The angle of your drag defines the angle of the "mirror" about which FreeHand reflects the selected objects. Double-click the tool icon to display the Reflect panel in the Transform panel.

Scale: Drag up and to the right to enlarge selected objects; drag down and to the left to reduce them. Shift-drag to scale the objects proportionally. Double-click the tool icon to display the Scale panel in the Transform panel.

Skew: Drag with this tool to slant selected objects. More often, you will probably want to Shift-drag to slant the objects horizontally or vertically. Double-click the tool icon to display the Skew panel in the Transform panel.

Trace: Drag around some detail in a tracing template to automatically trace around its borders with an object-oriented line or shape. Double-click the tool icon to adjust how the tool works.

Zoom: Click to magnify your document so that you can see small details more clearly. Option/Alt-click to step back from the image and take in a broader view. Drag to enclose the specific portion of the image that you want to magnify.

Cross-Reference

Keep in mind that the preceding list is the briefest of all possible introductions to FreeHand's tools. Figure 2-4 segregates the tools by category and indicates the chapter that contains oodles of information on each.

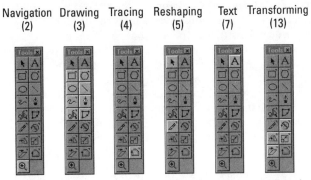

Navigation Drawing Tracing Reshaping Text Transforming
(2)   (3)   (4)   (5)   (7)   (13)

Figure 2-4: FreeHand's tools fall into the categories listed above the toolboxes. The highlighted tools belong to the labeled categories. The chapter in which I discuss the category appears in parentheses.

Floating Panels

FreeHand 8 offers at least 20 floating panels, which are organized in the Window menu under four categories: Toolbars, Inspectors, Panels, and Xtras. These panels contain many standard dialog box elements — pop-up menus, option boxes, and so on — as well as a few elements normally associated with windows. Although they are similar to dialog boxes, they differ in one important way; panels may remain open even after you are done using them.

First on our list of floating panels are the toolbars. Each toolbar, as the name implies, is a different collection of tools. Unlike the other floating panels, toolbars don't have a close box and they don't contain options. But, like the other panels, you can position them any where on-screen. Let's look at the five toolbars:

✦ **Main toolbar:** This toolbar contains many frequently accessed commands such as New, Open, Print, Undo, and so on. A real time-saver! You can turn this feature on or off by choosing Window ➪ Toolbars ➪ Main. A checkmark on the menu shows that it is currently displayed. (Sorry, there's no keyboard equivalent.)

✦ **Text toolbar:** This toolbar is positioned just below the Main toolbar. It contains all the frequently accessed text options like font, style, point size, leading, alignment, text effects, and so on. To turn on this feature, choose Window ➪ Toolbars ➪ Text. (This feature is explained in detail in Chapter 9.)

✦ **Toolbox toolbar:** This familiar tool set was explained earlier in this chapter. If you don't remember, flip back to the previous section. You can toggle the view of the toolbox with a quick press of ⌘/Ctrl-7 or by choosing Window @(Toolbars ➪ Toolbox.

✦ **Status toolbar:** The Status toolbar is new to FreeHand 8. In previous versions of FreeHand, all parts of this toolbar were integral parts of the Illustration window. The lower left corner of this toolbar features a pair of page-advance icons bordered on either side by a pop-up menu. Click a page-advance icon to advance from one page of a FreeHand document to the next. (Multiple-page documents are the subject of Chapter 17.) Press and hold the view size pop-up menu to magnify or reduce the drawing inside the illustration window. Press and hold the display mode pop-up menu to switch between the Preview and Keyline modes (as explained in the "Display modes" section later in this chapter). Hide or show the Status toolbar by choosing Window ➪ Toolbars ➪ Status.

Freehand 8.0

To increase redraw speeds, two new display modes are included in FreeHand 8: Fast Preview and Fast Keyline. Sure, these modes sacrifice some of your drawing's details, but with the time you save waiting for your screen to refresh, you can reread this book (and thoroughly savor every witticism) at least a couple of times.

✦ **Information toolbar:** The information toolbar displays a wealth of numerical data applicable to the current operation, including the coordinate location of the cursor, the angle of a drag, and the extent of an enlargement. Call it into view by choosing Window ➪ Toolbars ➪ Info. (For complete information on this feature, read Chapter 6.)

Freehand 8.0

FreeHand 8 lets you show or hide all of the toolbars with the View ➪ Toolbars command. Choosing this command toggles you between viewing and not viewing the toolbars. When a check mark appears to the left of the command, the toolbars are concealed. The best part about this command is that it includes a shortcut: ⌘/Ctrl-Option/Alt-T. A preference setting lets you decide whether this command includes the Toolbox toolbar as well.

With the black sheep of the floating panels family — the toolbars — out of the way, let's proceed to a rundown of the rest of the panels offered in FreeHand 8. All the non-toolbar panels possess regular (either Macintosh or Windows) close boxes, title bars, and collapse boxes. An example of one, the Text Inspector, is shown in Figure 2-5. Click the close box to hide the panel; drag the title bar to move the panel, and click the collapse box to hide everything but the title bar. To restore the entire panel, just click the collapse box again (or the Windows restore button) or use its shortcut. (See "Navigating Panels" later in this chapter, for information on panel shortcuts.)

Figure 2-5: The Text Inspector includes the common FreeHand panel elements.

The following list briefly describes each of FreeHand's "Inspector" type floating panels:

✦ **Object Inspector:** This panel shows what type of object you have selected and gives you the ability to change its attributes. You can resize rectangles and circles in this panel.

✦ **Stroke Inspector:** This panel contains all your stroke related needs. You're given a pop-up menu from which you can choose colors right from your Color List. You can also apply line weight from a pop-up menu, dash attributes, cap and join, overprinting, and arrowheads to a selected object.

✦ **Fill Inspector:** With this panel you can apply fills such as none, basic, custom, gradient, lens, pattern, PostScript, textured, and tiled attributes to selected closed paths.

✦ **Text Inspector:** Here you can change character, paragraph, spacing, columns and rows, and adjust columns of selected text or choose options from the pop-up menus. From within the Text Inspector you can access what I call *subinspectors* that provide additional options. (Confusing, eh?)

✦ **Document Inspector:** This panel is where you view thumbnails and set multiple pages, page size, page bleed, page orientation, and printer resolution.

Just to give you an idea of how many different aspects of FreeHand are wrapped up in the Inspectors, various bits and pieces are covered in Chapters 5, 6, 7, 8, 9, 10, 11, 12, 17, and 18. (Wowsers!)

The following list contains brief explanations of each of FreeHand's "Panel" type panels:

✦ **Layers:** This panel creates independent drawing layers and assigns objects to them. The Layers panel contains all options that affect layering and no miscellaneous junk. (If all FreeHand panels were as thoughtful or well organized, I wouldn't be able to have so much fun ridiculing them.)

✦ **Styles:** FreeHand allows you to define graphic and text styles. After applying the desired fill and stroke attributes to a selected object, choose New from the Styles panel's Options pop-up menu. You can then apply those same attributes and type styles over and over to other objects or text in your drawing.

✦ **Color List:** While the Inspector panel is out there trying to be the one-stop center for all your editing needs, FreeHand's straightforward supply of color options spans two panels (ignoring for a moment the vast Inspector itself). The first and most important among these is the Color List panel, which lists all colors you've created in the current document. This panel also displays the colors applied to a selected object.

✦ **Color Mixer:** The second color options panel is the Color Mixer panel, where you define the colors in your document using one of three color models: CMYK (cyan, magenta, yellow, black), RGB (red, green, blue), or HLS (hue, lightness, saturation). Color Mixer also gives you access to the appropriate (Mac or Win) system software defined colors. After you define a color, just drag it into the Color List panel or simply click the Add to Color List button (new in FreeHand 8) and give it a name.

✦ **Tints:** FreeHand 8 has spun the Version 7 Tint option into its own Tints panel. It lets you create shades of brand-name inks and other spot colors. One hundred percent is solid color; any smaller value is a lighter tint. Add tints you create to the Color List panel just as you would add any color.

✦ **Halftone:** Look closely at a color image in a magazine or other publication and you'll see patterns of tiny dots. These dots are halftone patterns. In FreeHand, you can change the halftone pattern applied to a selected object by using the options in the Halftone panel. FreeHand makes mincemeat of Illustrator in this area.

✦ **Align:** This panel lets you align objects and distribute them. These options are useful for creating schematic drawings and aligning text blocks. To use the options in the Align panel, you must first select two or more objects in the illustration window. To apply your settings to the selected objects, click the Apply button.

✦ **Transform:** The Transform panel offers five panel icons. From left to right, these are Move, Rotate, Scale, Skew, and Reflect. These icons let you transform selected objects numerically and are close cousins to the rotate, scale, skew, and reflect tools in the toolbox. At least one object must be selected in the illustration window before you can use these options. Click the Apply button or press Return/Enter to apply your changes. The Transform panel contains precise information about the objects selected and the type of transformation.

The following list briefly defines each of FreeHand's "Xtras" type panels:

✦ **Xtra Tools:** To access this panel, choose Window ➪ Xtra ➪ Xtra Tools. New features added to this panel in Freehand 8 include graphic hose, shadow, and mirror. This panel contains tools exclusively. These tools can be used to create special objects, edit existing objects, or offer new functionality.

✦ **Operations:** You can access this panel by choosing Window ➪ Xtra ➪ Operations. It contains all of the options from the Modify ➪ Alter Path submenu, among many others. The options let you apply operations to selected objects in your document. The contents of this panel vary depending on the contents of the Xtras folder on your hard drive.

Tip

All panels can be combined into one huge panel by dragging the name tabs together. Why you would ever want to do this is beyond me, but you can. Align, Transform, Xtra Tools, and Operations won't cooperate because they don't have one of those tabs at the top. Toolbars also won't work. Caution: On Macs, some of these lack resize windows in the lower left corner of the panel.

Freehand 8.0

Just as you can toggle the view of the toolbars, FreeHand 8 lets you show or hide all of the non-toolbar panels with the View ➪ Panels command, or its handy little shortcut: ⌘-Shift-H on Macs and Ctrl-Alt-H on PCs. One other feature with panels: they snap to logical alignments to better organize your on-screen space.

Working in the illustration window

Like any program worth its weight in dollar bills — which is about what these suckers cost — FreeHand provides a variety of navigational tools and functions that enable you to toodle around the illustration window. This section explains how to change the view size, scroll the document inside the illustration window, and switch between the Preview and Keyline display modes.

View size

FreeHand provides a nearly infinite supply of *view sizes*, which are the levels of magnification at which the illustration appears on screen. Magnified view sizes provide great detail but allow you to see only small portions of your drawing at a time. Reduced view sizes allow you to look at a large portion of your drawing but may provide insufficient detail for creating and manipulating objects. Because

FreeHand makes it easy to change quickly between various view sizes, you can accurately edit your artwork and still maintain overall design consistency.

When you create a new illustration, FreeHand displays the document at *fit-in-window* size, which means that an entire page just barely fits inside the confines of the illustration window. The exact level of magnification required to pull off this feat depends on the size of the document and the size of your monitor. In the case of Figure 2-6, the T-Rex fits in the window at 60 percent, as witnessed by the value in the view size pop-up menu in the lower left corner of the window.

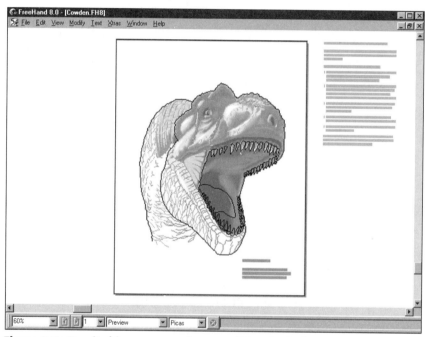

Figure 2-6: Despite his enormous size, even T-Rex fits in the window.

You can change the view size by choosing commands from the view size pop-up menu. In Figure 2-7, for example, I chose the 100% command to magnify T-Rex to *actual size*, which is the size at which the terrifying animal will print. This view size generally provides the most natural and reliable feedback concerning the progress of your artwork.

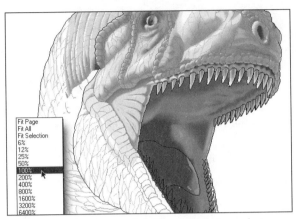

Fit Page
Fit All
Fit Selection
6%
12%
25%
50%
100%
200%
400%
800%
1600%
3200%
6400%

Figure 2-7: The same T-Rex illustration viewed at actual size.

Tip

You can highlight the text in the view size box (when any old cursor is active) and type the desired view percentage. Press Return/Enter, and FreeHand zooms to that percentage. Typing a value in the view size box provides access to thousands of incredibly accurate view sizes not offered in the view size pop-up menu.

The numerical sizes in the view size pop-up menu also appear in the View ⇨ Magnification submenu. Unfortunately, although they are more accessible in the pop-up menu, only the submenu lists the keyboard equivalents. For example, to switch to actual size you can press ⌘/Ctrl-1; to enlarge the current selection to as large as possible, use the keyboard shortcut ⌘/Ctrl-0 for the Fit Selection command. To fit the active page in the window, press ⌘/Ctrl-Shift-W; to fit all of the pages in the document in the window, press ⌘/Ctrl-Option/Alt-0. Other useful keyboard equivalents are ⌘/Ctrl-5 for 50 percent (half actual size), ⌘/Ctrl-2 for 200 percent (twice actual size), ⌘/Ctrl-4 for 400 percent (four times actual size), and ⌘/Ctrl-8 for 800 percent.

Note

The magnification limit is a whopping 25,600 percent. Once you exceed 6,400 percent, you increase the magnification in 100 percent increments. So, for example, you can magnify to exactly 6,395 percent but not 6,495 percent. If you enter 6,495 percent, FreeHand rounds you to the nearest 100 percent increment and displays 65x in the view size box. If you find this confusing, when you see an "x" in view size box, mentally replace it with "00."

Freehand 8.0

You can now save and name custom view sizes. Simply magnify your art to a view that you want to be able to return to time after time and choose View ⇨ Custom ⇨ New. The New View dialog box will prompt you to type in an appropriate name. The new view size will appear in both the View ⇨ Custom submenu and the view size pop-up menu. Incidentally, your custom view also will save the display mode information (discussed shortly) that was in effect when you saved your view.

The zoom tool

The other way to change view sizes is to use the *zoom tool*, the one that looks like a magnifying glass in the lower right corner of the toolbox. The zoom tool is more flexible than the view size commands because it gives you access to more than just the preset view sizes. Here's how it works:

✦ Click in the illustration window with the zoom tool to magnify the drawing to twice the previous view size, centered around the point where you click.

✦ Option/Alt-click with the zoom tool to reduce the drawing to half its previous view size, centered around the point where you click.

For both of these methods, if you were not at one of the preset view options, FreeHand takes you to the next preset view option instead of doubling or halving your view size.

✦ Drag a rectangular marquee (dotted line) around the portion of the drawing that you want to magnify. FreeHand magnifies the image so the marqueed area just fits inside the image window. For the top illustration in Figure 2-8, I dragged with the zoom tool around the dinosaur's eye. FreeHand then magnified the marqueed area to 307 percent, as demonstrated in the bottom illustration.

✦ For zooming out, Option/Alt-drag with the zoom tool to specify the space in which the windowed portion of the drawing should fit. In other words, when you Option/Alt-drag a marquee, FreeHand reduces the visible portion of the drawing so it fits inside your marquee.

For the previous two methods, if the horizontal and vertical proportions of the marquee do not match those of the illustration window — for example, if you draw a tall, thin marquee or a short, wide one — FreeHand favors the smaller of the two possible view sizes to avoid hiding any detail inside the marquee.

To temporarily access the zoom tool when some other tool is selected, press and hold ⌘/Ctrl-spacebar. Release both to return control of the cursor to the selected tool. To temporarily access the zoom out cursor, press ⌘-Shift-S on Macs and Ctrl-Alt-S on PC.

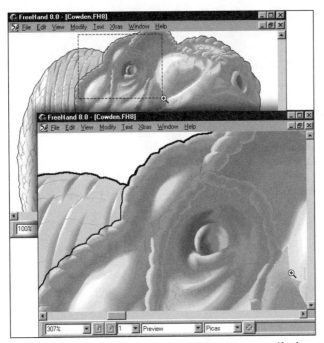

Figure 2-8: Drag with the zoom tool (top) to magnify the marqueed area so it consumes the illustration window.

Tip

Okay, so if you've ever used FreeHand before, you know about that shortcut. What you may not know is that you can magnify the view size to its absolute maximum — 25,600 percent — by pressing ⌘-Control-spacebar (or Ctrl-Shift-spacebar on a Windows machine) and clicking with the zoom tool. To reduce the view size to its absolute minimum (6 percent), press ⌘-Control-Option-spacebar (or Ctrl-Shift-Alt-spacebar for Windows) and click with the zoom tool. You may have to take off your shoes and use a toe or two to make that one work!

Dragging the scroll box

Like almost every other application, FreeHand employs scroll bars, boxes, and arrows. As a general rule, scroll bars are not the most efficient method for maneuvering around. In particular, clicking in the scroll bar and clicking a scroll arrow are unpredictable and slow methods for navigating in FreeHand. The only scroll bar standout is the scroll box. In fact, FreeHand is unusually well suited to tracking scroll box movements. Try pressing and holding on a scroll box and moving it around a bit. FreeHand responds to your movements immediately and predictably. Only after you release the scroll box does FreeHand take time out to redraw the hidden portions of the document. If you want FreeHand to redraw continuously as you scroll, choose File ➪ Preferences and, from the Redraw panel, select the Redraw While Scrolling check box. Realize though, that by choosing this option, you're increasing the time it takes for FreeHand to perform this operation.

Note   If FreeHand doesn't respond to your scroll box movements the way I say it will, it's because the Dynamic Scrollbar option is turned off. To fix this calamity, choose File ➪ Preferences, select the General panel, and select the Dynamic Scrollbar check box.

Using the grabber hand

An even better way to scroll is to use the grabber hand. And the only way to access the grabber hand is to press the spacebar. As long as a text block or option box is not active, pressing and holding the spacebar changes the cursor to a hand. Drag while pressing the spacebar to scroll the document. Releasing the spacebar returns control of the cursor to the selected tool.

Display modes

Look back at Figure 2-8. The drawing, like any created in FreeHand, is composed of many individual lines and shapes. In the case of this particular drawing, each shape is filled with a single, flat color. The shading you see is the result of hundreds of shapes piled on top of one another, each slightly lighter or darker than its immediate neighbor. Though you may never attempt anything so complex — few of us have the patience — your drawings will have fundamentally the same characteristics: one shape filled with one color stacked on top of another shape filled with a different color.

The drawing in Figure 2-8 is shown in the *Preview* mode, which is one of four *display modes* offered by FreeHand. When the Preview mode is active, FreeHand shows the document on-screen as similar as possible to the way it will look when printed. It shows all fills and all colors associated with the lines and shapes in your document. All this filling and coloring requires a lot of hard-core computing. In fact, the Preview mode can be exasperatingly slow, especially when you're actually working on a drawing, not just looking at it.

If your artwork contains blends and text, you may wish to employ one of FreeHand 8's new display modes: the *Fast Preview mode*. In Fast Preview, FreeHand limits the number of steps in every blend to ten for each. This limitation applies to the on-screen display of blends only and will not affect printing. Additionally, all text that use a point size less than 50 will appear as gray blocks. Once again, only the display of your work is affected.

Tip   To switch between the Preview and Fast Preview modes either choose the Fast Preview command from the Display Mode pop-up menu or choose the Fast Mode command from the View menu. Even better, simply press ⌘/Ctrl-Shift-K.

To speed things up considerably, you can instruct FreeHand to show only the skeletal framework of lines and shapes, and bag the fills and colors. Figure 2-9 shows the drawing from Figure 2-8 in this minimalist display mode, called the *Keyline mode*. Every shape gets a thin outline; its interior appears transparent. As you become more familiar with FreeHand and start creating more complicated artwork, you'll rely on the Keyline mode more and more. With this outline mode, you can construct drawings with greater precision and speed.

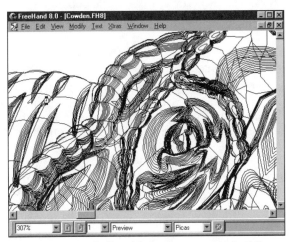

Figure 2-9: A unbelievably intricate network of lines and shapes is exposed in the Keyline mode.

To access the Keyline mode, choose the Keyline command from the Display Mode pop-up menu. It's located to the left of the Measures pop-up menu at the bottom of the window (as shown in Figure 2-9). You can also choose View ➪ Preview to turn off that command (the check mark disappears) or better yet, just press ⌘/Ctrl-K. This useful keyboard equivalent lets you toggle back and forth between the Keyline and Preview modes.

Note

FreeHand lets you assign the Preview and Keyline options on a layer-by-layer basis using the Layers panel. See Chapter 8 for thorough instructions for doing so. The big difference between assigning display modes using the pop-up menu rather than the Layers panel is that the pop-up menu lets you temporarily override your individual layer display mode settings. You can put the entire document into Keyline mode in one fell swoop. However, the reverse is not true: Choosing Preview from the pop-up menu does not necessarily preview your entire document; it simply returns you to your current layer settings. So, for example, if you had set layer three to Keyline, choosing Preview from the pop-up menu still displays layer three in Keyline mode.

Finally, if you want FreeHand to redraw the screen just as fast as it possibly can, you'll want to use its other new display mode: *Fast Keyline*. Utilizing all the time-saving techniques in the Keyline mode, the Fast Keyline mode hastens redrawing by displaying text smaller than 50 points as gray blocks.

Tip Just as with the two Preview modes, you switch from the Keyline mode to the Fast Keyline mode by choosing Fast Keyline from the Display Mode pop-up menu or by choosing View ➪ Fast Mode. If you prefer using the shortcut, just press ⌘/Ctrl-Shift-K.

Canceling the screen redraw on Macs

If you're using a Mac, you can press ⌘-period to cancel FreeHand's redraw, whether you're working in the Preview or Keyline mode. Note that if you press ⌘-period too quickly after scrolling or performing some other operation, FreeHand may think you're trying to cancel the operation. For best results, wait for the screen redraw cycle to begin before pressing ⌘-period.

The great thing about canceling the screen redraw is that it allows you to view a specific detail and then move on. Suppose you want to see how the back of the dinosaur's neck looks at a certain view size, but you don't care about the face and other details. FreeHand redraws the document starting with the rearmost shapes and works its way toward the front, so the neck is redrawn before forward items such as the eye and scales. After the neck comes into view, you can press ⌘-period to prevent the redraw from progressing any farther. This enables you to keep working with shorter interruptions. In time, you'll be pressing ⌘-period and ⌘-K on an almost continual basis.

Tip To reinitiate a screen redraw, either change view sizes or display modes, or click with the zoom tool.

Using Shortcuts

Shortcuts enable you to access commands and other functions without resorting to the laborious task of choosing commands from menus or clicking on some fool icon until your arm falls off. Many shortcuts are fairly obvious. For example, FreeHand lists keyboard equivalents for its commands next to the command name in the menu. You can choose File ➪ New by pressing ⌘/Ctrl-N, Edit ➪ Undo by pressing ⌘/Ctrl-Z, View ➪ Preview by pressing ⌘/Ctrl-K, and so on. But many of FreeHand's shortcuts are either hidden or can easily be overlooked. If you're a longtime user of FreeHand and you think you know all this, think again.

Table 2-1 lists my favorite FreeHand shortcuts. Some of these I've already mentioned, but they're worth repeating. Memorize them, photocopy and tack them to a wall, write them on the backs of your hands. But whatever you do, use them.

Table 2-1
FreeHand's Most Extraordinary Hidden Shortcuts

Operation	Shortcut
Navigation tricks	
Scroll document with grabber hand	Press the spacebar and drag
Fit Selection	⌘-0 (zero) or Ctrl-0 (zero)
Fit to Page	⌘-Shift-W or Ctrl-Shift-W
Zoom in to next preset view size	⌘-spacebar-click or Ctrl-spacebar-click
Zoom out to previous preset view size	⌘-Option-spacebar-click or Ctrl-Alt-spacebar-click
Fit all pages in window	⌘-Option-0 (zero) or Ctrl-Alt-0 (zero)
Go to previous page	⌘-Page Up or Ctrl-Page Up
Go to next page	⌘-Page Down or Ctrl-Page Down
View document at actual size	⌘-1 or Ctrl-1
Zoom in all the way (25,600%)	⌘-Control-spacebar-click or Ctrl-Shift-spacebar-click
Zoom out all the way (6%)	⌘-Control-Option-spacebar-click or Ctrl-Shift-Alt-spacebar-click
Switch display modes	⌘-K or Ctrl-K
Toggle fast mode	⌘-Shift-K or Ctrl-Shift-K
Cancel the screen redraw Text tricks	⌘-period or Ctrl-period
Select text tool*	T or A
Activate text block and select text	Double-click text block with arrow tool
Open Text Editor	Option-drag or Alt-click text with text tool
Draw text block outward from center	Option-drag or Alt-drag with text tool
Select word	Double-click word with text tool
Select paragraph	Triple-click in paragraph with text tool
Select all text across links blocks	⌘-A or Ctrl-A when a text block is active

(continued)

Table 2-1 *(continued)*

Operation	Shortcut
Adjust column width	Drag corner handle of text block with arrow tool
Stretch or compress type	Option-drag or Alt-drag corner handle of text block with arrow tool
Scale type proportionally	Shift-Option-drag or Shift-Alt-drag corner handle of text block with arrow tool
Adjust leading	Drag top or bottom handle of text block with arrow tool
Adjust letter spacing	Drag side handle of text block with arrow tool
Adjust word spacing	Option-drag or Alt-drag side handle of text block with arrow tool
Join selected type to selected line	⌘-Shift-Y or Ctrl-Shift-Y
Flow selected type inside selected shape	⌘-Shift-U or Ctrl-Shift-U
Convert selected text to editable shapes	⌘-Shift-P or Ctrl-Shift-P
Formatting text (one or more characters selected with text tool)	
Highlight text effect	⌘-Option-Shift-H or Ctrl-Alt-Shift-H
Strikethrough text effect	⌘-Option-Shift-S or Ctrl-Alt-Shift-S
Underline text effect	⌘-Option-U or Ctrl-Alt-U
Increase type size 1 point*	⌘-Option-2 and ⌘-Option-Shift- ↑ or Ctrl-Alt-2 and Ctrl-Alt-Shift-↑
Decrease type size 1 point*	⌘-Option-1 and ⌘-Option-Shift- ↓ or Ctrl-Alt-1 and Ctrl-Alt-Shift- ↓
Justify text	⌘-Option-Shift-J or Ctrl-Alt-Shift-J
Left align text	⌘-Option-Shift-L or Ctrl-Alt-Shift-L
Right align text	⌘-Option-Shift-R or Ctrl-Alt-Shift-R
Center align text	⌘-Option-Shift-M or Ctrl-Alt-Shift-M
Kern characters together 1% em	⌘-Option- ← or Ctrl-Alt- ←
Kern characters apart 1% em	⌘-Option- → or Ctrl-Alt- →
Kern characters together 10% em	⌘-Shift-Option- ← or Ctrl-Shift-Alt- ←
Kern characters apart 10% em	⌘-Shift-Option- → or Ctrl-Shift-Alt- →
Increase baseline shift 1 point	⌘-Option- ↑ or Ctrl-Alt- ↑
Decrease baseline shift 1 point	⌘-Option-↓ or Ctrl-Alt-↓

Operation	*Shortcut*
Drawing lines and shapes	
Draw oval outward from center	Option-drag or Alt-drag with oval tool
Draw circle	Shift-drag with oval tool
Draw circle outward from center	Shift-Option-drag or Shift-Alt-drag with oval tool
Draw rectangle outward from center	Option-drag or Alt-drag with rectangle tool
Draw square	Shift-drag with rectangle tool
Draw square outward from center	Shift-Option-drag or Shift-Alt-drag with rectangle tool
Draw diagonal or perpendicular line	Shift-drag with line tool
Auto-remove calligraphic/variable pen overlap	Control-calligraphic/variable pen
Create a straight segment while drawing	Press and hold Option or Alt key with freehand tool
Constrain a straight segment to multiples of 45° while drawing	Press and hold Shift-Option or Shift-Alt key with freehand tool
Erase while drawing with freehand tool	Press and hold ⌘/Ctrl key
Add a corner between straight segments	Click with pen or bézigon tool
Add a corner between curved segments	Press Option or Alt midway into dragging with pen tool
Add an arc	Drag with pen tool or Option-click with bézigon tool
Selecting objects (arrow tool active, all text blocks inactive)	
Select all objects in document	⌘-Shift-A or Ctrl-Shift-A
Deselect all objects in document	Tab key
Add object to selection	Shift-click object
Select single object inside group	Option-click or Alt-click object
Select points in grouped object	Option-drag or Alt-drag around points
Select points in geometric shape	Click on shape, ⌘-U or Ctrl-U, click point
Select group that contains selected object	Grave key (`)
Editing selected objects (arrow tool active)	
Move horizontally or vertically	Shift-drag with arrow tool

(continued)

Table 2-1 (continued)

Operation	Shortcut
Move in predefined increments	Any arrow key
Rotate in 45-degree increments	Shift-drag with rotate tool
Rotate and clone	Option-drag or Alt-drag with rotate tool
Flip horizontally or vertically	Shift-drag with reflect tool
Flip and clone	Option-drag or Alt-drag with reflect tool
Scale proportionally	Shift-drag with scale tool
Scale and clone	Option-drag or Alt-drag with scale tool
Slant horizontally or vertically	Shift-drag with skew tool
Slant and clone	Option-drag or Alt-drag with skew tool
Repeat the last transformation	⌘-Shift-G or Ctrl-Shift-G
Editing selected objects (arrow tool active)	
Join two lines or shapes into one	⌘-J or Ctrl-J
Split composite path into independent shapes	⌘-Shift-J or Ctrl-Shift-J
Mask selected objects inside shape	⌘-X or Ctrl-X, click shape, ⌘-Shift-V or Ctrl-Shift-V
Separate masked objects from a	⌘-Shift-X or Ctrl-Shift-X selected shape*
Coloring objects (drag from color swatch in Color List panel)	
Change color inside object	Drag color onto object
Change color of stroke	Drag color onto stroke
Change gradient fill to flat fill	Shift-drag color onto object
Change a fill to a linear gradient fill	⌘-drag or Ctrl-drag color onto object (or change angle of existing gradient fill)
Change a fill to a radial fill	Option-drag or Alt-drag color onto object (or change center of existing radial fill)

* New to Version 8

Customizing your shortcuts

One of the handiest new interface features in FreeHand 8 is you can change each and every one of its shortcuts. You can even add shortcuts to commands that don't have any. This means you can change FreeHand's shortcuts so that they conform to your personal bias or even your handed-ness. FreeHand 8 also ships with four other shortcut settings that reflect the shortcuts of a few other drawing programs—CorelDRAW 7, Illustrator 7 and QuarkXPress 3.3 and 4.

To dive-in and change FreeHand's shortcuts to your heart's content, just follow these easy steps:

1. Choose File ➪ Customize ➪ Shortcuts (⌘-Option-Shift-Control-K on Macs and Ctrl-Alt-Shift-Y on Windows).

2. Click on the big plus-sign button that's next to the Keyboard Shortcuts Setting pop-up menu. This brings up the Save Keyboard Shortcuts Setting dialog box. Here you name your custom keyboard setting file. I named mine "Deke's Grand Old Shortcuts Plan for Better Living." Your new settings file will be based on the shortcut scheme that appeared previously in the Keyboard Shortcuts Setting pop-up menu. Now, whatever changes you make will not affect any of the preset settings.

3. The next step is to add or change a command's shortcut. From the Commands scrolling field, double-click on the menu's name where the command appears. For example, if you want to change the Redo shortcut, double-click on Edit in the Command scrolling field.

4. Next, click on the command's name. Make sure the Go To Conflict On Assign checkbox is active and enter a shortcut in the Press New Shortcut Key option box. Continuing with the example, click on the Redo in the Command scrolling field and press, say, the ⌘ (or Ctrl), Shift, and Z keys. Click the Assign button and your shortcut will be added to the command's Current Shortcut Keys scrolling list.

5. If a conflict does exist with your new shortcut and a preexisting shortcut, you'll be given a change to assign a new shortcut to the command that previously used that shortcut. Again with that example, if you're working on a Windows machine, FreeHand will inform you that this shortcut is already assigned to the Snap To Point command and will prompt you to add a new shortcut to the Snap To Point command. Mind you, you don't have to add a shortcut to the other command, you just have that option.

6. FreeHand will also display your new shortcut inside the appropriate menu next to the command's name, but only if it is the first shortcut in the Current Shortcut Keys scrolling field. If other shortcuts appear above your new shortcut, you can click on those shortcuts and delete them via the Remove button.

7. If you're dissatisfied with all the changes you've made to your shortcut list, click the Reset button. Click Close to end your shortcut customizing adventure. Then, get out of there and use your new shortcuts.

Selecting tools

FreeHand allows you to select most of its tools from the keyboard rather than having to click on an icon inside the toolbox. Pressing keys may not sound particularly more convenient than clicking on an icon, but as you delve deeper into the heart and soul of FreeHand wizardry, you'll discover that there are times when you want to switch tools without moving your cursor.

Suppose you want to begin a rectangle at the exact spot where you just finished drawing a line with the freehand tool. Rather than moving the cursor and losing your place, you can simply press the 1 key or the R key and start drawing.

Figure 2-10 shows the keyboard equivalents required to select FreeHand's tools. Notice that most tools have more than one shortcut. To select one of the drawing tools, for example, you can either press a single number key or letter key that, it is hoped, you will associate with the name of the tool.

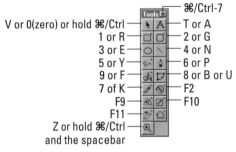

Figure 2-10: The toolbox labeled with all default keyboard equivalents.

One note about the labels in Figure 2-10: If the label indicates that you hold a key, it means that the tool only remains active as long as the key is down. For example, you can either access the arrow tool temporarily by pressing and holding the ⌘/Ctrl key, or select the arrow tool permanently by pressing either the V or the 0 (zero) key.

Tip

To show or hide the toolbox, press ⌘/Ctrl-7. Why 7? Well, perhaps FreeHand's programmers were thinking of the toolbox as the program's Agent 007, ready for any emergency. Or perhaps the toolbox is a 7th-heaven of functionality and potential. But more likely, it's because the toolbox is a veritable 7-Eleven of tools and gadgets, admittedly minus the Big Gulps and microwave burritos.

Navigating panels

The last thing you can do from the keyboard is display, hide, and navigate panels, as listed in Table 2-2. FreeHand's Window menu displays many of these keyboard equivalents.

Incidentally, I segregated these keyboard equivalents from those in Table 2-1 primarily so I could make fun of them. Although you at least stand a chance of memorizing the basically logical collection of keyboard shortcuts covered so far, those in Table 2-2 are almost nonsensical. Case in point: What's with ⌘/Ctrl-6 for the Layers panel? This shortcut and many others are leftovers from FreeHand 3. In addition to ⌘/Ctrl-6 for Layers, the others include ⌘/Ctrl-3 for Color List, ⌘/Ctrl-9 for Styles, and ⌘/Ctrl-M for Transform.

Anyway, do your best to learn these shortcuts and try not to get all stressed out when you don't.

Table 2-2
Displaying, Hiding, and Navigating Panels

Operation	Shortcut
The Inspector panel	
Object Inspector	⌘-I or Ctrl-I
Columns and Rows panel of the Text Inspector	⌘-Option-R or Ctrl-Alt-R
Copyfit panel of the Text Inspector	⌘-Option-C or Ctrl-Alt-C
Fill Inspector	⌘-Option-F or Ctrl-Alt-F
Stroke Inspector	⌘-Option-L or Ctrl-Alt-L
Text Inspector	⌘-T or Ctrl-T
Paragraph panel of the Text Inspector	⌘-Option-P or Ctrl-Alt-P
Spacing panel of the Text Inspector	⌘-Option-K or Ctrl-Alt-K
Document Inspector	⌘-Option-D or Ctrl-Alt-D
All those other panels	
Display Align panel	⌘-Option-A or Ctrl-Alt-A
Display/hide Color List panel	⌘-9 or Ctrl-9
Display/hide Color Mixer panel	⌘-Shift-9 or Ctrl-Alt-9 or double-click a color in the Color List panel*

(continued)

Table 2-2 *(continued)*	
Operation	*Shortcut*
Display/hide Halftone panel	⌘-H or Ctrl-H
Display/hide Layers panel	⌘-6 or Ctrl-6
Display/hide Styles panel	⌘-3 or Ctrl-3
Display Transform panel	⌘-M or Ctrl-M
Display/hide Operations panel	⌘-Option-O or Ctrl-Alt-O
Display/hide Xtra Tools panel	⌘-Option-X or Ctrl-Alt-X
Display/hide all Toolbars	⌘-Option-T or Ctrl-Alt-T
Display/hide all other Panels	⌘-Option-H or Ctrl-Alt-H
Activate first option box in next panel	⌘-grave (`) (no Windows equivalent)
Activate next option box in same panel	Tab
Activate previous option box in same panel	Shift-Tab

* New to Version 8

Customizing Your Work Environment

Everyone draws differently. For those who draw to a different drummer — in other words, all of us — FreeHand provides *preference settings*, which permit you to customize your work environment. FreeHand ships with certain preference settings already in force, called *factory default settings*, but you can change the settings to reflect your own personal preferences.

You can change the preference settings in two ways. You can make environmental adjustments by choosing File ➪ Preferences and mucking about with the 9 panels of options inside the Preferences dialog box. Or you can change the operation of specific tools by double-clicking the tool icon of any tool that contains a preference indicator in its top right corner. FreeHand remembers all preference settings by saving them to a file called FreeHand Preferences.

The FreeHand Preferences file

On Macs, the FreeHand Preferences file resides in the System Folder, inside the Preferences folder. On Windows machines, the preferences file — FHPrefs.txt — is located in the main FreeHand 8 directory. From here on, I'll simply refer to both of these files as the FreeHand Preference file. It's not that I'm playing favorites (or showing a preference, so to speak) for the Mac name for this file, it's just that the term *FreeHand Preference* readily conveys a bit more information and rolls off the tongue slightly better than does FHPrefs.txt. This file contains your settings for panel positions and option settings, as well as all settings from the Preferences dialog box. Whenever you make changes to these items, your changes are saved in the FreeHand Preferences file. Possibly you prefer not to change these settings, but to return to FreeHand's original settings. To restore FreeHand's factory default settings, delete the Preferences file.

Try this: When FreeHand is *not* running, drag the FreeHand Preferences file out of the Preferences folder and onto the Finder desktop if you're using a Mac; or on a Windows computer, drag the FreeHand Preferences file (FHPrefs.txt) from the FreeHand main directory onto the desktop. Then launch FreeHand. After the launch cycle completes, notice that only the Inspector, Color List, and Color Mixer panels are visible. These are the factory default panels. The other panels are hidden, whether you had them up last time you used the software or not. Tools and other settings have likewise reverted to their factory defaults.

Now quit the program. The last thing FreeHand does before quitting is update the FreeHand Preferences file in either the Preferences folder (for Macs) or the FreeHand main directory (Windows). Because no such file is available to update, FreeHand creates a new one.

Caution

Because FreeHand updates the FreeHand Preferences file only once per session during the quit cycle, it cannot update the file if the program bombs or if your computer crashes. Just as you lose any unsaved changes to your document during a crash, you also lose all preference adjustments made throughout the session. When you restart FreeHand, it loads the preference settings from the previous session because those were the last settings saved.

After quitting FreeHand, drag the FreeHand Preferences file that you moved back into its original location. Your computer will ask you if you want to replace the new file that FreeHand just created. Respond positively by whacking that Return/Enter key. Now relaunch FreeHand and see how your old preference settings have been restored.

The FreeHand Defaults file

The other haven for preference settings is the FreeHand Defaults file (known as the Defaults.ft8 file on Windows machines), which resides in the FreeHand 8 main folder or directory. This file determines the composition and contents of every new file you create in FreeHand. In fact, when you choose File ➪ New, FreeHand actually opens the FreeHand Defaults file and puts it in a new window.

Every setting that is saved with the current document rather than with the FreeHand Preferences file can be stored in the FreeHand Defaults file. These include the following:

✦ **Document setup:** All settings that you can access from the Document Inspector (⌘ /Ctrl-Option/Alt-D). These options affect multipage settings, thumbnail views, page orientation, bleed, and printer resolution.

✦ **Output options:** All settings from the Output Options dialog box, which you access by choosing File ➪ Output. These options affect how a document is printed and exported in the EPS format.

✦ **Default formatting attributes:** Settings from the Text Inspector (accessed by pressing ⌘/Ctrl-T) and the various Text Inspectors (⌘/Ctrl-Option/Alt-P and ⌘/Ctrl-Option/Alt-K). These default attributes include font, style, type size, leading, horizontal scale, kerning, baseline shift, paragraph spacing and indents, letter and word spacing, hyphenation (on or off), alignment, and a few more obscure options, such as effects, rules, and flush zone. In fact, just about every option that can be found in the Text Inspector is saved in the FreeHand Default file. One notable exception is the hyphenation dictionary option. The hyphenation dictionary is saved with the FreeHand Preferences file.

✦ **View menu settings:** Settings from the View menu, including the Preview, Rulers, Info Bar, Guides, Snap to Point, and Snap to Guides commands. The selected view size is also saved.

✦ **Colors and Layers:** All the settings in the Color List, Halftone, Styles, and Layers panel, as well as the Fill and Stroke panels of the Inspector panel.

✦ **Illustration window:** Size and position of the illustration window. If for no other reason than convenience, be sure to create your own defaults document in which you resize the illustration window so that it doesn't fill the entire screen.

✦ **Units:** Units of measure, which are easily accessed from the Units pop-up menu at the bottom of your illustration window.

Note

If you haven't seen FreeHand since the 5.5 days, you'll want to note the newish Modify menu. The constrain option that had been in the Document Setup of the Inspector palette in FreeHand 5.5 has moved to the Modify menu. Another change with the constrain option is that it is no longer a settable preference. If you change the constrain angle to let's say 30 degrees, the next time you launch FreeHand 8, the constrain will be 0 degrees.

You can also create objects that you want to appear in every new document. For example, if you want to include a copyright statement or logo inside each of your drawings, just add the necessary text blocks, lines, and shapes to the defaults file as you would add them to any drawing. Also, you can use the Set Note function, which allows you to attach a nonprinting note to any or all objects on your screen. These could be notes to yourself or revision marks.

When the default settings and objects are in place, save your document inside the FreeHand 8 folder under the name FreeHand Defaults or Defaults.ft8. (If you use a different name, be sure to change the name in the Document panel of the Preferences dialog box. Regardless of name, the file must be inside the FreeHand 8 folder.) Also select the FreeHand Template option from the Save as Type pop-up menu in the Save Document dialog box.

To restore FreeHand's factory default settings, quit FreeHand, throw away the FreeHand Defaults (or Defaults.ft8) file, and relaunch FreeHand. FreeHand does not automatically create a new FreeHand Defaults (or Defaults.ft8) file as it does the FreeHand Preferences file. If you want to customize the document-level settings, you have to make a new defaults file.

The Preferences command

Man, who would have thought customizing your onscreen environment could be so complicated? Or so shamefully prolonged and exhausting? Well, we're not done yet. Now that I've discussed every backdoor method I know for specifying preference settings, it's time to resort to the most obvious solution — the Preferences command (⌘/Ctrl-Shift-D).

The look of the Preferences dialog box has changed from FreeHand 7. A few of the options have been improved with more choices to enable the user to be in total control. Some of the categories have been merged in hopes of streamlining the whole preference experience.

Choosing File ➪ Preferences displays the Preferences dialog box shown in Figure 2-11. The dialog box either features 11 categories along the left (Macs) or 9 panel tabs along the top (Windows). Clicking a category name or a panel tab reveals the corresponding panel. The General panel appears first.

The General panel

The options in this panel let you set preferences pertaining to FreeHand's general behavior when editing your artwork. The following explanations cover the General panel options and all of their gory details:

✦ **Undo's:** FreeHand's versatile Undo command enables you to undo several consecutive operations. You can specify the maximum number of consecutive undos by entering any value between 1 and 100 for this option. Keep in mind that by increasing this value, you decrease the amount of application RAM available to other FreeHand operations. If you change this setting when a file is open, you must save the file, close it, and reopen it for your change to take effect. If you change this setting when no file is open, your change takes effect when you open a new or existing file.

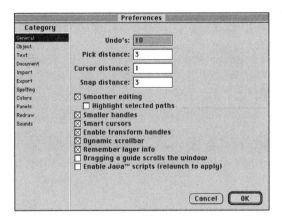

Figure 2-11: The Preferences dialog box showing all the General options.

✦ **Pick Distance:** This option is just the thing for the sloppy selector. It lets you click outside an object and still select it, as long as your click falls within a specified range. For example, the default value of 3 ensures that as long as the arrow cursor is within 3 screen pixels of an object, clicking selects that object. If selecting isn't your forte and you frequently find yourself missing objects, raise the value (5 is the maximum). However, if you're used to precise work and you anticipate creating complex artwork, lower this value to 2, which requires you to click more or less exactly on the objects you want to select.

Caution

Don't lower the Pick Distance value to less than 2, or you'll have a heck of a time manipulating Bézier control handles (the levers that accompany points in a free-form line or shape). A Pick Distance value of 0 makes control handles downright impossible to select. (Too bad this option is a program-level preference instead of a document-level one. Otherwise, you could use it to keep other folks from editing your artwork.)

✦ **Cursor Distance:** FreeHand enables you to move any selected object by pressing one of the four arrow keys. Each keystroke moves the selection the distance entered in the Cursor Distance box, as measured in the units specified in the pop-up menu at the bottom of the illustration window.

✦ **Snap Distance:** This option controls the distance at which a dragged object moves sharply toward — or *snaps* to — a stationary point, grid dot, or guide, as measured in screen pixels. For example, if the Snap Distance value is 3, a dragged object snaps to a guideline any time the object comes within 3 pixels of it. This option also affects how close endpoints must be to each other for you to fuse them together by choosing Modify ➪ Join (⌘/Ctrl-J) and how accurately you must click or drag to select and modify points and handles. You can enter a value from 0 to 5. In my opinion, the default setting is fine.

✦ **Smoother Editing:** This option allows you to edit paths in a more elegant manner. Back in FreeHand 5.5 you had black ugly lines to look at while you were dragging to adjust paths. In FreeHand 8, you have the option to work in that 5.5 view, or check the Smoother Editing box and edit with a cyan colored path, anchor points, and handles. If you choose to uncheck the Highlight Selected Paths option, only the point you have selected will be in color, the path is not highlighted.

✦ **Smaller Handles:** When this option is on, as it is by default, all points (hollow or filled) appear the same size. More to the point, all Bézier handle endpoints display in their smaller version. Turn off this option, and all selected points (hollow) are a bit larger than normal. Also, Bézier handle endpoints become slightly enbiggened (television gave me that word), making them proportionally easier to manipulate.

✦ **Smart Cursors:** FreeHand offers a number of *smart cursors*. These are special cursors that convey a wee more information by augmenting their normal counterparts with little additions in the lower right corner. Smart cursors include the *continue cursor* (the pen cursor with a little spike) that appears when you move the pen tool to a selected endpoint in an open path, and the *snap-to-point cursor* (the arrow cursor with a small square in the lower right corner) that appears when you move the arrow tool over a path's point (provided that the View ⇨ Snap to Point command is active). Turn this option off to see all cursors in their most generic form. But, hey, you might as well leave this option selected — you get more feedback from FreeHand with basically no reduction in performance.

✦ **Enable Transform Handles:** *Transform handles*, a new feature in FreeHand 8, allow you to do a couple of different transformations on the fly. When this option is selected, simply double-click a path and the transform handles appear. When you're done transforming, double-click again and they disappear. If you find this new implementation too intrusive, turn off this option and transform only when you choose a transformation tool or command.

✦ **Dynamic Scrollbar:** Remember the "Dragging the scroll box" section earlier in this chapter? I wrote that when you drag a scroll box, "FreeHand responds to your movements immediately and predictably." My exact words. If you deselect the Dynamic scrollbar option, you make a liar out of me. The scroll box moves without the illustration window updating one iota. So leave this option checked. You pay slightly in performance speed for this convenience, but it's worth it.

✦ **Remember Layer Info:** When active, this option instructs FreeHand to include a tag with every object that tells from which layer it comes. Then, when you copy an object and paste it, FreeHand pastes it to the layer from which it was copied, not to the active layer. If you paste an object into a different document, and that document doesn't include the required layer, FreeHand adds the layer along with the object to the document. This option also affects groups and composite paths. When you group or join two shapes, FreeHand is forced to send them to the same layer. However, when you ungroup or separate them, FreeHand recalls the original layers assigned to the objects and sends them there.

When the Remember Layer Info option is turned off, FreeHand doesn't tag objects. Regardless of where a cut or copied object was originally located, FreeHand pastes it onto the active layer. When you ungroup or separate a group or composite path, the individual objects stay on the same layer.

✦ **Dragging a Guide Scrolls the Window:** When active, this option causes FreeHand to scroll the window when you drag a guide line or guide object. When not active, you can remove a guide line by simply dragging it to a ruler.

✦ **Enable Java Scripts:** Use this to automate complex or repetitive functions such as file conversion.

✦ **Right Mouse Button Magnification (Windows only):** Activate this option and clicking with the right mouse button will toggle your view between actual size (100%) and the Fit Page view. By doing so, you loose the ability to access the content sensitive menus that normally appear when you click with the right mouse button. If you ask me, the benefits of leaving this option off greatly outweigh the advantage of turning it on.

The Object panel

Well, that one wasn't so bad was it? Are you ready to try the second panel? Look at it in Figure 2-12.

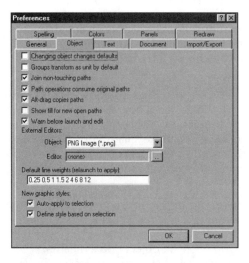

Figure 2-12: Select the Object panel to display options that affect how objects respond to your changes.

For the most part, the options in this panel control how you draw and edit objects. That one near the bottom only looks scary because of all those numbers, but it's really very straightforward. Pull up a chair and let me tell you about all these options:

✦ **Changing Object Changes Defaults:** This option controls the default attributes assigned to all objects in the current illustration. When the option is selected, changing the formatting of text or the fill or stroke of an object also changes the default setting within the document. The next object you create is formatted, filled, or stroked identically. If you deselect this option, the default attributes remain the same as those in the FreeHand Defaults file. (If you are trying to set up a new Defaults file, definitely select this option.)

✦ **Groups Transform as Unit by Default:** The first time you use FreeHand, this check box is off; it ought to be on. When active, the option ensures that all objects in a group rotate, scale, slant, and otherwise transform as a single unit — as if they are part of a collective being, like the Borg. (You know, from *Star Trek: The Next Generation*. Huh? Oh yeah?? Well, *you're* a nerd for *not* watching it.) By contrast, when you turn off this option, FreeHand transforms all objects independently. The result is usually fairly chaotic. (For more information, read the "Grouping and Protecting Objects" section of Chapter 6.)

In the application, this option is associated with the Transform as a Unit check box in the Object Inspector. Your setting here determines the status of that check box by default. However, the check box enables you to override the default setting on a group-by-group basis.

✦ **Join Non-Touching Paths:** The Modify ➪ Join (⌘/Ctrl-J) command joins lines in one of two ways. If two endpoints — one from each line — are close enough to each other, it fuses the two points into one. If the endpoints are separated by a greater number of pixels than are specified in the Snap Distance option box (in the General panel) (described previously), the command draws a segment between the points — that is, as long as the Join Non-Touching Paths option is checked. If you turn the option off, the Join command either fuses two endpoints into one or it ignores you.

✦ **Path Operations Consume Original Paths:** Boy, it must be getting close to lunchtime. This option just reminded me that I'm hungry. Basically, what this obscurely worded option means is that, if this option is checked, path operations, such as those listed in the Operations panel, and the Modify ➪ Combine & Modify ➪ Alter Path submenus are performed on the selected objects, leaving them altered. If you do not check this option, FreeHand creates copies of the original objects and performs the path operations on the copies, leaving the originals directly underneath the copies, and intact.

✦ **Option/Alt-Drag Copies Paths:** When active, you can drag away a clone of an object, leaving the original intact, by holding down the Option/Alt key and dragging the object. Go ahead and leave this option on as a nifty way to bypass the Clipboard when making a copy of an object.

Tip

If you want to clone an entire group of objects, make sure you first begin dragging and then hold down the Option/Alt key. If you hold down the Option/Alt key before you start dragging, FreeHand thinks that you are selecting one item within the group. You then end up cloning only one object when you drag.

✦ **Show Fill for New Open Paths:** In FreeHand 7, fills for open paths would not display onscreen. Not a real strong point for old FreeHand. But, fear not, things are better in FreeHand 8. Open path fills show up just as expected, that is, provided you leave this option selected. If you do choose to turn this option off, only open paths created after you turn it off are affected.

✦ **Warn Before Launch and Edit:** Logically, this option should follow the next option, External Editors, since its functionality is contingent on whether you choose to have an external editor. Anyhow, provided you've selected an external editor, checking this option guarantees that FreeHand will prompt you for permission to launch that editor whenever you choose the Edit ➪ External Editor command.

✦ **External Editors:** Select the particular application you want FreeHand to automatically launch (or at least attempt to) when you choose Edit ➪ External Editor. For example, TIFFS could launch Photoshop, or XRes LRG image could launch Xres.

✦ **Default Line Weights:** This item lets you edit the contents of the Width pop-up menu in the Stroke Inspector. The text field's contents are the nine preset line weights. You can add as many line weights as you want, as long as each number is separated by a space. You can delete line weights you don't want as well. Your edits here take effect after you relaunch FreeHand. Keep in mind that these values are measured in points ($\frac{1}{72}$ inch). A value of 0.25 appears in the submenu as Hairline.

✦ **New Graphic Styles: Auto-Apply to Selection:** Stay with me on this one because it makes sense once you understand the choice. When you create or select an object, be it either a text block or a graphic element, FreeHand tags that object with a style. So let's say, for example, that you select an object that FreeHand associates with a style called Fred. Now, you modify the selected path. It looks wa-a-a-ay different. You then choose New from the Style panel's Options pop-up menu — say that one a few times fast. FreeHand creates a new style that's based on your selection's attributes. You call your new style Lestat. This poses some questions: What style is associated with your original selection? Is it a Fred or a Lestat? You have the power to make this decision. If you enable the Auto-Apply to Selection option, your original selection will now have the new Lestat style. If you do not enable this option, your selection is remembered as a modified Fred — an outcast in all societies.

✦ **New Graphic Styles: Define Style Based on Selection:** This is another one of those leave-it-on items. Normally, when you create a new graphic style in the Styles panel, FreeHand bases the style on the selected object. If you disable this option however, FreeHand just copies the default style, requiring you to manually change the new style later on down the line.

The Text panel

Don't start lagging behind now; we've only scratched the surface of the world of preferences! The Text panel is next on the agenda and appears, in all of its glory, in Figure 2-13. The options in this panel pertain to FreeHand's defaults for creating and manipulating text blocks.

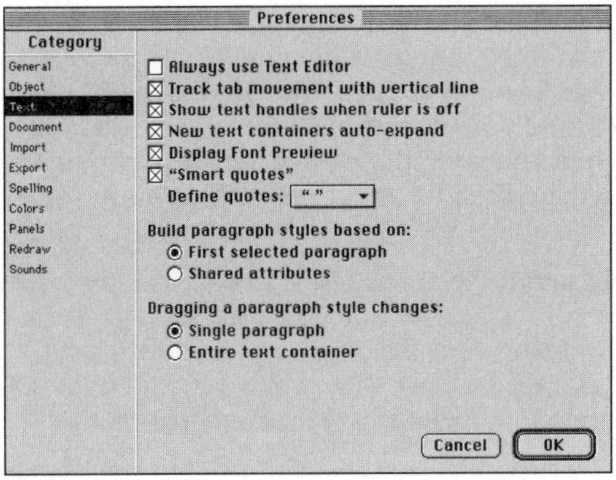

Figure 2-13: The Text panel controls FreeHand's defaults for working with text blocks.

The following explanations should assist you in determining which settings can best facilitate your text work. Base your decisions on the type of text work that you do.

✦ **Always Use Text Editor:** When this option is active, whenever you create a new text object or edit an existing one, FreeHand automatically brings up the Text Editor for text entry. When this preference is not active, you enter and edit text directly in your document. Although the Text Editor is very useful if you work a lot with small type, I think it is easier to leave the option off and choose the Text Editor from the Text menu as you need it .

The trouble with making this option active is that you cannot use the Text Editor in conjunction with the text ruler, which makes setting tabs a bear. It's one or the other. However, with this option not active, you can always invoke the Text Editor by pressing ⌘/Ctrl-Shift-E. Another factor to consider is that enabling this option does slightly slow FreeHand's performance.

✦ **Track Tab Movement with Vertical Line:** When this option is active, FreeHand displays a vertical line in your document as you drag to place a tab. The vertical line enables you to see where the tab lines up with your text. The vertical line disappears after you release the mouse button. Activating this preference does slightly slow down FreeHand's performance. Nevertheless, I keep this option selected because I enjoy the feature. It's your choice.

✦ **Show Text Handles When Ruler Is Off:** FreeHand surrounds a selected text block with a bounding box that has text handles attached to it. Your setting for this option determines whether Freehand displays this bounding box around the text block when you type.

If your View ➪ Text Rulers command is active, then FreeHand displays the bounding box regardless of your setting here. Also, if you select a text block, FreeHand displays the bounding box. Your setting here is only considered when you are not showing your text ruler and are typing text. In this situation, FreeHand displays only the text if this option is not active, and the text and bounding box when it is active. The only purpose the bounding box serves in this situation is to visually remind you of your text block's borders. You cannot edit these borders while you are typing. However, displaying the bounding box does slow down FreeHand's performance. Therefore, you probably want to leave this one off.

✦ **New Text Containers Auto-Expand:** FreeHand offers two methods for creating text blocks. The first method is most useful when creating paragraph text. You drag with the text tool to define your margins and then begin typing. FreeHand then automatically wraps the text when you reach the right margin. This preference has no bearing on this method of creating text blocks.

The second method is good for creating captions or single-line text blocks. You click the text tool in your document where you want the top left corner of the text block to appear, and begin typing. If this option is selected, FreeHand does not wrap the text. It continues to expand the text block to accommodate your typing. To wrap the text you must press Return/Enter. If you deselect this option, FreeHand makes all text blocks 3 inches wide and 2 inches tall. Because you can edit these dimensions after creating the text object, I would leave this preference on.

✦ **Display Font Preview:** New to FreeHand 8 and more handy than a dog trained to answer the phone and take messages, this option, when selected, displays an example any font highlighted in the Font pop-up menu—true for both the Text toolbar's and the Text inspector's.

✦ **Smart Quotes:** This option lets FreeHand use the popular curly typographer's quotes instead of inch marks when you type the "and" keys on the keyboard. You have six types of pop-up quotes to choose from.

✦ **Build Paragraph Styles Based on:** This option's setting affects how paragraph styles are defined when you create a new style that's based on your current text selection. If you choose the First Selected Paragraph option, then the new style reflects the attributes of the first paragraph in the current selection. If you choose Shared Attributes, then the style comprises only the attributes that are the same for all paragraphs in the current selection. So, if all paragraphs in the current selection have different leadings, then the new style will have no setting for leading. When you apply the style to text, the text's leading will remain unchanged.

✦ **Dragging a Paragraph Style Changes:** Your selection for this option determines what happens when you apply a text style to a multiparagraph text block. If you select Single Paragraph, then you can apply a different text style to each paragraph in the text block. If you select Entire Text Container, then when you apply a text style to any paragraph in the text block, you affect all paragraphs in the text block.

The Document panel

Next on the agenda is the Document panel, which you can plainly see in Figure 2-14. The options give you control over page related issues such as how FreeHand displays a page upon opening, how you navigate around with multiple pages and where page attributes are saved.

The following explanations should assist you in setting your document preferences.

✦ **Restore View When Opening Document:** Leave this item checked if you want FreeHand to open your documents at the magnification under which they were last saved. If you deselect this option, FreeHand opens a document so that its first page fits in the FreeHand window.

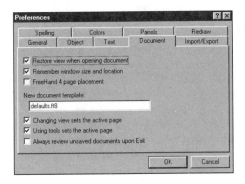

Figure 2-14: Just as you wouldn't want to mess with Texas, don't you go messing with the Document pane; but do feel free to change any of the options as you see fit.

✦ **Remember Window Size and Location:** When working on a document, you can change the size of the illustration window by dragging the size box in the lower right corner. You can also move the window by dragging the title bar. Normally, FreeHand saves the size and location of the illustration window along with the document so that the window appears in the same place when you next open the document. But if you deactivate this preference, FreeHand doesn't save this information with the document. Files without this information open inside a window with the same dimensions and positioning as a new document. You probably want to leave this preference selected.

✦ **FreeHand 4 Page Placement:** The pasteboard in FreeHand 8 is gigantic — an astounding 22 × 22 feet. This is much larger than FreeHand 4's pasteboard, which was a paltry 56 × 56 inches. If you plan to open your documents in

FreeHand 4, then make sure you select this preference. Enabling it causes FreeHand to place a colored rectangle on your pasteboard that delineates the FreeHand 4 acceptable reaches of your pasteboard. This rectangle appears in the bottom left corner of your pasteboard. On noncolor systems, it appears black. When you choose to add a new page, FreeHand automatically places the new page within these limits. After that, it's your responsibility to leave them there.

✦ **New Document Template:** Earlier in this chapter, I talked about the FreeHand Defaults file. But, in case you missed that part, FreeHand ships with a file called FreeHand Defaults (or Defaults.ft8 on Windows systems), which it uses as a template every time you create a new document. This file includes information such as page size and unit of measure. You can customize your work environment and save it as a defaults file. After doing so, enter the name of the new file here that is to be used as a template when creating new files.

✦ **Changing View Sets the Active Page:** Your setting here establishes how FreeHand determines which page is active — as displayed in the Inspector's Page panel — when more than one page is visible at a time. Enable this item if you want FreeHand to switch active pages when you scroll your document so that a different page dominates your view.

✦ **Using Tools Sets the Active Page:** This option is a close cousin of the preceding option. This one lets you make a page active by using a tool in it. Once again, I recommend that you leave this one active.

✦ **Always Review Unsaved Documents Upon Quit/Exit:** If you have unsaved documents open when you choose to quit FreeHand, you will be reminded about that fact, regardless of your setting here. The difference is that when you have this option selected, FreeHand alerts you before closing each unsaved document and asks if you want to save the document. If you do not have this option checked, FreeHand alerts you that you have unsaved documents and asks you if you want to review them. At that point, you can either choose to review them and have FreeHand alert you for each document — as if you had checked this option — or you can choose to quit anyway. FreeHand quits without alerting you for each and every open unsaved document.

The Import/Export panel (Windows)

This is the "turning point" panel. Once you finish the Import/Export, shown in Figure 2-15, you're more than halfway through the preference panels. Oh, right, you don't care. I forgot that you're reading this stuff out of order. You're fresh back from a game of golf or a particularly yummy lunch, and this is probably the first paragraph you've looked at all day. But me — I've been writing about preference settings for so long I'm starting to dream about them. More like bone-chilling nightmares, really. As in, quoth the raven, "preference settings!" Dig?

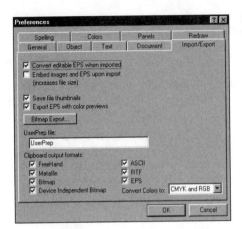

Figure 2-15: The Import/Export panel, for those Windows users who dare.

But before they lock me up, let me quickly explain the Import/Export panel. It contains options that affect the previews associated with *EPS files*. Briefly, an EPS file is designed to be placed into a page-layout program such as PageMaker or QuarkXPress. The EPS file includes two parts, a PostScript definition of the drawing that gets downloaded to the printer and a TIFF preview that you can see on-screen inside the page-layout program.

Here's how the options work:

✦ **Convert Editable EPS When Imported:** When you open an EPS graphic using File ➪ Open, FreeHand does its best to convert the graphic into an editable document. However, when you import the graphic using File ➪ Import (⌘/ Ctrl-R), FreeHand imports it as a static picture. Oh sure, you can transform the picture by moving it, rotating it, and so on, but you can't change the location of individual points and objects inside the graphic. If you want FreeHand to tear apart imported EPS graphics into FreeHand objects so that you can edit them, enable this item. (If FreeHand can't tear apart the graphic, as in the case of EPS documents created in previous versions of FreeHand, it imports it as a static picture.) I leave this option active so that I can combine and edit objects from different documents.

✦ **Embed Images and EPS Upon Import (Increases File Size):** To save space, FreeHand references imported TIFF (as well as other bitmaps) and EPS artwork on disk rather than saving them in their entirety with the rest of the document. However, this means that you need access to the original TIFF and EPS files any time you open the FreeHand document. If you enable this item, FreeHand includes the full code from an imported EPS graphic with a saved document. The program also converts imported TIFF images to embedded EPS code. Your FreeHand files will be much larger, but you won't need access to the original EPS and TIFF files. What's more, placing is slower with this preference enabled. Enable this item only if you own a big hard drive with a large amount of free space.

✦ **Save File Thumbnails:** This feature creates a thumbnail used by other applications, and by Freehand. The thumbnail is displayed in the Open or the Import dialog box when the filename is selected so you can see it before selecting.

✦ **Export EPS with Color Previews:** If you don't select this option, any artwork that you export from FreeHand as an EPS file will have a black-and-white PICT or TIFF associated with it.

✦ **Bitmap Export:** Click the Bitmap Export button to display the Bitmap Export Defaults dialog box. Here you can set the default resolution and anti-aliasing values for exporting a bitmap. You can also decide whether to include an alpha channel and if that alpha channel will, in turn, include a background.

✦ **UserPrep File:** A UserPrep file contains PostScript routines to download to the printer with your document. In general, this file fixes a problem FreeHand has discovered with a particular printer. FreeHand 8 ships with a number of UserPrep files. They install into a folder called UserPrep Files, located in your FreeHand 8 folder or directory. FreeHand also installs a UserPrep ReadMe into this folder. This ReadMe gives detailed information on what each of these files offers and at what price. If you experience output problems, read through the UserPrep ReadMe to determine if a UserPrep file exists that resolves this problem. If one does, then enter its name in this option box.

If you're a PostScript wiz — which includes two or three folks out of FreeHand's nine billion users — you've possibly written your own UserPrep file. If so, place the file in the UserPrep Files folder and enter its name in this option box.

✦ **Clipboard Output Formats:** This preference comes into play when you're switching between FreeHand and other applications (including the Mac or Windows desktop). If the Clipboard contains any of these formats, FreeHand requires additional time to perform behind-the-scenes Clipboard maintenance when switching between applications. If you deselect these options, FreeHand doesn't copy the formats to the Clipboard, resulting in a Clipboard with no contents.

Here's the short of it: If you are copying and pasting between FreeHand and other applications, by all means leave the options for formats that you are using selected. If you are switching between FreeHand and other applications, but not copying and pasting between them, you can speed up your application switching time by turning these puppies off. This preference does not affect copying and pasting within FreeHand.

✦ **Convert Colors To:** When you copy and paste objects between FreeHand and some other application, you can opt to have the objects' colors preserved as they appear in FreeHand or to convert them. For example, if you're using both RGB and CMYK colors in the items that you cut from FreeHand and you want the items' original colors preserve once you paste them into another program, choose the CMYK And RGB option from the Convert Colors To pop-up menu. If you want all the colors to show up as their RGB equivalents, choose the RGB option.

The Import panel (Macs)

The Import/Export panel, shown in Figure 2-16, is the import version of the Windows' Import/Export panel. On the Mac, the import options are separated from the its export options.

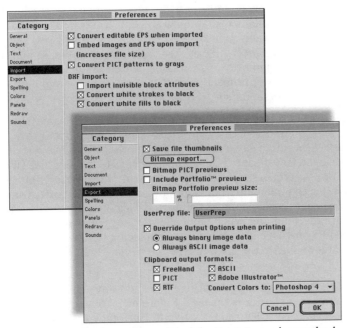

Figure 2-16: The Import panel and the Export panel, smushed together for the discriminating Mac user.

As with its Windows counterpart, the Import panel contains options that affect the previews associated with EPS files. Briefly, an EPS file is designed to be placed into a page-layout program such as PageMaker or QuarkXPress. The EPS file includes two parts, a PostScript definition of the drawing that gets downloaded to the printer and a PICT preview that you can see on-screen inside the page-layout program.

PICT is part of the QuickDraw screen-display language used by the Macintosh system software. Generally, DOS- or Windows-based applications don't support PICT, so an EPS file for the Windows platform gets a TIFF preview, which is always bitmapped.

Here's how the options work:

✦ **Convert Editable EPS When Imported:** When you open an EPS graphic using File ➪ Open, FreeHand does its best to convert the graphic into an editable document. However, when you import the graphic using File ➪ Import (⌘/Ctrl-R), FreeHand imports it as a static picture. Oh sure, you can transform the picture by moving it, rotating it, and so on, but you can't change the location of individual points and objects inside the graphic. If you want FreeHand to tear apart imported EPS graphics into FreeHand objects so that you can edit them, enable this item. (If FreeHand can't tear apart the graphic, as in the case of EPS documents created in previous versions of FreeHand, it imports it as a static picture.) I leave this option active so that I can combine and edit objects from different documents.

✦ **Embed Images and EPS Upon Import (Increases File Size):** To save space, FreeHand references imported TIFF (as well as other bitmaps) and EPS artwork on disk rather than saving them in their entirety with the rest of the document. However, this means that you need access to the original TIFF and EPS files any time you open the FreeHand document. If you enable this item, FreeHand includes the full code from an imported EPS graphic with a saved document. The program also converts imported TIFF images to embedded EPS code. Your FreeHand files will be much larger, but you won't need access to the original EPS and TIFF files. What's more, placing is slower with this preference enabled. Enable this item only if you own a big hard drive with a large amount of free space.

✦ **Convert PICT Patterns to Grays:** MacDraw Pro and Canvas let you to fill objects with bitmapped patterns (as does FreeHand). You can either import these drawings (via the PICT format) with patterns intact, or you can convert the patterns to gray. This option has no effect on the exporting of bitmapped patterns or the speed at which the screen redraws. As a rule, bitmapped patterns are hideously ugly, so leave this option turned on.

✦ **DXF Import:** Choose whether certain features of the 3-D file format DXF are incorporated. Objects imported from 3-D are often modeled with a white surface, and when imported into FreeHand as white, they would have very little volume shading. Two selections, Convert White Surface to Black and Convert White Fills to Black, solve this problem. They assign a dark fill to DXF data so that it will be correctly shaded. If your DXF file contains transparent portions, click Import Invisible Block Attributes to have FreeHand preserve the file intact.

The Export panel (Macs)

The Export panel, also shown in Figure 2-16, provides you with a bull-hunking lot of export options. They work as follows:

✦ **Save File Thumbnails:** This feature creates a thumbnail used by other applications, and by Freehand. The thumbnail is displayed in the Open or the Import dialog box when the filename is selected so you can see it before selecting.

✦ **Bitmap Export:** Click on the Bitmap Export button to display the Bitmap Export Defaults dialog box Here you can set the default resolution and anti-aliasing values for exporting a bitmap. You can also decide whether to include an alpha channel and if that alpha channel will, in turn, include a background.

✦ **Bitmap PICT Previews:** FreeHand allows you to generate object-oriented PICT previews. This means that you can accurately view an EPS file at any view size in PageMaker or QuarkXPress. However, it also means the artwork takes longer — sometimes much longer — to display. To speed things up, select the Bitmap PICT Previews option, which saves a static, bitmapped version of your drawing as it appears at actual size.

✦ **Include Portfolio Preview:** If you use your EPS file with Portfolio, you may want to save a second preview especially for Portfolio.

✦ **Bitmap Portfolio Preview Size:** To enable this option you must select both Bitmap PICT Previews and Include Portfolio Preview. You can then use the slider or text box to adjust the size of the bitmapped Portfolio preview. For best results however, leave the Bitmap Portfolio Preview Size value set to 100 percent. This way, Portfolio accurately reports the file size.

✦ **UserPrep File:** A UserPrep file contains PostScript routines to download to the printer with your document. In general, this file fixes a problem FreeHand has discovered with a particular printer. FreeHand 8 ships with a number of UserPrep files. They install into a folder called UserPrep Files, located in your FreeHand 8 folder or directory. Freehand also installs a UserPrep ReadMe into this folder. This ReadMe gives detailed information on what each of these files offers and at what price. If you experience output problems, read through the UserPrep ReadMe to determine if a UserPrep file exists that resolves this problem. If one does, then enter its name in this option box.

If you're a PostScript wiz — which includes two or three folks out of FreeHand's nine billion users — you've possibly written your own UserPrep file. If so, place the file in the UserPrep Files folder and enter its name in this option box.

✦ **Override Output Options When Printing:** Wow, we're really delving into TechnoDweeb city here folks. (You know, "Two brains for every boy.") But it's not my fault. I'm just covering these suckers in order. Okay, first some background: The settings in the File ⇨ Output Options dialog box affect both how a FreeHand drawing is printed and how it's exported to the EPS format. One set of options in this dialog box, Image Data, controls how TIFF images are encoded. The default option, Binary, is the most efficient. But if you select a different option, ASCII or None, FreeHand changes the encoding when saving the EPS file as well. If you enable the Override Output Options When Printing option, however, you can specify separate settings for printing and exporting. For exporting, FreeHand uses your Output Options dialog box's Image Data setting. For printing, FreeHand uses your Override Output Options When Printing preferences setting. You must choose between Always Binary Image Data and Always ASCII Image Data. Fair warning: Choosing Always ASCII Image Data prints slow as molasses.

✦ **Clipboard Output Formats:** This preference comes into play when you are switching between FreeHand and other applications (including the Mac or Windows desktop). If the Clipboard contains any of these formats, FreeHand requires additional time to perform behind-the-scenes Clipboard maintenance when switching between applications. If you deselect these options, FreeHand doesn't copy the formats to the Clipboard, resulting in a Clipboard with no contents.

Here's the short of it. If you are copying and pasting between FreeHand and other applications, by all means leave the options for formats that you are using selected. If you are switching between FreeHand and other applications, but not copying and pasting between them, you can speed up your application switching time by turning these puppies off. This preference does not affect copying and pasting within FreeHand.

✦ **Convert Colors To:** When you copy and paste objects between FreeHand and some other application, you can opt to have the objects' colors preserved as they appear in FreeHand or to convert them. For example, if you're using both RGB and CMYK colors in the items that you cut from FreeHand and you want the items' original colors preserved once you paste them into another program, choose the CMYK and RGB option from the Convert Colors To pop-up menu. If you want all the colors to show up as their RGB equivalents, choose the RGB option.

The Spelling panel

The Spelling panel gives you two calls on how the spell checker works and one for adding new words to the dictionary. Figure 2-17 displays the panel with its original default settings. Although I retained the default settings for the spell checker, I changed my setting for the method used to add words to the dictionary.

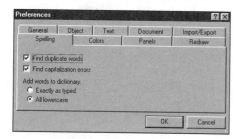

Figure 2-17: The Spelling panel preferences determine how the spell checker works.

Based on the following explanations, make your own setting decisions.

✦ **Find Duplicate Words:** Leave this option enabled if you want the FreeHand spell checker to alert you when it finds the same word twice in a row, such as *the the* in the following sentence: I went to the the store.

✦ **Find Capitalization Errors:** Leave this option enabled if you want FreeHand to alert you if it finds that the first word after a period begins with a lowercase letter.

✦ **Add Words to Dictionary:** You can choose between two options here. When you choose Exactly as Typed, then FreeHand adds a word to the dictionary exactly as it appears in your document. So, if you choose to add *FreeHand*, then the word goes into the dictionary with both the *F* and the *H* in uppercase. If you choose the All Lowercase option, then the word goes into the dictionary as *freehand*. I'm sure you can understand this feature's worth when writing about anything computer-related.

The Colors panel

This panel, shown in Figure 2-18, offers several procedures that ease color organization. These features are understated, yet extremely considerate of a user's needs. They seem to be genuinely directed at eliminating tedious, repetitive tasks.

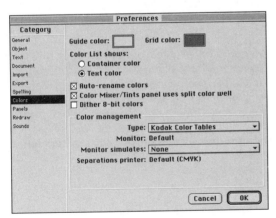

Figure 2-18: The Color panel dictates what and how colors are used in the FreeHand environment.

The options in the Color panel work as follows:

✦ **Guide Color/Grid Color:** To change the color of ruler guides or grid dots, click the corresponding color swatch. After the color picker surfaces, make the desired changes.

✦ **Color List Shows:** Text objects possess a color for the actual letters and a background color for the object that contains the text. This is definitely a good thing. If the two colors were the same, you wouldn't be able to read the text. Your selection here determines which of these two colors the Color List displays in its upper left corner when a text object is selected.

✦ **Auto-Rename Colors:** When this option is checked and you change a Color List color, FreeHand updates the name of the new color to correctly show the new color's components. This becomes important when using automatically generated color names (brought to you by the Xtras ⇨ Colors ⇨ Name All Colors command) and then changing them either by using the Color Mixer or by choosing the Xtras ⇨ Colors ⇨ Randomize Named Colors command. Boy, would I leave this one checked. Unchecked, it can lead to some serious confusion or outright lies, to be more honest.

✦ **Color Mixer/Tints Panel Uses Split Color Well:** When this option is checked, the left side of Color Mixer or the Tints panel maintains the original color before you began tweaking it, while the right side reflects your changes. This enables you to compare the two. When it's not checked, the entire box reflects your changes. I've tried but cannot come up with one good reason to deselect this option.

✦ **Color Management:** FreeHand supports the Kodak Digital Science Color Management System (CMS) for color matching. What this means is that your Color Management System can calibrate your monitor to the Kodak software (if it has been loaded) so what you see on your screen matches what you print.

Here's how it works: Choose a monitor profile from the Monitor pop-up menu. In the Monitor simulates pop-up you have three choices: None, Composite printer, and Separations printer. You then choose from a pop-up menu available composite printer profiles as well as separations printer profiles. To have the composite printer's color output match the separations printer, check the box for Composite simulates separations. The RGB image default allows you to choose the monitor display of an RGB image to match how the image was created.

The Panels panel

Let's keep the momentum going. This preference panel, appearing in Figure 2-19, concerns how panels will behave. Most of you will eventually adjust these settings to conform with how you work.

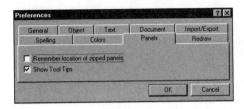

Figure 2-19: Without meaning to repeat myself, I must say that the Panels panel is the panel to direct the behavior of panels.

The following panel preferences give you more options for conforming your setup to your tastes.

✦ **Remember Location of Zipped Panels:** This is an interesting option. If you like to keep your panel collapsed and out of the way when you don't need it, you select this option. It causes FreeHand to remember two separate locations for each panel: one for when it's open, and one for when it's collapsed. Then, whenever you need to use the panel, press its keyboard shortcut. The panel pops open where you last used it. After you finish working with it, click the top right corner to collapse it. The panel collapses and hops right back to the last position held in its collapsed state.

✦ **Show Tool Tips:** This feature has FreeHand updating tool tips as you select various shortcuts to modify their performance, like pressing Option/Alt to drag-copy.

The Redraw panel

The check boxes in the Redraw panel, portrayed in Figure 2-20, are designed to accelerate the pace at which FreeHand redraws objects in the Preview mode. As a general rule of thumb, fewer options checked means a faster redraw speed and a lower quality screen representation

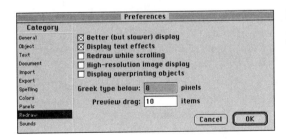

Figure 2-20: The options in the Redraw panel impact the speed with which FreeHand handles in the preview mode.

The options in the Redraw panel work as follows:

✦ **Better (But Slower) Display:** This option controls the display of linear, logarithmic, and radial gradations in the preview mode. When selected, gradations appear to contain up to 256 steps on a 24-bit monitor and 33 dithered steps on an 8-bit monitor or lower. If the option is deselected, only nine steps are assigned to a gradient. If the issue here were appearance alone, it would be a no-brainer. You would activate this option. However, what you gain in appearance, you lose in performance speed. Set your priorities and then decide on your setting for this preference. This option has no effect on blends, which always display at maximum quality.

✦ **Display Text Effects:** When turned on, FreeHand displays its predefined inline, shadow, strikethrough, underline, and zoom effects as closely as possible to the way they will print. When you turn the option off, the text looks as if no effect is applied. In either case, the text prints accurately. Again, turn the option off to speed up screen display.

✦ **Redraw While Scrolling:** This should be called the MTV-Generation Immediate Gratification option. When it is selected, FreeHand redraws the screen continuously as you drag a scroll box or drag the page with the grabber hand. Keep this option off for faster scrolling, assuming you can stand the suspense.

✦ **High-Resolution Image Display:** This option controls the onscreen appearance of imported images in the Preview mode. When the option is selected, FreeHand displays imported images at their full resolution. When High-Resolution Image Display is turned off, FreeHand simplifies the image, displaying fewer pixels. Turning the option off greatly speeds up screen redraw time but diminishes clarity and detail in the image. This option's setting does not affect the image's printed appearance. Large TIFFS or LRG images from XRes can completely disable FreeHand.

✦ **Display Overprinting Objects:** When this option is active, FreeHand fills objects that you have chosen to overprint with tiny little white O's. Don't worry, they don't print. FreeHand puts them there to help you to keep track of which objects you've set to overprint. Incidentally, you set an object to overprint in the Inspector's Basic Fill panel.

✦ **Greek Type Below ___ Pixels:** This option controls the perceived type size at which FreeHand no longer tries to display type accurately on-screen and instead replaces lines of text with thin gray bars — a feature known as *greeking*. For example, if you enter a value of 8 for this option (the default setting), text set to 8 points or smaller appears gray at actual size; 16-point type and smaller appears gray at 50 percent view size; 32-point type and smaller appears gray at 25 percent view size; and so on. The benefit of greeking text is that FreeHand can display gray bars faster than it can generate individual characters. To turn off the greeking feature completely, enter a value of 0 for this option.

✦ **Preview Drag ___ Items:** If you select and immediately drag an object in the illustration window, FreeHand shows you a rectangular dotted outline that demonstrates the boundaries of the object. By contrast, if you hold down your mouse button, pause for a second or two, and then begin dragging, FreeHand displays the object accurately throughout the drag. This is called a *drag preview*. By default, however, FreeHand dumps the drag preview when you drag more than ten objects, regardless of whether you pause or start dragging right away. FreeHand does this because it takes more time to animate multiple objects than to animate just one. By entering a higher number in the Preview Drag option (say, 16), you tell FreeHand to preview drags as long as that number (16) or fewer objects are selected.

Tip

An even better alternative for previewing dragged objects is to press the Option/Alt key any time while dragging. Regardless of how many objects are selected or what the Preview Drag value is, pressing Option/Alt displays the objects in their entirety. So leave the Preview Drag value set to 1 and use the Option/Alt key to preview. This way, you get quick drags on a regular basis. When you want to be able to see what's going on, press the Option/Alt key. Just remember to release the Option/Alt key *before* you let go of the mouse button or you'll end up with a copy of the objects.

The Sounds panel (Macs)

FreeHand 3.1 introduced this hidden feature, which I like to call *sonic snapping*. The feature plays a sound whenever a point snapped to another point, grid dot, or guideline. However, you had to use ResEdit to get to it. Now you can access it inside the Preferences dialog box by selecting Sounds, shown in Figure 2-21, which is really great because it makes it easier to turn the feature off once you get sick of it.

Here's how it works. Go to the Sounds panel. Select the sounds that you want to associate with each kind of snap from the pop-up menus. Each pop-up menu lists sounds loaded into your System file. Click the Play button if you can't remember what a selected sound sounds like (or if you simply want to amuse yourself). Select the None option from the pop-up menu if you don't want to hear a particular snap. You also have two other options:

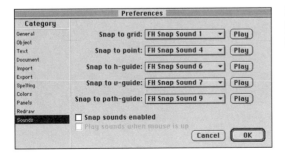

Figure 2-21: Accessing the Sounds panel inside the Preference dialog box.

✦ **Snap Sounds Enabled:** Select this option to instruct FreeHand to play the sounds. Now every time a snap occurs, you'll hear a chirp, whistle, explosion, car crash, cult movie quote, or whatever sound you selected.

✦ **Play Sounds When Mouse Is Up:** Only available when the Snap Sounds Enabled option is checked, this option allows you to hear sounds even when you're just moving your mouse around without dragging. What a nuisance! Leave this option off.

In fact, if you want my opinion, leave this entire feature off. If you activate it, you'll quickly learn it turns your computer into a noise machine. If you spend any amount of time on the phone, talking to clients, listening to music or news, or just plain enjoying the little bit of silence left in the industrialized world, you'll go nuts within eight minutes — plus or minus 15 seconds — after selecting Snap Sounds Enabled.

A concluding remark about setting your preferences

Finally, I have a word to the wise about changing your preferences. After you've weighed my words of wisdom, deliberated carefully, gone through deep soul-searching, and selected each of your preferences, quit FreeHand and relaunch it. One reason for doing so: a couple of preferences require the relaunch. But also, you've been mucking around with many settings. If anything went wrong at this point and you crashed, you would need to read through this entire section and choose your settings again. Why tempt fate like that? Just quit and restart. Please. FreeHand then writes all of your new settings to your Freehand Preferences file, and they'll be safe.

✦   ✦   ✦

Drawing in FreeHand

Constructing Paths

Venturing Down the Garden Path

Now that you've got a feel for the layout of FreeHand 8, it's time for you to develop a sense for how to use this powerful little drawing program. Let's start with the basics: the tools and commands that allow you to jump right into the creation process. More to the point, you learn how to use FreeHand's drawing tools and a few of their related commands. I think you'll find it considerably more satisfying than staring at the screen and just visualizing your drawing.

Half of FreeHand's tools are devoted to the mundane and sometimes unnerving task of drawing. I describe seven of these toolbox tools — rectangle, oval (or ellipse), polygon, line, freehand, pen, and bézigon — in this chapter. In addition, I discuss two Xtras: the arc and spiral tools — but you won't find them in the toolbox. They reside in your Xtra Tools panel (⌘/Ctrl-Option/Alt-X). The lone drawing-orientated holdout from the toolbox — the trace tool — is discussed in Chapter 4.

To keep things as straightforward as possible, I've divided this chapter into three major sections:

✦ **Geometric Shapes:** This section discusses the prosaic rectangle and oval tools, as well as the slightly more interesting polygon tool. I also introduce you to the arc and spiral tools. Although most newborns could sit down and use these tools without my help, I feel duty-bound to explain them. However, one entry — "Geometric shapes at an angle" — bears quick reading by one and all.

✦ **Straight and Free-Form Paths:** This section covers the line and freehand tools. The line tool takes all of three or four seconds to explain, but the freehand tool is remarkably capable and lends itself to a variety of drawing situations.

✦ **The Subterranean World of Bézier Curves:** If you're a beginner, you may want to skip this section for now. Although Bézier curves are incredibly powerful, you may find them somewhat bewildering at first. Like single-malt Scotch and Tom Waits, Bézier curves are an acquired taste. But once you learn to love them, you'll never go back.

Geometric Shapes

FreeHand offers five tools for creating geometric shapes: the rectangle, oval, arc, spiral, and polygon tools. You operate each tool by dragging with it from one location to another. The points at which you begin and end the drag signify the boundaries of the rectangle, oval, arc, spiral, or polygon. Although limited in utility, these geometric shapes are very easy to draw because they involve no planning and little guesswork.

Drawing a rectangle

Consider the rectangle tool. After selecting this tool, drag inside the illustration window to create a rectangle. This process is the same one you use to create a rectangle in all graphics applications that run on the Mac and Windows.

One corner of the rectangle is determined by the point at which you begin to drag; the opposite corner occurs at the point at which you release (see Figure 3-1). The two remaining corners line up vertically and horizontally with their neighbors. A fifth point, called the *center point*, is created at the center of the shape. The center point of a rectangle is always visible in the keyline mode but is visible in the Preview mode only when you are moving or transforming the shape.

If you press the Option/Alt key while drawing with the rectangle tool, the beginning of your drag becomes the center point of the rectangle, as shown in Figure 3-2. As before, the release point becomes one of the rectangle's corners; it also determines the distance and direction from each of the remaining three corners to the center point.

Rectangle tool

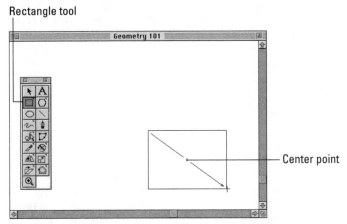

Figure 3-1: Operate the rectangle tool by dragging from one corner to the opposite corner of the desired shape, as indicated by the arrow.

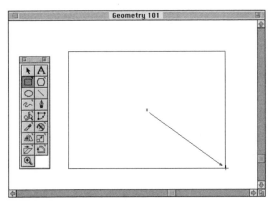

Figure 3-2: Option/Alt-drag with the rectangle tool to draw a rectangle from the center outward.

Notice that the length of the drag in Figure 3-2 is the same as that in Figure 3-1, but because the Option/Alt key is pressed in Figure 3-2, the drag results in a rectangle that is four times as large as the one in Figure 3-1. So if you want to expend less mouse-moving energy when you're drawing, use an Option/Alt-drag instead of a plain old drag. This technique comes in handy when you're creating several rectangles at a time, or when your wrist is starting to ache from overuse.

If you press the Shift key while drawing with the rectangle tool, you constrain the resulting shape. To constrain the creation or manipulation of an object is to attach certain guidelines to the effects of your mouse movements. In this case, pressing Shift constrains the rectangle to a square. Pressing both Shift and Option/Alt while drawing with the rectangle tool creates a square from center to corner.

Tip

Press the 1 key — either in the standard key set or on the keypad — or the R key (R for Rectangle) to select the rectangle tool.

Drawing a rectangle with rounded corners

By default, rectangles drawn in FreeHand have perpendicular corners (which simply means that one side meets another to form a 90-degree angle). But you can also draw rectangles with rounded corners. To do so, double-click the rectangle tool icon in the toolbox to display the dialog box shown in Figure 3-3. Enter a value into the Corner Radius option box (or drag the knob inside the slider bar) to specify the radius of the rounded corner.

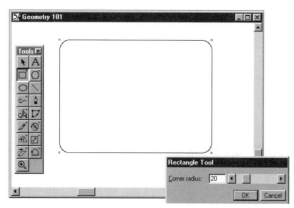

Figure 3-3: Double-click the rectangle tool icon in the toolbox to round off the corners in a rectangle.

As you may recall from your junior-high geometry class, the *radius* is the distance from the center of a circle to any point on its outline. Think of a rounded corner as one-quarter of a circle, as shown in the first example in Figure 3-4. The arrows in the figure show the radius of the circle.

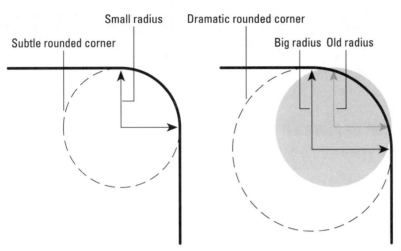

Figure 3-4: A small corner radius (left) results in a more subtle rounding effect than a larger corner radius (right).

The size of the circle increases as the radius increases, so a large Corner Radius value rounds off the corners of a rectangle more dramatically than a smaller value. To demonstrate this idea, the second example in Figure 3-4 shows the result of increasing the radius. I superimposed a grayed version of the radius from the first example for comparison.

By default, the Corner Radius value is measured in points. Not to be confused with points on a path, these points are very tiny increments of measure equal to $1/72$ inch. (Because most monitors display 72 screen pixels per inch, one point is equal to one screen pixel at actual size.) You can change the unit of measure by selecting a new option from the Units pop-up menu at the bottom of the illustration window. For more information, see the "Changing the unit of measure" section of Chapter 6.

Drawing an ellipse

You use the oval (or ellipse) tool very much like the rectangle tool. One difference, of course, is that you use the oval tool to create ellipses and circles instead of rectangles and squares. Another difference is that the points at which you click and release with the oval tool do not reside on the path of the ellipse; they are merely reference points. An ellipse drawn with the oval tool fits inside the area of your drag.

To understand this concept, it helps to imagine an invisible bounding box forming as you drag with the oval tool, as illustrated in Figure 3-5. The ellipse exists entirely within the boundaries of this bounding box, as it does when you draw with an oval tool in most other Macintosh applications.

Ellipse tool

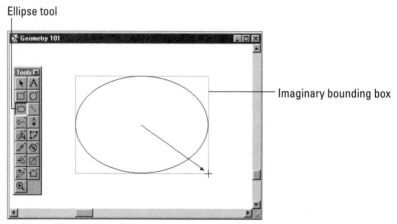

Imaginary bounding box

Figure 3-5: An ellipse fits entirely inside the area of your drag.

If you press Option/Alt while drawing with the oval tool, the beginning of your drag becomes the center point of the ellipse. The release point becomes the corner of the bounding box, thereby determining the size and shape of the ellipse.

Press Shift and drag with the oval tool to create a perfect circle. Press both Shift and Option/Alt to draw a circle outward from the center point.

Tip

You can access the oval tool from the keyboard by pressing the 3 key in the standard key set or on the keypad. Or, if you prefer, press the E key (E for Ellipse).

Drawing an arc

You must have both the Xtra Panels and the Arc Xtras in your Xtras to access the arc tool. If this is indeed the case, the arc tool appears as a very generous slab of pie in your Xtra Tools panel. In case you forgot how to open that panel, let me save you the trouble of scrambling through this book. Choose Xtra Tools from the Window ⇨ Xtras submenu or press ⌘/Ctrl-Option/Alt-X. The functionality for creating arcs is contained in the Xtra titled Arc.

You use the arc tool to create 90-degree arcs that can be open or closed and concave or convex. The points at which you click and release with the arc tool determine the end points of your arc. When you press Shift and drag with the arc tool, you create a perfect quarter circle.

Double-click the arc tool to display command central for arc creation—the Arc dialog box—pictured in Figure 3-6. Here FreeHand presents several options and a nifty preview box that shows how an arc will look based on your current settings. The neat thing about your selections in this dialog box: You can reverse them whenever you want by holding down the appropriate key when creating the arc.

Figure 3-6: All of the Arc dialog box settings can be reversed by holding down the appropriate key while creating the arc.

The first option—Create Open Arc—is pretty straightforward. When creating a closed arc, you get a hefty slice of pie. When creating an open arc, you get just the crust—or a curve to be more geometric. To reverse this setting, hold down the ⌘/Ctrl key while creating your arc.

The second option—Create Flipped Arc—is a bit less straightforward. It's easier to see the difference that your setting for the Create Flipped Arc option makes if you draw a closed arc, especially inside the Arc dialog box's preview. Whether or not this option is selected, you can always extend the arc in any orientation you choose, it just may not curve in the direction you wish. That's where the handy Option/Alt key comes into play. To reverse the direction of the arc's curve—that is, to reverse the Create Flipped Arc option setting—hold down the Option/Alt key while creating your arc.

The third option—Create Concave Arc—is best explained by viewing the preview box after selecting this option. Enabled, the Create Concave Arc option is sort of the opposite of a closed arc, which brings up an important point: If you select Create Concave Arc, then FreeHand ignores your setting for the first option, Create Open Arc. To reverse the Create Concave Arc setting, hold down the Option/Alt key while creating your arc.

Drawing a spiral

As with the arc tool, the spiral is an Xtra. As such, you must load both the Xtra Panels and the Spiral Xtras to access the spiral tool. Then a cute coil icon appears in the Xtra Tools panel. That curly little thing is the spiral tool. The functionality for creating spirals is also contained in an Xtra. In this case, it's the one titled Spiral.

You use this tool to create proportional spiral paths. Creating spirals is similar to creating ellipses. The points at which you click and release with the spiral tool are merely reference points for defining an invisible bounding box. The spiral fits within the boundaries of this bounding box. You determine the spiral's appearance by setting one of two parameters. If you tell FreeHand the number of rotations you want to fit within the bounding box, FreeHand calculates the space between the rings. Or, you can tell FreeHand the distance you want between the rings and — you guessed it — FreeHand calculates the number of rotations that can fit within the bounding box.

The only key with an impact on spiral creation is the Shift key, which affects the alignment of the spiral's center and end points. The Shift key constrains this alignment to an angle of 45 degrees, or any multiple of 45 degrees.

Before I continue, I bet you've discovered that the spiral tool icon has a preference indicator in its top right corner. Tell the truth — you're probably exploring the Spiral dialog box, pictured in Figure 3-7, without me — aren't you? Fine. But I want to go over this dialog box anyway.

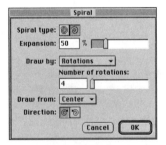

Figure 3-7: Double-clicking the spiral tool displays the Spiral dialog box.

The first choice you encounter concerns the spiral type. You can choose between two icons. The left one is a tight little coil, and the right one appears to be in the process of uncoiling. Your choice here affects the distance between the spiral rings. If you choose the left one, FreeHand creates spirals with a constant distance between the rings. If you choose the right one, FreeHand creates a nautilus-type spiral, where the distance between the rings expands outward. If you choose the nautilus spiral, an additional option appears in the dialog box. This option enables you to specify the rate of expansion as a percentage. You specify this value by typing a number between 1 and 200 in the text box or by dragging the adjacent slide bar.

I hinted to you about the next option, Draw By. Remember when I mentioned that you can tell FreeHand either the number of rotations or the distance between the rings? Well, here is your opportunity to do so. If you choose Rotations, then specify how many. If you choose Increments, specify the space between rings. If you are creating expanding spirals, enter the size of the initial space at the center of the spiral.

Next, for the Draw From option, you decide how to drag to create the spiral. You have several choices (refer to Figure 3-8 for the visuals that accompany these descriptions):

✦ **Center:** For this option, you define a radius of the spiral from the center outward. The point where you begin to press the mouse button becomes the center of the spiral. Continue to hold down the mouse button and drag to where you want the spiral's outer edge. See the left spiral in Figure 3-8.

✦ **Edge:** Just reverse the explanation for Center. In this case, you describe a radius of the spiral from the outer edge to the center. See the center spiral in Figure 3-8.

✦ **Corner:** With this option selected, you drag diagonally to describe the spiral's bounding box, just as you do to create an ellipse or a rectangle. See the right spiral in Figure 3-8.

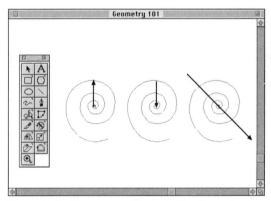

Figure 3-8: The arrows illustrate the three Draw From options: Center (left), Edge (center), and Corner (right).

Finally, the Direction option lets you choose to swirl your spiral clockwise or counterclockwise. This option is invaluable when drawing water going down the drain in Australia.

Drawing a polygon

When you drag with the polygon tool inside the illustration window, FreeHand draws an equilateral polygon — a shape with multiple straight sides, each of which are the same length and meet each other at a consistent angle. The hexagon in

Figure 3-9 is an example of an equilateral polygon. Pentagons, octagons, and even squares are other examples.

Polygon tool

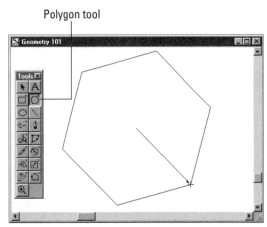

Figure 3-9: Shapes drawn with the polygon tool have a set number of straight sides, all of which are the same length.

As indicated by the arrow in Figure 3-9, the polygon tool always draws outward from the center; the Option/Alt key is not required, nor does it have any influence. It's also worth noting that FreeHand does not assign center points to polygons. This is because FreeHand doesn't treat polygons as special shapes as it does rectangles and ellipses. For example, you don't have to ungroup a polygon to edit it as Bézier free-form paths. In this sense, polygons are just like free-form paths drawn with the freehand and pen tools.

The other difference between the polygon tool and its geometric counterparts is the impact of the Shift key. When you press Shift while drawing with the rectangle or oval tool, FreeHand keeps the shape proportional. (Just thought I'd recap that little bit of information in case you plumb forgot.) But by definition, equilateral polygons are already proportional. So when you Shift-drag with the polygon tool, FreeHand limits your drag to four different angles for each side in the shape.

For example, if you set the polygon tool to draw a triangle, you can Shift-drag in 12 directions—3 sides × 4 angles. There are 360 degrees in a circle, so you can drag in 30-degree increments—360 degrees ÷ 12 directions. If you set the polygon tool to draw a hexagon, which has 6 sides, Shift-dragging constrains your movements to 24 different directions.

I realize that all this sounds a tad bit confusing, so let me oversimplify things a little: By pressing the Shift key, you can draw a shape with at least one side that is oriented horizontally, vertically, or diagonally. That's not the whole story, but it's close enough.

Tip   To select the polygon tool, press the 2 key. If pressing 2 doesn't work for you, and you feel those darn uppity number keys get enough attention already as it is, feel free to give the G key a thunk (G is for polyGon).

Sides and stars

To specify the number of sides you want in your polygon, double-click the polygon tool icon in the toolbox. FreeHand displays the Polygon Tool dialog box shown on the left in Figure 3-10. To add or subtract sides, enter any number between 3 and 20 into the Number of Sides option box.

You can also create stars with the polygon tool. To do so, select the Star radio button in the Polygon Tool dialog box. The Star Points options appear, as shown on the right dialog box in Figure 3-10. By default, the Automatic radio button is selected, which results in the kind of stars featured in the top row of Figure 3-11. The opposite arms of these stars are perfectly aligned with each other. For example, in the five-point star, the tops of the right and left arms form a horizontal line.

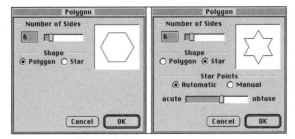

Figure 3-10: The Polygon Tool dialog box as it appears when the Polygon (left) and Star (right) options are selected.

Figure 3-11: Three stars subject to the Automatic option (top), and the same three with acute stars inset (bottom).

To override this option, you don't need to select the Manual radio button — just drag the knob inside the slider bar below the radio buttons, and FreeHand automatically selects the Manual radio button. Drag left (toward Acute) to reduce the angles at which the sides in a star meet; drag right (toward Obtuse) to enlarge the angles. Acute stars have sharp points; obtuse stars have dull ones. The bottom row of Figure 3-11 shows several acute stars inset inside their automatic companions. Notice that the arms of the acute stars — created with the Manual option — do not align with each other.

Geometric shapes at an angle

In the course of drawing with one of the geometric shape tools, you may find that your path rotates at some odd angle, as demonstrated by the rectangle in Figure 3-12. Don't blame yourself — it's not happening because you're misusing the tool. It's happening because you — or someone else using your copy of FreeHand — altered the angle of the constraint axes. The constraint axes control the angle at which you can manipulate objects while pressing Shift. They also control the creation of geometric shapes.

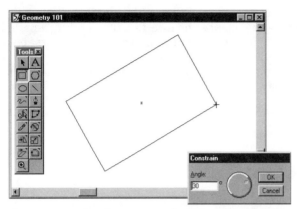

Figure 3-12: Drawing a rectangle with the Angle value in the Constrain dialog box set to 30 degrees.

You change the angle of the constraint axes by entering a value into the Angle option box in the Constrain dialog box (Modify ➪ Constrain). If the Angle value is anything but 0, rectangles and ellipses are rotated to that degree. The Angle value also affects polygons that you create while pressing the Shift key.

Cross-Reference

For more information on the Constrain command, read the "Constrained movements" section of Chapter 5. This can be very useful when you are reshaping and transforming objects.

Straight and Free-Form Paths

With the geometric shape tools, you create simple shapes quickly and easily. However, FreeHand's true drawing prowess is rooted in its capability to define free-form paths. A free-form path can be simple, such as a wedge or a crescent, or it can be an intricate polygon or naturalistic form that meets the most complex specifications.

Drawing straight segments

Because of its simplicity and limited utility, the straight line may seem more like a geometric path than a free-form path. But in FreeHand, the straight line shares more similarities with paths drawn with the freehand and pen tools than with rectangles or ellipses. Though a straight line is simple to create, you can manipulate its path and the points without first ungrouping it, just like a shape drawn with the polygon tool. But unlike polygons, straight lines are open, enabling you to quickly integrate them into more complex paths.

To draw a straight line, select the line tool and drag in the illustration window. (See Figure 3-13 if you're stumped.) The distance and direction of your drag determine the length and angle of the line. The beginning of your drag marks the first point in the line; the release location marks the final point. Both points are called *endpoints* because they appear at either end of the path and they are both associated with only one segment. Endpoints have special properties that are explored later in this chapter.

Line Tool

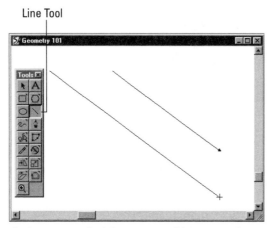

Figure 3-13: Admit it—you would never understand how to use the line tool without this figure.

If you press Shift and drag with the line tool, FreeHand constrains the line to a horizontal, vertical, or diagonal angle. Keep in mind that you can change the effect of pressing the Shift key by entering a value other than 0 into the Angle option box in the Constrain dialog box (Modify ➪ Constrain) as described in the previous section. Pressing Option/Alt while drawing with the line tool creates a line from the center outward.

Tip

Pressing the 4 key selects the line tool. When it doesn't, press N (N is for liNe). If that doesn't work, beg, plead, and resort to bribery. Just because your computer doesn't respect you doesn't mean it won't pity you.

Drawing freehand lines

The next tool we visit in our wonderland of tools is the freehand tool, is used for real-time drawing. After selecting this tool, you click and drag as if you were drawing with a pencil on a sheet of paper. FreeHand tracks the exact movements of your mouse onscreen, creating a free-form line between the locations at which your drag begins and ends. After you release, FreeHand automatically determines the quantity and location of points and segments and creates the freehand path.

Consider the example of the apple shown in Figure 3-14. This figure shows the progression of the freehand tool cursor. I started by dragging with the tool from the upper left corner of the apple's stem down to the beginning of the leaf. I then dragged up and back down in two opposite arcs to create the leaf. After dragging downward to finish the stem, I swept around in a great rightward arc and down to the lower tip of the core, as shown in the third window in the figure. Finally, I dragged back up and around to the left, eventually meeting the first point in a single continuous movement.

Figure 3-14: Drawing an apple with the freehand tool in four steps.

Notice that the apple in Figure 3-14 exhibits some jaggedness along its lower right side. This jagged area exists for two reasons. First, I drew this figure with a mouse. The mouse is not a precise drawing instrument. When you move a mouse, a ball within its chamber rolls about against the surface of the table or mouse pad. The ball in turn causes two internal tracking wheels to move, one vertically and one horizontally. Based on the activity of these two wheels, the mouse conveys movement information to the computer.

No matter how thoroughly you clean a mouse, there will be some interference between the ball and the wheels, even if it's only small particles of dust. For example, if you draw a 45-degree diagonal line, both the vertical and horizontal tracking wheels should move at exactly the same pace. If some interference comes between the ball and the horizontal wheel, causing the wheel to remain motionless for only a moment, the mouse sends purely vertical movement information to the computer until the interference has passed. The result is a momentary jag in an otherwise smooth diagonal line.

Second, most people — even skilled artists — are not very practiced at drawing with a mouse. It takes time to master this skill. You may find that your first drawing efforts look much different than you had planned — possibly far worse than Figure 3-14, for example. Luckily, the freehand tool is capable of smoothing out many imperfections.

Tip

Press the 5 key to access the freehand tool. If that doesn't strike your fancy, press the Y key. (Y is for "why not use the F key?" Well, the F key is the shortcut for the freeform tool, a new tool that you'll meet in Chapter 5.)

Freehand curve fit

After you complete the process of drawing a path and release your mouse button, FreeHand performs some calculations to determine how many points to assign to your path and where to locate those points. It bases these calculations on the following criteria:

✦ **Consistency:** FreeHand assigns a point to every location at which your drag changes direction. Thus, smooth, consistent mouse actions produce smooth, elegant paths; jerky or unsteady mouse actions produce overly complex lines.

✦ **Speed:** The speed at which you draw may also affect the appearance of a freehand path. If your mouse lingers at any location, FreeHand is more likely to assign a point there. However, if you draw too quickly, FreeHand ignores many of the subtle direction changes in your drag. A slow but steady technique is the most reliable.

✦ **Curve fit:** FreeHand enables you to control the sensitivity of the freehand tool by using the Tight Fit check box in the Freehand Tool dialog box. (To access this dialog box, double-click the freehand tool icon in the toolbox.) Selecting this option instigates a tight curve fit, which results in a freehand path that more accurately matches your drag. Deselecting the option results in a looser curve fit, which instructs FreeHand to smooth over inaccuracies in your drag.

Figure 3-15 shows how FreeHand interprets my apple path depending on the selection of the Tight Fit option. The path on the left was created with Tight Fit on; the path on the right is the result of turning Tight Fit off. The two paths are similar, but a few differences are obvious. With Tight Fit off, FreeHand missed two key corners around the leaf. The stem is overly gooey, and the left side of the apple lacks sufficient definition. I recommend that you keep Tight Fit selected unless you consider yourself a total spaz with a mouse or have little confidence in your overall drawing ability.

Figure 3-15: The points and segments assigned to the apple path when the Tight Fit option is selected (left) and deselected (right).

Note

You can't alter the curve fit for a path after the path is created, because FreeHand calculates the points for a path only once — after your release. For each of the two paths in Figure 3-15, therefore, I had to change the curve fit and then draw a new apple from scratch.

Tip

You can give an existing path the *appearance* of a looser curve fit. To do this, select the path and then simplify it by choosing Modify ➪ Alter Path ➪ Simplify. (You can also choose Simplify from the Operations panel or from the Xtras ➪ Cleanup submenu.) Enter an Amount value, from 0 to 10, in the Simplify dialog box, which appears when you choose this command. The number you enter establishes an acceptable variation between the new and original paths. Smaller numbers remove fewer points but result in paths that more closely resemble the original paths. The reverse is true for larger numbers. When you press OK, FreeHand automatically removes points within the limits you set that it considers excessive. The effect is similar to changing from a tight curve fit to a looser one.

Another option in the Freehand Tool dialog box, Draw Dotted Line, enables you to specify the manner in which FreeHand displays your freehand path while you're drawing it. When this option is off, FreeHand displays your path as a solid line, as shown back in Figure 3-14.

If you want to draw more quickly and FreeHand isn't keeping up with your mouse movements, turn this option on. FreeHand then displays your path as a broken dotted line, which takes less time to draw and track on-screen. The downside to this setting is that FreeHand barely provides you with enough visual feedback to figure out what you've drawn. Personally, I prefer to leave the Draw Dotted Line option deselected and draw carefully.

Erasing with the freehand tool

Normally, FreeHand tracks every movement you make with the freehand tool, creating a continuous path. If you press the ⌘/Ctrl key while drawing, however, you can erase a mistake. In the middle of a drag, press ⌘/Ctrl — don't release the mouse button! — and trace back over a portion of the path that you just drew. Be sure to trace your steps exactly. As you do, the path disappears in chunks. Each chunk represents a segment being deleted.

This technique enables you to fix mistakes as you go. You can draw a path with the freehand tool, immediately "undraw" part of it while pressing the ⌘/Ctrl key, and then release ⌘/Ctrl and continue drawing.

Drawing freeform polygons

Now, instead of ⌘/Ctrl-dragging back over your path, ⌘/Ctrl-drag away from it and then release the ⌘/Ctrl key and continue to draw. Notice that FreeHand does not display your path between the point where you pressed the ⌘/Ctrl key and the point where you released it. At the end of your drag, FreeHand calculates the quantity and position of the points necessary to represent your freehand path in the usual manner and displays the formerly invisible segment. The only difference is that any portion of your path that was created while the ⌘/Ctrl key was down is represented by a single segment.

This feature is a fluke, but it's a fun fluke. The official way to create a straight segment with the freehand tool is to press Option/Alt while dragging. FreeHand creates a straight segment between the points at which you press and release the Option/Alt key, just as it does when you press ⌘/Ctrl. However, when you press Option/Alt, you can see the straight segment between the two points as you draw. The following steps show how to use this powerful function:

1. Throughout these steps, keep the mouse button down. Begin by drawing a common, everyday, garden-variety squiggle.

2. With the mouse button still down — don't you dare release it — press the Option/Alt key and drag to a different location. As illustrated in Figure 3-16, a straight segment follows the movements of your cursor.

3. Release the Option/Alt key but don't release the mouse button. Then draw another squiggle. As shown in Figure 3-17, your movements are interpreted exactly as they were before you pressed Option/Alt.

4. Release your mouse button. The completed path contains a single, straight segment between the points at which you pressed and released the Option/ Alt key.

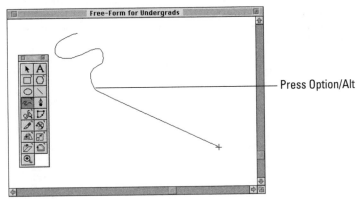

Figure 3-16: The freehand tool draws a straight segment as long as Option/Alt is pressed.

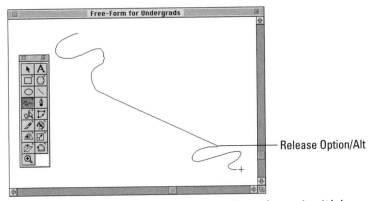

Figure 3-17: Continue drawing after you release the Option/Alt key.

If you press Shift and Option/Alt together when dragging with the freehand tool, FreeHand constrains the straight segment to a 45-degree angle. Keep in mind that you can alter the effects of pressing the Shift key by rotating the constraint axes — which you accomplish by using the Constrain command, as described in the "Geometric shapes at an angle" section earlier in this chapter.

Extending a line

You can also use the freehand tool to extend an open path. Suppose you drew a line with either the line tool or the freehand tool some time ago, but now you want to make the line longer or close the path. Select the path with the arrow tool, switch to the freehand tool, and then drag from one of its endpoints with the freehand tool, as shown in Figure 3-18. FreeHand treats the line you create by dragging with the tool as an extension of the existing open path. To close the path, drag from one endpoint to the other.

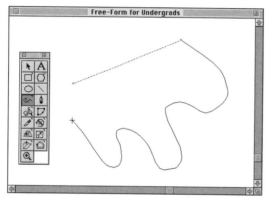

Figure 3-18: You can extend a selected straight line drawn with the line tool by dragging from its endpoint with the freehand tool.

You'll see the freehand cursor (a big plus sign) with a little plus sign to the lower right indicating that you are directly over the anchor point on which you want to continue. When you are closing the path, your cursor will show a square in the lower right to indicate you are closing this path. If you don't see the square, your path is still open, even though it may look closed. You'll see these augmented cursors only if the Smart Cursors option on the General panel inside the Preference dialog box is selected; otherwise, you'll see only the plain, old big plus sign of the freehand cursor.

Sketching complicated paths

You can use the freehand tool to sketch complicated objects, especially line drawings. If you are skilled in drawing with the mouse or tablet, you may find the immediacy of producing high-resolution images in real time very appealing. Drawing with the freehand tool can soften the computer-produced appearance of an illustration and may convey a sense of informality and spontaneity to those who view your work.

However, regardless of your drawing ability or preferences, the freehand tool seldom results in paths that look just the way you want them to right off the bat. You need to manipulate most freehand paths to some degree or other in order for them to print acceptably. Like taking photographs with a Polaroid camera, drawing with the freehand tool provides immediate satisfaction. But you sacrifice accuracy and elegance. For this reason, I recommend that you use the tool primarily for sketching and prepare yourself to spend some time properly reshaping your paths (as described in Chapter 5).

Drawing calligraphic lines

FreeHand provides a pressure-sensitive freehand tool that offers both variable-weight and calligraphic options. Double-click the freehand tool icon in the toolbox to display the Freehand Tool dialog box. Then select either the Variable Stroke or Calligraphic Pen radio button. Figure 3-19 shows the options associated with each.

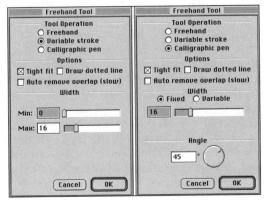

Figure 3-19: By using the Variable Stroke and Calligraphic Pen options, you can create variable-weight paths as closed shapes.

Pressure-sensitive input

The Variable Stroke option is designed to make the freehand tool compatible with pressure-sensitive drawing tablets such as the Wacom ArtZ, one of the most essential pieces of hardware available to computer artists.

The ArtZ includes a pen-like stylus that feels and behaves like a felt-tip pen. When the Variable Stroke option is active, FreeHand responds to the amount of pressure you apply to the stylus. As you bear down on the stylus while drawing with the freehand tool, FreeHand thickens the line; as you let up, the line becomes thinner. Figure 3-20 shows the freehand tool caught in the act of drawing a Japanese character using the Variable Stroke option.

The Variable Stroke Freehand tool

Figure 3-20: When the Variable Stroke option is active, the freehand tool reacts dynamically to pressure-sensitive input.

The thickness of the line varies between the weights you enter into the Min and Max option boxes in the Freehand Tool dialog box. Any values between 0 and 72 are accepted. If you enter a value into the Min option box that is higher than the Max value, FreeHand is smart enough to simply reverse the values rather than irritating you with a bone-headed error message.

After you complete the line, FreeHand calculates the points required to express it as an object-oriented path. This is nothing out of the ordinary. What *is* unusual is that the path is automatically closed, because FreeHand has to trace around the line to produce the variable-weight effect. In doing so, FreeHand creates some strange overlapping areas that can interfere with reshaping. You can eliminate this problem by enabling the Auto Remove Overlap option in the Freehand Tool dialog box.

To understand the true greatness of the Auto Remove Overlap feature, you need to experience what happens if you do not enable it — then, trust me, you'll never work without it. Figure 3-21 shows the path from the previous figure expressed as an object. In the second example, I made the fill transparent so that you can more easily see the object's outline. Notice how the path wraps around the corners in the Japanese character? This wrapping ensures that the path follows the motion of your freehand cursor as closely as possible. However, it also makes the path very difficult to edit. The third example shows the same object created with the Auto Remove Overlap option enabled. It's the little things that make a relationship between you and your application work. This feature shows that FreeHand genuinely cares about you. Features such as this one make it so much more meaningful when you and FreeHand create art together.

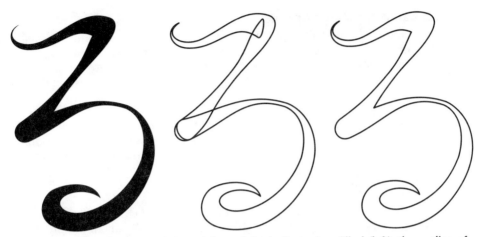

Figure 3-21: Though my variable-weight path looks fine when filled (left), the outline of the path overlaps to express the corners in my drag (center). Using the Auto Remove Overlap feature eliminates this problem (right).

Pressure without the tablet

Confession is good for the soul. So I'm here to tell you, I lied. The paths from Figure 3-20 and 3-21 were not drawn with a pressure-sensitive tablet. They could have been, of course, but I decided to make things a little more challenging and test FreeHand's keyboard controls instead. The truth is, by pressing the following keys as you draw, you can create variable-weight paths without the aid of a Wacom ArtZ or other tablet:

- ✦ To make the line thicker, press the → key. If you sinned in a previous life and were therefore born right-handed, you'll probably prefer to use the 2 key, which serves the same purpose. You can also press the right-bracket key (just above Return/Enter), but why would you?

- ✦ To make the line thinner, press the ← key. Alternatively, you can press the left-bracket or 1 key.

These keyboard controls are fantastic. Each press of an arrow, number, or bracket key increases or decreases the thickness of the path by ⅛ of the difference between the Min and Max values in the Freehand Tool dialog box. For example, if the default Min and Max values are 0 and 16 respectively, each whack of a key changes the weight by 2 points. The only way to get a feel for this feature is to experiment. Have at it, and have a ball.

The Calligraphic Pen option

When you select the Calligraphic Pen radio button in the Freehand Tool dialog box, the freehand tool draws a path that looks like it was created with a broad-tipped pen. You specify the angle of the pen tip by entering a value into the Angle option box or by dragging the knob inside the circle just above the OK button (refer back to Figure 3-19).

If the Fixed radio button is selected (it's located right there below the word Width), the calligraphic line conforms to a fixed weight. But if you select the Variable option, the freehand tool responds to pressure-sensitive input and keyboard controls just as it does when the Variable Stroke option is active. In my humble opinion, there's no reason not to select Variable.

The problem with the Calligraphic Pen option — and I'm talking opinion, not fact (although I'm generally pretty sure the two are identical) — is that it produces rather artificial results. Take the line in Figure 3-22 as an example. If I were to draw this character with a real flat-tipped pen, I could revolve the pen between my fingers to adjust the angle of the tip on the fly. But in FreeHand, the angle is fixed. Even if you had an iron grip and the steadiest hand on earth, you couldn't keep a pen tip this stationary. Only a machine could produce this line.

I'm not saying that FreeHand dropped the ball here — Illustrator offers a similar function that's equally inflexible — it's just that it doesn't measure up to the humanizing touch supplied by the Variable Stroke option and the freehand tool in general.

The Subterranean World of Bézier Curves

All right, so much for the easy stuff. If you've come this far, you're ready to get serious about drawing in FreeHand. The tools I've discussed up until now are laughably rudimentary and imprecise compared with the elemental machinery covered throughout the remainder of this chapter. Here's where you address the world of points and segments on an intimate basis. It's just you and your path, friend. Time to snuggle up. Armed with this knowledge, you'll be able to create absolutely any line or shape you need to begin or complete an illustration.

The math of the Bézier curve

Underneath the surface of each and every path you draw in FreeHand is a complex mathematical structure. As the story goes — and I tell you, it's an absorbing one — a French mathematician named Pierre Bézier (pronounced *bez-ee-ay*) discovered that you can define irregular curves by inventing two *control handles* (x_1,y_1 and x_2,y_2 for the algebra enthusiasts in the audience) for every fixed point (x,y) in a curve. In case you don't have the vaguest idea what I'm talking about, Figure 3-23 shows an aerial view.

The Calligraphic Pen freehand tool

Figure 3-22: When the Calligraphic Pen option is active, the freehand tool draws more or less like a broad-tipped pen.

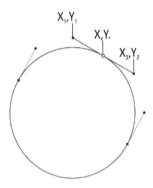

Figure 3-23: The world according to Pierre Bézier.

These handles (our good buddies x_1,y_1 and x_2,y_2) act as levers. As a curve passes from one point (x,y) to another (Pierre was a little vague on this one, so I'll call it "Sam"), it is magnetically attracted to the control handles. One handle tells the curve how to enter the point; the other tells the curve how to exit the point. The fact is, these curves get bossed around a lot.

Now don't you feel newly educated? Can you sense your brains wanting to just bust out of your head? Kind of like the scarecrow, after he stumbled on the Great and Powerful Oz, huh? Pretty soon, you'll be spouting off Bézier curve theory at dinner parties and making your friends flee in terror.

Well, whatever your feelings, these so-called *Bézier curves* are at the heart of FreeHand's graphics capabilities, as well as those of the PostScript page-description language. Don't worry if you don't fully understand the whole Bézier craze yet; I don't really expect you to. Throughout what remains of this chapter, I'll ease you into Bézier curves one limb at a time until, before you know it, you're fully immersed and wallowing around helplessly. It's the only way, trust me.

Using the bézigon and pen tools

FreeHand offers two tools for drawing Bézier curves. One is the bézigon tool, which incorporates the capabilities of the old corner, curve, and connector tools. And the other is the pen tool, which is slightly more difficult to use but provides you with more control.

Regardless of which tool you use, you build a path by creating individual points. FreeHand automatically connects the points with segments. The following list explains the specific kinds of points and segments you can create in FreeHand and how to create them. (Refer to Figure 3-24 for examples, and keep in mind that each of these techniques is described in more detail in an upcoming section.)

✦ **Corner point:** Click with the bézigon or pen tool to create a corner point, which represents the corner between two straight segments in a path.

✦ **Straight segment:** Click at two different locations to create a straight segment between two corner points. Shift-click to draw a horizontal, vertical, or diagonal segment between the new corner point and its predecessor.

✦ **Curve point:** Option/Alt-click with the bézigon tool or drag with the pen tool to create a curve point with two symmetrical Bézier control handles. A curve point ensures that one segment meets with another in a continuous arc.

✦ **Curved segment:** Option/Alt-click (bézigon tool) or drag (pen tool) at two different locations to create a curved segment between two curve points.

✦ **Connector point:** After creating a corner point, Control-click (or Alt-right click, as described in the following Note) with the bézigon tool or Control-drag (or Alt-right drag) with the pen tool to create a connector point with one control handle pointing away from the corner point. A straight segment joins the corner and connector points. Then Option/Alt-click (bézigon tool) or drag (pen tool) to create a curve point, which appends a curved segment to the connector point. The connector point ensures a perfectly smooth transition between this curved segment and the straight segment before it.

Note

Because you Windows people don't have a key that is equivalent to the Macintosh Control key—the Ctrl key on a PC keyboard is equivalent to the ⌘ key on a Macintosh's and not the Control key—you'll have to employ a slightly odd operation. Whereas Mac people Control-click with the bézigon tool to create a connector point, you Windows folk will need to Alt-right-mouse-button-click (or, more succinctly, Alt-right click). That's correct, click with the right mouse button when the Alt key is pressed. Be sure that the Alt key is pressed or clicking with the right mouse button will call-up the content-sensitive menu. To create a connector point with the pen tool, Windows users will need to Alt-right-mouse-button-drag, also known as Alt-right drag.

✦ **Straight segment followed by curved:** After creating a corner point, Option/Alt-drag at a new location with the pen tool to create another corner point with one control handle pointing away from its predecessor. A straight segment joins the two points. Then drag at a third location to append a curved segment to the end of the straight segment.

✦ **Curved segment followed by straight:** After creating a curve point, drag at a new location with the pen tool to create another curve point. Midway into the drag, press the Option/Alt key and move the control handle back to its point. Pressing Option/Alt converts the curve point to a corner point; dragging the handle back to its point deletes the handle. Then click again at a different location to append a straight segment to the end of the curved segment.

✦ **Cusp point:** After creating a curve point, drag at a new location with the pen tool to create another curve point. Midway into the drag, press the Option/Alt key — beginning to sound familiar? — only this time, move the control handle in some other direction of your choosing. Pressing Option/Alt converts the curve point to a corner point; dragging the handle without deleting it retains two independent handles. A corner point with two handles is sometimes called a cusp point. Finally, drag again at a new location to append a curved segment that proceeds in a different direction than the previous curved segment.

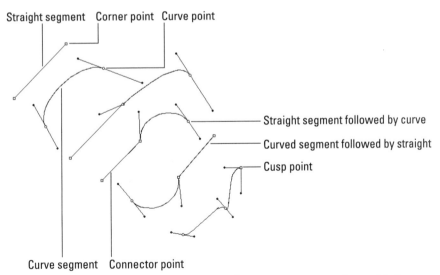

Figure 3-24: The various kinds of points and segments you can draw with the bézigon and pen tools.

To complete your path, you can either close it to create a shape or leave it open to create a line. Close the outline by clicking or dragging on the first point in the path. Every point will then have one segment coming into it and another segment exiting it. Remember, as long as you're using smart cursors, the black square to the lower right of the cursor signals a closed path.

Tip

To leave the path open, press the Tab key to deactivate it. Then click in the illustration window with either the bézigon or pen tool to begin a new path.

Moving points as you create them

Before I begin my long diatribe about the many ways to use the bézigon and pen tools, I want to tell you about a special function built into each. Both the bézigon and the pen tools let you move points while creating them. In the case of the bézigon tool, just drag with the tool rather than clicking. As you drag, the point moves around beneath your cursor. FreeHand draws a segment between the point in motion and its predecessor, giving you a feel for what the segment will look like subject to different point placements.

Tip

To move a point while using the pen tool, press the ⌘/Ctrl key. For example, try this: Drag with the pen tool to create a curve point with two symmetrical Bézier control handles. The handles follow the motion of your cursor, while the point itself remains stationary. To move the point and handles simultaneously, press the ⌘/Ctrl key as you continue to drag. As long as the key is pressed, the point moves. Release ⌘/Ctrl to fix the point in place.

Test-driving the bézigon tool

It's one thing to read and even understand a list of ways to use FreeHand's Bézier curve tools; it's another to actually put one of them to use. Because the bézigon tool is more automated than the pen tool, I'll demonstrate how to use it first. The following steps walk you through a simple bézigon tool scenario, where you'll create a free-form polygon composed entirely of corner points. (In later sections, you'll create curves and add connector points.)

1. Select the bézigon tool and click at some location in the illustration window to create a corner point, which will represent a sharp corner in your path. The corner point appears as a tiny hollow square to show that it is selected. It is also open-ended, meaning that it doesn't have both a segment coming into it and a segment going out from it. In fact, this new corner point — I'll call it point A — is associated with no segment whatsoever. It is a lone point, open-ended in two directions.

Tip

To select the bézigon tool from the keyboard, press the 8 key or the B key or, even, the U key. (I don't really get that last one, either.) As you become more familiar with these tools, you'll probably find yourself regularly switching back and forth between the bézigon and pen tools. To access the pen tool, press 6 or the P key.

2. Click at a new location in the illustration to create a new corner point — point B. FreeHand automatically draws a straight segment from point A to point B, as illustrated in Figure 3-25. Notice that point A now appears solid rather than hollow. This shows that point A is the member of a selected path but is itself deselected. Point B is selected and open-ended. FreeHand automatically selects a point immediately after you create it and deselects all other points.

Bézigon tool

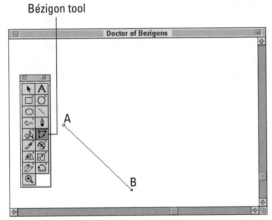

Figure 3-25: Draw a straight segment by clicking at two separate locations with the bézigon tool.

3. Click a third time with the bézigon tool to create yet another corner point — point C. Because a point can be associated with no more than two segments, point B is no longer open-ended, as verified by Figure 3-26. Such a point is called an *interior point*.

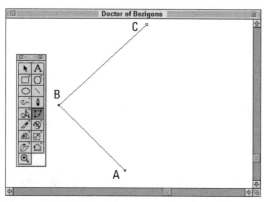

Figure 3-26: Point B is now an interior point, incapable of receiving additional segments.

4. You can keep adding points to a path one at a time for as long as you like. (Actually, FreeHand 8 does limit you to about 32,000 points per path. If anyone would like to actually count these and let me know for sure, I'll include it in the next edition.)

5. Click a fourth time and create point D, much as I did in Figure 3-27. Let's now end this particular bit of fun here and close this path. Click again on the original point, point A. Notice that your smart cursor displays the additional little black box when you move it over point A, indicating that you're about to close the path.

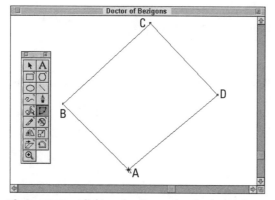

Figure 3-27: Clicking the first point (point A) in a path closes the path and deactivates it. The next point you create begins a new path.

6. All points in a closed path are interior points. Therefore, the path you just drew is no longer active, meaning that FreeHand will draw no segment between the next point you create and any point in the closed path. To verify this, click again with the bézigon tool. You create a new, independent point that is selected and open-ended in two directions, as shown in Figure 3-28. Meanwhile, the closed path becomes deselected. The path-creation process is begun anew.

Drawing perpendicular segments

To constrain a point so that it is created at a multiple of 45 degrees from its predecessor, press Shift as you click with the bézigon tool. This technique allows you to create horizontal, vertical, and diagonal segments. In Figure 3-29, for example, I actually clicked at the location shown by the cross-shaped cursor. However, because I pressed the Shift key, point F was constrained to a 180-degree angle from point E, resulting in a horizontal segment.

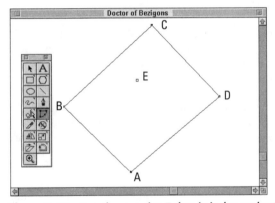

Figure 3-28: Creating a point E that is independent of the previous path deselects that path and begins a new one.

You can alter the effect of pressing the Shift key by rotating the constraint axes. Just enter a value into the Angle option box in the Constrain dialog box (Modify ➪ Constrain), as described in "Geometric shapes at an angle," earlier in this chapter.

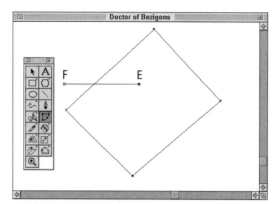

Figure 3-29: Shift-click with the bézigon tool to create a horizontal, vertical, or diagonal segment.

Drawing curved segments

When you Option/Alt-click with the bézigon tool, you create a curve point, which ensures a smooth arc between one curved segment and the next. A curve point sports two crosslike control handles. These handles act as levers, bending segments relative to the curve point itself.

Figure 3-30 shows a curve point bordered on either side by corner points. All three points are shown as they appear when selected. You can recognize the curve point because FreeHand displays it as a hollow circle, whereas the corner points are hollow squares. When not selected, both curve and corner points appear as black squares.

The small crosses are the Bézier control handles belonging to all three points. Each control handle is perched on the end of a lever. As you can see, the levers for the control handles associated with the curve point form a straight line. It is this alignment that forces the two segments on either side of the curve point to form an even, smooth arc.

Option/Alt-click

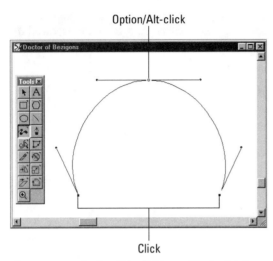

Click

Figure 3-30: Option/Alt-clicking with the bézigon tool creates a curve point, which ensures a smooth arc between segments.

Cross-Reference

Each corner point in Figure 3-30 also has a Bézier control handle. A curve point created with the bézigon tool always attaches a control handle to each of its neighboring points, regardless of identity. This is a function of FreeHand's automatic curvature function, which is described in more detail in the "Why the pen tool is so great" section later in this chapter as well as the "Automatic curvature" section of Chapter 5.

Curve points act no differently than corner points when it comes to building paths. You can easily combine curve and corner points in the same path by alternatively clicking and Option/Alt-clicking. If the first point in a path is a curve point, just click on it to close the path; you don't have to Option/Alt-click. If the first point is a corner point, Option/Alt-clicking on the point closes the path but does not convert the point from corner to curve. In other words, you can't change the identity of an existing point using the bézigon tool.

Creating smooth transitions

The connector point is a special point offered by FreeHand that ensures a smooth transition between straight and curved segments. As I mentioned earlier, you can create a connector point by Control-clicking (or, for those of you of the Windows persuasion, Alt-right clicking) with the bézigon tool.

Although some people will go their entire lives without once using these creatures, connector points can be very useful in specific situations, as demonstrated in Figure 3-31.

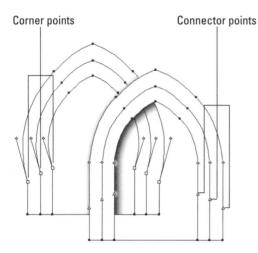

Corner points   Connector points

Figure 3-31: Corner points result in corners (left); connector points ensure smooth transitions between straight and curved segments (right).

Here, I created two archways, one of which features corner points near its base, and the other of which features connector points. (Connector points show up as hollow triangles when selected.) Each of the shapes in the archway features straight segments on the left and right sides of the base and curved segments near the top. When I positioned corner points at the intersections of the straight and curved segments, as in the rear example in the figure, FreeHand's automatic curvature routine caused the curves to bulge outward, resulting in definite corners. But when I redrew the archway using connector points, as in the forward example, I eliminated these corners.

FreeHand ensures these smooth transitions by locking the Bézier control handle belonging to any connector point into alignment with the straight segment that precedes it. In the case of the archways, the straight segments associated with the connector points are vertically oriented, so the connector-point control handles are locked into vertical alignment. If I were to reshape these paths, I could move the connector point handles up and down, but not side to side.

Tip

Use connector points to create any straight path that ends in a rounded tip, such as a finger, bullet, or other cylindrical object. Connector points can also be useful for creating rounded corners.

The versatile pen tool

Like the bézigon tool, the pen tool is capable of creating corner points, curve points, and connector points. But unlike the bézigon tool, it also enables you to precisely determine the placement and quantity of Bézier control handles. The pen tool offers less automatic software control and turns over more control to you. This means more freedom as well as more responsibility. It's just like growing up.

If you click with the pen tool, you create a corner point with no control handle. In this one respect, the pen tool works identically to the bézigon tool. If you drag with the pen tool, however, you create a curve point. The point at which you begin dragging determines the location of the curve point; the point at which you release becomes a Bézier control handle that affects the next segment you create. A second handle appears on the opposite side of the curve point that's a mirror image of the first. This handle determines the curvature of the most recent segment, as demonstrated in Figure 3-32.

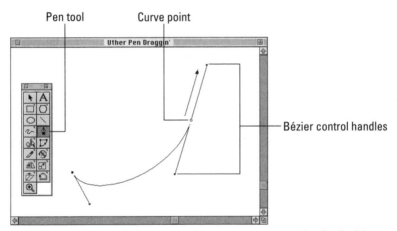

Figure 3-32: Drag with the pen tool to create a curve point flanked by two Bézier control handles.

You might think of a curve point as the center of a small seesaw, with the Bézier control handles acting as opposite ends. If you move one handle, the other handle moves in the opposite direction, and vice versa.

You can also create connector points by Control-dragging or Alt-right dragging with the pen tool, but quite frankly, the bézigon tool is almost always better for this purpose. The problem with using the pen tool is that *you* have to do the work. *You* have to identify where the straight segment is and where the curved segment is going to be, or vice versa. *You* have to position the Bézier control handle. *You* have to make sure you don't install the darn thing upside down. *You're* in charge of everything. Because a connector point serves such a small and specific function, there's no sense in mucking around with it. Just Control-click or Alt-right click with the bézigon tool and let FreeHand figure it out. Even super-advanced users will be glad they did.

Creating cusps

As I think I've mentioned a few times now — not sure, gettin' kinda senile — a curve point has two Bézier control handles, each positioned in an imaginary straight line with the point itself. A corner point, however, is much more versatile. It can have zero, one, or two handles.

To create a corner point that has one or two Bézier control handles — commonly called a *cusp* — press the Option/Alt key as you drag with the pen tool. If you press Option/Alt before dragging, you create a corner point with just one control handle that affects the next segment you create. If you press Option/Alt after you begin to drag but before you release the mouse button, you create a corner point with two independent control handles.

Suppose that you're dragging with the pen tool. As shown in the first example in Figure 3-33, the result is a curve point. The handle beneath your cursor controls the next segment that you create; the handle on the opposite side of the point controls the preceding segment. After correctly positioning the opposite handle — but before releasing the mouse button — you press the Option/Alt key. This changes the round curve point to a square corner point, as shown in the second example in Figure 3-33. While pressing Option/Alt, you can move the handle beneath your cursor independently of the handle for the preceding segment. This latter handle remains motionless as long as the Option/Alt key is pressed.

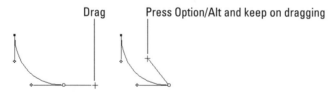

Drag   Press Option/Alt and keep on dragging

Figure 3-33: Pressing Option/Alt while dragging with the pen tool changes the curve point (left) to a corner point with two independent Bézier control handles (right).

Tip

If, while Option/Alt-dragging with the pen tool, you decide that you want to return the Bézier control handles to their original symmetrical configuration, simply release the Option/Alt key and continue dragging. The current corner point immediately changes back to a curve point.

Three cusp point vignettes

To try out a few cusps on your own, check out the following steps, which provide three different examples of FreeHand's cusp-creation capabilities. In this first example, you'll create a cusp point that consists of two independent control handles.

1. Begin by drawing the path shown in Figure 3-34. You do so by dragging three times with the pen tool. First, drag downward from the right point (A). Then drag leftward from the bottom point (B). Finally, drag upward from the left point (C) — as shown in the figure — but do *not* release the mouse button.

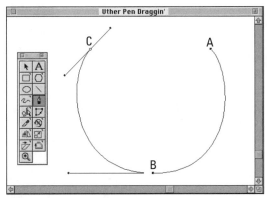

Figure 3-34: Caught in the act of creating a curve point in a semicircular path with the pen tool.

2. Suppose that you want to close the path with a concave top, resulting in a crescent shape. All segments in this shape are curved, and yet the upper segment meets with the lower segments to form two cusps. This means that you must change the two top curve points to corner points with two Bézier control handles apiece — one controlling the upper segment and one controlling a lower segment.

With the mouse button still down, press and hold the Option/Alt key. Now move your cursor downward, as indicated by the arrow in Figure 3-35, and release the mouse button and then the Option/Alt key. The handle affecting the next segment moves with your cursor while the other handle remains stationary. The result is a corner point with two control handles, each fully independent of the other.

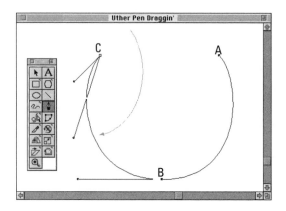

Figure 3-35: Press the Option/Alt key and continue
your drag downward to convert the curve point to
a cusp.

3. Closing the path is a little bit tricky. In fact, what I'm about to show you is one
   of the least known and most useful tricks for closing a path. See, FreeHand's
   pen tool is generally very capable, except when it comes to closing paths. If
   you drag with the pen tool on the first point in the path, you're liable to make
   a mess of it. And if you only click the first point, you sacrifice all control over
   the way in which the path closes. So don't do either. Instead of dragging on
   the first point, drag very near to it, at the location indicated by point D in
   Figure 3-36. As you drag upward, the control handle for the new segment
   moves downward, creating the concave portion of the segment. When your
   segment looks more or less like the one in the figure, pause your cursor but
   do not release the mouse button.

4. Remember that tip a few pages back about moving a point by ⌘/Ctrl-dragging
   with the pen tool? Well, now's your chance to try it. With the mouse button
   still down, press and hold the ⌘/Ctrl key. Then move point D so that it exactly
   covers point A. As soon as the two points overlap, release the mouse button
   and then the ⌘/Ctrl key. Whenever two endpoints in the same path overlap,
   FreeHand automatically fuses the two into a single point and closes the path.
   In this case, fusing points A and D results in the conversion of point A to a
   cusp point with two independent control handles, as shown in Figure 3-37.

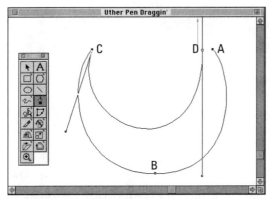

Figure 3-36: Drag upward from a location near —
but not directly on — the first point in the path.

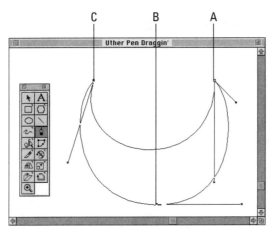

Figure 3-37: Press the ⌘/Ctrl key and drop point
D onto point A to close the path.

For more information on automatically joining endpoints in a path, see the "Auto joining" section of Chapter 5.

For the next example, I'd like to show you one method for retracting a control handle from a point resulting in a cusp that consist of only one control handle.

1. Begin again by drawing the path shown in Figure 3-34, as described in the first step of the previous section.

2. In this set of steps, you close the path with a flat top, resulting in a bowl shape (see Figure 3-39). Because curve points and Bézier control handles produce curved segments, you must convert points A and C to corner points and lop off one control handle from each point.

With the mouse button still down, press and hold the Option/Alt key. Then drag the control handle beneath the cursor back to point C, as shown in Figure 3-38, and release the mouse button and Option/Alt key. Notice that the Bézier control handle that would otherwise affect the next segment has disappeared. This technique is known as retracting a control handle.

If the control handle that you just tried to retract is still partially visible, press ⌘/Ctrl-I to display the Object Inspector. Then click on the right-hand Curve Handles icon.

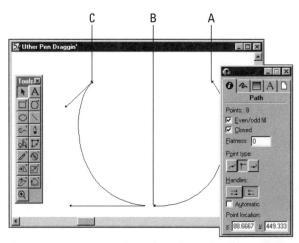

Figure 3-38: Press Option/Alt and continue your drag back to point C, thereby retracting a control handle.

3. Again, you'll be closing your path with the assistance of the ⌘/Ctrl key. Click and hold the mouse button at the location of point D in Figure 3-39. Do *not* move your mouse. With the mouse button still down, press and hold the ⌘/Ctrl key. Then drag point D onto point A and release the mouse button and then the ⌘/Ctrl key. FreeHand fuses points A and D into a single point, closing the shape. The new segment is flat, bordered on both sides by corner points with one Bézier control handle apiece.

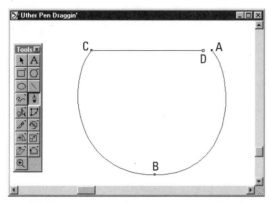

Figure 3-39: Press and hold the mouse button at point D. Then press the ⌘/Ctrl key and drag point D onto point A.

In this final exercise, we create a cusp point that only has one control. This differs from the last endeavor in the fact that, instead of creating a point that has two control handles and then removing one of the handles, we will create this point with only one control in the first place.

1. This third exercise demonstrates how to create a corner point with only one Bézier control handle by pressing Option/Alt before dragging with the pen tool. Begin by creating a straight-sided path like the one shown in Figure 3-40. It doesn't matter how many points are in the path, just as long as they're all corner points.

2. To prepare for the curved segment, press the Option/Alt key and drag to create a new corner point, like the selected point in Figure 3-40. Because the Option/Alt key is pressed, the pen tool automatically creates a corner point with only one Bézier control handle. The segment that connects the new point to its predecessor is straight because the control handle is positioned to affect the next segment you create. When you position the control handle where you want it, release the mouse button and then the Option/Alt key.

3. To close the shape, drag near the first point in the path, as demonstrated in Figure 3-41. As in the previous path-closing steps, do not release the mouse button. You have created a new curve point that is linked to the most recent corner point by a curved segment.

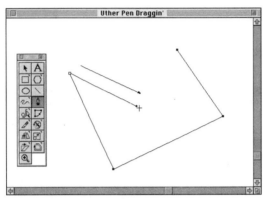

Figure 3-40: Option/Alt-drag to create a corner point with one control handle that will affect the next segment.

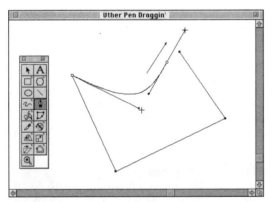

Figure 3-41: Create a curved segment by dragging with the pen tool near the first point in the path.

4. With the mouse button still down, press the ⌘/Ctrl key and move the curve point onto the first corner point in the path. FreeHand closes the shape and fuses the two points into a single corner point with a single Bézier control handle. The result is shown in Figure 3-42.

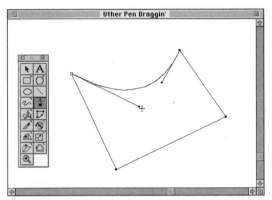

Figure 3-42: Press the ⌘/Ctrl key and drop the new curve point onto the path's first point.

Why the pen tool is so great

In time, you'll probably find that the pen tool is the tool of choice for creating complex paths, as opposed to tinkering with the bézigon tool. The reason is control. Take the fish shapes shown in Figures 3-43 and 3-44, for example. The top fish in each figure is the product of five corner points and five curve points, all created with the pen tool. By clicking, dragging, and Option/Alt-dragging, I manually specified the placement of each point and every Bézier control handle in the shape.

The bottom example in each figure shows the same shape drawn with the bézigon tool. Though each and every point is positioned identically to its pen-tool counterpart, the result is a rather malformed specimen, thanks to the repositioning and removing of key Bézier control handles. The culprit is FreeHand's built-in automatic curvature routine, which governs the placement of all control handles created with the bézigon tool. Automatic curvature encompasses a set of rules that guide the placement of Bézier control handles. The two simplest rules are as follows:

✦ Each point that neighbors a curve point gets one Bézier control handle pointing toward the curve point. The segment between the curve point and its neighbor is formed according to the definition of a circle and according to the locations of other neighboring points.

✦ If a corner point neighbors another corner point, the segment between the two points gets no Bézier control handle whatsoever and is therefore absolutely straight.

The first rule results in the distortion of the tail by exaggerating the curvature of its segments so they appear like arcs in a circle. The second rule straightens out the mouth because the mouth is defined using corner points only.

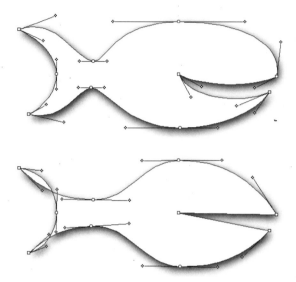

Figure 3-43: The points in a fish created with the pen tool (top) and the bézigon tool (bottom).

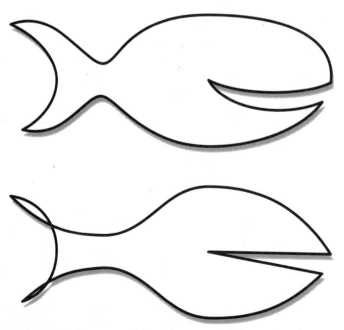

Figure 3-44: The same fish as they appear when printed.

I am not suggesting that by using the bézigon tool, you limit yourself to producing ugly results. In fact, automatic curvature has some real benefits, as discussed in Chapter 5. However, the results may not exactly suit your needs. The second example in each figure is, after all, a fish, but the first example shows the fish I wanted to create. The pen tool is the only tool among FreeHand's arsenal that is proficient enough to get the job done right the first time.

✦   ✦   ✦

Tracing an Imported Template

It Pays to Cheat

I know, that's not what your elementary school teacher taught you, but it's one of life's lessons that everyone must eventually learn. Simply put, starting from scratch is for those proverbial birds. The folks who reap the big rewards in the shortest time are those who give themselves a boost up. They're looking out for number one. All that malarkey about a level playing field is a conspiracy cooked up years ago by a now-defunct Communist fifth column. The fact is, if you lift from a known quantity, you can't go wrong. It's the American way.

I'm speaking, of course, of cheating in FreeHand by introducing a tracing template. Wait, you thought I meant . . . and you were sitting there nodding your head in agreement? Oh, you are sick! You and your kind are exactly what's wrong with this great country.

Where'd I put that soapbox? (Ahem.) I am not condoning going around stealing artwork from your friends and neighbors. Okay, sure, 2 Live Crew showed us all that you can steal a Roy Orbison song and call it a parody. But don't be scanning copyrighted artwork, converting it in FreeHand, and calling it your own. That's absolutely verboten. Well, more or less verboten, anyway. I mean, there's the old criticism-and-commentary loophole. And artists have been seeking "inspiration" from other artists since the beginning of time.

On second thought, you look to me like you need a good lawyer.

A trace of tradition

What I really have in mind is tracing from noncopyrighted material as well as original sketches and compositions. It's a cheat, I grant you, but it's the kind of cheat that artists have been relying on for years. You think that Edouard Manet just started slapping paint on the canvas when he created his revolutionary *Le Déjeuner sur l'Herbe*? No way. First, he sketched a bunch of folks enjoying a picnic. Then he thought, "You know, what this picture really needs is a naked woman." Manet was a big believer that a naked woman spiced up any environment. So he dug through his vast collection of bordello sketches and found an appropriate subject, one who looked like she could go for some KFC and coleslaw. Doubtless, he combined a few other sketches and maybe even tried out an egg tempura treatment or two. Finally, after he had successfully assembled all his elements, he embarked on the final painting.

I'm guessing that's how it went, anyway. I wasn't there, so I have to rely on the testimony of the few witnesses who are still available. Considering that this all happened in 1863, the number of reliable witnesses is kind of limited. And they all spoke French.

But that's not the point. The point is that although few of us can live up to Manet's artistic prowess, we can all mimic his approach. Not the naked woman part, necessarily — misogyny is best left to experts like 2 Live Crew — but the tradition of preliminary sketch followed by final execution.

FreeHand enables you to trace scanned images and artwork created in painting programs. It also automates the conversion process by providing a trace tool. Even skilled computer artists are well advised to sketch their ideas on paper or in a painting program before executing them in FreeHand. The following section explains why.

Why trace a bitmap?

It's not easy to draw from scratch in FreeHand. Even if you draw exclusively with the freehand tool, you frequently have to edit your lines and shapes, point by point (as I discuss in the next chapter).

Also, to build an image in FreeHand, you have to do just that: build. You have to combine heaps of mathematically defined lines and shapes and layer them much like girders at a construction site. (Don't you just love these analogies? I've got tons more.)

In fact, you'll probably have the most luck with FreeHand if you're part artist and part engineer. But for those of us who aren't engineers and can't even imagine how engineers think, a painting application such as Photoshop or Painter provides a more artist-friendly environment.

Painting programs provide straightforward tools such as pencils and erasers that work like their real-life counterparts. Your screen displays the results of your mouse movements instantaneously. You can draw, see what you've drawn, and make alterations in the time it takes the appropriate neurons to fire in your brain.

But despite the many advantages of painting programs, their single failing — grainy output — can be glaringly obvious, so much so that people who have never used a computer can recognize a bitmapped image as computer-produced artwork. Object-oriented drawings, on the other hand, are always smooth.

The jagged nature of images produced with painting programs is particularly noticeable in the case of black-and-white artwork. For example, the bitmapped fish in Figure 4-1 was fairly easy to create. The fish is well executed, but its jagged edges are far too obvious for it to be considered professional-quality artwork. By introducing a few shades of gray to the image, I softened much of its jaggedness, as illustrated in Figure 4-2. However, the fish now looks muddy and out of focus. Continuous-tone bitmaps are better suited to representing photographs than line art.

Figure 4-1: A typically jagged black-and-white bitmapped image.

Figure 4-2: Gray pixels soften the edges but also obscure details.

Only in a drawing program such as FreeHand can you create pristine line art. The fish in Figure 4-3 for example, required more time and effort to produce, but the result is a smooth, highly-focused, professional-quality image.

Figure 4-3: By tracing the bitmapped fish image in FreeHand, I was able to create this smooth, exemplary drawing.

Importing Tracing Templates

Whether you sketch your idea on paper and then scan it into your computer or sketch it directly in a painting application, you can import the sketch as a tracing template into FreeHand. FreeHand can import any bitmapped image that is saved in one of the following standardized graphic formats:

✦ **MacPaint:** MacPaint documents may originate not only from MacPaint itself but also from other low-end painting programs (such as Color It! and SuperPaint) and from scanning applications such as ThunderWare. The MacPaint format is one of the most widely supported graphics formats for the Mac. Unfortunately, it is also the most limited. The MacPaint format accommodates monochrome (black-and-white) images on vertically oriented, 7½ × 10½-inch pages containing a maximum of 72 dots per inch.

✦ **PICT:** The PICT format, commonly associated with moderately powerful drawing applications such as MacDraw and Canvas, is much more flexible. PICT is the original file-swapping format developed by Apple for transferring both bitmapped and object-oriented pictures from one graphics application to another. PICT can accommodate any size graphic, including resolutions of more than 300 dots per inch, and over 16 million colors. For this reason, nearly all scanning and image-editing applications support the PICT format.

Don't be surprised if you encounter an out-of-memory error when you import a color bitmap saved in the PICT format. Because FreeHand provides much more reliable support for the TIFF format, avoid most memory problems by saving your color scans and paintings as TIFF documents. I recommend the use of 8-bit TIFFs because they compress well. Considering that you won't need 32-bit color for tracing purposes, the TIFF format can save a bundle in file size.

✦ **TIFF (Tagged Image File Format):** The TIFF format is exclusively a bitmapped format, used widely in programs such as Photoshop and other applications mentioned in Chapter 1. But, like PICT, it is otherwise unrestricted, accommodating graphics of any size, resolutions exceeding 300 dots per inch, and over 16 million colors. Aldus developed TIFF in an attempt to standardize images created by various scanners, and provide a reliably-defined gray-scale image of more consistent laser prints. Nearly all scanning and image-editing programs support the TIFF format. On the Windows platform, they are named "TIF."

✦ **EPS (Encapsulated PostScript):** The EPS format combines a pure PostScript-language description of a graphic with a PICT-format screen representation. Altsys (the developers of FreeHand) created the EPS format in cooperation with Aldus and Adobe. It's designed for swapping high-resolution images from one PostScript-compatible application to another. It is not, however, an efficient format for saving bitmaps. A color EPS bitmap, for example, is typically two to three times as large as the same bitmap saved in the TIFF format.

The PICT and TIFF formats offer compression options to save space on disk. If QuickTime is running on your computer, many applications can apply JPEG compression to PICT files. Regardless of QuickTime, you can compress TIFF files using the LZW method. FreeHand does not support the PICT format with JPEG compression, but it does support the TIFF format with LZW compression.

Due to the poor performance of the PICT and EPS formats, I heartily recommend that you save all images in the TIFF format (with LZW compression, if available) before importing them for tracing.

Kinds of tracing templates

Tracing templates fall into three broad categories:

✦ **Scans:** Scans are electronic images of photographs, prints, or drawings. Old black-and-white scans lying on dusty, forgotten disks are commonly saved as MacPaint documents. Grayscale and color scans are typically saved in the PICT and TIFF formats. Scans offer exceptionally accurate tracing backgrounds, especially when taken from photographs. All parts of the image have position and scale accurately represented. They are useful for detail work such as producing schematic drawings, medical illustrations, and other documents that require the utmost accuracy. Scans also are useful for people who want to draw but don't consider themselves very skilled at it. Scans can be the perfect bridge between an amateur effort and a professional product. Follow the directions for Importing or Pasting a PICT image depending on your image source.

✦ **Drafts:** Drafts include CAD (computer-aided design), schematic, or structured drawings created in MacDraw, MacDraft, Claris CAD, and similar applications. Such drafting programs rarely provide the array of free-form illustration tools and sophisticated transformation and special-effects capabilities available in FreeHand. Draft templates are typically transported via the PICT format. Follow the directions in the next section for importing PICT images.

✦ **Sketches:** All great works of art begin with sketching — its roots are deep in the artistic tradition. If you were creating an oil painting, for example, you might make several sketches before deciding how the finished piece should look. Like oil paint, FreeHand is ill-suited to sketching, as the creative process is based on a metaphor of building your illustration. The act of sketching is best suited to painting applications, which provide environments conducive to spontaneity. You can scribble, erase, and create much as you do when you use a pencil — quickly and freely. The good news is you can combine the two, traditional sketching and precision FreeHand drawing. Simply sketch in the paint program, or sketch on paper and scan the image. An alternative would be to use a pressure sensitive tablet especially if you are a traditional artist using FreeHand as a new tool. The steps for turning your sketched images to templates are explained next.

Placing a template file

To import a template — whatever its format — into an open FreeHand illustration, follow these steps:

1. Choose File ➪ Import (⌘/Ctrl-R) or use the Import Icon at the left of the Main toolbar, or press ⌘/Ctrl-O. FreeHand displays the Import Document dialog box.

It's a good idea to name template images with a template suffix such as ".PICT" or integrate something like "temp" into their name so you can tell them apart from your other scans. Color scans can also be used as templates when saved as EPS files.

2. Select a template file from the scrolling list and press Return or Enter. FreeHand reads the file from disk and displays the place cursor, as shown in the first example in Figure 4-4.

3. Click with the place cursor to specify the location of the upper left corner of the template. Click once and it is placed. FreeHand places placed templates in the illustration at their actual size. (Bitmap image dimensions are different from their resolution.) All previously selected objects become deselected.

Place cursor

Figure 4-4: Click with the place cursor (left) to position the upper left corner of an imported template (right).

An important alternative to clicking with the place cursor is dragging with the place cursor. Instead of simply plopping down your template (as you do when you click with the place cursor), dragging with the place cursor allows you to place a graphic and scale it at the same time. Once you've marqueed the appropriate area with the place cursor and released the mouse button, FreeHand scales the imported graphic to fill the area surrounded by your drag. The resizing is always proportional, so the horizontal and vertical dimensions of the imported graphic are equally affected.

For best results, send the template image to a Background layer. (If the Layers panel is not available, press ⌘/Ctrl-6.) To do this, click Background in the Layers panel while the template (imported image) is selected. The template then appears dimmed or grayed, as shown in Figure 4-5, which makes it easier to distinguish from paths and other objects in your illustration. Also, you can display imported artwork on a Background layer in both the Preview and Keyline modes, while you can display imported artwork that's on a Foreground layer only in the Preview mode. And background artwork does not print, so you can isolate it from the actual illustration.

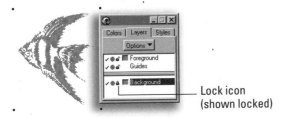

Lock icon
(shown locked)

Figure 4-5: A tracing template appears dimmed or grayed when placed on a Background layer, making it easier to trace.

After positioning the template on the Background layer, be sure to deselect the template by clicking on an empty portion of the screen and then click Foreground in the Layers panel. Otherwise, you will end up tracing your object-oriented paths on the Background layer along with the template.

Tip

To protect the template so that you don't accidentally move or otherwise alter it, click the lock icon in front of the Background option in the Layers panel. The lock icon changes from unlocked (open) to locked (closed). With the template locked, you'll also have fewer problems selecting and manipulating objects in your illustration.

Pasting a template file

You can also import a template via the Clipboard. You just use the Cut, Copy, and Paste commands common to the Edit menus of all Mac and Windows applications. The following steps explain how:

1. While inside a painting program (such as Photoshop), select the portion of the picture you want to use as a template and choose Edit ➪ Copy (⌘- on Macs and Ctrl+C).

2. Switch to the FreeHand application. If FreeHand is currently running, choose the FreeHand icon from the list of running applications in the Applications menu or on the Taskbar. If FreeHand is not currently running, double-click the FreeHand icon at the Finder level to launch the program.

3. After FreeHand is running, (remember to select the Background layer) choose Edit ➪ Paste (⌘/Ctrl-V). FreeHand displays the copied template image in the center of the illustration window (not necessarily in the center of the page).

Caution

As is the case when placing a graphic, you may encounter an out-of-memory error when pasting a color bitmap from the Clipboard, thanks to FreeHand's less reliable handling of the PICT format. So my earlier recommendation still stands: The most successful method for importing a grayscale or color template is to save it as a TIFF document and import it into FreeHand using the Import command in the File menu.

Automated Tracing

You can use any of the drawing tools I discussed in Chapter 3 to trace a bitmapped image. Just follow the outline of the bitmap using the tools as directed in that chapter. However, if the process seems too complicated, or if you just want to speed things up, FreeHand provides an additional drawing tool that automates the tracing process: the trace tool. The remainder of this chapter tells you everything you need to know to use this amazing device.

The trace tool

You can use the trace tool to trace the borders of a template image. To operate the trace tool, just drag to create a rectangular marquee around the portion of the template that you want to trace. FreeHand does the rest.

Using the trace tool is certainly easier than tracing a template image by hand. Unfortunately—you knew there had to be a catch, didn't you?—the results are less precise and require more adjustments than paths you create with the pen tool or even the freehand tool.

Take a look at the angelfish in Figure 4-6. The following steps explain how to use the trace tool to convert a low-resolution, jagged-as-all-get-out image like this one to a mathematically precise, object-oriented one.

Figure 4-6: No amount of retouching in a paint program equals the sharp edge created by FreeHand's automatic trace tool.

1. Import your bitmap image using either the Import or Paste command, as explained earlier in this chapter.

2. With the imported image selected, click the Background option in the Layers panel to send the template to the Background layer. The image then appears dimmed or grayed in the illustration window. You're now ready to convert the image with the trace tool. (To trace another layer, use the trace tool options.)

3. Deselect the template and lock the Background layer. Then click Foreground in the Layers panel to make sure that FreeHand doesn't send your traced paths to the Background layer.

4. Drag with the trace tool as if you were drawing a rectangle around the template image. A marquee tracks the movements of your cursor, as shown in Figure 4-7. After the marquee entirely surrounds the template, release the mouse button. Several seconds later—or, if the template is very detailed, several lifetimes later—FreeHand produces a collection of selected closed paths that trace the various outlines of the template, as shown in Figure 4-8.

Note

The trace tool always produces closed paths. Even if you drag the marquee around the template image of a line, FreeHand traces entirely around the line to create a long and very thin shape.

Trace tool

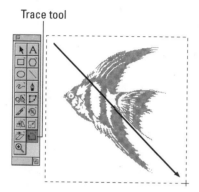

Figure 4-7: Drag with the trace tool to marquee the entire template image.

Figure 4-8: FreeHand automatically produces several closed paths that trace the outline of the marqueed image.

The trace tool options

The trace tool has a number of options for tracing both color and grayscale images; images of various resolutions, including high resolution scans, and screen resolution (normal) templates. Before you trace, you can choose the layer you wish to trace, and are not limited to the Background layer. Deselecting one of these layer controls made the tool insensitive to templates in that layer.

An overview of using the tool has some basic steps: select the imported image you would like to trace, select the trace tool, double-click and set the tool options for this image, and then drag the tool across the selected image. The following descriptions of the tracing options can all be referenced by Figure 4-9.

Okay, so let's get into these tracing options:

✦ **Color Mode:** In previous versions, a color template was perceived by tracing tools as all black. It's a relief that this is not longer the case! Be sure to tell FreeHand if your scan is color, or grayscale (including black and white). The difference between the two settings is that choosing color causes FreeHand to detect the relative lightness and darkness of the colors in template. Choose the bit-depth for the selected template. Common settings include 24-bit color (RGB), 32-bit color (CMYK), 8-bit color (Index Color for Web graphics), 8-bit grayscale (black-n-white photo), or 1-bit grayscale (black and white line art).

Figure 4-9: The "way fab" options of the trace tool: Color mode, Resolution, Trace Layers , Path Conversion, and Noise Tolerance.

✦ **Resolution:** Getting a good template in the past required enough experience and skills to figure out how to scan your image so the file was not too small, or too large, and you didn't lose edge detail when used as a template. Those lucky artists with Photoshop skills could manipulate the scan to create a good template! Present day FreeHand can be sensitized to the image resolution, and use all the available pixel data in the scan for a good quality autotraced object. Extra edge smoothing is applied to low-resolution images.

✦ **Trace Layers:** The trace tool can be set to trace any layer that is created in advance. Freedom from the Background layer is possible if you feel constrained. More on this feature later in the chapter.

✦ **Path Conversion:** This feature tells the tool what types of shapes to create when it detects edges on the template, and which edges to trace around. Four options are available for Path Conversion: Outline (outlines each shape separately, and paths can overlap to complete a shape); Centerline (places a centered line within each shape, with an option to make each line uniform, or the same weight); Centerline/Outline (combines outline and center line functions as needed, and you can tell the trace tool to leave certain image areas open) and Outeredge (allows for tracing outer edge only — great for silhouettes!). These options make the tracing tool on par with Adobe's Streamline.

✦ **Trace Conformity:** Here, you can instruct FreeHand on how closely the traced path follows the contours of the template. The next section addresses this in greater detail.

✦ **Noise Tolerance:** The trace tool's noise tolerance setting adjusts the tool's sensitivity to stray pixels at the edge of a traceable area. Increase the tolerance for rough-edged templates. The minimum setting of 0 tolerance will produce highly irregular edges. The default is 5 with a maximum tolerance of 20, which creates overly smooth paths.

Trace curve fit

Changing the Trace Conformity setting from loose to tight results in the tool exaggerating every pixel in the edges of the template — this creates a rough, imprecise path with a great many anchor points. The Trace conformity control has a low setting of 0 and a high, tight setting of 10. Smoother paths require fewer anchor points, and good results are usually achieved by leaving the Trace Conformity function at a value of 5.

Figure 4-10 shows how FreeHand's trace tool interprets the angelfish image differently depending on the selection of the Trace Conformity option. I created the path on the left with a Trace Conformity of 9 selected; and I traced the path on the right with a Trace Conformity of 1. The two circled areas in each angelfish highlight major differences between the two images.

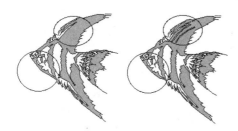

Figure 4-10: The results of tight and loose settings in the trace tool dialog box. Circled areas highlight major differences.

If you compare these images to those back in Figure 3-15, you can see that the Trace Conformity option of the tracing tool is similar to the freehand tool's Tight Fit option. However, with the trace tool, you can compensate for edge inaccuracies in the image you are tracing. With the Freehand tool, you adjust the controls to compensate for the inaccuracies a person encounters while attempting to draw freehand with a computer mouse.

All paths that you create with the trace tool are filled and stroked with the default attributes. To complete a traced image, you need to apply your desired fill and stroke to each path, as explained in Chapters 11 and 12. Figure 4-11 shows the end result of a properly stroked and filled angelfish.

Image size

More important than curve fit is the size of your tracing template. Your image should be as large as necessary. You probably guessed as much — after all, it only makes sense that FreeHand can trace a bitmapped template image containing a lot of detail better than one that contains very little detail. As of yet, FreeHand isn't smart enough to make up detail on its own, so it has to rely on the image to provide as much information as possible.

Figure 4-11: The final result.

Tip

You will get better results from an image by scaling it within FreeHand. The trace tool is most accurate when each and every pixel of the template image is visible at the 100 percent view size. For a template to trace well, I use Photoshop to resize the image to about 10 inches × 10 inches. I find it easier to manage the letter-sized page on the screen and then proof it as I work on a laser printer. Once the template is traced, artwork can be scaled up within FreeHand without loss of quality. The best way to accomplish this is to save the image to disk—whether from Photoshop or some other application—at a resolution of exactly 72 dots per inch, which is the resolution of a standard monitor. (Even if your screen's resolution is slightly different, 72 works just fine.) Regardless of what you've heard about images looking better at higher resolutions, they trace better in FreeHand at low resolutions.

Cross-Reference

When in doubt, use the scale tool or Transform panel to increase the size of the image. For complete information on this tool and panel, see Chapter 13.

Tracing layer control

The trace tool dialog box enables you to tell FreeHand which layers within a trace tool marquee should be evaluated. The options are incredibly straightforward, but here's an explanation just in case. Select exactly the layer you want the tool to recognize, then select the imported template on that layer, and drag the tool across—voilà! It helps to make a new layer in advance for each template.

Here's an example. Suppose that your illustration involves two bitmapped images, one directly in front of the other. If one image is positioned on a Background layer and the other is on some Foreground layer, you can use the options in the trace tool dialog box to trace one image without tracing the other. (For more information about layering, read the section "Layering Objects" in Chapter 6.)

Note FreeHand traces everything surrounded by a marquee—not just the imported image but objects created directly inside FreeHand as well. When you're working inside a complicated illustration, play it safe: Place the tracing template on the Background layer, lock that layer, and execute your trace on a Foreground layer.

Improving shapes created with the trace tool

After tracing is complete, FreeHand has a nifty feature for improving the automatically detected shapes. The Simplify command is found under the Modify ➪ Alter Path submenu. Use this feature to reduce the number of points in a path, for example if it is too rough. This feature is a great time saver since it not only removes extra points, it puts the remaining points in the optimum position along the path, and will add points if needed. Pretty smart, huh?

To apply this feature, select the path you want to improve, and apply the Simplify command. The exact steps are as follows:

1. Select the path you wish to improve or simplify.
2. Choose Modify ➪ Alter Path ➪ Simplify or Xtra ➪ Cleanup ➪ Simplify, or click Simplify in the Xtra Operations panel.
3. Enter a value from 1 to 10 (with .25 point adjustment) in the Amount option box in the Simplify dialog box. Large numbers eliminate lots of points!
4. Click OK.

Tracing Grayscale and Color Images

FreeHand imports a whole slew of files formats including PICT, TIFF, JPEG, PDF, GIF, Targa, BMP, PNG (Portable Network Graphic images), Photoshop, EPS, and a number of others. They can all be used as templates because FreeHand's trace tool is sensitive to different color and gray levels—256 of them. This makes tracing seemingly troublesome color and gray levels a snap. Simply select the appropriate settings, from 2 levels (black and white) to 256 levels. Drag the trace tool across the selection and—Zowee! It's a miracle! You have a beautiful image tailored to your specifications. I recommend trying a few traces with different settings. Once you've traced an image to your satisfaction, all that's left to do is reshape your newly formed paths to perfection. Coincidentally, that's the focus of Chapter 5.

✦   ✦   ✦

Reshaping and Combining Paths

The Forgiving Medium

Sometimes I think Michelangelo made a mistake when he decided to take up marble sculpting. It's got to be the world's least forgiving medium. The integrity of the stone is inconsistent—one moment impervious, the next moment fragile. You have to swing the hammer like a pick ax to shave away small details from the body of the piece, while all it takes is a misplaced tap to knock off a delicate extremity. Chink. Oops, there goes the nose. Pang. Uh oh, there goes a finger. Fwack. Oh, David, buddy, that's got to hurt. Then again, maybe I can use it in my next piece, Josephine and What's Left of Napoleon. Okay, to keep things proportional, I'd have to make Josephine over 200 feet tall, but hey, waste not, want not.

Meanwhile, getting back to Michelangelo, I just don't think that he had the temperament for the whole sculpting scene. The city of Florence is teeming with his half-finished masterpieces, works that he either abandoned in disgust or willfully attacked in fits of rage. It wouldn't surprise me to find out that the guy who whacked off David's toe in the Galleria dell' Accademia a few years back was the reincarnation of Michelangelo intent on wreaking further damage on his work.

Okay, I guess that might surprise me. But if Michelangelo were to come to me today, I'd certainly feel compelled to put my hand on his shoulder and gently counsel him to stick with pencil and paper. "You can erase a pencil mark," I'd tell him. "No need to hack the paper to bits or burn it or anything. Just rub, rub, rub, and the mistake vanishes like a bad dream.

"Better yet, Michel . . . can I call you Mike? You should try out FreeHand. Really, it's a great program. You got a Mac, Mike? Windows? Well, then, you're set. You see, after you create a graphic object in FreeHand, the object is by no means permanent. You can reshape any path. Obviously, if you do most of your drawing with the freehand and trace tools, your paths are going to need some reshaping. But even if you're a pen tool master, you'll probably end up adjusting most of the paths you create. Reshaping in FreeHand is like painting over the same area on a canvas. . . . Well, then, it's like painting on a fresco, Mike. The point is, it's a fine-tuning process."

You never know. Michelangelo might not have listened to me. By the time the guy was my age, he had polished off two of the world's great masterpieces and was getting ready to start on the Sistine Chapel. So fine, if the guy wants to waste his life on marble, that's his funeral. I just think that maybe he could have really amounted to something if he had given FreeHand a chance.

But enough about Michelangelo. What you're really interested in is developing your artistic talents, not those of some long-gone Italian. To that end, this chapter shows you how to fine-tune your FreeHand masterpieces by reshaping and combining paths. (Note that the illustrations in this chapter were created with the smaller handles preference deselected.)

Selecting and Deselecting

Before you can reshape a path, you have to select it. Selecting a path in FreeHand is not unlike selecting an element in some other object-oriented program on a computer. You just position your arrow tool cursor over part of an object and click. Points or corner handles appear on the selected object to indicate that the next action you perform will affect it.

If an object has no fill, you must click an object's stroke to select it. Otherwise, you can click the object's stroke or fill.

Selecting paths

Like most manipulations covered in this chapter, selecting is performed with the arrow tool (which some folks call the *selection* or *pointer* tool) — the first tool in the toolbox. Clicking a point or segment with the arrow tool selects the path that contains the element.

You can access the arrow tool when any drawing tool is selected by pressing and holding the ⌘/Ctrl key. As soon as you release the ⌘/Ctrl key, FreeHand returns control to the selected tool. To permanently access the arrow tool, press V (V is for pointy little arrow).

Different kinds of paths have different ways of showing that they're selected. For example, if you click a rectangle or ellipse, four small, corner handles surround the shape, as illustrated in Figure 5-1. These handles signify that the selection comprises grouped objects that may be subject to special manipulations, as described in the "Reshaping Rectangles and Ellipses" section later in this chapter.

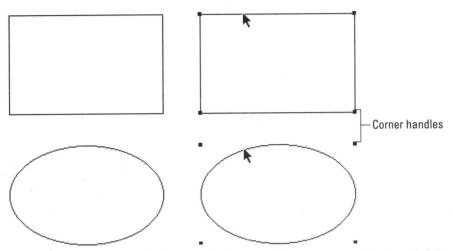

Corner handles

Figure 5-1: A rectangle and ellipse, each shown as it appears when deselected (left) and after selecting it with the arrow tool (right).

When you click a polygon, straight line, or other free-form path, FreeHand displays all points as small squares, as shown in Figure 5-2. This indicates that the path is selected but the individual points in the path are deselected. Any manipulation you perform affects all portions of the path equally.

To select multiple paths, click the first path you want to select and then Shift-click each of the others. Or drag a marquee around portions of several paths and press the grave key (`). I discuss this second method in slightly more depth in the next section.

Selecting points

To select a specific point in a path, first select the path and then click directly on the desired point with the arrow tool. A selected point appears hollow, as shown in Figure 5-3. A selected corner point is a hollow square; a selected curve point is a hollow circle, and a selected connector point is a hollow triangle. All Bézier control handles associated with the selected point and the two neighboring segments also display. Deselected points in the path appear as small filled squares.

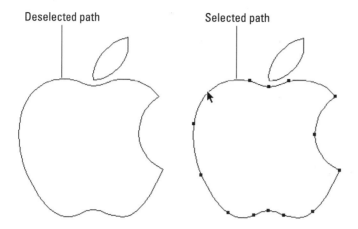

Deselected path   Selected path

Figure 5-2: Normally invisible (left), the points in a free-form path display when you select the path with the arrow tool (right).

Figure 5-3: After selecting a free-form path, you can select a specific point in the path by clicking it.

To select multiple points in a selected path, click the first point you want to select and then press Shift and click each point you want to add to the selection. Another way to select multiple points is to marquee them. Drag with the arrow tool in an empty portion of the illustration window to create a rectangular marquee with a dotted outline, as shown in the first example in Figure 5-4.

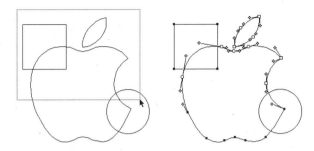

Figure 5-4: All points surounded by a marquee (left) becomes selected (right). A rectangle or ellipse must be entirely surrounded to be selected.

FreeHand positions one corner of the marquee at the spot where you begin to drag. The opposite corner of the marquee follows the movements of your cursor as you drag. All points within the marquee that belong to free-form paths become selected when you release your mouse button, as illustrated in the second example in the figure.

To select a grouped object, such as a rectangle or ellipse, you must surround the entire group with your marquee. Notice in the second example in Figure 5-4 that the square is selected, but the circle is not. The square fit entirely inside the marquee; the circle was only partially marqueed.

Tip

Marqueeing is possibly the most convenient means for selecting multiple objects. However, marqueeing selects not only paths, but also their points. If you drag a path in which specific points are selected, you end up stretching the shape rather than moving it (as explained in the "Moving Elements" section later in this chapter). If you want to manipulate whole paths and speed up the screen display, press the grave key (upper left key on the keyboard) or choose the Edit ⇨ Select ⇨ Superselect command to deselect all points while leaving their paths selected.

Figure 5-5 shows the result of choosing the Edit ⇨ Select ⇨ Superselect command or pressing grave (`)(pronounced grahauv — like the accent, not the tomb) after marqueeing the points shown in the second example in Figure 5-4. Notice that all hollow points turn solid and all Bézier control handles disappear. Now you can drag these shapes without stretching them.

Figure 5-5: The paths from the previous figure after I pressed the grave (`) key.

You can combine marqueeing with Shift-clicking to select multiple paths and points. You can also marquee while pressing the Shift key, which adds the marqueed points and paths to the existing selection.

Selecting everything

The only remaining selection methods to mention are the Select All command (⌘/Ctrl-A) and the Select All in Document command (⌘/Ctrl-Shift-A), both in the Edit ⇨ Select submenu. When you choose the Select All command, FreeHand selects every path, group, and other object on the current page (as long as the objects reside on unlocked layers, discussed in Chapter 6). Choose the Select All in Document command to select every path, group, and other object in the entire document including the pasteboard. The one exception is when a text block is active, in which case either Select command highlights all text inside the text block only.

Note

This differs from version 5.5 where Edit ⇨ Select All selected all objects on documents and pasteboard and Select All on Page selected only the objects on the current page. So it is reversed from the previous version to make sense.

Deselecting objects

If you don't want an object to be affected by a command or mouse operation, you need to deselect it. To deselect all objects, simply click with the arrow tool in an empty portion of the illustration window.

If the entire window is filled with objects, and you can't find an empty portion to click in, press the Tab key or use the Edit ⇨ Select ⇨ None submenu. Tab deselects all objects in an illustration except when a text block is active . In fact, you probably want to get in the habit of pressing Tab even when an empty portion of the window is available; it's much faster than using the arrow tool.

FreeHand also deselects all currently selected objects when you do any of the following:

◆ Select an object that was not previously selected by clicking on it with the arrow tool.

◆ Click or drag with the rectangle, oval, polygon, line, or trace tool.

◆ Click or drag with the freehand, bézigon, or pen tool in an empty portion of the illustration window.

◆ Click or drag with the text tool.

◆ Choose Paste (⌘/Ctrl-V), Paste Behind, Duplicate (⌘/Ctrl-D), or Clone (⌘-= on Macs and Ctrl-Shift-C on PCs) from the Edit menu.

Deselecting specific points and paths

You don't have to deselect every object in an illustration; you can deselect specific paths and points without affecting other selected objects. To deselect a single selected point, for example, Shift-click it with the arrow tool. To deselect an entire path, Shift-click any of its segments.

You can also deselect points and grouped objects by Shift-marqueeing. If you press the Shift key and then marquee a portion of your illustration, all selected points and grouped objects within the marquee become deselected. At the same time, all deselected points and grouped objects in the marquee become selected. It's a role reversal kind of thing.

Note

Shift-marqueeing deselects points and grouped objects only. The method does not work for deselecting entire free-form paths. To deselect a path, you have to Shift-click one of its segments.

Reshaping Rectangles and Ellipses

Try this little experiment: Draw a rectangle with the rectangle tool. The shape and size don't matter. Now select the arrow tool and try to select a specific point in the shape.

Can't do it, huh? When you click a point, it doesn't become hollow, as it would in a free-form path. If you Shift-click a point, the entire rectangle becomes deselected. That's because rectangles and ellipses are created as grouped objects, or simply groups. FreeHand fuses all elements in a group into a single object, locking points into relative alignment so that the path cannot be reshaped.

Using handles

Grouped objects are not entirely immutable, however. The easiest way to alter a geometric shape is to *scale* it — change its size — by dragging one of its four corner handles. As shown in the first example in Figure 5-6, FreeHand displays the group's original size and shape during your drag for reference. The center point of the shape updates throughout the operation so that you can more precisely align the shape with other objects in the illustration window.

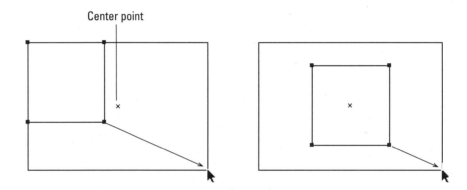

Center point

Figure 5-6: Scale a geometric shape by dragging (left) or Option/Alt-dragging (right) one of its corner handles with the arrow tool.

If you Option/Alt-drag a corner handle, you scale the path with respect to its center point, as illustrated in the second example in Figure 5-6. Press Shift while dragging to constrain a rectangle to a square or an ellipse to a circle.

Tip

To scale a rectangle or oval exclusively horizontally or vertically, press the ⌘/Ctrl key while Shift-dragging. Press ⌘/Ctrl while Shift-Option/Alt-dragging to scale the path about its center point.

To scale a rectangle or ellipse *proportionally* — that is, to maintain a constant ratio between height and width — Shift-drag with the scale tool as described in the "Constrained scaling" section in Chapter 13.

Handle coordinates

One of the most basic ways to manipulate any object in FreeHand is to adjust the options in the Object Inspector. Press ⌘/Ctrl-I to access the Object Inspector.

Figure 5-7 shows the Object Inspector as it appears when a rectangle and ellipse is selected. The Dimensions option boxes control the size and location of the selected shape. The X and Y options list the coordinates of the shape's upper left corner handle in relation to the ruler origin, which is the point at which the horizontal and vertical coordinates equal zero (as described in the "Using the rulers" section in Chapter 6).

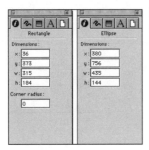

Figure 5-7: The Object Inspector as it appears when a rectangle (left) or ellipse (right) is selected.

By default, the ruler origin is located in the lower left corner of the page. Positive X values are to the right of the origin; negative X values are to the left. Positive Y values are above the origin; negative Y values are below.

The W and H options control the width and height of the selected shape. All values are measured in the unit of measure specified in the Object Inspector. The default unit is points.

When a rectangle is selected, the Object Inspector displays an additional option box, Corner Radius. This option controls the extent to which the corners of the selected shape are rounded. The radius of a rectangle with perpendicular corners is 0. As you increase the corner radius values, the rounded corner consumes a larger portion of the rectangle. For more information, read the "Drawing a rectangle with rounded corners" section in Chapter 3. After changing any of the values in the Object Inspector, press the Return/Enter key to implement your changes. (The panel really ought to have an Apply button.)

Note

If two or more objects are selected, the Object Inspector appears blank. This happens because FreeHand can't communicate size and location information for more than one object at a time.

Ungrouping geometric shapes

As I described in the preceding pages, FreeHand gives you a number of ways to modify rectangles and ellipses. But none of these methods allows you to move one point in a path independently of its neighbors. The only way to truly reshape a geometric shape is to ungroup it by selecting it and choosing Modify ➪ Ungroup (⌘/Ctrl-U). Ungrouping frees the points in a geometric path so that you can manipulate them independently, just like you can manipulate points in a free-form path. Figure 5-8 shows the effect of ungrouping three geometric shapes.

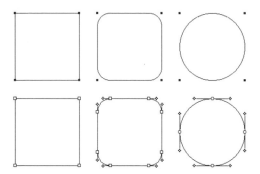

Figure 5-8: Three geometric shapes before (top) and after (bottom) choosing the Ungroup command.

When you ungroup a geometric shape, its corner handles and center point disappear, and you gain access to points, segments, and Bézier control handles. So that you can see all these items, I took the liberty of selecting all points in the ungrouped paths. Notice that the selected points in the two rectangles are corner points (hollow squares), while those in the circle are curve points (hollow circles). This gives you maximum flexibility in reshaping the paths, as you discover in later sections.

Caution

After you ungroup a rectangle, you can never again access the Corner Radius option shown in Figure 5-7 — not even if you regroup the path by choosing the Group command — unless you choose Edit ➪ Undo Ungroup (⌘/Ctrl-Z) immediately after ungrouping the path. To change the curvature of the corners of an ungrouped rectangle, you have to reshape the path manually, just as if it were created with one of the free-form drawing tools. Also, you can't scale an ungrouped path by dragging at its corner as you can with a standard grouped rectangle.

It's not necessary to ungroup paths created with the arc, spiral, polygon, or line tool. Like paths created with free-form drawing tools, arcs, spirals, polygons, and lines are created as ungrouped objects. You can reshape them immediately.

Moving Elements

The most common method for reshaping a path is moving some element — whether it is a point, segment, or Bézier control handle — in the path. Moving selected points independently of deselected points stretches the segments that connect the points. You can also stretch curved segments by moving a Bézier control handle, which changes the curvature of the path.

Cross-Reference

The following sections explain how to reshape paths by moving elements in the path. For information on moving entire paths, including a full-blown description of the Move panel in the Transform panel, read Chapter 13, "The Transformations and the Xtras," which is based on the escapades of a Motown group that never quite got off the ground.

Moving points

To move one or more points in a path, select the points you want to move and then drag any one of them. FreeHand moves all selected points the same distance and direction. When you move a point while a neighboring point remains stationary, the segment between the two points shrinks or stretches to accommodate the change in distance, as illustrated in Figure 5-9. If a point has any Bézier control handles, the handles move with the point, unless the point is governed by automatic curvature — as is the case with points created with the bézigon tool. When automatic curvature is in effect, the handles move independently according to how FreeHand thinks the path should look. Either way, the curved segment not only shrinks or stretches, but also bends to accommodate the movement of a point.

Figure 5-9: Dragging the selected point (left) stretches the segments between the point and its deselected, stationary neighbors (right).

When you move multiple points, any segment located between two deselected points or between two selected points remains unchanged during the move, as illustrated in Figure 5-10. FreeHand allows you to move multiple points within a single path, as in Figures 5-9 and 5-10, or in separate paths, as in Figure 5-11. This means that you can reshape more than one path at a time.

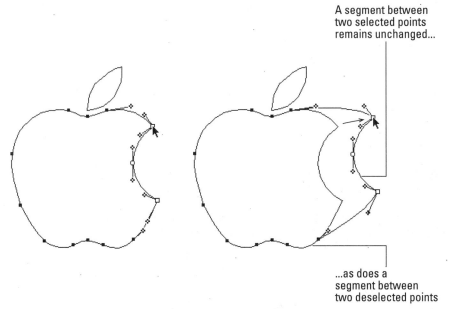

A segment between
two selected points
remains unchanged...

...as does a
segment between
two deselected points

Figure 5-10: Dragging at any selected point in a shape (left) moves all selected points an identical distance and direction (right).

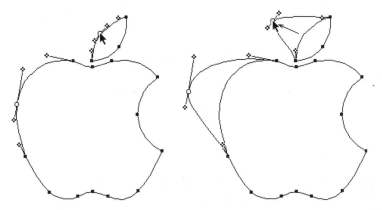

Figure 5-11: You can even move multiple points when selected points reside in different paths.

As you can see from the figures, FreeHand displays both the previous and current locations of points and segments as you drag them. This useful feature lets you gauge the full effect of a move as it progresses.

Constrained movements

You can constrain the movement of selected points to any angle that is a multiple of 45 degrees. Just press the Shift key after you begin your drag and hold the key down until after you release the mouse button. (If you press and hold Shift before beginning your drag, you run the risk of deselecting the point which you click.) You can alter the effects of pressing the Shift key by rotating the constraint axes. You do this by entering a value into the Angle value in the Constrain dialog box . Then press Enter. Figure 5-12, for example, shows the result of entering a value of 15 into the Angle option box and Shift-dragging a few selected points.

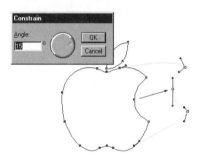

Figure 5-12: By entering a new value into the Angle option box in the Constrain dialog box, you can change the angle of a Shift-drag.

The constraint axes specify the eight directions in which you can move an element by Shift-dragging. By default, these directions are as follows:

✦ **0 degrees:** Directly to the right

✦ **45 degrees:** Diagonally up and to the right

✦ **90 degrees:** Straight up

✦ **135 degrees:** Diagonally up and to the left

✦ **180 degrees:** Directly to the left

✦ **225 degrees:** Diagonally down and to the left (same as -135 degrees)

✦ **270 degrees:** Straight down (same as -90 degrees)

✦ **315 degrees:** Diagonally down and to the right (same as -45 degrees)

Each direction differs from its neighbor by an angle of 45 degrees. By entering a number between -360 and 360 in the Angle option box of the Constrain dialog box, you rotate the constraint axes. The second example in Figure 5-13 illustrates the effect of rotating the axes 15 degrees. If you were to Shift-drag an element under these conditions, your movements would be constrained to the directions labeled in the figure. You wouldn't be able to Shift-drag in a horizontal or vertical direction until you changed the Angle value back to 0.

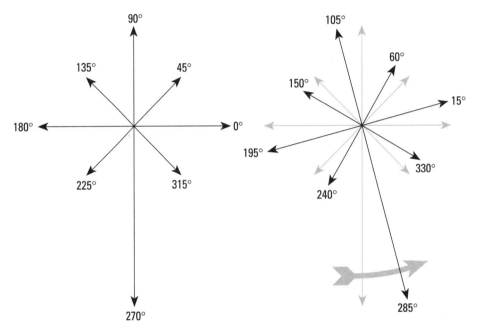

Figure 5-13: The default constraint axes (left) and the axes as they appear when rotated 15 degrees (right).

The Angle value in the Constrain dialog box also affects the following:

✦ Rectangles, spirals, and ellipses (as explained in the "Geometric shapes at an angle" section of Chapter 3). The angle of the constraint axes affects these shapes whether or not you press the Shift key.

✦ Polygons and straight lines created by Shift-dragging.

✦ The angle of straight segments that you draw by Shift-clicking with the pen or bézigon tool or Shift-Option/Alt-dragging with the freehand tool.

Note   Unlike rotated constraint axes in Illustrator, rotated constraint axes in FreeHand do not affect the performance of transformation tools or the angle at which text blocks are drawn.

Snapping

While dragging an element, you may find that it has a tendency to move sharply toward another element. Called *snapping*, this effect is one of FreeHand's ways of ensuring that elements belonging together are positioned flush against each other to form a perfect fit.

When you drag an element within 1 to 5 pixels of any point on your illustration window — you specify the exact distance in the Snap Distance option box found on the General panel in the File ⇨ Preferences dialog box — your cursor snaps to the point. Both point and cursor then occupy an identical horizontal and vertical location.

One of the most useful applications for snapping is to align a point in one path with a point in another, as shown in Figure 5-14. However, if you drag a point in a selected free-form path, you end up moving only that point, which reshapes the path instead of moving it.

To move the entire path by dragging at a single point, you must first select all points in the path prior to dragging. To do this, simply click on the path with the arrow tool. Then, click on the point from which you wish to drag the entire path, but don't drag. This will select the point. Now, Shift-click on that same point. Release the Shift key but don't release the mouse button. The entire path is once again selected and you can now drag the path by that point.

Figure 5-14: The result of dragging an entire path by one of its points.

Your cursor snaps to stationary points as well as to the previous locations of points that are currently being moved. Snapping also occurs in proximity to text block handles and to points in geometric shapes, even if the paths have not yet been ungrouped.

You can turn FreeHand's snapping feature on and off by choosing View ➪ Snap to Point or pressing ⌘/Ctrl-Shift-Z. FreeHand puts a check mark by the command name in the menu when the feature is active.

Using arrow keys

You can also use the four arrow keys to move selected elements. Each arrow key moves a selection in the direction of the arrow. The → key, for example, moves all selected elements a specified increment to the right. When using the arrow keys to move elements, snapping is ignored.

To specify the distance by which a single keystroke moves a selected element, enter a value into the Cursor Distance option box in the General panel of the Preferences dialog box. The value that you enter is measured in points, picas, inches, or millimeters, depending on the current unit of measure specified in the Measures pop-up menu on the Status toolbar.

You can use arrow keys to move selected points and whole paths. However, you cannot use arrow keys to move a selected Bézier control handle independently of its point. You can only move segments and Bézier control handles by dragging them, as described in the next sections.

Stretching segments

You can also reshape a path by Option/Alt-dragging one of its segments. When you Option/Alt-drag a segment, you stretch it as shown in Figure 5-15. You can Option/Alt-drag curved and straight segments alike. When reshaping a straight segment, FreeHand automatically adds Bézier control handles to the neighboring points.

When you Option/Alt-drag a curved segment, the Bézier control handles extend and retract with your cursor movements. However, they do so along established lines, constant with their original inclination. In other words, although the length of a control handle lever changes as you Option/Alt-drag a curved segment, the angle of the lever remains fixed. As Figure 5-16 illustrates, the lever can flip in the opposite direction, but never, no never, will it sway back and forth. This guarantees that the segment moves in alignment with neighboring stationary segments.

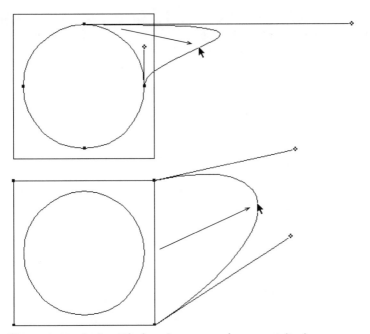

Figure 5-15: Option/Alt-dragging a curved segment (top)
and a straight segment (bottom).

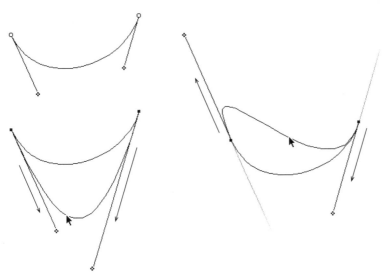

Figure 5-16: When you drag a curved segment, each control handle
extends and retracts, but its angle remains fixed.

Note that the bit about constant handle angles only applies to curved segments. When you Option/Alt-drag straight segments, the handles are free to fly about willy-nilly. It makes the results a little less predictable, but it also makes for a more flexible editing atmosphere.

Dragging Bézier control handles

The only element I've neglected so far is the Bézier control handle. I saved it until last because it's the most difficult element to manipulate. So far, I've only introduced and briefly discussed the qualities of Bézier control handles, those pesky elements that control the curvature of segments as they enter and exit points. It's time we went all the way.

The way of the Bézier

To display a Bézier control handle, select the point to which the handle belongs and then drag the handle you want to move. That's all there is to it. But learning to predict the outcome of your drags can be a little more difficult.

That's where Figures 5-17 through 5-21 come in. Each figure features four curve points. Each point is located in the exact same position in each figure; from one figure to the next, only the labeled control handles have moved. However, these simple adjustments have a dramatic impact on the appearance of each path.

I've lettered the active handles to show the exact manner in which a handle is relocated from one figure to the next. For the record, handle A controls the left segment, handles B and C control the middle segment, and handle D controls the right segment.

When you move one Bézier control handle for a curve point, the other handle for that point moves in the opposite direction. Hence, the two handles of a curve point form a constant lever. Compare Figure 5-18 with Figure 5-17. In Figure 5-18, handles C and D have been moved only slightly, while handles A and B have been moved dramatically. I dragged handle A in a clockwise sweep, sending handle B upward. Figure 5-19 shows the path as it appears during the drag. The arrow shows the motion of my drag. You can see how the control handle stretches the segment like taffy on a pull.

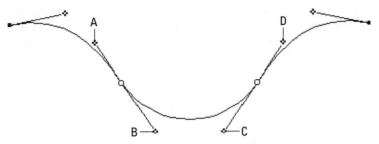

Figure 5-17: A path composed of four curve points, two of which are selected to display their Bézier control handles.

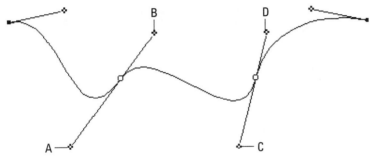

Figure 5-18: The path from Figure 5-17 after I dragged handle A in a clockwise sweep.

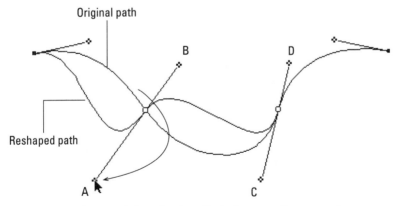

Figure 5-19: The act of dragging handle A shown as it appears in progress.

In Figure 5-18, handle B forces the center segment to ascend as it exits the left curve point. But because of handle C, the segment also ascends as it enters the right curve point. So somewhere between the two points, the segment has to change direction. Hence, the segment slopes up, and then down, and then up again.

The farther I moved the two opposite handles away from each other, the more desperately the segment between them stretched to keep up. In Figure 5-20, I've moved handles B and C a few inches from each other. Now the segment proceeds leftward both as it exits point B and as it enters point C. Somewhere in between, it has to go rightward. (After all, what goes left must go right, right?) The result is a segment that bulges in three directions — left, right, and downward.

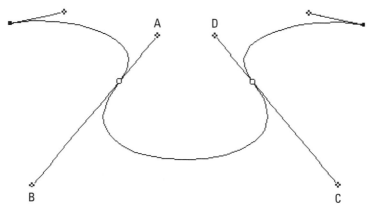

Figure 5-20: Dragging handles B and C far away from each other forces the center segment to bulge outward.

The final example, shown in Figure 5-21, shows that there is absolutely no limit to how far you can drag a Bézier control handle from its point or how severely you can stretch a curved segment. The segment always stretches to keep up, turning around only when necessary to meet the demands of the opposite point and its Bézier control handle.

Certainly, I could come up with all kinds of analogies at this point. Segments stretch like taffy attached to rubber bands between two nails mounted on a medieval rack in a dark dungeon lifted off a comics page onto a piece of Silly Putty fortified with pieces of well-chewed gum spit out onto blacktops where they were thoroughly warmed just in time for you to step on them and mush them into the treads of your silicon sneakers . . . but I think that you already get the idea. These things are so flexible that they make Mr. Fantastic look like he was made out of plywood. And you can stretch them to your heart's content using Bézier's Believe-It-Or-Not control handles.

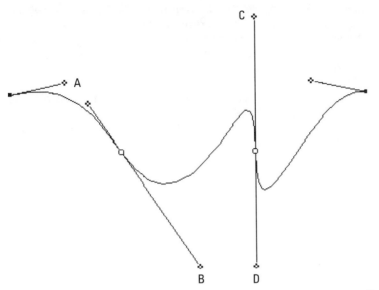

Figure 5-21: There is no limit to the extent that you can drag a handle or stretch a segment.

Rules of the Bézier road

Although you can stretch segments from here to the Pleistocene era, there's little reason you'd want to (unless you'd like to check out the origins of primitive man). As in all of life's pursuits, segment-stretching is best done in moderation. The art of dragging Bézier control handles is not so much a question of what can you do as when you should do it and to what extent.

One of the most common problems people have when learning to use FreeHand is trying to determine the placement of Bézier control handles. Several rules have been developed over the years, but the best are the *all-or-nothing rule* and the *30-percent rule*.

The all-or-nothing rule states that every segment in your path should be associated with either two Bézier control handles or none at all. In other words, no segment should rely on only one control handle to determine its curvature. The 30-percent rule says that the length of any control handle lever should be approximately 30 percent of the length of the segment it controls.

Figures 5-22 and 5-23 feature a pair of Gufus and Gallants of our Bézier curve rules.

The top path in Figure 5-22 violates the all-or-nothing rule. Its two curved segments are controlled by only one handle apiece, resulting in weak, shallow arcs. In the case of both segments, you have no control over the way the segments attach to the base of the path. So one segment begins flat, and the other flattens out at the end. Flat curves are like flat tires; they don't fulfill their intended purpose.

The second example in Figure 5-22, however, obeys the all-or-nothing rule. As the rule states, its straight segment is associated with no handle and both curved segments have two handles apiece. The result is a full-figured, properly pumped-up dome, a credit to any illustration.

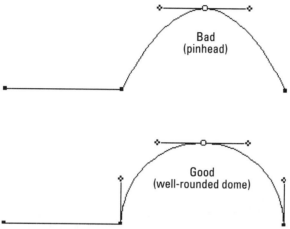

Figure 5-22: The all-or-nothing rule states that every curved segment should be controlled by two handles, one for each of its points.

The first path in Figure 5-23 violates the 30-percent rule. The control handle levers for the central point are much too long, about 60 percent of the length of their segments, and the two outer levers are too short, about 15 percent of the length of their segments. The result, quite frankly, is an ugly, misshapen mess. In the second example, the two levers belonging to the left segment each measure about 30 percent of the length of the segment. The right segment is shorter, so its levers are shorter as well. The curvature of this path is smooth and consistent, giving the path an organic appearance.

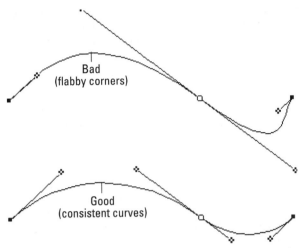

Figure 5-23: The 30-percent rule states that every Bézier lever should extend about a third of the length of its segment.

Adding, Deleting, and Converting

Moving points and adjusting control handles are fundamental ways to change the shape of a path. But sometimes, no matter how much time you spend adjusting the placement of its points or the curvature of its segments, a path fails to meet the requirements of your illustration. When that happens, you may want to expand the path by adding points or to simplify the path by deleting points.

The number and identity of points and segments in a path is forever subject to change. Whether the path is closed or open, you can reshape it by adding, deleting, and converting points. Adding or deleting a point forces the addition or deletion of a segment. And the conversion of a point — whether from corner to curve or from curve to corner — frequently converts a segment from curved to straight or from straight to curved. The following sections describe how you can apply all these reshaping techniques to any existing path.

Adding points and other elements

Adding elements to a path is sort of like finishing a basement or adding a room above the garage, except that it's free and you don't need a building permit. It's a great way to expand upon a geometric shape or extend something you've drawn with the freehand or trace tool.

In the upcoming "Adding points inside a path" section, for example, I walk you through the process of converting a simple circle into something a little more meaningful by merely throwing in a few additional points. First, however, I need to show you how to add points to the end of an open path.

Appending endpoints

As discussed in Chapter 3, a point associated with less than two segments is an *endpoint*, because it represents one end or the other of a path. An open path always has two endpoints. A closed path contains no endpoint; each point is connected to two other points by segments.

An active endpoint is waiting for a segment to be drawn from it. To activate an endpoint in a passive path so that you can draw a new segment from it, select the point with the arrow tool. Then you can click or drag anywhere else on your screen with either the bézigon or pen tool to create a segment between the selected endpoint and the newly created point. After you do this, the one-time endpoint is bound by segments on both sides — meaning that it's no longer an endpoint. It relinquishes its endpoint title to the newest point in the line.

You can use the same technique to close an existing path. Just select one endpoint and then click or drag the other endpoint with the bézigon or pen tool. FreeHand draws a segment between the two endpoints, closing the path to form a shape. Both endpoints are eliminated and converted to interior points.

This brings up an interesting question: What happens to an endpoint when you close the path using a different method than you used to create the point? For example, if you Option/Alt-click a corner point with the bézigon tool, does the point remain a corner point or convert to a curve point? In this case, it remains a corner point. A closing point retains its original identity any time you close the path with the bézigon tool. But when using the pen tool, you can convert an endpoint in the course of closing a path, as follows:

✦ Click the closing point to make it a corner point.

✦ Drag on the closing point to change it to a curve point.

✦ Drag on the closing point and press Option/Alt before completing the drag to change the point to a cusp point with two independent control handles.

✦ Press Option/Alt and then drag on the closing point to change it to a corner point with only one Bézier control handle.

✦ Control-drag (or Alt-right drag) on the closing point to change it to a connector point with a single control handle.

The moral of the story is this: If you don't want to run the risk of changing the identity of the closing point, use the bézigon tool to close the path (or simply select the Closed check box in the Object Inspector). If you'd rather have full control over the final endpoint as you close the shape, use the pen tool. And finally, you can define a new point in the path and ⌘/Ctrl-drag it onto the first point to automatically join the points as described in the "Three cusp point vignettes" section in Chapter 3.

Tip   If you've activated the Smart Cursors option on the General panel in the Preferences dialog box, notice the cursor change when you are exactly over another point. If you are closing the path, a small black square shows up at the bottom right of the cursor. To continue on a line without selecting it, place your pen tool over the point you want to continue on. Notice the hollow square to the lower right of the cursor, click or click and drag to continue.

As if you didn't already have enough options, you can also lengthen an open path by drawing from one of its endpoints with the freehand tool. To close a path, drag from one endpoint to the other. To close it with a straight segment, Option/Alt-drag from one endpoint to the other.

Adding points inside a path

Endpoints aren't the only kinds of points you can add to an existing path. You can also add an interior point to open and closed paths by clicking existing segments with the bézigon tool.

First, select the path to which you want to add a point. Then click with the bézigon tool on some segment in the path. A new corner, curve, or connector point appears at that location, depending on the method you used. What was once one segment becomes two.

You can use the pen tool to insert points in a path as well. Click an existing segment to insert a corner point; drag on a segment to insert a curve point, and Control-drag (or Alt-right drag) to insert a connector point. Dragging with the pen tool allows you to determine the precise placement of Bézier control handles.

Suppose that you want to change an ordinary, ungrouped circle that's composed of four curve points into a crescent. You can get the job done by adding points within the path. The following steps describe one way to perform this task.

1. Draw a circle by Shift-dragging with the oval tool. Then choose Modify ➪ Ungroup (⌘/Ctrl-U) to ungroup the shape.

2. Select the path. Press the 8 or B or U key to select the bézigon tool and then click in the middle of each of the right-hand segments. Each click inserts a curve point, as illustrated in Figure 5-24.

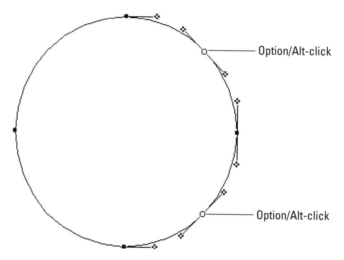

Option/Alt-click

Option/Alt-click

Figure 5-24: Use the bézigon tool to add a curve point in the middle of each of the two right-hand segments of an ungrouped circle.

3. Press and hold the ⌘/Ctrl key to access the arrow tool. While pressing the key, drag the rightmost point toward the center of the shape, as shown in Figure 5-25.

4. Release the ⌘/Ctrl key to restore the bézigon cursor. Click in the middle of each of the two segments between the crescent tips and the dragged point, as indicated by the two selected curve points in Figure 5-26.

5. Finally, move the most recently created points outward from the center of the shape, in the direction indicated by the arrow in Figure 5-27. The Bézier control handles of the point at the center of the mouth will require some adjustment as well. Figure 5-28 shows the completed path as it appears when printed from FreeHand.

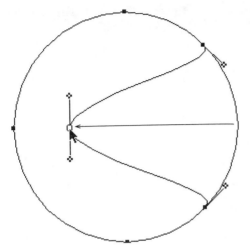

Figure 5-25: Drag the rightmost point toward the center of the shape.

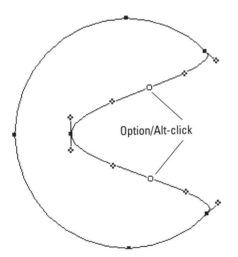

Figure 5-26: Add a point to the middle of each of the segments that form the mouth of the shape.

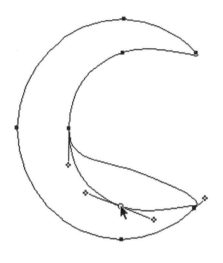

Figure 5-27: Drag the most recent points into position.

Figure 5-28: The finished path as it appears when printed from FreeHand.

Caution

Although it is possible to click with the bézigon or pen tool directly on a point in a selected path, I recommend that you avoid doing so. FreeHand will add a new point to the path and position it directly in front of the previous point. It's unlikely that you will want two points in the same path to be positioned so close to each other. You will probably have to zoom in to separate them.

Adding Bézier control handles

If you want to bend an existing straight segment, or if a curved segment doesn't curve sufficiently, you need to add a Bézier control handle to a neighboring point. In FreeHand, you can add control handles to a corner point or connector point long after the point was created. You cannot add a control handle to an existing curve point or to any other point that already has two control handles — such points are already at full capacity.

To add a control handle, first select the desired point, and then Option/Alt-drag from the point with the arrow tool. The effect of your Option/Alt-drag depends on the following criteria:

✦ If no control handle yet exists for the point, the new control handle affects the more recent of the two neighboring segments.

✦ If one control handle already exists for the point, the new control handle affects the opposite segment.

✦ If two control handles already exist for the current point, Option/Alt-dragging simply moves the point to a new position.

You can't always predict which of two neighboring segments will be affected when you add a Bézier control handle, because you can't simply look at a path and recognize its direction. As a result, you just have to adopt a trial-and-error attitude when Option/Alt-dragging a point.

If the first control handle does not affect the desired segment, Option/Alt-drag the point again to produce another control handle. This second handle will, by necessity, be the one you want, because no more than two control handles can exist for a point. Delete the unwanted handle by dragging it back to the point until it snaps into place or by clicking the second of the two Curve Handle icons in the Object Inspector. (Both techniques are described in the "Retracting Bézier control handles" section later in this chapter.)

Tip
Better yet, use the Reverse Direction command, which changes the direction in which the path travels. After Option/Alt-dragging the unwanted Bézier control handle, choose Edit ➪ Undo Move (⌘/Ctrl-Z) to put it away. Then click the Reverse Direction icon in the Operations (⌘/Ctrl-Option/Alt-O) panel. Now click the point again to select it, Option/Alt-drag from the selected point, and — lo and behold — there's the control handle you were looking for.

To make things a little more predictable, click the Correct Direction icon in the Operations panel. This command makes all selected paths progress in a clockwise direction, regardless of how you drew them. You can also choose Reverse Direction or Correct Direction from the Modify ➪ Alter Path submenu or the Xtras ➪ Cleanup submenu.

Deleting points and other elements

The simplest way to delete points is to select them and press the Delete or Backspace key. The selected points disappear, as do the segments associated with the points. To prevent gaps in the outline of the paths to which the points belonged, FreeHand connects the points that neighbored the deleted points with new segments.

The first example in Figure 5-29 shows the familiar ungrouped circle path with the right point selected. The second example shows how the path changed after I pressed the Delete or Backspace key. FreeHand fused the two segments surrounding the deleted point into a single segment. The segment's curvature is determined by the remaining points in the path. The result is a path that remains closed and selected, although all points are deselected.

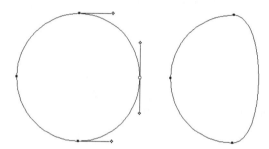

Figure 5-29: Selecting an interior point (left) and pressing the Delete or Backspace key removes the point but retains a segment (right).

If you delete an endpoint from an open path, you delete the single segment associated with the point. FreeHand doesn't draw a new segment in its place. Also, the new endpoint in the path becomes selected, enabling you to extend the path using the freehand, bézigon, or pen tool or further shorten the path by pressing the Delete key again.

Avoid deleting a point from a line that consists of only two points. You'll end up with a single-point path, which is almost completely useless unless you intend to build on it immediately. Lone points are hard to find once deselected, tend to clutter up the illustration window, and needlessly increase the size of your document when it's saved to disk.

Removing a segment

FreeHand prevents breaks in the outline of a path by drawing new segments in place of deleted ones. If you want to delete a segment *and* create a break in the path — whether to open a closed path or to split an open path in two — you have to do a little additional work. Although FreeHand provides no direct means for deleting a segment, you can get the job done by following these steps:

1. Select the path that you want to open or split.

2. Press the 7 or the K key to select the knife tool. Then click the segment that you want to delete, as shown in the first example in Figure 5-30. You have now split the segment and inserted two endpoints into the path.

3. To ensure that both new endpoints are selected, press the ⌘/Ctrl key to access the arrow tool and marquee the points, as shown in the second example in Figure 5-30. Because the selected points overlap, they disappear, as shown in the first example in Figure 5-31. This is FreeHand's way of showing that overlapping points are selected.

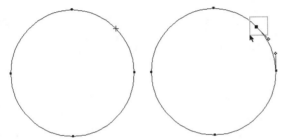

Figure 5-30: Click a segment with the knife tool (left) to split the segment and insert two endpoints (right).

4. Press the Delete key. Both points disappear, as shown in the second example in Figure 5-31, leaving a break in the outline of the path.

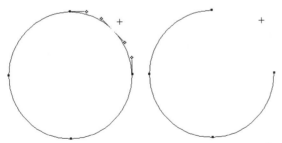

Figure 5-31: After selecting the two coincident points (left), press the Delete key to open the path.

For a complete discussion of the knife tool, see the "Splitting and slicing" section later in this chapter.

Deleting a whole path

As shown back in Figure 5-29, deleting a point from a closed path causes the remaining path to become selected. If you press the Delete key a second time, you delete the entire path. This means that if a closed path — in the course of its creation — ends up deviating so drastically from your original intention that there is no sense in attempting a salvage, you can delete the entire object by selecting any point in the path and pressing Delete twice in a row.

You can also delete any path, whether it's open or closed, by selecting the entire path and pressing Delete. Or, if you prefer, choose the Clear command from the Edit menu.

The Clear command deletes entire selected paths, whether or not one or more points in the path are also selected. To perform the same operation from the keyboard, press the grave key to deselect all points while leaving their paths selected and then press the Delete key.

Retracting Bézier control handles

To put away, or retract, a Bézier control handle, drag the control handle back to its point and release. If the Snap to Point command (⌘/Ctrl-Shift-Z) is active in the View menu, the control handle snaps to its point as you retract it. If you want to retract the corresponding control handles for multiple selected points at the same time, click the Handles icon in the Object Inspector.

Take a look at Figure 5-32. Suppose that you wanted to retract each of the control handles associated with the leftmost point in the crescent shape. In each case, you can either drag the handle back to its point or click the spotlighted icon in the Object Inspector. How do you know which icon goes with which handle? Again, it's a function of the direction of the path.

The crescent in the figure was based on a circle created with the oval tool, which always travels in a clockwise direction. So the segment below the leftmost point enters it, and the segment above the point exits it. If you clicked the right icon in the panel (labeled *Retract exit handle* in the figure), you would delete the upper handle, which controls the exiting segment. If you clicked the left icon, you would delete the *entrance* (or in this case, lower) *handle*.

Retract exit handle

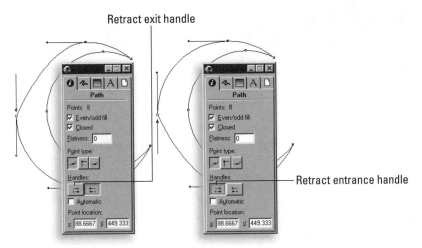

Retract entrance handle

Figure 5-32: In each example, the spotlighted icon performs the same effect as dragging the control handle, as indicated by the arrows.

Tip

To make any path behave like the crescent in Figure 5-32 — that is, so that all segments travel in a clockwise direction — select the path and choose either Modify ⇨ Alter Path ⇨ Correct Direction or Xtra ⇨ Cleanup ⇨ Correct Direction. You can even click the Correct Direction icon in the Operations panel. The left Curve Handles icon then retracts the Bézier control handle pointing in the counterclockwise direction, and the right icon retracts the handle pointing clockwise. Complicated paths can be tricky because they can loop all over the place, but you'll eventually get the hang of it.

Generally, you'll only want to retract control handles belonging to corner and connector points. But as illustrated in the figures, it is possible to retract a curve point handle. Doing so ruins the purpose of the point by eliminating the seesaw lever. If you delete a handle from a curve point, I suggest that you convert the point to a corner point by clicking the Corner Point icon in the Inspector panel (as described in the next section). If you leave the points as is, you're likely to confuse yourself in later editing stages because you may end up with curve points at obvious corners in the path.

Converting points

FreeHand lets you change the identity of any interior point within an existing path to a curve, corner, or connector point. You convert a point by using the Point Type icons in the Object Inspector, as shown in Figure 5-33. You just select the point that you want to change and click the appropriate icon in the panel.

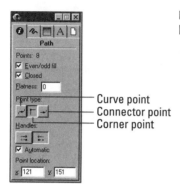

Curve point
Connector point
Corner point

Figure 5-33: The three Point Type icons let you change the identity of a point.

When a single point is selected, or when two or more points of the same type are selected, a Point Type icon appears highlighted to identify the points. If you select two or more dissimilar points, no icon appears highlighted. However, you can make the selected points similar by clicking an icon.

Automatic curvature

When you create a point with the bézigon tool, FreeHand automatically determines the location of any Bézier control handle for the point — a feature called *automatic curvature*. FreeHand bases its decision on the identity and location of the point with respect to the identities and locations of its immediate neighbors.

Any time you move, add, or retract a Bézier control handle, the affected point deviates from FreeHand's perception of automatic curvature. To restore the control handles of a selected point to their predetermined locations, select the Automatic check box below the Handles icons in the Object Inspector.

Perhaps the best way to understand automatic curvature is to think of a line made up of three points — a corner, a curve, and another corner. Suppose you drew this line with the pen tool, manually positioning the control handles of the points to create a path like the one shown in the first example in Figure 5-34.

Now imagine there is a center spot equidistant from all three points. This center spot is shown in the figure as a small x. If you select the three points and select the Automatic option, FreeHand moves the control handles so that the path curves symmetrically about the imaginary center spot, as shown in the second example in Figure 5-34. In other words, the automatic curvature function moves the control handles of selected curve points and their neighbors to mimic the arc of a circle.

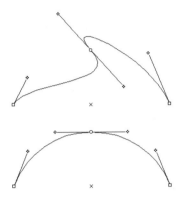

Figure 5-34: A curve point created with the pen tool (top) and subjected to automatic curvature (bottom).

After you turn on the Automatic option, the rules of automatic curvature guide the manipulation of a point. In the first example in Figure 5-35, I selected the curve point in my path. When I moved the point to the left, as shown in the second example, FreeHand automatically repositioned the control handles belonging to the dragged point as well as both of its neighbors. With the automatic curvature function in force, you can move a point and reshape its segments in a single operation.

But as I demonstrated with the fish way back in Figures 3-43 and 3-44, automatic curvature is not always the best solution. You can remove automatic curvature from a selected point in two ways:

✦ Move at least one control handle for that point.

✦ Select the point and deselect the Automatic check box in the Object Inspector.

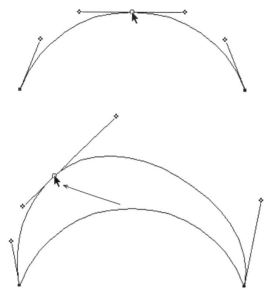

Figure 5-35: Dragging a point when automatic curvature is active simultaneously moves the point and reshapes its segments.

Path Information

If you want to make several changes to a point or path at once, FreeHand provides a one-stop path manipulation headquarters: the Object Inspector.

After selecting an ungrouped path, press ⌘/Ctrl-I to display the Object Inspector shown in Figure 5-36. The options in the panel apply to any free-form path, whether you created it with the polygon, line, freehand, bézigon, pen, or trace tool. They also affect any ungrouped rectangle or ellipse.

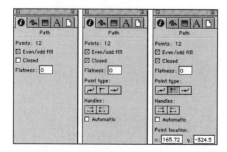

Figure 5-36: The Object Inspector as it appears when a path (left), multiple points (middle), and a single point (right) are selected.

Note

If more than one path is selected, the Object Inspector is blank. You have to deselect all but one path to adjust the options described in the next few paragraphs.

Assuming that a freeform path is selected, the Object Inspector always lists how many points make up the path. This information is particularly useful if the selected path is complicated or contains tightly packed points, which is often the case with paths created with the freehand or trace tool. The other items in the Object Inspector include the following:

✦ **Even/Odd Fill:** The Even/Odd Fill option controls the manner in which overlapping portions of a selected closed path are filled. Generally speaking, selecting this option makes overlapping areas transparent; deselecting the option fills overlapping areas according to the specifications in the fill panel of the Inspector panel.

✦ **Closed:** If you select the Closed check box, FreeHand inserts a segment between the two endpoints of the selected path. The identities of the endpoints dictate the curvature of the new segment. Because closed paths support fills, closing a path displays its fill. Deselecting the Closed option opens the selected path by eliminating the segment between the first and last points, which is a function of the order in which the points were created.

✦ **Flatness:** The Flatness option controls the manner in which the selected path is printed to a PostScript output device such as a LaserWriter or imagesetter. PostScript printers imitate curves as a collection of hundreds or even thousands of tiny, straight lines. The Flatness option determines the greatest distance, in device pixels, that any of these lines can stray from the mathematical definition of the curve. Enter any number between 0 and 100 for this option. Higher values permit fewer straight lines and therefore result in more jagged curves. Leave this option set to 0 unless you experience problems printing the current illustration. For complete information on this option, read the "Splitting long paths" section in Chapter 18.

✦ **Point Type:** These icons only appear when one or more points are selected. Click an icon to change the identity of the points. Read the "Converting points" section a couple of pages back if this doesn't make sense.

✦ **Handles:** Again, these icons only appear when at least one point is selected. Click the left icon to retract the Bézier control handle associated with the segment that enters a selected point; click the right icon to retract the handle that controls the segment that exits the point. Then read the "Retracting Bézier control handles" section earlier in this chapter to figure out what I'm talking about.

✦ **Automatic:** Select this check box and your life becomes fully functioning, just like you always dreamed it would. Your dishes will wash themselves, your roof will stop leaking, and your spouse and loved ones will behave themselves.

Oh, wait, wrong Automatic option. I was thinking of that one I saw advertised on QVC. (You mean you don't have one?) The Automatic option included with FreeHand subjects a selected point to the rules of automatic curvature, as described in the "Automatic curvature" section earlier in this chapter. Sadly, your roof will still leak.

✦ **Point Location:** When a single point is selected, two Point Location option boxes appear at the bottom of the panel, listing the horizontal (X) and vertical (Y) coordinates of the point as measured from the ruler origin. These values are very useful for aligning points. Say, for example, that you want to align point A horizontally with point B. Click point A and note the coordinate in the X option box. Then click point B, replace the value in the X option box with the coordinate for point A, and press Return/Enter. Bingo, the points are perfectly aligned.

Freeform for All

Finally, in the quest to reshape a path just perfectly, we come to the least precise and easiest to ignore method: the use of the freeform tool. It's Macromedia's answer to Adobe's poorly conceived and lamely implemented reshape tool — debuting in Illustrator 7. To its credit, Macromedia did design the freeform tool with a number of options, giving you more control over the tool's use. Because the freeform tool lets you mold paths and segments by pushing and pull them, its also easier to use than the Illustrator counterpart. But, nevertheless, both tools leave you wondering if the abilities gained by their use outweigh the loss of control you will suffer. After all, there is nothing that you can do with these tools that you can't do via the other path reshaping methods outlined throughout this chapter. Furthermore, the traditional methods give you exacting control over your adjustments, resulting in changes as precise as you desire.

The freeform tool has two modes, Push/Pull and Reshape Area, which I talk about next.

Pushing and pulling a path

The Push/Pull mode (the default mode) lets you change the shape of a selected path by either clicking anywhere on the path — point or segment — and pulling the path around, or clicking just inside or outside the path and pushing the path into a new shape. Provided you've activated the Smart Cursors option in the General panel of the Preference dialog box, FreeHand shows you which process you're about to execute by augmenting the freeform cursor with a jagged little line for a pull and a hollow little diamond for a push. Although both the pulling and pushing methods may sound as though they deliver similar results, pushing a path with the freeform tool gives a sloppy and unpredictable outcome.

Pulling a path with the freeform tool allows you to quickly and easily modify the sections of your path. As you drag on a selected segment, FreeHand alters the shape of the path by changing the size and orientation of the Bézier control handles of the two points that flank the segment. No additional points are added to the path. In Figure 5-37, I started with the polygon that appears on top and reshaped it into the happy little mammal on the left by pulling on the polygon's segments with the freeform tool.

When you push a path with the freeform tool, you curve the path to fit the shape of the freeform tool. The freeform tool acts essentially like a ball that, quite unceremoniously, sinks into your path, as shown on the right in Figure 5-37. As you drag into your path, FreeHand adds new points to the path, giving it a more rounded appearance. The thing about pushing a path with the freeform tool is that, because the tool is designed to just slightly curve the path at the point where you push the path, you don't want to drag the cursor farther into the path than a distance equal to half of the tool's size. If you do drag farther, the freeform will carve a channel into your path.

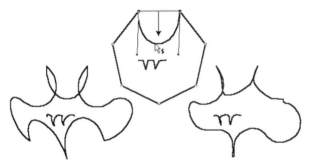

Figure 5-37: Reshaping a path with the freeform tool can produce reasonably good results when you pull on the path (the left version) and horrendously bad when you push on the path (as on the right).

Double click the Freeform icon in the toolbox to display the Freeform Tool dialog box, as shown in Figure 5-38. Here you decide in which capacity the tool will function and how it will behave. The left portion of the figure shows the options for the Push/Pull mode of the freeform tool.

The Push/Pull options work as follows:

✦ **Tool Operation:** Here you choose the tool's mode. The mode you choose impacts both how the tool operates and what options are displayed in this dialog box — in this case, the Push/Pull mode and options. (For information about the Reshape Area mode functions and options, jump to the next section.)

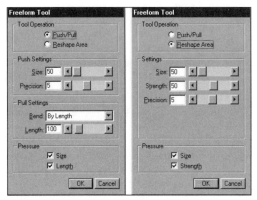

Figure 5-38: Inside the Freeform Tool dialog box, you decide the mode of the tool and how it will impact a path.

The Push/Pull options work as follows:

✦ **Push Settings:** When you push on a path with the freeform tool — by dragging from just inside or outside a selected path — the path contorts to fit the freeform tool. The Push Settings options allow you to determine how much of the path is affected and the number of points that FreeHand will add to the path. With the Size option box, you can choose to have to the freeform tool impact anywhere from 1 to 1,000 points on a path. (Just in case you're curious, 1,000 points is just shy of 14 inches. Tell me that isn't the perfect setting for subtle adjustment of detailed artwork.) The setting in the Precision option box dictates how many points FreeHand adds to your altered path. The higher the setting, the more points your path gets.

Tip Press the [or] keys — that's left and right brackets — to change the Size option on the fly while you're pushing with the freeform tool. The [key decreases the value and] increases it.

✦ **Pull Settings:** When you pull on a path — by clicking directly on it with the freeform tool — the affected portion is either bounded by the two closest points or determined by arbitrary length. To stretch the path between two of the path's points, choose the Between Points options from the Bend pop-up menu. This is easily the most useful setting for the freeform tool. When this option is active, pulling on a segment with the freeform tool allows you to smoothly stretch the path between its two points. If you prefer to dictate the length of the affected segment, choose the By Length option from the Bend pop-up menu. This enables the Length slider bar, where you choose how much of the path will stretch.

Tip

Get this for fantastic: you can press the [or] keys to change the Length while you're pulling with the freeform tool. Once again, the [key decreases the value and] increases it.

✦ **Pressure:** If you're using a pressure-sensitive drawing tablet — as described in the "Pressure-sensitive input" section of Chapter 3 — the Freeform Tool dialog box gives you access to two special settings: Size and Length. With either of these options activated, the pressure that you apply to your stylus will directly determine how much of the path is affected. If you want a large portion of the selected path to stretch as you push it, check the Size checkbox. Activate the Length option to vary the affected portion of a selected path as you pull it.

Reshaping an area

The other mode for the freeform tool is the Reshape Area mode. This mode lets you reshape the entire outline of selected path all at once. Instead of just pushing or pulling on part of a path — which is what happens when you use the freeform tool on a path when the tool is in the Push/Pull mode — you can reshape large sections of a selected path by stretching the path with the freeform tool while it's in the Reshape Area mode.

Provided you've activated the Smart Cursors option in the General panel of the Preferences dialog box, the cursor for the freeform tool in the Reshape Area mode consists of three concentric circles. The outer circle limits how much of the selected path is effected and its size is determined by the Size value in the Freeform Tool dialog box. The middle circle represents the degree to which the freeform tool will alter the selected path and it's size is determined by the Strength value set in the Freeform Tool dialog box. The larger the circle, the more the path will stretch to accommodate you drag. The inner circle simply tracks the center of the cursor and doesn't impact the selected path.

In the Reshape Area mode, the freeform tool's behavior is specified by settings in the Freeform Tool dialog box. These settings are shown in the right side of Figure 5-38.

The Reshape Area options work as follows:

✦ **Size:** Choose a value between 1 and 1000 to determine how large of an area you want to affect. If you've opted to use smart cursors, this value directly determines the diameter of the outer circle of the tool's cursor.

I bet you've already guessed this little tidbit, but I might as well go ahead and throw it in: Press the [or] keys to change the Size option while you're using the freeform tool in the Reshape Area mode. The [key decreases the value and] increases it.

✦ **Strength:** Here you decide how much of an impact the freeform tool will have on a selected path. The greater the percentage you enter in this option box, the more the path will stretch as you drag with the freeform tool.

You can change the Strength value by pressing Shift-[or Shift-] while you drag with the freeform tool. Them bracket key are just super; they ask so little and, yet, they give so much.

✦ **Precision:** This value dictates how many points FreeHand will add to your path as you reshape it. Once again, the larger the value, the greater number of points your new path will have.

✦ **Pressure:** If you a have pressure-sensitive drawing tablet — discussed in the "Pressure-sensitive input" section of Chapter 3 — you can activate these settings to reflect your stylus' behavior. Selecting the Size option will change the affected area of the selected path as a function of how hard you press with your stylus. When the Strength checkbox is in effect, the harder you press with your stylus, the more the path will respond to your drag. If you have both these option checked, the Size setting takes precedence since you can only indicate one of the attributes as you draw with your stylus.

Combining and Splitting Paths

Many of the reshaping techniques I've described so far are available in some form or another in just about every drawing software on earth. ClarisDraw, for example, allows you to move elements, add and delete points, play around with control handles, and convert straight segments to curved segments. Yet ClarisDraw is commonly considered too remedial for tackling a complex illustration.

This section discusses two areas in which FreeHand stands well above the common drawing crowd: the combining and splitting of points and segments in one or more paths. These features make it possible to break up portions of a path like pieces in a tailor-made puzzle and then assemble them in any way you see fit.

Joining open paths

The Join command in the Modify menu (⌘/Ctrl-J) enables you to combine both closed and open paths. It combines multiple closed paths into a special kind of object called a *composite path*, as described in Chapter 15. But first and foremost, this command joins endpoints from two different open paths to form a single free-form line.

Fusing endpoints from separate paths

If two endpoints from two separate paths are *coincident* — that is, if one point is positioned exactly on top of the other in the illustration window — issuing the Join command fuses the two into a single interior point. The following steps show how this works, should you be inclined to try it.

1. Select an endpoint in the first path and drag it onto an endpoint in the second path using the arrow tool, as illustrated in Figure 5-39. The points snap together if the Snap to Point command in the View menu is active.

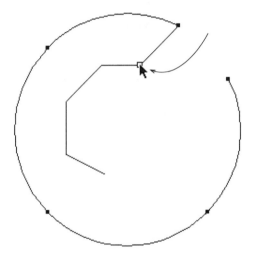

Figure 5-39: Drag the endpoint of one path so it snaps to the endpoint of another.

2. Currently, only one path is selected. To use the Join command, both paths must be selected. So Shift-click with the arrow tool on the second path to add it to the selection, as illustrated in Figure 5-40.

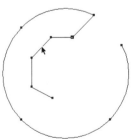

Figure 5-40: Shift-click the second path before choosing the Join command (⌘/Ctrl-J).

3. Choose Modify ➪ Join (⌘/Ctrl-J). FreeHand fuses the two endpoints into a single interior point inside a longer open path. As long as you select the two paths that you want to join, FreeHand is smart enough to figure out which endpoints — if any — are coincident.

Joining two lines with a straight segment

If none of the endpoints in two open paths are coincident when you choose the Join command, Freehand joins the closest pair of endpoints — one point from each path — with a straight segment. In the first example in Figure 5-41, I selected two open paths. None of the endpoints overlapped. The two endpoints on the left side of the example are closer together than the endpoints on the right. So when I chose Modify ➪ Join, FreeHand joined the left endpoints with a straight segment, as shown in the second example in the figure.

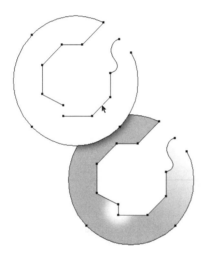

Figure 5-41: After you select two open paths (top) and choose Join, FreeHand draws a straight segment between the nearest endpoints (bottom).

In order for this feature to work, the endpoints must be at least five pixels apart. (Actually, the exact minimum distance is determined by the value in the Snap Distance option box in the General panel of the Preferences dialog box.) If the points are closer, FreeHand moves them together and fuses them into a single interior point. Also, the Join Non-Touching Paths check box in the Object panel of the Preferences dialog box must be turned on. If this option is off, and the endpoints are separated by more than five pixels, FreeHand ignores you when you choose Join. (What an uppity program.)

Auto joining

You don't need to use the Join command when you're joining two endpoints in a single path. Endpoints in an open path will *auto join* when made coincident. Simply select one endpoint and drag it in front of the other endpoint in the same path, as shown in the first example in Figure 5-42. The two points automatically bond to form a selected interior point, as illustrated in the second example. If you turn to the Object Inspector, you find the Closed check box selected, confirming that the path is closed.

Regardless of their original identities, endpoints auto join to form a corner point. The original Bézier control handles are retained.

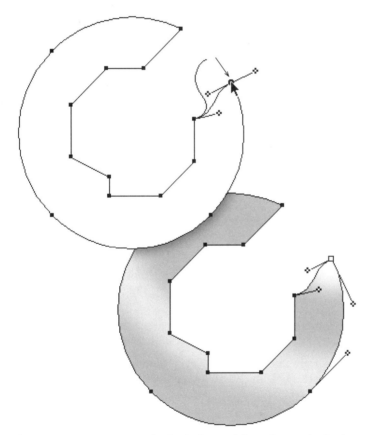

Figure 5-42: Drag one endpoint in front of the other endpoint in the same path (top) to automatically fuse the two points into one (bottom).

Combining path outlines

The Operations panel provides several ways to combine paths in ways that the Join command can't even begin to match, poor thing. Six of these — Intersect, Transparency, Punch, Crop, Union, and Divide (new to FreeHand 8) — make it easier to draw complex paths by combining more rudimentary shapes.

The Intersect, Transparency, Punch, Crop, Union, and Divide commands share many of the following characteristics and parameters:

✦ To use any of these commands, you must select two or more paths.

Now that FreeHand 8 allows you to add fills to open path, these six path operations also work equally well on any path. The paths you select may be open or closed, filled or unfilled. You also can mix and match your selections; select a closed path with a gradient fill and an open path with a flat fill. The choice is yours.

✦ You can apply all the commands to rectangles and ellipses without first ungrouping the shapes. You also can apply them directly to free-form paths.

✦ Intersect, Punch, Crop, Divide, and Union delete the selected paths and replace them with a new path or paths. If you want to retain the original paths, be sure to either first clone the selection by choosing Edit ➪ Clone (⌘-= on Macs and Ctrl-Shift-C on PCs), or if you prefer to have FreeHand automatically perform the command on a copy of the original objects, deselect Path Operations Consume Original Paths in the Object panel of the Preferences dialog box before applying Intersect, Punch, Divide or Union.

✦ The Punch and Divide commands can create multiple paths. Punch, Divide, Crop, and Union can result in a composite path.

✦ The new paths move to the front of the current layer.

✦ When you choose the Intersect, Crop, or Union command, FreeHand fills and strokes the new shape according to the attributes of the rearmost path in the selection.

✦ Applying Divide fills each new shape with the attributes of the foremost path that was involved in the creation of the new path.

✦ When you choose the Punch command, FreeHand fills and strokes each path according to the path's original attributes; only the frontmost shape is deleted.

✦ All of these commands are most accessible from the Operations panel. However, they are also available from the Modify ➪ Combine submenu and the Xtras ➪ Path Operations submenu. To keep things simple, I'll only refer to the Operations panel throughout this section.

With these little morsels of information in mind, read on for details about each command.

Intersect

The Intersect command retains the area in which all selected paths overlap. Consider Figure 5-43. In the first example, I selected two overlapping paths, a not-yet-ungrouped ellipse and a free-form path drawn with the pen tool. When I chose Intersect from the Operations panel, FreeHand deleted all portions of the path that did not overlap and drew a new path around the overlapping area. The result is a hand shape, the outside of which curves in a perfect oval. Drawing this shape from scratch would require considerable toil and Bézier tinkering, but building it by combining paths is easy.

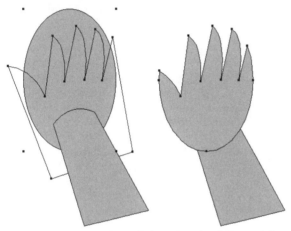

Figure 5-43: Two selected closed paths (left) and the single combined path formed by choosing the Intersect command (right).

Intersections abound in real life. The intersection of your body and your shoe is your foot; the intersection of the contents of a box of Arm & Hammer and a spilled jar of vinegar is a childhood volcano; the intersection of a cowboy and a bucking bronco is a bruised behind.

Caution

It is very important that all selected paths overlap when you choose Intersect. If any two paths in the selection do not overlap, the Intersect command merely deletes the paths. Suppose that you select three shapes: a circle, a square, and a triangle. The circle and square overlap, the square and triangle overlap, but the triangle and circle do not overlap. When you choose the Intersect command, FreeHand looks at the paths and determines that the three paths don't share any common space. The Intersect command turns up empty-handed. Rather than delivering an error message, FreeHand simply deletes the selection.

Transparency

The Transparency command is the only command capable of retaining your original shapes in the course of creating new ones. Not only will you retain your original shapes, you can also mix the fills of the shapes. When you click the Transparency icon in the Operations panel, FreeHand displays the Transparency dialog box. Use the option box or adjacent slider to set the transparency percentage for the front object. If you want to use the fill of the rearmost object, enter a value of 100. To lift the fill from the frontmost object, enter a value of 0. To mix the colors, enter a value in between. After you press Return/Enter, FreeHand creates a new shape and leaves the originals intact. The resulting shape lacks a stroke. Furthermore, the command can't mix gradations. If you attempt to, FreeHand performs the Transparency operation using the From color for graduated fills and the Outer color for radial fills. And, here's the final gripe: the Transparency dialog box doesn't have a preview option. In other words, the only way to gauge your color mixing is to move the slider and click OK. If you don't like the result, you have to choose Undo (⌘/Ctrl-Z) and try again.

Punch

When using the Punch command, try to keep in mind that it has no bearing whatsoever to funny-looking, big-nosed, bat-wielding, psychotic puppets who speak in falsetto. Instead, this command takes one selected path and uses its outline to punch a hole in any and all selected paths behind it.

The following steps explain how to create the familiar Apple logo by using Control-dragging, the Join and Punch commands, and a few techniques I have yet to properly introduce.

1. Begin the graphic by drawing half of the apple as an open path using the freehand or pen tool — whichever makes you most comfortable. This is the only step that takes any talent. If you can draw even a rude approximation of half an apple, as shown in the first example in Figure 5-44, you'll breeze through the remaining steps.

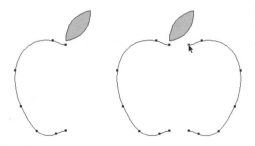

Figure 5-44: After drawing half of the apple (left), I cloned the path and flipped it horizontally (right).

2. Make sure that the two endpoints line up vertically. To do this, use the Point Location options in the Object Inspector. Select the first endpoint, copy its X option box value, select the second endpoint, paste the coordinate of the first endpoint in the X option box, and press Return/Enter.

3. Select the arrow tool. If any points in the path are selected, press the grave (`) key. Then choose Edit ⇨ Clone (⌘-= on Macs and Ctrl-Shift-C on PCs) to make a copy of the selected line.

4. Flip the path horizontally. The best way to accomplish this is to display the Transform panel (⌘/Ctrl-M), click the Reflect icon in the panel (far right), enter 90 into the Reflect Axis option box, and click the Reflect button inside the Transform panel.

5. The flipped clone no doubt overlaps the original. Drag it off to the side a bit so that you can better see what you're doing. Then Control-drag the path by one of its endpoints (see the second example in Figure 5-44) so that it snaps onto the corresponding endpoint in the original path.

6. The result should look like an apple, but the path isn't closed yet. To do the honors, Shift-click the original path so that both halves are selected. Then choose Modify ⇨ Join (⌘/Ctrl-J). FreeHand joins one pair of coincident endpoints. Then, because the other two endpoints are also coincident, FreeHand auto joins them to form a closed path. (This is why it was so important to align the endpoints vertically in step 2.)

7. Shift-drag with the oval tool to draw a circle, which will represent the bite out of the apple. Then use the arrow tool to drag the bite into position, as shown in the first example in Figure 5-45.

8. Shift-click the apple shape so that both apple and bite are selected. Then click the Punch icon in the Operations panel. Because the circle is in front, FreeHand punches the circle out of the apple, as shown in the second example in Figure 5-45.

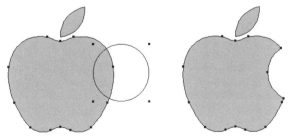

Figure 5-45: Draw a circle to represent the bite (left), then select both shapes and choose the Punch command (right).

When two or more paths are selected, FreeHand punches the frontmost selected path out of each of the other paths. If a rear shape entirely surrounds the front shape, FreeHand combines them into a composite path. For more information, check out Chapter 15.

Crop

The Crop command operates like a "cookie cutter" on the selected objects. Crop takes two or more objects and crops the bottom path (or paths) to the shape of the topmost path in the stacking order. The result is the opposite of Punch.

Here's another method for taking a bite out of the apple.

1. Begin the graphic by drawing the apple and the oval used in the Punch section and again position them as shown in Figure 5-45.

2. Select both objects.

3. Click the Crop icon in the Operations panel. Because the circle is in front, FreeHand crops away the apple leaving only the "bite" portion, just the opposite of Punch.

Union

The Union command traces an outline around all selected shapes. Like a silhouette or a chalk line around a corpse, the Union command eliminates overlapping details and retains only the overall outline. The first example in Figure 5-46 shows three simple shapes I created using the rectangle, ellipse, and pen tools. (Can you see how I created the gray shape by overlapping a rectangle and ellipse and applying the Intersect command?) I selected all three shapes, clicked the Union icon in the Operations panel to fuse the outlines of the path into a single shape, and filled the new shape using the fill of the rearmost object. The result is shown in the second example in Figure 5-46.

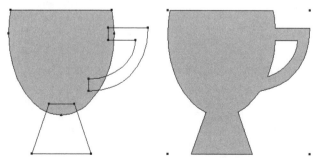

Figure 5-46: Three selected shapes (left) brought together using the Union command (right).

Notice how the shape in the second example in the figure contains two outlines, one around the cup — or whatever it is — and one inside the handle. The outline inside the handle is transparent. Only one kind of path can accommodate a transparent outline inside a filled shape, and that's a composite path. Again, for more information on these wonders of FreeHand drawing, read Chapter 15.

Just for fun, Figure 5-47 shows the paths created using Intersect, Punch, and Union.

Figure 5-47: The paths from Figures 5-43, 5-45, and 5-46 as they appear when printed from FreeHand.

Divide

New to FreeHand 8 is the wildly useful Divide command. You can think of the Divide command as the Ginsu knife of the FreeHand world. It slices and dices any overlapping portions of the selected objects to create new shapes. It works much like the Punch command, except that the Divide command retains all paths after its execution. If I had applied the Divide command instead of the Punch command to the left portion of Figure 5-45, then, in addition to the apple (that appears on the right of that figure), FreeHand would have created both a path for the extracted bite and the remaining, hungry little circle. The big difference between the Divide and Punch command is that, with the former, the stacking order of the selected paths doesn't matter. All that FreeHand does is create new paths based on how the selected paths' outlines overlap each other. To get an idea of how the Divide command will impact your artwork simply view your overlapping paths in the Keyline mode.

Just like the Punch command, the Divide command can create either regular old paths or them hi-tech composite paths. As you've probably guessed by now, for more composite path information, you can read Chapter 15.

Splitting and slicing

The knife tool is used to split a point or segment. By selecting the knife tool and clicking at some location on a selected segment, you insert two endpoints into the segment — each associated with one segment — which splits the segment in two. If you click with the knife tool on an interior point, you split the point into two endpoints. Either way, using the knife tool opens a closed path or splits an open path into two lines.

Pressing the 7 key — either in the standard key set or on the keypad — selects the knife tool. Or, you can always press the K key (K is for Knife).

Double-clicking the knife icon displays the Knife Tool dialog box, as shown in Figure 5-48. Here you can choose to cut either Freehand or Straight paths. The Freehand option enables you to use the knife to cut lines the same way you would use the freehand tool to draw paths. Straight lets you cut straight paths only. Width lets you specify how wide a swath you cut. It uses your current document units, as specified in the Document Inspector. The Width option is only used when you drag the knife, not when you click with it. Next you can choose whether to Close Cut Paths. I love this feature. When enabled, it closes the paths along both sides of your cut. Finally, you can choose Tight Fit, which causes the cut to more closely reflect your mouse movements.

Figure 5-48: The Knife Tool dialog box displaying the setting you must match for the following steps.

You can drag with the knife tool to slice through multiple segments at a time. Imagine — the knife tool actually behaves like a knife instead of a pair of scissors.

Suppose that you want to split an ordinary circle into the three shapes shown in Figure 5-49. The following steps describe how you can accomplish this feat using the knife and bézigon tools.

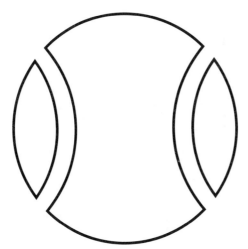

Figure 5-49: The completed tennis ball-looking thing printed from FreeHand.

Because your life would be empty without this information, here's how you draw a tennis ball.

1. Draw a circle with the oval tool.

2. Double-click the knife tool icon in the toolbox and match the settings shown in Figure 5-48.

3. Select the circle and Shift-drag the knife tool to create a vertical slice through the right side of the circle. This splits the circle into two closed paths as shown in Figure 5-50.

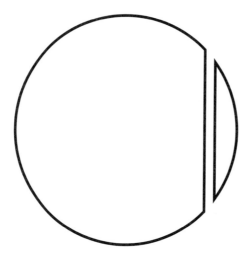

Figure 5-50: Shift-dragging with the knife tool slices through the circle and splits it into two closed shapes.

4. Select the right-hand path and press 8, B, or U to select the bézigon tool. Then click halfway down the vertical cut to place a curve point. With the point selected, go to the Object Inspector and enable the Automatic option. Repeat this for the left-hand path.

5. Drag the point you just created on the right-hand path to a location that mirrors the center curve point of the right-hand path. Your goal is to form a leaf-shaped path like the one that appears in Figure 5-51.

6. Drag the point you added to the left-hand path so that the curve of the left-hand shape parallels the right-hand shape. The result is shown in Figure 5-51.

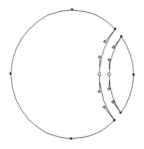

Figure 5-51: Drag segments to create the tennis-ball effect.

7. Repeat steps 1 through 6 on the left side of the circle to complete the tennis ball effect.

You can use the knife tool on a point or segment in any selected, ungrouped path. You can also split elements in a grouped or composite path, provided that you selected one or more individual paths by clicking the path with the arrow tool (as described in the "Selecting elements within groups" section of next chapter). Watch out, though — the cut paths are removed from the group. The knife tool produces no effect if no path is selected or if you click or drag in an empty portion of the window.

You can also split an interior point into two endpoints by selecting the point and choosing the Split command from the Modify menu (⌘/Ctrl-Shift-J). The only advantage this command has over the knife tool is that you can use it to split multiple points simultaneously. Otherwise, the knife tool is typically more convenient.

Reneging the Past

Because we all make mistakes, especially when drawing and tracing complicated paths, FreeHand provides you the ability to nullify the results of previous operations. In fact, FreeHand offers a greater capacity to nullify past actions than the overwhelming majority of applications running on the Mac and Windows. So, when drawing anxiety sets in, remember this simple credo: *Undo, redo, revert.* That's Latin for "Chill, it's just a computer, not a crazed brain-sucking creature from another planet (much as it might resemble one)."

Undo

If you are familiar with other Mac or Windows programs such as PageMaker, Photoshop, or CorelDRAW, you are no doubt familiar with the Undo command in the Edit menu (⌘/Ctrl-Z). This command allows you to negate the last action you performed. Suppose that you add a point to a path and then decide that you don't like how it looks. Choose the Undo command, and the new point disappears. You will, in fact, be returned to the moment before you added the point. Any previous selections are selected again, and so on. It's like a miniature time machine.

You can even undo such minor alterations as changing an option in a dialog box — which is a level of precision unmatched by most other applications. And you can always undo the last action, even if you have since clicked on-screen or performed some minor action that the Undo command does not recognize. FreeHand is truly amazing in this respect.

Tip

Get this: FreeHand goes so far as to allow you to undo an operation that you performed before the most recent Save operation (although you cannot undo the Save command itself). You can delete an element, save the illustration, and then choose Undo to make the element reappear. It's an absolutely phenomenal, life-saving capability. Oh, if only real life were so forgiving!

The Undo command, however, does have its limits. You cannot undo an operation that you performed in a previous FreeHand session. FreeHand displays the name of the operation that you're about to undo in the Edit menu, following the word Undo. Examples include Undo Freehand and Undo Move Elements. If you're not sure what action you're about to undo, check the menu first.

Multiple undos

In a typical application, after you undo an operation, the Undo command changes to a Redo command, providing a brief opportunity to reperform an operation — just in case you decide that you didn't want to undo it after all. In FreeHand, the Undo command remains available so that you can undo the second-to-last operation, and the one before that, and so on. In fact, you can undo up to 99 consecutive operations. This power-user feature takes a great deal of the worry out of using FreeHand. Even major blunders can be whisked away.

You adjust the number of possible consecutive undos by entering any value from 1 to 100 for the Number of Undo's option in the General panel of the Preferences dialog box (accessed by choosing File ➪ Preferences, ⌘/Ctrl-Shift-D). The default value is 10. To make a new value take effect, you must close the document and reopen it. This gives FreeHand the opportunity to create an adequately sized undo buffer in the application RAM.

Tip Conventional wisdom suggests that your machine must assign at least 8MB of application RAM to FreeHand to support the maximum 100 consecutive undos. If FreeHand cannot build a buffer large enough when launching, you may be presented with an out-of-memory error and find that FreeHand refuses to launch. In this worst-case scenario, you can reset the preference settings by throwing away the FreeHand Preferences file, found in the Preferences folder inside System Folder. Then relaunch FreeHand. To save RAM limit the number of Undo steps to eight or less.

After you undo the maximum number of operations, the Undo command appears dimmed in the Edit menu. Pressing ⌘/Ctrl-Z produces no effect until a new operation is performed.

Redo

Just as you can undo as many as 100 consecutive actions, you can redo up to 100 consecutive undos by using the Redo command in the Edit menu (⌘/Ctrl-Y). You can choose Edit ➪ Redo only if the last command you issued was the Undo command. Otherwise, the Redo command appears dimmed. Also, if you undo a series of actions, perform a new series of actions, and then undo the new series to the point where you had stopped undoing previously — are you following me here? — you can't go back and redo the first series of undos. Instead, you can simply continue to undo from where you left off.

Tip

You may have noticed that the keyboard shortcut for the Redo command (⌘/Ctrl-Y) is not all that convenient, especially compared to the one for Undo (⌘/Ctrl-Z). To undo and then redo an action a number of different times is a downright pain in the butt with the default shortcuts. Although ⌘/Ctrl-Y is the standard shortcut for Redo in such mainstay applications as Microsoft Word, I'd have to say that Illustrator has the right idea with the vastly superior shortcut ⌘/Ctrl-Shift-Z. Do yourself a favor and switch ⌘/Ctrl-Y to ⌘/Ctrl-Shift-Z, as explained in Chapter 2.

Repeat

You can repeat the Xtra last performed on the same selected objects, or you can select new objects on which to perform the exact same Xtra.

The Xtras ➪ Repeat command lets you to reapply the last Xtras menu or the Operations panel command. It saves you from multiple excursions into the Xtras submenus. Its keyboard shortcut is ⌘-Shift-+ on Macs and Ctrl-Alt-Shift-X on PCs

Whenever you perform a command that appears in either the Xtras menu or the Operations panel, the Repeat command wording changes to include that command. For example, if the last command you performed from the Xtras menu or the Operations panel was Punch, the Repeat command reads Repeat Punch. Choosing commands from other FreeHand menus does not change the Repeat command. Do whatever you want. When you're good and ready, come back to the Xtras menu, and Repeat Punch will still be waiting for you.

Although Punch isn't a true Xtra, its command is located in the Xtras menu. You know what they say about location. You don't? The three most important factors for a business are location, location, and location. The same holds true for the Repeat command. True Xtras, impostor Xtras, Illustrator, Photoshop plug-ins — they all work with the Repeat command.

Revert

Suppose that you revise your illustration by performing a series of actions. After making these changes, you decide that the illustration looked better before you started. You may be able to use the Undo command to reverse all your changes one operation at a time. However, not only would that take a lot of time, there's no guarantee that you have enough undos at your disposal.

A better solution is to use the Revert command in the File menu. The Revert command returns your illustration to the state it was in immediately following the last save operation. This command is useful when you have made major changes in your illustration that you now regret, such as deleting important elements or editing text.

To revert to the version of the current illustration saved to disk, choose File ⇨ Revert. FreeHand displays an alert box to make sure that you haven't lost your mind and you really do want to dispose of all changes made since the last Save command.

After you revert to the last version of the illustration saved to disk, you cannot return to the previous version. If you want to go ahead and revert to the last saved version, click the OK button or Alt-R; if not, click Cancel, or press ⌘-period or Alt-C.

If you have not saved your illustration since opening it, or if you are working on a new illustration that has never been saved to disk, the Revert command is dimmed.

If you're not sure what the last saved version of your file looks like — or whether it's any better than the mess you just created — choose File Í Save As (⌘/Ctrl-Shift-S) and save the new file under a different name than the last saved version. Then open the old file and compare the two versions.

✦   ✦   ✦

The Regimental Approach

FreeHand Eliminates Drafting Nightmares

Are you ready for a tiresome personal story? If not, skip to the next section, where I finally manage to impart some information that may actually help you use FreeHand.

In my junior high school — you are ready for this, aren't you? In my junior high school, the boys — that's right, only the boys — had to take wood shop one semester and drafting another. (I forget what the girls had to take. Mending or "Learning to Love Baking Soda" or something like that. Oh, and the obligatory "How to Act Dumber than Your Prospective Husband," which I hear was actually a very challenging course.)

In seventh grade, I started off with shop class and came to hate it almost immediately. I was so awful at working with power saws and sanders that I finally just molded my spice rack out of putty. But all the eighth-graders assured me that although shop was admittedly terrible, drafting was worse. You just sat there and drew boring geometric stuff, and nobody could talk except the teacher, who nagged you about your uneven lines and sloppy corners, like maybe someone was really going to build something based on your dweeb-esque drawing. Only a total nerd could tolerate it.

Being an avid nerd, I naturally took to drafting like a fish takes to chowing down flies. I got an A on every project, easily earned an A in the class, and was generally the envy of those with poor fine-motor skills. It was a very successful experience. For me, anyway.

But I was, after all, a scrub. I may have been better than most kids in the class, but I'm relatively certain that I wasn't perfect.

(If I was, I'd like to know where I went wrong, because I've sure as heck managed to wander several figurative miles from the mark since.) Later in life, I had the opportunity to test what an incompetent I really was. I was hired to create a series of precision drawings for this so-called professional directory. It was really just a cheap magazine composed exclusively of paid advertisements from doctors, lawyers, and a host of Boulder's stereotypical New Age companies, including a few out-and-out charlatans who have since gone under, much to my general amusement. (Oh, man, that felt good. If you're a freelance artist, I heartily recommend that you write a book someday and openly ridicule some old client. Truly cathartic.)

The point is, the drawings were a constant source of irritation. Every undesirable burp of ink from my drafting pen required an application of white ink, which was supposed to cover the mistake. But the white ink, of course, created a bump in the paper surface over which it was nearly impossible to draw a straight line or adhere that sticky halftone-dot transparency stuff without forming a slight shadow. I eventually created pieces that I was happy with, but the process was exasperating and incredibly time-consuming.

Don't you just love these personal stories? They allow us to bond. I mean, I really feel close to you right now.

So, where was I? Yeah, okay, so the problem was, I was trying to draw like a machine. Like arithmetic and automobile assembly, drafting is one of those tasks that machines can accomplish quickly, efficiently, and accurately. The machine needs a human to guide it; I'm not trying to imply that you're out of the loop. But the machine greatly improves your chances of a timely success.

In the case of drafting, FreeHand (yes, it all comes back to that) combined with a Mac or PC is the machine of choice. FreeHand provides grids, ruler tracking, automatic object distribution, and improved locking capabilities. But more important, FreeHand makes a mockery of drafting with conventional tools. Every corner is sharp, every line weight is absolutely consistent, every angle is accurate, and, if you make a mistake, absolution is no farther away than the Undo command or Delete key.

And don't think that you have to be an architect or engineer to take advantage of FreeHand's precision controls. These functions are designed with illustrators and designers in mind. If you've ever hoped to align two objects exactly, lock a path to prevent it from being altered, or organize objects onto separate layers, this chapter is essential reading.

Controlling Movement

Now that we've gotten my sordid history out of the way—really, (sniff) thanks for listening—I have a chapter of information just itching to be conveyed. If you read the previous chapter, you've already had a taste of some of the precision techniques that FreeHand offers. Shift-dragging, rotating the constraint axes, snapping, and nudging points via the arrow keys all qualify as means for making controlled adjustments to an illustration. The following sections explain additional drawing and editing functions that enable you to make precise changes to your illustration.

Using the rulers

FreeHand provides access to one vertical and one horizontal ruler. These rulers track the movement of your cursor or, if you're dragging an object, the movement of the object. Choose View ➪ Page Rulers (⌘/Ctrl-Option/Alt-M) to display the rulers, which appear at the top and left-hand edges of the illustration window, as shown in Figure 6-1. When the rulers are visible, a check mark precedes the Page Rulers command in the View menu. Choose the command again to hide the rulers.

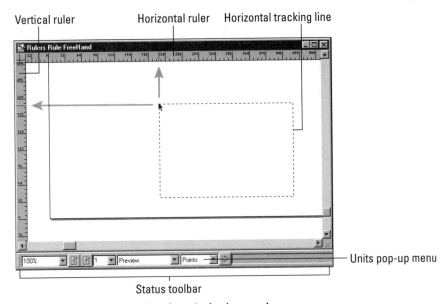

Figure 6-1: The horizontal and vertical rulers as they appear when the unit of measure is points.

Changing the unit of measure

The units displayed on both rulers can be points, picas, inches, or millimeters. For the record, a *pica* is almost exactly ⅙ inch, and there are 12 *points* in every pica (so, about 72 points in an inch). To change the unit of measure, select a new option from the Units pop-up menu in the Status toolbar, located, by default, at the bottom of the illustration window.

Whole picas, inches, or millimeters are indicated by long tick marks; fractions are indicated by short tick marks. As you magnify the view size, the units on the rulers become larger and more detailed. As you zoom out, units become smaller and less detailed. Numbers on each ruler indicate the distance from the *ruler origin*, the location in the illustration window at which the horizontal and vertical coordinates are zero. By default, the ruler origin is located in the bottom left corner of the page, as illustrated in Figure 6-1. All ruler measurements are made relative to this origin.

When you go to choose a unit, you'll notice that the Units pop-up menu offers two inches options: Inches and Decimal. If you select Inches, FreeHand divides each inch using a series of differently sized tick marks, placing the longest tick mark at the half inch, two shorter marks at the quarter inches, four still shorter at eighth inches, and so on, just like on a conventional drugstore ruler. Select Decimal to display a maximum of ten tick marks, all sized equally, per inch. It's purely a matter of preference.

As I alluded to in previous chapters, the unit of measure you select affects the way values in several of FreeHand's option boxes are measured. These option boxes include the following:

✦ Cursor Distance in the General panel of the Preferences dialog box

✦ All measurements listed in the Info toolbar

✦ Baseline Shift in the Character panel of the Text Inspector (⌘/Ctrl-T)

✦ All Paragraph Spacing and Indents option boxes in the Paragraph panel (⌘/Ctrl-Option/Alt-P) of the Text Inspector

✦ Width in the Stroke Inspector (⌘/Ctrl-Option/Alt-L)

✦ All Dimensions option boxes in the Object Inspector (⌘/Ctrl-I)

✦ All option boxes in the Document Inspector (⌘/Ctrl-Option/Alt-D)

✦ All option boxes in the Column & Row panel (⌘/Ctrl-Option/Alt-R) of the Text Inspector

You can override the unit of measure in any of these option boxes by adding the following abbreviations after the value that you enter: i for inch, m for millimeter, and *p* for *pica*, with any value following p indicating points. For example, *1.125i* means 1⅛ inches; *40m* means 40 millimeters; *12p6* means 12 picas, 6 points (12½ picas), and *p60* means 60 points (the same as *5p*, 5 picas).

Tracking lines

As long as the cursor is inside the illustration window, FreeHand tracks its movement on the horizontal and vertical rulers. It displays small dotted tracking lines to indicate the precise location of your cursor, as shown in Figure 6-1. For example, the cursor in Figure 6-1 is 212 points above and to the right of the ruler origin. (Each tick mark equals 8 points, and each tracking line in the figure is 2½ marks past the 192 mark, hence 212.)

Cross-Reference

Don't worry, you don't have to make these kinds of computations in your head. You can view the coordinates in the Info toolbar, displayed by choosing Window ➪ Toolbars ➪ Info, as explained in the "Using the Info toolbar" section later in this chapter.

When you drag a path or text block, FreeHand indicates the size of the dragged object in the horizontal and vertical rulers. This function is especially useful if you are trying to move an object to a specific location on the page. Too bad it's not in force during other transformations as well, such as scalings and rotations.

Changing the ruler origin

As I mentioned a moment ago, the ruler origin is located at the bottom left corner of the page by default. What I didn't mention was that you can relocate the ruler origin by dragging from the *ruler origin box*, which is the square created by the intersection of the horizontal and vertical rulers. Figure 6-2 illustrates the process of relocating the ruler origin. The black lines that extend from the arrow cursor indicate the prospective position of the new origin. If you drag very near to a point (and provided you've activated the Snap to Point command), the ruler origin snaps to the point, enabling you to make all measurements from a specific portion of an object. Furthermore, if you've selected the Smart Cursor option in the General panel of the Preference dialog box, the snap-to-point cursor will display. Notice that the movement of the ruler origin is tracked by the rulers.

At the end of the drag, the ruler origin moves to the location occupied by the cursor. All ruler measurements are then made from the new ruler origin. To return the ruler origin to its default location, double-click the ruler origin box.

Using grids

In addition to rulers and tracking lines, FreeHand provides a *grid*, which is a network of imaginary, regularly spaced horizontal and vertical lines that constrain the operation of tools within the illustration window. The grid affects the creation of points and the placement of control handles. The segments themselves can snake along as they please, but points align to grid intersections. This feature helps you to line up objects and elements inside objects as you draw.

You can display the grid by choosing the Grid ➪ Show command from the View menu. However, just because the grid is visible doesn't mean that it will have any effect on your cursor — and just because it's invisible doesn't mean it won't. To make your cursor snap to grid intersections, choose View ➪ Snap to Grid. When either of these commands is active, you see a check mark next to the command name; the check mark disappears when you hide the grid or turn off the Snap to Grid command.

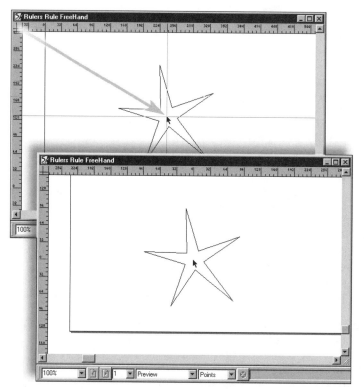

Figure 6-2: Drag from the ruler origin box (top) to relocate the point at which the horizontal and vertical coordinates are zero (bottom).

To specify the space between the imaginary horizontal and vertical grid lines, enter a value into the Edit Grid dialog box by choosing the Grid ⇨ Edit command from the View menu (see Figure 6-3). By default, the value is 6 points, or ¹⁄₁₂ inch. When you make the grid visible, however, FreeHand always spaces the lines about 1 inch apart, regardless of view size. This helps to avoid screen clutter. As Figure 6-3 illustrates, the window would get pretty busy if FreeHand displayed each and every grid line.

The individual dots in the grid lines represent the amount of space between the actual grid intersections. For example, if FreeHand displays 11 dots between visible grid lines — which is the default setting — then there are 11 actual grid lines between one inch and the next, for a total of 12 grid increments per inch.

When you turn on the Snap to Grid feature, FreeHand snaps your cursor, or any object or element that you drag, to the nearest grid intersection. This affects the creation and manipulation of all points and handles in a path, whether you're working with a free-form or geometric path. Suppose that the grid is turned on and set to ½ inch. Any time you drag with any tool, the cursor jumps in ½-inch increments. As a result, you can't create a rectangle that is, say, ¾-inch wide; it must measure ½ inch or 1 inch. FreeHand provides no means for automatically aligning existing objects to the grid. You have to drag them manually.

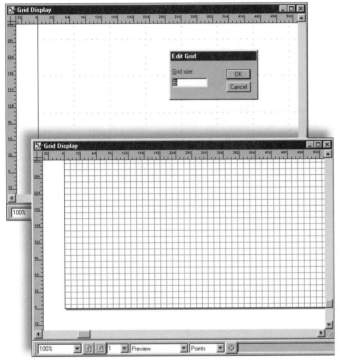

Figure 6-3: How FreeHand displays the grid on-screen (top) and the actual grid network that controls the movement of the cursor (bottom).

You can control the color of the visible grid using the Grid Color option in the Colors panel of the Preferences dialog box (⌘/Ctrl-Option/Alt-D).

Creating guidelines

If the grid is too regular for your tastes, you can create your own custom *guidelines* by dragging from one of the rulers:

✦ Drag downward from the horizontal ruler to create a horizontal guideline that spans the width of the active page, as illustrated in Figure 6-4.

✦ Drag to the right from the vertical ruler to create a vertical guideline that is the height of the active page.

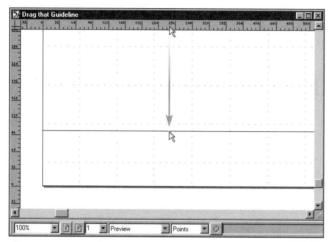

Figure 6-4: Drag from one of the rulers to position a horizontal or vertical guideline.

You use guidelines to mark a particular horizontal or vertical location inside the illustration window. You can then align points or segments in an object to the guideline and create perfect rows or columns of objects. When the Snap to Guides command is active in the View menu (⌘-, on Macs and Ctrl-Shift-G on PCs), as it is by default, your cursor snaps to a guideline. When the command is active, FreeHand puts a check mark by the command name.

Using objects as guides

Any object in FreeHand can be made into a guide. This feature is great because it enables you to align objects to any path. Its implementation is very sweet; I did it right in one try just by guessing. Here's what you need to do. First, if your Layers panel isn't open, press ⌘/Ctrl-6 to display it. Then simply select an object and click the Guides layer in the Layers panel. That's all. You did it right if the object's color changes to your current guide color.

The Guide Color option in the Colors panel of the Preferences dialog box (⌘/Ctrl-Shift-D) lets you change the color of your guides.

After you place the object on the guide layer, it becomes a path-guide. You can align an object to a path-guide, just as you would to a guideline. That's really all you need to know about it. However, this is one of those features for which a better technical understanding is very useful. Here's an exercise that illustrates what happens when you snap to paths that are not horizontal or vertical.

To set the stage, choose the View ➪ Snap to Guides command (⌘-, on Macs and Ctrl-Shift-G on PCs). Make sure that a checkmark appears to the left of the command in the View menu. Then, in the Preferences dialog box, set the Snap Distance to 5 and activate the Smart Cursors option in the General panel. You may want to zoom in for a detailed view when snapping to the guide object as you try out this exercise.

1. Create a 45-degree line by Shift-dragging with the line tool.

2. With the line selected, click the Guides layer in the Layers panel. The line's color changes to indicate that it's on the Guides layer and is now a path-guide.

3. Create a circle by Shift-dragging with the ellipse tool.

4. Slowly drag the circle toward the path-guide. As you drag, a bounding box appears around the circle's perimeter. Notice that the snap occurs when the corner of the bounding box touches the path-guide, which is before the circle's edge ever touches the guide object. Also notice that the arrow cursor gets a hollow circle to the lower right of the arrow to indicate a snap. Now, slowly continue dragging until the edge of the circle touches the path-guide. No snap. The snap is to the object's bounding box, not to its path. That's the first case I wanted to point out to you.

5. Go ahead and delete the circle but leave the path guide intact.

6. Select the rectangle tool and slowly create a rectangle as shown in Figure 6-5. Pay close attention to when the snap occurs. Also notice that the arrow cursor gets a hollow circle to the lower right of the arrow to indicate a snap. Notice that the top right corner of the rectangle is already past the edge of the path-guide before the snap occurs. That's because when creating objects, FreeHand snaps when the path of your drag crosses the path-guide. This is not necessarily the first time the object's path touches the path-guide.

7. Shift-drag with the oval tool to create a circle and send it to the Guides layer. The circle's color changes to indicate that it is a path-guide.

8. Select the rectangle tool.

9. Create a rectangle as in Figure 6-6, where the bottom left corner snaps to the path-object. Notice when the snap occurs. Also notice that the arrow cursor gets a hollow circle to the lower right of the arrow to indicate a snap. The snap occurs when the corner of the rectangle touches the path-guide. When an object becomes a path-guide, FreeHand does not consider its bounding box.

To recap briefly:

✦ When repositioning objects, you can snap any of the four corners of an object's bounding box to any point along the path of a guide object.

✦ When creating objects, you snap to a guide object when your drag touches any place along a guide's path.

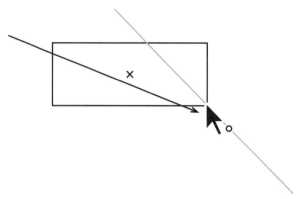

Figure 6-5: Drag as the arrow indicates to create a rectangle that snaps to the path-guide.

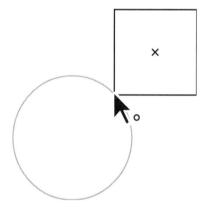

Figure 6-6: You can snap to any spot along a path-guide.

Editing guides

Choosing View ➪ Guides ➪ Edit displays the Guides dialog box, pictured in Figure 6-7. Here FreeHand lists all guides in your document by pages. At the top of this dialog box, you specify the page for which you want to list guides. Click the pages icons or enter a page in the option box for the page of your choice. Below that is a scrolling field that displays the guides for that page. FreeHand lists locations for horizontal and vertical guides using the current ruler units, and the current ruler origin. Each path-guide is listed merely as a path, which isn't extremely informative. In fact, if you have more than one path-guide on a page, listing them in the Guides dialog box becomes almost useless.

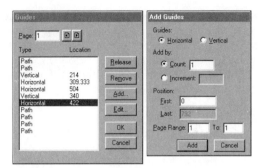

Figure 6-7: The Guides dialog box and its little buddy, the Add Guides dialog box.

Several buttons along the right of the dialog box let you manipulate the contents of the list box. These buttons are as follows:

✦ **Release:** Converts all guides currently selected in the list box into objects and places them on the active layer. Guidelines become actual lines in your document.

✦ **Remove:** Removes all guides currently selected in the list box from your document. (This button was called Delete in previous versions of FreeHand.)

✦ **Add:** Opens the Add Guides dialog box. This dialog box, shown on the right in Figure 6-7, lets you create a single guide or an array of guides. You specify whether the guides are horizontal or vertical. When creating an array of guides, enter the number of guides to add in the Count option box, or specify the distance between the guides in the Increment option box. Whichever number you enter, FreeHand calculates the second. This calculation is also based on your entries under Position. Here you enter the location of the first and last guidelines. Finally, if you want to repeat the same guide array over multiple pages, enter the desired page range.

✦ **Edit:** Enabled only when a single horizontal or vertical guide is selected in the list box. It opens a dialog box that lets you enter a new position for the selected guide. You can also open this dialog box by double-clicking the guide name in the list box.

Tip

You can also move and delete guides manually. To move an existing guideline, use the arrow tool to drag it to a new location in the illustration window. To delete a guideline, drag it back to the horizontal or vertical ruler. This can be a frustrating task, because FreeHand has a tendency to scroll as you drag beyond the confines of the illustration window. You eliminate the scrolling problem when you disable the Dragging a Guide Scrolls the Window option in the General panel of your Preferences dialog box. You can access the Guides dialog box by double-clicking on a guide as well. This automatically highlights the guide's name in the Guides dialog box.

Choose View ➪ Guides ➪ Lock to protect existing guidelines from being moved or deleted. To hide or display the guidelines, choose View ➪ Guides ➪ Show. Hidden guidelines do not affect the creation or manipulation of objects. FreeHand puts a check mark next to Lock or Show when the command is active. Oddly enough, you can still create new guides when existing guides are locked or hidden. The new guides will display the same characteristics as the other guides — they will also be locked or hidden.

Tip

You can more conveniently control guidelines from the Layers panel. Click the little lock icon that precedes the Guides layer name to lock and unlock the guidelines. Click the check mark to hide and display the guidelines. Best of all, you can move the guidelines so that they're positioned in front of objects on a certain layer. Just drag the Guides option to a different location in the list included with the Layers panel. For more information on the Guides layer, read the "Layering Objects" section later in this chapter.

You can alter the interval at which a dragged element snaps toward a guideline. Just enter a new value in the Snap Distance option in the General panel of the Preferences dialog box. You can enter any value from 1 to 5; values are measured in screen pixels. The default value is 3. Entering 1 is a bad idea, because the snap is practically undetectable.

Using the Info toolbar

When you choose Window ➪ Toolbars ➪ Info, FreeHand displays the Info toolbar directly below the Main and Text toolbars. This thin horizontal strip provides all kinds of interesting and useful data about the current operation. The Info toolbar constantly tracks the movement of your cursor in the illustration window and analyzes all changes that occur as a result of your clicks and drags.

For example, Figure 6-8 shows the Info toolbar as it appears when you drag an object with the arrow tool. The first item in the Info toolbar tells you either the type of path you're dragging or the number of paths you're moving. The second and third items (x and y) represent the horizontal and vertical coordinates of the cursor with respect to the ruler origin.

The fourth and fifth items (dx and dy) list the horizontal and vertical components — better known as the width and height — of the move. The sixth and seventh items (dist and angle) tell the distance and direction of the move. The latter is measured in degrees, relative to the 0-degree mark in a 360-degree circle. If the circle was a clock, the 0-degree mark would be 3 o'clock. (Refer back to lucky Figure 5-13, which shows the constraint axes and the directions associated with several common degree readings.)

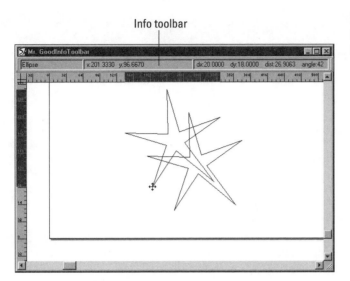

Info toolbar

Figure 6-8: The Info toolbar as it appears when moving an object.

The Info toolbar also displays valuable information when you are creating geometric and free-form paths and when you are transforming selections with the arrow, scale, reflect, rotate, or skew tool. All position and distance items are listed in the unit of measure specified in the Status toolbar. Table 6-1 lists all the items that you may see in the Info toolbar and describes their meanings. I've listed the items in the order that they appear in the Info toolbar.

Table 6-1
A Guide to the Info Toolbar

Item	Current Action	Meaning
tab	Dragging a tab stop or indent marker in the tab ruler	Horizontal distance from the left edge of the text block to the position of the tab stop or insertion marker
x	Using any tool other than a transformation tool	Horizontal distance from the cursor to the ruler origin
y	Using any tool other than a transformation tool	Vertical distance from the cursor to the ruler origin
xscale	Scaling, reflecting, rotating, or skewing a selection	Horizontal distance from the transformation origin to the ruler origin
yscale	Scaling, reflecting, rotating, or skewing a selection	Vertical distance from the transformation origin to the ruler origin

(continued)

	Table 6-1 *(contined)*	
Item	*Current Action*	*Meaning*
w	Dragging with the rectangle, ellipse, trace, or zoom tool	Width of drag
h	Dragging with the rectangle, ellipse, trace, or zoom tool	Height of drag
dx	Dragging a selection with the arrow tool or dragging with the line or pen tool	Width of drag
dy	Moving a selection with the arrow tool or dragging with the line or pen tool	Height of drag
dist	Moving a selection with the arrow tool or with the line or pen tool	Direct measurement of distance dragged
angle	Moving a selection with the arrow tool or dragging with the polygon, line, or pen tool	Direction of drag
OR	Reflecting a selection	Angle of reflection axis
OR	Rotating a selection	Angle of rotation
radius	Dragging with the polygon tool	Direct measurement of distance dragged
sides	Dragging with the polygon tool	Number of sides in the shape
xscale	Scaling or skewing a selection	Horizontal extent of the transformation expressed as a ratio (for example, 1.0 equals 100%)
yscale	Scaling or skewing a selection	Vertical extent of the transformation expressed as a ratio (for example, 1.0 equals 100%)

Alignment and Distribution

FreeHand's alignment and distribution functions enable you to adjust the locations of two or more selected objects with respect to one another. These functions are most useful when you're creating schematic drawings and want to line up objects in rows, columns, or other visual patterns.

To align or distribute (adjust the spacing between) two or more objects, select the objects and display the Align panel — shown in Figure 6-9 — by choosing either Modify ➪ Align or Window ➪ Panels ➪ Align (⌘/Ctrl-Option/Alt-A) or by clicking the Apply button in the Main toolbar. Then select the desired options from the Horizontal and Vertical pop-up menus and click the Align button.

Modify ⇨ Align or Window ⇨ Panels ⇨ Align (⌘/Ctrl-Option/Alt-A) or by clicking the Apply button in the Main toolbar. Then select the desired options from the Horizontal and Vertical pop-up menus and click the Align button.

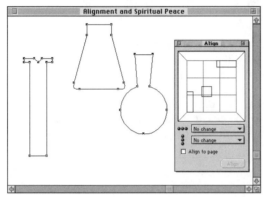

Figure 6-9: The Align panel enables you to align and distribute selected objects with respect to each other.

FreeHand 8 uses a graphical element to illustrate Horizontal and Vertical inside the Align panel. It's easy to see; just look for the six billiard balls seemingly lined up for an amazing trick shot. However, the horizontal line of balls is the Vertical option and the vertical line of balls is the Horizontal option—rather confusing so watch out. (If the Apply button is dimmed, it's because you haven't selected enough objects—"enough" being two.)

Aligning selected objects to each other

Each of the pop-up menus in the Align panel offers three alignment options and four distribution options. The alignment options line up selected objects according to their left or right edges, their tops or bottoms, or horizontally or vertically by their centers. FreeHand 8 gives you the ability to align selected points. Points are aligned in the same manner as alignment of objects.

Here's an example. Suppose that you've drawn a series of silhouetted soldiers marching down a road. But you were naturally so busy concentrating on making the shapes look like soldiers against an eerie twilight sky that you entirely neglected to line them up properly. So rather than marching on a flat road, they bob up and down. To align their feet along a perfectly horizontal surface, you select all the soldier shapes, select the Align Bottom option from the Vertical pop-up menu, and press the Align button.

Note   You don't have to select options from both the Horizontal and Vertical pop-up menus. When aligning the soldiers along the road, for example, you would leave the Horizontal pop-up menu set to No Change. In fact, you will more often than not select an option from only one pop-up menu. Otherwise, the shapes bunch up on each other.

If, instead of aligning with respect to the points or objects you've selected, you wish to use the border of the page as the guide for alignment, then activate the Align to Page checkbox at the bottom of the Align panel.

Rather than run through every possible alignment permutation, I've included the following exercise, which begins with the three paths shown in Figure 6-10. The steps will only take you two or three minutes to complete—this is pretty easy stuff—so give them a whirl.

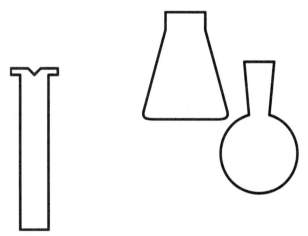

Figure 6-10: Three beakers that want desperately to be aligned.

1. Draw three beaker shapes. Spend hours on this step and make your beakers look exactly like the ones in Figure 6-10. Or just draw three rectangles. It doesn't really matter; FreeHand is capable of dealing with non-beaker shapes.

2. Select all three objects and choose Modify ➪ Align (⌘/Ctrl-Option/Alt-A) to bring the Align panel forward.

3. Select the Align Left option from the Horizontal pop-up menu. Just to be safe, make sure that the Vertical pop-up menu is set to No Change.

4. Click the Apply button in the lower right corner of the panel. FreeHand then performs a two-step operation. First, it determines the leftmost point within each of the three selected shapes. For the sake of discussion, I'll call these key points A, B, and C. FreeHand notes that point A is farther to the left than B or C.

The shape to which point A belongs, therefore, remains stationary. In the second step, FreeHand moves the shapes containing points B and C until all points — A, B, and C — line up in a vertical formation, as shown in Figure 6-11.

Figure 6-11: The eager beakers horizontally aligned by their left edges.

5. Ick, the beakers look terrible aligned by their left edges. Who in the world thought this would be a good idea? Choose Undo Align Objects from the Edit menu (⌘/Ctrl-Z) to restore the objects to their original locations.

6. Back inside the Align panel, select No Change from the Horizontal pop-up menu. Notice how the panel remembers your last setting? Then select Align Top from the Vertical pop-up menu.

7. Press Apply to produce the result shown in Figure 6-12. FreeHand finds the topmost point in each shape, makes the tippy-top shape stationary, and moves the others into position so that the tops of the shapes are aligned in horizontal formation. This configuration produces a better effect than Figure 6-11 because the beakers were positioned in a vaguely horizontal formation to begin with.

 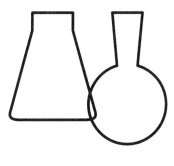

Figure 6-12: The beaker boys aligned vertically by their tops.

Note

In case you're wondering why FreeHand's Horizontal alignment options don't result in horizontal formations, as the option name might suggest, here's the reason: The Horizontal options align objects by their left or right edges, which results in a vertical column of objects. Likewise, the Vertical options align objects by their top and bottom edges, which creates a neatly aligned horizontal formation.

As demonstrated in the exercise, the Align Left and Align Top options work by moving key points in the selected paths into alignment with a model key point that remains stationary. The same is also true for the Align Right and Align Bottom options. However, the two Align Center options work a little differently. Each option first examines the equations that define all the selected paths. After plotting a few points along the outlines of the paths, the option averages the locations of these points to find a central horizontal and vertical coordinate. Finally, the option moves each path so that its center is located at the average coordinate.

Objects that are aligned horizontally fall into a linear column; objects that are aligned vertically fall into a straight row. If you want to align two objects by their exact centers, so that the smaller object is inset inside the larger one, select the Align Center options from both the Horizontal and Vertical pop-up menus.

Spacing objects evenly

To *distribute* objects is to place them so that the distance between object A and its neighbor, object B, is equal to the distance between object B and its neighbor, object C. For example, if a series of objects is distributed to the left, the leftmost point in each object is an equal distance from the leftmost point in each of its neighbors.

To use FreeHand's distribution options, you have to select at least three objects. FreeHand allows you to apply distribution options to two objects, but the options have no effect. This is because FreeHand compares the space between objects when distributing. Therefore, you must select a minimum of three objects to have two spaces to compare.

The following steps give you a quick introduction to the distribution options. Again, the steps involve the three beakers from Figure 6-10.

1. Select all three objects and press ⌘/Ctrl-Shift-A to bring up the Align panel.

2. Select the Align Bottom option from the Vertical pop-up menu. As you know — you *were* paying attention earlier, weren't you? — this option repositions the bottoms of two of the paths to align with the bottom of the lowest path.

3. Select the Distribute Widths option from the Vertical pop-up menu. The Distribute Widths option instructs FreeHand to put an equal amount of

horizontal space between each object. You see a preview of the option's effect in the top half of the panel.

4. Press Align. As shown in Figure 6-13, FreeHand's distribution feature automatically spreads the paths in an aesthetically pleasing formation. FreeHand's distribution options are a guaranteed hit.

Figure 6-13: The bleak beakers aligned by their bottom edges and distributed horizontally according to width.

If you're not sure what results your alignment or distribution settings will produce, refer to the small icons inside the rectangle at the top of the Align panel. These icons move to represent the effects of your selections. Keep in mind, however, that the icons may not bear a whole lot of resemblance to the selected objects in the illustration window, so you have to use a little bit of imagination. You can click in the quadrants of the icon window to "automatically" set the alignment. It's fun to watch the icons scurry around repositioning themselves, but it's not very useful and may even be frustrating. Play around with this feature or just apply a few options and then undo the operation if you don't like it.

Tip

To gain additional control when aligning objects, try locking one — and only one — of the objects by choosing Modify ➪ Lock (⌘/Ctrl-L) before you apply options from the Align panel. The locked object remains stationary, while other selected objects are aligned to it. (For more information on the Lock command, keep reading.)

Grouping and Protecting Objects

With the Group and Lock commands, you can protect objects from editing danger. Both commands make it difficult to access individual points in a path. And the Lock command goes so far as to prevent you from moving or otherwise transforming whole objects.

Both commands build on FreeHand's assortment of precision functions by enabling you to put some objects off limits. It's as if you could tell a bottle of ink, "No matter what I do — whack you, elbow you, or fling you across the room — don't spill all over this one drawing." To rope off entire collections of objects, check out the "Protecting layers" section later in this chapter.

Making many objects into one

A section or two ago, I asked you to imagine drawing silhouetted soldiers. You probably thought that I was just trying to stimulate your interest by setting a mood. But there was actually a modicum of method behind my madness.

You see, you can create a silhouette using a single shape. If, however, each of your soldiers comprised multiple shapes, the Align options would present a problem: They would align each and every object individually. Figure 6-14, for example, shows a soldier made up of 15 shapes. When I align the shapes along the bottom, the soldier falls apart, as in the second example. This is because FreeHand aligns the bottom of each and every shape.

Figure 6-14: A soldier before (left) and after (right) I aligned its various paths by their bottoms.

To prevent this from happening, you need to make FreeHand think of all 15 shapes as a single object — which you can do by grouping the shapes. To do this, select the shapes and choose Modify ➪ Group (⌘/Ctrl-G) or click the Group button in the Main Toolbar. All shapes in the group then behave as a single, collective object. To align your platoon of soldiers, you group the shapes in each soldier independently and then apply the desired options from the Align panel.

General grouping facts

When you choose the Group command, you achieve the same results whether you select only a single point or segment or an entire path. All objects that are even partially selected become grouped in their entirety.

You can apply the Group command to a single path to safeguard the relationship between points and segments. You can even group multiple groups and groups of groups. (But you can't group a grouper; you have to catch it with a rod and reel like everyone else.) In fact, you can apply the Group command to any type or graphic object that you can create or import into FreeHand.

After you group one or more objects, all points within the group disappear. When the group is selected, four corner handles define the perimeter of the group, much like those associated with a geometric shape. Using the arrow tool, you can drag any of these corner handles to scale a group, as discussed in the "Using handles" section of Chapter 5. Shift-drag a handle to scale the group proportionally.

You can scale a group with respect to its center by pressing the Option/Alt key. And you can scale a group horizontally or vertically by Shift-dragging and then pressing and holding the ⌘/Ctrl key midway into the operation.

Transforming as a unit

When a group is selected, the Object Inspector relates information about the group as a whole. The first two Dimensions option boxes display the location of the lower left corner handle of the group in relation to the ruler origin. The second pair of options controls the width and height of the group.

Below the option boxes is the Transform as Unit check box, which enables you to predetermine how a transformation will affect the attributes of the selected group. If you want certain aspects of a group — such as type orientation, fill, and stroke — to remain constant throughout a transformation, leave this option deselected. Although this is the default setting, it is generally not the setting you'll want to use.

Take a look at Figure 6-15, for example. To create the image on the right, I grouped the objects in the Slug-Man Clothiers logo on the left and then skewed the entire group. Because Transform as Unit was deselected, the stroke remained constant and the type simply rotated around its transformed ellipse. The relationship between paths in the cartoon has become hopelessly jumbled. I fixed the problem by transforming attributes along with the group, as shown in Figure 6-16. To do this, select the Transform as Unit check box before performing the transformation.

Figure 6-15: After grouping several objects (left), I skewed the group (right), completely destroying every relationship the original group possessed.

Figure 6-16: Select the Transform as Unit check box to distort both the attributes of a group and the objects in a group equally when applying a transformation.

Note Fans of Bill Amend's hilarious syndicated comic strip FoxTrot will recognize young Jason Fox's inspiring creation, the awesomely powerful Slug-Man, in these two figures. I'm certain that if this astonishingly gifted superhero had a line of baggy Slug-Pants, his logo would look exactly like this.

For more information on transformations, including the skewing operation demonstrated here, read Chapter 13. For more information on Slug-Man, buy every *FoxTrot* collection you can get your hands on.

Selecting elements within groups

To select a whole group, click any path in the group with the arrow tool. You can also select an individual object in a group by Option/Alt-clicking it with the arrow tool. Option/Alt-clicking with the arrow tool displays individual points in the path, allowing you to fill, stroke, reshape, or transform a single path within a group without affecting other objects in the group.

To select multiple paths in a group, Shift-Option/Alt-click on each path. Or press the Option/Alt key while marqueeing with the arrow tool and then press the grave key (`) to deselect the points and leave just the paths selected.

After selecting a single path in a group, you can select groups within groups by pressing the grave key (our friend in the upper left corner of the keyboard). Each time you press grave, you select the group that includes the previously selected group. The following steps demonstrate how this works:

1. Draw four separate paths with the freehand tool. After drawing each path, choose Modify ➪ Group (⌘/Ctrl-G) to group that single path.

2. Select two of the grouped paths and again choose Modify ➪ Group. Select the other pair of paths and group them as well.

3. Select both grouped pairs and choose Modify ➪ Group. The result is four groups (the original free-form paths) within two groups (the pairs) within a single group.

4. Using the arrow tool, Option/Alt-click any one of the paths. This selects the entire path and displays its points. Then click a single point in the selected path to select the point.

5. Press the grave key. FreeHand deselects the point but leaves the path selected. (I first introduced this technique in the "Selecting points" section of Chapter 5.)

6. Press the grave key a second time. The points disappear, and four corner handles appear around the selected path, indicating that you have now selected the grouped object that contains this lone path.

7. Press the grave key a third time. The larger group, containing two grouped paths, becomes selected.

8. Press grave a fourth time. The highest-level group becomes selected, which includes all four free-form paths.

Although Option/Alt-clicking enables you to select elements inside objects that you combined with the Group command, you cannot Option/Alt-click to access segments or points inside a rectangle or ellipse. To select a point in a geometric shape, you must first ungroup the shape, as described in the next section.

Ungrouping

You can ungroup any group by choosing Modify ➪ Ungroup (⌘/Ctrl-U) or click the Ungroup button in the Main Toolbar. Okay, that's obvious. But here are a few less obvious facts you may want to know about ungrouping:

✦ You can ungroup multiple groups simultaneously, but only one level at a time. In other words, if a group contains groups, you must ungroup the most recently created group first. You can then ungroup the member groups by choosing Modify ➪ Ungroup again while all groups are still selected.

✦ If a selection contains both grouped and ungrouped objects when you choose the Ungroup command, FreeHand deselects the ungrouped paths and leaves only those objects that were previously grouped selected.

✦ You cannot ungroup a member of a group — at least, not from the group — that you selected by Option/Alt-clicking. You must always ungroup objects sequentially.

✦ You can ungroup a geometric path created with the rectangle or oval tool, even while it's part of a larger group. If it is part of a larger group, only the geometric path will ungroup; the larger group will remain grouped.

Ungrouping is sometimes an essential part of the reshaping process. Most notably, before you can join two elements that are contained in different groups, you have to ungroup the paths that contain the two elements. For example, if one endpoint in an open path is part of a group and an endpoint from another path belongs to a different group, you can't join the two endpoints. (In fact, if you choose Modify ➪ Join, FreeHand ignores you.) You must ungroup the paths before choosing the Join command.

Distinguishing groups from composite paths

What if ungrouping a path doesn't produce the desired effect? Then perhaps the object wasn't a group in the first place. Instead, it may be a composite path that was created using Modify ➪ Join or Text ➪ Convert to Paths.

To determine whether a combined object is a group or a composite path, display the Object Inspector (⌘/Ctrl-I). If the words *Composite Path* appear below the Inspector title bar, the selection is a composite path (like you needed me to tell you that). You can break apart a composite path by choosing Modify ➪ Split (⌘/Ctrl-Shift-J).

Avoiding accidental alterations

While working on a complicated illustration, you will probably create several objects that overlap. In the process of reshaping and transforming some of those objects, you may inadvertently select and alter an overlapping object that was positioned exactly where you wanted it to be. Fixing an object that was correct to begin with can be exceedingly frustrating. Unfortunately, the more complicated your drawing becomes, the greater the likelihood that you will disturb one or more perfectly positioned objects.

Luckily, FreeHand gives you a couple of ways to make sure that you don't ruin an object that you've spent hours slaving to create and position. In FreeHand, if an object is locked or if the object is hidden from view, it's safe from harm. The first method entails the use of the Lock and Unlock commands in the Modify menu. You can also click the Lock and Unlock buttons in the Main Toolbar. Either way, you can protect text blocks and graphic objects from being upset or altered. These two commands are the subjects of the following sections.

Locking objects

Locking a path prevents the path or any of its points from being moved. You can't drag or transform a locked object in any way. A locked object, however, is not entirely unalterable. You can still select it and change its fill or stroke attributes.

To lock an object, select it and choose the Lock command from the Modify menu (⌘/Ctrl-L). You cannot lock a single point independently of other points in a path. If you specifically select one point in a path and choose the Lock command, FreeHand locks the entire path.

The first example in Figure 6-17 displays two paths, one of which is selected. The following exercise demonstrates how you can use the Lock command to protect the selected path.

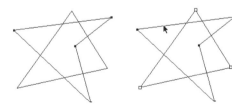

Figure 6-17: After locking the selected path (left), I marqueed both paths and poised my arrow cursor to drag a segment in the locked path (right).

1. Draw a couple of free-form paths. Make them pathetically simple. You don't want to waste too much time on this exercise.

2. Select one of the paths, as shown in the first example in Figure 6-17. Choose Modify ⇨ Lock (⌘/Ctrl-L) to lock the selection.

3. Drag a marquee around both shapes with the arrow tool. FreeHand selects all points in the unlocked path but selects none of the points in the locked one, as in the second example in Figure 6-17.

4. Drag a segment in the locked path. As you drag, only the unlocked shape moves, as shown in Figure 6-18, despite the fact that your cursor is not positioned over any part of that path. When an object in the current selection is locked, FreeHand treats the manipulation just as it would normally, except that it does not allow any point in the locked object to move.

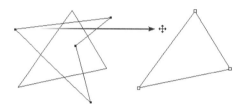

Figure 6-18: If you drag a locked object, all unlocked objects in the current selection move and the locked object remains stationary.

Though you can't delete locked objects by pressing the Delete key, you can delete them by removing the layer on which the objects appear. For more information on this function, read the upcoming "Deleting an existing layer" section.

Unlocking objects

To unlock an object, select the object and choose Modify ➪ Unlock (⌘/Ctrl-Shift-L) or click the Unlock button in the Main Toolbar. If the selected object is not locked, the Unlock command is dimmed.

FreeHand saves an object's locked status with the document. Therefore, when you open an existing file, all objects that were locked during the previous session will still be locked.

Out of sight, out of mind

As I mentioned just a couple of sections ago, in addition to offering the lock command, FreeHand provides you another method of security: hiding your artwork. That's right, grab your artwork and ditch it under that big pile of clothing in your closet. No, wait, that's not right. That's what one does when trying to hide a tin of processed piggy-meat, packed generously with pork flavored gelatin. That reminds me, I really need to do my laundry.

Anyway, to hide your FreeHand art, select it with the arrow tool and choose the View ➪ Hide Selection command. Presto, the selected items disappear. You can even hide some objects one moment, and then, say, five minutes later, select a whole new batch of objects and hide them as well. All objects hidden via the Hide Selection command form a single collection of hidden objects.

The advantage of hiding objects is that once hidden, you can do absolutely nothing to alter the hidden objects. Nothing, that is, short of deleting the layer on which the objects reside — more about that in "Layering Objects" — or changing the object style upon which any hidden object is based, as discussed in Chapter 10. The disadvantage is that, unlike locked objects that remain in sight, allowing you to see how they work in the grand scheme of things as you proceed to manipulate the rest of your artwork, you can't see hidden objects. Yeah, I know, you're saying "Duh, kind of a no-brainer there." But really, you can't see what part the hidden objects play as you make adjustments to your visible artwork and that can be rather inconvenient. Alas, there's always a tradeoff.

To reveal the hidden objects, all you need to do is choose the View ⇨ Show All command. All objects hidden by way of the Hide Selection command suddenly pop back into view. No matter when you hid the objects, whether you hid a few one minute and then hid a bunch later, choose Show All and they are all back in view. That's the other rub about this method of hiding objects. Since you cannot select hidden objects and thus cannot specify which hidden objects you wish revealed, if you want to view one hidden object, you must reveal them all.

Layering Objects

When you preview or print an illustration, FreeHand describes it one object at a time, starting with the first object in the illustration window and working up to the last. The order in which the objects are described is called the *stacking order*. The first object described lies behind all other objects in the illustration window. The last object sits in front of its cohorts. All other objects exist on some unique tier between the first object and the last.

Left to its own devices, layering would be a function of the order in which you draw. The oldest object would be in back; the most recent object would be in front. But FreeHand provides a number of commands that enable you to adjust the stacking order of existing graphic objects and text blocks.

Using the Layers panel, you can create self-contained *drawing layers* (or simply *layers*) that act like transparent pieces of acetate. You can draw an object on any layer and see it clearly through all layers in front of it. An illustration can contain any number of layers; each layer can contain any number of objects; you can name layers and alter their order as you see fit.

Suppose that you want to create a complex illustration of a frog, complete with internal organs, skeleton structure, googly eyes, and so on. To keep the objects that make up the organs from getting all jumbled together, you could isolate them on separate layers. For example, you might put the heart on one layer, the spleen on another, and the lungs on a third. Then, if you discover that you've accidentally gone and drawn a rat's heart instead of a frog's heart, you can replace or refine the heart without endangering the perfect little froggy spleen and lungs you created. You can even print all the layers to different pages, which is ideal for publishing your own visible frog inserts for encyclopedias.

Working with drawing layers

To display the Layers panel, choose Window ➪ Panels ➪ Layers (⌘/Ctrl-6) or click the Layers button in the Main toolbar. FreeHand displays all existing drawing layers in the foreground document as options in a scrolling list inside the Layers panel, as shown on the left in Figure 6-19. You can define and manipulate the layers using the options in the Options pop-up menu, which appears on the right in Figure 6-19.

Figure 6-19: The Layers panel (left) and the contents of the Options pop-up menu (right).

Layers in FreeHand fall into one of two categories: foreground and background. Any foreground layer is a printing layer and any background layer is a nonprinting layer. Three premade layers are included by default in all FreeHand documents and, conveniently enough, two of the layers' names reflect their type:

✦ **Foreground:** This foreground layer contains the objects that will print. The other two layers are reserved for nonprinting objects.

✦ **Guides:** This layer contains the nonprinting guidelines and guide objects, as described earlier in the "Creating guidelines" section. By default, the Guides layer is located in back of the Foreground layer. Any free-form objects that you send to this layer become guides.

✦ **Background:** The last layer — as the name implies, a background — is separated from its predecessors by a bar. This bar indicates that any layer appearing underneath it will not print. Conversely, all layers that print appear above. The Guides layer is the exception. It never prints despite where it appears. A background layer is a good place for positioning tracing templates and other visual guides. The Background layer is located in back of all layers above it in the list.

You can create as many foreground or background layers as you want. Any objects on foreground layers will print; objects on the background layers won't.

Tip

If you want to create additional default layers that FreeHand will include with every new document, create the new layers and rename and reposition them as desired, as described in the upcoming sections. Then save your document as the new FreeHand Defaults file, as described in "The FreeHand Defaults file" in Chapter 2.

When you select an object in the illustration window, FreeHand highlights the name of the object's drawing layer in the scrolling list. If you select multiple objects from different layers, no layer name appears highlighted. If no object is selected, the highlighted layer name is the default drawing layer, on which all future objects will be created.

Assigning objects to layers

To send one or more selected objects to a different layer, simply click a layer name in the scrolling list. You can send only whole objects to a different layer. If a path is only partially selected when you click a layer name, FreeHand moves the entire path to the selected layer. Any objects you send to the Guides layer become guides, and you cannot move locked objects. Objects that you send to the Background layer appear screened and do not print.

Tip

You may find that every time you send an object to a different layer, you also change the default layer. This happens when the Changing Objects Changes Defaults check box in the Object panel of the Preferences dialog box is selected. To send a selection to a layer without affecting the default layer, you must deselect this option. (However, by doing so, you also prevent FreeHand from changing other default settings — such as the fill or stroke of an object — in keeping with your last operation.)

The following sections explain the various ways you can adjust layers from the Layers panel. Note that all these changes apply to the foreground document only; they do not affect all open documents, for example. The only way to make changes that affect multiple documents is to alter the FreeHand Defaults file, which changes all future documents created in FreeHand but does not affect existing documents.

Creating and naming a new layer

To introduce a new drawing layer to the foreground document, select the New option from the Options pop-up menu. (I recommend that you press the Tab key before selecting this option, to prevent any objects in the document from being sent to the new layer.) FreeHand creates a new foreground layer in front of all the other layers in the document and names it something meaningless like Layer-5. To rename the layer, double-click its name in the list. Then enter the new name and press Return/Enter to accept it.

You can rename any layer in the Layers panel except the Guides layer. FreeHand is very possessive of this layer and hates to see you do much of anything with it except move it around.

Another method for creating a new layer is to clone an existing one. Select the layer that you want to clone and then select the Duplicate option from the Options pop-up menu. FreeHand clones all objects on the existing layer and sends the clones to a new layer. FreeHand names the new layer something stupid like *Copy of Layer-5*, so it's up to you to rename it. Why clone an existing layer instead of creating a brand new one? Primarily because it enables you to experiment with reshaping and otherwise editing a collection of objects without risking permanent damage to your drawing.

To transfer a new layer from document A to document B, send an object to the new layer in document A and then copy the object to the Clipboard. Next, switch to document B and paste. FreeHand pastes not only the object, but also its layering information. This technique assumes that you selected the Remember Layer Info check box in the General panel of the Preferences dialog box.

Reordering layers

The order in which layer names appear in the Layers panel determines the stacking order of your document. The first name in the list represents the foremost layer; the last name is the rearmost layer.

To change the order of layers in the foreground document, simply drag a layer name to a different position inside the scrolling list of the Layers panel. FreeHand takes objects assigned to that layer and repositions them behind or in front of objects on other layers, according to your drag. Drag a layer name below the line in the Layers panel to make the layer a nonprinting background layer. All objects on that layer then appear dimmed. Drag a layer above the line to make it a printing foreground layer.

You can even drag the bar that separates the foreground layers from the background ones up or down in the Layers panel. This enables you to change multiple layers to background or foreground layers at the same time.

By default, the Guides layer is in front of all background layers but in back of all foreground layers. You can reorder it in any way you see fit. However, because the Guide layer is designed as a nonprinting layer in spite of whether it appears with the foreground or background layers, guidelines never print.

Showing and hiding layers

A check mark in front of a layer name indicates that all objects on that layer will be displayed onscreen. Objects on foreground layers that are checked will print. Click on the check mark to hide it and, by so doing, hide all objects on that layer in the illustration window. This technique enables you to isolate a detail on another layer so that you can examine it more closely or make corrections to it. To display objects on a hidden layer, click on in front of the layer name to redisplay the check mark.

Tip

To specify whether objects on hidden layers print, choose File ➪ Output Options to display the Output Options dialog box, shown in Figure 6-20. Then select or deselect Include Invisible Layers. When this option is selected, hidden layers print — as long as they are foreground layers. For more information on printing, read Chapter 18.

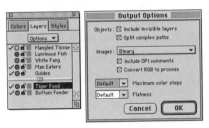

Figure 6-20: Hidden foreground layers like White Fang and Luminous Fish print, as long as the Include Invisible Layers check box in the Output Options dialog box is selected.

To hide all layers in the foreground document, select the All Off option from the Options pop-up menu or ⌘/Ctrl-click any check mark in the Layers panel. Then click in front of specific layer names that you want to display. To display all layers, select the All On option or ⌘/Ctrl-click in front of a layer name that is hidden.

Note

The View ➪ Hide Selection and View ➪ Show All commands work independently of the hiding functionality of the Layers panel. In other words, if you wish to reveal an object that you hide via the Hide Selection command, you must use the Show All command.

Setting a layer's display mode

In Chapter 2 you learned about display modes and how to use the Display Mode pop-up menu inside the Status toolbar to set a document to Preview or Keyline mode. You can also set display modes on a layer-by-layer basis using the Layers panel. Doing so allows you to set more complicated layers to Keyline mode, while leaving others in Preview mode. The display modes option is found in the Layers panel, thereby enabling you to set different display modes for different layers.

By default, FreeHand creates new layers set to Preview mode. The Layers panel indicates this with the gray circular button, which appears to the left of the lock symbol by each layer's name. To change a layer to Keyline mode, click this button. The button loses its gray fill and displays an x in its center, just as objects in Keyline mode lose their fills and display x's in their centers. In Figure 6-20 (in the previous section), the Layers panel indicates that Luminous Fish is in Preview mode, whereas Mangled Tissue is in Keyline mode.

To view all layers in Keyline mode, ⌘/Ctrl-click any gray-filled preview buttons. To view all layers in Preview mode, ⌘/Ctrl-click, any open, x-in-its-center keyline icon.

Protecting layers

Just as you can protect a selected object from being altered (by choosing Modify ➪ Lock), you can protect entire layers of objects. One way to protect a layer is to hide it as described in the preceding section. You cannot manipulate objects on a hidden layer, because you have no way to get to them.

You can also protect objects on a layer by locking the layer. To do so, click the tiny lock icon in front of the layer name in the Layers panel. When the lock appears to be open, the layer is unlocked; when the lock appears closed, all objects on the corresponding layer are off limits. To unlock a layer, click its icon again.

To lock all layers in a document, ⌘/Ctrl-click any open lock icon. To unlock all layers, ⌘/Ctrl-click any closed lock icon.

Deleting an existing layer

You can delete any existing drawing layer — even if it's chock-full of objects, including locked objects — by selecting the layer name in the Layers panel and choosing the Remove option from the pop-up menu. If the layer is indeed filled with objects, FreeHand displays an alert box and warns you that all objects on the layer will be deleted from your illustration. If the layer is absolutely empty, no alert box appears.

Before deleting a layer, hide all layers except the layer you want to delete and then choose View ➪ Fit All, or press ⌘/Ctrl-Option/Alt-0 (zero). From this vantage point, you can view all objects that you intend to delete, including those in the area outside the boundaries of the page.

If you delete a layer by mistake, choose the Undo Remove Layer command from the Edit menu (⌘/Ctrl-Z) to restore the layer and all its objects. Note that the Guides layer cannot be deleted.

Changing the stacking order within layers

You also can reorder objects on a single layer. Among the commands that FreeHand provides for this purpose are the common Bring To Front (⌘/Ctrl-F) and Send To Back (⌘/Ctrl-B) commands, which reside in the Modify ➪ Arrange submenu.

If you select an object and choose Bring To Front, FreeHand moves the object to the front of its layer and then treats the object exactly as if it were the most recently created path in the layer. Therefore, the object is the last in the layer to be described when you preview or print the drawing. If you choose Send To Back, FreeHand treats the selected object as if it were the first path in the layer, describing it first when you preview or print.

You can apply both commands to whole objects only. If a path is only partially selected when you choose either command, FreeHand moves the entire path to the front or back of its layer. If you select more than one object when choosing Bring To Front or Send To Back, the relative stacking order of each selected object is retained. For example, if you select two objects and choose Modify ➪ Arrange ➪ Bring To Front, the forward of the two objects becomes the frontmost object on its layer. The rearward of the two objects becomes the second-to-frontmost object.

Forward and backward

When you're creating complicated illustrations, it's not enough to be able to send objects to the absolute front or back of a layer. Even a simple illustration can contain over 100 objects. Changing the layering of a single object from, say, 14th-to-front to 46th-to-front would take days using Bring To Front and Send To Back.

Fortunately, FreeHand provides two commands that make relative layering manipulations possible: Move Forward (⌘- [on Macs and Crtl-Alt-Shift-F on PCs) and Move Backward (⌘-]on Macs and Ctrl-Alt-Shift-K on PCs), also under the Modify Í Arrange submenu. Each command scoots a selected object one step forward or one step backward within its layer.

Figure 6-21 demonstrates the Bring Forward command. The first example shows four layered shapes. If you select the black shape and choose Modify ➪ Arrange ➪ Move Forward, the selected path moves one step forward, as shown in the second example. The third example shows the results of choosing Move Forward a second time.

Figure 6-21: The effects of selecting the rearmost path (left) and choosing Bring Forward twice (center and right).

Paste in back or in front

FreeHand also enables you to send one object, call it A, directly in back of another, which — though I'd like to name it "Smelly Elephant" — I'll call B purely for the sake of consistency. To accomplish this, select object A, choose Edit ➪ Cut (⌘/Ctrl-X), select object B, and choose Edit ➪ Paste Behind. FreeHand places object A at the exact horizontal and vertical location from which it was cut, directly in back of object B.

If multiple objects are selected when you choose the Paste Behind command, FreeHand places the contents of the Clipboard in back of the rearmost selected object. If no object is selected, the Paste Behind command is dimmed.

For those of you who feel that the Paste Behind command is just not quite your style, you're in luck. FreeHand 8 now offers the vastly differently command, Paste In Front. It works exactly like the Paste Behind command, except that it pastes objects in front of the selected objects. So, to continue the above scenario, select object C, choose Edit ➪ Cut (⌘/Ctrl-X), again select object B, and finally, choose Edit ➪ Paste In Front. This time, FreeHand places C, again in its exact horizontal and vertical location, directly in front of B. I bet you didn't see that one coming.

The effect of grouping and joining on layering

Because they combine selected objects, the Group and Join commands also affect the layering of objects in an illustration. All elements in a group or joined path are fused into a single object. Therefore, they can't have any objects stacked between them. FreeHand handles this issue by automatically moving the elements you group to the front of a layer, as follows:

✦ If all selected paths are on the same layer, FreeHand sends them to the front of their layer when you choose Modify ➪ Group or Modify ➪ Join.

✦ If the selected paths are on different layers, FreeHand sends them to the front of the active layer, even if none of the paths were on that layer before you chose the command.

✦ Provided that the Remember Layer Info check box in the General panel of the Preferences dialog box is selected, choosing Modify ➪ Ungroup or Modify ➪ Split restores the original paths to their original layers.

Although you basically have to fork over control when using the Group and Join commands, you can adjust the relative layering of objects inside groups and composite paths. Press the Option/Alt key and click an object with the arrow tool. Then choose any of the four stacking order commands at the top of the Modify ➪ Arrange submenu.

✦   ✦   ✦

Adding Text

Entering and Editing Text

Text Is a Drawing's Best Friend

Some guy who was hoping to get his name in one of those books of pithy quotes once ventured that a picture is worth a thousand words. Judging by the relative earnings of artists and writers, I'd say that a picture is worth more like 2,500 words. Regardless of the current rate of exchange, a picture doesn't take the place of a thousand words. Otherwise, I wouldn't have to write these endless pages of text; I'd just show you a few choice pictures and call it a day.

Text explains pictures; pictures accompany text; and in the best of documents, pictures and text suggest complementary but unique information. That's why type and graphics are such bosom buddies in FreeHand. In fact, FreeHand has more than bolstered its text-handling capabilities; it's broken away from the pack. Nearly all of FreeHand's text functions rival their counterparts in dedicated text wranglers such as PageMaker and QuarkXPress.

Isn't this a job for PageMaker?

I've heard some users of earlier FreeHand versions make comments to the effect of, "What's with all the new text stuff? Isn't this supposed to be a drawing program? If I want to create a newsletter, I'll use a page-layout program."

Well, if that sums up your opinion, you and I have a bone to pick. Page-layout and drawing programs are twins separated at birth. Both rely on discrete objects to represent page elements. (Hint: Has anyone noticed that both QuarkXPress and FreeHand use a rectangular box-like container for text?)

Both hinge on the capabilities of the PostScript page-description language. And both enable you to combine text and graphic objects.

The differences between page-layout and drawing programs are entirely a matter of emphasis. Page-layout programs provide only the minimal drawing tools and include a large supply of functions for manipulating text and importing artwork. Drawing programs generally emphasize drawing functions and downplay text editing and importing. Yet both types of programs have equal controls for specifying spot and process colors.

FreeHand, meanwhile, has a proud history of blurring the lines between page layout and drawing. It has long provided top-notch importing capabilities and respectable text handling. Back in version 5, it merely went a step further by introducing spell checking, search-and-replace capabilities, general speedup, text styles, and a host of other features that may sound Greek to you now but will eventually be music to your ears.

Furthermore, FreeHand is alone in providing a sufficient number of capabilities to create professional-quality text and graphics within the same program. There's no need to switch out of the program to draw some complex graphic and then switch back to surround the graphic with text. You can see how the graphic looks on the page as you draw and edit it. FreeHand eliminates the guesswork and broadens your design options by supplying everything you need within easy reach. If you've ever heard yourself say, "Gee whiz, I'd like to add a special design element here, but it's too much effort," the new FreeHand is for you.

Come on, FreeHand can't do everything

You're right, FreeHand hasn't lifted *every* option from PageMaker and QuarkXPress. When creating a small document in FreeHand, you have to live without the following features:

✦ **Master pages:** That's right, you can't use master pages for positioning repeating elements such as page numbers and logos. But you can duplicate pages very easily by selecting Duplicate from the Options pop-up menu in the Document Inspector. (See, wasn't that easy?) For more information, read Chapter 17.

✦ **Automatic page numbering:** Okay, so you're not going to be able to format the *Encyclopedia Britannica* in FreeHand. But you can lay out an eight-page newsletter and number the pages manually. And in FreeHand, you can create a page that is double-width when you layout a photo-spread in the centerfold.

✦ **Automatic indexing and table of contents generation:** Get serious.

✦ **Kerning tables:** Yeah, yeah, this ultra high-end function and several others are missing from FreeHand. But it's taken PageMaker and QuarkXPress several years to hone these functions, so you can't expect FreeHand to master them overnight.

Introducing Text Objects

Rather than floating freely on your page, type in FreeHand is housed inside boundaries called *text objects*, which can be rectangles, ellipses, polygons, or free-form paths. These text objects define the shape formed by your type, as illustrated by the three examples in Figure 7-1. Many of FreeHand's general functions, including the transformation and duplication techniques described in Chapters 13 and 14, are as applicable to text objects as they are to graphic objects. For example, after creating a text object in the shape of a star, you can rotate it to any angle you please. However, FreeHand also offers a world of functions that apply exclusively to type, as explained throughout this chapter and the two that follow.

Creating a text block

The most common variety of text object is the rectangular *text block*, which you create with the text tool. Text blocks are the most formal as well as the most capable kinds of text objects. Most important, text blocks are equipped with special editing handles that other text objects lack. These handles allow you to experiment with formatting attributes, as explained in the "Manipulating text block handles" section later in this chapter.

After selecting the text tool in the upper right corner in the toolbox, you can use it to create a new text block in the following ways:

✦ Click anywhere on the page to indicate the placement of the upper left corner of the text block. Provided you have New Text Containers Auto-Expand enabled in the Text panel of your Preferences dialog box, your text block expands in width to include all of your text on one line. To force FreeHand to continue onto the next line, press Return/Enter. This feature is great for adding caption text to your artwork.

✦ If you do not have New Text Containers Auto-Expand enabled, FreeHand automatically sizes the text block to three inches wide and two inches tall, as is the case with the text block shown in the background of Figure 7-2.

✦ It could not be easier to specify custom text-box dimensions: Drag with the text tool, and release the mouse when you see the dimensions needed. The width of your drag defines the width of the text block; the length of the drag defines the height.

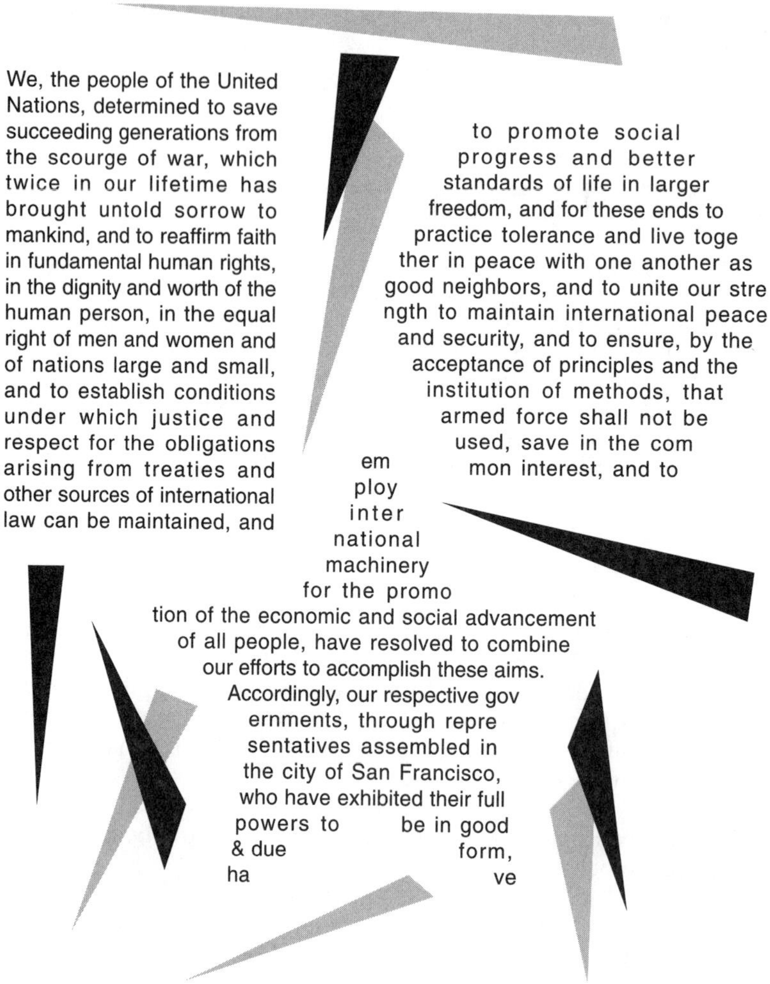

We, the people of the United
Nations, determined to save
succeeding generations from
the scourge of war, which
twice in our lifetime has
brought untold sorrow to
mankind, and to reaffirm faith
in fundamental human rights,
in the dignity and worth of the
human person, in the equal
right of men and women and
of nations large and small,
and to establish conditions
under which justice and
respect for the obligations
arising from treaties and
other sources of international
law can be maintained, and

to promote social
progress and better
standards of life in larger
freedom, and for these ends to
practice tolerance and live toge
ther in peace with one another as
good neighbors, and to unite our stre
ngth to maintain international peace
and security, and to ensure, by the
acceptance of principles and the
institution of methods, that
armed force shall not be
used, save in the com
mon interest, and to

em
ploy
inter
national
machinery
for the promo
tion of the economic and social advancement
of all people, have resolved to combine
our efforts to accomplish these aims.
Accordingly, our respective gov
ernments, through repre
sentatives assembled in
the city of San Francisco,
who have exhibited their full
powers to   be in good
& due   form,
ha   ve

Figure 7-1: Three differently shaped text objects, with a lot of wacky
triangles to keep them company.

✦ To create a text block that is a specific numerical size, move the ruler origin to
  the point at which you want to position the upper left corner of the text block.
  Then begin dragging with the text tool at the ruler origin and monitor the
  movement of your cursor using the horizontal and vertical rulers.

✦ Shift-drag with the text tool to draw a perfectly square text block. (But then
  you already knew this, from the chapter on the drawing tools — right?)

Text tool   Insertion marker

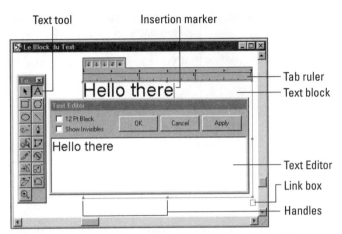

Tab ruler

Text block

Text Editor

Link box

Handles

Figure 7-2: Entering text using the Text Editor dialog box, with a default text block (in the background) created by clicking with the text tool.

✦ Option/Alt-drag to force the text block to 'grow' the box from the center outward.

Tip

Pressing the T or A key selects the text tool at any time *except* when a text block or option box is active.

The Text Editor dialog box

The Text Editor dialog box gives you the option to either enter and edit text directly on the page, just as in every other drawing program on earth, or use the Text Editor dialog box to enter your text. The Text Editor dialog box lets you enter and edit text at a legible size, even when working in the fit-in-window view size. When the text tool is selected you can choose Text ➪ Editor from the menu or press ⌘/Ctrl-Shift-E to display the Text Editor, superimposed in Figure 7-2.

This dialog box looks and operates in a pretty straightforward manner. It displays the text from the active text block with all of its current formatting intact. If you prefer to see text in its unadorned state, enable the 12 Pt Black check box in the top left corner of the dialog box. If you wish to view the invisible elements in you text (such as spaces, carriage returns, tabs, and line breaks), then click the Show Invisibles check box.

While in the Text Editor, you still have access to many of the commands in the Text menu. Easily change the text attributes by applying text styles from the Styles panel or by adding color to the text using the Color List or Color Mixer. You can even preview copy changes in your document while working in the Text Editor by clicking the Apply button.

If you prefer to always use the Text Editor when entering and editing text, enable the Always Use Text Editor option in the Text panel of the Preferences dialog box. I recommend against doing this, however. When you use the Text Editor, you have no access to the text ruler, which means that you cannot set tabs in your text. Considering that FreeHand provides a keyboard shortcut to invoke the Text Editor, I suggest that you take advantage of it.

The mysteries of the text block

If you're not using the Text Editor, after you draw a text block, FreeHand displays the various elements previously shown in Figure 7-2. Although I describe each element in more detail later in this chapter, here are a few brief introductions to get you started:

✦ **I-beam cursor:** Appearing any time the text tool is selected, or a text block is active, this cursor will create a new text block or highlight text inside an active text block for editing.

✦ **Insertion marker:** The blinking insertion marker indicates the location at which text you enter from the keyboard will appear inside the text block. Some folks call this the insertion point, but what with the word "points" meaning everything from dots in a path to ½-inch increments, I think it's high time we gave that word a break.

✦ **Tab ruler:** If you have View ⇨ Text Rulers enabled, a check mark appears in the menu to the left of this command, and a big, huge, clunky ruler adorns the top of every text block. Its sole purpose is to let you position tabs and indent text. Never mind that nine out of ten text blocks you create won't include tabs, and only a small percentage more will require indents — the tab ruler is standard equipment on every text block. The keyboard shortcut for toggling this command on and off is ⌘-/ on Macs and Ctrl-Alt-Shift-T on PCs. You care about the tab ruler when creating bullet lists, or setting up columns of information, like menus in a restaurant. Tabs with leaders help your eye follow the food across the column to the price. Double-click a tab and the convenient Edit-Tab window offers alignment control, precise position and a choice of leaders. FreeHand also lets you show or hide the text ruler.

✦ **Handles:** These guys let you stretch and squish text blocks and change some formatting attributes while you're at it.

✦ **Link box:** Click this box and learn about the origins of primitive man. No, wait, that's just a joke. You folks who believe in creationism, take a deep breath and count to ten before you try to get this book banned. The real purpose of the link box is to enable you to send excess text to another text object. You just drag from the link box to another text block, and zip! — the excess text flows into place. If you have no idea what I'm talking about, skip to the "Flowing text from one block to another" section later in this chapter.

Pressing keys to enter text

Enter text from the keyboard to fill the text block with letters. As you type, the insertion marker moves rightward. When a word threatens to extend beyond the right side of the text block, FreeHand wraps the word and insertion marker down to the next line.

When you're entering text, most keys fulfill the same purpose as they do in a typical word processor such as Microsoft Word. Each letter and number key inserts the character that appears on the key. The Caps Lock key, Shift key, and spacebar also work just like they do in a word processor. The following keys perform special functions:

✦ **Option (Macs only):** Accesses special characters when pressed with letter and number keys. You can press the Shift and Option keys together to access still more special characters. To view these special characters, choose the Apple menu ➪ Key Caps. Refer to your Apple documentation for instructions, if necessary.

✦ **Delete:** Removes the character to the left of the insertion marker.

✦ **Tab:** Inserts a tab character, which creates a user-definable space between two words.

✦ **Return/Enter:** Inserts a carriage return, which moves the insertion marker, along with any text to the right of the marker, to the next line of type. (Also separates type along the top of an ellipse from type along the bottom of an ellipse, as explained in Chapter 9.)

✦ **Arrow keys:** Arrow keys move the insertion marker inside the text block.

Special characters and keyboard options

Did I just hear you say, "Duh," like maybe this isn't the most amazing information you've ever learned? Well, then, here are a few keyboard options you might not know about:

✦ **Esc:** This key combination inserts a nonbreaking space that prevents two words from wrapping to separate lines. You can also get this character by pressing ⌘/Ctrl-Shift-H or choosing Text ➪ Special Characters ➪ Nonbreaking Space.

✦ **Forward Delete:** Labeled Del on a Macintosh extended keyboard, this key removes the character to the right of the insertion marker. (I bet you thought that the Forward Delete key only worked in a word processor.) PC users will be at home on this one, because this is how the Delete key works under Windows.

✦ **Shift-Return/Enter:** When you press the Return/Enter key by itself, you finish off one paragraph and begin a new one. But when you press Shift-Return/Enter (or choose Text ➪ Special Characters ➪ End of Line), you create a line break inside the paragraph. The text after the line break appears on the next line but remains part of the same paragraph as the line above it, which means that it isn't subject to new indents and paragraph spacing. Use a line return when you want to knock a word down to the next line without creating a new paragraph.

✦ **Shift-Enter (this shortcut works on Macs only):** Press the Shift-Enter — that's Enter from the keypad — key combination or choose Text ➪ Special Characters ➪ End of Column — the command appears on both Macs and Windows computers — to insert a column break. A column break moves all text to the right of the insertion marker to the top of the next column or to the next text block in a story. Like a carriage return, a column break results in a new paragraph.

✦ **⌘-hyphen (this shortcut works on Macs only):** This key combination creates a discretionary hyphen, which is a hyphen that only appears when FreeHand needs to break the word at the end of a line. When the hyphen is not required, FreeHand does not display it. For more information, read "Hyphenating words" in the next chapter.

✦ **Shift-Option-hyphen (this shortcut works on Macs only):** The em dash — like the dashes that surround this little remark you're reading now — is a standard part of the Macintosh character set. But for the sake of Windows users, FreeHand makes the character available from the Text ➪ Special Characters submenu. You can also create an en dash, usually used to represent minus signs, by pressing Option-hyphen.

✦ **⌘-arrow key (Macs only):** If you press ⌘ with the ← or → key, you move the insertion marker to the beginning of the previous word or the beginning of the next word, respectively.

✦ **Home:** Pressing the Home key moves the insertion marker to the beginning of the text block. If the block is part of a chain of linked text objects, Home moves the insertion marker back to the beginning of the very first block in the chain.

✦ **End:** Pressing End moves the insertion marker to the end of the text block. Note that Home and End are not exact opposites. In a chain, Home moves the insertion marker all the way to the beginning of the chain, but End moves it to the end of the active text block.

✦ **⌘/Ctrl-Tab(another of the Macs only shortcuts):** Pressing this key combination deactivates the text block. Memorize this keyboard equivalent and be prepared to use it often.

Fixed spaces

This information doesn't deserve its own section. But I couldn't figure out for the life of me where else to put it, so here it is. Both the spacebar (and Option-spacebar on Macs) create *variable-width* space characters, meaning that FreeHand can automatically vary their widths depending on word spacing and justification settings. To create a *fixed-width* space whose width is dependent solely on type size, choose one of the Space commands from the Text ➪ Special Character submenu. Or press one of the following key combinations:

✦ **⌘/Ctrl-Shift-M:** This key combo creates a fixed space the width of the letter M. Called an em space, it is as wide as the type size is tall. For example, a 12-point *em space* is 12 points wide.

✦ **⌘/Ctrl-Shift-N:** This combination creates an *en space*, which is half the width of the type size. In other words, a 12-point en space is 6 points wide or roughly as wide as a standard lowercase letter such as n.

✦ **⌘/Ctrl-Shift-T:** Use this key combination to create a *thin space*, which is $\frac{1}{10}$ of the width of the type size — even thinner than the letter *i*. We're talking super, ultra thin.

All these characters are breaking spaces, which means that FreeHand can break two words separated by one of these characters across two lines.

Creating a free-form text object

If a rectangular text block is too conventional for your purposes, FreeHand enables you to enter type inside any closed path, whether it was drawn with one of the geometric shape tools or with a free-form path tool. To do this, select the path and choose Flow Inside Path from the Text menu (⌘/Ctrl-Shift-U). FreeHand creates a blinking insertion marker inside the path and, provided View ➪ Text Rulers is active, even displays a tab ruler above the path. Enter text from the keyboard to fill the path with type, as shown in Figure 7-3. (I know, the cadence of the poem is way off, but it fits inside the star, which is more than I can say for most poems.)

Alternatively, you can create your text inside a standard text block before assigning it to a free-form text object. If your text will require a fair amount of editing, you may want to try out this technique, because FreeHand can redraw text inside a standard text block faster than it can flow the text inside the nooks and crannies of a complex object. When you finish editing, select both the text block and path and choose Text ➪ Flow Inside Path.

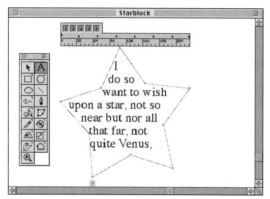

Figure 7-3: Choose Text ➪ Flow Inside Path to convert a path into a text object, complete with a tab ruler.

Hiding the path outline

If you fill and stroke your path before you choose Text ➪ Flow Inside Path, FreeHand retains the fill and stroke attributes when it converts the path to a text object. You can quickly remove them without changing any fill or stroke settings by deselecting a single option. With a text block selected, switch to the Object Inspector (⌘/Ctrl-I), and deselect the Display Border check box. The fill and stroke disappear, as shown in Figure 7-4. You can also remove both fill and stroke using the options in the Fill and Stroke Inspectors, as described in Chapters 11 and 12.

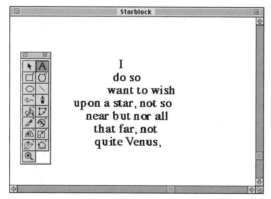

Figure 7-4: Use the Display Border check box to show and hide the outlines around text objects, whether you're working with rectangular or free-form objects.

Tip

To display the rectangular border around a standard text block, first select the Display Border check box. Then assign the desired stroke attributes using the options in the Stroke Inspector (⌘/Ctrl-Option/Alt-L). If either the Display Border check box is turned off or the pop-up menu in the Stroke Inspector is set to None, the border will be invisible (except in the Keyline mode).

Separating text and path

To separate text from a path, select the free-form text object and choose the Remove Transforms command from the Text menu. FreeHand creates a new text block for the type and converts the text object back to a geometric shape or free-form path, as illustrated in Figure 7-5.

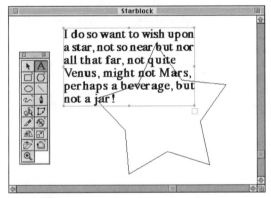

Figure 7-5: Choose Text ⇨ Remove Transforms to convert text and path into separate objects.

The rectangular text block is the lowest form of container available to type in FreeHand. Therefore, you cannot apply the Remove Transforms command to a lowly text block.

Importing Stories

Much — if not most — of the text you'll use in FreeHand will be entered directly in FreeHand. But there may be times when you want to create complete pages or mix graphics with large amounts of text, particularly because the program accommodates multipage layouts. When long documents (called *stories*) are required, FreeHand enables you to import text documents created in a word processor. After all, word processors are faster for text entry and allow luxuries such as thesauruses and glossaries.

Preparing text

When importing text, FreeHand reads the file from disk and copies it to the foreground illustration. FreeHand 8 can import text stored in two formats:

✦ **Plain text:** If you save a word processing document in the plain text or ASCII (pronounced *ask-ee*) format, no formatting is retained. Font, type size, style, and all other attributes are thrown by the wayside during the saving process. All you get are the actual characters of text.

✦ **RTF (*Rich Text Format*):** If you want to retain formatting, save your document in the RTF format. Designed by Microsoft, RTF is basically plain text with a bunch of formatting codes thrown in. It's not the most efficient or reliable format in the world, but it is common and it works with FreeHand.

If your word processor does not support RTF, you may be able to convert the file using a file-conversion utility such as Apple File Exchange or MacLink from DataViz. On the Windows side, there's Conversions Plus, also from DataViz. Short of that, save the file as a plain text file, which sacrifices all formatting. You can then reformat the text in FreeHand, as described in Chapter 8.

Some formatting attributes may get confused in the process of exporting the file to the RTF format and importing the file into FreeHand. The following list describes how FreeHand handles the most common formatting attributes. Formatting options not included in this list are most likely not supported by FreeHand and are therefore ignored.

✦ **Typefaces:** All text retains the font specified in the word processor. If one or more fonts are not available to the system software, FreeHand displays a list of the missing fonts in a dialog box. FreeHand suggests changing all fonts to your machine's default font. To specify your own replacements, click the Replace button. Select a substitute font from the pop-up menu and click the Change button to replace the font. Click the Don't Change button to skip a single missing font and let FreeHand change it to the default font. Click the Cancel button to change all remaining missing fonts to the default font.

✦ **Type size and leading:** FreeHand retains the type size and *leading* (line spacing) specified in the word processor. The only exception is so-called *automatic leading*, which converts to some fixed value that may not match the leading of the original document.

✦ **Type styles:** FreeHand converts bold and italic type to their equivalent stylized screen fonts. If no stylized screen font is available for a particular style, FreeHand substitutes the plain style. Styles that are ignored include underline, strikethrough, small caps, and hidden. Outline text is assigned a hairline stroke and a transparent fill. Shadow is converted to the FreeHand shadow effect. Superscript and subscript styles remain intact.

✦ **Colors:** In my tests, FreeHand usually handled colors accurately. Sometimes, in imported text, when the first line of type was assigned a different color from the rest of the text, FreeHand enthusiastically applied the first-line color throughout the rest of the imported story.

✦ **Line and column breaks:** Although FreeHand correctly recognizes carriage returns and line breaks, it misinterprets column and page breaks as carriage returns.

✦ **Alignment:** FreeHand recognizes paragraph alignment on imported text that is aligned left, center, and right, as well as justified.

✦ **Paragraph spacing:** FreeHand can handle paragraph spacing accurately, whether you assign spacing before or after a paragraph, or both.

✦ **Indents:** FreeHand correctly transfers all indents, including first-line indents, left indents, right indents, and hanging indents. Margin settings that you establish in a Page Setup dialog box don't transfer. Your indents, therefore, are relative to the margins you set in FreeHand.

✦ **Tabs and tab leaders:** Tabs characters convert correctly; FreeHand even retains the locations of tab stops. However, tab leaders such as dots or dashes do not transfer successfully.

✦ **Special characters:** Word processors provide access to special characters not included in the standard Apple-defined or Windows-defined character set. These include em spaces, nonbreaking hyphens, automatic page numbers, and so on. Of these, only discretionary hyphens and nonbreaking spaces transfer successfully.

✦ **Headers, footers, and footnotes:** FreeHand ignores these types of weird extraneous items in imported text.

Using the Import command with text

To import a story, choose File ➪ Import or press ⌘/Ctrl-R. FreeHand displays the Import Document dialog box, which works just like the Open Document dialog box. Locate the file you want to import and press the Return /Enter key. After waiting a few moments for FreeHand to load the file into memory — or, if it's a long story, after waiting several minutes — you will be rewarded with a place cursor. Click with the cursor to import the text into a text block that is as wide as the original word-processing document. Drag with the cursor to define the width and height of the new text block.

If the story is too long to fit inside the text block, FreeHand puts a black circle inside the link box off the lower right corner of the block. To display the rest of the story, you can enlarge the path or pour the story into additional paths as described in the upcoming section, "Flowing text from one block to another."

Tip   To cancel a place operation before clicking or dragging with the place cursor, select any tool from the toolbox or press its function key equivalent. For example, you could select the arrow tool or simply press the 0 (zero) or the V key.

Adjusting Text Objects

Text objects are very much like paths, in that you can reshape them to make them fit your needs. You can drag a text block handle, adjust the points in a free-form text object, and flow excess text from one text object into another. The following sections describe all these techniques.

Manipulating text block handles

Unlike other kinds of text objects, text blocks drawn with the text tool are bordered by eight handles, one at each corner and one centered along each side. By dragging these handles, you can change the dimensions of a text block to permit more or fewer words per line, change the amount of vertical space between lines of text, and change the horizontal space between letters and words.

Enlarging or reducing a text block

When creating a text block, you don't have to accept the default dimensions provided by FreeHand or even the dimensions you specified by dragging with the type tool. At any time, you can change the size of an existing text block by selecting the block and dragging one of its four corner handles with the arrow tool. Notice the friendly overflow symbol at the lower right corner? When it is just an empty square, all the text you have typed is visible, and it is not necessary to enlarge the text box.

Suppose that a text block is too narrow to hold one of your words on a single line. Even though the word is not hyphenated, FreeHand is forced to break it onto two lines, as it did with the word *determined* in Figure 7-6. This problem generally occurs only if the path is very narrow or the type is very big. To remedy the problem, you can do the following:

✦ Reduce the size of the type (as described in the "Changing the type size" section of Chapter 8).

✦ Hyphenate the word by inserting a discretionary hyphen (Text ⇨ Special Characters ⇨ Discretionary Hyphen), as in *deter-mined*.

✦ Increase the width of the text block as demonstrated in Figure 7-7.

Figure 7-6: If a single word is too long to fit on a single line, FreeHand arbitrarily breaks it onto two lines.

By changing the size of a text block, you can fit long words on a single line, include more or less text on each line, or display more or fewer lines of text inside the text block. To make the transition from Figure 7-6 to Figure 7-7, I just selected the arrow tool and dragged one of the corner handles in the text block. When you change a text block size, a rectangle representing the size of the altered text block tracks the movements of your cursor. When you release the mouse button, FreeHand rewraps the text to fit the new dimensions.

Caution

If you're familiar with other drawing or desktop publishing applications, you may be tempted to adjust the size of the text block by dragging the top or bottom handle or one of the side handles. Avoid this urge, no matter how strong it may be. In FreeHand, dragging one of these handles changes both the size of the block and the formatting of the text inside. Only drag *corner* handles to adjust the dimensions of the text block and rewrap text.

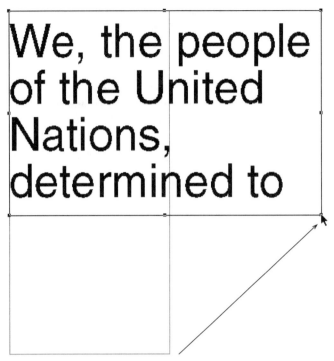

Figure 7-7: After I dragged the lower right corner handle of the text block, FreeHand rewrapped the text to fit inside the new text block dimensions.

Automatically expanding text blocks

When a text block is selected, additional methods for changing the size of a text block are available from the Object Inspector (⌘/Ctrl-I). These methods enable you to automatically expand text blocks horizontally or vertically to accommodate all of the text within the block. Figure 7-8 shows the two icons that give you these capabilities.

Choosing the icon that expands the *width* of a text block forces all of the text in a selected text block onto a single line, expanding the text block horizontally. This feature is useful for creating caption text. Double-clicking the center handle on the right side of the text block also automatically expands a text block.

Figure 7-8: When a text block is selected, the Object Inspector lets you automatically expand a text block.

Choosing the icon that expands the *height* of the text block increases a selected text block's height to accommodate any text that does not fit within the current confines of the text object, or decreases the height of the text block if it's too large for the text it contains. If you recall, when all text does not fit within a text block's borders, a black circle appears inside the link box off the lower right corner of the text block. Use this option to automatically increase a text block's height to a size that displays all of its text.

Deactivating a text block

There's something interesting going on here that you may have missed. While you're entering or editing text inside any text object, the blinking insertion marker is your visual cue that the text block is active. When you select the arrow tool, the insertion marker remains visible, meaning that the text block is still active. You can continue entering text just as before. However, if you click or drag with the arrow tool, you deactivate the text block. As long as you click or drag on the text block, the corner handles remain available, but the insertion marker immediately goes into hiding.

This information is especially good to know when you want to delete a text block. When a text block is active, pressing the Delete key removes one or more characters of type. But if you press and hold the ⌘/Ctrl key (to access the arrow tool), click on the text block to deactivate it, and then press Delete, you delete the entire text block.

This may seem like a strange little trick, but believe me, you'll end up creating a lot of text blocks you don't need when working in FreeHand. Temporarily switching to the Keyline mode is a good way to spot these extra text blocks — they appear as empty rectangles. A single click of the text tool can result in a new text block, and unlike most programs, FreeHand doesn't automatically delete empty text blocks. So remember, if you accidentally click with the text tool, ⌘/Ctrl-click on the offending text block and press Delete to eliminate it.

FreeHand has an easy method for deleting all empty text blocks at once. Simply choose Xtras ⇨ Delete ⇨ Empty Text Blocks, and you remove all empty text blocks from your document in one fell swoop.

Another way to delete an empty text block is to double-click on the link box with the arrow tool (or ⌘/Ctrl-double click with some other tool). I prefer to ⌘/Ctrl-click and press Delete because the link box is a smaller target than the entire text block. Furthermore, the link box may be offscreen or otherwise difficult to access.

Note

Keep in mind that *deactivating* a text block is different from *deselecting* it. When a text block is deactivated, you can still see its handles. When the text block is deselected, the handles and the insertion marker disappear. (You can deselect a text block by clicking outside the block with the arrow or some other tool.)

Now, no doubt, somebody out there is wondering how to reactivate an inactive text block. Easy. Just click inside the text block with the text tool or double-click on the text block with the arrow tool. You can then enter or edit text. For more information on this topic, skip ahead to the "Selecting and Editing Text" section near the end of this chapter.

Spacing out your text

Earlier I warned you against dragging the top, bottom, and side handles of a text block. In FreeHand, dragging these noncorner handles doesn't change the size of the text block so that more or less text will fit inside the block. Instead, your drag changes the space between the lines, letters, and words that are already visible. FreeHand also adjusts the size of the text block to accommodate the new spacing. The top, bottom, and side handles work as follows:

✦ **Drag the top or bottom handle:** Drag either the top or bottom handle to change the amount of vertical space — called *leading* — between lines of type. If you drag down on the top handle or up on the bottom handle, you reduce the leading. If you drag up on the top handle or down on the bottom handle, you increase the leading, as shown in Figure 7-9.

✦ **Drag a side handle:** Drag the handle on the left or right side of a text block to change the amount of space between characters of text, called *letterspacing*. Drag the left handle farther to the left or the right handle to the right to increase the letterspacing (see Figure 7-10); drag the left handle to the right or the right handle leftward to decrease letterspacing.

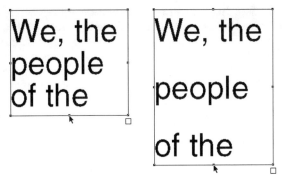

Figure 7-9: Drag the bottom handle of a text block (left) to change the amount of vertical space between lines (right).

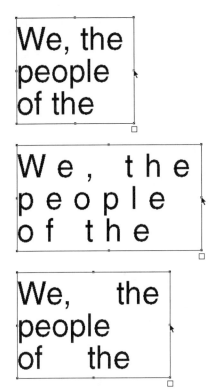

Figure 7-10: Drag the side handle of a text block (top) to change the amount of horizontal space between letters (middle). Option/Alt-drag the handle to change the width of space characters between words.

✦ **Option/Alt-drag a side handle:** If you press the Option/Alt key while dragging a side handle, you change the amount of space between words, which is called — you guessed it — *word spacing*. The space between characters within each word remains unchanged. In FreeHand, the space between two words depends on the width of the space character between them. When you Option/Alt-drag a side handle, only variable-width space characters are affected. FreeHand doesn't change the size of any fixed-width em spaces, en spaces, or thin spaces. If your text includes a lot of fixed-width spaces mixed in with variable-width spaces, Option/Alt-dragging can result in awkwardly spaced text.

Scaling text on the fly

You can also change the size of characters in a text block by pressing modifier keys while dragging a corner handle. If you Option/Alt-drag a corner handle, FreeHand scales the characters inside the text block relative to the block itself. You can make characters short and fat, as in the bottom right example in Figure 7-11, or tall and thin, as in the bottom left example. If you want to scale the text proportionally — so that horizontal and vertical proportions are affected uniformly — Shift-Option/Alt-drag a corner handle.

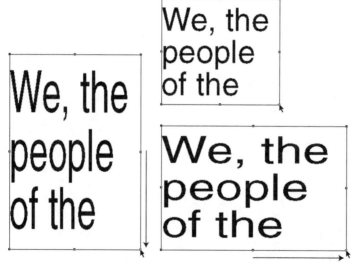

Figure 7-11: Option/Alt-drag the corner handle of a text block (top) to scale the characters inside the text block (bottom two examples).

Reshaping geometric and free-form text objects

If you created a text block by choosing Text ⇨ Flow Inside Path instead of dragging with the text tool, you can reshape the path just as if it were a standard graphic object. For example, if you created the path with the rectangle or oval tool, drag one of its corner handles to enlarge or reduce the path. FreeHand rewraps the text inside the path, just as it does when you drag the corner handle of a standard text block.

Tip

If you have created a geometric text object from a rectangle or oval and want to be able to drag the points in independently of one another, you must first ungroup the path. Using the arrow tool, Option/Alt-click on the outline of the path. Then choose Modify ⇨ Ungroup (⌘/Ctrl-H) and drag the points. The following steps explain the process in more detail.

1. Draw a text block with the text tool and enter some completely random text.

2. Draw an ellipse with the oval tool.

3. Shift-click on the text block with the arrow tool to select both the ellipse and text block. Then press ⌘/Ctrl-Shift-U or choose Text ⇨ Flow Inside Path. The first example in Figure 7-12 shows one possible result.

Figure 7-12: After combining a text block and ellipse into a single text object (top), I Option/Alt-click on the ellipse to select the shape and deselect the text (bottom).

4. Option/Alt-click the ellipse to select the shape independently of the text. As you can see in the second example in Figure 7-12, the baselines — those horizontal lines below the characters — disappear, showing that the text is no longer selected.

5. Press ⌘/Ctrl-U or choose Modify ➪ Ungroup. The individual points in the free-form path are now visible.

6. Click on a point to select it and display its Bézier control handles, as shown in the first example in Figure 7-13.

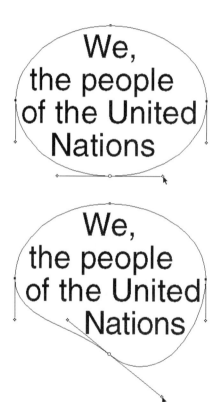

Figure 7-13: Ungroup the path to display its points (top) and drag a Bézier control handle to reshape the path (bottom).

7. Drag one of the control handles associated with the point to reshape the path. You can also drag the point itself. The text moves with the new curvature of the path, as illustrated in the second example in Figure 7-13.

If you construct a text object using a free-form path drawn with the polygon, freehand, trace, bézigon, or pen tools, you can reshape the path by dragging points and Bézier control handles without first ungrouping the path. In fact, you don't even have to Option/Alt-click on the path to select it independently of its text. Just start right in — with a few exceptions, you can use any of the techniques discussed in Chapter 5 that are applicable to closed paths. The only reshaping commands that you can't apply to a text object are those under the Modify ➪ Alter Path submenu.

Otherwise, you can do as you please. Move points, drag Bézier control handles, Option/Alt-drag segments to bend them, add points and control handles, delete points and retract control handles, and convert points from curve to corner, corner to connector, and so on. You can even open a text object or use the knife tool to split it into two separate paths. Doing so, however, permanently removes all text from inside the object (unless you choose Edit ➪ Undo, that is).

Changing the dimensions of a free-form text object

The problem with free-form text objects is that when you scale them, you scale the text inside them as well. You can't scale the whole object and force the text to rewrap inside the new boundaries. For example, try this: Select a free-form text object and group it by pressing ⌘/Ctrl-G. Then drag the corner handle. Whether or not the Transform as Unit check box in the Object Inspector is selected, FreeHand scales text and object together.

There is a solution, but it's a bit circuitous. You have to join the text object to another closed path to create a composite path. The following steps explain how this technique works.

1. If you already created a free-form text object, split it apart by selecting the object and choosing Text ➪ Remove Transforms. If you haven't created a free-form text object yet, draw a free-form path and then create a separate text block.

2. Draw a very slim rectangle — skinnier than a single character of text — with the rectangle tool. (It's not absolutely essential that you draw a rectangle, but a rectangle is about the easiest shape to draw. And why work any harder than you have to?) The rectangle should be in close proximity to the free-form path, but it should not overlap the path.

3. Select the arrow tool and Shift-click on the free-form path to select it and the already-selected rectangle. Then press ⌘/Ctrl-J or choose Modify ➪ Join to combine the two paths into a composite path, complete with four corner handles.

4. Now Shift-click on the text block to add it to the selection and press ⌘/Ctrl-Shift-U (Text ➪ Flow Inside Path). FreeHand fuses the text block and composite path into a single free-form text object, as illustrated in the first example in Figure 7-14.

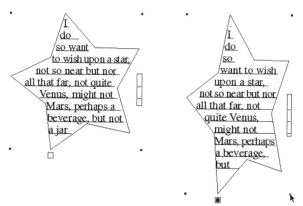

Figure 7-14: After combining a text block and composite path (left), you can drag the corner handle of the text object to scale the text object independently of the characters inside it (right).

5. Now drag one of the corner handles of the text object. The text object grows or shrinks according to your drag. But this time, rather than scaling the characters inside the path, FreeHand leaves the size of the letters unchanged and rewraps the words onto new lines, as illustrated in the second example in Figure 7-14.

See how the baselines of the text object in Figure 7-14 extend from the star into the rectangle? This is because FreeHand thinks of the star and rectangle as isolated portions of the same path. When I widen the rectangle by Option/Alt-clicking it with the arrow tool, selecting the two points on the right side of the path, and dragging outward, words appear inside the path, as shown in Figure 7-15. Notice that these aren't words from the end of my marvelous little poem, but rather from the middle. The words actually extend from the star out into the rectangle. This is why I instructed you to draw a slim rectangle in step 2 — to prevent the rectangle from filling with type.

Of course, there's one problem with the technique that I described in these five steps: You're left with this extra rectangular path. If you want to display the border around the free-form text object, the border around the rectangle is also visible. Ah, but I have a solution in the form of Top Secret step 6!

6. Press the Option/Alt key and marquee around the rectangle, *without enclosing any other paths*, including the free-form text object. If it's impossible to avoid other paths, Option/Alt-click on the rectangle, click on one of its points, and Shift-click each of the three remaining points. Either way, you will have selected all points in the rectangle. Then press the Delete key. This deletes the rectangle and leaves the free-form text object as a composite path that you can enlarge or reduce independently of the type inside.

Figure 7-15: Because the star and rectangle are combined into a composite path, FreeHand flows the text horizontally from one shape to the other.

I know it sounds weird, but it works every time. And believe it or not, there's presently no better solution. If you try to delete the rectangle without first selecting its points, you delete the text object as well. You can't make a single object into a composite path, so you have to join the text object and rectangle and then turn around and delete the rectangle.

Cross-Reference

For complete information on composite paths, read Chapter 15, "Blends, Masks, and Composite Paths."

Using Inset values

One of the major difficulties in filling complex objects with type is getting the characters to accurately fill the little nooks and crannies. Multisyllabic phrases like *nationwide gubernatorial bipartisanship* always seem to coincide with the tiniest corners in your objects.

Rather than wasting huge amounts of time reshaping your path so that the text fits, experiment with the Inset values inside the Object Inspector (⌘/Ctrl-I) when the text block that's in need of adjusting is selected. The Inset option boxes are labeled L, T, R, and B, for left, top, right, and bottom. Positive values create margins between the free-form path and the text, which is generally only useful if you plan on displaying the path outline and want the margins for aesthetic purposes.

If you want to squish more text into the path, negative values are the ticket. Negative values allow the text to extend beyond the boundaries of the free-form path. For example, if you can't seem to get a string of text to fit on a line—even though it looks like there's tons of room to spare—enter a negative value into the R option box. FreeHand then lets the text extend beyond the right edge of the text object.

Flowing text from one block to another

If a story contains more than a couple of paragraphs, you'll probably want to do more than simply reshape the text object to make the entire story visible in the illustration window. You can *flow* long stories across text objects to create multiple columns or even multiple pages of text. Figure 7-16 shows a story flowed into three paths. A story like this is called a *chain* because each text block in the story is *linked* to another.

We, the people of the United Nations, determined to save succeeding generations from the scourge of war, which twice in our lifetime has brought untold sorrow to mankind, and to reaffirm faith in fundamental human rights, in the dignity and worth of the human person, in the equal right of men and women and of nations large and small, and to establish conditions under which justice and respect for the obligations arising from treaties and other sources of international law can be

maintained, and to promote social progress and better standards of life in larger freedom, and for these ends to practice tolerance and live together in peace with one another as good neighbors, and to unite our strength to maintain international peace and security, and to ensure, by the acceptance of principles and the institution of methods, that armed force shall not be used, save in the common interest, and to employ international machinery for the promotion of the

economic and social advancement of all people, have resolved to combine our efforts to accomplish these aims.

Accordingly, our respective governments, through representative assembled in the city of San Francisco, who have exhibited their full powers to be in good and due form, have agreed to the present Charter of the United Nations and do hereby establish an international organization to be known as the United Nations.

Figure 7-16: A single story flowed between three text blocks.

If you enter or import too much text to fit inside a single text object, the link box just outside the lower right corner of a text block contains a black circle. You can display the excess text — also called *overflow* text — in the following two ways:

✦ If the text appears inside a standard text block, drag a corner handle to enlarge the block. If you're working with a free-form text object, reshape the object as described earlier in this chapter.

✦ Send the overflow text to another text object by creating a link.

To use the second method, you must first create a new container for the overflow text. Click or drag with the text tool to create a new text block or use the drawing tools to create a new closed path. Then drag from the link box that contains the black circle into your new text object, as shown in Figure 7-17. The next time you select the original text block, you'll see that the link box symbol has changed from a black circle to a double-headed arrow (as in the second example in the figure), showing that a link has been established.

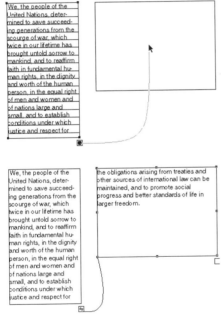

Figure 7-17: Drag from a link box into a new text block (top) to link the two blocks and flow text between them (bottom).

Tip

When linking text blocks, you'll generally want to work in the Keyline mode. This way, you'll be sure to see the outlines of the text blocks. In the Preview mode, any deselected text blocks that are not stroked—which is the default setting—are invisible.

You can even flow type into a text object that already contains type. As shown in Figure 7-18, FreeHand simply shoves the existing type in the receiving text object forward to make room for the type being flowed from the other text object. Flowed type and existing type are fused into a single story.

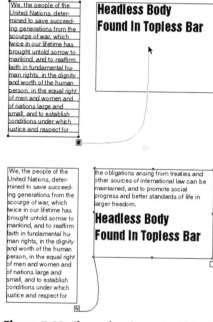

Figure 7-18: If you drag into a text block that already contains type (top), FreeHand flows the incoming type into the beginning of the text block and pushes the existing type to the end (bottom).

Cross-Reference

To create evenly sized, evenly spaced columns of type, you may want to establish a series of guidelines, as described in the "Creating guidelines" section of Chapter 6. You can also use the Align panel to even up the tops or bottoms of the text objects and distribute them evenly by selecting the Distribute Widths option from the

Horizontal pop-up menu. See the "Alignment and Distribution" section of Chapter 6 for more information.

Reflowing a story

Chains of text objects in FreeHand are as flexible as they are in QuarkXPress (meaning that they're a heck of a lot better than they are in PageMaker). To change the order in which text flows from one object to another, you simply redrag from a link box that contains a double-arrow symbol.

For example, Figure 7-19 shows a chain comprising three text blocks. I numbered the blocks to show the order in which the text flows. If I drag from the link box associated with the first text block and release the mouse button inside the third text block, as illustrated in the figure, FreeHand reflows the text as shown in Figure 7-20. What was once the second text block has now been removed from the chain.

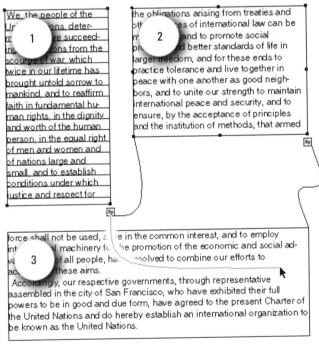

Figure 7-19: By dragging from the link box for text block #1 into text block #3 . . .

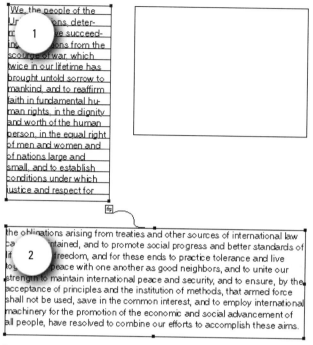

Figure 7-20: . . . I instruct FreeHand to reflow the text and bypass the block in the upper right corner.

Other ways to reflow text inside a chain include:

✦ Select a text block in the chain and delete it or cut it to the Clipboard. Removing a text block leaves the text itself intact. The text reflows around the missing text block. For example, if you deleted the second block from Figure 7-19, the text would automatically flow between the first and third blocks, as shown in Figure 7-20.

✦ If you reduce the size of a text block by dragging its corner handle, text flows out of that block and into the next block in the chain.

✦ If you enlarge a text block — again by dragging a corner handle — text flows into that block and out of the next block in the chain. This may have the effect of sucking up the entire contents of the last text object in a chain. However, FreeHand doesn't delete the text object or remove it from the chain. If you want to delete the last text object, you have to do the job manually (by clicking the object with the arrow tool and pressing the Delete key).

Separating a text block from a story

Separating a text block and the type inside it from the rest of a chain is a cumbersome operation in FreeHand, on par with extracting Estonia, Latvia, Lithuania, and Belarus from the Russian Federation. You can't simply cut the text block and paste it, as in QuarkXPress or Illustrator. If you try, FreeHand simply removes and pastes the block without affecting any of the type inside it (as I explained a brief moment ago). So what's the solution? Read the following steps to find out.

1. Select the text object that you want to separate. We'll call this object *Azerbaijan.*

2. Copy it to the Clipboard by pressing ⌘/Ctrl-C.

3. Select the text tool and double-click the very first word inside Azerbaijan. We'll call this word *Baku.* (Actually, I'm getting a little carried away here. You can call the word *Tbilisi* if you want to, even if it is in Georgia.)

4. Press Shift-End to select all remaining words in the text object — words like *Sungait* and *Gyandzha.*

5. Press the Delete key to get rid of the selected text. Unless it's the last text object in the chain, Azerbaijan fills with all new words. (Don't worry, Azerbaijan's on the Clipboard, so *Baku, Sungait,* and all the rest of them are safe and sound. Isn't geography fun?)

6. Click on an empty portion of your document to deselect the text block. Then press V to select the arrow tool.

7. Select Azerbaijan and press Delete. The text object disappears and the words flow back into the original positions.

8. Select one of the other text blocks in the chain — Kazakhstan, Tajikistan, Uzbekistan, or one of them other Stans — and then choose Edit ➪ Paste Behind. FreeHand pastes Azerbaijan back into its original location. Finally, Azerbaijan is free of the chain!

9. Shout "Hooray" and start a war with one of your neighbors. Armenia looks vulnerable.

Breaking the link between text blocks

To unlink text objects in a chain, drag from a link box into an empty portion of the illustration window. FreeHand empties the type out of all the later text blocks in the chain, but those text blocks remain linked to each other. For example, if I dragged from the link box associated with the first text block back in Figure 7-19, I would destroy the link between blocks #1 and #2. Meanwhile, blocks #2 and #3 — now empty — would remain linked. If I then dragged from block #1's link box into block #2, I would reestablish the entire chain and fill blocks #2 and #3 with text.

Selecting and Editing Text

I mentioned this earlier, but just to recap, you can activate an existing text object by double-clicking it with the arrow tool. FreeHand automatically selects the text tool and displays an insertion marker inside the text object and a tab ruler over it. After the text object is active, you can replace characters inside the object by selecting them and entering new characters from the keyboard.

You can use the text tool to select the contents of any text object as follows:

✦ **Drag over the characters that you want to select:** Drag to the left or to the right to select characters on the same line of type; drag upward or downward to select characters on multiple lines; and drag across columns in a chain to select large portions of a story. The selected text becomes highlighted.

✦ **Double-click a word to select the word and the space after it:** Hold down the mouse button on the second click and drag to select several words at a time.

✦ **Triple-click within a paragraph to select the paragraph:** Hold down the mouse button on the third click and drag to select additional paragraphs.

✦ **Click at one end and Shift-click at the other:** Click to set the insertion marker at the beginning of the text you want to select. Then Shift-click at the end of the desired selection. All text between the two clicks becomes highlighted.

✦ **Press ⌘/Ctrl-A to select everything:** Choose Select All from the Edit menu (⌘/Ctrl-A) to select all text throughout the entire story, including any text objects linked to the active block.

You can also select text using the arrow keys. Click to set the insertion marker at one end of the text you want to select and extend the selection using the keyboard equivalents listed in Table 7-1.

Table 7-1
Extending a Selection with the Arrow Keys

To Extend the Selection	Press These Keys
One character to the left	Shift-←
One character to the right	Shift-→
One word to the left	⌘ -Shift-← (Macs only)
One word to the right	⌘ -Shift-→ (Macs only)
One line up	Shift-↑

To Extend the Selection	Press These Keys
One line down	Shift-↑
To beginning of text block	Shift-Home
To end of text block	Shift-End

In addition to replacing highlighted text, you can:

✦ Apply formatting attributes to it, as discussed in the following chapter.

✦ Delete the text by pressing the Delete key.

✦ Send a copy of the text to the Clipboard by choosing Edit ➪ Copy or pressing ⌘/Ctrl-C.

✦ Remove the text and send it to the Clipboard by choosing Edit ➪ Cut (⌘/Ctrl-X).

✦ Replace the selected text with text that you copied earlier by choosing Edit ➪ Paste (⌘/Ctrl-V).

Pasted text always retains its original character formatting, although it assumes the paragraph-level formatting of the paragraph into which it is pasted. You can even copy text from a different application and paste it into FreeHand, or vice versa.

Spell Checking Text

If you're familiar with any other application's spell-checking functions, you can probably figure out how to use FreeHand's in no time flat. In addition to checking for misspelled words, FreeHand can also alert you when it finds duplicate words or capitalization errors. To check for these as well, make sure that you enable Find Duplicate Words and Find Capitalization Errors in the Spelling panel of the Preferences dialog box.

FreeHand's spell-checking capabilities inhabit the Spelling (Check) panel. Open this panel by choosing Text ➪ Spelling or by pressing ⌘-Shift-G on Macs and Ctrl-Alt-S on PCs. But, before I launch into the intricacies of the Spelling (Check) panel, let's discuss the Show Selection check box that appears in the bottom right corner of this panel. When you consider that this is a preference setting, it seems odd that it appears in the Spelling (Check) panel and not in the Spelling panel of the Preferences dialog box. It works a bit oddly, as well. Enabling it scrolls your document to the misspelled word. However, FreeHand doesn't take the Spelling (Check) panel into account. I found that too often, the Spelling (Check) panel obscured my view of the misspelled word. Later, under "Proceeding with a spell check," I explain that FreeHand displays the text surrounding the misspelled word in the Spelling (Check) panel. I find this display to be sufficient, and I recommend leaving Show Selection disabled.

Selecting the text to check

The Spelling (Check) panel can check as little or as much text as you wish. Clicking the Start button causes FreeHand to begin spell checking. Exactly what FreeHand spell checks when you choose Start depends on your current text selection.

✦ To spell check your entire document, have no text selection.

✦ To spell check either a single word or a portion of a text block, highlight the text you want to check.

✦ To spell check one or more text blocks, select the block or blocks with the arrow cursor.

✦ To spell check only an active text block, place the insertion marker in it.

When your selection includes a text block that is linked to other text blocks, FreeHand also spell checks all text blocks linked to the selected one, including text that has not yet been flowed.

Proceeding with a spell check

After you select the text to be checked, choose Text ➪ Spelling (⌘/Ctrl-Option/Alt-S) and click Start to begin the spell check. When FreeHand encounters a possible error, it displays the suspect text at the bottom right corner of the Spelling (Check) panel. As Figure 7-21 shows, this display includes the type of error, the error itself, and the text that surrounds the error in the document. The most likely correction appears in the word-entry field and other possible corrections appear in the suggestions list. Clicking an item in the suggestions list places it in the word-entry field.

FreeHand needs a response from you concerning the first error it flags. At this point you have several options:

✦ **Ignore:** While a spell check is in progress, the Start button changes to its alter ego, the Ignore button. When you click the Ignore button, FreeHand skips the currently flagged word. Subsequent occurrences of the work also are flagged when you click Ignore.

Word-entry field   Suggestions list

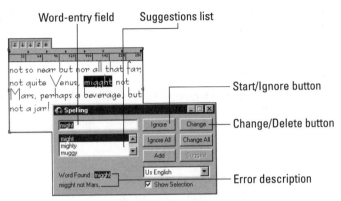

Start/Ignore button

Change/Delete button

Error description

Figure 7-21: The Spelling (Check) panel in action.

✦ **Ignore All:** Ignores the currently flagged word as well as all subsequent occurrences of it that FreeHand encounters during the current spell-checking session.

✦ **Change:** Replaces the flagged word in your document with the text in the word-entry field.

✦ **Change All:** Replaces all occurrences of the flagged word in your document with the text in the word-entry field.

✦ **Add:** Adds the flagged word to the current user dictionary. The capitalization that FreeHand uses when entering the word depends on your setting for Add Words to Dictionary in the Spelling panel of your Preferences dialog box. When adding words, include the appropriate hyphenation to the word in the word-entry field. This ensures that FreeHand properly hyphenates the word when hyphenation is necessary.

Note

You can add words to the dictionary that are not in your document. To do so, just type the word into the word-entry field and choose Add.

✦ **Delete:** The alter ego of Change. When FreeHand finds duplicate occurrences of a word, the Change button becomes the Delete button. Clicking Delete removes the extra occurrence of the word from your document.

Note

You also have one other option. You can manually type a correction into the word-entry field and then click the Change button.

After you respond, FreeHand moves on to the next error it encounters, and the fun continues. When FreeHand reaches the end of the selection, a big, chipper alert appears informing you of the fact. At this point, if you intend to do a great deal of text work, you may want to collapse the panel and pull it off to the side. In this case, it's nice to enable the Remember Location of Zipped Panels option on the Panels panel of the Preferences dialog box.

Requesting suggestions

The Spelling (Check) panel also lets you check the spelling of words that aren't in your document. If you type a word into the word-entry field and click on Suggest, FreeHand lists possible correct spellings in the suggestions list.

Finding and Changing Text

FreeHand's find-and-change text capabilities are easy to use and understand. If you have used a find-and-change text feature in other applications, FreeHand's will seem familiar. If you aren't familiar with find and change, here's a brief scenario of what a lifesaver they can be.

Consider the following situation. You have just completed a handout for a meeting that will take place in half an hour, and all you have left to do is print it. The handout tells all about John Doe, who will be speaking at the meeting. Suddenly you find out that the speaker's name is Jane Doe, not John Doe (gasp!). The Text Find feature lets you change all occurrences of John Doe to Jane Doe with the click of one button.

FreeHand's find-and-change capabilities can be found in the Find Text panel, pictured in Figure 7-22. You open to this panel by choosing Edit ➪ Find & Replace ➪ Text or by pressing ⌘/Ctrl-Shift-F.

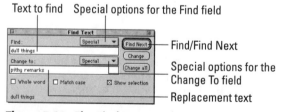

Figure 7-22: The Find Text panel.

Another similarity between this feature and the Spelling (Check) is the Show Selection check box in the bottom right corner of the panel. Enabling it scrolls your document to the found word. It also has the same flaw as its counterpart in the Spelling (Check) panel. It does not take floating panels into account, so in too many instances, the Find Text panel obscures the found word. Later in this section, under

"Proceeding with a find-and-change operation," I explain that FreeHand displays the text surrounding the found word in the Find Text panel. Therefore, I recommend leaving Show Selection disabled.

Selecting text to search

Your first step in finding and changing text is to indicate the text you want to search. As with spell checking, no selection causes FreeHand to search your entire document. If you prefer to limit your selection, highlight or select the text that you want to search. When your selection includes a linked text block, FreeHand searches through all of the text linked to the selected text block.

Setting your search criteria

After you select the text to be searched, you need to indicate the text you want to find by choosing Edit ➪ Find & Replace ➪ Text. You do so by typing the text into the Find field. You can enter up to 255 characters. However, you can't paste into this field. Go figure.

Next, you need to enter the replacement text in the Change To field. To simply delete the Find text, leave the Change To field blank. As with the Find field, you can enter up to 255 characters in the Change To field.

You can also enter special characters into both the Find and Change To fields. For detailed instructions, see "Finding and changing to Special options" later in this section.

You still have two more choices that further define your search criteria:

✦ **Whole Word:** When this option is enabled, FreeHand only finds instances where the entire word matches the Find entry, as opposed to finding a portion of a word. For example, if the text in the Find field is *man* and Whole Word is enabled, FreeHand will not find the word *mansion*. If Whole Word is not enabled, FreeHand will find the word *mansion*.

✦ **Match Case:** When enabled, FreeHand finds only instances where a word in the document matches the Find text both in spelling and in capitalization. For example, if the text in the Find field is *FreeHand* and Match Case is enabled, FreeHand will not find the words *freehand* or *Freehand*. If Match Case is not enabled, FreeHand will find *FreeHand*, *freehand*, and *Freehand*.

Proceeding with a find-and-change operation

Now that you've selected the text to search and set your search criteria, you're ready to begin your quest. Click Find, and FreeHand locates the first occurrence of the Find text. In the bottom of this panel, FreeHand displays the Find text and the text surrounding it. At this point you need to respond by selecting one of the following options.

✦ **Find/Find Next:** Leaves the currently found text intact and finds its next occurrence.

✦ **Change:** Changes the currently found text and finds its next occurrence.

✦ **Change All:** Changes all occurrences of the found text.

After you respond, FreeHand continues to search for other occurrences of the Find text, and you keep responding. When FreeHand reaches the end of the selection, you're greeted by an alert that informs you of the fact.

Finding and changing to Special options

Probably the coolest thing about the Find Text panel is the ability to enter special characters into the Find and Change To fields. This can be a godsend when importing text from other applications or platforms. When importing text, special characters, such as tabs, can be misinterpreted due to differences in the character maps used by different platforms. Being able to replace them all with one click can save you from the very tedious task of searching for each occurrence and manually correcting it.

The Find Text panel contains two almost-identical pop-up lists of Special options, one corresponding to the Find text and the other to the Change To text. Simply choose the Special option you want from the appropriate list. FreeHand then enters an identifying character into the corresponding field.

If you were observant, you noticed that in the last paragraph I said "almost identical." This is because three options appear in the Special pop-up menu for the Find text that do not appear in the pop-up menu for the Change To text. These three are *wild card* options. A wild card option gets its name from its similarity with a wild card in poker — it can be anything. There are three types of wild card options. They are listed below with examples of when to use each.

✦ **Any Single Character:** Use this to find both text and numbers; an alphanumeric search. For example, say you have to remove all references to General 800 company — which is also referred to by its code, GEN800 — from your document. To quickly find both types of references to this company, enter "gen" in the Find option box and choose "Any Single Character" from the

Special Find field and then disable Whole Word and Match Case. Keep clicking Find/Find Next to find all references to the company.

✦ **Any Single Letter:** If you only want to find text, you'll want to do an alpha search. For example, say your document contains only numbers. You know in advance that some of these numbers will change, but you want to enter them anyway as placeholders to get the document's layout correct. In this case, you could add a letter to each of the placeholder numbers. That way, when you do get the correct data, you can quickly find the ones to update by choosing the Any Single Letter option from the Special Find pop-up menu. Keep clicking Find/Find Next to find all the bogus data.

✦ **Any Single Number:** If you have a hankering to find a number, you'll love this option. For example, say you just received an update for a sales figure that you mentioned in your document. To quickly find the reference to this sales figure, select the Any Single Number option from the Special Find field. Keep clicking Find/Find Next to browse through all of the numbers in your document until you find the old sales figure.

Changing Case

The final bit of text-smithing that FreeHand 8 offers is the new case-changing ability. The Text ➪ Convert Case submenu offers five commands that will change the uppercase or lowercase status of every letter in your selected text according to a few simply rules. This is great when you have, say, accidentally entered an entire block of text with the Caps Lock key depressed. In previous versions of FreeHand, the only option you would have would be to re-enter all the text correctly. Now, you can select all the faulty text, and correct it via the commands in the Convert Case submenu.

Settings

Before we look at the individual Convert Case commands, let's look at the Convert Case Settings command. Choose Text ➪ Convert Case ➪ Settings to display the Settings dialog box pictured in Figure 7-23. The first option, Small Caps: ___% of Point Size, allows you to decide just how tall you wish your small caps to be. *Small caps* are simply capital letters that are smaller than usual. They look just like capital letters except that they're diminutive in stature. Kind of like how amebas look just like we humans except that they are shorter and really don't have our good fashion sense. Also in the Settings dialog box you can specify which words are immune to the five Convert Case commands. To include a word in your Exceptions list, click the Add button and type away. Click the Add button for each new word. If you ever change your mind about one of the words in the list, all you do is click the word and then click the Delete button. You will also need to decide for which cases you wish your exceptions to be honored.

Figure 7-23: In the Settings dialog box you set the size for small caps and compose a list of words that are exempt to the Convert Case commands.

Convert Case commands

The Convert Case commands are relatively straight forward. To use these commands you need to use the text tool to select the text you wish to change. You can select anywhere from one letter to an entire story. The five commands work as follows:

✦ **Upper:** Choose the Upper command to change all selected text to uppercase (capital) letters.

✦ **Lower:** This command changes all selected text to lowercase letters.

✦ **Small Caps:** When you choose Small Caps, all the lowercase letters (and only the lowercase letters) in the selected text are converted to small caps. These are smaller versions of normal uppercase letters that have been reduced to the percentage specified in the Small Caps:___% of Point Size option box in the Settings dialog box.

✦ **Title:** If you wish to capitalize the first letter of every word, then choose the Title command.

✦ **Sentence:** The Sentence command will capitalize the first letter of every sentence and change every other letter to its lowercase version.

✦   ✦   ✦

Formatting and Copyfitting

My Newest Office Caper

You wouldn't believe what just happened. Just this minute. You know those little Cappio thingies? They're little bottles of iced cappuccino that are marketed to beatnik wannabes (like me). I love them and heartily recommend them; they're great for caffeine addicts trying to wean themselves off of Mountain Dew.

Well, anyway, you have to shake them. To mix the contents, I mean. It says so right on the label: "Shake well." So there I was, engaging in some vigorous agitation — *shicka shaka* (a couple of sound effects for you) — when I noticed this stuff squirting all over my desk.

Okay, so the lid was off. But can you believe these labels? If they mean "Shake well before removing lid," why don't they say so? This is a clear case of planned obsolescence. They want you to throw your cappuccino all over the room so that you have to buy more. I think I'll sue. I'm a member of the Don't Take Responsibility for Your Actions generation. I'll sue Maxwell House until its lawyers weep openly. Desk damage and related trauma, $6 million.

Meanwhile, I have quite the mess on my desk. Luckily, I didn't get the stuff on either of my computers. Talk about your minor miracles. There's always the chance I'll be canonized for it. Check out Saint Deke, he squirts liquid out of open bottles without hitting his computers. But I really soaked everything in between. Half of my library is sitting here in puddles of sugary, coffee-y, milky goop, the perfect recipe to stick, stain, and stink. Really, I couldn't be happier.

This Will Help Me Use FreeHand, Won't It?

There we go. All cleaned up. So, without further ado, back to FreeHand. Text in FreeHand, in fact. For you folks who like to learn without a bunch of true life-stories nonsense, skip to here. I should have told you earlier, but now you know.

The thing is, the importance of text can't be understated. You have to make your message clear — "Shake well before removing lid, you taffy-brained ferret" — and you have to format it so that the taffy-brained ferrets of the world (I must count myself among them) read your words. I can't help you with the making-your-message-clear part, but I can explain all the options that FreeHand gives you for sizing, spacing, and styling the words that you use.

As far as pure formatting power is concerned, you've hit the jackpot. FreeHand offers a number of formatting options. FreeHand is the only program that lets you modify the distance between the first line of type and the top of a text block, the distance between the last word in a line and the right edge of a text block, the order in which text flows inside rows and columns, and a bunch of other stuff that probably won't make a whole lot of sense to you this early in the game.

What is formatting?

First, what is *formatting* and what is that other thing that I alluded to in the title of the chapter but haven't bothered to so much as mention yet, *copyfitting*? Well, formatting options determine how individual characters look, how big they are, how far apart they are, the distance between lines of type — in short, formatting defines the appearance of text. FreeHand breaks formatting attributes into three categories: those that affect individual characters, those that affect entire paragraphs, and those that affect entire text blocks. Here's how they work:

✦ Character-level formatting attributes include font, type size, style, leading, horizontal scale, kerning, baseline shift, and a few special effects. To change the formatting of one or more characters, you first select the characters in the text object and then apply the desired options. FreeHand modifies the selected characters only.

✦ Paragraph-level formatting attributes include tabs and indents, letterspacing and word spacing, hyphenation settings, and alignment options. To change the formatting of an entire paragraph, you need only position the insertion marker inside that paragraph and then apply the desired paragraph-level formatting options. To change the formatting of several consecutive paragraphs, select at least one character from each of the paragraphs you want to modify.

✦ Block-level formatting includes a few options that I discussed in the previous chapter, such as the physical dimensions of the text object and the Inset values, as well as the number of rows and columns in a text object. To change the formatting of an entire text object, select the object with the arrow tool or click inside it with the text tool. Then apply the desired block-level formatting options.

Figure 8-1 shows the panels that contain all the formatting attributes offered by FreeHand. Except for the handful of options in the Text toolbar and tab ruler, all of FreeHand's formatting options are found in one of the panels of FreeHand's formatting Inspectors.

Character-level attributes

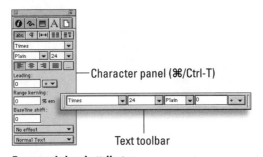

Paragraph-level attributes

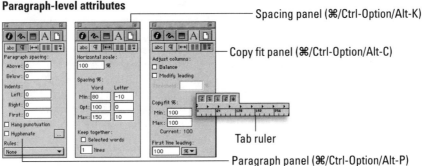

Block-level attributes

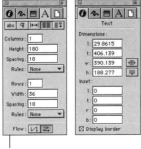

Columns and Rows panel (⌘/Ctrl-Option/Alt-R)

Figure 8-1: FreeHand's formatting options at a glance.

None of FreeHand's formatting panels include Apply buttons (but they all should). In order to apply changes that you enter into option boxes, you have to press the Return or Enter key. If you want to cancel an option, simply click in the illustration window with the arrow tool.

You can also specify the formatting attributes for a new text block before typing it. After clicking or dragging with the text tool, specify the formatting options you want and then begin typing.

What is copyfitting?

Copyfitting refers to FreeHand's ability to change formatting attributes automatically so that a story exactly fits into an allotted space. You can balance the amount of text inside two columns, increase the leading in a column to fill the vertical space, and expand or reduce the type size and leading to fill several text objects in a chain. These options enable you to give FreeHand some of the formatting responsibility instead of micromanaging the document all by yourself.

Character-Level Formatting

Some folks hate desktop-publishing and design programs because they provide complete nincompoops with the power to create ugly type. I studied fine art in college, and I learned a variety of techniques while serving a brief stint as an assistant art director for a local newspaper. But I've never taken a single design course in my life. For what it's worth, I learned my own personal brand of design on the job largely by trial and error. As a result, some of my early work met with disapproval. "Ugly, ugly, ugly," was one reviewer's reaction. Unfortunately, I can't say that the commentary was completely without merit. My first designs looked as if I was afraid that if I didn't use every typeface and shred of clip art at my disposal, I might hurt their feelings.

But so what? My early encounters with desktop publishing were a transitional learning phase just like any other. The fact that I was able to successfully print my documents didn't make my experimentation any less odious than if I had created them using conventional tools. The same goes for you. You may be an expert designer or an absolute novice. But either way, I encourage you to experiment with FreeHand's formatting capabilities as much as possible. Only through experimentation can you grow as a designer. And FreeHand is about the most forgiving environment I can think of for developing a mastery of your craft.

All about fonts

In computer typography, the term *font* is frequently used as a synonym for *typeface*. But back in the days of hot metal type, a clear distinction existed. Because characters had to be printed from physical hunks of lead, you needed an entirely separate font of characters to express a change in typeface, style, or size.

Things have changed quite a bit since then. In FreeHand (or any other Mac or Windows program), you can access scaleable fonts, which are mathematical definitions of character outlines. In its most fundamental form, each character is expressed as one or more paths, just like the ones you draw in FreeHand. You can scale these paths to any size, independent of the resolution of your screen or printer.

Type styles and families

Although a single font can satisfy any number of size requirements, it can convey only a single *type style*. The plain and bold styles of a typeface, in other words, are supplied as two separate fonts. So, in computer typesetting, every font carries with it both unique typeface and type style information.

Helvetica and Times, for example, can each be displayed in four type styles, as shown in Figure 8-2. Each type style is a separate font. Together, each set of four type styles makes up a *type family*.

Helvetica
Helvetica Bold
Helvetica Oblique
Helvetica Bold Oblique

Times Roman
Times Bold
Times Italic
Times Bold Italic

Figure 8-2: Members of the Helvetica and Times type families.

Different type styles emphasize text in different ways. Plain text — sometimes called Roman, meaning upright with serifs — is by far the most common variety. It is used to display body copy, the large blocks or columns of text that represent the heart and soul of information contained on a page. The italic (cursive) or oblique (slanted) style may be used within body copy to highlight a foreign or unfamiliar phrase or simply to stress a word. The bold style is relegated to special text such as captions and headlines. You can even italicize bold text to create a ***bold italic*** style.

Applying typeface and type style

To assign a typeface to all selected characters use the Text toolbar. Then select an option from the font pop-up menu, labeled in Figure 8-3. To access the pop-up menu, be sure to click and hold on the down-pointing arrowhead rather than on the font name itself.

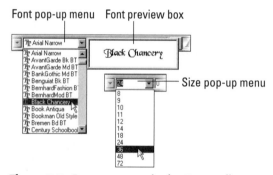

Figure 8-3: Pop-up menus in the Text toolbar.

As you scroll through your fonts in the Fonts pop-up menu, you notice a font preview box appears to the side of the pop-up menu. I can't tell you how much I love this feature. I don't know about you, but I've got a bunch of fonts that I'm not sure how they found their way into my fonts folder and have even less of a clue of what they look like. Now I can quickly tell what a particular font looks like without having to first use it in a drawing.

To change the type style, you have one of two options. First, if you have more than one font in a font family, you can choose to use one of the stylized members of a particular font family. For example, if you have all four styles of the Times family loaded on your machine — Plain, Bold, Italic, and BoldItalic — then all four fonts are available in the fonts pop-up menu. Second, you can have FreeHand apply styles — Bold or Italic — to a font. Simply select the text you wish to affect and click on either the bold or italic button in the Text toolbar..

Note

Typeface and style options are also available under the Text menu in the Font submenus. But as long as the Text toolbar is available, there's no use in bothering with these menus. Anyway, the Text ➪ Font submenu isn't equipped with the font preview feature.

Using the Text toolbar option boxes

An even better way to apply typefaces and styles is to enter text into the respective Text toolbar option boxes. You don't have to enter the full name of a typeface or style, just the first few letters. For example, if you place the insertion marker at the beginning of the leftmost option box in the toolbar and enter an A, FreeHand automatically selects Avant Garde, because Avant Garde is the only typeface in the pop-up menu that begins with an A (refer to Figure 8-3). If more than one typeface begins with the same letter, as in the case of Chicago, Cooper Black, and Courier, pressing C selects the first typeface in alphabetical order.

Tip

But what happens when the first several characters in the names of two or more fonts are the same? That's where the ↑ and ↓ keys come in. Press ↓ again to select the next font in the list. The ↑ selects the previous one. This technique also works in the Size pop-up menu.

After you change the values in the font and/or style option boxes, press the Return or Enter key to apply them to the selected text. If you want to cancel your selection, just click in the illustration window.

Enlarging and reducing type

After choosing a font to govern the fundamental appearance of your text, you can further enhance and distinguish individual characters and words by changing their size. But to enlarge or reduce type, you first need to understand how it's measured. To begin with, there are four basic kinds of characters. The horizontal guidelines that serve as boundaries for these characters are labeled in Figure 8-4.

Figure 8-4: Type is measured using a series of horizontal guidelines.

Here's a quick rundown of the naming conventions for the different types of characters:

✦ *Capital letters* extend from the *baseline* upward to the *cap height* line. Examples include *A*, *B*, and *C*. Numerals (*0123456789*) also qualify as capitals because they typically stay within the same boundaries as caps.

✦ *Medials* fit entirely within the space between the *baseline* and the *x-height* line. Examples include *a*, *c*, and *e*.

✦ *Ascenders* are lowercase characters that extend above the cap height line. Examples include *b*, *d*, and *k*.

✦ *Descenders* are lowercase characters that extend below the baseline. Examples include *g*, *j*, and *p*.

Not every character fits snugly into one of these categories. For example, the lowercase characters *i* and *t* violate the x-height line but are nonetheless considered medials. This is because the dot of the *i* is not viewed as an integral part of the character, and the *t* does not usually extend to the cap height line. Other times, a letter qualifies as both an ascender and a descender, as is the case for the italic *f* in a serif font. Nonletters — such as %, #, and & — are generally considered capitals. But there are several exceptions, such as $, §, and many forms of punctuation, including parentheses.

Changing the type size

Hot stuff, huh? Well, for those of you who are worried that we're delving too deeply into the territory of typo-dweebology, let me get straight to the point, which is this: The type size of a character is measured from the topmost point of the tallest ascender to the very lowest point of the deepest descender. Type size is always measured in points, regardless of the current unit of measure, which is why you frequently see type size called *point size*.

You can change the type size by selecting an option from the size pop-up menu in the Text toolbar (refer back to Figure 8-3) or by entering a value into the size option box. FreeHand accepts any value between 1 and 5,000 points (over 6 feet!) in 0.001-point increments. If you enter a value in the option box, make sure to press the Return or Enter key to implement it.

Tip

If you're not sure what type size to use, you can enlarge and reduce selected characters incrementally from the keyboard. Press ⌘-Option-Shift-< on Macs and Ctrl-Alt-1 on PCs or ⌘/Ctrl-Option/Alt-Shift-↓ to reduce the type size by 1 point. Press ⌘-Option-Shift-> on Macs and Ctrl-Shift-2 on PCs or ⌘/Ctrl-Option/Alt-Shift-↑ to make the selected type 1 point larger.

Horizontal scale

When you change the type size, you scale the width and height of each character by equal amounts. But you can also scale the width of a character independently of its height. Just enter a value into the Horizontal Scale option box in the Spacing panel of the Text Inspector (⌘/Ctrl-Option/Alt-K). As illustrated in Figure 8-5, any value below 100 percent puts the characters on a weight-loss program; any value over 100 percent fattens them up. Fashion models probably like compressed type, but sumo wrestlers prefer expanded type.

48-point Helvetica compressed to 60%

The same font & size expanded to 140%

Figure 8-5: The same type size compressed (top) and expanded (bottom) by changing the Horizontal Scale value.

If you're familiar with the range of commercial fonts available on the market, you probably know that you can purchase typefaces that are already compressed or expanded. And you may wonder why you would want to do that, if you can simply compress or expand the font in FreeHand. The truth is that using the Horizontal Scale option can make your text look pretty weird.

Figure 8-6 shows two characters that are identical in height and width. The left character was set in Helvetica and compressed in FreeHand. The right character was set in Helvetica Condensed, a specially designed font. Notice that the vertical stems in the left character are much skinnier than the arches that join the stems, which is exactly the opposite of the way it's supposed to be. By compressing the letter, I reduced the width of the stems without changing the thickness of the arches one iota. In the condensed character on the right, the designers of the font resolved this problem. They also squared off the arches slightly to make the font more legible.

Figure 8-6: Two characters, one compressed inside FreeHand (left) and the other set in a condensed typeface (right).

The moral is, don't squish your characters too much. As a general rule of thumb, stick to Horizontal Scale values between 80 and 125 percent. Anything beyond this range really upsets the design of the characters.

Tip

Expanding the width of characters also expands the spaces between characters — so much so that the text can have as many gaps as David Letterman's dental work. To offset this effect, you can reduce the spacing by entering a negative Range Kerning value in the Character panel. As a general rule of thumb, enter one negative percentage point of Kerning/Range Kerning for every 10 percent added to the Horizontal Scale value. For example, to create the 140 percent expansion shown in Figure 8-5, I entered a Range Kerning value of -14 percent. If only braces worked this quickly.

Vertical and horizontal spacing

The remainder of the character-level formatting options are located in the Character panel of the Text Inspector, which appears back in Figure 8-1.

Three character-level formatting attributes control the amount of space between selected characters:

✦ *Leading* is the amount of vertical space between one line of text and the next (as illustrated back in Figure 8-4).

✦ *Kerning* (or range kerning, depending on how many characters you've selected) controls the amount of horizontal space between neighboring characters of text.

✦ *Baseline shift* raises or lowers selected characters with respect to the baseline, bringing them closer to neighboring lines of type. The primary purpose for this option is to create superscript and subscript type.

Increasing and decreasing leading

Back in the old days, printers actually shoved little pieces of lead between lines of type to increase the vertical spacing. Then they presumably licked their fingers and went crazy from lead poisoning, which is how they came up with the term *leading* (pronounced ledd-ing, not lee-ding), a word no sane person would invent. A few recent typographers have tried to rename it line spacing, but leading has managed to stick it out as the preferred term of the trade.

FreeHand gives you a choice of three ways to measure leading, each of which is represented by an option in the pop-up menu to the right of the Leading option box in the Character panel of the Text Inspector (displayed in Figure 8-1). Two of the options, Extra represented by the plus sign and Percentage represented by the percentage symbol, measure leading relative to the type size of the selected characters. These options are most useful when the type size varies from one line to the next, and you want to make sure that FreeHand compensates for this fact. Fixed leading, which is represented by an equal sign, remains unchanged when you enlarge or reduce the type size, whereas the other two options let the leading grow and shrink with type size adjustments. The options work as follows:

✦ **Extra (+):** By default, the leading value is identical to the type size. To insert a few additional points of leading, select the Extra option.

✦ **Fixed (=):** To measure leading as the distance from the baseline of one line of type to the baseline of the next, use this option.

✦ **Percentage (%):** To measure leading as a percentage of the type size, select this option. This option improves on the old "automatic" leading setting, which was always 120 percent.

Regardless of which pop-up menu option you select, you change the leading by entering a value into the option box and pressing the Return or Enter key. Like type size, leading is always measured in points, regardless of the current unit of measure.

Generally, you should select entire lines of type when changing the leading. If a single line contains characters with two different leading specifications, the larger leading value prevails. When making a large initial capital letter, for example, you might have a 24-point character on the same line as several 12-point characters. If the leading for all characters is set to 120 percent, the entire line is set at 29-point leading, which is 120 percent of the 24-point type size. You can access the leading pop-up menu and option box in the Text toolbar as well.

Tip

Remember, you can adjust the leading of a text block by dragging on the top-center or bottom-center handle of that text block, as described in the "Spacing out your text" section of Chapter 7.

Pair and range kerning

The title of the second option box in the Character panel of the Text Inspector is either *Kerning* or *Range Kerning*. The former title appears when the insertion marker is positioned between two characters of type; the latter appears when one or more characters are selected. Both Kerning and Range Kerning control the amount of space between each pair of selected characters.

Normally, FreeHand accepts the dimensions of each character stored in the font definition and places the character flush against its neighbors. The font defines the width of the character as well as the amount of space that is placed before the character and after it. This "flank space" is called side bearing, as illustrated in the first example in Figure 8-7. FreeHand arrives at its normal letterspacing by adding the right side bearing of the first character to the left side bearing of the second.

However, font designers can specify that certain pairs of letters, called *kerning pairs*, should be positioned more closely together than the standard letter normally allows. Whenever the two characters of a kerning pair appear next to each other, as in the case of the *W* and *A* shown in the second example in Figure 8-7, they are spaced according to special kerning information contained in the font.

If you don't like the default amount of kerning between two characters of type, you can adjust the space. Position the insertion marker between the characters and enter a new value into the Kerning option box in the Character panel of the Text Inspector. If you want to change the kerning between multiple characters, select those characters and enter a value into the Range Kerning option box. Then press the Return or Enter key.

Both the Kerning and Range Kerning values are measured in $\frac{1}{100}$ths of an em space (an em space, introduced in Chapter 7, is a character that's as wide as the type size is tall). A value of 25 is roughly equivalent to a standard space character. Enter any number between -200 and 1000, in 0.01 increments. A negative value squeezes letters together; a positive value spreads them apart.

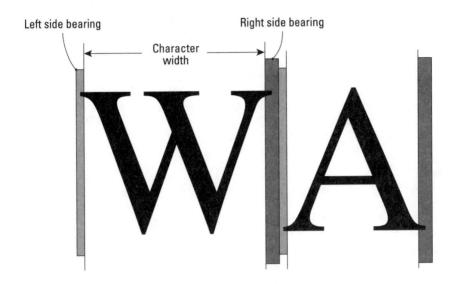

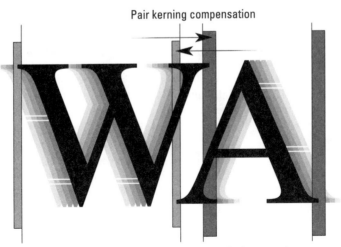

Figure 8-7: A kerning pair is a set of two letters that looks better when spaced close to each other than when set shoulder to shoulder as prescribed by the default side bearings.

Tip

If you don't know what kerning value to use, you can adjust the kerning from the keyboard. Press ⌘/Ctrl-Option/Alt-← to squeeze letters together by ⅟₁₀₀ (1 percent) em space; press ⌘/Ctrl-Option/Alt- → to spread them apart by the same increment. To adjust letters by ⅟₁₀ (10 percent) em space, press ⌘/Ctrl-Option/Alt-Shift-← or ⌘/Ctrl-Option/Alt-Shift- →. The Kerning value in the Character panel of the Text Inspector tracks your changes.

When kerning small type, you may not be able to see any difference as you add or delete space, because the display is not accurate enough. If that happens, use the zoom tool to magnify the drawing area while kerning or tracking characters from the keyboard. (If you're using PostScript fonts, you must have ATM installed to see any difference when you zoom.)

Baseline shift

The value in the Baseline Shift option box determines the distance between the selected type and its baseline. You can use this option to create superscripts and subscripts or to adjust the vertical alignment of text on a path (as discussed in the following chapter). Enter any value between negative and positive 1,000 points (nearly 14 inches) or the equivalent in another unit of measurement. Unlike type size and leading, the Baseline Shift value is measured in the unit specified in the Status toolbar. A positive value shifts the text upward; a negative value shifts it downward. Press Return or Enter to apply the value to the selected text.

One of the most popular uses for the Baseline Shift option is to create fractions. You don't have to put up with pseudo-fractions like 1/2, where the numerator and denominator sit clumsily on either side of a slash, almost as though the slash was accidentally placed between them. In FreeHand, you can create real fractions — the kind that would make your old math teacher proud. The following steps explain how:

1. Enter the fraction from the keyboard. Windows people will have to use the standard slash (/). Unfortunately, this isn't the best character for the job, but if you're using Windows, this is your only choice. If you're on a Mac, you do have a better option — use the special fraction symbol, accessed by pressing Shift-Option-1.

2. Select the numerator. Change the size value in the Text toolbar to half its current size. If the type size is 12 points, for example, make it 6.

3. Enter a Baseline Shift value equal to about one-third the original type size. In the 12-point example, the Baseline Shift value would be 4.

4. Select the denominator and match its type size to that of the numerator, but do not change the Baseline Shift.

That's all there is to it. Amazingly easy, huh? The result will be a fraction like the ones shown in Figure 8-8. This fraction was originally set in 120-point type. I changed the numerator (35) to 60-point type and shifted it 40 points upward. I changed the denominator (38) to 60-point type as well but did not shift it.

Figure 8-8: A fraction created by varying the type size of all numbers and the baseline shift of the numerator. The fraction on the left uses the special Macintosh fraction symbol (Option-Shift-1) while the one on the right gets the most out of the standard slash.

Tip

You can adjust the baseline shift from the keyboard in 1-point increments. Press ⌘/Ctrl-Option/Alt-↑ to raise the selected text; press ⌘/Ctrl-Option/Alt-↓ to lower it.

Stylistic effects

FreeHand provides several predefined special effects for text. To apply an effect to a few selected words, select an option from the Effect pop-up menu at the bottom of the Character panel of the Text Inspector.

In all likelihood, the current option shown in the pop-up menu is No Effect. You can customize six of the effects by choosing Edit from the pop-up menu.

Tip

For best results, apply these effects only to very large text — say, 48-point text or larger. You must select the Display Text Effects check box in the Redraw panel of the Preferences dialog box to view the effects in the Preview mode — although not in the Fast Preview mode. Needless to say, the effects don't display correctly in the Keyline mode.

You can apply only one Effect option to a character at a time. However, you can combine stylized effects with type styles. For example, the bold type style and the inline effect can coexist quite happily.

And now, without further ado, the following sections explain FreeHand's stylistic effects.

Cross-Reference

With just a smidgen of ado, I'd like to mention that you can also create stylistic effects by selecting characters with the text tool and specifying attributes from the Fill and Stroke Inspectors. For more information, read the first few pages of Chapters 11 and 12.

The highlight effect

Selecting the Highlight Effect option positions a rectangular highlight behind selected text. By default, the highlight is a solid pale gray rectangle, centered behind the text block, with its width equal to the point size of the selected text. If you assumed that you can change these settings, you're right. Choosing Edit from the effects pop-up menu in the Character panel of the Text Inspector or choosing Text ➪ Effect ➪ Highlight reveals the Highlight Effect dialog box pictured in Figure 8-9.

Figure 8-9: The Highlight Effect dialog box at its default setting for 36-point text.

All units in the Highlight Effect dialog box are measured in points, regardless of your current document units setting. The settings offered here work as follows:

✦ **Position:** The center of the highlight. FreeHand defines the text block's baseline as the zero position. Negative values move the highlight down; positive values move it up.

✦ **Dash:** The stroke of the highlight. FreeHand treats the highlight as a line. Therefore, a thick, dashed highlight appears as vertical stripes.

✦ **Width:** The line-weight value of the highlight. This value defines the thickness of the highlight rectangle.

✦ **Color box:** The color of the highlight. To change the color of the highlight, drag a color from the Color List or Color Mixer panel (both explained in detail in Chapter 10) and drop it on the color box above the Overprint option or choose a color from the pop-up menu to the right of the color box. To edit the color, make sure you open the Color Mixer or Color List panel (also described in Chapter 10) before you open the Highlight Effect dialog box. Although you can use the color panels while you are in the Highlight Effect dialog box, you cannot open them while the dialog box is open.

✦ **Overprint:** Overprints the highlight bar when enabled. See Chapter 11 for detailed information concerning overprinting.

The inline effect

Select the Inline Effect option from the Text ➪ Effects submenu to assign multiple outlines to selected type. An example of inline type appears in Figure 8-10.

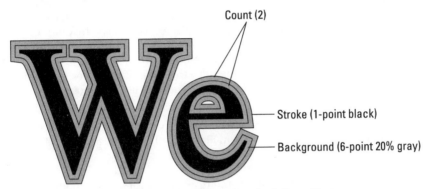

Count (2)

Stroke (1-point black)

Background (6-point 20% gray)

Figure 8-10: A block of large text subjected to the inline effect.

To customize the effect, choose Edit from the Effect pop-up menu in the Character panel of the Text Inspector or choose Text ➪ Effect ➪ Inline, which displays the Inline Effect dialog box shown in Figure 8-11.

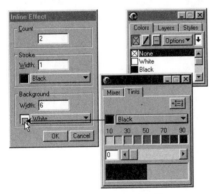

Figure 8-11: Drag a swatch from one of the color panels to change the color of the outlines or the spaces between outlines in the inline effect.

The options in this dialog box work as follows:

✦ **Count:** This number tells FreeHand how many outlines to draw around each selected character.

✦ **Stroke:** Under Stroke, enter a line-weight value into the Width option box. This value defines the thickness of each outline drawn around the selected characters. To change the color of the outlines as well as the color of the selected characters, drag a color from the Color List or Color Mixer panel (as shown in Figure 8-11) and drop it on the color box below the Width option or choose a color from the pop-up menu to the right of the color box. You can also click and hold on the associated pop-up menu and choose from any of the colors in your color list panel.

✦ **Background:** The Background options specify the thickness and color of the areas between the outlines. Back in Figure 8-10, I used a 6-point, 20 percent gray Background.

 Cross-Reference For complete information on defining and dragging colors, read Chapter 10. Chapter 12 explains line weight and other stroke attributes.

The shadow effect

Drop shadows are immensely popular, though indisputably overused. Unfortunately, you don't have any way to control this effect in FreeHand. To apply a drop shadow to selected type, select the Shadow Effect option from the Effect pop-up menu. That's it. The Edit selection is dimmed, so you can't change the color or position of the drop shadow — it's always gray and offset slightly down and to the right.

The strikethrough effect

Selecting the Strikethrough Effect option lets you position a line on top of the selected text. By default, this line is solid black and centered through your text. The strikethrough effect also offers a dialog box that lets you change the strikethrough line's appearance. Choosing Edit from the Effects pop-up menu in the Character panel of the Text Inspector or Text ⇨ Effect ⇨ Strikethrough displays the Strikethrough Effect dialog box pictured in Figure 8-12.

Figure 8-12: The Strikethrough Effect dialog box at its default settings for 72-point text.

This dialog box looks remarkably like the Highlight Effect dialog box. In fact, only the default settings differ. The difference between these two effects is that the highlight is placed behind the text and the strikethrough is placed on top of the text. For the record, though, I'll go over the settings offered:

✦ **Position:** The center of the strikethrough. FreeHand defines the text block's baseline as the zero position. Negative values move the strikethrough down; positive values move it up.

✦ **Dash:** The stroke of the strikethrough. FreeHand treats the strikethrough as a line. Therefore, a thick, dashed strikethrough appears as vertical stripes.

✦ **Width:** The line-weight value of the strikethrough.

✦ **Color box:** The color of the strikethrough. To change the color of the strikethrough, drag a color from the Color List or Color Mixer panel and drop it on the color box . Again, make sure that you open the color panels before opening the Strikethrough Effect dialog box to have access to these panels from within this dialog box.

✦ **Overprint:** Overprints the strikethrough when enabled. See Chapter 11 for detailed information concerning overprinting.

All units in the Strikethrough Effect dialog box are measured in points, regardless of your current document units setting.

The underline effect

Selecting the underline effect lets you position a line below the selected text. By default, the underline is a solid black line positioned just below the baseline of your text. The underline effect also offers a dialog box to let you change its appearance. Choosing Edit from the Effects pop-up menu in the Character panel of the Text Inspector or Text ➪ Effect ➪ Underline displays the Underline Effect dialog box pictured in Figure 8-13.

Figure 8-13: The Underline Effect dialog box at its default setting for 48-point text.

If this isn't the darnedest thing—this dialog box looks just like the Highlight Effect and the Strikethrough Effect dialog boxes. In fact, other than the default settings, this dialog box is the same as the Highlight Effect dialog box. The underline is placed behind the text when the underline and text overlap. As usual, all of the units in the Underline Effect dialog box are measured in points, regardless of your current document units setting. This is what each option means:

✦ **Position:** The center of the underline. FreeHand defines the text block's baseline as the zero position. Negative values move the underline down; positive values move it up.

✦ **Dash:** The stroke of the underline. FreeHand treats the underline as a line. Therefore, a thick, dashed underline appears as vertical stripes.

✦ **Width:** The line-weight value of the underline.

✦ **Color box:** The color of the underline. To change the color of the underline, drag a color from the Color List or Color Mixer panel and drop it on the color box . Again, make sure that you open the color panels before opening the Underline Effect dialog box to have access to these panels from within this dialog box.

✦ **Overprint**: Overprints the underline when enabled. See Chapter 11 for detailed information concerning overprinting.

The zoom effect

And finally, select the Zoom Effect option to create a continuous gradation that trails away from the text, as illustrated in Figure 8-14. After applying the effect, choose Edit from the Effects pop-up menu in the Character panel of the Text Inspector or Text ⇨ Effect ⇨ Zoom to display the Zoom Effect dialog box shown in Figure 8-15.

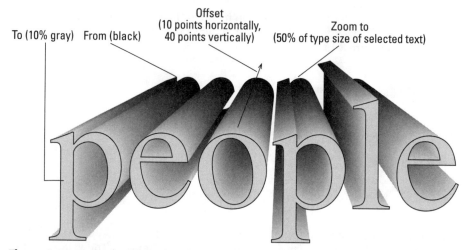

Figure 8-14: A word subjected to the zoom effect. The central arrow shows the direction of the offset.

Figure 8-15: The Zoom Effect dialog box lets you size and position the rear portion of the gradation.

The options in the Zoom Effect dialog box work as follows:

✦ **Zoom To:** The zoom effect works by creating several clones of the selected text, layering them one in front of another, and filling each with a slightly different color. The Zoom To value determines the type size of the rearmost clone, measured as a percentage of the type size of the selected type.

✦ **Offset:** Enter values into the Offset option boxes to specify the distance between the selected text and the rearmost clone. The X value is measured from the center of the selected text. Positive is right; negative is left. The Y option is measured from the baseline. Positive is up; negative is down. Both values conform to the current unit of measure.

✦ **From:** Drag a color swatch from the Color List or Color Mixer panel and drop it onto the From color box to define the color of the rearmost clone or choose a color from the pop-up menu to the right of the color box. You can also click and hold on the color pop-up menu and select any color that's included in your Color List. This option also determines the color of the outline that surrounds the selected text. Again, make sure that you open the color panels before opening the Zoom Effect dialog box to have access to these panels from within this dialog box.

✦ **To:** Drag a color onto the To color box to define the color of the selected text.

FreeHand automatically assigns an intermediate size, position, and color to each of the clones between the selected text and the rearmost clone, creating a smooth gradation. The result is an effect that takes forever to display on-screen and even longer to print.

Paragraph Style pop-up menu

The last pop-up menu in the Character panel of the Text Inspector applies a paragraph style to a selected paragraph. Highlight the paragraph and select a style to apply. Only styles that have been added to the Styles panel may be selected in this pop-up menu.

Paragraph-Level Formatting

Nearly all of FreeHand's paragraph-level formatting options are located in three panels of the Text Inspector. These panels are the Paragraph panel, Spacing panel, and Character panel, accessed by pressing ⌘/Ctrl-Option/Alt-P, ⌘/Ctrl-Option/Alt-K and ⌘/Ctrl-T, respectively. (Refer back to Figure 8-1 if you forgot what these panels look like.)

A few options in these panels bear more than a passing resemblance to those I've discussed already:

✦ The Paragraph panel options in the Paragraph panel add vertical space between paragraphs, much as the Leading option adds space between lines.

✦ In the Spacing panel, the Spacing values add horizontal space between characters and words, much like the Kerning and Range Kerning values.

✦ The Keep Together option boxes near the bottom of the Spacing panel — pay attention, because this is the only place I discuss these options — specify the minimum number of lines that must appear in each half of a paragraph that is broken between two columns or linked text blocks. The Selected Words option prevents lines from breaking between certain words. The Lines value prevents paragraphs from breaking between certain lines. It's just the thing for eliminating those single-line orphans that have a habit of popping up so mournfully at the tops of columns. "If you plaise, sa', I'd lak to be wit the rest of me pa'graph." Gosh, this topic always brings a tear to my eye.

Tabs and indents

Although FreeHand devotes an unprecedented three panels to paragraph formatting, its most essential formatting options are found in the tab ruler that hovers above the active text object when View ➪ Text Rulers is active (pressing ⌘-/ on Macs and Ctrl-Alt-Shift-T on PCs toggles Text Rulers on and off). With the tab ruler, you can control tabs and paragraph indents. You can also modify paragraph indents inside the Paragraph panel of the Text Inspector.

Why tabs are so great

For folks who grew up using a typewriter, tabs and tab stops can be the single most difficult typesetting concept to understand. It's not that typewriters don't provide these features; it's that few folks feel any need to use them. Most conventional typewriters provide movable tab stops for indenting text and creating tables. After moving a tab stop to a point along the carriage, you press the Tab key to advance the carriage so that the next character you enter begins at the tab stop. Although simple in structure, tab stops require a degree of planning that most occasional typists aren't willing to expend. As a result, they don't change the tab settings on their machines to fit the document they're trying to create; instead, they use the same tab stops for everything. If they need to create columns of text, they hit the Tab key, see where that takes them, and if they need to move farther across the page, they press the spacebar.

Suppose that you're working on a typewriter that has tab stops set at half-inch intervals — a typical default setting — and you want to create the three-column table shown in Figure 8-16. Ideally, you would reset your tab stops so that you could type the entry description, press Tab, enter the dollar value in the second column, press Tab again, and enter the dollar value in the third column. But you're short on time and energy, so you decide not to set the proper tab stops for the table and use the default settings instead. Although the values are roughly the same width, ranging between $2.99 and $200.00, the descriptions run as long as Top Grain Italian Leather Attache and as short as Attache Case. So to account for a short description, you have to press the Tab key two or more times in a row to advance even with the first column of dollar values.

```
Item                                      List Price    Our Price

- - - - - - - - - - - - - - - - - - - - - - - - - - - - - - - - - - - - - -

Business Credit Card Case                     4.00        2.99

Card File Binder                             28.50       21.99

Business Card File                            5.50        3.99

Leather Card Case                            27.00       19.99

Attache Case                                 43.00       18.99

Dome Top Attache                            120.00       69.99

Executive Leather Attache                   109.00       59.99

Expandable Leather Attache                  130.00       79.99

Top Grain Italian Leather Attache           200.00      129.99

Business Clip Folder                          7.00        4.49

Steno Notebook                               16.00       11.99
```

Figure 8-16: A typical table created on a typewriter using multiple tabs and spaces.

Furthermore, to match the figure, you need to align the right sides of the dollar values so that ones, tens, and hundreds line up regardless of the number of digits in each number. You determine that you can accomplish this feat by taking a few whacks at the spacebar. For example, to properly align the value 4.49 with 129.99 above it, you press the spacebar twice in a row before entering 4.49 to account for the two-digit difference in the values.

Produced on an ordinary typewriter, your table looks fine. No one but you knows that you didn't set up the ideal tab stops for the document. But suppose you make the mistake of using this same approach in creating a table inside FreeHand, which also provides you with default tab stops spaced ½ inch apart. You use multiple tabs to align values after descriptions, and you use spaces to align digits within the second and third columns. Everything looks fine on-screen. And although the numbers tend to weave slightly when printed, as illustrated in the first example in Figure 8-17, you figure that the table is good enough (especially after an attempt to remedy the alignment by adding and deleting spaces only worsens the situation).

In fact, everything's smooth sailing until you decide to subject the table to a different font or a larger type size. That's when the table goes haywire. As shown in the second example in Figure 8-17, entries that belong in the second column start nudging toward the third, forcing third-column entries onto their own lines. Your previously aligned digits now weave back and forth dramatically, making a mess of your fastidious spacing efforts. You're faced with the unpleasant alternative of going through your text and manually removing tabs and spaces.

Why does a change in font or size wreak so much havoc? The reason is that FreeHand treats tabs and spaces as modifiable characters. A tab character — created by pressing the Tab key — is constantly on the prowl for a tab stop. If a new font or size enlarges the first-column entry to the extent that it overlaps the second column, the next tab character abandons the second-column tab stop — which it can no longer reach — and makes a beeline for the third-column tab stop. Like a domino, the third-column tab character is sent looking for a fourth-column tab stop; finding none, it instead knocks the last entry onto a new line of type.

Spaces are even more problematic, because you can't depend on a space character to adhere to a constant width. On a typewriter, all characters, including spaces, are the same width. By contrast, most Macintosh and Windows fonts — with the exception of Courier, Monaco, and a few others — are variable-width fonts, meaning that different characters have different widths. An *i*, for example, is narrower than an *M*. Depending on the font, a space character may be as narrow as an *i* or as wide as a *t*. So when you change selected spaces to a new font, you are likely to increase or reduce the width of each space, thereby upsetting the alignment of any letters or numbers that follow space characters.

Suffice it to say that using spaces is absolutely forbidden when you're aligning table entries. Never ever use them for this purpose. As far as tabs are concerned, you are well advised to conserve tab characters and instead rely on tab stops to align columns. When creating table entries, press the Tab key no more than once in a row. After you finish entering a few lines, select what you've written so far and add, subtract, and move the tab stops in the tab ruler as explained in the next section.

Item	List Price	Our Price
Business Credit Card Case	4.00	2.99
Card File Binder	28.50	21.99
Business Card File	5.50	3.99
Leather Card Case	27.00	19.99
Attache Case	43.00	18.99
Dome Top Attache	120.00	69.99
Executive Leather Attache	109.00	59.99
Expandable Leather Attache	130.00	79.99
Top Grain Italian Leather Attache	200.00	129.99
Business Clip Folder	7.00	4.49
Steno Notebook	16.00	11.99

Item Our Price	List Price	
Business Credit Card Case 2.99	4.00	
Card File Binder	28.50	21.99
Business Card File	5.50	3.99
Leather Card Case	27.00	19.99
Attache Case 18.99	43.00	
Dome Top Attache	120.00	69.99
Executive Leather Attache	109.00	59.99
Expandable Leather Attache 79.99	130.00	
Top Grain Italian Leather Attache	200.00	129.99
Business Clip Folder 4.49	7.00	
Steno Notebook 11.99	16.00	

Figure 8-17: A tabbed and spaced table set in Times (top) reveals its unstable construction when changed to Helvetica (bottom).

Positioning tab stops

The tab ruler enables you to set tab stops in one or more selected paragraphs. As shown in Figure 8-18, the tab ruler is divided into three strips: the *icon strip*, the *marker strip*, and a *horizontal ruler*.

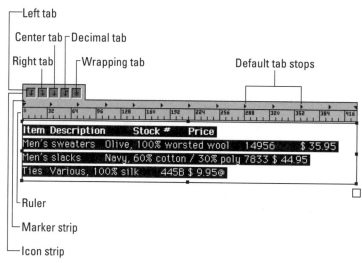

Figure 8-18: The fully annotated tab ruler, with some accompanying selected type.

The icon strip includes five tab icons, each of which produces a different kind of tab stop. Every tab stop controls the alignment of a clump of text between two tab characters or between a tab character and a carriage return. Several of these clumps result in a column. The icons are described below in the order they appear in the tab ruler:

✦ **Left tab:** The left edge of a selected clump of text aligns to this tab stop.

✦ **Right tab:** The right edge of a selected clump aligns to this tab stop.

✦ **Center tab:** The middle of a selected clump aligns to this tab stop.

✦ **Decimal tab:** The decimal character in numbers (such as $25.95) in a selected clump aligns to this tab stop.

✦ **Wrapping tab:** This one's a little different. Wrapping tab stops are always used in pairs. The left edge of a selected clump aligns to the first wrapping tab stop. If the right edge of the clump extends beyond the second wrapping tab stop, the text wraps down to a second line of type. (For an example of this tab stop in action, keep an eye out for Figure 8-20, which I explain in a moment.)

As I mentioned earlier, FreeHand supplies every new text block you create with a series of default tab stops: left tab stops spaced ¹/₂ inch (36 points) apart. To assign tab stops to a paragraph of text, select the paragraph with the text tool — FreeHand does not provide you with access to the tab ruler when you select a block with the arrow tool — and drag from one of the five tab icons into the marker strip. Any default tab stops to the left of the new tab stop disappear. You can track the movement of tab stops in the Info toolbar.

FreeHand has another method for tracking your tab stops. To use it, enable the Track Tab Movement with Vertical Line option in the Text panel of your Preferences dialog box. When this option is enabled, FreeHand displays a vertical line the length of your screen that demarcates your movements as you drag a tab stop into position.

In Figure 8-19, I dragged a center tab stop from the icon strip into the marker strip. This centers the text that follows the first tab character in each selected line. The figure also shows the effects of right and decimal tab stops, which align text following the second and third tab characters. I've included gray lines and gradations so that you can see the alignment more clearly.

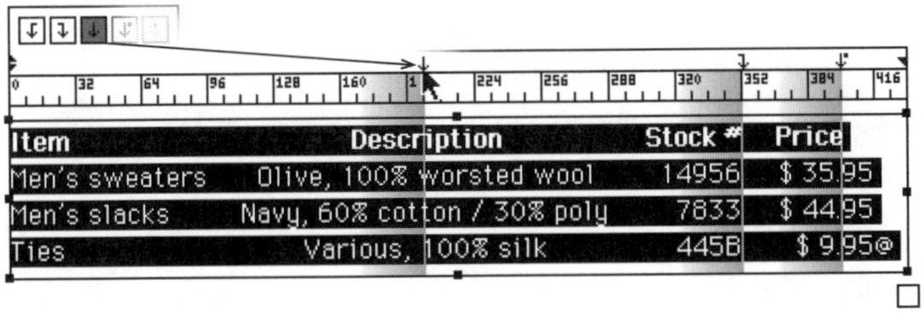

Figure 8-19: Examples of how center, right, and decimal tab stops affect a tabbed paragraph.

Wrapping tab stops are a little more difficult to use. You begin by positioning a wrapping tab stop on the left side of the column of text you want to align. You then position a second wrapping tab stop on the right side of the text. As shown in Figure 8-20, the column of text between the corresponding tab characters stays inside the boundaries represented by the two tab stops. In the figure, I lengthened the third row of text so that it no longer fits inside these boundaries. The wrapping tab stops send the leftover text to a fourth line. If it weren't for the wrapping tab stops, the extended clump of text would nudge its neighbors to the right, forcing them to search for new tab stops.

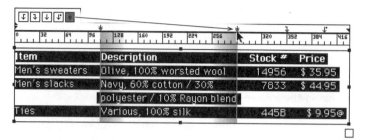

Figure 8-20: Text wraps between two wrapping tab stops.

Note

Any time you add a tab stop, as in the case of the second wrapping tab stop, you have to add a corresponding tab character to each line of type. Therefore, to align the text as shown in Figure 8-20, I needed two tab characters to separate each clump in the Description column from its neighbor in the Stock # column. This is the only circumstance in which you should enter two tab characters in a row.

To move a tab stop, simply drag it inside the marker strip. To delete an existing tab stop, drag it off the marker strip. The tab stop disappears and ceases to affect the selected paragraph. Depending on which stop you delete, some default tab stops may reappear. You can adjust tab stops only after selecting text with the type tool.

Editing tab stops

FreeHand offers a more exact method for repositioning tabs with the Edit Tab dialog box, pictured in Figure 8-21. To gain access to this dialog box, double-click the tab stop in the tab ruler that you want to edit. The Edit Tab dialog box provides two word processing features. You can position tabs by numerical values and add tab leaders. The Edit Tab dialog box appears, showing the characteristics of the tab that you double-clicked.

Figure 8-21: Use the Edit Tab dialog box to add a leader to a selected tab.

The options in the Edit Tab dialog box work as follows:

✦ **Alignment:** This option displays the current tab type. The pop-up menu lists all tab types available from the text ruler. You can change the tab to any other tab type by choosing a different type from this pop-up menu.

✦ **Position:** This option box displays the tab stop's current position using the current document units. You can reposition the tab by entering a new value in this option box. The values are accurate to four decimal places.

✦ **Leader:** A *leader* is a character that is repeated throughout the length of a tab. For example, a table of contents usually shows an item on the far left and a row of dots leading to the page number for the item on the far right. The dots are the leader. FreeHand offers four leader options from this pop-up menu, including None for no leader. You can also enter your own leader character by typing in the option box. Choose the option you want from the pop-up menu or type one in the option box.

Paragraph indents

In addition to the many tab icons, the tab ruler offers three *indent markers* that control the left and right boundaries of lines inside a text block. These markers, labeled in Figure 8-22, work as follows:

✦ First-line indent specifies the indentation of the first line of type in each selected paragraph.

✦ Left indent positions the left edges of all lines except the first one in each selected paragraph.

✦ Right indent positions the right edges of all lines — including the first one — in each selected paragraph.

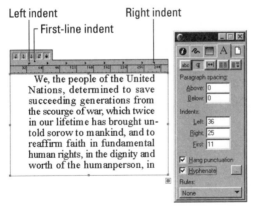

Figure 8-22: The three indent markers (left) and their corresponding options in the Text Paragraph panel (right).

To access the indent markers, you have to select your paragraphs with the text tool; otherwise, the tab ruler is not available. When you drag the first-line indent marker, it moves independently of the other indent markers. But when you drag the left indent marker, you move both it and the first-line marker simultaneously. The two are so frequently together that you may at first mistake them for one marker.

FreeHand also provides three Indents options in the Paragraph panel of the Text Inspector (⌘/Ctrl-Option/Alt-P), as shown in Figure 8-22. The beauty of these options is that you can access them even when you use the arrow tool to select the text block. Each option performs the same function as one of the indent markers. The value in the Left option box is measured from the left edge of the selected text block. The Right value is measured from the right edge. But the First value is measured from the position of the left indent marker. So if the first-line indent marker is to the right of the left indent marker, the First value is positive; if the first-line marker is left of the left indent marker, the First value is negative.

Types of indents

If you drag the first-line indent marker to the right of the left indent marker (as shown previously in Figure 8-22) or enter a positive value into the First option box, you create a standard paragraph indent, as shown in the first example in Figure 8-23. To make your paragraphs more flexible, use this technique to create indents rather than pressing Tab at the beginning of every paragraph. If you later want to get rid of your indents, you can do it globally rather than deleting a bunch of tabs one by one.

> We the people of the United Nations, determined to save succeeding generations from the scourge of war, which twice in our lifetime has brought untold sorrow to mankind, and to reaffirm faith in fundamental human rights, in the dignity

1.   We the people of the United Nations, determined to save succeeding generations from the scourge of war, which twice in our lifetime has brought untold sorrow to mankind, and to reaffirm faith in fundamental human

Figure 8-23: Two paragraphs, one formatted with a standard indent (top) and the other formatted with a hanging indent (bottom).

If you drag the left indent marker to the right and then drag the first-line indent back to the left edge of the tab ruler, you create a hanging indent, as shown in the second example in Figure 8-23. You can achieve the same effect by entering a positive value (say, 24) into the Left option box and the opposite of that value (-24) in the First option box.

Tip

Hanging indents are perfect for creating numbered lists, bulleted items, and other special text blocks. Be sure to enter a tab character after the bullet or number. For example, a tab separates the *1.* from *We* in second example in Figure 8-23. Then drag a left tab stop exactly onto the left indent marker to complete the effect. The tabbed text in the first line aligns with the indented text in the remaining lines of the paragraph.

Changing the alignment

I'm willing to bet a quarter that every computer program that supplies a text tool lets you change the alignment of a paragraph. (And I usually limit my gambling to a dime.) You can align a paragraph so that all the left edges line up (called *flush left, ragged right*); so that all the lines are centered; or so that all the right edges line up (*flush right, ragged left*). You can also justify a paragraph, which stretches the lines so that they entirely fill the width of the text object. Only the last line in a justified paragraph is allowed to remain flush left.

Examples of all four alignment settings are shown in Figure 8-24. To access any of these settings, switch to the Character panel of the Text Inspector (⌘/Ctrl-T) and select one of the Alignment icons. From left to right, the Alignment icons are flush left, centered, flush right, and justified.

You can control the minimum width of any line in a nonjustified paragraph. This is an ideal solution if you don't want to use justified type, which can make text blocks look overly square. It also keeps your text from weaving in and out dramatically. The effect is like partially justifying a paragraph; it's a happy medium between ragged right and fully justified text.

To specify the minimum width, enter a value into the Ragged Width % option box from the Edit Alignment dialog box (which you access by clicking the Edit icon — the one with the ellipses on it — just to the right of the justify icon in the Character panel). The value is measured as a percentage of the width of the text block. A value between 80 and 90 percent produces the most legible results while retaining the informal appearance of nonjustified text.

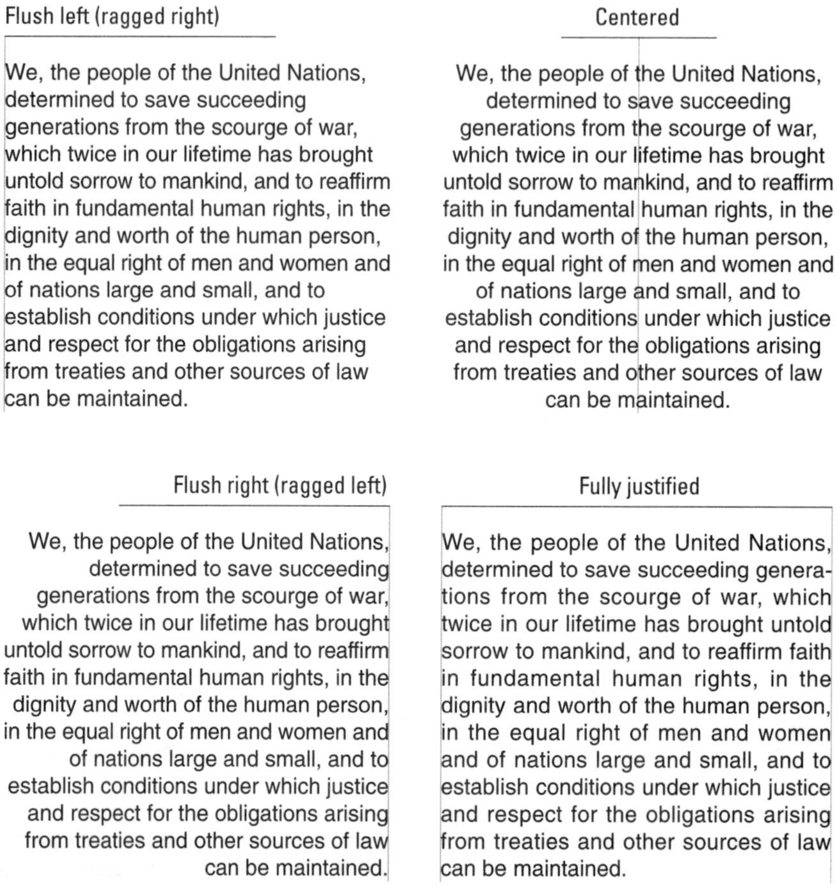

Flush left (ragged right)

We, the people of the United Nations,
determined to save succeeding
generations from the scourge of war,
which twice in our lifetime has brought
untold sorrow to mankind, and to reaffirm
faith in fundamental human rights, in the
dignity and worth of the human person,
in the equal right of men and women and
of nations large and small, and to
establish conditions under which justice
and respect for the obligations arising
from treaties and other sources of law
can be maintained.

Centered

We, the people of the United Nations,
determined to save succeeding
generations from the scourge of war,
which twice in our lifetime has brought
untold sorrow to mankind, and to reaffirm
faith in fundamental human rights, in the
dignity and worth of the human person,
in the equal right of men and women and
of nations large and small, and to
establish conditions under which justice
and respect for the obligations arising
from treaties and other sources of law
can be maintained.

Flush right (ragged left)

We, the people of the United Nations,
determined to save succeeding
generations from the scourge of war,
which twice in our lifetime has brought
untold sorrow to mankind, and to reaffirm
faith in fundamental human rights, in the
dignity and worth of the human person,
in the equal right of men and women and
of nations large and small, and to
establish conditions under which justice
and respect for the obligations arising
from treaties and other sources of law
can be maintained.

Fully justified

We, the people of the United Nations,
determined to save succeeding generations from the scourge of war, which
twice in our lifetime has brought untold
sorrow to mankind, and to reaffirm faith
in fundamental human rights, in the
dignity and worth of the human person,
in the equal right of men and women
and of nations large and small, and to
establish conditions under which justice
and respect for the obligations arising
from treaties and other sources of law
can be maintained.

Figure 8-24: The four alignment settings available to every program on earth.
The gray lines represent the axes of the alignments.

You can also instruct FreeHand to justify the last line in a fully justified paragraph.
But you don't accomplish this by turning the function either on or off, as you do in
a program such as Illustrator. Instead, you enter a relative value into the Flush Zone
% option box in the Edit Alignment dialog box. Again, this value is measured as a
percentage of the width of the text block. If the last line exceeds this length,
FreeHand justifies it. Otherwise, the line remains flush left. (Note that the Flush
Zone % option only affects the last line in fully justified paragraphs.)

The last option that affects alignment isn't found in the Character panel of the Text
Inspector. FreeHand's programmers tucked the Hang Punctuation check box away
in the Paragraph panel (⌘/Ctrl-Option/Alt-P). Select this check box to make

punctuation such as commas, quotation marks, hyphens, and so on hang outside the edge of a selected paragraph, as shown in Figure 8-25. If two adjacent punctuation symbols occur at the beginning or end of a line, only the first or final symbol hangs outside the paragraph, as illustrated by the period and closing quote in the second example in Figure 8-25. You can apply this option to flush left, flush right, or justified paragraphs.

"We, the people of the United Nations, are determined to save succeeding generations from the scourge of war, which twice in our lifetime has brought untold sorrow to mankind."

"We, the people of the United Nations, are determined to save succeeding generations from the scourge of war, which twice in our lifetime has brought untold sorrow to mankind."

Figure 8-25: The quotation mark hangs outside the flush left paragraph (top). The closing quotation mark and some commas hang outside the flush right paragraph (bottom).

Paragraph spacing

Just as you can change the vertical and horizontal spacing of characters, you can change the vertical and horizontal spacing of whole paragraphs. For vertical spacing, use the two Paragraph Spacing option boxes in the Paragraph panel of the Text Inspector. The Above value determines the amount of space between the first line in each selected paragraph and the last line in the paragraph above it. The Below value determines the amount of space between the last line in each selected paragraph and the first line in the paragraph below it.

Together, these values make up the paragraph spacing of a document. The paragraphs in this book, for example, are typically separated by one pica of paragraph spacing. Like the popular first-line indent, paragraph spacing is a form of visually separating one topic from another. It loosens up the page and makes it more readable. Generally speaking, however, you should use either a first-line indent or paragraph spacing in your designs. Although I have been known to use both in a single paragraph — there's no law against it — many professional designers consider one or the other to be sufficient. Anything more may be construed in some circles as overkill.

At this point, you may be wondering why FreeHand provides both Above and Below options. Isn't one or the other sufficient to space out paragraphs? There are two reasons for this. One is to accommodate style sheets (see "Using Text Styles" later in this chapter). The second reason that FreeHand includes two options is to accommodate paragraph rules — those thin lines that are sometimes used as paragraph borders.

The Below value determines the space between the rule and the paragraph above it; the Above value determines the space between the rule and the paragraph below it. (I know that it sounds backward, but this is the way it works.) For more information on paragraph rules, read the upcoming "Creating paragraph rules" section.

Spacing letters and words

You can control the amount of space between all characters in a paragraph by adjusting the *letterspacing*. You can also control the amount of space between words in a text block by changing the *word spacing*. Press ⌘/Ctrl-Option/Alt-K to display the Spacing panel of the Text Inspector, wherein the Spacing % options appears.

Note

You may be thinking to yourself, "How is letterspacing, which controls the amount of space between individual characters, different from kerning, which controls the amount of space between individual characters? It sounds like the same thing to me." Well, you've brought up a good point. (Actually, I brought it up, but I thought I'd be generous and give you the credit.) The outcome of kerning and letterspacing is frequently the same. But kerning applies to selected characters, and letterspacing affects entire paragraphs. Also, the two are measured differently. Kerning is measured in fractions of an em space; letterspacing is measured as a percentage of the standard character spacing. But most important, kerning is fixed, while letterspacing is flexible. FreeHand is allowed to automatically vary letterspacing according to guidelines that you establish.

There are two primary reasons for manipulating letterspacing and word spacing:

✦ To give a paragraph a tighter or looser appearance. You control this general spacing using the Opt (for Optimum) options.

✦ To determine the range of spacing manipulations that FreeHand can use when trying to fit text on a line, especially inside a justified paragraph. FreeHand has to tighten up some lines to get them to fit exactly inside the column; it must loosen up other lines. You specify how much FreeHand can shrink or expand spacing by using the Min and Max options.

Letterspacing values are measured as percentages of standard character spacing; word spacing values are measured as percentages of a standard space character. The exact character spacing and space character width depend on the font you select.

The values for the Spacing % options can range as follows:

✦ The Min Word value must be 0 percent or greater. The Min Letter value may range from -100 to 1,000. Neither values be larger than the Max value.

✦ The Max value must be larger than the Min value but can't be greater than 1,000 percent, or 10 times standard spacing.

✦ The Opt value can be no less than the Min value and no more than the Max value.

Figure 8-26 shows a single justified paragraph under various word and letterspacing conditions. In the first column of paragraphs, only the word spacing changes; all letterspacing values are set to 100 percent. In the second column, only the letterspacing changes; all word spacing values are set to 100 percent. The headlines above each paragraph indicate what values were changed. The percentages represent the values entered in the Min, Opt, and Max options, respectively.

If you have trouble making the spacing of a paragraph look like you want it to, it's probably because you're giving FreeHand too much latitude. To gain absolute control over word spacing or letterspacing, enter the same value in the Min, Opt, and Max option boxes. In other words, make all the word spacing values the same, or make all the letterspacing values the same, or both. This way, FreeHand has to conform exactly to the values you give it. The only exception arises when you're working inside a justified paragraph, in which case FreeHand overrides your settings and increases the spacing as required. For example, if you set all six Spacing % values to 100 percent and then justify the selected paragraph, you're asking FreeHand to do the impossible. It has to change the spacing somehow, and it does so without your consent.

Hyphenating words

FreeHand offers full automatic hyphenation. Its automatic hyphenation functions are similar to those provided by PageMaker and QuarkXPress. FreeHand recognizes that it can break a word across two lines at a hyphen character. But that's only the beginning. You can also instruct FreeHand to automatically hyphenate words according to a dictionary that's installed along with the software.

Word: 75%, 100%, 150%

We, the people of the United Nations, determined to save succeeding generations from the scourge of
war, which twice in our lifetime has
brought untold sorrow to mankind,
and to reaffirm faith in fundamental
human rights, in the dignity and

Letter: 95%, 100%, 110%

We, the people of the United Nations, determined to save succeeding generations from the scourge of
war, which twice in our lifetime has
brought untold sorrow to mankind,
and to reaffirm faith in fundamental
human rights, in the dignity and

Word: 25%, 50%, 100%

We, the people of the United Nations,
determined to save succeeding
generations from the scourge of war,
which twice in our lifetime has brought
untold sorrow to mankind, and to
reaffirm faith in fundamental human
rights, in the dignity and worth of the

Letter: 75%, 85%, 100%

We, the people of the United Nations,
determined to save succeeding generations from the scourge of war, which
twice in our lifetime has brought untold
sorrow to mankind, and to reaffirm faith
in fundamental human rights, in the
dignity and worth of the human person,

Word: 150%, 150%, 200%

We, the people of the United Nations, determined to save succeeding generations from the
scourge of war, which twice in our
lifetime has brought untold sorrow
to mankind, and to reaffirm faith
in fundamental human rights, in

Letter: 100%, 125%, 150%

We, the people of the United Nations, determined to save succeeding generations from the
scourge of war, which twice in our
lifetime has brought untold sorrow
to mankind, and to reaffirm faith
in fundamental human rights, in

Figure 8-26: Examples of different word spacing and letterspacing values. In the left
column, letterspacing is constant. In the right column, word spacing is constant.

To activate the automatic hyphenation function, select the paragraph that you want
to hyphenate, press ⌘/Ctrl-Option/Alt-P to display the Paragraph panel of the Text
Inspector (shown in Figure 8-27), and select the Hyphenate check box. FreeHand
then adds hyphens and breaks words across lines as it deems necessary.

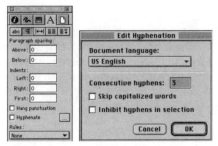

Figure 8-27: FreeHand's automatic hyphenation options share a dialog box with the Paragraph spacing panel.

Automatic hyphenation controls

In addition to automatic hyphenation, FreeHand provides three other hyphenation options found in the Edit Hyphenation dialog box. To access it, click the Edit button to the right of the Hyphenate box:

✦ **Document Language:** If you own a non-English version of FreeHand or you have access to non-English hyphenation dictionaries, you can select a different language from the Document Language pop-up menu.

✦ **Consecutive Hyphens:** By default, FreeHand doesn't allow any more than three consecutive lines to end in hyphens. The reasoning behind this practice is that more than three hyphens can distract readers from your text and make them say, "Whoa, do you think they used enough hyphens in this paragraph, or what? It's like every single line has a hyphen in it. This document is really starting to make me grouchy" — or words to that effect. In truth, hyphens do indeed make a paragraph more difficult to read, so the fewer hyphens you use, the better. I personally set the Consecutive Hyphens value to 2. Then, if I think more hyphens are warranted for a specific paragraph, I add them by hand.

✦ **Skip Capitalized Words:** Select this option to instruct FreeHand not to hyphenate words that include capitalized letters. This not only prevents the program from hyphenating special capitalized words such as *FreeHand*, but also everyday run-of-the-mill words that are capitalized because they appear at the beginning of sentences. I suggest that you leave this option off and manually turn off hyphenation for special words, as discussed in the next section.

✦ **Inhibit Hyphens in Selection:** To unhyphenate — or is it dehyphenate? — a word, select the offending word and select the Inhibit Hyphens in Selection check box. From this point on, FreeHand will know that the selected word is hands-off in the hyphenation department. "Absolutum wordis non gratis," is the Latin phrase, I believe. "Et tu hyphenatum?"

Manual hyphenation controls

Just like FreeHand's other automated functions — the freehand tool, the trace tool, automatic curvature, power steering, and antilock brakes — automatic hyphenation doesn't always deliver the way you want it to. This is where you — the manual hyphenation engine — come in. You can remove hyphens from words that you don't want to hyphenate, as explained previously, and add hyphens to words that either are not hyphenated or are not hyphenated to your satisfaction.

To add a hyphen, you can simply enter a hyphen character to the offending text. But doing so can turn around and bite you. If you edit the text, for example, you may end up with stray hyphens between words that no longer break at the ends of lines. A better idea is to insert a discretionary hyphen, which disappears any time it's not needed. You can access the discretionary hyphen by choosing Text ➪ Special Character ➪ Discretionary Hyphen. If no hyphen appears when you enter this character, it simply means that the addition of the hyphen does not help FreeHand break the word. You can try inserting the character at a new location, or you can tighten the word spacing and letterspacing slightly to allow room for the word to break.

Creating paragraph rules

You can append a rule (horizontal line) to the end of a selected paragraph in FreeHand using the options in the Rules pop-up menu in the Paragraph panel of the Text Inspector. But the implementation involves so many steps that it's almost easier to add a rule by drawing it with the line tool. For the record, though, here's the four-step process required to create a paragraph rule:

1. Select the paragraph (with the arrow tool) to which you want to apply the rule. FreeHand will place the rule under the last line in the paragraph. (There's no way to put the rule at the top or sides of the paragraph.)

2. Switch to the Paragraph panel (⌘/Ctrl-Option/Alt-P) and select an option from the Rules pop-up menu at the bottom.

3. If you're in the Preview mode, you won't see any paragraph rule. Why not? Because you haven't assigned a stroke yet. Silly you. Switch to the Stroke Inspector (⌘/Ctrl-Option/Alt-L) and assign a stroke as described in Chapter 12.

4. Aaugh. Now you can see your paragraph rule, but you've also outlined the text block. Switch to the Object Inspector (⌘/Ctrl-I) and deselect the Display Border check box.

But wait, there's more. You create a rule by selecting one of two options — Centered or Paragraph — from the Rules pop-up menu. The Centered option centers the rule below the paragraph; the Paragraph option aligns the rule flush left, flush right, or whatever, depending on the alignment of the paragraph. The trouble is, the first time you apply either option, you get the same effect — a rule stretched across the entire length of the last line. To change this, choose the Edit option from the Rules pop-up menu. The Paragraph Rule Width dialog box appears, as shown in Figure 8-28, which allows you to specify the length of the line as a percentage value. Select an option from the pop-up menu to decide whether the percentage is measured relative to the length of the last line or the entire text block (the Column option). Then press Return or Enter. Figure 8-29 shows the results of applying several different settings to two paragraphs at a time. All examples feature a hairline rule.

Figure 8-28: Choose the Edit option from the Rules pop-up menu in the Paragraph panel of the Text Inspector to display this dialog box.

Tip

To increase the amount of space between a paragraph and its rule, enlarge the Below value at the top of the Paragraph panel of the Text Inspector. To adjust the space between the rule and the next paragraph, select the next paragraph and change the Above value.

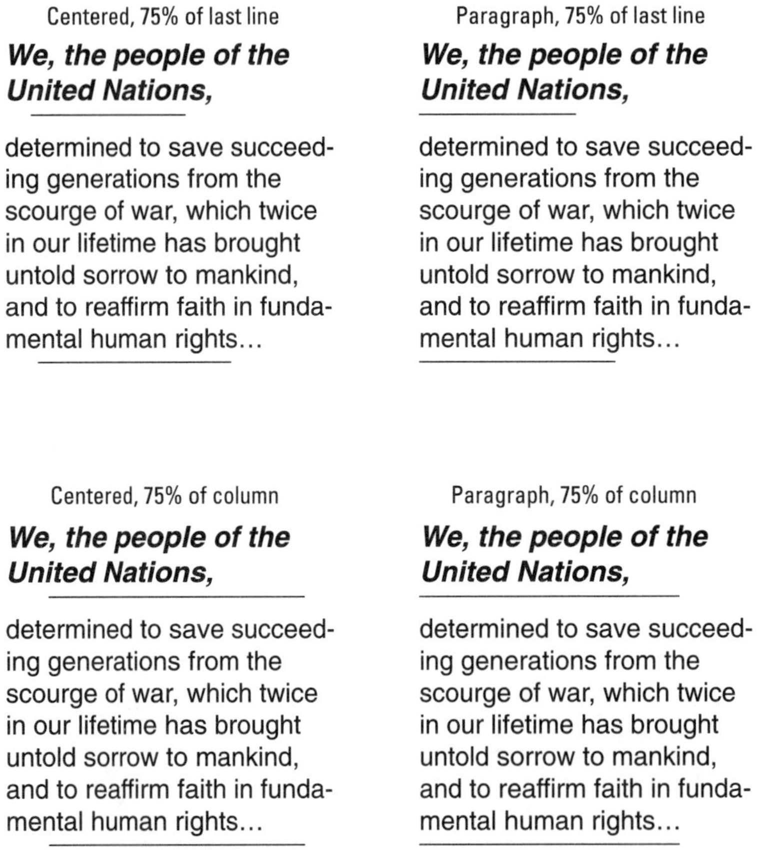

Centered, 75% of last line

We, the people of the United Nations,

determined to save succeeding generations from the
scourge of war, which twice
in our lifetime has brought
untold sorrow to mankind,
and to reaffirm faith in fundamental human rights...

Paragraph, 75% of last line

We, the people of the United Nations,

determined to save succeeding generations from the
scourge of war, which twice
in our lifetime has brought
untold sorrow to mankind,
and to reaffirm faith in fundamental human rights...

Centered, 75% of column

We, the people of the United Nations,

determined to save succeeding generations from the
scourge of war, which twice
in our lifetime has brought
untold sorrow to mankind,
and to reaffirm faith in fundamental human rights...

Paragraph, 75% of column

We, the people of the United Nations,

determined to save succeeding generations from the
scourge of war, which twice
in our lifetime has brought
untold sorrow to mankind,
and to reaffirm faith in fundamental human rights...

Figure 8-29: The effects of four different rule settings.

Using Text Styles

You can create text styles as well as object styles in FreeHand 8. Most of the information concerning text styles is also applicable to object styles. There are two major differences. First, in the case of text styles, FreeHand is focused on character and paragraph attributes, whereas with object styles, it's all stroke and fill. Second, you cannot apply a text style to a graphic object, nor can you apply an object style to a text block. (Refer to Chapter 10 for more information on object styles.)

First a word about the concept of text styles. Here's a true story from my past. I remember when I was learning AutoCAD, deep in the dark ages of "human" interface design. The lab assistant was showing me a few things. And I remember that he told me, "If you want to get good at this, you've got be a lot lazier." The following discussion is in the spirit of that advice.

If you haven't yet, I guarantee you will reach a point in life where you always assign text styles at the outset. Initially this will happen because you want to avoid reworking all text in a document paragraph by paragraph. Eventually, though, you'll do so in appreciation of the freedom and power that using text styles gives you. In short, working with text styles is just more fun.

FreeHand's text style capabilities are made available to you through the Styles panel, pictured in Figure 8-30. You can display this panel by pressing ⌘/Ctrl-3, and it is also found under Window ⇨ Panels ⇨ Styles. In the Styles panel, you have two different view options: small icons with names and large icons without names. The small icons give no detail of the style while the large icons impart as much font, style, and color information as they can. To switch between the two views, choose the Show/Hide Names command from the Options pop-up menu in the Styles panel.

Object Style icon

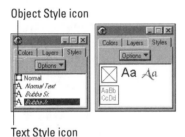

Text Style icon

Figure 8-30: The Styles panel with a whole mess of text styles.

Creating text styles

By creating a text style, you can apply a complex set of character and paragraph attributes with a single click of the mouse button. If you later decide that you want to change the attributes, you just edit the style. FreeHand automatically applies the new attributes to all text to which you had applied the original style.

Creating and manipulating styles

To create a new style, apply the desired character and paragraph attributes to a text block. Then select the text block and select New from the Options pop-up menu in the Styles panel. FreeHand adds a new style name, which it calls *Style-1* or something along those lines, to the scrolling list in the panel. To the left of its name is the Text Style icon, as labeled in Figure 8-30. You can rename the style by double-clicking it, entering a new name, and pressing Return or Enter.

If no object is selected when you select the New option, the Styles panel grabs the default character and paragraph attributes. You can use this technique to set up text styles for the different categories of text in your document. For example, you can set up styles for headings, captions, and body text.

Duplicating attribute styles

You can duplicate styles in two ways:

✦ Click a style name and select the Duplicate option from the Options pop-up menu in the Styles panel.

✦ Click a style name and select New from the Options pop-up menu.

That's right — both techniques produce identical results. In either case, you create a new style based on an existing one. What's more, the new style — I'll call it *Bubba Jr.* as back in Figure 8-30 — is tagged to the style you duplicated — *Bubba Sr.* What we've got here is a classic parent-child relationship.

The connection between a parent style and its child is the same as that between a style and a tagged text block. When you change the parent style, all child style attributes that match the parent style attributes — bold text, hanging indents, hairy arms — change as well. If you want to break the bond between parent and child — you heartless home-wrecker — click on the child in the Styles panel and select the Set Parent option from the pop-up menu. A dialog box asks you to select a new adoptive parent, such as Charles H. Maudlin III. When you press Return/Enter, FreeHand juggles the family structure and replaces Bubba Sr. with Charles III. FreeHand also changes any attributes that Bubba Jr. shared with Bubba Sr. so that they match Chaz. For example, if both Bubbas had blue text, and Chaz has green text, Bubba Jr.'s text changes to green as well.

It's really sad, actually. When Bubba Jr. visits the old homestead these days, the family hardly recognizes him. He doesn't even watch football anymore.

Cutting and copying styles

You can transfer text styles from one document to another by cutting or copying text blocks. Just select one or more text blocks that are tagged to one or more text styles, cut or copy the text blocks (⌘/Ctrl-C or ⌘/Ctrl-X), switch to another open document, and paste the text blocks (⌘/Ctrl-V).

To delete a style without sending it to the Clipboard, click on the style and select Remove from the Options pop-up menu in the Styles panel. All text blocks tagged to the style are then tagged to the parent style.

Editing text styles

Editing styles is slightly more involved than creating them. There are two basic approaches. You can redefine the style, or you can use the one-stop-shopping Edit Style dialog box.

Redefining styles

Here are the steps for redefining a text style:

1. Press Tab to deselect all objects.

2. Click on the style you want to edit. FreeHand makes the character and paragraph attributes the default attributes. (If the style was already selected but it has a plus sign next to it, click on some other style and then click on the desired style. I explain the significance of the plus sign in the next section.) This provides you with a starting point.

3. Edit the character and paragraph settings.

4. Select the Redefine option in the Options pop-up menu of the Styles panel. A dialog box appears, asking you which style you want to redefine. Click on the style name and press the Return or Enter key. The style is now redefined.

Or, you can edit the character and paragraph settings of a text block to which the style is already applied and then select the Redefine option. However, this strategy can lead to some weirdness on FreeHand's part. Suppose you select a text block that is tagged to Style A and use it as a jumping off point for redefining another style, Style B. After you define Style B, FreeHand reapplies Style A to the text block, which upsets the edits you've made to the text block's attributes. You then have to apply Style B to the text block to restore the edits. It's not the end of the world, but it can be disconcerting, which is why I prefer to redefine styles while no text block is selected.

The Edit Style dialog box

Using the Edit Style dialog box is my very favorite way of editing a style. Click on the text style that you want to edit in the Styles panel. Next, choose Edit Style from the Options pop-up menu to display the dialog box pictured in Figure 8-31. What a work of art! It shows you the selected style's settings for all possible text style attributes. You're free to reset them all at once.

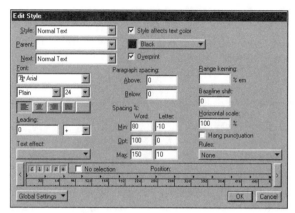

Figure 8-31: The Edit Style one-stop-shopping dialog box.

Other than the Global Settings pop-up menu at the bottom left corner of the dialog box, I have already covered all of the options found in this dialog box in this chapter. So, without any further ado, let's go over the options in the Global Settings pop-up menu:

✦ **No Selection:** If you currently have an object selected in your document and don't want the changes you're about to make to affect that object one iota, choose this option.

✦ **Restore Original Values:** This is the bail-out option. It lets you reset all values in the dialog box to what they were when you first opened the dialog box.

✦ **Restore Program Defaults:** This one resets all the values to their settings at the start of your current working session in FreeHand.

Applying a style

To apply your new style — or any other style — to another text block in the document, select the text block and click on the text style name in the panel. You can also apply a style from the Character panel of the Text Inspector — a new feature in FreeHand 8. Not only does the text block immediately gain all character and paragraph attributes assigned to the text style, it becomes tagged to the text style. From now on, any changes you make to the text style affect the tagged text block as well. The next section explains how this process works.

The effect of style changes on tagged text blocks

Editing a style has the added effect of reformatting every text block tagged to that style, which is a great way to make global changes. Let's say that you created a newsletter that uses several different text styles. All of these text styles have paragraph spacing and indent settings that are based on a style called Stretch It Out. You were a little short on material for the newsletter, so you were generous with both the margins and the paragraph spacing. Suddenly you realize that by switching from standard to legal-size paper and decreasing the margins and paragraph spacing, you can fit the entire newsletter on one page instead of two. You can edit the paragraph spacing and margins in Stretch It Out to change these settings for all text in your newsletter, thereby fitting it all on one page. You're lauded as a hero. You get chosen as employee of the month. Congratulations!

This brings up an interesting phenomenon: Every text block you create in FreeHand is tagged to some style or other. When you create a text block, FreeHand tags it to the default style, which is generally the last style used. If you've never touched the Styles panel, all your text blocks are tagged to the factory-default style, Normal Text. Notice that as you assign other character and paragraph attributes to text blocks, FreeHand displays a plus sign to the left of the words Normal Text, showing that the text block is still tagged to the style but does not subscribe to all of the style's attributes.

If the tagged text block matches the style in some respects and not others, what happens when you redefine the style? The answer is that the similar attributes change and the different ones don't. Suppose that a text block tagged to the Normal Text style is aligned center and uses 24-point blue text. The only difference between the text block and the style is the blue text. If you edit the Normal Text style to include a left alignment and a 36-point text, the object updates to include a left alignment and 36-point text, but the color of the text remains blue.

Importing and exporting styles

Not only can you create and edit text style in FreeHand, you can also import and export text styles. Once you create a text style that you really like, you simply need to export it and you're ready to share it with all your FreeHand-using friends or add it to your styles library that lives on your hard drive. To export a text style, choose the Export command in the Option pop-up menu in the Styles panel. FreeHand will ask you to select the text style that you wish to export from a list of all the text styles presently cohabiting in your open document. Select the intended style and click the Export button — FreeHand whisks you to the Export Styles dialog box that functions just like the Save dialog box. Later down the road, when you're creating a new document and think that a style that you've previously created and exported would do perfectly in your current work, all you have to do is import that style. To import a style, choose the Import command in the Options pop-up menu in the

Styles panel and find your saved style on disk. The only thing with imported and exported styles is that FreeHand will only import styles that have been exported from FreeHand. In other words, if you wish to import a style, you must know of a preexisting text style file that was created and exported in FreeHand.

Block-Level Formatting

The only formatting options that I haven't yet discussed are found in the Columns and Rows panel of the Text Inspector (⌘/Ctrl-Option/Alt-R). With these options, you can subdivide a text block into vertical columns and horizontal rows and affect entire selected text blocks at a time. You can either click inside a text block with the text tool or select it with the arrow tool to prepare it for modification.

Columns and rows

As you can see in Figure 8-1, the Columns and Rows panel of the Text Inspector includes three sets of options — Columns, Rows, and Wrap Order (Flow). The Columns and Rows options work as follows:

✦ **Columns/Rows:** In this option box, enter the number of columns or rows you want to create. You can enter any number between 1 and 100, though it's unlikely that you'll want to go quite that high.

✦ **Height/Width:** Enter the height of a column or the width of a row into the option box. These options are only available when you're editing a standard text block. If one or more free-form text objects are selected, the Height and Width options are unavailable.

✦ **Spacing:** Enter the amount of space that separates one column or row from its neighbors into this option box. As with the Height and Width options, FreeHand interprets the value in the current unit of measure.

✦ **Rules:** You can select from two kinds of rules to separate columns and rows. Both Rules pop-up menus offer Inset options, which break the rule into several free-floating lines, one for each row or column of text. You can also select the Full Height or Full Width option, which extends the rule across the entire height or width of the text block. Figure 8-32 shows examples.

Press the Return or Enter key to apply your values to the selected text block. Figure 8-32 shows the result of applying Columns and Rows settings as well as the results of applying them to a large text block. By creating two columns and three rows, I've partitioned the text block into six independent cels (one of which is labeled in the figure).

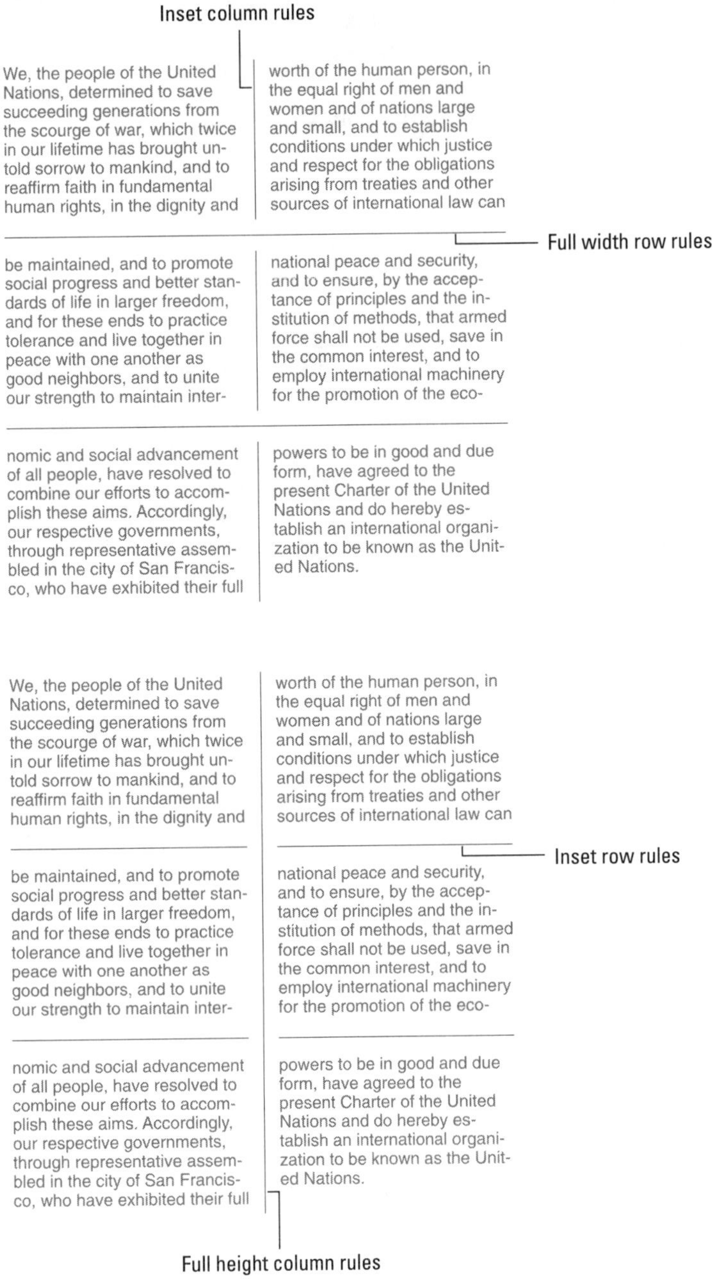

Inset column rules

We, the people of the United Nations, determined to save succeeding generations from the scourge of war, which twice in our lifetime has brought untold sorrow to mankind, and to reaffirm faith in fundamental human rights, in the dignity and

worth of the human person, in the equal right of men and women and of nations large and small, and to establish conditions under which justice and respect for the obligations arising from treaties and other sources of international law can

Full width row rules

be maintained, and to promote social progress and better standards of life in larger freedom, and for these ends to practice tolerance and live together in peace with one another as good neighbors, and to unite our strength to maintain inter-

national peace and security, and to ensure, by the acceptance of principles and the institution of methods, that armed force shall not be used, save in the common interest, and to employ international machinery for the promotion of the eco-

nomic and social advancement of all people, have resolved to combine our efforts to accomplish these aims. Accordingly, our respective governments, through representative assembled in the city of San Francisco, who have exhibited their full

powers to be in good and due form, have agreed to the present Charter of the United Nations and do hereby establish an international organization to be known as the United Nations.

We, the people of the United Nations, determined to save succeeding generations from the scourge of war, which twice in our lifetime has brought untold sorrow to mankind, and to reaffirm faith in fundamental human rights, in the dignity and

worth of the human person, in the equal right of men and women and of nations large and small, and to establish conditions under which justice and respect for the obligations arising from treaties and other sources of international law can

Inset row rules

be maintained, and to promote social progress and better standards of life in larger freedom, and for these ends to practice tolerance and live together in peace with one another as good neighbors, and to unite our strength to maintain inter-

national peace and security, and to ensure, by the acceptance of principles and the institution of methods, that armed force shall not be used, save in the common interest, and to employ international machinery for the promotion of the eco-

nomic and social advancement of all people, have resolved to combine our efforts to accomplish these aims. Accordingly, our respective governments, through representative assembled in the city of San Francisco, who have exhibited their full

powers to be in good and due form, have agreed to the present Charter of the United Nations and do hereby establish an international organization to be known as the United Nations.

Full height column rules

Figure 8-32: The four kinds of rules you can use to visually separate columns and rows.

Columns, rows, and cels are great for creating tables, lists, and stories. For example, by partitioning a text block, you can create several columns of text without resorting to linking separate text objects into a chain. A chain is more flexible, because you can move and independently resize separate text blocks to your heart's content, but columns and rows are easier to create.

Wrapping order

Normally, FreeHand bumps text from one cel to the next in the same way it wraps a word to the next line. When the word exceeds the boundaries of one cel, off it goes to the next. If you don't like how FreeHand divides your text, you can insert a manual column break by pressing Shift-Enter on a Mac or Ctrl-Shift-Enter on a PC. The text after the column break character goes to the next cel in the *wrapping order*.

The wrapping order, called Flow in FreeHand, determines whether excess text flows from the first cel in a text block to the cel in the next row or the cel in the next column. Select the first of the two Flow icons at the bottom of the Column & Rows panel to send text from one cel to the cel in the next row, as shown in the first example in Figure 8-33. When the text reaches the bottom of the column, it breaks to the first cel in the next column. Select the second wrapping icon to send text from one cel to the cel in the next column, as illustrated by the second example in the figure. When the text reaches the end of a row, it goes to the next row down.

Copyfitting

FreeHand's copyfitting controls are located in the Copyfit panel of the Text Inspector (shown in Figure 8-1), which you can access by pressing ⌘/Ctrl-Option/Alt-C. This panel offers two varieties of copyfitting controls. The first controls — Balance and Modify Leading — are specifically designed to accommodate text blocks that include multiple columns. The second variety, represented by the Copyfit % option boxes, affect an entire story, even if the story flows between multiple linked text blocks. All these options instruct FreeHand to automatically adjust type size and/or leading to make type better fit inside its text object.

Tip

To approach the problem from the opposite angle — that is, to resize a text block so that it fits its text — select the text block and double-click inside the link box. This technique only works if the link box is empty, meaning that there is no overflow text. Also, you can only shrink a text block by double-clicking in the link box; you can't enlarge it. And finally, you can't use this method on free-form text objects or text blocks with more than one column or row.

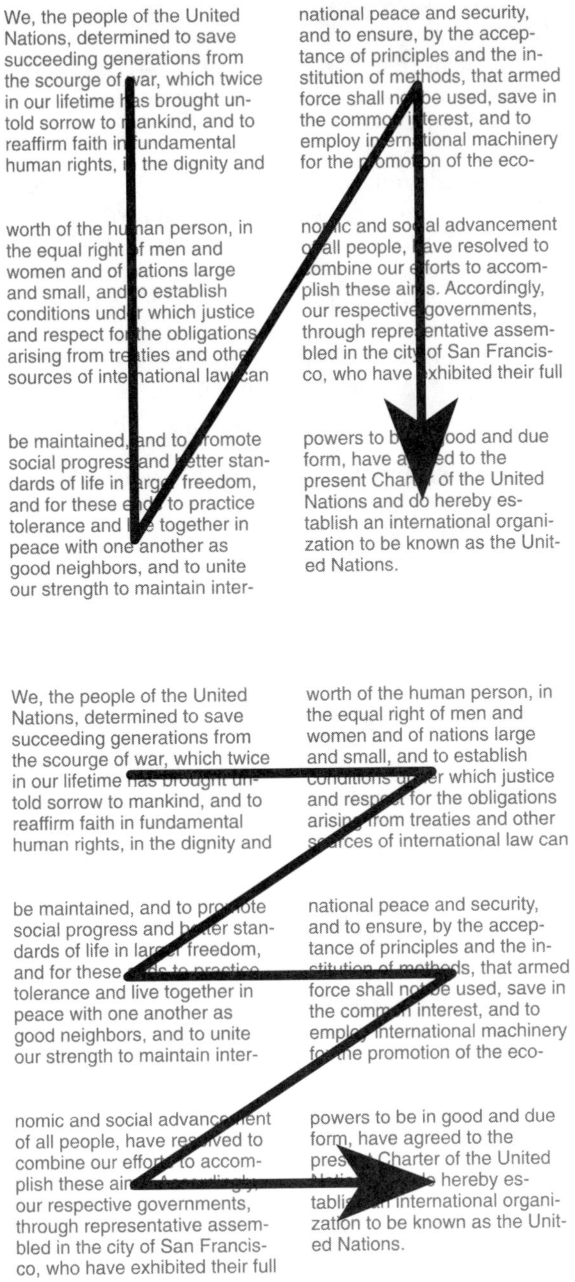

We, the people of the United Nations, determined to save succeeding generations from the scourge of war, which twice in our lifetime has brought untold sorrow to mankind, and to reaffirm faith in fundamental human rights, in the dignity and worth of the human person, in the equal right of men and women and of nations large and small, and to establish conditions under which justice and respect for the obligations arising from treaties and other sources of international law can be maintained, and to promote social progress and better standards of life in larger freedom, and for these ends to practice tolerance and live together in peace with one another as good neighbors, and to unite our strength to maintain international peace and security, and to ensure, by the acceptance of principles and the institution of methods, that armed force shall not be used, save in the common interest, and to employ international machinery for the promotion of the economic and social advancement of all people, have resolved to combine our efforts to accomplish these aims. Accordingly, our respective governments, through representative assembled in the city of San Francisco, who have exhibited their full powers to be in good and due form, have agreed to the present Charter of the United Nations and do hereby establish an international organization to be known as the United Nations.

We, the people of the United Nations, determined to save succeeding generations from the scourge of war, which twice in our lifetime has brought untold sorrow to mankind, and to reaffirm faith in fundamental human rights, in the dignity and worth of the human person, in the equal right of men and women and of nations large and small, and to establish conditions under which justice and respect for the obligations arising from treaties and other sources of international law can be maintained, and to promote social progress and better standards of life in larger freedom, and for these ends to practice tolerance and live together in peace with one another as good neighbors, and to unite our strength to maintain international peace and security, and to ensure, by the acceptance of principles and the institution of methods, that armed force shall not be used, save in the common interest, and to employ international machinery for the promotion of the economic and social advancement of all people, have resolved to combine our efforts to accomplish these aims. Accordingly, our respective governments, through representative assembled in the city of San Francisco, who have exhibited their full powers to be in good and due form, have agreed to the present Charter of the United Nations to be hereby establish an international organization to be known as the United Nations.

Figure 8-33: The effects of selecting each of the two Flow icons.

Balancing columns

The two Adjust Column options — Balance and Modify Leading — enable you to adjust the length of type in a text block with multiple columns. You can only apply these options to one text block at a time.

Select the Balance option to equalize the number of lines of type in a multicolumn text block. For example, consider the three-column text block shown at the top of Figure 8-34. The first two columns contain 19 lines apiece, while the last contains only seven. If you select the Balance option, FreeHand adjusts all columns so that they each contain 15 lines, as in the second example in the figure. Of course, you could achieve the same effect by adding up the total number of lines, dividing them by 3, and dragging the corner handle of the text block until the columns balanced — but why go to all that trouble when you can just select an option? Save your energy for more important things.

Select the Modify Leading option to increase the leading of the type inside a text block so that the type exactly fits the height of the column. By default, FreeHand doesn't adjust columns that are less than 50 percent full. You can include or exclude columns by changing the value in the Threshold % option box of the Copyfit panel of the Text Inspector. If you enter large values, you prevent FreeHand from adjusting short columns; if you enter small values, FreeHand adjusts even short columns.

If you select both Balance and Modify Leading, FreeHand equalizes the number of lines and stretches them to fit the text block height. For example, Figure 8-35 shows two text blocks. In the first one, I selected the Modify Leading option and left the Threshold % left at 50, which slightly increased the leading of the first two columns and ignored the third because it is less than 50 percent full. If you compare the first example in Figure 8-34 to the first one in Figure 8-35, you'll see that the first two columns in the latter are a few points longer. FreeHand increased the leading to make the lines fit the column length, and, thus, the last line in Figure 8-35 is slightly lower than in Figure 8-34.

The second example in Figure 8-35 shows the result of selecting both the Modify Leading check box and the Balance check box. As in Figure 8-34, FreeHand pours 15 lines into each column. But this time, since every column is more than 50 percent filled with text, FreeHand loosens the leading to fill the text block completely.

We, the people of the United Nations, determined to save succeeding generations from the scourge of war, which twice in our lifetime has brought untold sorrow to mankind, and to reaffirm faith in fundamental human rights, in the dignity and worth of the human person, in the equal right of men and women and of nations large and small, and to establish conditions under which justice and respect for the obligations arising from treaties and other sources of international law can be maintained, and to promote social progress and better standards of life in larger freedom, and for these ends to practice tolerance and live together in peace with one another as good neighbors, and to unite our strength to maintain international peace and security.

We, the people of the United Nations, determined to save succeeding generations from the scourge of war, which twice in our lifetime has brought untold sorrow to mankind, and to reaffirm faith in fundamental human rights, in the dignity and worth of the human person, in the equal right of men and women and of nations large and small, and to establish conditions under which justice and respect for the obligations arising from treaties and other sources of international law can be maintained, and to promote social progress and better standards of life in larger freedom, and for these ends to practice tolerance and live together in peace with one another as good neighbors, and to unite our strength to maintain international peace and security.

Figure 8-34: A text block before (top) and after (bottom) selecting the Balance check box.

We, the people of the United Nations, determined to save succeeding generations from the scourge of war, which twice in our lifetime has brought untold sorrow to mankind, and to reaffirm faith in fundamental human rights, in the dignity and worth of the human person, in the equal right of men and women and of nations large and small, and to establish conditions under which justice and respect for the obligations arising from treaties and other sources of international law can be maintained, and to promote social progress and better standards of life in larger freedom, and for these ends to practice tolerance and live together in peace with one another as good neighbors, and to unite our strength to maintain international peace and security.

We, the people of the United Nations, determined to save succeeding generations from the scourge of war, which twice in our lifetime has brought untold sorrow to mankind, and to reaffirm faith in fundamental human rights, in the dignity and worth of the human person, in the equal right of men and women and of nations large and small, and to establish conditions under which justice and respect for the obligations arising from treaties and other sources of international law can be maintained, and to promote social progress and better standards of life in larger freedom, and for these ends to practice tolerance and live together in peace with one another as good neighbors, and to unite our strength to maintain international peace and security.

Figure 8-35: The result of selecting the Modify Leading check box (top) and both the Modify Leading and Balance check boxes (bottom).

Automatic size and leading adjustments

The Copyfit % options automatically adjust type size and leading values so that selected type exactly fits inside the text blocks you've provided for it. The Min and Max values provide FreeHand with a range of percentages by which to scale type size and leading. (The program always scales both size and leading by the same amount.) To use these options, select a single text block with the arrow tool or click inside a text block with the type tool. If the text is too small to fit inside its text blocks, as shown in the first example in Figure 8-36, increase the value in the Max option box. The Max value represents the largest percentage by which FreeHand can scale your text. In the case of Figure 8-36, I entered a value of 150 percent, but FreeHand only had to scale the type size and leading by 120 percent to achieve the second text block in the figure.

If your text is too large to fit inside a text object, reduce the Min value. In Figure 8-37, I filled a free-form path with text sized to 9 points and spaced with 10.8-point leading. The text is too large to fit inside the text object, so the link box contains a black circle. I selected the text object and changed the Min value in the Copyfit panel to 50 percent. In the second example in Figure 8-37, FreeHand reduced the type size and leading to 70 percent of their original values, which was enough to get the text to fit entirely inside the path. As you can see, copyfitting is extremely useful for fitting text inside complex paths. When you enter a Min value, set it lower than you think may be necessary; that way, you give FreeHand an ample margin to work in.

Size: 7.5/ leading: 9

We, the people of the United Nations, determined to save succeeding generations from the scourge of war, which twice in our lifetime has brought untold sorrow to mankind, and to reaffirm faith in fundamental human rights, in the dignity and worth of the human person, in the equal right of men and women and of nations large and small, and to establish conditions under which justice and respect for the obligations arising from treaties and other sources of international law

can be maintained, and to promote social progress and better standards of life in larger freedom, and for these ends to practice tolerance and live together in peace with one another as good neighbors, and to unite our strength to maintain international peace and security, and to ensure, by the acceptance of principles and the institution of methods, that armed force shall not be used, save in the common interest, and to employ international machinery for the promotion of the economic and social advancement of all people, have resolved to combine our efforts to accomplish these aims. Accordingly, our respective governments, through representative assembled in the city of San Francisco, who have exhibited their full powers to be in good and due form, have agreed

to the present Charter of the United Nations and do hereby establish an international organization to be known as the United Nations.

Size: 9/ leading 10.8

We, the people of the United Nations, determined to save succeeding generations from the scourge of war, which twice in our lifetime has brought untold sorrow to mankind, and to reaffirm faith in fundamental human rights, in the dignity and worth of the human person, in the equal right of men and women and of nations large and small, and

to establish conditions under which justice and respect for the obligations arising from treaties and other sources of international law can be maintained, and to promote social progress and better standards of life in larger freedom, and for these ends to practice tolerance and live together in peace with one another as good neighbors, and to unite our strength to maintain international peace and security, and to ensure, by the acceptance of principles and the institution of methods, that armed force shall not be used, save in the common interest, and to

employ international machinery for the promotion of the economic and social advancement of all people, have resolved to combine our efforts to accomplish these aims. Accordingly, our respective governments, through representative assembled in the city of San Francisco, who have exhibited their full powers to be in good and due form, have agreed to the present Charter of the United Nations and do hereby establish an international organization to be known as the United Nations.

Figure 8-36: To fill three text blocks in a chain (top), FreeHand automatically increases the type size and leading values by 120 percent (bottom).

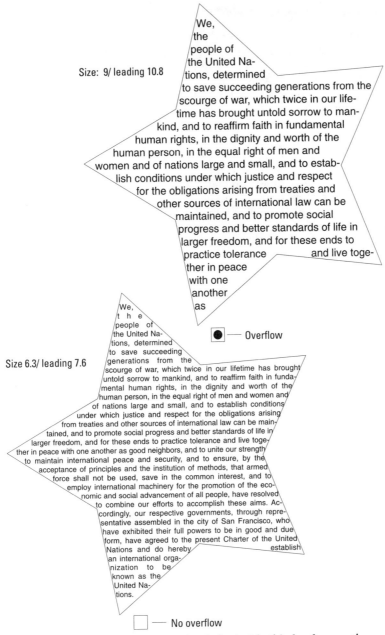

Figure 8-37: To shrink the text so that it fits inside this freeform path without overflowing (top), FreeHand reduces size and leading to 70% (bottom) of their original values.

First-line leading and drop caps

One option inside the Copyfit panel of the Text Inspector that has nothing to do with copyfitting is First Line Leading, which affects the vertical placement of the very first line of type in a story. The value you enter is measured from the top of the text block to the baseline of the first line of type. You have access to the same options as when specifying standard leading; that is, you can enter a value into an option box and select one of three leading types — Extra (+), Fixed (=), or Percentage (%) — from a pop-up menu.

The idea behind this option is that every line of type is spaced from another line of type according to the specified leading. But the first line of type has no preceding line from which to be measured. You can use this option to set up drop caps and prevent tightly leaded text from extending beyond the top of the block. You'll probably only use it once in a blue moon, but when that blue moon occurs, the option comes in pretty handy.

✦   ✦   ✦

Special Text Effects

Aren't We Done with Text Yet?

Chapter 8 provided about 50 reasons why you can feel free to stop using your current page-layout program and rely on FreeHand for small-document creation. In fact, you probably thought that Chapter 8 was so long that there just couldn't be anything more to say about text. But the truth is, you've learned about only some of FreeHand's text-handling features so far. This chapter shows you a few text features that even the most adept page-layout program can't begin to match. As you're about to discover, FreeHand is not only as good at handling text as any page-layout program, it's also much better in the special-effects department.

The ability to put text on a path is a prime example. FreeHand has offered this feature since Version 1. In fact, FreeHand was the second drawing program in Macintosh history to offer text on a path. The first was Cricket Draw, but believe me, the less said on that subject, the better. I almost swore off computers because of that program. (If you haven't noticed already, I have a low threshold for program peculiarities, and that program was one big peculiarity.)

FreeHand lets you wrap text around graphic objects. In other words, if a graphic object intrudes into the space occupied by a text block, the type inside the block can skirt around the graphic according to your specifications. This is the one thing covered in this chapter that you can do in PageMaker and QuarkXPress. But thanks to FreeHand's expert Bézier-curve control, you can create wraps in FreeHand that are much more precise than in those other programs.

FreeHand also enables you to convert characters of text into graphic objects. You can actually edit the shapes of the characters, which is an essential feature if you want to create logos and other customized type treatments. In addition, you can pass along documents to friends and associates who don't use the same fonts as you do, without any fear of typeface mismatches. You aren't likely to find this capability in a page-layout program for the simple reason that such programs don't usually offer the tools required to edit Bézier curves, which are at the heart of all PostScript typefaces. (In case you're curious, FreeHand also converts TrueType faces to Bézier curves, although that's not exactly how they're originally constructed.)

Binding Text to a Path

Just as you can create text inside a path in FreeHand, you can create text on a path. Figure 9-1 shows a path I created using the pen tool and the same path with text bound to it. Notice in the second example that the text adheres to every twist and turn in the path. In fact, the baseline of the text actually becomes the path.

To create text on a path, select the path, choose Text ➪ Attach to Path (⌘/Ctrl-Shift-Y) or click the Attach to Path button on the Text toolbar, and start typing. The text you enter appears on the path. Or if you prefer, you can create the text separately in a standard text block. Then select both the text block and free-form path with the arrow tool and press ⌘/Ctrl-Shift-Y. You can bind text to both open and closed paths, as illustrated in Figures 9-2 and 9-3.

Note

In earlier versions of FreeHand, the Join command allowed you to join text objects in addition to graphic objects. Now, the Join command only joins graphic objects and has no effect on text.

Here are a few quick tidbits of information that you might find useful when binding text to a path:

✦ You can link text on a path to other text objects just as you can a standard text block. As shown in Figure 9-2, text bound to a path does indeed include a link box. If the link box is filled with a black circle, the path contains overflow text that can be linked to another path.

✦ If you drag from a link box to an open path, FreeHand automatically binds the overflow text to that path. If you drag to a closed path, FreeHand fills the path with text, creating a free-form text object. If you want to bind overflow text to a closed path, link it normally so that the text appears inside the path. Then choose Text ➪ Detach From Path or click the Detach From Path button on the Text toolbar to return the text to its original path to its own text block, Shift-click on the closed path with the arrow tool so that both text and path are selected, and press ⌘/Ctrl-Shift-Y to bind the text to the path. The link remains intact throughout.

Figure 9-1: A free-form path before (top) and after (bottom) binding text to it.

✦ A carriage return produces two different effects depending on what kind of path is involved. If you press Return/Enter within text that is bound to a closed path, the carriage return separates type along the top of the path from type along the bottom of the path, as illustrated in Figure 9-3. When you press Return/Enter within text bound to open paths, the characters after the carriage return disappear and are treated as overflow text. A black circle appears inside the link box.

Link box

Figure 9-2: After selecting a standard text block and a path (top), choose the Bind to Path command to force the baseline of the text to follow the path (bottom).

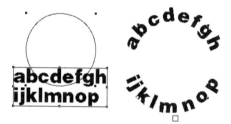

Figure 9-3: When joining text to an ellipse (left), you can use a carriage return to separate type along the top of the ellipse from type along the bottom (right).

✦ Paths composed exclusively of curve and connector points — no corners — are well suited to binding text. When type has to flow around a corner, it may interrupt a word. FreeHand is not smart enough to keep whole words together in path text. Also, type may overlap inside sharp corners. I avoided both these pitfalls back in Figure 9-1 by inserting em and en spaces to spread apart overlapping letters. I also kerned the text between corner points to fit the text exactly.

✦ Unlike Illustrator, FreeHand does not automatically kern text on a path. As a result, the characters spread along convex areas and squeeze together in concave areas. Take another look at Figure 9-2 to see what I mean. To account for this spreading and squeezing, select the characters and kern them manually.

✦ You select text on a path with the text tool in the same ways that you select normal text. But because the characters bob up and down and rotate around, you may find yourself missing a character while clicking or dragging with the text tool and accidentally creating a new text block. If this happens, press ⌘/Ctrl-Z to undo the mistake, and try to keep your patience in check.

Tip

If you keep having problems, especially when trying to position the insertion marker after the last character on the path, click in the middle of a nearby word or on some other easy target. Then use the arrow keys to position the insertion marker exactly where you want it. (Remember Mac users, you can press ⌘/Ctrl-← or ⌘/Ctrl-→ to scoot the insertion marker one word at a time.)

✦ When you bind text to a path, FreeHand hides the stroke of the path by default. You can view the path at any time by switching to the Keyline display mode (⌘/Ctrl-K). To print the path and display it in the Preview mode, select the Show Path check box in the Text on a Path panel in the Object Inspector (⌘/Ctrl-I).

✦ To remove text from a path, select the path and choose Text ⇨ Detach From Path. FreeHand sends the text to a standard text block.

Reshaping a path of bound text

A standard text block is capable of displaying several lines of type. With the exception of text on an ellipse, text bound to a path can only accommodate one line. A word either fits on the path, or it becomes part of the overflow. If the path is too short to accommodate all words bound to it, the excess words fall off the end of the path and the link box displays the familiar black circle, as shown in Figure 9-4.

Figure 9-4: The words *United* and *Nations* refuse to fit on their path and are therefore assigned to overflow.

You have several choices for displaying excess type along a path that's too short:

✦ Reduce the size of the type or kern it more tightly. (Both options are discussed in Chapter 8.)

✦ Edit the text by deleting a few words or characters until it fits on the path.

✦ Link the path to a fellow text object.

✦ Reshape the path by adding points and stretching segments until all text is visible.

To lengthen a path that has type fixed to it, you can drag points and Bézier control handles with the arrow tool. After each drag, FreeHand refits the text to the new shape of the path.

Dragging and converting elements

Suppose that you want to lengthen the path shown in Figure 9-4 so that the missing words fit completely on the path. The following steps demonstrate a few reshaping methods.

1. Click on the path to select it. Then click the rightmost endpoint in the path to select it.

2. Drag the right endpoint, as shown in the first example in Figure 9-5. The type immediately adjusts to follow the altered path, as shown in the second example. (Depending on how you define "immediately," of course. On my machine, it takes several seconds.)

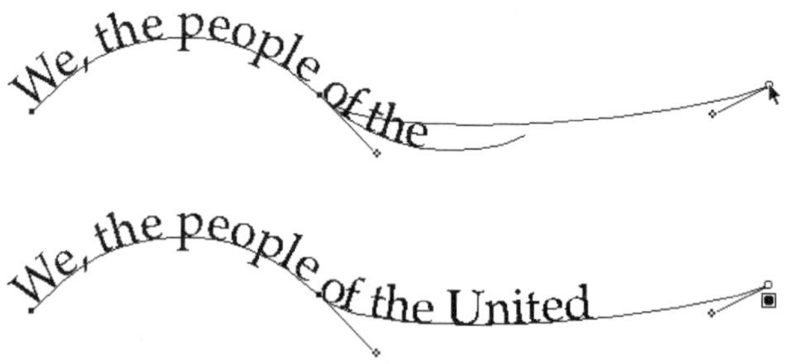

Figure 9-5: After you drag the endpoint of the path (top), FreeHand redraws the text to fit (bottom).

3. Notice that the new path doesn't curve as fluidly or symmetrically as it did in Figure 9-4. To compensate, drag down on the rightmost Bézier control handle to adjust the segment, as shown in Figure 9-6.

You can even change the identity of a point in the path, but it involves slightly more work. For example, the middle point in Figures 9-4 through 9-6 is a curve point. If you select the point and press ⌘/Ctrl-I to display the Object Inspector, FreeHand displays a special panel — called the Text on a Path panel — of bound text options, all of which I will address in just a moment. The familiar point options that you get when reshaping a free-form path are nowhere in sight. To access those options, move on to step 4.

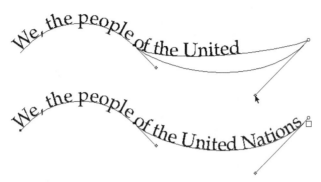

Figure 9-6: You can also drag the control handles associated with type on a path.

4. Click in an empty portion of your document. Then Option/Alt-click on the path with the arrow tool to select the path independently of the text bound to it. Now click the middle point and press ⌘/Ctrl-I to display the more familiar Object Inspector, featured in Figure 9-7.

5. Select the middle of the three Point Type icons to convert the selected curve point to a corner point. You can now drag its Bézier control handles independently, as illustrated in Figure 9-7.

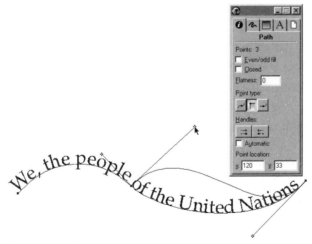

Figure 9-7: After converting the middle point from a curve point to a corner point, you can drag the control handles independently of each other to create a cusp in the path.

Tip

Remember, to access any of the point-by-point options available to free-form paths in the Object Inspector, you have to select the path independently of the text by Option/Alt-clicking on it.

Other reshaping options and limitations

FreeHand does not let you use certain reshaping techniques with bound text. The following rules cover what you can and cannot do.

You can do the following:

✦ You can extend an open text path using any of the free-form drawing tools. Figure 9-8, for example, shows the result of dragging from the endpoint of a line of bound text with the freehand tool.

✦ You can insert a point into a path of bound text using the bézigon or pen tool.

However, you can't do the following:

✦ You can't use the Join command to join an open path with bound text to another open path — bound text or no bound text.

✦ You can't create a break in a path of bound text by clicking or dragging with the knife tool or by choosing the Split command.

✦ And, as you may have already guessed, you can't apply any of the commands under the Modify ⇨ Alter Path submenu to a path with text all over it.

If you want to use any of the techniques mentioned in the preceding three bullets to reshape a path, you must first remove the text from the path by choosing Text ⇨ Detach From Path. After you make your changes to the path, recombine the text and path by selecting them both and choosing Text ⇨ Attach To Path.

Vertical distribution of path text

When you first join a line of type to a path, the text is joined by its baseline. Just in case you need a refresher, the baseline is the imaginary line on which characters sit, as illustrated on the top Figure 9-9. The figure also shows the *ascender* and *descender* lines, which mark the tops of tall letters (*b, d, f,* and so on) and the bottoms of hangy-down ones (*g, j, p,* and others). When you bind text to a path, these ascender and descender lines bend with the path just as surely as the baseline (check out the second example in the figure).

Figure 9-8: By dragging from an endpoint in an open path of bound text with the freehand tool (top), you can extend the length of the path and make room for more text (bottom).

Ascender

Baseline

Descender

Figure 9-9: When you join the text to a path, the baseline, ascender line, and descender line (top) curve to follow the exact form of the path (bottom).

You can change the way your text sits on a path by opting for a different *vertical distribution*, which adheres characters to the path by their ascenders or descenders instead of by the baseline. FreeHand calls this concept *text alignment* (a bit of misnomer). To access the Text Alignment options (the ones that I would call *vertical distribution options*), select the path that holds your text and press ⌘/Ctrl-I. FreeHand displays the specialized Object Inspector shown in Figure 9-10. For reasons I'll never divulge, I call this the Text on a Path panel. The Top pop-up menu offers access to three Text Alignment options (four, if you include None). The Bottom pop-up menu provides the same options, but is only applicable to text on an ellipse, as explained later.

Figure 9-10: The Text on a Path panel of the Object Inspector provides access to three Text Alignment options in both the Top and Bottom pop-up menus.

By way of example, suppose that you want to create two lines of type that follow the same path, but place one above the path and one below it. This is a job for the Ascent and Descent options. Try it out for yourself by working your way through the following steps.

1. Create two text blocks of related information. One block of text will ride on top of the path, the other underneath.

2. Draw a free-form path similar to the one shown in Figure 9-11. You need one path for each text block, but you want the two paths to be identical. Select the path and choose Edit ⇨ Clone (⌘-= on Macs and Ctrl-Shift-C on PCs). FreeHand creates a duplicate of the path directly in front of the original.

Armed force shall not be used

save in the common interest.

Figure 9-11: After creating two text blocks, draw a free-form path and clone it, providing identical paths for both text blocks.

3. Using the arrow tool, Shift-click in the first text block to add it to the current selection.

4. Press ⌘/Ctrl-Shift-Y (Text ⇨ Attach To Path) to bind the first block of text to the path.

5. Press ⌘/Ctrl-B or choose Modify ⇨ Arrange ⇨ Send to Back to place the bound text behind all other objects in the illustration.

6. Press Tab to deselect the bound text. Click on the remaining path and Shift-click in the second text block to select both objects.

7. Press ⌘/Ctrl-Shift-Y again. The second text block binds to its path, overlapping the first text and its path. This makes for an extremely illegible effect, as shown in Figure 9-12.

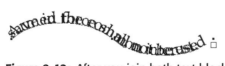

Figure 9-12: After you join both text blocks to their paths, the two lines of type overlap.

8. Press ⌘/Ctrl-I to display the Text on a Path panel of the Object Inspector. The selected path contains the second line of type, which should be positioned below the first line of type. With this in mind, select the Ascent option from the Top pop-up menu. FreeHand then adheres the uppermost boundary of the characters to the path.

9. Press ⌘/Ctrl-K to switch to the Keyline mode so that you can see the paths. Then ⌘/Ctrl-click on the path that contains the *second* line of type to select the path that contains the *first* line of type. (As you may recall from Chapter 6, ⌘/Ctrl -clicking selects the object in back of the previously selected object.)

10. To position the selected line of type above its path, select the Descent option from the Top pop-up menu in the Text on a Path panel. The result appears in Figure 9-13.

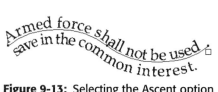

Figure 9-13: Selecting the Ascent option forces the second line of type downward; selecting the Descent option forces the first line upward.

Tip

The Top and Bottom options in the Text on a Path panel in the Object Inspector move text vertically with respect to a path in three gross increments. But you can also fine-tune the Text Alignment you've chosen in the Text on a Path panel by using baseline shift. To take advantage of this feature, select some text with the text tool and press ⌘/Ctrl-Option/Alt-↑ to raise the text in 1-point increments; press ⌘/Ctrl-Option/Alt-↓ to lower the text by a point. Or enter a value into the Baseline Shift option in the Character panel of Text Inspector (⌘/Ctrl-T) and press Return/Enter. (Positive values shift the text upward; negative values shift it downward.)

In Figure 9-14, I shifted the words *Armed force* and *save in the* 12 points above the baseline. I also shifted the words *be used* and *interest* 12 points downward.

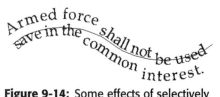

Figure 9-14: Some effects of selectively applying baseline shift to bound text.

Type on an ellipse

Because folks have expressed more interest in joining text to circles and ovals than to any other kinds of shapes, FreeHand provides some special options for type on an ellipse. If you have a keen memory, you'll recall that earlier I mentioned that you can use a carriage return to separate type along the top of an ellipse from type along the bottom of the ellipse. (Look back at Figure 9-3 if your synapses need a jog.)

FreeHand also allows you to manipulate these two portions of text separately. After you join type to an ellipse, press ⌘/Ctrl-I to display the Text on a Path panel in the Object Inspector. Here, you can access Text Alignment settings for both the upper and lower lines of type by selecting options from the Top and Bottom submenus.

Characters before the carriage return ride the top of the ellipse; characters after the carriage return hang from the bottom. To create the text shown in Figure 9-15, press the Return/Enter key after entering *Something* (and before entering *Incredible*). By default, the top text is aligned by its descent line and the bottom text is aligned by its ascent line (as you can see in the panel in the figure). This ensures that both lines of type align with each other exactly.

Figure 9-15: The first word is aligned by its descent line and the second by its ascent line.

There's really no reason to change these settings unless you want to position the text inside the ellipse rather than outside it. To accomplish this, select Ascent from the Top pop-up menu in the Text on a Path panel of the Object Inspector and then select Descent from the Bottom pop-up menu. You'll also need to increase your kerning dramatically to account for FreeHand's extreme character crowding.

Changing the orientation

In addition to the Text Alignment options, the Text on a Path panel of the Object Inspector offers an Orientation pop-up menu with four options that control the angle of individual characters as they follow a path. Figure 9-16 shows how each option affects a sample path of text.

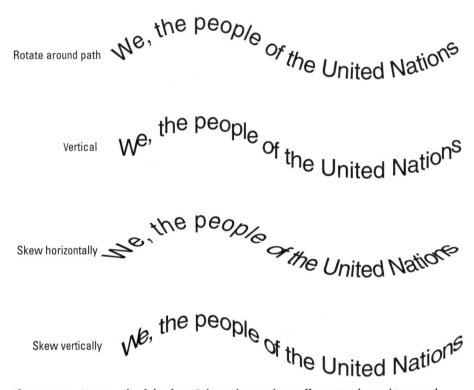

Figure 9-16: How each of the four Orientation options affects text bound to a path.

The Orientation options work as follows:

✦ **Rotate Around Path:** The baseline of each character is tangent to its position on the path. In English, that means that characters tilt back and forth as the path twists and turns. This option—the default setting—is far and away the most common, the most legible, and the most useful.

✦ **Vertical:** Though the baseline curves with the path, each character is positioned straight up and down, as it would appear if it were in a standard text block. Characters frequently overlap when you select this worst of all possible options.

✦ **Skew Horizontally:** When you select this option, characters slant with the inclination of the path. Though the name of this option implies that the type slants only horizontally, letters may slant both horizontally and vertically, like slats in a Japanese fan.

✦ **Skew Vertically:** This option results in vertical skewing only and is useful for creating exciting three-dimensional effects such as those shown in Figure 9-17. Characters remain upright instead of leaning from side to side, ensuring limited overlap (if any). Select this option any time you're tempted to select Vertical. In fact, it's second only to Rotate Around Path in usefulness.

How formatting affects bound text

I've discussed the effect of baseline shift on bound text, but what about other formatting options? It depends on which option you want to use. Type size, for example, has the same effect on bound text as it does on standard text blocks. But leading has no effect because most paths can't accommodate two lines of text, and those that can don't permit you to specify a numerical distance between the two lines. The following list explains how FreeHand's formatting attributes affect text bound to a path.

✦ **Font, style, type size, and horizontal scale:** These attributes affect bound text the same way they do text in a standard text block. Select the characters you want to change and format away.

✦ **Leading:** Leading has no effect whatsoever on bound text.

✦ **Kerning:** When creating standard text blocks, you may want to try out kerning occasionally. But when you're binding text to a path, kerning is a must. If a path contains any bumps and dips, your text will look like heck—and I do mean heck—until you kern it.

✦ **Baseline shift:** Use baseline shift to move text up and down with respect to the path.

✦ **Keep on Same Line and Lines Together:** These options—one from the Character panel and the other from Paragraph—just make more text fall off into the overflow pile. Don't mess with them.

✦ **Stylistic effects:** You can apply the highlight, inline, shadow, strikethrough, or underline style to bound text without any problem. The zoom effect, however, evaluates each character independently and results in shadows that overlap neighboring characters. Besides, it's ugly and it takes forever to print. Don't just avoid the zoom effect; run away from it screaming.

Figure 9-17: Vertically skewed type can be useful for creating 3-D effects, such as type around a globe.

✦ **Paragraph spacing:** Like leading, paragraph spacing doesn't work with bound text.

✦ **Tabs and indents:** FreeHand treats tab characters in bound text exactly like carriage returns, and you can't even access tab stops. You can change indents, however, using the options in the Paragraph panel, which have the effect of pushing text farther along on the path.

✦ **Rules:** You can apply rules, but they won't have any effect.

✦ **Word spacing and letterspacing:** These options work just as explained in Chapter 8. But you're better off sticking with kerning, which enables you to make more precise changes.

✦ **Hyphenation:** This will only result in hyphenating the last word of text bound to a path as it flows into a text block. But I can't imagine any reason you'd actually *want* to use hyphens in bound text.

✦ **Alignment:** The alignment options in the Character panel of the Text Inspector have a big effect on text bound to a path. Normally, when you bind text, FreeHand aligns it flush left with the first point in the path. The exception is text on an ellipse, which is automatically centered. You can, however, change the alignment of any path to flush left, center, or flush right. If you select the Justification icon, FreeHand spreads the text across the entire length of the path.

✦ **Block-level formatting and copyfitting:** These options aren't available when you're formatting bound text. Although it wouldn't make much sense to use columns and rows in bound text, it's too bad you can't access the copyfitting options. They could come in especially handy for fitting overly long text to a path.

Horizontal alignment and direction

Before I close my discussion of bound text, I need to prepare you for a couple of things that can go wrong. Text on an ellipse is basically never a problem because FreeHand automatically centers the first line along the top and the second line along the bottom. But text on other kinds of paths can experience two problems. The text can start at the wrong point in a closed path, and it can flow in the wrong direction along both open and closed paths.

The best way to demonstrate these problems is by way of an example. Suppose that you want to join the text block and path shown in Figure 9-18 in order to create a logo like the one shown in Figure 9-19. (I inserted em spaces between the words *Hills* and *Research* to account for the valley in the path.)

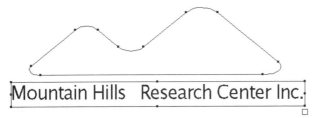

Figure 9-18: A closed path and a block of text just itching to be bound to it.

Figure 9-19: The results of binding text and path.

But just because you want your text to look like Figure 9-19 doesn't make it so. Type begins at the first point in the path, and it flows in the same direction that the path flows. For example, in the case of an ellipse, the direction of a path is clockwise, so text on an ellipse reads in a clockwise direction. The direction of a free-form path is determined by the order in which you added points with the pen or bézigon tool or the direction in which you drew the path with the freehand or line tool.

Unless the leftmost point in the path from Figure 9-18 was the first point created, the text doesn't bind as shown in Figure 9-19. Figure 9-20 shows how the text binds if the top point is the first one in the path. And when the path is drawn in a counterclockwise direction, things get even weirder. The text flows inside the path rather than outside it and also appears upside down, as shown in Figure 9-21.

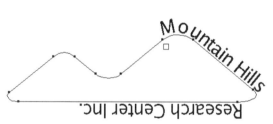

Figure 9-20: Type may begin at an undesirable point in a path.

Figure 9-21: If the path was drawn counterclockwise, the type flows in an undesirable direction.

Both problems are easily remedied. The following steps show how to establish a different first point in a closed path, correcting the situation of Figure 9-20.

1. First, confirm that the text is aligned flush left by displaying the Character panel of the Text Inspector (⌘/Ctrl-T) and make sure that the first Alignment icon is selected. This alone may be enough to align the text the way you want it.

2. But if it isn't, choose ⌘/Ctrl-I to display the Text on a Path panel of the Object Inspector. Use the Inset options at the bottom of the panel to adjust the positioning of the text on the path. The values are in the current ruler units. Edit the value in the Left option box for left-aligned text or edit the Right option box value for right-aligned text.

If the text is flowing on the inside rather than the outside of the path, these steps solve only half of your problem. To change the direction of a path, thereby remedying the problem of Figure 9-21, do the following:

1. Press Tab to deselect the text bound to a path, as well as everything else in your illustration.

2. Option/Alt-click on the path — not the text — with the arrow tool to select the path independently of the text. (If you can't see the path, switch to the Keyline mode by pressing ⌘/Ctrl-K.)

3. Choose Reverse Direction from either the Modify ⇨ Alter Path ⇨ Reverse Direction or the Xtras ⇨ Cleanup submenu. You can also click the Reverse Direction icon from the Operations panel. FreeHand changes the direction of the path and reflows the text in a clockwise direction. The Correct Direction command would also fulfill this purpose.

Wrapping Text in and around Graphics

Yea, that's it for text on a path! Now onward to wrapping text in and around graphic objects, a feature that allows a graphic to sit inside a text block without the two overlapping and creating a great big illegible mess. You can also put text wrapped within a closed path using the path as a boundary.

First, let's wrap some text around graphics. Using FreeHand's wrapping feature, you can flow type around the boundaries of one or more graphic objects, as shown in Figure 9-22. Using the Standoff Distances options in the Run Around Selection dialog box (displayed by choosing Text ⇨ Run Around Selection), you can even specify the minimum distance between type and graphic objects.

We, the people of the United Nations, determined to save succeeding generations from the scourge of war, which twice in our lifetime has brought untold sorrow to mankind, and to reaffirm faith in fundamental human rights, in the dignity and worth of the human person, in the equal right of men and women and of nations large and small, and to establish conditions under which justice and respect for the obligations arising from treaties and other sources of international law can be maintained, and to promote social progress and better standards of life in larger freedom, and for these ends to practice tolerance and live together in peace with one another as good neighbors, and to unite our strength to maintain international peace and security, and to ensure, by the acceptance of principles and the institution of methods, that armed force shall not be used, save in the common interest, and to employ international machinery for the promotion of the economic and social advancement of all people, have resolved to combine our efforts to accomplish these aims. Accordingly, our respective governments, through representative assembled in the city of San Francisco, who have exhibited their full powers to be in good and due form, have agreed to the present Charter of the United Nations and do hereby establish an international organization to be known as the United Nations.

Figure 9-22: In FreeHand, you can wrap type around the boundaries of one or more graphic objects.

The following steps explain how to wrap text around graphic objects in FreeHand.

1. Determine which text block you want to wrap. (Generally, this technique is better suited to text inside blocks and other objects than text bound to a path.)

2. Select the graphic objects around which you want your text to wrap and position them relative to the text block. The whale in the figure comprises ten free-form paths. You don't have to group the objects, nor should you. FreeHand is perfectly capable of wrapping text around multiple objects, but it can't wrap around a group.

3. Choose Modify ➪ Arrange ➪ Bring To Front (⌘/Ctrl-F). The graphic objects must be in front of the text block to wrap properly.

4. Choose the Run Around Selection command from the Text menu or press ⌘/Ctrl-Option/Alt-W to display the dialog box shown in Figure 9-23.

Figure 9-23: Click the icon on the right to wrap text around the selected graphics.

5. Select the right icon at the top of the dialog box. This icon instructs FreeHand to wrap text around all selected objects. The Standoff option boxes appear when you select the icon.

6. Enter values into the option boxes to define the amount of space between the graphic and the text surrounding it, called the *standoff*. To create the wrap shown back in Figure 9-22, I entered small Left and Right values but set the Top and Bottom values to 0 (as in Figure 9-23). FreeHand applies these values according to the current unit of measure. Press the Return/Enter key to apply your changes.

Text wrapping can be a frustrating prospect. You have to play around with it for a long time before you get it right. You'll probably find yourself dragging the paths around to see where they look best. (Each time you drag the paths, FreeHand automatically readjusts any overlapping text to wrap around them. This happens because wrapping is an attribute assigned to the graphic objects, not to the text.) You'll no doubt have to experiment with the values inside the Run Around Selection dialog box a few times as well. Too bad FreeHand's programmers didn't think to include an Apply button so that you could try out values without leaving the dialog box.

When you are more or less happy with the standoff, go ahead and group the objects if you like. By grouping the objects, you can more easily select them later without clicking and Shift-clicking repeatedly. FreeHand can retain your text wrapping settings after you apply the Group command; however, you can't apply new standoff values to a group.

If you decide later that you want to change the standoff, select the group, ungroup it, choose Text ⇨ Run Around Selection, and make your adjustments. After the standoff problems are remedied, regroup the paths.

Alignment and spacing

The Run Around Selection command is pretty straightforward. What's not straightforward is getting your results to look moderately attractive. Here are a few rules of thumb:

✦ **Justify your text.** This ensures that the text is equally close to the left edges of your graphic objects as it is to the right edges. If you format the text flush left, FreeHand typically allows relatively large gaps to form to the left of the graphics. You can compensate by entering a negative value into the Left option box in the Run Around Selection dialog box, but that sometimes results in the text overlapping the graphics.

✦ **Raise the ragged width value.** If you absolutely have to use flush-left text, at least bump up the value in the Ragged Width % option in the Edit Alignment dialog box of the Character panel of the Text Inspector. Use a value in the neighborhood of 90 percent. This setting gives your text a looser look without permitting large gaps. Figure 9-24 shows close-ups of the text from Figure 9-22 aligned flush left. In the first example, the Ragged Width % value is set to 0; in the right example, the value is set to 90. I've added a gray bar to emphasize the difference. The effect of the high Ragged Width % value is subtle, but it helps make the gap look less arbitrary.

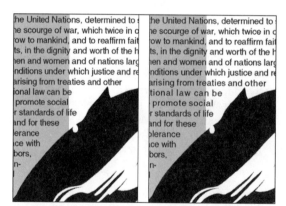

Figure 9-24: Wrapped, flush-left text subject to a Ragged Width % value of 0 (left) and 90 (right).

✦ **Increase the letterspacing.** FreeHand's default letterspacing and word spacing values result in huge gaps between words, while the letterspacing remains relatively tight. If you raise the Max value in the Letter column in the Spacing panel of the Text Inspector to about 150 percent, you'll get better results.

✦ **Turn on automatic hyphenation.** By all means select the Hyphenation check box in the Paragraph panel of the Text Inspector. This provides FreeHand with greater latitude when breaking words between lines and around the graphic.

Establishing a standoff dummy

You can also establish a standoff by creating a special path to act as a dummy for the actual graphic object. Make the fill and stroke of this path transparent (by selecting None from the pop-up menus in the Fill and Stroke Inspectors, as described in Chapters 11 and 12). This way, the path will be invisible when previewed or printed.

You then wrap the type around the invisible path rather than around the graphic objects. Select the standoff dummy in the Keyline mode (so that you can see it) and use the Run Around Selection command to make text wrap around it. Then position the graphic object as desired. This technique offers more flexibility than wrapping text around the actual objects, because you can reshape the standoff dummy to change the gaps between text and graphics without affecting the appearance of the graphics one whit.

When working with a standoff dummy, justify the text and set all the Standoff option values in the Run Around Selection dialog box to 0. The text will abut right up against the dummy, making your edits more predictable.

Unwrapping text blocks

To allow text to cover your graphic objects, select the objects, press ⌘/Ctrl-Option/Alt-W, and select the left icon in the Run Around Selection dialog box. Then press the Return/Enter key. You can turn off the text wrap for a single path at a time or all paths at once. At the risk of stating the obvious, you turn off the text wrap for a standoff dummy in the same way.

Wrapping text inside a graphic

If you want to flow text inside a path, it is simply a click away. Select a text block and a path, then choose Flow Inside Path from the Text menu (⌘/Ctrl-Shift-U) or use the Flow Inside Path button on the Text toolbar. Text flowed inside a closed path starts at the top of the path and flows to its edges. The path acts as a boundary. Use the Inset options at the bottom of the Object Inspector to specify how far the text is inset from the edge of the path. You can edit the text flowed inside a path directly without removing it from the path. The text can be rotated, reflected, scaled and skewed. To unflow the text choose Text ➪ Detach From Path. It's that easy. Saying any more about this feature would simply be wasting valuable space so let's continue on with the final text command.

Converting Type to Paths

If you're interested in creating logos or other very specialized character outlines, you need to know about this last command. By choosing the Convert to Paths command from the Text menu (⌘/Ctrl-Shift-P) or the Convert to Paths button on the Text toolbar, you convert any selected text block into a collection of editable paths. For FreeHand to successfully implement the Convert to Paths command, the following conditions must be met:

✦ The selected type must be set in a PostScript or TrueType font.

✦ The printer font for the current typeface must be available to your system software.

The first example in Figure 9-25 shows a three-character text block set in Helvetica Black and selected using the arrow tool. The second example shows the characters after I chose the Convert to Paths command. The characters are now grouped paths. If you ungroup the selection by pressing ⌘/Ctrl-U, you can access the individual character outlines.

Figure 9-25: Select the text block with the arrow tool (top) and press ⌘/Ctrl-Shift-P to convert the characters to a group of editable paths.

If a character contains more than one outline, FreeHand converts it to a composite path, which permits some outlines to create holes in the outline behind them. For example, the ampersand (&) in Figure 9-25 has been converted into three outlines. The fact that these outlines have been combined into a composite path allows the two interior outlines to cut transparent holes into the larger, outer outline behind them. This enables you to see through the character to paths behind it, as discussed in Chapter 15.

To reshape a composite path, you first have to Option/Alt-click on it with the arrow tool. The four corner handles disappear, and all points and segments in the selected path display. You can now manipulate these points just as if they belonged to a standard path. To select multiple paths in a composite path, Shift-Option/Alt-click each additional path. Figure 9-26 shows the result of selecting the outlines of the converted letters from Figure 9-25.

Figure 9-26: Here the *T* and *G* are expressed as standard paths; the ampersand is a composite path because it includes two holes.

After you convert the characters to paths, you can edit them using any of the techniques described in Chapter 5. The final logo doesn't have to bear any resemblance to the original characters. My completed logo appears in Figure 9-27. I retained the basic shape of the *T*, reshaped the *G* considerably, and completely altered the shape of the ampersand. After you convert a few characters of your own, you'll soon discover that converted text is as easy to integrate and edit as any line or shape drawn with the freehand or pen tool.

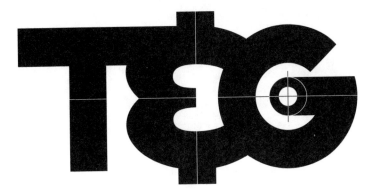

Figure 9-27: The logo for my little company, based on the font Helvetica Black.

After you convert your text to paths, you can't go back and edit it. So before choosing Text ⇨ Convert to Paths, make sure that your text is in the desired font, type size, and so on. And for heaven's sake, check your spelling. Of course, if you spot an error right after converting the characters to paths, you can undo the conversion and correct the problem.

✦   ✦   ✦

Applying Color and Form

◆ ◆ ◆ ◆

◆ ◆ ◆ ◆

Defining Colors and Styles

Color Me Beautiful

In this chapter, I cover automatic name-coding of colors.
This is the best kind of advancement — it doesn't change your
color modus operandi one bit. After you become accustomed
to having this feature around, you'll learn to truly love it —
wonder how you ever lived without it, even.

Chapter 11 covers commands for manipulating colors of
existing objects. These commands are fun. Being able to
quickly shade multiple objects lets you produce some
interesting shadows, and the commands are a great vehicle for
creating some nice custom panels.

Well, now that I have thoroughly whetted your appetite for
color information, we'll start off with a discussion of monitors.

Displaying Colors On-screen

FreeHand's color capabilities are available to anyone who can
run the software; they aren't limited by the monitor you use or
by the printer on which you proof your work. When you're
using a monochrome or grayscale monitor, for example,
FreeHand substitutes colors with corresponding shades of
gray. It's like a black-and-white television that displays *The
Wizard of Oz* as if Dorothy never quite got out of Kansas. But
just because you don't see the colors doesn't mean that they
aren't there.

When you use a color monitor, FreeHand takes full advantage of it and displays as many colors as your monitor allows, depending on the sophistication of your computer's video capabilities. Most computer systems that you can buy off the shelf can display up to 24 million colors, provided that you have upgraded the computer to its maximum 2MB of VRAM. (VRAM — or *video RAM* — is a special kind of memory designed specifically to enhance video display.)

The size of your monitor has an inverse effect on the number of colors your computer can display, because the computer has to hold the entire screen image in memory at any one time. More colors take up more space in VRAM, as do more screen pixels. If you increase the size of the monitor, the computer has to deal with a larger number of screen pixels. To make room in VRAM, it cuts back on the number of colors it displays. For example, equipped with original factory VRAM, the LC could display 256 colors on a 10-inch monitor and only 16 colors on a 13-inch monitor. Most desktop computers top out at 2MB of VRAM, which is enough to display 16 million colors on 16-inch screens and smaller, and 32,000 colors on larger devices.

Bit depths

VRAM enables your computer to devote a certain amount of data to each pixel on the monitor, as measured in bits. A *bit* is the absolute smallest unit of measurement. It may be either 0 or 1, off or on. For this reason, the number of colors your screen can display is called the *bit depth*. For example:

✦ **1-bit:** If a computer devotes only 1 bit per pixel, the result is a black-and-white screen display. Each pixel is either off or on, white or black.

✦ **4-bit:** That's 2 to the 4th power, or 16 colors, each of which is a *gray value* — a shade of gray. In other words, you see only variations of gray, not blues, greens, reds, and so on. This display is more appealing because you get smoother color transitions.

✦ **8-bit:** Any Mac or PC with a built-in video port lets you access at least 256 colors (2 to the 8th power). If you use an 8-bit screen, be sure to turn on the Dither 8-bit Colors option in the Colors category of the Preferences dialog box.

✦ **16-bit:** You would think that 16-bit video translates to 2 to the 16th power, or 65,536 colors. But 16-bit and higher video signals must divide evenly into thirds — one each for the red, green, and blue color channels (hence *RGB video*). So the video card devotes 15 bits to color (5 bits per channel) and reserves the leftover bit for color overlay. In practice, therefore, you get only 32,768 colors (2 to the 15th power).

✦ **24-bit:** Most folks need to purchase a separate 24-bit (or *full-color*) video board to access the 16 million-color range (2 to the 24th power = 16,777,216 colors).

Preparing your color monitor

You change the number of colors that your computer shows on-screen by using the Monitors control panel. To access the control panel, either choose Apple ⇨ Control Panels (on Macs) or Taskbar Start ⇨ Settings ⇨ Control Panels (on Windows), which displays the Control Panels folder. Then double-click the Monitors icon (Macs) or the Display icon (Windows) in the directory window. On a Mac, the Monitors & Sound control panel appears, as shown on the left in Figure 10-1 — select the number of colors you want to display from the Color Depth scrolling list. On a Windows machine, the Display Properties dialog box appears — click the Settings panel and then select the number of colors from the Color Palette, as shown on the right in Figure 10-1. The system software immediately changes the number of colors displayed on-screen. Click the Close/OK button to accept your changes.

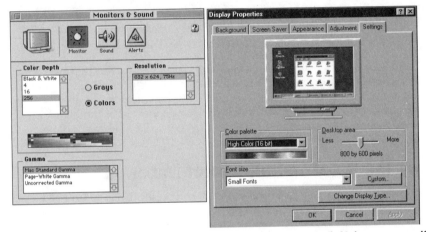

Figure 10-1: The Monitors & Sound control panel on a Mac (left) lets you specify the number of colors that can be displayed simultaneously on your monitor. The Settings panel of the Display Properties control panel (right) is the Windows' counterpart.

If your computer can handle 256 or fewer colors, set the bit depth to its maximum. If your computer can handle 32,000 or 16 million colors, you probably want to change the bit depth periodically while working in FreeHand. Screen colors best match printed colors when you use 24-bit color, but using fewer colors can significantly speed screen display. Third-party video boards sometimes supply shortcuts so that you can change bit depths without having to repeatedly display the Monitors & Sound or Display Properties control panel.

Creating and Organizing Colors

FreeHand's color capabilities have always been a little difficult to understand, but they've seen slow but steady improvement. The first drawing program to offer color, FreeHand 1 supplied an entire menu devoted exclusively to defining colors. The arrangement was needlessly complicated and involved a lot of to-ing and fro-ing between dialog boxes. FreeHand 3 simplified things greatly by introducing a Colors panel and integrating all color-definition functions into a single dialog box. But the interface didn't always make sense when you applied colors, especially to gradations.

FreeHand 4 introduced drag-and-drop colors, which means you can actually drag a color directly onto an object. This feature makes applying colors much easier. But it relies on two panels—Color List and Color Mixer—where a panel and a dialog box used to suffice. I hoped that FreeHand 5 would sport a single panel with easy access to all color application and definition functions. Unfortunately, it only merged the Tints panel into the Color Mixer.

FreeHand 8 allows you to combine the Color List panel, the Color Mixer panel, and the Tints panel using the tear-off panels feature. This places all of the color controls in one panel sporting three panels, although you can't access all of the controls at once. However, that's a minor inconvenience when viewed in the big picture of what FreeHand has done to facilitate using color in the world of bytes and mice.

Using the Color List and Color Mixer panels

The central headquarters for FreeHand's coloring options is the Color List panel, which appears labeled to the gills in Figure 10-2. To display this panel, press ⌘/Ctrl-9. From the panel, you can fill objects, stroke objects, name colors, and arrange colors created in the Color Mixer panel.

The following items explain how to perform a few general operations from this panel. Later sections in this chapter explain many operations in greater detail.

✦ **Filling an object:** Select the object, click the Fill icon, and click a color name in the scrolling color list. (You have to click a name; clicking the color swatch itself produces no effect.) Or, you can drag a color swatch from the panel and drop it onto an object.

✦ **Stroking an object:** Again, you select the object, click the Stroke icon, and click a color name in the scrolling list. You can also drag from a color swatch and drop it onto the outline of a path, though this can be a little tricky.

Fill icon
Stroke icon
Both icon   New Color icon

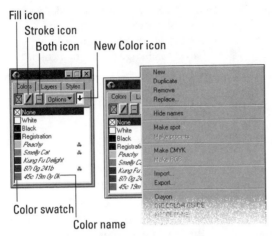

Color swatch

Color name

Figure 10-2: The Color List panel with the Options menu hidden (left) and displayed (right).

✦ **Stroking and filling:** When a selected object's stroke and fill are different colors, the Both selector displays a —. Drag your desired color over the Both selector and both the stroke and fill will be the same.

✦ **Creating a new color:** Select the New option from the Options pop-up menu to take the color you have mixed defined in the Color Mixer panel and make it a new item in the scrolling list. FreeHand automatically assigns the color a name that lists its RGB or CMYK values — for example, 75r 100g 25b or 0c 23m 65y 0k. Whether FreeHand names the color by its RGB or CMYK values depends upon your setting in the Color Mixer panel.

✦ **Cloning a color:** Click a color name in the scrolling list and select the Duplicate option from the Options pop-up menu to clone a color. Or just drag a swatch from the scrolling list to the New Color icon. You can then rename the color and edit it, if desired.

✦ **Renaming a color:** Double-click a color name to highlight it, enter the new name from the keyboard, and press Return/Enter. Make sure to deselect all paths before double-clicking in the Color List to avoid changing the color of a selected object. You cannot rename the White, Black, None, or Registration colors. (For more information on Registration, see Chapter 18.)

✦ **Editing a color:** To change a named color in the list — as well as all objects filled or stroked with that color — ⌘/Ctrl-click the color swatch to transfer the color to the Color Mixer panel. (This assumes that the Color Mixer panel is available. If it's not, double-click the color swatch.) Then edit the color as desired and drag it from the Color Mixer panel onto the color swatch in the scrolling color list, as demonstrated in Figure 10-3.

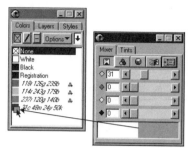

Figure 10-3: Drag from the color area in the Color Mixer panel onto an existing color swatch in the scrolling color list to change the named color.

✦ **Rearranging the order:** To change the order of names in the scrolling color list, drag a name up or down in the list.

✦ **Deleting a color:** First, deselect all objects. Then click a color name in the scrolling list and select Remove from the Options pop-up menu to delete the color. If an object is filled or stroked with the color, or if the color is part of a *tint* or *style* (both defined later in this chapter), FreeHand warns you that you're about to delete a color that's in use.

✦ **Getting a color back:** You can retrieve a deleted color — or undo any other color operation — by pressing ⌘/Ctrl-Z.

✦ **Hiding color names:** You can hide the names of the colors by choosing Hide Names from the Options pop-up menu. This results in a panel of color swatches resembling an aerial view of a crayon box. Kind of cute but not real useful.

Naming colors

My vote for FreeHand's most impressive feature is its automatic naming of new colors. We're not talking about names like Mary or Jim, either. FreeHand generates a color name comprising either the color's RGB or CMYK values. Consider this automatic generation as a name-coding of all colors in a document's Color List panel.

Name-coding colors is a powerful feature. Several commands based on this feature appear in FreeHand. These are located in the Xtras ⇨ Colors submenu.

✦ **Name All Colors:** Names all colors in the Color List. When you import a color panel, this command is a quick way to generate name codes for all the colors at once.

✦ **Randomize Named Colors:** Randomly changes the values of all colors in the Color List (other than None, Black, White, and Registration). Maybe you'll find this command useful. It's a little too pet-rockish for my taste.

✦ **Sort Color List by Name:** Reorganizes the Color List's contents by name. One would think that, due to the character of name-coding, sorting by name would list all of the components in numerical order, leading to a nice spectral progression. Not so! For example, when colors are named by their CMYK components, FreeHand first lists all the 100 cyans, next lists the 10–19 cyans, then the 1 cyans, followed by the 20–29 cyans, and so on.

✦ **Delete Unused Named Colors:** Deletes all colors in the Color List that have not been applied to an object in the document. OK, I lied earlier when I wrote that all of these commands are in the Xtras ⇨ Colors submenu. I meant all but this one, which is in the Xtras ⇨ Delete submenu.

If you change the color, its name changes as well. If your color names do not update correctly, then somehow the Auto-Rename Changed Colors option got disabled in the Colors panel of the Preferences dialog box.

Dragging (and dropping) colors

In FreeHand, you can drag a color swatch from a panel and drop it onto an object or another color swatch in some other panel. To *drop* a color, incidentally, simply means to release the mouse button over a target. For example, if you were creating a flier for a dinner theater production of *Dumbo*, and your boss told you to drag the color pink and drop it onto a drawing of an elephant, you would drag the pink color swatch, position it over the elephant, and release the mouse button. It's like a little color bomb. *Feeeooo kaboom.* One pachyderm made psychedelic.

This drag-and-drop technique has two advantages: first, you can transfer colors between panels quickly; second, you can apply colors to objects without first selecting them. The limitation of dragging and dropping is that you can only color one object at a time. If you want to change multiple objects, select them, click the Fill or Stroke icon, and click a color name in the scrolling list.

Personally, I think that the term *drag and drop* is a waste of words. Why say "Drag A and drop it onto B" when you can say "Drag A onto B" and save a few words? With that in mind, the following list describes a few ways to drag color swatches in FreeHand. Unless otherwise noted, these techniques work for dragging colors from any panel, including the Color List and Color Mixer panels, as well as the Fill and Stroke Inspectors.

✦ **Filling paths:** Drag a color from any panel into the middle of a closed path to fill the path with that color.

✦ **Filling type:** Drag a color swatch onto a text character to fill the type. If no type is selected, the color fills all characters in the text block. If one or more characters are selected with the text tool, only the selected characters are filled.

✦ **Filling a text block:** Drag a color swatch and drop it inside a text block — but not directly onto a character — to change the color of the interior of the text block. If the text block is active, you will not see your changes until you deselect the block.

✦ **Filling with a directional gradation:** Drag a color swatch and press the ⌘/Ctrl key before dropping the color to change a flat fill to a gradient fill. Use the same process to change the direction of an existing gradient fill. This technique does not work with characters of type, but it does work with text blocks. Just be sure to select the text block with the arrow tool.

✦ **Filling with a radial gradation:** Press the Option/Alt key before dropping the color to change the fill to a radial gradation or change the center of an existing radial gradation. The same limitations that apply to directional gradations govern radial ones.

✦ **Changing to a flat fill:** Press the Shift key before dropping a color to replace a gradation with a flat fill.

✦ **Stroking paths:** Drag a color onto the outline of a path to stroke the outline with the color. For some reason, this technique does not work with individual characters of type. But you can stroke a text block (provided that the Display Border check box in the Object Inspector is selected as discussed in Chapter 7).

✦ **Filling and stroking selections:** After selecting objects with the arrow tool or selecting characters with the text tool, drag a color swatch onto the Fill icon in the Color List panel to change the fill of all selected objects or characters. Drag a color onto the Stroke icon to change the stroke of the selection or to add a 1-point stroke of that color if the object is strokeless. Drag a color onto the Both selector to change the fill and stroke simultaneously.

✦ **Adding a color to the scrolling color list:** After defining a color in the Color Mixer panel, drag the color from the Color Mixer panel into an empty portion of the scrolling color list in the Color List panel. If the visible portion of the scrolling color list is full, drag the color onto the New Color icon, as shown in Figure 10-4. (You can also drag from a color swatch in the Fill or Stroke Inspectors.)

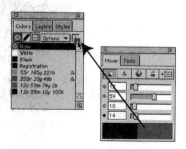

Figure 10-4: Drag from the color area in the Color Mixer panel onto the New Color icon in the Color List panel to add a new color to the scrolling list.

No doubt I'm overlooking some variation on the drag-and-drop motif, but you get the idea. You can replace any color inside or around an object or in a panel by simply dragging some other color around the screen.

Using the eyedropper tool

The eyedropper tool adds a special twist to dragging and dropping colors. This tool is available from your Xtra Tools panel. Press ⌘-Shift-+ on Macs and Ctrl-Alt-Shift-X on PCs to open the Xtra Tools panel and click the Eyedropper icon. The cursor changes to a cute little eyedropper.

Just position the tip of the eyedropper cursor over a color that you want to grab. Hold down the mouse button and drag and drop the color onto either another object or a color well.

Here's the best part about the eyedropper: You can use it on imported images. In plain English, if you import a bitmapped image, the eyedropper lets you pick up the color of any pixel in the image, provided that the image is not locked (or on a locked layer).

Mixing colors

The Color Mixer panel lets you define colors by mixing primary hues in various quantities. It's like accidentally spilling some yellow paint and some blue paint on your kitchen floor, only to discover the perfect shade of avocado for painting your fridge and other major appliances. Except, of course, that you mix the colors on purpose and they aren't nearly so messy. Oh, and I suppose that FreeHand is more of an enamel than a semigloss.

Tip

You can show and hide the Color Mixer panel by pressing ⌘/Ctrl-Shift-9. But perhaps more useful, you can show the Color Mixer and transfer a color to the panel by double-clicking any color swatch in another panel. If the first double-click hides the panel, just double-click the color swatch again to display the panel. (Hey, kids, it's a double-double-click!)

Double-clicking a color swatch in either the Stroke or the Fill Inspector, incidentally, hides and shows both the Color Mixer and Color List panels. I'm not sure how useful this is, but it's certainly worth a "Gee whiz."

Tip

An even quicker and less click-intensive method of transferring a color into the Color Mixer panel is to ⌘/Ctrl-click a color swatch. This technique works from inside the Color List panel as well as from the Fill and Stroke Inspectors.

You can access different *color models* by clicking the first three icons along the top of the panel. (Color models are different ways to define colors both onscreen and on the printed page.) Figure 10-5 shows how each of the three color models defines a particularly ugly shade of green.

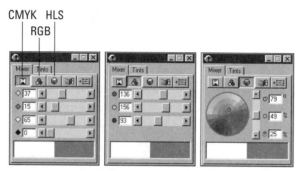

Figure 10-5: The Color Mixer as it appears when each of the three color model icons is selected.

The following sections explain each color model in detail.

Using the CMYK color model

In nature, our eyes perceive pigments according to the *subtractive color model.* Sunlight contains every visible color found on Earth. When sunlight is projected on an object, the object absorbs (subtracts) some of the light and reflects the rest. The reflected light is the color that you see. For example, a fire engine is bright red because it absorbs all nonred colors from the white-light spectrum.

Pigments on a sheet of paper work the same way. You can even mix pigments to create other colors. You might recall from second grade or thereabouts that you can mix red and yellow to make orange, yellow and blue to make green, and red and blue to make purple.

But what you learned in elementary school is only a rude approximation of the truth. Did you ever mix a vivid red with a canary yellow, only to produce a disappointingly drab orange, completely unrelated to the vibrant orange that your teacher had displayed? Talk about false advertising. The reason that you didn't achieve the vibrant orange you were hoping for is obvious if you stop and think about it. The fact that red starts out darker than bright orange means that you have to add a heck of a lot of yellow before you arrive at orange. And even then, you had better use an incredibly bright, lemon yellow, not some deep canary yellow that already has a lot of red in it.

The real subtractive primary colors used by commercial printers—cyan, magenta, and yellow—are for the most part very light. Cyan is a light blue; magenta is only a shade or two darker than pink, and yellow, well, you're probably familiar with yellow. Unfortunately, on their own, these colors don't do a very good job of producing dark colors. In fact, at full intensities, cyan, magenta, and yellow all mixed together don't get much beyond a muddy brown. That's where the nonlight color, black, comes in. Black helps to accentuate shadows, deepen dark colors, and, of course, print real blacks.

The colors in the CMYK (cyan, magenta, yellow, black) model mix as follows:

✦ **Cyan and magenta:** Full-intensity cyan and magenta mix to form a deep blue that tends toward violet. Subtract some cyan to make purple; subtract some magenta to make a dull medium blue. All of these colors assume a complete lack of yellow.

✦ **Magenta and yellow:** Full-intensity magenta and yellow mix to form a brilliant red. Subtract some magenta to make vivid orange; subtract some yellow to make rose. All of these colors assume a complete lack of cyan.

✦ **Yellow and cyan:** Full-intensity yellow and cyan mix to form a medium green with a surprising amount of blue in it. Subtract some yellow to make a deep teal; subtract some cyan to make chartreuse. All of these colors assume a complete lack of magenta.

✦ **Cyan, magenta, and yellow:** Full-intensity cyan, magenta, and yellow mix to form a muddy brown.

✦ **Black:** Black pigmentation added to any other pigment darkens the color.

✦ **No pigment:** No pigmentation results in white (assuming that white is the color of the paper).

When the CMYK icon is selected in the Color Mixer panel, FreeHand provides one option box and one slider bar each for cyan, magenta, yellow, and black ink. The values represent percentages from 0 for no color (or white) to 100 for full-intensity color.

Using the RGB color model

RGB is the color model of light. It comprises three primary colors—red, green, and blue—each of which can vary in *intensity* from 0 (no hue) to 65,535 (full intensity). The RGB model is also called the *additive primary model* because a color becomes lighter as you add higher levels of red, green, and blue light. All monitors, projection devices, and other items that transmit or filter light—including televisions, movie projectors, colored stage lights—rely on the additive primary model.

Red, green, and blue light mix as follows:

✦ **Red and green:** Full-intensity red and green mix to form yellow. Subtract some red to make chartreuse; subtract some green to make orange. All of these colors assume a complete lack of blue.

✦ **Green and blue:** Full-intensity green and blue with no red mix to form cyan. If you try hard enough, you can come up with 65,000 colors in the turquoise/jade/sky blue/sea green range.

✦ **Blue and red:** Full-intensity blue and red mix to form magenta. Subtract some blue to make rose; subtract some red to make purple. All of these colors assume a complete lack of green.

✦ **Red, green, and blue:** Full-intensity red, green, and blue mix to form white, the absolute brightest color in the visible spectrum.

✦ **No light:** Mixing low intensities of red, green, and blue plunges a color into blackness.

When you select the RGB icon in the Color Mixer panel, FreeHand provides option boxes and slider bars for red, green, and blue light. The values represent percentages from 0 for no light (or black) to 100 for full-intensity color.

Using the HLS color model

If you click the HLS icon in the Color Mixer panel, FreeHand provides access to the HLS color model, which stands for hue, lightness, and saturation.

In either case, *hue* is pure color — the stuff rainbows are made of — measured on a 360-degree circle. Red is located at 0 degrees, yellow at 60 degrees, green at 120 degrees, cyan at 180 degrees (midway around the circle), blue at 240 degrees, and magenta at 300 degrees. It's basically a pie-shaped version of the RGB model at full intensity.

Saturation represents the purity of the color. A zero saturation value equals gray. White, black, and other shades of gray have no saturation. Full saturation produces the purest version of a hue.

Brightness is the lightness or darkness of a color. A brightness value of zero equals black. Full brightness combined with full saturation results in the most vivid version of any hue. *Lightness* (also called *luminosity*) — the *L* in *HLS* — is slightly but significantly different from brightness. Zero luminosity still equals black, but full luminosity turns any hue or saturation value to white. Therefore, medium luminosity is required to produce the most vivid version of any hue.

When you select the HLS icon in the Color Mixer panel, FreeHand provides three options boxes — one each for hue, lightness, and saturation — along with a wheel and a slider bar. The perimeter of the wheel measures hue, and the interior portions control saturation. The slider bar adjusts lightness.

Process colors, spot colors, and tints

Normally, every color you define in the Color Mixer dialog box is a *process color*. This means that FreeHand ends up separating the color into its cyan, magenta, yellow, and black components during the printing process even if you defined the color using the RGB or HLS color model. After all, colors on paper must use pigments.

Process-color printing is a very economical solution because it enables you to create a rainbow of colors using only cyan, magenta, yellow, and black ink. But it's not sufficient for all jobs. Suppose you can only afford two inks — black and some other color. You don't want to use cyan, magenta, or yellow; in fact, you were thinking of forest green. It doesn't make sense to pay for cyan, magenta, and yellow just to mix one shade of green, especially when your printer can supply the precise shade of forest green ink that you want, already mixed and ready to go. These premixed inks are called *spot colors*.

Although process inks provide access to a wide range of colors, there's an equal number of colors that they can't produce. Some people are very picky and refuse to settle for a process-color approximation of the color they want to use. For example, if you turn over a six-pack of Miller Genuine Draft beer — not that I've ever swilled the stuff, of course — you'll see five color marks, one each for our friends cyan, magenta, yellow, and black, plus a fifth for a spot color, goldenrod. A casual glance suggests that this goldenrod is hardly different than the process yellow. Surely if you threw in a smidgen of magenta and a pinch of cyan, you could get a similar color. But the Miller Brewing Company apparently thought differently. Hence, the specialized goldenrod ink.

Using premixed spot colors

You can access spot colors in FreeHand in two ways. The first and most popular option is to load one or more spot colors from the libraries included with FreeHand. Pantone is the primary supplier of spot-color inks in the United States; Dainippon Ink and Chemicals (DIC) serves this same function in Japan.

If you're not familiar with either of these organizations, you're probably thinking, "There are companies out there that sell *colors*?" It's true, Pantone and DIC are in the business of providing professional spot-color inks. They've designed standardized collections of colors that any printer with access to their custom primary inks can mix using a list of recipes. This ensures standardization, so that whether you print a document in Milwaukee, Wisconsin, or Golden, Colorado, the homes of Miller and Coors, respectively, your beer boxes come out the same.

To add a spot color to the scrolling list in the Color List panel, select one of the options (know as libraries) from the bottom portion of the Options pop-up menu in the Color List panel. After you select a library, a dialog box filled with colors appears, as shown in Figure 10-6. You can scroll through the library by clicking in the scroll bar at the bottom of the dialog box. Click and ⌘/Ctrl-click or Shift-click on the colors you want to add to the scrolling list in the Color List panel. After you select all the colors you expect to use, press Return/Enter.

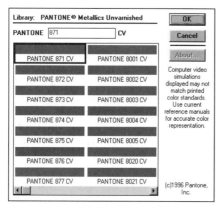

Figure 10-6: All colors you select from a color library will appear in the scrolling list in the Color List panel.

The second method for selecting a spot color is to create one yourself. This assumes that you know that your commercial printer can match the color with a premixed ink. Generally, you'll only use this option when working for clients who have had a few spot colors especially designed for their companies, as in the case of Miller's goldenrod.

To create your own spot color, first create a color in the normal fashion in the Color Mixer panel. Drag the completed color onto the New Color icon in the Color List panel, click the color name, and select the Make Spot option from the Options pop-up menu. FreeHand changes the formatting of the color name from italic type, which indicates a process color, to upright type, which indicates a spot color.

In an effort to streamline this process, FreeHand 8 includes a new button in the Color Mixer panel: the Add to Color List button. (This button appears all the way to the right, along the top of the Color Mixer.) After you create a color inside the Color Mixer panel, click the Add to Color List button. FreeHand displays a dialog box where you can name the color and decide if it should be a process or spot color. Click the OK button and your new color takes its place in the Color List panel.

For complete information on process-color and spot-color printing, read Chapter 18.

Creating tints

In FreeHand, a spot color isn't just one color, it's as many as 99 colors, each varying slightly in tint from 100 percent intensity down to 1 percent, so-light-it-probably-won't-print intensity. Tints can be especially useful for establishing shadows and highlights without having to purchase another color.

When creating black-and-white artwork, tints are your means for creating shades of gray. Simply use black as the base color, as shown in Figure 10-7. You can also create tints of process colors. These tints are separated into their CMYK components when printed from FreeHand, just like any other process colors.

To create a tint, first click the Tints panel tab or press ⌘/Ctrl-Shift-3. FreeHand displays the color on which you want to base the tint in the Base box in the Tints panel. In Figure 10-7, this color is Black, as it is by default. The Tints panel automatically creates nine variations on the color, ranging from 10 to 90 percent in 10 percent increments. You can specify some other tint by entering a value into the option box at the bottom of the panel or by using the slider bar.

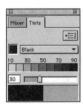

Figure 10-7: The Tints panel lets you create a shade of an existing color.

To add a tint to the scrolling color list, first select it so that you update the color well to the tint shade. Then click the Add to Color List button, name the color, decide whether it should be a process or spot color and press Return/Enter. Or, if you prefer the old-fashioned method, drag the color from the color well at the bottom of the Color Mixer panel and drop it onto the New Color icon in the Color List panel.

Using color libraries

Because the process of defining colors is time-consuming, and because you may want to use the same colors in many documents, FreeHand lets you organize colors into libraries that you can load into any illustration.

To give you a few examples, FreeHand includes 21 libraries in the Color folder inside the FreeHand 8 folder. Twelve are the spot-color libraries from DIC and Pantone, including the Pantone Hexachrome library for high-fidelity printing. Seven are process-color libraries from other color companies such as Trumatch, Focoltone, Munsell, and Toyo. (Pantone also includes two sets of process-color versions of its spot colors.) And the last two are just for fun. The Crayon library contains 64 colors including Aquamarine, Cornflower, Mulberry, and Seafoam. And Greys includes every possible tint of black expressed both as process and spot colors.

To open a library, select the desired option from the bottom portion of the Options pop-up menu in the Color List panel. A dialog box filled with a scrolling list of colors appears, as shown back in Figure 10-6. The Options pop-up menu lists every library inside the Color folder. If a library is located elsewhere on disk, select the Import option and locate the library file using the controls in the Select Color Library dialog box.

The following steps explain how to create your own library.

1. Select Export from the Options pop-up menu.

2. A dialog box appears, asking you to select the colors from the Color List panel that you want to save to the library. Click a color to select it. ⌘/Ctrl-click additional colors to add them to the selection. To select several colors at a time, click the first one to select it and then Shift-click the last color you want to select. FreeHand selects the first and last colors that you clicked, as well as all of the colors in between those two. You can then ⌘/Ctrl-click any colors within the selection that you don't want to deselect them. After you're satisfied with your selection, press Return/Enter.

3. FreeHand displays a dialog box like the one shown in Figure 10-8. In the Library Name option box, enter the name of the library as you want it to appear in the Options menu. In the File Name option box, enter the name under which you want to save the file.

4. The Preferences values control the number of columns and rows that appear in the dialog box when you open the library. For example, the Pantone library shown previously in Figure 10-6 was created by changing the Colors per Column value to 7 and the Colors per Row value to 2.

5. If you like, enter some general information into the Notes field. You can access this information later by clicking the About button in the Library dialog box.

6. To save the library with the other libraries in the Color folder, click the Save button. FreeHand adds the library to the bottom of the Options submenu.

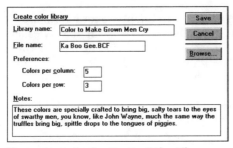

Figure 10-8: In the Create Color Library you can name, specify the size of and annotate a new color library that you construct.

After you finish saving the library, try selecting its option from the Options pop-up menu in the Color List panel. The contents of the library appear in a dialog box. You can now import colors from this library into other documents.

Using Object Styles

FreeHand's Styles panel, shown in Figure 10-9, is a time-saving feature that many people overlook. You can display this panel by pressing ⌘/Ctrl-3. The Styles panel contains a list of named object styles that you can use to control all aspects of the fills and strokes of paths. By creating an object style, you can apply a complex set of attributes with a single click of the mouse button. If you later decide that you want to change the attributes, you just edit the object style. FreeHand automatically applies the new attributes to all objects (in the current illustration) to which you had applied the original style.

Figure 10-9: The Styles panel as it appears normally (left) and with pop-up menu displayed (right).

The Styles panel also lists text styles. Refer to Chapter 8 for information about using text styles. Although many similarities exist between text styles and object styles, enough differences exist to warrant separate coverage of the two. If some of the following discussion seems repetitious, I apologize. However, because this topic can be a bit thick, I decided to err on the side of repetition rather than confusion.

Object styles automate the process of filling and stroking graphic objects. They make it possible to define a set of fill and stroke attributes only once and then use those attributes an unlimited number of times — a major time- and energy-saver. Without object styles, you must assign attributes again and again during the creation of a drawing, meaning several trips to FreeHand's many color panels, not to mention the Fill and Stroke Inspector. Using styles also ensures consistency throughout an illustration; every object to which a single object style is applied is colored identically.

Object styles also store custom halftone settings, which you specify in the Halftone panel. Because halftone settings specifically affect printing, they're covered in the "Halftone screens" section in Chapter 18. You may have also noticed that I have yet to discuss most fill and stroke options; these are the subjects of Chapters 11 and 12, respectively.

The Objects panel of your Preferences dialog box contains two options that affect object style creation. These two options are Auto-Apply to Selection and Define Style Based on Selection. I recommend you enable both of these options. Review the discussion on these options in Chapter 2, if necessary.

Creating and manipulating object styles

To create a new object style, apply the desired fill and stroke attributes to a graphic object. Then select the object and select New from the Options pop-up menu in the Styles panel. FreeHand adds a new style name, which it calls *Style-1* or something along those lines, to the scrolling list in the panel. You can rename the style by double-clicking it, entering a new name, and pressing Return/Enter.

If no object is selected when you select the New option, the Styles panel grabs the default fill and stroke attributes. You can use this technique to capture fill and stroke settings that you want to use later but that aren't applicable to the objects you've created so far.

To apply your new object style — or any other object style — to another object in the document, select the object and click the object style name in the panel. Not only does the object immediately gain all fill and stroke attributes assigned to the object style, it becomes *tagged* to the object style. From now on, any changes you make to the object style affect the tagged object as well. The remainder of this chapter explains how this process works.

Editing object styles

Editing object styles is slightly more involved than creating them. There are two basic approaches. You can redefine the object style or use the Edit Styles dialog box.

Redefining object styles

Follow these steps to redefine an object style:

1. Press Tab to deselect all objects.

2. Click the object style you want to edit. FreeHand makes the fill and stroke attributes the default attributes. (If the style was already selected but it has a plus sign next to it, click some other object style and then click the desired object style. I explain the significance of the plus sign in a little while.) This provides you with a starting point.

3. Edit the settings in the Fill and Stroke Inspectors as desired.

4. Select the Redefine option in the Options pop-up menu of the Styles panel. A dialog box appears, asking you which style you want to redefine. Click the object style name and press Return/Enter. The object style is now redefined.

Or, you can edit the fill and stroke attributes of an object to which the object style is already applied and then select the Redefine option. This strategy, however, can lead to some weirdness on FreeHand's part. Suppose that you select an object that is tagged to Style A and use it as a jumping off point for redefining another style, Style B. After you define Style B, FreeHand reapplies Style A to the object, which upsets the edits you've made to the object's attributes. You then have to apply Style B to the object to restore the edits. It's not the end of the world, but it can be disconcerting, which is why I prefer to redefine styles while no object is selected.

Using the Edit Style dialog box

The Edit Style dialog box, pictured in Figure 10-10, is a far more convenient means of editing a style. To bring up this dialog box, Option/Alt-click the style's name in the Styles panel or, if you like going the long way, click the style's name in the Styles panel and choose Edit Style from the Options pop-up menu. This dialog box lists all of the selected style's settings. The fill and stroke setting options contained here are subjects of Chapters 11 and 12.

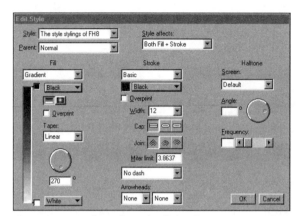

Figure 10-10: The Edit Style dialog box is a powerhouse for editing all aspects of an object style at one convenient location.

Make any attribute changes that you want and click OK. FreeHand updates the object style's definition and all objects tagged to the object style according to your changes.

The effect of object style changes on tagged objects

Editing a style has the added effect of refilling and stroking every object tagged to that object style, which is a great way to make global changes. Let's say that you drew several Norwegians sunbathing on a beach. The objects that make up their faces, arms, legs, belly buttons, and other exposed bits are tagged to an object style called Sickly Pale. If you change the fill of the style from greenish peach to golden brown, you give the sunbathers automatic tans. Change the fill to brick red, and you give them a nasty burn, all without so much as selecting a single object.

This brings up an interesting phenomenon: *Every* object you create in FreeHand is tagged to some object style or other. When you draw an object, FreeHand tags it to the default object style, which is generally the last object style used. If you've never touched the Styles panel, all your objects are tagged to the factory-default style, Normal. The original settings for Normal are a transparent fill and a 1-point black stroke. You'll notice that as you assign other fill and stroke attributes to objects, FreeHand displays a plus sign to the left of the word Normal, showing that the object is still tagged to the style but does not subscribe to all of the style's attributes.

If the tagged object matches the style in some respects and not others, what happens when you redefine the style? The answer is that the similar attributes change and the different ones don't. Suppose that an object tagged to the Normal style has a transparent fill with a 1-point red stroke. The only difference between the object and the style is the color of the stroke. If you edit the Normal style to include a yellow fill and a 13-point purple stroke, the object updates to include a yellow fill and a 13-point line weight, but the color of the stroke remains red.

Cross-Reference

You can also duplicate object styles and copy and paste them between documents. These procedures are identical for both text and object styles. Refer to these topics in Chapter 8 (under Duplicating attribute styles, Cutting and copying styles, and "Importing and exporting styles") for detailed procedures.

✦   ✦   ✦

Flat Fills and Gradations

The Benefits of Fill

If FreeHand didn't give you the ability to fill objects, your paths and character outlines would be without substance and form. Fill — the colors, textures, and patterns that you assign to the interior of your paths — is like the skin wrapped around the skeleton of a path. Without an opaque fill, no object could cover another. You could see through the bones of one object to the bones of the objects behind it. This is why the best drawing programs — including FreeHand — invest heavily in the core functions of path drawing, filling, and printing. If FreeHand were less capable in any one of these categories, the power of the program would be greatly diminished; functions beyond these qualify either as convenience features or special effects.

Why all this hoopla over assigning a color to the interior of a path? Think about it. Together, fill and stroke are all that separate the Etch-A-Sketch keyline mode from the preview mode. If push came to shove, you could do without stroke by drawing thin shapes — like those produced by the freehand tool when the Variable Stroke option is active — and filling them. But there's no getting around fill. It enables you to shade objects, create shadows and highlights, or simply add color to a document. Fill is what fools your viewer into perceiving your abstract objects as representations of real life.

How fill affects objects

In FreeHand, you can fill any path or text block. When a closed path is filled, its entire interior is affected. Figure 11-1 shows a closed path as it appears in the keyline and preview modes. The shape acts like a kind of malleable water balloon — the fill seeps into every nook and cranny of the outline.

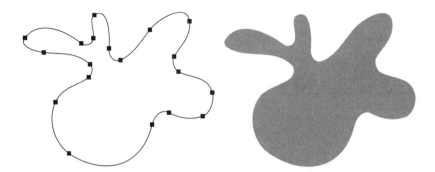

Figure 11-1: A filled shape shown in the keyline (left) and preview (right) mode.

 Unlike previous versions of FreeHand, in which you could not add fills to open paths, FreeHand 8 allows you to fill an open path in exactly the same way you have always been able to fill closed paths. One such open path is the subject of Figure 11-2. The only catch is that you must have the Show Fills for New Open Paths option in the Objects panel of the Preferences dialog box selected.

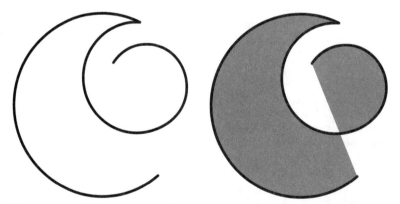

Figure 11-2: With the advent of FreeHand 8, an open path will now both preview and print any fill that you desire it to have. Just remember to select the Show Fills for New Open Paths option in the Object panel of the Preference dialog box.

There are a couple of things you need to know about the Show Fills for New Open Paths option. First, it is deactivated by default. This default setting is both odd and annoying. My natural inclination is to think that the opposite would be more convenient to most users since who would assign a visible fill to a path and, yet, not expect to see it preview or print? Also, if you forget to select this option, you may have the distinct pleasure of staring at you monitor and trying to figure out why your lovely open path will not take a gradient or some other fill as yours truly has now done twice.

This brings me to second point. As the option's name states (Show Fills for New Open Paths), only open fills that are created after you've selected the option are affected. In other words, if you create open paths in a document before you select the Show Fills for New Open Paths option, your old open paths will neither automatically acquire fills in response to your activating the option nor accept fills via any of the normal methods. You will have to recreate these open paths anew if you want them filled.

Let's all take a moment to thank Macromedia for finally adding the much needed capability to add fills to open paths. Now, let's all curse Macromedia for their donkey-backwards implementation of said option.

If you find yourself wondering what all the hubbub surrounding this new capability of FreeHand to fill open path is all about, consider the following. Filled, open paths with stroked or unstroked edges (as the case warrants) can be useful for establishing indefinite boundaries between shapes — boundaries that are implied by the surrounding shapes rather than spelled out with strokes. Notice in Figure 11-3 that the forward and rear wings on the port side of the plane (the side facing the viewer) are open paths. If either path were closed, after all, you'd see a closing segment at the junction of the wing and the plane. And yet the wings are obviously filled, because they cover the portions of the plane behind them.

Figure 11-3: With the use of filled, open path, the port wings suggest boundaries without relying entirely on stroke.

How fill affects text

You can also fill text objects. If you select a text object with the arrow tool and apply a fill, the fill affects the text object independently of the characters of type inside the object, as illustrated in Figure 11-4.

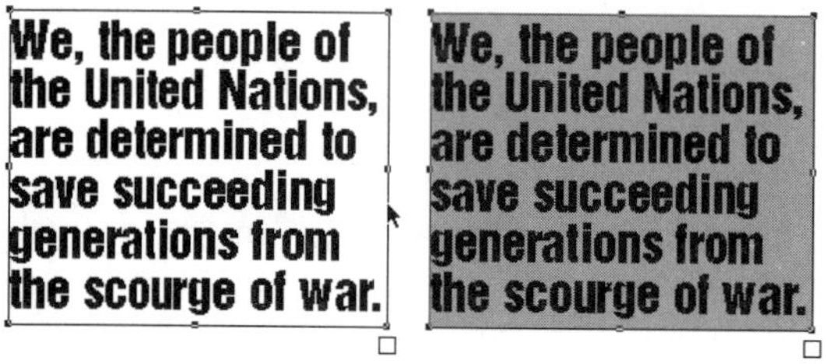

Figure 11-4: If you apply a fill to a text block that was selected with the arrow tool (left), the fill affects the block and not the text (right).

To fill one or more characters of text without affecting the text block, select the characters with the text tool and then apply the fill. Figure 11-5 shows the result of applying a white fill to a few characters after filling the block with gray.

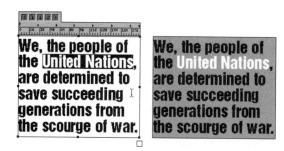

Figure 11-5: If you select characters with the text tool (left), you can fill them without affecting other characters.

You can't, however, apply special fill effects such as gradations and tile patterns to type. If you want to create an effect like the one shown in Figure 11-6, you have to first convert the text to composite paths by choosing Text ➪ Convert To Paths, as discussed in the last section of Chapter 9. You can then fill the character outlines as if they were any other graphic objects.

Figure 11-6: After converting a text block to composite paths, you can assign gradations to the characters.

Assigning Flat Fills

To fill an object, you can drag a color onto it as described in the last chapter. You can even use modifier keys such as ⌘/Ctrl and Option/Alt to create gradations. But to access textures, tiles, and other special fill patterns as well as gain full control over gradations, there's no substitute for the Fill Inspector.

To access this panel, press ⌘/Ctrl-Option/Alt-F. As shown in Figure 11-7, the panel sports a pop-up menu that lets you access different kinds of fills, all of which are covered in this chapter. When you select any of these menu options, FreeHand displays a new set of options that you use to design the particular fill.

Transparent fills

The first two options in the pop-up menu enable you to accomplish basically the same thing as dragging and dropping color swatches from the Color List panel. They apply a single flat fill, which can be either transparent or an opaque color. For example, to make the interior of a selected object transparent, you can use any of the following techniques with absolutely identical degrees of success:

Figure 11-7: Click on the pop-up menu in the Fill Inspector to access various fill patterns and gradations.

✦ Select the object and then select the None option from the pop-up menu in the Fill Inspector.

✦ Select the object, click on the Fill icon in the Color List panel, and click on the None color name in the scrolling list.

✦ Select the object and drag the None color swatch—the one that looks like a box with an inset X—onto the Fill icon in the Color List panel.

✦ Whether or not the object is selected, drag the None color swatch from the Color List panel onto the object.

Now, I don't know about you, but the last technique sounds the easiest to me. No selecting involved, no extra steps, just drag and drop. In fact, the only reason to use any of the other techniques is if you want to make multiple objects transparent. In that case, it's generally easier to select all the objects and apply the None option inside a panel.

Making the fill transparent is useful when you want to see only the stroke as well as see through the path to the objects behind it. You can even apply both a transparent stroke and a transparent fill to create an entirely transparent path that is visible in the keyline mode only. You can use such a path for alignment purposes or to surround an image that you intend to export as an EPS file, as described in the "Exporting an Illustration" section of Chapter 16.

Note

You can't make characters of type completely transparent. They have to have either a fill or a stroke. By default, the stroke is already transparent, so you can't make the fill transparent as well. If you apply the None option to type selected with the text tool, FreeHand ignores you. You have to convert the characters to paths before you can make them completely transparent.

Single-color fills

The second option in the Fill Inspector pop-up menu is Basic, which applies a single color to the interior of an object. When you select Basic, a color swatch and an Overprint check box appear in the Fill Inspector. As discussed in Chapter 10, you can change the color swatch by choosing a color from the pop-up menu to the right of the swatch or by dragging a swatch from the Color List or Color Mixer panel onto it — both of these actions are shown in shown in Figure 11-8. So why not, instead, drag the color directly onto the object and remove the middleman? The answer: There is no reason. Even if you want to apply colors to multiple objects, it's quicker to select the objects and drag the color swatch to the Fill icon in the Color List panel than to deal with the Basic option.

Tip

If an object is filled with a gradation or pattern, and you want to change it to a flat fill, drag a color swatch over the object, press and hold the Shift key, and drop the color. (Be sure to release the Shift key after releasing your mouse button.)

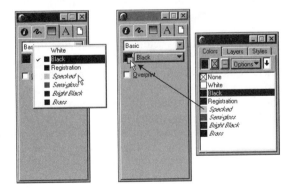

Figure 11-8: To change the color of a flat fill, drag a color swatch from some other panel onto the color swatch in the Basic panel of the Fill Inspector.

Overprinting colors

The only reason to so much as display the Fill Inspector when an object is filled with a uniform color is to access the Overprint check box. This option controls whether the color inside the selected object mixes with the colors of the objects behind it—known as overprinting. When this option is selected, an object is allowed to overprint the object behind it, provided that the colors of the overlapping objects are printed to different separations. For more information on color separations, see Chapters 10 and 18.

Suppose that your drawing consists of three spot colors: black, orange, and blue. Orange can overprint blue, blue can overprint orange, and either can overprint or be overprinted by black, because orange, blue, and black print to their own separations. However, a 30 percent tint of blue cannot overprint a 70 percent tint of blue, because all blue objects print to the same separation.

If the Overprint check box is deselected, as it is by default, portions of an object covered by another object are knocked out; that is, they don't print when the two objects are output to different separations.

Take a look at the faces in Figure 11-9. (Doesn't it just cheer you right up to see these happy faces? I thought that you might need a lift right about now.) Imagine that the faces are filled and stroked in tints of orange and that the little berets—these are French smiley faces—are colored in tints of blue. In the left example in the figure, the portions of the orange objects under the hat have been knocked out. In the right example, the objects overprint, allowing the blues and oranges to blend, giving the hat a translucent appearance. The diagrams under the faces show the hat and faces as they appear when printed to separate pages.

The Overprint option makes no difference in grayscale or black-and-white illustrations that don't require separations. If the selected object is filled with one or more process colors, only those colors on different separations overprint. For example, if you apply the Overprint option to Object A, which is filled with 100 percent cyan and 20 percent magenta, and the object behind it, Object B, is filled with 50 percent magenta and 100 percent yellow, the intersection of the two objects will be filled with 100 percent cyan, 20 percent magenta, and 100 percent yellow. The magenta value from Object A wins out—even though it's lighter than the magenta value in Object B—because overprinting doesn't affect colors on the same separation.

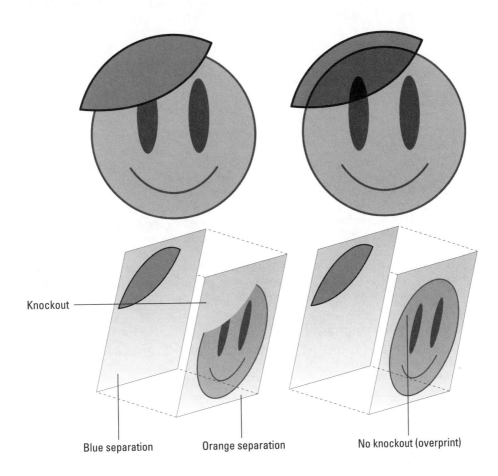

Figure 11-9: An orange face with a blue hat as it appears when the Overprint option is deselected (left) and selected (right).

The problem with the Overprint option is that it doesn't display correctly on-screen, nor does it proof correctly to color printers. When the Display Overprinting Objects option is enabled in the Redraw panel of the Preferences dialog box, Freehand fills over printing objects with Os. I recommend that you enable this option. At least with this option enabled, you can visually distinguish the overprinting objects.

Tip

If you want to mix the colors in overlapping objects and see the results, select the two objects and choose Transparency from the Operations panel. If necessary, press ⌘/Ctrl-Option/Alt-O to open the Operations panel. FreeHand displays the Transparency dialog box, described in Chapter 5. Better yet, use one of the new Lens fills, discussed in length in the "Lens Fills" section later in this chapter.

Transparency gives you added flexibility because it doesn't rely on color separations. For example, if you applied this technique to Objects A and B from a couple of paragraphs back, the new path created by the command would be filled with 100 percent cyan, 50 percent magenta, and 100 percent yellow.

The result is a heck of a lot more logical, and you can see it on-screen. The only downside is that you have to apply strokes to the new path manually because Transparency always produces a path with no stroke.

Lifting the color of a fill

Actually, the Basic panel of the Fill Inspector has one additional use. If you work like I do, you rarely name colors and put them into the Color List panel like you're supposed to. It's just too much work. It's so much simpler to mix a color and drag it directly onto an object from the Color Mixer panel.

But this kind of flagrant laziness can get you into a bind. For example, what do you do if you want to modify the color of an object slightly or take the color of one object and apply it to another? Because it's highly unlikely that you will be able to remember the ingredients of the color, it's a lucky thing that FreeHand offers three methods for lifting an object's color.

The eyedropper tool, covered in Chapter 10, should be your method of choice for dragging a color from one object and dropping it onto another. Remember, the eyedropper tool is located in the Xtra Tools panel. Press ⌘/Ctrl-Option/Alt-X to display this panel.

Here's another method. I recommend this one for modifying an existing color. Select the object, display the Fill Inspector, and ⌘/Ctrl-click on the color swatch in the panel. The color is immediately transferred to the Color Mixer. You can then edit the color or drag it onto the New Color icon in the Color List panel for future use.

I know that I already explained how ⌘/Ctrl-clicking transfers a color to the Color Mixer panel in the previous chapter. But this is a slightly different and sufficiently common way to use the technique that I figured it warranted another mention.

The final method is best when modifying several colors at once. For example, if you want to give several objects a warmer feel, select the objects and choose Xtras ➪ Colors ➪ Color Control to display the dialog box pictured in Figure 11-10. Choose CMYK and enter -50 in the Cyan, 25 in the Magenta, and 50 in the Yellow option boxes. See the following section, "Fine-tuning colors," for instructions on using this dialog box.

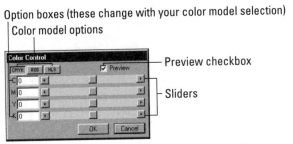

Figure 11-10: The Color Control dialog box, where you can fine-tune your colors.

Fine-tuning colors

I've never felt quite satisfied with manipulating colors in an electronic environment. Sure, it's a lot less messy and far more forgiving, but it's still bizarre to assign numerical values to something as intangible as color. Slowly, though, the electronic world is catching up to the world of paints and brushes — not by attempting to re-create real-life color mixing, but by enabling you to do things with colors electronically that you could never do in real life. Granted, the reverse is still true, but when in Rome. . . .

Remember, a computer is a tool. A very, very powerful tool. The same hardware and software combination is potentially, but hardly ever, equally as powerful to two different persons. Users who understand what a feature can do and arrange their tasks to take full advantage of the feature's capabilities get the most bang for their buck. Don't think I'm telling you to conform, like some pathetic android, to a computer's way of thinking — far from it. I'm suggesting that you plan your tasks to take full advantage of what your computer can do for you. The following color fine-tuning features are a good example. Mixing different shades for every color you are using in a piece of real-life artwork would be a tedious task. FreeHand makes it a breeze.

Most powerful of all of the methods for fine-tuning colors is the Color Control dialog box, which you display by choosing Xtras ⇨ Colors ⇨ Color Control. It takes a bit more work to master, but it lets you be a lot more specific. Just as the Color Mixer lets you choose whether to use the CMYK, RGB, or HSL color model, so does the Color Control dialog box. Your color-selection choice affects the contents of the dialog box. It displays option boxes and sliders for the components of the color model you choose.

At first the appearance of the option boxes and sliders may seem a bit disorienting. All the values are listed as zero, while the pointers in the sliders are positioned in the center of the sliders. This is because you can enter either positive or negative values. The values are interpreted as percentages of change from the existing colors. You enter values from positive to negative 100 percent. When you enable the Preview check box, FreeHand updates the current selection as you make changes in the dialog box.

But if the Color Control dialog box is too much work for you, there are also several commands that modify colors' shades. They're available from the Xtras ⇨ Colors submenu. Certain rules apply to all of these commands (as well as to the Color Control dialog box). All of these commands affect selected objects' strokes and fills. All of these commands affect process colors only; they do not affect spot colors (except black).

These commands achieve their effects by manipulating either the lightness or saturation of your selection's colors. If necessary, refer back to the HSL color model discussion in Chapter 10 for a refresher on lightness and saturation. The following list explains what results you can expect when using these commands.

✦ **Darken:** Darkens colors of selected objects by decreasing the lightness factor by 5 percent.

✦ **Desaturate:** Makes colors of selected objects appear duller by decreasing their saturation by 5 percent.

✦ **Lighten:** Lightens colors of selected objects by increasing the lightness factor by 5 percent.

✦ **Saturate:** Makes colors of selected objects appear brighter by increasing their saturation by 5 percent.

All of these commands can be reapplied — provided that in the interim, you don't choose another command from the Xtras menu or the Operations panel — by pressing ⌘-Shift-+ on Macs and Ctrl-Alt-Shift-X on PCs. Just keep pressing that keystroke until you're satisfied with the resulting colors.

After you apply any of these commands to objects, you can use the eyedropper tool to drag and drop the resulting shades onto the Color List.

Applying Gradient Fills

A gradient fill (also called a gradation) fades from one color to another inside an object. FreeHand provides two type of gradients in the Gradient panel of the Fill Inspector: the graduated and radial gradients. You choose between the two by clicking on one of the two Gradient fill buttons in the Gradient panel of the Fill Inspector. The Graduated button creates gradations that fade in a constant direction, which can be from top to bottom (as in the top example in Figure 11-11), side to side, or whatever. The Radial button creates gradations that flow outward in concentric circles, as in the second example in the figure.

Figure 11-11: Gradations created by selecting the Graduated (top) and Radial (bottom) options.

Directional gradations

The Graduated button sounds as if it should give the selected object a high-school diploma or at least a certificate in VCR repair. But it really displays options for changing the colors and direction of a gradient fill. When you select the Graduated button from the Gradient panel of the Fill Inspector pop-up menu, as shown in Figure 11-12, FreeHand displays the following options:

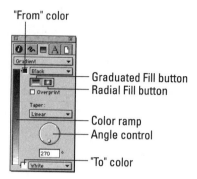

"From" color

Graduated Fill button
Radial Fill button

Color ramp
Angle control

"To" color

Figure 11-12: Select Gradient from the Fill Inspector pop-up menu to display options for specifying the colors, speed, and direction of a gradation.

✦ **Color swatches:** Drag colors onto the color ramp to specify the first, last, and intermediate colors in a gradation. In earlier versions of FreeHand no more than two colors were permitted in a single gradation. FreeHand 8 allows you to specify multicolor gradations. You can also now use different spot colors or create a gradation from a spot color to a gray value or process color.

✦ **Overprint:** The overprint check box overprints the fill of a selected path as described in detail in the previous section.

✦ **Graduated Fill/Radial Fill buttons:** These buttons allow you to choose a Graduated Fill or a Radial Fill from the Gradient panel of the Fill Inspector. Choosing a Graduated Fill using the button on the left changes colors along a straight line. The Radial Fill option, the button on the right, changes colors in a circular pattern from the center to the outer edges. Radial Fills will be discussed in the next section. The remainder of the options in the Gradient panel refer to the Graduated Fill.

✦ **Taper:** This pop-up menu provides two options that control the speed at which the first and last colors fade together. Select the Linear option to create a linear gradation in which every increment between the first and last colors is emphasized equally. Select the Logarithmic option to create a logarithmic gradation, which fades quickly at first and then more slowly as the gradation progresses. The result is a gradation that favors the last color over the first.

Figure 11-13 shows two shapes filled with black-to-white gradations that flow in identical directions. The only difference is that the top gradation is linear and the bottom is logarithmic. Rectangles highlight the locations of medium gray, which is the middle color in either gradation. The medium gray is smack dab in the middle of the shape in the linear gradation, but it's scooted toward the From color of the shape in the second gradation. Less space is devoted to colors darker than medium gray than to colors lighter than medium gray.

50% gray

50% gray

Figure 11-13: A shape filled with a linear gradation (top) and another filled with a logarithmic gradation (bottom).

✦ **Angle:** This option controls the direction of the gradation. You can enter a value in degrees into the Angle option box or drag the knob around the perimeter of the wheel. The option box value and knob work dynamically with each other. If you enter 90 into the option box, the knob moves around to the 12 o'clock position, and so on. The default angle is 270 degrees, which is straight down.

The top fill in Figure 11-14 shows the results of setting the Angle value to 45 degrees and using a From color of black and a To color of white. The lower path contains identical From and To colors, but the Angle value is changed to 225 degrees, forcing the gradation to progress in the opposite direction.

Figure 11-14: Shapes filled with a 45-degree angle gradation (top) and a 225-degree angle gradation (bottom).

Together, the options can be used to create just about any directional gradation. The following steps explain how you can use all the options in combination to change a black-to-white gradation that favors white to one that favors black.

1. Select a closed path and press ⌘/Ctrl-Option/Alt-F to display the Fill Inspector. Select Gradient from the pop-up menu at the top of the panel.

2. Drag the black color swatch from the Color List panel onto the top of the ramp in the Fill Inspector. Drag the white swatch from the Color List panel onto the bottom of the ramp. (This step may not be necessary because black and white are the default colors.) You can also click and hold on the top color name (black or white) and drag to the color listed since all colors you created in the Color List panel are listed in these pop up menus.

3. Select Logarithmic from the Taper pop-up menu.

4. Change the Angle value to 225 degrees and press Return/Enter. The result is a fill that fades from right to left, quickly at first and slowly toward the end, as seen in the first example of Figure 11-15. Suppose, however, that this effect isn't what you want. You're happy with the direction and the colors, but you

want to emphasize black and play down white. Unfortunately, the Logarithmic option always stresses the bottom color. So you're stuck, right? Not at all. You just have to flip the colors and flip the direction while leaving the Logarithmic option alone.

Figure 11-15: Two shapes filled with logarithmic gradations, each of which uses different first and last colors and flows in the opposite direction from the other.

5. Inside the Fill Inspector, change the Angle value to 45 degrees, the exact opposite of 225 degrees.

6. Swap the colors. Here's a fun way to do it: ⌘/Ctrl-click on the black swatch to transfer it to the Color Mixer. Now drag the white swatch onto the ramp to make the top color white. Finally, drag the black from the Color Mixer panel onto the bottom swatch.

Your path now contains a gradation that appears to flow in the same direction as before, and between the same colors. However, black now receives more emphasis than white.

Tip

To change the colors of a gradation without fussing with the ramp options, drag a color swatch and drop it onto the desired end of an object. If you drop the swatch onto the side of the shape favored by the first color, you replace the first color; if you drop it onto the neighborhood occupied by the last color, you replace the last color.

To change the direction of a gradation, press and hold the ⌘/Ctrl key while dropping the color. ⌘/Ctrl-dropping always replaces the bottom color in the Gradient panel of the Fill Inspector (so be sure not to ⌘/Ctrl-drop the color that appears in the top or From swatch, or you'll create what looks like a solid fill).

Cross-Reference

You can also create complex gradations by using the Blend command, as described in the "Creating custom gradations" section of Chapter 15. The process requires some extra effort but also affords more control and a wider range of color options than do graduated fills.

Radial gradations

To create a simple radial gradation, select the Radial button from the Gradient panel of the Fill Inspector. FreeHand displays the options shown in Figure 11-16.

Locate center box
Radial Gradient field

Figure 11-16: Select the Radial button from the Gradient panel of the Fill Inspector to display options for selecting the colors in a radial gradation.

The options work as follows:

✦ **Color swatches:** Drag a color onto the top of the ramp to specify the color around the perimeter of the gradation. Drag a color onto the bottom to specify the center color.

Figure 11-17 shows two objects filled with radial gradations. In the first fish, the perimeter color was set to black and the center color to white. A white center color usually creates a highlighting effect. In the second fish, the center and perimeter colors are reversed. This results in the black-vortex-of-despair effect that is all the rage these days, particularly inside fish shapes.

Figure 11-17: A radial gradation from black to white (top) and another from white to black (bottom).

✦ **Locate Center:** To reposition the center point of a radial fill you drag the Locate Center box around inside the Radial Gradient field — both of which are labeled in Figure 11-16. Figure 11-18 shows two black-to-white radial gradations with different center points. To create the first fish, I moved the Locate Center box to the upper right region of the Radial Gradient field. To achieve the second fish, I moved the Locate Center box down and to the left of the field.

Figure 11-18: The results of moving the center point —
represented by the white spot — to different locations.

Multicolor fills

So far, the gradations that I've shown have only included two color, but this
limitation is not a reflection of FreeHand's true capability. In fact, FreeHand allows
you to number colors in any gradient. It is simply a matter of dragging additional
color swatches onto the color ramp in the Gradient panel of the Fill Inspector.
Figure 11-19 shows the Gradient panel ready to fill a path with a rainbow of grays.

The color ramp displays how your fill will appear. To add a color ramp chip, drag a
color from the Color List, Tint, or Color Mixer panel. Observe the effect in the color
ramp and reposition the color ramp chip if necessary. Continue in this manner until
you are satisfied with the appearance of the fill.

Figure 11-19: The Gradient panel of the Fill Inspector lets you create gradients with a horde of different colors.

Lens Fills

New to FreeHand 8 is the Lens panel of the Fill Inspector, shown in Figure 11-20. Just as with any other fill, you enter a Lens fill by first selecting a path and then choosing the type of Lens fill from the first pop-up menu in the Lens panel of the Fill Inspector. I'll discuss the six type of Lens fills first. The three viewing settings that are common to all six Lens fills are discussed below in the "The viewing options" section.

Figure 11-20: The Lens panel of the Fill Inspector gives you access to six new Lens fills.

The looking glass

A Lens fill lets you view another part of your artwork (which I'll call the source) through a Lens filled path. Think of a Lens fill as, more or less, transforming your path into a piece of glass that allows you to see through the path to whatever source you wish. But, as we will see, more than simply a piece of ordinary glass, the Lens fills are instilled with some rather special properties. For example, if you opt to use the Magnify option from the Lens panel of the Fill Inspector, your path is metamorphosed into a magnifying lens that allows you to enlarge the source. Choose the Monochrome option and your path becomes a duel-tone viewer, showing the source in just two colors.

Transparency

Choose the Transparency option to turn your path into a piece of stained glass. Just as you can wear a pair of rose colored glasses to tint your view of the world, you can add this Lens fill to a path to tint the view of the sorce. Choose the color of the tint from the color pop-up menu and then decide how transparent you want the fill with the Opacity slider bar. In Figure 11-21, the leftmost circle shows the Transparency Lens fill with a black tint at 50% opacity.

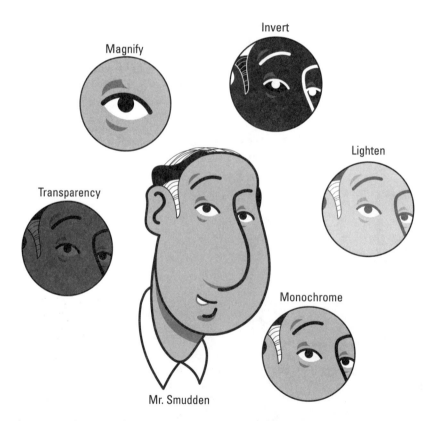

Figure 11-21: Using the center portrait as the source — a fellow I like to call Mr. Smudden — the five surrounding circles show different views that the different types of Lens fill can produce.

Magnify

With a Magnify Lens fill, you turn your path into a telescope. You can opt to have the path to magnify anywhere between double size up to a whopping 20 × normal. Just use the slider bar to set the magnification power. The second circle, moving clockwise, in Figure 11-21 shows a Magnify Lens fill with a 2 × power.

Invert

Choose the Invert Lens fill to invert all the colors of the source. The topmost circle in Figure 11-21 shows an example of the Invert Lens fill. All the colors that appear in the fill are just the opposite of those that appear in the source.

Lighten

Remember the Xtra ⇨ Colors ⇨ Lighten Colors command discussed in the "Fine-tuning colors" section of Chapter 11? Well, the Lighten Lens fill works very similarly. It manipulates the lightness of the color in the view of the source objects. But, instead of limiting you to increments of 5% as the Lighten Colors command does, you can choose any percentage from the % slider bar. The rightmost circle in Figure 11-21 shows a Lighten Lens fill with a 50% setting. Note that this is the exact same result of using a Transparency Lens fill with a white tint and a 50% opacity.

Darken

The flip side of the Lighten Lens fill is the Darken Lens fill. The same % slider bar here, giving you considerable more flexibility than does the related Xtra ⇨ Colors ⇨ Darken Colors command. In the grayscale Figure 11-21, the Darken option set to 50% would give the exact same result as the Transparency Lens fill with a black tint and a 50% opacity that appears in the leftmost circle.

Monochrome

With a Monochrome Lens fill you transform the source image into a two-tone view. The view consist of white and the full range of any other color you can create in the Color Mixer. The last circle in Figure 11-21 shows the Monochrome Lens fill in action. "But it looks exactly like the original!" you exclaim. That's because the source is grayscale and the Lens fill uses black as it's second color. If this was a color image, I could show you the same fill with only shades of blue or any other color I wish.

The viewing options

The Lens panel of the Fill Inspector in Figure 11-20 gives you access to its six fill types and three viewing settings. Although each type of Lens fills imparts a different effects, they all make use of the same three view controls. These three options (Centerpoint, Objects Only and Snapshot) appear at the bottom the Lens panel.

✦ **Centerpoint:** One of the most interesting features of a Lens fill is that, in additional to using the portion of your document that lies directly below the Lens filled path as your source, you have the freedom of using any part of your artwork as the source. To do so, simply select the Centerpoint option, and enter the new coordinates of what should appear through the Lens filled path in the X and Y option boxes of the Lens panel. In Figure 11-21, all five of the circular Lens filled paths that surround the portrait use the Centerpoint option to show different views of Mr. Smudden's right eye. You may also position the centerpoint manually. Click on the Centerpoint check box and a little clover-shaped marker appears in the center of the Lens filled path. Move this marker anywhere to designate the source of the filled path's view.

✦ **Objects Only:** If the source of the lens fill included some of the background of your document — a spot your artwork that contains no paths or images — FreeHand will add color to this in the view. If you wish that only objects of the source are affected when viewed in a lens filled path, select this check box.

✦ **Snapshot:** Select the Snapshot option to ensure that view through a Lens filled path remains the constant, despite what happens to the source. You can move, hide or ever delete the source that a Lens filled path views and, provided the Snapshot option is active, that path will still show a view of the source.

Applying and Editing Patterns

FreeHand provides two methods for applying patterns to shapes. You can either define simple and not particularly useful bitmapped patterns, or you can draw complex patterns using graphic objects. In either case, you create the pattern as a tile, sort of like a bathroom tile. Bitmapped tiles are always square; object-oriented tiles can be square or rectangular. FreeHand repeats the tile over and over again inside the filled shape.

Bitmapped patterns

Select the Pattern option from the Fill Inspector pop-up menu to fill a selected path with a bitmapped pattern similar to those offered by entry-level drawing applications. (In fact, the primary purpose for the inclusion of bitmapped patterns is to make FreeHand compatible with graphics created in MacDraw.)

When you select the Pattern option, you gain access to a scrolling collection of 64 patterns included with FreeHand. As shown in Figure 11-22, a slider bar appears along the bottom of the panel. Above the slider are six pattern boxes. To replace the patterns in these boxes with one of the others in the collection, drag the knob inside the slider.

Pattern editor

Pattern preview

Pattern boxes
Slider bar

Figure 11-22: Select the Pattern option from the pop-up menu to select and edit bitmapped patterns.

Select a pattern by clicking on one of the six pattern boxes. The selected pattern appears inside the larger boxes in the middle of the panel. The left box is the pattern editor. It contains an enlarged version of the pattern, which you can edit by clicking pixels on and off. The right box is the pattern preview, which shows the pattern repeated many times at actual size. (Clicking in this box produces no effect.)

Two buttons are also provided to enhance your editing abilities. The Invert button changes all black pixels in a pattern to white and all white pixels to black — in other words, you create a negative version of the current pattern. If you decide that you want to get a clean start and create an entirely new pattern, you can erase all pixels in a pattern by clicking on the Clear button.

The white pixels in a bitmapped pattern are always white and opaque. But you can change the color of the black pixels by dragging a color swatch from the Color List panel onto the swatch below the pop-up menu in the Pattern panel of the Fill Inspector or you can also click and hold on the color pop-up to select any color from your color list. Although the color does not appear in the pattern inside the Fill Inspector, it does appear in the selected object. You can't apply the None swatch to bitmapped patterns.

Note

Although you can apply any color that you want to a bitmapped pattern, a color that requires a screen value may not print correctly, depending on whether your printer is equipped with PostScript Level 1 or Level 2. Older model Level 1 printers — like my LaserWriter IINTX — can't print tints (including gray values) or process colors unless they are composed of 100 percent CMYK combinations. Level 2 printers handle tints and process colors just fine.

Also, regardless of whether you enlarge or reduce a path, the bitmapped fill pattern always prints at 72 dots per inch. The resolution doesn't even enlarge on-screen when you magnify the view size.

In other words, don't use bitmapped patterns. They are provided strictly to aid in the conversion of PICT graphics originally created in MacDraw for the Macintosh. This feature is more or less defunct and hardly anyone uses it. If you find a bitmapped pattern, replace it.

Object-oriented tile patterns

The Tiled option in the Fill Inspector pop-up menu enables you to define a tile pattern, which is a repeating rectangular design composed of other filled and stroked objects. Using the Tiled option is one of two techniques that you can use to fill an object with one or more additional objects. The other and more versatile technique is masking, which is discussed in Chapter 15.

Figure 11-23 shows the Fill Inspector as it appears when you select the Tiled option. The following list explains the function of each option in the panel. (Later sections examine the options in greater detail and show you how to use them to create a tile pattern.)

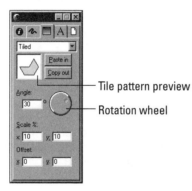

Tile pattern preview

Rotation wheel

Figure 11-23: Select the Tiled option from the pop-up menu to define and transform object-oriented tile patterns.

✦ **Paste In:** After selecting and copying the objects that make up your prospective tile pattern, click the Paste In button to paste the contents of the Clipboard into the tile pattern preview box (just to the left of the button).

✦ **Copy Out:** Click this button to transfer the contents of the tile pattern preview box to the Clipboard. You can then paste the objects into your illustration and edit them as desired.

The remaining options transform the repeating tiles inside the filled object. None of them affects the size of the object itself.

✦ **Angle:** Enter a value into the Angle option box or drag the knob inside the rotation wheel to rotate the tiles. Rotating can help eliminate the rectangular appearance of the tiles.

✦ **Scale %:** Enter values into the X and Y option boxes to scale the tiles horizontally and vertically, respectively. Values lower than 100 percent reduce the size of the tiles; values above 100 percent enlarge them.

✦ **Offset:** Enter values into these X and Y option boxes to move the tiles inside the object horizontally and vertically, respectively. Negative values move the tiles to the left or down. Positive values move them to the right or up.

Creating and assigning a tile pattern

In FreeHand, all tile patterns are rectangular. Even if you select a completely nonrectangular object to serve as a tile pattern, FreeHand spaces the tile from each of its neighbors as if it were sitting on an invisible rectangle. For example, Figure 11-24 shows a series of stars. The first star is filled with a gradation; the star below that appears inside its implied rectangular boundary. I defined the star as a tile pattern and used it to fill an enlarged version of itself. (I've also reduced the tile pattern to 30 percent of its former size so that you can see many repetitions of it.) No star tile overlaps another star, nor does it intrude inside its neighbors' rectangular space.

An interesting side note about Figure 11-24: Notice that because the star is the lone element in the tile, you can see through the cracks between the tiled stars to the drop shadow behind them. The only way to avoid this effect is to draw a rectangle without a stroke behind your object before making the object into a tile pattern.

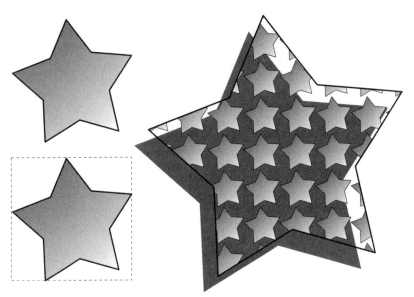

Figure 11-24: Even a nonrectangular shape like a star (left) is spaced as if it were sitting on an invisible rectangle when expressed as a tile pattern (right).

All right, enough tidbits. Time to see how this tile stuff really works. The following steps explain how to define a tile and use it to fill a graphic object.

1. Begin by drawing, filling, and stroking all objects that you want to have appear inside the tile. Then select the objects and send them to the Clipboard by pressing ⌘/Ctrl-C or ⌘/Ctrl-X (depending on whether or not you want the objects to remain available inside the illustration window).

2. Select the graphic object that you want to fill with the tile pattern.

3. Select the Tiled option from the pop-up menu in the Fill Inspector. The options shown in Figure 11-23 appear.

4. Click on the Paste In button to paste the contents of the Clipboard into the tile pattern preview box. This box shows you how a single tile will look. Meanwhile, you can see your tile pattern in all its splendor inside the selected object. (If not, you must be in the keyline mode. Press ⌘/Ctrl-K to enter the preview mode.)

5. Use the transformation options to rotate, scale, and move the tiles inside the object as desired.

Those are the basic steps. For some real-life practice in creating and using an actual tile, work your way through the following set of steps. In this exercise, you create a pattern that looks like a metal, nonslip surface, complete with raised edges. (You know, like on a fire-engine bumper. Didn't you ever want to be a firefighter?) Alternating horizontal and vertical ridges appear to stand up from a metal surface, as shown in Figure 11-25. The tile pattern includes a square behind all its other objects to ensure that the pattern is opaque (rather than periodically transparent, as in Figure 11-24).

Cross-Reference

I haven't yet covered a few of the operations included in the following steps. For more information on the Duplicate command, see Chapter 14. For more information on reflecting objects, read Chapter 13. And for complete information on masking, see Chapter 15. You don't need to study up on these techniques to complete the steps, however; they're used in only the most straightforward ways here.

1. Draw the first ridge as a combination of three paths, as shown on the left side of Figure 11-26. Each path comprises only two corner points, one at the top and one at the bottom. Each corner handle has a single control handle, extending toward the curved side.

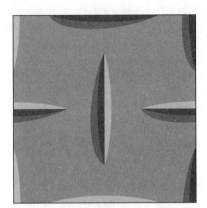

Figure 11-25: A single tile (top) and an object filled with reduced versions of the tiles (bottom), which mimic the metal ridges on a fire engine bumper.

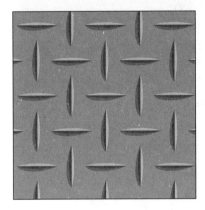

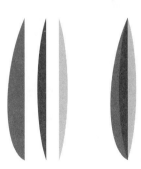

Figure 11-26: The three paths that make up the ridge (left), and the ridge as it appears when the three paths are combined (right).

2. Fill the paths with different shades of gray to impart a sense of depth and shadow. Fill the first path with 45 percent gray, the second with 60 percent gray, and the third with 15 percent gray.

3. After you draw the paths, bring them together as shown in the right half of Figure 11-26. The middle shape covers the left one. (You can use the Align panel to align the right edges of the two shapes.) The straight side of the right shape meets flush with the straight sides of the other two shapes.

4. Select the three paths and press ⌘/Ctrl-G to group them.

5. Choose the Clone command from the Edit menu (⌘-= on Macs and Ctrl-Shift-C on PCs) to create a clone of the group directly in front of the original.

6. Drag the cloned group while pressing Shift to move it an inch or so to the left.

7. Choose the Duplicate command from the Edit menu (⌘/Ctrl-D), which creates a second clone of the group that's spaced the same distance from the first clone as the first clone is from the original.

8. Now select the middle group. This ridge needs to be reflected so that it lies horizontally. Display the Transform panel by pressing ⌘/Ctrl-M. Click on the Reflect icon, which is the farthest icon to the right. Then enter 45 into the Reflect Axis option box and press Return/Enter. FreeHand flips the object about a 45-degree axis, which has the added effect of laying it on its side, as shown in Figure 11-27.

Figure 11-27: Clone two additional ridges and flip the middle one about a 45-degree axis.

9. The first row of ridges is now complete. Now, create the second row. First, select the two left ridges and press ⌘-= on Macs and Ctrl-Shift-C on PCs to clone them.

10. Click on the Move icon in the Transform panel, which is the icon farthest to the left. There are two Move Distance option boxes. The X option box should

contain a value; the Y value is 0. These values reflect your last move, which was entirely horizontal. To move the two clones to the second row, you want to match your last move to keep the spacing even. Leave the X value as is and enter that same value into the Y option box. Make sure that the X value is positive and that the Y value is negative. These settings move the cloned groups to the right and down by the same distance as your previous moves. Press Return/Enter to implement the transformation.

11. Now select only the horizontal ridge in the second row and press ⌘-= on Macs and Ctrl-Shift-C on PCs yet again to clone it. This time you want to move the ridge far to the left, twice the distance of the previous moves, to clear the vertical ridge. To do this, double the X value in the Move panel of the Transform panel and enter a negative sign in front of it. For example, my previous X value was 75 (points), so I changed it to -150. Then change the Y value to 0 and press Return/Enter. You should now have the ridges shown in Figure 11-28.

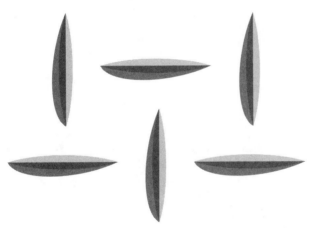

Figure 11-28: The completed second row, with all ridges evenly spaced horizontally and vertically.

12. To create a third row of ridges, select the three grouped objects in the top row and press ⌘-= on Macs and Ctrl-Shift-C on PCs for the bazillionth time. This time, you want to move the clones far enough down to clear the second row. So enter the same value in the Y option box of the Move panel that's currently in the X option box, negative sign and all. In my case, I entered -150. Then change the X value to 0 and press Return/Enter. The third row is now in place.

13. Draw a square surrounding the portions of the ridge objects that you want to repeat in the pattern. This square should intersect the top- and bottom-row ridges along their straight sides, as shown in Figure 11-29. The square represents the boundaries of the tile.

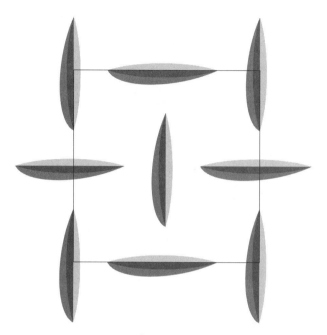

Figure 11-29: Draw a square to determine the boundaries of the tile.

14. While the square is selected, choose Modify ➪ Arrange ➪ Send to Back (⌘/Ctrl-B) to move it in back of the ridges. Then fill the square with 30 percent gray to act as a background for the ridges. The square should have no stroke. This is very important: A stroke would result in a border that would interrupt the transition between tiles.

15. The pattern objects can't exceed the boundaries of the square. Therefore, you must clip the excess ridges away before defining the pattern. You could accomplish this by applying the Intersect command 27 times, but an easier solution is to mask the ridges with the square. Select all nine ridge groups and choose Edit ➪ Cut (⌘/Ctrl-X) to send them to the Clipboard.

16. Next, select the square and choose Edit ➪ Paste Inside (⌘/Ctrl-Shift-V). All portions of the ridge objects that previously exceeded the boundary of the square are now clipped away, as shown back in the first example of Figure 11-25. (The one difference is that your path should not have a stroke surrounding the shape.)

17. While the square is still selected, press ⌘/Ctrl-X, sending the square and its contents to the Clipboard.

18. With nothing selected, press ⌘/Ctrl-Option/Alt-F to display the Fill Inspector. Then select the Tiled option from the pop-up menu and click on the Paste In button. The panel appears exactly as shown back in Figure 11-23.

19. To make sure you don't somehow lose this fill pattern — particularly because you haven't applied it to anything yet — make it into a style. Press ⌘/Ctrl-6 (if necessary) to display the Styles panel. Then select the New option from the Options pop-up menu. After FreeHand creates the new style, double-click on the style name, rename it Metal Ridges, and press the Return/Enter key.

20. Save your document so that you don't lose all of your hard work.

Congratulations, you have just created a tile pattern, one of the hardest things to do in FreeHand. I didn't tell you that at the beginning of the project because I didn't want you to wimp out on me. You can now fill any shape with the pattern using the Styles panel, as described in the previous chapter.

Transforming a tile pattern independently of a path

After applying a tile pattern, you can scale, rotate, or move the pattern inside the object it fills. Figure 11-30, for example, shows the results of transforming the metal ridges pattern inside a rectangle. The first example in the figure shows the pattern as it appears before any transformation. The second example on the left shows the pattern scaled to 200 percent. The first example on the right shows the pattern rotated 45 degrees. In the final example, both scaling and rotating have been applied to the pattern.

Notice that transformations applied from inside the Tiled panel of the Fill Inspector do not transform the filled object itself, only the tiles within the object. Also, a pattern is transformed only within the selected object. Transforming a pattern within one object does not transform that pattern within other objects filled with the same pattern.

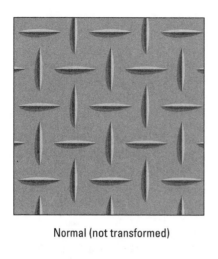

Normal (not transformed)

Rotated 45°

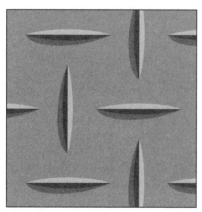

Scaled 200%

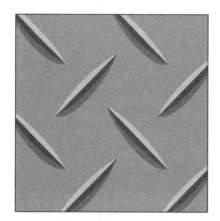

Rotated and scaled

Figure 11-30: The metal ridges pattern subject to various internal transformations.

Incidentally, when you fill an object with a pattern, the relative location of each tile is based on its distance from the lower left corner of the page. This location acts as the origin point for all tile patterns, even if an object filled with a pattern appears far from this origin. All manipulations performed in the Fill Inspector are performed with respect to this location. For example, when you rotate a pattern 45 degrees, you rotate it around the lower left corner of the page.

Cross-Reference

You can also transform a tile pattern along with a filled object when you move the object or apply one of the four transformation tools. To transform tiles and object alike, make sure that the Fills check box in any one of the panels in the Transform panel is selected before applying the transformation. For more information, read Chapter 13.

Tile pattern considerations

A few final notes: You can't apply tile patterns to type, as shown in Figure 11-31, unless you first convert the text block using the Convert to Paths command (⌘/Ctrl-Shift-P). Generally, large sans serif type is best suited to this purpose.

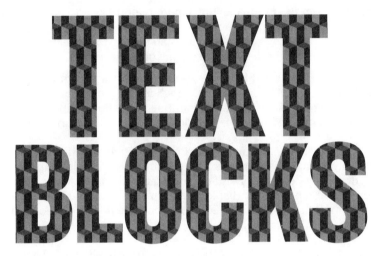

Figure 11-31: A tile pattern can only be applied to text that is converted to paths.

Also, you should know that although patterns may be beautiful to look at, they take a lot of effort to create and eat up disk space and printer memory like you wouldn't believe. For a more efficient filling technique that doesn't restrict you to using repeating images, create a mask as described in the "Creating a clipping path" section of Chapter 15. Or use FreeHand's collection of custom PostScript fills. They're easy to use, they print quickly, and they're introduced in the following section.

PostScript Fill Effects

FreeHand has long been the only drawing program on the Mac to offer special PostScript fill effects. (At least one program, CorelDRAW!, offers an even wider variety of PostScript fill effects for Windows users.) A good many FreeHand users don't take advantage of these effects, but in my opinion, they're definitely worth the old once-over.

Note

PostScript fill effects only print from PostScript printers. If you own a non-PostScript printer, you won't be able to print any of the effects covered throughout the remainder of this chapter.

You can apply FreeHand's special PostScript fill effects in three ways:

✦ **Select Custom from the Fill Inspector pop-up menu:** This option provides access to a bunch of weird fill patterns, most of which you can edit using additional options. Except for the noise effects, these patterns aren't particularly useful, but they're kind of fun.

✦ **Select Textured from the Fill Inspector pop-up menu:** The so-called Textured effects are similar to Custom fills, but resemble real-life fabric, gravel, paper patterns, and so forth. They're more useful than the Custom effects, but you don't have any control over the size or spacing of the texture tiles.

✦ **Select PostScript from the Fill Inspector pop-up menu:** If you know how to program in PostScript, you can select the PostScript option from the Fill Inspector pop-up menu. Then enter your routine in the PostScript Code field. Use spaces to separate code commands; don't use carriage returns.

Just as PostScript fill effects don't print on non-PostScript printers, they don't display correctly on your monitor because your monitor is also (at least, probably) a non-PostScript device. Instead, FreeHand demonstrates that an object is filled with a Custom or Textured pattern by displaying a bunch of Cs or — if you select the PostScript option — PSs inside the object. You won't see how the effect really looks until you print your illustration.

Call me a philistine, but I think that one of the reasons for using FreeHand is to avoid PostScript programming. Granted, you can create some interesting effects, but you have to be clever enough to master a computer language, figure out some interesting way to apply it, tear out your hair debugging code, and for what? So that you can create a bunch of little curlicues, different-size circles, or whatever. Meanwhile, you could have drawn the curlicues and circles by hand and saved about three years of research.

Like I said, call me a philistine, but I like to see my wife and engage in some noncomputer activities every once in a while, so PostScript programming is out.

The Custom fill effects

When you select Custom from the Fill Inspector pop-up menu, FreeHand displays a second pop-up menu filled with ten PostScript fill routines, as shown in Figure 11-32. Many of the options display additional options that enable you to customize the effect. A few effects, though, can only be applied as is. The following sections explain the effects in the order that they appear in the pop-up menu.

Figure 11-32: When you select Custom, FreeHand displays a second pop-up menu containing a list of ten PostScript fill routines.

A word about how the following sections are organized: When an effect offers lots of options — as in the case of bricks, circles, hatch, squares, and tiger teeth — the section that explains the effect includes two-part figures. (For an example, see Figure 11-34.) The first portion of the figure in each of these section shows two versions of the panel. The left panel contains the default settings (except for the colors, which depend on the last colors you used to fill other objects); the right panel contains my custom settings. The second half of these same figures show the default and custom settings applied to two fishy shapes. I created the top fish shape using the settings from the left panel (default settings); the bottom fish shape is the result of the right panel (custom) settings.

Now that I've explained this general format, I won't repeat it within each and every individual section. Believe me, this will make the text more readable. Not only that, you'll be able to flip through the pages without reading the text and still know what's going on.

Black & white noise

The black & white noise effect fills an object with a random pattern of black and white single-point pixels. FreeHand doesn't let you manipulate this effect, so no additional options display when you select Black & White Noise from the pop-up menu. An example of the black & white noise effect is shown in Figure 11-33.

Bricks

The bricks effect fills an object with rows of offset rectangles that produce a brick pattern. Selecting Bricks from the pop-up menu displays the options shown in Figure 11-34.

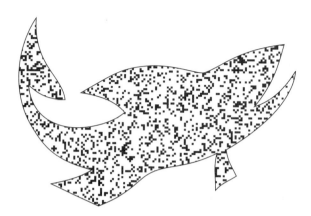

Figure 11-33: You can't edit the black & white noise effect.

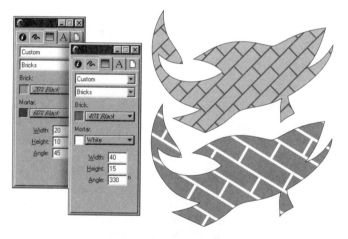

Figure 11-34: Selecting the Bricks effect displays the options shown in these panels. The left panel contains the default settings; the right panel shows my custom settings. On the right are two variations of the brick effect created using the options from the panels.

The options work as follows:

✦ **Brick:** Drag a color onto this swatch to specify the color of the background bricks.

✦ **Mortar:** This swatch controls the color of the 1-point lines between bricks. (The lines are always 1-point thick.)

✦ **Width:** Enter a value into this option box to specify the width of each rectangle in points.

✦ **Height:** This value determines the height of each rectangle, again measured in points.

✦ **Angle:** The value in this option box controls the angle of each row of rectangles in degrees.

Circles

The circles effect fills an object with rows and columns of evenly spaced circles. Selecting Circles from the pop-up menu displays the options shown in Figure 11-35. These options work as follows:

✦ **Color:** Drag a color onto this swatch to specify the color of the outline of each circle. The interiors of the circles are always transparent.

✦ **Radius:** Enter a value into this option box to determine the radius of each circle, measured in points.

✦ **Spacing:** The value in this option box controls the distance between the center of a circle and the center of each of its neighbors, again measured in points.

Tip

To prevent circles from overlapping, make the Spacing value at least twice as large as the Radius value. If the Spacing value is exactly twice the Radius value, the circles touch, as in the top fish in Figure 11-35. In this case however, if the strokes are wider than one point, the strokes of the circles will overlap each other.

✦ **Angle:** This value controls the angle of each row of circles in degrees.

✦ **Stroke Width:** Enter a value into this option box to determine the thickness of the outline of each circle in points.

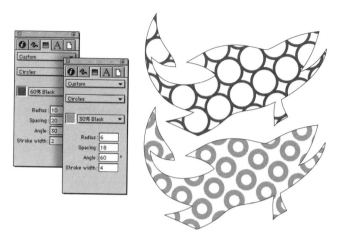

Figure 11-35: Selecting the Circles effect displays the options shown in these panels. The two fishys are filled according to these settings.

Hatch

The hatch effect fills an object with hatch marks created by overlapping two sets of parallel lines. Selecting Hatch from the pop-up menu displays the options shown in Figure 11-36. These options work as follows:

✦ **Color:** Drag a color onto this swatch to specify the color of the hatch lines. The areas between the lines are always transparent.

✦ **Angle 1:** Enter a value into this option box to specify the angle of the first set of parallel lines in degrees.

✦ **Angle 2:** This value controls the angle of the second set of parallel lines, again in degrees.

✦ **Spacing:** The value in this option box controls the distance, in points, between parallel lines in each set.

✦ **Stroke Width:** Enter a value into this option box to determine the line weight of all lines in points.

✦ **Dashed Lines:** Select this check box to create dashed hatch lines, as in the bottom fish of Figure 11-36. Deselect the option to create solid lines, as in the top example.

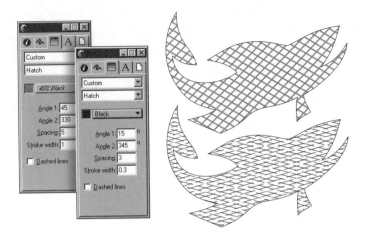

Figure 11-36: Selecting the Hatch effect displays the options shown in these panels. Two variations of the hatch effect bloat these swimming varmints.

Noise

The noise effect fills an object with a random pattern of single-point pixels, randomly colored with a range of gray values. Selecting Noise from the pop-up menu displays two Whiteness Value % option boxes, which control the range of gray values permitted in the pattern. These options work as follows:

✦ **Min:** Enter a value into this option box to specify the darkest gray value assigned to a pixel. The default value is 0, which is black. (Note that this is the opposite of how normal screen values work; with screen values, 100 percent indicates a solid color such as black.)

✦ **Max:** This value controls the lightest gray value assigned to a pixel. The default value is 100, which is white.

Figure 11-37 shows two examples of the noise effect. The default effect, shown in the top example, permits the widest possible range of gray values. In the second example, I condensed the range, creating a more uniform, less grainy effect.

Figure 11-37: Two variations of the noise effect, one using Min and Max values of 0 and 100 (top) and the other using Min and Max values of 50 and 80 (bottom).

Random grass

The random grass effect fills an object with a specified number of randomly placed, black-stroked curves. As shown in Figure 11-38, this effect is perhaps the least interesting of FreeHand's PostScript fill routines.

When you select Random Grass from the pop-up menu, FreeHand displays the Number of Blades option box. Enter any value from 0 to 1,000 to specify the number of curved lines spread over the selected area. An example containing 200 curves is shown in Figure 11-38. Note that the lines are always black and 1 point thick.

Random leaves

The random leaves effect fills an object with a specified number of leaf shapes, which are randomly sized and positioned. The leaves are always filled with white and stroked with 1-point black outlines. Selecting Random Leaves from the pop-up menu displays the Number of Leaves option box. Enter any value from 0 to 1,000 into this option box to specify the number of leaf shapes spread over the selected area. An example containing 150 leaves is shown in Figure 11-39.

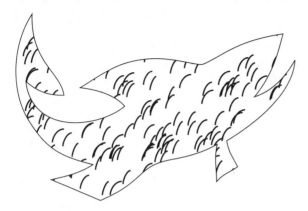

Figure 11-38: The random grass effect filled with 200 blades.

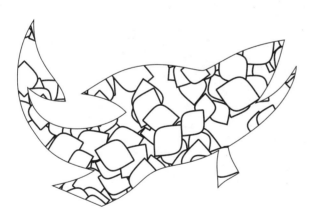

Figure 11-39: The random leaves effect filled with 150 leaves.

Squares

The squares effect fills an object with rows and columns of evenly spaced squares. Selecting Squares from the pop-up menu displays the options shown in Figure 11-40. These options work as follows:

✦ **Color:** Drag a color onto this swatch to specify the color of the outline of each square. The interiors of the squares are always transparent.

✦ **Side Length:** Enter a value into this option box to determine the length of every side of each square in points.

✦ **Spacing:** The value in this option box controls the distance between the center of each square and the center of any of its neighbors, measured in points.

Similar spacing rules to prevent overlapping apply for the squares effect as for the circles effect. The Spacing value should be at least twice as large as the Side Length value, plus the Stroke Width.

✦ **Angle:** This value controls the angle of each row of squares in degrees.

✦ **Stroke Width:** Enter a value into this option box to determine the thickness of the outline of each square in points.

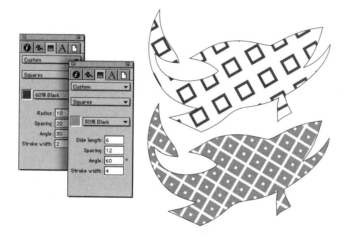

Figure 11-40: Selecting the Squares effect displays the options shown in these panels. Two variations of the squares effect appear as large as fish tend to appear on the right of this figure.

Tiger teeth

The tiger teeth effect fills an object with two sets of dovetailed triangles that resemble a closed mouth of sharp teeth. Selecting Tiger Teeth from the pop-up menu displays the options shown in Figure 11-41. These options work as follows:

✦ **Tooth:** Drag a color onto this swatch to specify the color of half the triangles. When the Angle value is set to 0 degrees, the Tooth swatch controls the color of the left teeth.

✦ **Background:** This swatch controls the color of the remaining triangles. When the Angle is 0, this swatch colors the right teeth.

✦ **Number of Teeth:** The value in this option box controls the number of Tooth-colored triangles that fill the selection.

✦ **Angle:** The value in this option box controls the angle of the triangles in degrees.

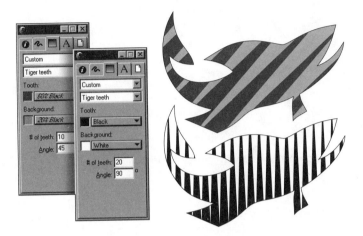

Figure 11-41: Selecting the Tiger Teeth effect displays the options shown in these panels. Two variations of the tiger teeth effect make these piranhas gnash. OK, not really. Never mind. Please move along.

Top noise

The top noise effect fills the selection with a random pattern of single-point pixels, colored according to your specifications and set against a transparent background. Selecting Top Noise from the pop-up menu displays a Gray Value option box, which controls the gray value assigned to the pixels. A value of 100 equals white; 0 equals black. An example of the top noise effect colored with 50-percent gray is shown in Figure 11-42.

Transparent fill routines

Five Custom fill routines have transparent backgrounds. These include circles, hatch, random grass, squares, and top noise. A sixth pattern, random leaves, is partially transparent, because the leaves themselves are filled with white. Any of these PostScript routines can be stacked in front of an object, allowing the background object to partially show through.

The top fish in Figure 11-43 comprises three shapes stacked on top of one another. The rear shape is filled with flat 50 percent gray, the middle shape is filled with the top noise effect set to 80 percent (which is the same as 20 percent gray), and the front shape is filled with the random leaves effect set to 100. The bottom of the figure shows the three shapes as they appear when separated.

Figure 11-42: The top noise effect with a gray value of 50 percent.

Now, you may think that you can make other routines, such as bricks and tiger teeth, transparent by dragging the None swatch onto one of the colors in the Custom panel of the Fill Inspector. But this strategy doesn't work. The color swatches included with Custom routines accept process color, spot colors, and tints, but you can't apply the None option.

PostScript textures

Selecting the Textured option from the pop-up menu at the top of the Fill Inspector provides access to FreeHand's nine PostScript texture routines. Regardless of which routine you select from the pop-up menu in the middle of the panel, FreeHand displays the same options, shown in Figure 11-44. A color swatch lets you change the color applied to the texture, but the background is always white and opaque. A preview box shows an enlarged version of the texture. This preview is designed to help you predict how the texture will look when applied to an object, because PostScript textures don't preview in the illustration window. You should keep in mind, however, that the textures appear about three times larger in the preview box than they do when applied to objects. Figure 11-45 shows every one of the textures applied to my familiar fish shape.

Figure 11-43: Three shapes—two of which contain Custom routines— stacked in front of one another (top) and offset slightly (bottom).

Figure 11-44: When you select the Textured option, a second pop-up menu contains a list of PostScript fill routines (right).

Burlap

Coarse gravel

Coquille

Denim

Fine gravel

Heavy mezzo

Light mezzo

Medium mezzo

Sand

Figure 11-45: The nine PostScript textures included with FreeHand.

Assigning Strokes

Every Good Object Deserves Strokes

Stroke is the PostScript-language term for the attribute that controls the appearance of the outline of a path. In early versions of FreeHand, however, this attribute was called "line." Even though lots of computer artists were already familiar with stroke from Adobe Illustrator, I suppose that FreeHand's designers thought that "line" sounded a little bit friendlier.

In Version 3, FreeHand's terminology was in a state of flux. The attribute was called line when it applied to a graphic object and stroke when it applied to text. (You used to have to use separate dialog boxes to stroke paths and text, a foible that Version 4 remedied.)

FreeHand 5 embraced the industry standard stroke and completely abandoned line. Almost completely, anyway. Want to know the one remnant of old terminology left in FreeHand 8? Press ⌘/Ctrl-Option/Alt-L — L for line — and up pops the Stroke Inspector.

How stroke affects objects

Deciding whether to stroke an object is one of the most painless choices you can make in FreeHand. If you want to see a path's outline, apply a stroke; otherwise, don't.

The principle behind stroking is equally straightforward. The stroke is centered on the path. Half of the stroke resides on the inside of the path, and the other half resides on the outside. Figure 12-1 shows an identical stroke applied to an open path and to a closed path. In both cases, I've displayed the path in white to show how the stroke is centered.

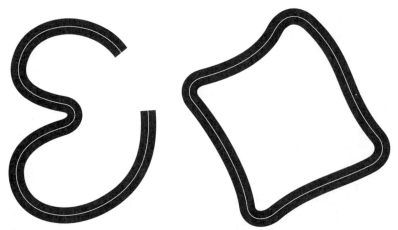

Figure 12-1: An open path (left) and a closed path (right), each stroked with a heavy line. The actual paths appear in white.

It's important to keep this centering in mind when you're trying to determine the amount of space the stroke will occupy when you print your artwork. You can also exploit this feature to create interesting effects, as described in the "Mixing Stroke Attributes" section later in this chapter.

How stroke affects text

Stroking text is slightly more complicated than stroking an ordinary path. If you select a text block or text bound to a path with the arrow tool and apply a stroke, the stroke affects the path, not the text itself, as shown in Figure 12-2.

Figure 12-2: When you apply a stroke to a text object selected with the arrow tool, FreeHand strokes the path, not the text.

If the stroke does not appear in the preview mode after you apply it, it's because you haven't told FreeHand to display the path. If the text is inside a text object, press ⌘/Ctrl-I to display the Object Inspector. Then select the Display Border check box. If the text is bound to a path, press ⌘/Ctrl-I to display the Object Inspector, and then select the Show Path check box.

To stroke characters of type, select the characters with the text tool and then apply the stroke. The stroke has the effect of thickening the characters. In Figure 12-3, for example, I selected and stroked the words *we the people*. Stroking is a great way to make text bolder if the font doesn't offer a sufficiently bold style.

Figure 12-3: You can stroke text separately from its path.

To see only the stroke, apply a transparent fill by dragging the None color swatch onto the characters. Because the characters are stroked, FreeHand allows you to make the interior of the characters transparent. (For some reason, FreeHand prevents you from making both the fill and stroke of text transparent at the same time.) In Figure 12-4, you can see through the characters to the bound path behind them.

Figure 12-4: After you stroke the characters, you can make their fills transparent.

Just as FreeHand doesn't allow you to apply certain kinds of fills to text objects, it won't let you apply two stroking attributes — line caps and arrowheads — to type. If you want to create an effect like the one shown in Figure 12-5, you must first convert the text to composite paths by Text ⇨ Convert to Paths (⌘/Ctrl-Shift-P), as described at the end of Chapter 9. You can then stroke the character outlines just like any other graphic object.

Figure 12-5: After converting character outlines to paths, you can assign round line joins, dash patterns, and arrowheads, all shown here.

Assigning a Stroke

Just as you can assign colors to the interiors of paths by dragging color swatches from the Color List and other panels, you can assign color to the outline of paths by dragging and dropping. The problem is, the target is typically much smaller. Although the interior of a path may be vast and expansive, the stroke might be a slim hairline. It's like trying to hit the side of a barn with a snowball one minute and then shooting for a tin can resting on the weather vane the next.

Luckily, FreeHand helps you out a little. As long as you drop the color within three or so pixels of the stroke — you specify the exact number of pixels using the Snap

Distance option box in the General panel of the Preferences dialog box — FreeHand changes the stroke and not the fill.

This is not the case when you're stroking characters of text. In fact, FreeHand simply does not allow you to stroke characters by dragging and dropping. You have to use the Stroke icon in the Color List panel or rely on the options in the Stroke Inspector.

Furthermore, dragging and dropping only changes the color of a stroke. And as you'll soon learn, there's much more to stroke than just color. In fact, FreeHand's stroking options rival its filling options in terms of variety and quantity.

To access these additional stroking options, bring up the Stroke Inspector by pressing ⌘/Ctrl-Option/Alt-L, which stands for loopy. You can choose the variety of stroke by selecting an option from the pop-up menu at the top of the Inspector, as shown in Figure 12-6. Three of the options — None, Pattern, and PostScript — are very similar to their counterparts in the Fill Inspector. They work as follows:

✦ **None:** Select the None option to make the stroke transparent. You can also select the None color swatch from the Color List panel and drag it onto an object.

✦ **Pattern:** Select this option to apply a bitmapped pattern. If you've lost your sanity, that is. Otherwise, select a different option.

✦ **PostScript:** If you're a card-carrying propeller head, select this option and enter your own PostScript code. Better yet, define your illustration entirely by entering PostScript code into a word processor. That way, you won't have to spend any money on FreeHand, and you can amaze all your friends in Mensa.

Figure 12-6: Select an option from the pop-up menu in the Stroke Inspector to determine the variety of stroke applied to an object.

Upcoming sections explain two other options, Basic and Custom, in a little more detail. Basic is far and away the most common variety of stroke you'll use in your illustrations. Custom provides access to predefined PostScript routines that are sufficiently different from their Fill Inspector counterparts to warrant further explanation in the "Custom PostScript strokes" section of this chapter.

Single-color strokes

Selecting Basic from the pop-up menu in the Stroke Inspector displays the options shown in Figure 12-7. These options allow you to stroke a selected path or character outline with a uniform color and thickness. You can also specify how the ends and corners of the stroked path will look, select dash patterns, and assign arrowheads.

Figure 12-7: The Basic options control the color, thickness, cap, join, dash pattern, and arrowheads applied to the selected object.

The first two options in Figure 12-7 work exactly like their identical twins in the Fill Inspector:

✦ **Color swatch:** Change the color of a stroke by dragging a color swatch from the Color List or Color Mixer panel onto the swatch in the Stroke Inspector. Or, use the eyedropper tool to drag and drop a color from your document into the color swatch. You can also click and hold on the default color (black) and choose any of the colors in that pop-up menu from your color list.

✦ **Overprint:** You can print the stroke from one separation on top of the fills and strokes in another separation by selecting the Overprint check box. For the full story (and accompanying intrigue), see the "Overprinting colors" section of Chapter 11.

Nothing out of the ordinary; you've done it a billion times. But everything else in this Inspector may look a little foreign. The following sections explain how these options work.

Line weight

Directly below the Overprint check box is the Width pop-up menu, which controls the thickness, or line weight, of a stroke. Line weight in FreeHand is specified in points, picas, inches, or millimeters, depending on the unit of measure set in the Units pop-up menu in the Status toolbar.

You can enter a line weight value — $\frac{1}{10,000}$-point increments are permitted — into the Width box to apply it to the selected object. There is a Width pop-up menu with preset widths to choose from as well.

Figure 12-8 shows the nine line weights included in the Width pop-up menu by default. Keep in mind that you can change these line weights by editing the option box for Default Line Weights in the Object panel of the Preferences dialog box, as discussed in Chapter 2.

Generally, I advise against specifying a line weight value smaller than 0.15 point. FreeHand defines a hairline — the thinnest line weight traditionally available — as 0.25 point. So a 0.15-point line is just over half the weight of a hairline. As an example, suppose that you specify a 0-point line weight. This setting instructs FreeHand to print the thinnest line available from the current output device. The thinnest line printable by 300-dpi laser printer is 0.24-point thick ($\frac{1}{300}$ inch), approximately equal to a hairline. But higher-resolution printers, such as Linotronic and Compugraphic imagesetters, easily print lines as thin as 0.03 point, or eight times thinner than a hairline. Because any line thinner than 0.15-point is almost invisible to the naked eye, such a line will probably drop out when reproduced commercially.

Line caps

The next option in the Stroke Inspector is the Cap option. Using this option, you can select a line cap, which determines the appearance of a stroke at an endpoint. Line caps are generally useful only when you're stroking an open path. The only exception is when you use line caps in combination with dash patterns, as described in the "Dash patterns and line caps" section later in this chapter.

From left to right, the three Cap icons represent the butt cap, round cap, and square cap.

✦ **Butt cap:** Notice the black line that runs through the center of each of the Cap icons. This line denotes the position of the path relative to the stroke. When the Butt Cap icon is selected, the stroke ends immediately at either endpoint and is perpendicular to the final course of the path.

✦ **Round cap:** Giving a stroke a round cap is like attaching a circle to the end of a path. The endpoint acts as the center of this circle, and its radius is half the line weight, as illustrated in Figure 12-9. For example, if you have a 4-point line weight with round caps that follows a horizontal path, a 2-point portion of the stroke is on top of the path and the other 2-point portion is underneath. (Because the path is itself invisible, the two halves of the stroke meet with no break between them.) Upon reaching the end of the path, the top half of the stroke wraps around the endpoint in a circular manner and continues on to form the bottom half of the stroke. The end of the path, then, is a semicircle with a 2-point radius.

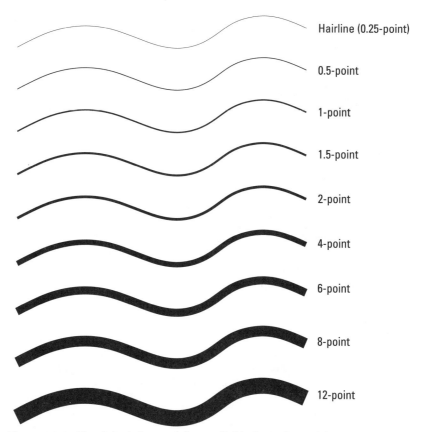

Hairline (0.25-point)

0.5-point

1-point

1.5-point

2-point

4-point

6-point

8-point

12-point

Figure 12-8: The default line weights available from the Width pop-up menu.

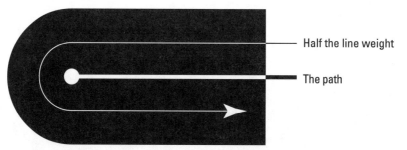

Half the line weight

The path

Figure 12-9: When the Round Cap icon is selected, the stroke wraps around each endpoint in a path to form a semicircle.

Tip Butt caps sometimes look as if they were abruptly cut short, especially when combined with thick line weights. Round caps give exposed endpoints a more finished appearance. Figure 12-10 shows several open paths. The first set of paths is stroked with butt caps, and the second is stroked with round caps. (The actual paths appear inset with thin white strokes.) Round caps are like childproof corners — the other objects can run into them without hurting themselves.

Figure 12-10: A set of five open paths stroked with butt caps (left) and round caps (right).

✦ **Square cap:** When you select the third icon, FreeHand attaches a square to the end of a line. The endpoint is the center of the square. As with the round cap, the size of the square depends on the line weight. The width and height of the square are equal to the current line weight, so that the square projects from the endpoint a distance equal to one-half the line weight, as illustrated in Figure 12-11. If a path has a 4-point line weight, for example, the end of the stroke would extend 2 points beyond the endpoint.

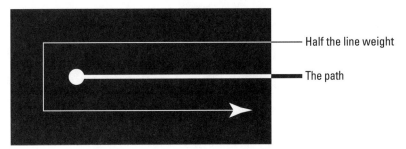

Figure 12-11: When the Square Cap icon is selected, the stroke extends half the line weight beyond the endpoint.

Line joins

Below the Cap radio buttons are the three Join radio buttons. Using these options, you can select a line join, which determines the appearance of a stroke at corners in a path. (Assuming that you followed my recommendations in Chapters 3 and 5, corners should occur exclusively at corner points, not at curve or connector points.)

From left to right, the Join icons represent the miter join, round join, and bevel join options, which work as follows:

✦ **Miter join:** If a corner has a miter join, the outside edges of a stroke extend until they meet, as shown in the top star in Figure 12-12. An uninterrupted miter join always forms a crisp corner. You can, however, cut a Miter join short by using the Miter Limit option, as explained in the next section.

✦ **Round join:** When this icon is selected, half the line weight wraps around the corner point to form a rounded edge, as in the middle star in the figure. Round joins and round caps are so closely related that they are almost always paired together. I recommend that you don't use round joins in combination with butt caps. This goes doubly if any dash pattern is involved, because round joins actually form complete circles around corner points.

✦ **Bevel join:** The bevel join is very similar to a butt cap. Instead of allowing the outer edges of a stroke to meet to form a crisp corner, as in the case of a miter join, the stroke is sheared off at the corner point, as in the lower right star in Figure 12-12. The result appears to be two very closely situated corners on either side of each corner point.

Cutting short overly long miter joins

Below the Join icons is the Miter Limit option box, which lets you bevel excessively long miter joins on a corner-by-corner basis. In Version 3, the Miter Limit was measured as an angle in degrees. Since Version 4, this value has been changed to represent the largest allowed ratio between the miter length and the line weight, both labeled in Figure 12-13. As long as the miter length divided by the line weight is less than the Miter Limit value, FreeHand creates a miter join. But if the miter length grows (or the Miter Limit value shrinks) enough that the miter length divided by the line weight is more than the Miter Limit value, FreeHand lops off the miter and makes it a bevel join.

The primary use for this option is to hack off miter joins associated with curved segments. As shown in Figure 12-14, miter joins can become extremely long when a corner point is associated with one or more inward-curving segments. What's worse, the join doesn't curve along with the segment; it straightens out after the corner point. The result is an unbecoming spike that appears to have little to do with the rest of the path.

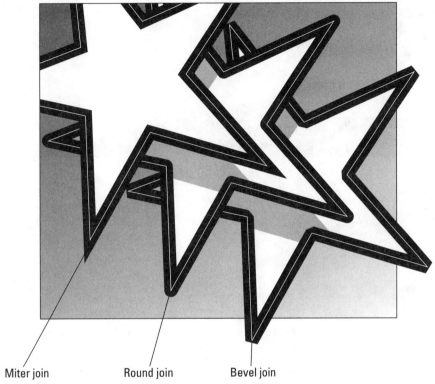

Miter join   Round join   Bevel join

Figure 12-12: Three stars, each stroked with a different kind of line join. Notice the appearance of the inward-pointing corners as well as the outward-pointing corners in each path.

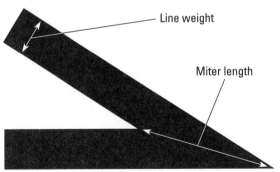

Line weight

Miter length

Figure 12-13: If the miter length divided by the line weight is more than the Miter Limit value, FreeHand bevels the join.

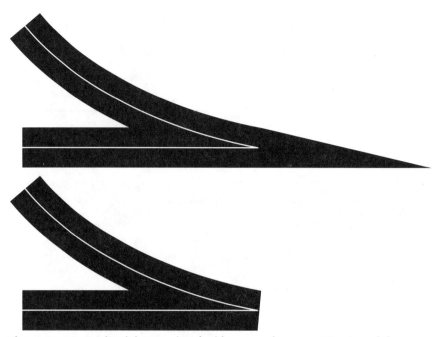

Figure 12-14: A miter join associated with a curved segment (top), and the same join beveled (bottom).

Note

The solution — clipping the join as in the second example in Figure 12-14 — is a harsh compromise. In fact, it's not a compromise at all. FreeHand either gives you a ridiculously long miter or it bevels it completely. If you want to preserve the attractive quality of a miter join without allowing it to take over too large a portion of your drawing, manually adjust your path to increase the angle between a pair of segments, thus decreasing the miter length. If that fails, experiment with the round join to see if it looks better. Consider the Miter Limit option a last resort.

The Miter Limit value can range from 0 to — of all numbers — 57. Though it's never dimmed, the Miter Limit option is applicable only to miter joins. If either the Round Join or Bevel Join icon is selected, the Miter Limit value has no effect.

Dash patterns

The pop-up menu below the Miter Limit option box gives you a choice of eleven dash patterns, which are repetitive interruptions in a stroke. For example, a standard coupon border in an advertisement is a dash pattern.

The first dash pattern offered in the pop-up menu is No Dash, which results in a solid stroke. The default setting, No Dash ensures that the stroke remains uninterrupted throughout the length of the path.

All of the remaining patterns are dashed strokes. The most popular use of dashed strokes is to indicate cut-out lines for items that are meant to be clipped from a page: coupons, paper dolls, and so on. Dash patterns are also used to indicate a ghostly or translucent shape. If you were illustrating the scene from *A Christmas Carol* in which Marley comes back and scares the pants off Scrooge, for example, you might want to apply dash patterns to Marley. Or to the door nail, which, according to Dickens, Marley was as dead as. Or to Scrooge's dead cat, Phil, who was edited out of the story at the last minute on account of his smelling rather dead. (Few people know just how many dead characters there are in *A Christmas Carol*. Makes *The Wild Bunch* look pretty peaceful.)

For those of you currently working on Dickens projects, Figure 12-15 shows an example of each of FreeHand's predefined dash patterns. The labels that accompany the patterns show the length, in points, of the dashes and gaps. For example, in the second pattern, each dash is 8 points long, and each gap is 4 points wide. If a label contains more than two values, the subsequent numbers represent additional dashes and gaps. In the example 12-2-2-2 (Figure 12-15), the first dash is 12 points long, the first gap is 2 points, the second dash is 2 points long, and the second gap is another 2 points. FreeHand repeats the sequence over and over again.

Tip

Press the Option/Alt key while selecting any option from the pop-up menu except No Dash to display the Dash Editor dialog box shown in Figure 12-16. This dialog box displays the length of each dash and gap in the current dash pattern. Change the values to create a new dash pattern based on the existing one.

Each option box in the Dash Editor dialog box represents the interval — measured in the current unit of measure — during which a dash will be On or Off in the course of stroking a path. On values determine the length of dashes; Off values determine the length of the gaps between the dashes. All values can range from 1 to 200 points; decimal values and zeros are ignored (even though FreeHand shows a bunch of zeros in the dialog box).

Suppose you want to create a dashed line composed of a series of 6-point dashes followed by 3-point gaps. After displaying the Dash Editor dialog box, enter 6 in the first On option box and 3 in the first Off option box. Leave the remaining six option boxes set to 0. If a series of consecutive On and Off options are 0, FreeHand simply ignores them. Therefore, after FreeHand creates the first 6-point dash and its following 3-point gap, it repeats the sequence over and over throughout the length of the selected path.

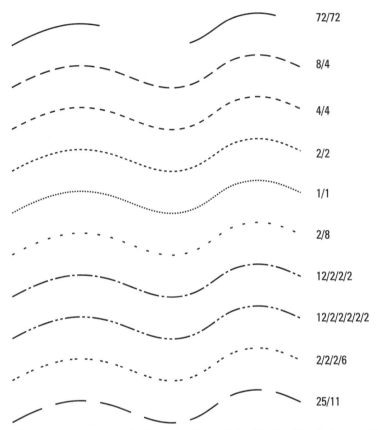

72/72

8/4

4/4

2/2

1/1

2/8

12/2/2/2

12/2/2/2/2/2

2/2/2/6

25/11

Figure 12-15: The ten dash strokes included with FreeHand, along with the patterns' dimensions listed in points.

Figure 12-16: Press Option/Alt when selecting a pattern to display this dialog box, which lets you design your own custom dash pattern.

You can establish the same dash pattern in several ways. For example, instead of leaving the last six options blank, you could fill them with 6-3-6-3-6-3. Many other variations produce the same effect.

When you press Return/Enter or click on the OK button, FreeHand adds the new dash pattern to the end of the pop-up menu. Therefore, you don't endanger an existing dash pattern when you Option/Alt-select it; FreeHand always applies your changes to a new pattern. All custom dash patterns are saved with the foreground document. They are transferred from one illustration to the next if you cut a line stroked with the pattern and paste it into another document.

Arrowheads

FreeHand offers editable arrowheads. You can either select from the predefined arrowheads included with the product or design your own. Arrowheads affect open paths only.

Apply an arrowhead by selecting an option from one of the two Arrowheads pop-up menus, shown in Figure 12-17. The first pop-up menu appends an arrowhead to the first endpoint in the path; the second menu appends an arrowhead to the last endpoint. (Remember that which endpoint is first and which is last depends on the order in which you drew the path.)

Arrowheads grow and shrink according to the line weight that you apply to the path. Figure 12-18 shows every one of FreeHand's predefined arrowheads applied to a column of 8-point lines and a column of 2-point lines. The arrowheads themselves are the same. But because FreeHand sizes the arrowheads according to the line weight, they appear four times larger on the left side of the figure than they do on the right.

Figure 12-17: Select an option from one of the Arrowheads pop-up menus to assign an arrowhead to an open path.

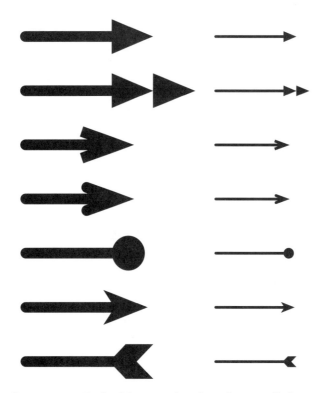

Figure 12-18: Each of the Arrowheads options applied to
8-point lines (left) and 2-point lines (right).

To create your own custom arrowhead, select the New option from either of the
Arrowheads pop-up menus. FreeHand displays the Arrowhead Editor dialog box
shown in Figure 12-19. The dialog box provides you with a little illustration window
(which I call the edit window), a set of drawing and transformation tools, and a
bunch of buttons and other options. This arrowhead designer is without a doubt
the best I've seen in any drawing program.

When you select the New option from the Arrowheads pop-up menu, the Arrowhead
Editor appears with an empty edit window. If you want to work from an existing
arrowhead rather than creating one from scratch, press the Option/Alt key and
select any one of the predefined arrowheads from the pop-up menu. FreeHand
displays an arrow in the edit window, as shown in Figure 12-19.

Another way to create an arrowhead is to design it in the standard illustration
window, where you have access to FreeHand's full suite of tools. Then copy the
object you want to use as an arrowhead—one object only—select the New option

from one of the Arrowheads pop-up menus, and click on the Paste In button (or press ⌘/Ctrl-V) inside the Arrowhead Editor dialog box. (If the Paste In button is dimmed, it's because an object already resides in the edit window, which can only handle one object at a time.) If the entire edit window turns black or some other color, your object is too large to fit in the window. ⌘/Ctrl-Option/Alt-Shift-spacebar-click on the screen to zoom out all the way to the edit window's minimum view size.

Tools   Edit window

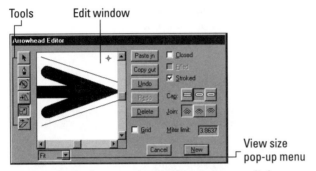

View size
pop-up menu

Figure 12-19: The Arrowhead Editor is its own little mini-program. Here I'm enlarging the arrowhead with the scale tool.

The elements of the Arrowhead Editor dialog box work as follows:

✦ **The toolbox:** The tools along the left side of the dialog box include, from top to bottom, the arrow, pen, rotate, reflect, scale, and skew tools. Each tool works exactly as it does in the standard illustration window. You can press the ⌘/Ctrl key to access the arrow tool, create and add points with the pen tool, and transform the arrowhead with the other tools.

If you're editing one of FreeHand's predefined arrowheads and you merely want to enlarge the arrowhead for use with thin line weights, don't edit the path with the arrow tool; use the scale tool instead. As shown in Figure 12-19, begin dragging at the center of the arrowhead and drag up and to the right to enlarge the shape.

✦ **Hidden tools:** They're not in the toolbox, but you can access the grabber hand and zoom tool using keyboard equivalents. Spacebar-drag to scroll with the grabber hand; press ⌘/Ctrl-spacebar or ⌘/Ctrl-Option/Alt-spacebar to get the zoom tool. ⌘/Ctrl-Shift-spacebar-click zooms you all the way in; ⌘/Ctrl-Option/Alt-Shift-spacebar-click zooms all the way out.

✦ **The view-size pop-up menu:** Select options from the pop-up menu to change the view size. Unfortunately, the standard keyboard equivalents — ⌘/Ctrl-1, ⌘/Ctrl-2 — don't work inside the Arrowhead Editor dialog box.

✦ **Paste In, Copy Out:** Click the Paste In button or press ⌘/Ctrl-V to paste an object from the Clipboard into the edit window, provided that an object is not already there. Click on the Copy Out button or press ⌘/Ctrl-C to copy the current contents of the edit window to the Clipboard.

✦ **Undo, Redo:** What would an edit window be without these two buttons? You can undo and redo the same amount of consecutive operations that you can throughout the rest of FreeHand. You can also use the familiar keyboard equivalents, ⌘/Ctrl-Z and ⌘/Ctrl-Y.

✦ **Delete:** Just press the Delete key or click on the Delete button to delete the contents of the edit window.

✦ **Grid:** If you want to constrain your edits using the grid, select the Grid check box.

✦ **Closed:** This check box ensures that the arrowhead is a closed path. Be sure that this check box is selected if you want your arrowhead to be filled rather than hollow.

✦ **Filled:** When this option is checked, FreeHand fills the arrowhead with the color applied to the stroke (not the fill) in the Inspector. To create a hollow arrowhead, deselect this option.

✦ **Stroked:** This option is certainly an unexpected one — it enables you to apply a stroke to a stroke attribute. When you select Stroked, FreeHand applies the same color and line weight to the arrowhead that you apply to the rest of the stroke. However, you can specify an independent line cap and line join using the Cap and Join icons and the Miter Limit option box.

When you finish creating or editing the arrowhead, press Return/Enter or click the New button. FreeHand adds the new arrowhead to the end of both Arrowheads pop-up menus in the Stroke Inspector. To transfer the arrowhead to another illustration, copy a path stroked with the arrowhead and paste it into the other document.

Custom PostScript strokes

All right, that's it for the Basic options. If you select Custom from the pop-up menu in the Stroke Inspector, FreeHand lets you select from 23 special PostScript routines, as shown in Figure 12-20. Just like the custom fill effects, custom stroke effects don't preview, only print. Even worse, FreeHand doesn't give you any indication that a path includes a custom stroke. Cool, huh? Unlike the Custom fill effects covered in Chapter 11, 22 of the 23 Custom stroke effects are remarkably similar, so much so, in fact, that if you know how to use one, you know how to use them all. The only exception is the neon effect, which is described at the end of this section.

To explain all stroking effects except neon, I'll use the arrow effect as an example. Like the others, the arrow effect repeats a series of objects — in this case, a stylized arrowhead motif — along the length of a selected path. Choosing the Arrow option from the Effect pop-up menu displays the options shown on the left side of Figure 12-20. Here's how they work:

✦ **Color:** Drag a color onto this swatch to specify the color of the outlines of the arrowheads. The interior of each arrowhead is transparent.

✦ **Width:** Enter a value into this option box to specify the thickness of the custom stroke in points.

✦ **Length:** This value controls the length of each arrowhead, measured in points.

✦ **Spacing:** This value determines the distance between the end of one arrowhead and the beginning of another, again measured in points.

Custom stroke preview

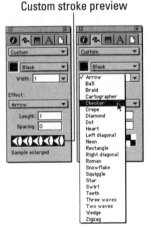

Figure 12-20: When you select the Custom option, a second pop-up menu presents a list of 23 PostScript stroke routines (right).

Figure 12-21 shows the arrow pattern and the other 21 custom patterns that use these options. In each case, I set the color to black, the width and length to 20, and the spacing to 0, all of which are default settings. The only exception is the rectangle effect (lower left corner), which uses a Spacing value of 2 to keep the rectangles from butting up against each other. All the Custom strokes look fine on a straight line, but as you can see in the figure, some lend themselves to curved lines better than others.

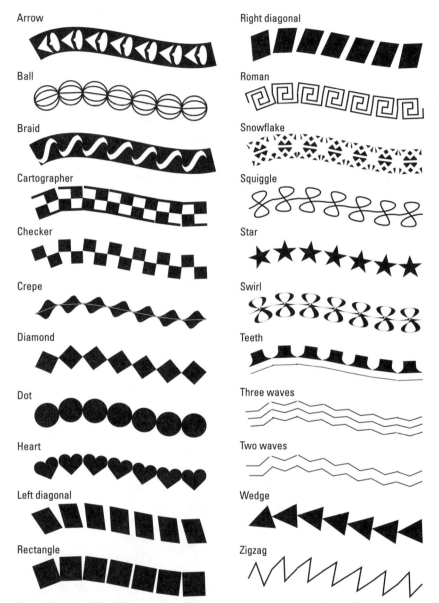

Figure 12-21: You can access these custom stroke patterns from the Custom pop-up menu in the Stroke Inspector.

The neon effect

The only unusual Custom stroking effect is neon, which combines three lines — one stroked with white, in front of another stroked with black, in front of a third stroked with 50 percent gray. Selecting Neon from the Effect pop-up menu leaves only one option box available, Width. Enter a value to specify the line weight of the 50 percent gray line. The black line will be half this weight. The white line is always 1 point thick. Figure 12-22 shows an example of the neon stroke.

Regardless of which Custom effect you select, FreeHand previews the effect in the illustration window as a solid line with the color and line weight specified in the Stroke Inspector.

Figure 12-22: A path stroked with a 20-point version of the neon effect.

Other patterned strokes

Custom PostScript routines aren't the only kinds of repeating patterns that you can apply in FreeHand. In fact, there's a much more flexible way that provides more options and displays correctly on-screen. Create a block of text set in Zapf Dingbats, the wacky symbol font designed by Hermann Zapf back in the seventies, when wacky symbols were the happenin' scene. You can make all the characters identical or mix it up a bit, as shown in the first example of Figure 12-23.

After you create your text, draw a path, select both text and path, and combine the two by choosing Text ➪ Attach To Path (⌘/Ctrl-Shift-Y). The text becomes a stroke, as shown in the second example of Figure 12-23. Color the text by selecting the characters with the text tool and applying a fill color. The type size serves as the line weight. You can even kern the text if you don't like the spacing. Try doing that with the Custom effects!

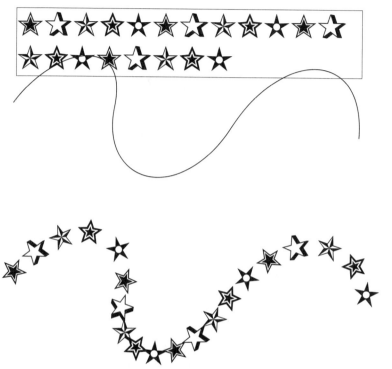

Figure 12-23: After creating a text block of Zapf Dingbats stars (top), bind the text to a path to create a patterned stroke (bottom).

Mixing Stroke Attributes

You can create interesting effects by mixing dash patterns with caps, joins, and line weights. You can also stack clones of an object, one in front of another, and stroke each with a slightly different line weight and color. Provided that the weight of each stroke is thinner than the weight of the stroke behind it, portions of each stroke show through, an effect that's ideally suited for creating hollow or gradient outlines.

Stacking strokes

I'll start things off by showing a few ways to stack strokes. The following steps demonstrate how to apply an inline effect to some converted text. If you read Chapter 8, you're probably thinking, "Inline? Isn't that the wimpy little effect you access from the Text ➪ Effect submenu?" Yes, it is. The problem isn't really with the inline effect itself, but rather with the way that FreeHand's automated Inline option implements it. If you're willing to spend some time experimenting with stacked strokes, you can create some pretty cool inline effects that are well beyond anything the Inline option can do. If you take a peek at Figures 12-25 and 12-26, you'll see what lies in store for you.

1. Convert some text to paths or draw simple shapes. Figure 12-24 shows a combination of the two. The X is a Zapf Dingbats character — the number 8 in Zapf Dingbats; I drew the O to match. For the best results, make sure that the paths are large — say, a few inches tall.

Figure 12-24: Two paths stroked with 12-point outlines.

2. Apply a thick stroke and no fill to the paths. In the case of Figure 12-24, I applied a 12-point line weight with round joins. You can use any color you want (except white).

3. Select the paths and clone them (⌘-= on Macs and Ctrl-Shift-C on PCs). This creates duplicates of the paths right in front of the originals.

4. Change the stroke to a slightly thinner white outline. I used a 9-point line weight. You now have a standard inline effect, in which a white outline is bordered on either side by colored outlines peeking out from the rear stroke.

5. To give the effect a three-dimensional feel, offset the clones slightly. With the cloned paths selected, press the ↑ key once and the ← key once. Assuming that the Cursor Key Distance value in the General panel of the Preferences dialog box is set to 1, you have nudged the clones one point up and one point left, resulting in the effect shown in Figure 12-25. The offset clones make the paths look as if they have engraved edges.

Figure 12-25: Clone the paths, apply a 9-point white stroke, and offset them one point up and one point left.

6. You can keep cloning, applying thinner strokes, and offsetting till you're blue in the face. To create the characters shown in Figure 12-26, I cloned the paths, applied 5-point black strokes, and offset the clones another one point up and one point left. I then cloned them a third time, stroked them with 2-point white outlines, and offset them again. Finally, I selected the original paths way in back — it helps to switch to the keyline mode and zoom in — and filled the originals with gradations.

You can create other stroking effects by stacking clones with progressively thinner line weights and lighter tints. By lightening the color of a stroke each time you reduce the line weight, you can create neon type. In Figure 12-27, for example, the rearmost paths are stroked with a 100 percent black, 12-point line weight. I then cloned the paths and changed the line weight to 11-point and the tint to 90 percent. I cloned again, changed the line weight to 10-point and the tint to 80 percent, and so on. The tenth clone is stroked with a white, 2-point outline. All paths were given round joins to emulate the curves associated with neon tubes.

Figure 12-26: The result of two more sets of offset clones, one with 5-point black strokes and the top with 2-point white strokes. I also filled the original paths with a very subtle gradation.

Figure 12-27: You can create neon strokes by repeatedly cloning paths and stroking each clone with a thinner, lighter outline than the path behind it.

If you want to add some depth to the effect, offset each set of paths immediately after you clone it, as in the previous set of steps. To create Figure 12-28, I offset each clone one point up and one point to the left. The result looks less like neon lights and more like letters sculpted in relief.

Figure 12-28: The paths from Figure 12-27 offset from each other — point vertically and horizontally.

Actually, there's a quicker way to achieve the neon effect: Use the Blend command, described in Chapter 15. For example, to make a neon X, stroke the original path with a 12-point black line weight, clone the path, offset the clone if necessary, and apply a 2-point white stroke. Then select one point in each path — if the paths are coincident (right on top of each other), marquee the points with the arrow tool — and choose Blend under Modify ⇨ Combine ⇨ Blend or ⌘/Ctrl-Shift-B.

Dash patterns and line caps

You can combine dash patterns with line caps to create effects such as the one shown in Figure 12-29. Because FreeHand treats the beginning and ending of each dash in a pattern as the beginning and ending of a stroke, both ends of a dash are affected by the selected line cap. This allows you to create round dashes as well as rectangular ones.

To produce the pattern shown in Figure 12-29, you create a black stroke with round caps and joins and a 12-point line weight. You then Option/Alt-select an option from the dash pattern pop-up menu in the Stroke Inspector. When the Dash Editor dialog box appears, enter 1 for the On value (the smallest value permitted for a dash) and 18 for Off. Then press Return/Enter.

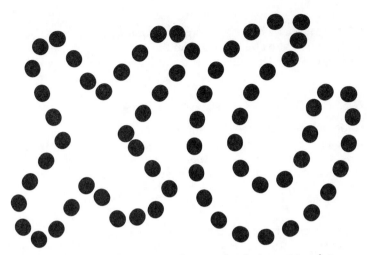

Figure 12-29: A dash pattern with a 1-point dash, an 18-point gap, a 12-point line weight, and round caps and joins.

The diagram in Figure 12-30 shows how each dash is constructed. By setting the length of each at 1, you instruct FreeHand to allow only one point between the center of the round cap at the beginning of the dash and the center of the round cap at the end of the dash, which results in an oval. (The endpoints of the dashes appear as small white circles in Figure 12-30.) The cap of each oval has a 6-point radius, so the complete oval measures 13 points wide. Because 13 points of each 19-point sequence (1-point dash plus 18-point gap) is consumed by a round cap oval, a distance of only six points separates each oval.

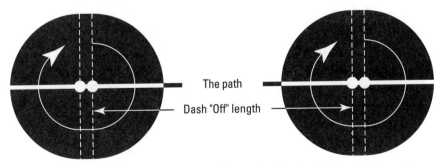

Figure 12-30: Round caps wrap around the ends of each dash in a dash pattern. Small dashes result in near-perfect circles.

Tip The moral of the story is that when you're creating round dashes, the Off value in the Dash Editor dialog box must be greater than the line weight to prevent the dashes from overlapping. The On value must be 1 to achieve near-circular dashes.

Stacking dash patterns and line caps

You can create more interesting effects by stacking round-cap dash patterns in front of other dash patterns. Using a technique similar to stacking solid strokes, you make the line weight of each path thinner than the line weight of the path behind it. Although you can vary the line caps, keep the dash pattern constant throughout all layered paths; that is, the length of each dash and length of each gap — what I call the periodicity of the pattern — should not vary.

The following steps begin with the stroke pattern shown back in Figure 12-29. The periodicity of this pattern is 19 points — a 1-point dash plus an 18-point gap. The stroke also includes a 12-point line weight. In the exercise, you layer two clones in front of these paths to create a pattern of inline circles.

1. Follow the process described in the preceding section to create the dash patterns shown in Figure 12-29. Then clone the paths by pressing ⌘-= on Macs and Ctrl-Shift-C for PCs.

2. Change the stroke color to white with a 9-point line weight.

3. Offset the paths one point left and one point up by pressing the ← key and then the ↑ key. The result is shown in Figure 12-31.

Figure 12-31: Clone the paths from Figure 12-29, apply a 9-point white stroke, and offset the paths one point up and one point left.

4. Clone, stroke, and offset some more, as desired. I created Figure 12-32 by creating two more clones, each offset one point left and one point up from its predecessor. I applied a black 5-point stroke to the second clone and a white 2-point stroke to the third clone. The effect is rather like a string of shimmering jewels. Or perhaps they're a bunch of disembodied eyeballs, staring at something stage left. Now if we could only make them blink, that'd be really cool. (Insert a Beavis and Butthead laugh here.)

Figure 12-32: The result of two more sets of offset clones with 5-point black and 2-point white strokes, respectively.

Converting a Stroked Line to a Filled Shape

The last features I cover in this chapter convert strokes into paths, in much the same way that Text ➪ Convert To Paths converts character outlines to paths. By converting your strokes to paths, you can reshape each edge along a stroke — inside and outside — and apply fill effects such as gradations and patterns that you can't apply to strokes.

FreeHand provides two commands for converting strokes to paths. Both are available from the Operations panel. Choose ⌘/Ctrl-Option/Alt-O, if necessary, to open the panel. Choose Expand Stroke to trace two paths around a stroke, one along the inside edge and the other around the outside edge. Choose Inset Path to trace around the inside or outside edges of a stroke, which results in only one path instead of two.

Expanding the stroke

Neither of these commands pays any attention to the existing stroke applied to a path. You specify the stroke inside a dialog box after you choose the command. For example, when you choose Modify ➪ Alter Path ➪ Expand Stroke, FreeHand displays the Expand Stroke dialog box shown in Figure 12-33. Enter the line weight for the traced stroke in the Width option box or drag inside the slider. You can also specify line cap and line join, complete with a Miter Limit value.

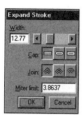

Figure 12-33: Use this dialog box to specify the thickness of the stroke that FreeHand converts to a composite path.

After you press Return/Enter, FreeHand creates two paths along the inside and outside edges of the stroke. (This assumes that you're converting a stroke associated with a closed path, which is the more complex scenario. The command traces a single closed path around strokes associated with open paths.) The two paths are combined into a composite path so that the smaller path knocks a hole into the larger path. FreeHand also converts the old stroke color to the fill color. This means that you can apply a different fill to create a special stroking effect.

Figure 12-34 shows examples of the different effects you can achieve. Both sets of paths were created using the Width value shown in Figure 12-33. To create the first star graphic, I applied the burlap textured PostScript fill routine to get what appears to be a textured stroke. This isn't necessarily an amazing effect, but it is one that you can't get without first converting the strokes to paths.

The second example in Figure 12-34 is a little more exciting. To create this effect, I Option/Alt-clicked on the inside shape with the arrow tool to select it independently from the outside shape. I then offset the shape by dragging it up and to the left, resulting in what appears to be a variable-weight stroke. I also applied real 0.5-point black strokes to each shape to add definition.

To create the thick black stripes, I resorted to masking (discussed in detail in Chapter 15). First I drew a squiggly line with the freehand tool and stroked it with a 24-point black line weight. I cut the path (⌘/Ctrl-X), Option/Alt-clicked with the arrow tool on the larger of the two star shapes to select it, and chose Edit ➪ Paste Inside (⌘/Ctrl-Shift-V) to mask the freehand line with the star. For now, just let it wash over you. As you'll see in Chapter 15, there's absolutely no end to the fill patterns you can achieve using masking.

Figure 12-34: Two graphics created by first converting the strokes to composite paths and filling and stroking the paths.

Tip

You can retrieve your original path by using the Blend command, discussed in Chapter 15. Select the composite path that you created with the Expand Stroke command by Option/Alt-clicking and Option/Alt-Shift-clicking on each path. Choose Blend from the Operations panel. FreeHand creates a slew of intermediate paths between the two shapes in the composite path. Press ⌘/Ctrl-I to display the Object Inspector. Then enter 1 into the Number of Steps option box. Voilà—there's your original path.

Creating an inset path

The Expand Stroke command traces new paths around either side of your selected path. The expanded stroke is centered on the original path, just like a standard stroke. The distance between the new paths and the original equals half the Width value in the Expand Stroke dialog box. So, if the Width value is 12, FreeHand traces one path six points inside the selected path and another path six points outside the selected path.

The Inset Path command works differently. When you choose Inset Path from the Operations panel, FreeHand displays the Inset Path dialog box, shown in Figure 12-35. Here, instead of the Width option box, you have the Inset option box. This is the total distance between the selected path and the new inset paths. If you enter an Inset value of 12, a new path is placed 12 points inside of the selected one.

Furthermore, you can enter either a negative or positive value into the Inset option box. A positive value traces inside the path; a negative value traces outside the path.

Figure 12-35: Here you decide the number of new paths with which FreeHand surrounds the selected path and how far away from it that they appear.

You can also choose the number of new paths that FreeHand creates in the Steps option box. Lastly, you decide how those new paths are distributed. Choose Uniform from the pop-up menu just to the right of the Steps option box in the Inset Path dialog box if you want each new path created the same distance away from the original path, as shown on the left of Figure 12-36. Select Farther from the pop-up menu to place the first path the inset distance away from the original path. Each additional path is placed incrementally closer to the last path. The third option, Nearer, creates the first path right next to the original path. Each new path is placed a little farther away.

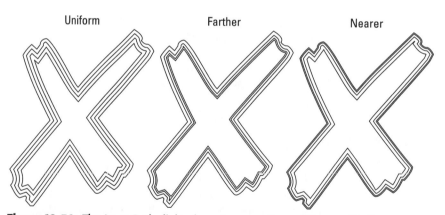

Figure 12-36: The Inset Path dialog box gives you three different distribution choices for your inset paths.

Generally, you'll want to apply the Inset Path command to clones of a path. With both clone and original to work with, you can create inline effects and variable weight strokes. You can also use fills to emulate fancy strokes, as in Figure 12-34.

✦   ✦   ✦

Special Effects

The Transformations and the Xtras

Simply Not Just the Same Old Object

FreeHand offers several methods for taking objects and giving them a whole new look. These methods fall into two groups. First, you have *The Five Transformations*. They're the group available from the Transform panel that you first danced to back in FreeHand 4. At that time, they seemed so wild. Now they're more of an established, essential group. The second group is *The Xtras*, part of the new FreeHand beat. Based on the philosophy that "being essential has been done already," they've got novelty appeal. They may seem fun, but they'll probably never replace *The Five Transformations* on your list of all-time favorites. So, without any further ado . . .

The Miracle of FreeHand's Transformations

Emcee: Ladies and gentlemen, tonight's guests are those kings of object manipulation, those movers and shakers, twisters and quakers, benders and breakers: Please welcome Move, Scale, Reflect, Rotate, and Skew—The Five Transformations!

Viewer 1:	*(Claps once, hesitantly.)* Who?
Viewer 2:	*(Sleepily.)* Wake me up for the Kingston Trio.
Viewer 1:	Who?
Viewer 2:	*(Snores loudly.)*

All right, I suppose that you might be able to find more miraculous transformations than those you can accomplish in FreeHand. The transformations from water to wine, demons into swine, Madonna to Momma, 8-tracks to CDs, Andrew Dice Clay to a complete absence of Andrew Dice Clay . . . all these qualify as more miraculous, in fact. But the ability to take an object and stretch it, spin it, and slant it in various directions is not to be scoffed at. These transformations are at the root of FreeHand's special effects capabilities and are absolutely essential to creating digital illustrations.

The transformations themselves aren't likely to elicit much in the way of screaming or fainting. You can move objects, enlarge or reduce them, flip them, rotate them, and slant them, all of which FreeHand has enabled folks to do since Version 1. But thanks to the precision, immediacy, and predictability of the controls, transformations double as practical solutions to everyday problems and inspirational ways to experiment with objects.

Transforming Objects

As shown on the left side of Figure 13-1, FreeHand still provides the four transformation tools that it has offered since the old days. To use any of these tools, you drag in the illustration window to transform one or more selected objects. The only transformation tool not labeled in the figure is the arrow tool, which — in addition to its seven million other functions — lets you move selected objects.

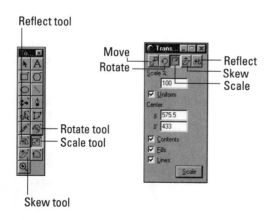

Figure 13-1: The transformation tools in the toolbox (left) and the corresponding icons in the Transform panel (right).

Shown on the right side of the figure is the Transform panel, which you display by pressing ⌘/Ctrl-M. The panel contains five separate panels of options, one for each of the five transformations. You display the panels by clicking on the appropriate icons.

The Transform panel makes numerical transformations very convenient, especially if you need to perform a certain kind of transformation several times in a row. Instead of having to Option/Alt-click with a tool over and over to display and redisplay a specialized dialog box, you simply click inside an option box, enter a new value, press Return/Enter, examine the results, adjust the value, press Return/Enter again, and so on, until you get the desired results.

Here are a few things that both new and experienced users should know about working with the transformation tools and Transform panel:

✦ To transform an entire path, select the path but not its points. If any of the points are selected, FreeHand transforms the segments between those points independently of other points in the path.

✦ To transform a text object independently of the characters inside it (or bound to it), Option/Alt-click on the path with the arrow tool to select only the path. Then apply the desired transformation. The type rewraps to fit the transformed text object. (If you apply a transformation to a text block without first Option/Alt-clicking, FreeHand transforms text and object equally.)

✦ When you're dragging with a transformation tool, FreeHand allows you to drag outside of the illustration window (as long as you start dragging inside the window and do not drag past the window's edge). This can be useful for enlarging and reducing an object dramatically with the scale tool or rotating an object with extreme precision using the rotate tool.

✦ Double-click on a transformation tool icon in the toolbox to switch to the corresponding panel in the Transform panel. Alternatively, provided nothing is selected, you can Option/Alt-click with the tool in the illustration window. (Because there is no specific move tool, you can access the Move panel only by clicking on its icon in the Transform panel.)

✦ The point at which you begin dragging with any of the four transformation tools serves as the center of the transformation. For example, when you drag with the rotation tool, FreeHand rotates the object around the point at which you pressed the mouse button.

✦ Whether you double-click or Option/Alt-click, FreeHand records the coordinates for the center of the selection into the two Center option boxes in the Transform panel. These coordinates serve as the center of the transformation. To change the Center coordinates, you can enter new values or just click with the transformation tool in the illustration window. (This doesn't apply to using the Move panel because there is no center for a move.)

✦ To use the selection's center as the center of the transformation, click with a transform tool. Just be careful to click without moving the mouse. FreeHand records the coordinates of the selection center into the two Center option boxes in the Transform panel.

✦ All panels in the Transform panel include Contents and Fills check boxes. These options enable you to transform masked objects and tile patterns, respectively, along with an object. If you deselect the Contents check box, FreeHand transforms the selected object independently of the elements pasted inside it (if any such objects exist). If you deselect Fills, FreeHand transforms the object independently of its tile pattern (again, if the object is filled with such a pattern). For more information on masking, skip ahead to Chapter 15.

✦ You can click inside one of the Transform panel's option boxes to activate the panel, or press the Tab key one or more times to cycle through to the panel. When the panel is active — the title bar appears highlighted — you can press the Return/Enter key to apply your changes. If the panel is not active, you have to click on the apply button.

✦ Both techniques have the added effect of deactivating the panel. So to apply a transformation a second time, you have to reactivate the panel by pressing the Tab key and then press Return/Enter. (Or you can leave the panel inactive and simply click on the apply button.)

✦ Pressing ⌘/Ctrl-Tab always takes you back to the panel you used last. So, if you're using the Transform panel several times in a row, a single press of ⌘/Ctrl-Tab reactivates the panel.

✦ If you used some other panel last, you have to press the keyboard combination two or more times in a row.

✦ To bring the Transform panel forward so that no other panel is covering it, press ⌘/Ctrl-M once or twice (depending on whether the panel is displayed).

That's good enough for now. Don't worry if a few of the finer points of these operations — such as "Why should I care?" — escape your understanding for the moment. All are covered in greater detail in later sections.

Moving Whole Objects

The "Moving Elements" section of Chapter 5 described several techniques for moving points, segments, and Bézier control handles inside a path. However, it didn't say much about moving entire objects, because I was saving this information for this chapter. Aren't you glad that you stuck it out?

In many ways, moving is the odd transformation out. If the five transformations really were a band, Move would be the guy who played the drums, never wrote any of the songs, got paid less than the other members, and was generally considered to be a no-talent jerk who got incredibly lucky. You know, sort of like Ringo Starr, or Oates in Hall and Oates. Then again, maybe Hall is the no-talent one. It's pretty hard to tell.

Anyway, moving is the odd transformation: FreeHand doesn't give you a special tool for doing the job; if you don't do things right, you can end up deselecting the object; there's no shortcut for accessing the Move panel; and the panel lacks a couple of options that would make it more useful. Some folks don't even think of moving as a transformation because it doesn't in any way alter the appearance of an object — it just changes its location.

Manual movements

On the other hand, you can use all kinds of techniques to move objects that aren't applicable to other kinds of transformations. It's as if — wait a second, maybe Ringo was the best Beatle after all. He had a great solo album. He got the most fan mail. He had the sense not to marry Yoko Ono, he didn't write an opera about Liverpool, he didn't join the Traveling Wilburys. By gum, it was those other guys that were no-talent jerks.

The following list explains all the ways that you can move selected objects in FreeHand. A few may be familiar to you from Chapter 5, but it never hurts to recap.

✦ **Drag with the arrow tool:** Drag on a selected object to move it. This information may sound ridiculously remedial, but if you don't drag on the object when moving it, you deselect the object. When you perform other transformations, you don't have to begin dragging on the object. Instead, you drag from the point that will serve as the center of the transformation, which can be literally anywhere in the illustration window.

When moving an open or unfilled path, you have to begin dragging on a segment in the path. When moving a filled path in the preview mode or a text block in either display mode, you can begin dragging inside the object.

✦ **Press and hold to preview:** If you start right in dragging an object, FreeHand displays a rectangular dotted outline to show you the object's approximate location. This outline isn't very useful for gauging the position of an object during a move, but it doesn't take any time for FreeHand to draw, so the program can easily keep up with your movements. If you want to see an exact outline when working in the preview mode, click and hold for a moment before beginning your drag. This tells FreeHand that you want to preview the object with accurate outlines and proper fill and stroke colors throughout the move.

Tip

If you find yourself dragging a selected object too quickly and getting stuck with the not-so-helpful rectangular bounding box outline instead of the path's true outline, tap the Option/Alt key while you're dragging — don't press and hold the Option/Alt key, just press and release it. FreeHand will reward you with the true outline of the path. This also works when you are moving more objects than is allowed by the value entered in the Preview Drag option box inside the Redraw panel of the Preference dialog box.

✦ **Press Option/Alt to preview:** Assuming you haven't changed the Preview Drag value in the Redraw panel of the Preferences dialog box, the above technique only works when a single object is selected. You can bump up the Preview Drag value in the Preferences dialog box to accommodate the press-and-hold technique when more than one object is selected.

✦ **Double-click to display transformation handles:** New to FreeHand 8 is another method of moving selected objects. After you have selected the paths that you want to move, double-click on any one of the selected paths and FreeHand will display the transformation handles — eight black boxes, equally distributed around the selected items collective bounding box. As you drag the selected items via the transformation handles, FreeHand displays the true outline of the paths despite how quickly you start the drag or whether the number of items exceeds the value in the Drag Preview option box. Make sure the Enable Transformation Handles option in the General panel of the Preference dialog box is selected. For more information on the transformation handles, see the "Transformation handles" section later in this chapter.

✦ **Drag a path by one of its points:** You can drag a single object by one of its points, as described in the "Snapping" section of Chapter 5.

✦ **Snap to points:** Drag onto a point in a stationary path to snap to it. (For this to work, the Snap to Point command under the View menu must be active.)

✦ **Press Shift after you drag to constrain**: It's important that you press Shift after beginning your drag. If you press Shift before dragging — as you can when using any of the transformation tools — you deselect the object. To constrain the movement of an object along the constraint axes, start dragging, press and hold the Shift key, release the mouse button, and release Shift.

✦ **Press an arrow key:** This moves the selected objects by the amount specified in the Cursor Key Distance option box in the General panel of the Preferences dialog box.

Moving by the numbers

You can also specify the movement of a selected object numerically via the Move panel of the Transform panel, shown in Figure 13-2. As I mentioned earlier, you have to click on the Move icon.

Figure 13-2: The Move panel of the Transform panel lets you specify a move numerically.

To use the Move panel, enter values into each of the Move Distance option boxes. The values are measured in the unit specified in the Status toolbar and are accurate to $\frac{1}{10,000}$ point or the equivalent in other units.

✦ The X value moves the selection horizontally; the Y value moves it vertically.

✦ Positive values move the selection to the right or up; negative values move it to the left or down.

✦ If you want to move an object exclusively up or down, enter 0 for the X value. If you want to move it directly left or right, enter 0 into the Y option box.

After you enter the X and Y values, press Return/Enter or click on the Apply/Move button to apply the transformation.

Moving in direct distances

What's missing are direct distance and angle options. For example, what if you want to move an object 20 points along a 30-degree axis? Rotating the constraint axes has no effect on the performance of options in the Move panel. So what do you do?

Well, there are two possible solutions. One is to drag the object manually while monitoring your progress in the Info toolbar. If you really want to be precise, enter the angle of your drag into the Angle option box in the Constrain dialog box — displayed when you choose Modify ➪ Constrain. Then press the Shift key while dragging the object to constrain the movement to the axes and monitor the distance (Dist) in the Info toolbar.

The other and even more precise solution is to do the math. Don't be afraid; as long as you have a calculator with Cos, Sin, and ∏ buttons (pronounced co-sign, sign, and pie), you can handle it. On the other hand, if your calculator is strictly the generic business variety, you're out of luck. There's no way to do those equations in your head.

What you need to do is convert a direct distance and angle to horizontal and vertical distance values. Together, these items make up a triangle, as illustrated in Figure 13-3. All it takes to compute the X and Y values for the Move panel is a little geometry.

Note

Figure 13-3 diagrams the movement of an object up and to the right. But it doesn't matter which direction you want to move. If you move down and to the right, flip the triangle vertically in your head. If you want to move up and to the left, flip it horizontally.

The first step is to convert your angle from degrees to a fraction of ∏. It's sort of like converting a temperature from Fahrenheit to Celsius. To make the conversion, use this equation:

A ° 180 × ∏

where A is the angle. For example, if the angle is 30 degrees, divide it by 180 to get ⅙, or 0.1667. Then multiply that times ∏, which gives you ⁱ⅙, or 0.5236.

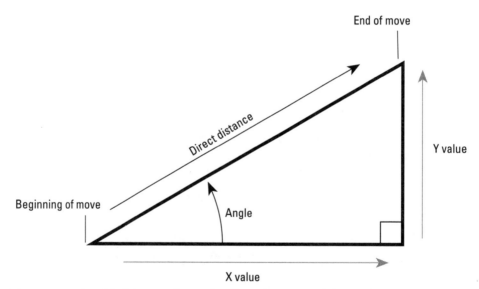

Figure 13-3: Provided that you know the direct distance and the angle you want to move an object, you can calculate X and Y values for the Move panel.

Now that you have the converted angle, which I'll call *C*, you can figure out the X and Y values. To calculate the X value, use this equation:

X = Cos C × D

where D is the direct distance value. In other words, after calculating the converted angle C, press the Cos button on your calculator. In the case of my 30-degree example, Cos 0.5236 equals 0.8660. Then multiply the result times the direct distance. I wanted to move my object 300 points, so I multiplied 0.8660 by 300 to get approximately 260 points. Enter the final answer — in my case 260 — into the X option box.

To calculate the Y value, use this equation:

$$Y = \text{Sin } C \times D$$

This time, take your converted angle and press the Sin button. In my case, I calculated Sin 0.5236, which equals exactly 0.5. Then multiply this answer times the direct distance value and enter it into the Y option box. In the example, the Y value is 150 ($300 \times 0.5 = 150$).

Let FreeHand do the simple calculations for you. Any option box you find in FreeHand is capable of doing arithmetic. FreeHand can do multiplication, division, addition, and subtraction with the use of the appropriate symbol (*, /, +, -). For example, you can either do the calculation mentioned above manually or just enter 300 * .5 in to the Y option box of the Move panel. In the later case, FreeHand converts the multiplication into 150.

Other things you should know

If a selected path is being used to mask other objects, as explained in Chapter 15, select the Contents check box to move the masked objects along with the path. Deselect the option to move the selected path independently of the masked objects. This forces FreeHand to mask a different portion of the objects.

If a selected path is filled with a tile pattern, select Fills to move the pattern with the object. Deselect the option to move the path and leave the tile pattern in place. This has the effect of offsetting the pattern inside the path (much as if you entered values into the Offset options in the Fill Inspector).

The X and Y options in the Move panel record past moves. After you move an object by hand, the X and Y option boxes display the exact horizontal and vertical components of the move, accurate to $\frac{1}{10,000}$ point. This information makes it possible for you to repeat or nullify all or part of the most recent move, regardless of how long ago the move was made. Simply take the values in the X and Y option boxes, enter their opposites, and press Return/Enter or click on the Apply/Move button. (In other words, if there is a negative sign before the value, delete it; if there isn't a negative sign, add one.)

Suppose that you move one object until it snaps onto another object. In doing so, you move the object up and slightly to the right. But you didn't actually want to change the horizontal position; you *had* to change it because that was the only way to make the snap work. (Sometimes, Shift-dragging an object can interfere with snapping, so it's best to drag without the Shift key.) To nudge the object leftward to its previous horizontal position, you'd change the X value from plus to minus and enter 0 for the Y value.

The only kinds of moves that the X and Y options don't record are moves made with the arrow keys. This is a feature, not a bug. FreeHand rightly assumes that you can keep track of arrow key movements.

One more thing: The Move panel isn't only applicable to whole objects. You can also use the X and Y options to move selected points independently of other points in a path.

Scale, Reflect, Rotate, and Skew

Now for the real transformation tools, the tools with heart, soul, and spunk. Every one of these tools changes the appearance of an object, sometimes in addition to changing its placement. Okay, I know what you're thinking. "Hey, if Ringo is FreeHand's move functions, who are the other transformations? Aren't we short a Beatle?" Not at all. Let me explain:

✦ The scale tool is Paul, because it's remarkably capable and possibly the most popular of the bunch. You'll find yourself using it more often than you hum "Yesterday."

✦ The reflect tool is Stuart Sutcliffe — one of the early Beatles — because Paul can do everything he can do. And just as there's no point in having Stuart if you have Paul — you just don't need two bass players, after all — you don't need the reflect tool as long as the scale tool is around. Why? Because the scale tool can just as easily flip objects as resize them. On the other hand, the reflect tool is there if you need it, unlike Stu, who is, unfortunately, dead.

✦ The rotate tool is John because it's the hippest transformation tool, if not quite so popular with the teenyboppers as the scale tool. It's the musical equivalent of "Strawberry Fields Forever," sending objects spinning and reeling into trippy, far-out scenes. Also, the farther you drag the rotate tool away from its origin, the better it performs. John goes to the Middle East and comes up with the poetic "Dear Prudence;" he moves back to the Dakota and shouts "Mother" at the top of his lungs. The connection is so uncanny that it's scary.

✦ The skew tool is George because you hardly ever use the thing and it works more predictably when it's constrained. On his own, George sang a bunch of sappy stuff and droned away on his sitar as melodically as if he were playing a power mower. With a little help from Eric Clapton, he came up with "While My Guitar Gently Weeps." As we'll see, the skew tool needs the same kind of adult supervision, which you apply by pressing the Shift key.

I also have this thing about how the Transform and Inspector panels are like The Captain and Tennille, but I doubt that you want to hear it. It's a "Muskrat Love" kind of thing.

Enlarging and reducing objects

Use the scale tool to reduce and enlarge paths and text objects. It's not the only way to scale; you can group objects and scale them by dragging a corner handle with the arrow tool, for example. But the scale tool works more precisely than other techniques, and you can apply it to any number of objects whether they are grouped or not.

After selecting the objects that you want to scale, drag with the scale tool to enlarge or reduce them. The direction in which you drag determines whether an enlargement or reduction takes place:

> ✦ Drag up to enlarge an object vertically.
>
> ✦ Drag to the right to enlarge an object horizontally.
>
> ✦ Drag down to reduce an object vertically.
>
> ✦ Drag to the left to reduce an object horizontally.

In both examples in Figure 13-4, I dragged up and to the right in order to enlarge the selected object both vertically and horizontally. You can track the extent of your scaling by keeping an eye on the XScale and YScale values in the Info toolbar. The values are expressed as ratios of the new size over the previous size. Move the decimal point two digits to the right to make the conversion to percents. For example, the XScale value in Figure 13-4 is 1.82, which is the same as 182 percent. The YScale value, 1.95, is 195 percent. Any value over 1.00 indicates an enlargement; a smaller value indicates a reduction.

The point at which you begin dragging also has an effect on the scaling of an object. This point determines the center of the enlargement or reduction, called the transformation origin. Both examples in Figure 13-4 show identical enlargements, but they begin at different origins. As a result, the objects in the two examples move to different locations as they increase in size. Enlarging an object always moves it away from the origin, as the figure demonstrates. Reducing an object moves it toward the origin. Because the origin in the first example is close to the object, the object hardly moves at all as it enlarges. Meanwhile, the origin in the second example is high above the object, so the object moves dramatically in the opposite direction as it increases in size.

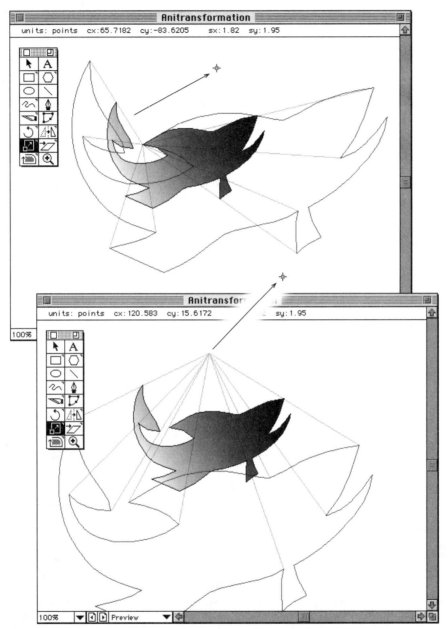

Figure 13-4: Enlarging an object by dragging with the scale tool.

The following steps give you a chance to experience the scale tool up-close and personal. Figure 13-5 displays two paths representing a telephone. The path of the receiver is selected; the path below it is not. In the steps, you enlarge the receiver, reduce it, and flip it upside down.

1. Draw two paths that look something like the ones in Figure 13-5. Don't sweat it if they don't look exactly like my phone paths; you're not going to be graded on accuracy. Just draw some rough approximation and be done with it. Then save your document, because you use these paths three more times in this chapter.

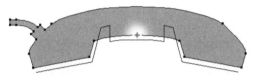

Figure 13-5: Begin dragging with the scale tool near the middle of the selected shape to establish a transformation origin.

2. Select the top path with the arrow tool. Then switch to the scale tool and begin dragging at the location of the small cursor in Figure 13-5. This establishes the transformation origin.

3. Drag up and to the right, as demonstrated in Figure 13-6. As you drag away from the transformation origin, the path of the receiver grows larger. Both the previous and current size of the selected path are displayed throughout your drag, allowing you to gauge the effect of the enlargement. Release your mouse button to complete the scaling operation.

4. Press ⌘/Ctrl-Z to undo the enlargement and return the path to its original size. We're just playing around here; no permanent progress made.

5. Again, using the scale tool, drag from the same spot in the middle of the receiver to establish the transformation origin. But this time, drag down and to the left to reduce the selected object, as shown in Figure 13-7. As you drag, the selected path shrinks. Release the mouse button to complete the reduction.

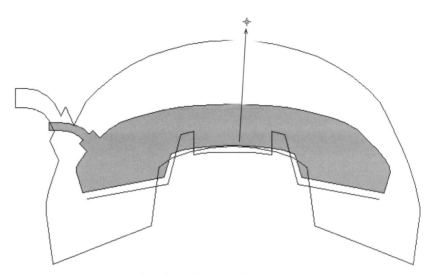

Figure 13-6: Drag up and to the right from the transformation origin to enlarge the selected object.

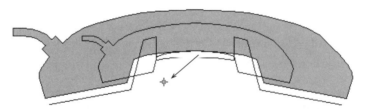

Figure 13-7: Drag down and to the left to reduce the selected object.

6. Press ⌘/Ctrl-Z again. I hate to bore you with such recent history, but in the previous steps, you enlarged the receiver both horizontally and vertically. Then you reduced it both horizontally and vertically. This time, however, you'll enlarge the path one direction and reduce it the other.

7. Starting at the same old transformation origin, drag with the scale tool up and to the left. FreeHand stretches the object vertically and squishes it horizontally, as shown in Figure 13-8.

You can enlarge a selected object as much as you want, but it can't exceed FreeHand's maximum page size. You can also reduce an object into virtual invisibility. If you drag past the point at which a selection is reduced into nothingness, you flip the selected object.

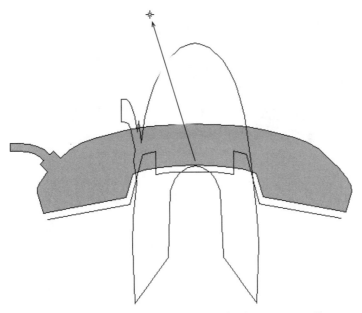

Figure 13-8: Drag up and to the left to make the receiver taller and narrower.

8. Press ⌘/Ctrl-Z to undo the previous scaling. Then drag downward from the familiar origin, which reduces the size of the shape. Keep dragging downward until the receiver flips, as shown in Figure 13-9. After the shape flips, it stops shrinking and begins growing as you continue to drag. In the figure, for example, the receiver is bigger than it was when I started, even though I'm dragging downward, a direction normally associated with reductions.

This little known feature of the scale tool allows you to reflect and scale objects at the same time. However, you can only flip objects horizontally and vertically with the scale tool. To flip an object across an angled axis, you have to use the reflect tool, as described in the "Flipping objects" section later in this chapter. (I guess maybe Stu had something on Paul after all.)

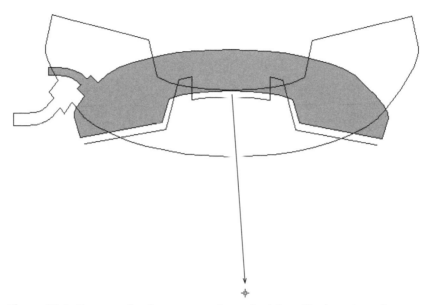

Figure 13-9: Drag very far down or very far to the left to flip the selected object, and even eventually enlarge it.

Constrained scaling

To constrain the scale tool so that it affects the height and width of a selected object equally, Shift-drag with the tool. Shift-drag up and/or to the right to enlarge an object proportionally. I say "and/or" because either action produces the same result when the Shift key is down. Shift-drag down and/or to the left to reduce the object proportionally.

Although you can combine operationally opposite directions by Shift-dragging up and to the left or down and to the right, it isn't a particularly good idea. The scale tool can't both enlarge the width and reduce the height, or vice versa, when the Shift key is pressed, so it treats the 135-degree axis as a border between the worlds of proportional reductions and proportional enlargements (see Figure 13-10). If you drag in one of these directions, you may find yourself crossing these boundaries and switching from enlargement to reduction to reflection with disconcerting frequency.

You can constrain an exclusively horizontal or vertical resizing, but you can't do it with the scale tool. Select an object, group it, and then drag a corner handle with the arrow tool. While dragging, press and hold the Shift and ⌘/Ctrl keys to make the resizing purely horizontal or vertical.

Better yet, double-click on the selected path to display the transformation handles and drag on one of the horizontal or vertical handles. Dragging on the horizontal or vertical handles constrains the scaling to an exclusively horizontal or vertical scaling. For more information, see the "Transformation handles" section later in this chapter.

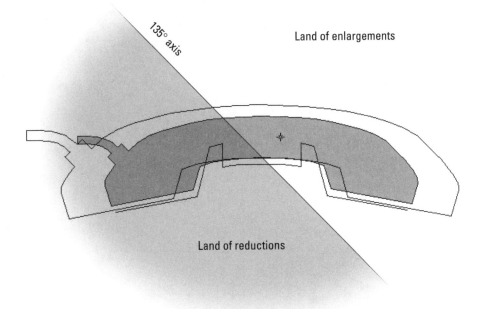

Figure 13-10: Shift-dragging with the scale tool divides the illustration window in half. Drag in one half to enlarge the selection; drag in the other half to reduce it.

As for *why* FreeHand devotes more control to scaling groups with the arrow tool than performing the same task with the scale tool, I have no idea. But that's the way it is.

Scaling partial paths

In addition to scaling whole objects, you can scale selected elements inside a path independently of their deselected neighbors. Simply select the points that you want to enlarge or reduce and use the scale tool as directed in the previous sections.

For example, only six points are selected in the skyline path shown in Figure 13-11. The segments that border each of these points are the only segments that will be affected by the scale tool. In Figure 13-12, I dragged down and to the left with the scale tool to reduce the selected elements. This had the effect of shrinking the segments between selected points and stretching those between a selected point and a deselected point.

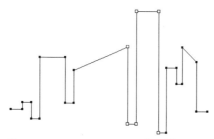

Figure 13-11: An open path with six points selected.

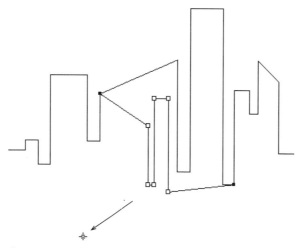

Figure 13-12: Dragging down and to the left reduced the selected elements while leaving segments between the deselected points unchanged.

Dragging points with the scale tool can be very much like dragging them with the arrow tool. But when you use the scale tool, each selected point moves a different amount, depending on its proximity to the transformation origin. If you look closely at Figure 13-12, you'll notice that the points close to the transformation origin move much less than those farther away. For example, the two selected points on the left side of the base of the tower move a few picas apiece, while the points at the top of the tower move a full inch.

Tip

For this reason, the scale tool can prove very useful for moving specific points in ways that the arrow tool does not allow. For example, to move two selected segments equal distances in opposite directions about a central point, drag from the point with the scale tool. In the left example of Figure 13-13, I selected the points bounding each of two horizontal segments in a hexagonal shape. By positioning the scale cursor midway between the points and dragging upward, I moved the points in opposite directions, as illustrated in the right example.

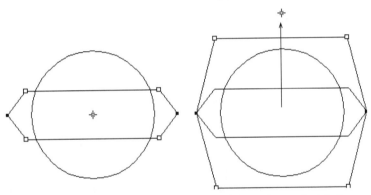

Figure 13-13: After selecting a few points (left), I dragged with the scale tool to move the points away from one another (right).

Using the Scale panel options

Double-click on the scale tool icon in the toolbox or Option/Alt-click with the scale tool in the illustration window to display the Scale panel of the Transformation panel, shown in Figure 13-14. (If worse comes to worst, you can always click on the scale icon in the Transform panel itself.) This panel enables you to scale selected objects with numerical precision.

To scale the width and height of an object proportionally, select the Uniform check box and enter a value into the Scale % option box. Values less than 100 percent reduce the size of a selected object; values greater than 100 percent enlarge the object; a 100 percent value leaves the object unaltered.

Figure 13-14: The Scale panel lets you specify percentages by which to enlarge or reduce selected objects.

To scale the width and height of an object independently, deselect the Uniform check box, which splits the Scale % option box into two option boxes, H and W, as shown in Figure 13-14. The X value makes the object fatter or thinner; the Y option box makes it taller or shorter.

Below the Uniform check box are two Center option boxes, which determine the location of the transformation origin, as measured from the ruler origin. By default, FreeHand automatically stores the coordinate of the exact center of the selection. If you click on the Apply/Scale button without changing these values, FreeHand scales the selected objects with respect to their shared center.

If you want FreeHand to record a click point, you have to click with the scale tool (or some other transformation tool) in the illustration window. FreeHand immediately records the coordinates of the click point in the two Center option boxes. Then enter the desired percentages in the Scale % option boxes and click on the Apply/Scale button as usual.

The Contents and Fills check boxes work as they do in other panels, scaling masked elements and tile patterns along with the selected objects when applicable. The Lines check box, however, is unique to the Scale panel. It enables you to choose whether to scale the line weights of selected objects. For example, if you reduce a path stroked with a 4-point line weight to 25 percent of its original size, and the Lines check box is selected, FreeHand reduces the stroke to a 1-point line weight.

If the scale is not proportional (Uniform is turned off), FreeHand runs through a strange and complicated procedure (which you may or may not care about). It divides the X and Y values by 100 percent, takes their square roots, and multiplies them times the line weight. Suppose that you scale the 4-point line weight 300 percent horizontally and 50 percent vertically. FreeHand divides both values by 100 to get 3 and ½. The square roots of these numbers are roughly 1.732 and 0.707, which, when multiplied together and then by 4, yield a new line weight of 4.898 points.

Incredibly complex and deadly boring. That's the way computer books were meant to be, right?

Flipping objects

Flipping objects with the scale tool is a nifty parlor trick and even useful on rare occasions, but you can achieve better control if you flip with the reflect tool. The reflect tool—the one that looks like two triangles—flips an object around a reflection axis, which acts like a pivoting mirror. The selected object looks into this mirror; the result of the flip is the image that the mirror projects.

To use the reflect tool, drag in the illustration window to define the angle of the reflection axis. As you drag, FreeHand previews the effect of the transformation so that you can easily predict the results of different axis angles.

Suppose that you want to flip the receiver path from Figure 13-5 around an angled axis. The following exercise explains how to do this:

1. Select the reflect tool and begin dragging from the center of the receiver (at the spot indicated by the star cursor in Figure 13-5). This establishes the transformation origin, which is the first point in the reflection axis.

2. Drag with the tool to determine the angle of the reflection axis, which forms a straight line between the cursor and the origin.

3. Drag above and to the left of the origin, as shown in Figure 13-15. FreeHand displays the reflection axis as a solid line across the illustration window.

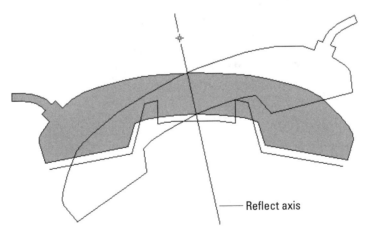

Reflect axis

Figure 13-15: Drag with the reflect tool to tilt the reflection axis and flip the selected object accordingly.

It also shows both original and current positions of the selected object on-screen. Release the mouse button when you've reflected the object as desired.

You can monitor the angle of the reflection axis in the Info toolbar by watching the Angle value. To constrain the reflection axis in 45-degree increments — so that the selection is flipped vertically, horizontally, or diagonally — Shift-drag with the reflect tool. (The performance of the tool is not in any way influenced by the angle of the constraint axes.)

Flipping partial paths

Just as you can scale selected elements independently of their deselected neighbors, you can also flip them. Simply select the points that you want to flip and use the reflect tool as usual.

Figure 13-16 shows the result of dragging with the reflect tool while the points from Figure 13-11 are selected. The effect is a little rough-and-tumble, but you can see that each selected point is flipped to the opposite side of the reflection axis. Segments between selected points are rotated but not stretched. Meanwhile, segments between selected and deselected points are stretched dramatically.

This technique generally produces the most satisfactory results when you Shift-drag with the reflect tool. The segments are less likely to overlap in the spider-web mess shown in Figure 13-16.

Using the Reflect panel options

Double-click on the reflect tool icon in the tool box, Option/Alt-click with the reflect tool in the illustration window, or click on the Reflect icon in the Transform panel to display the Reflect panel, shown in Figure 13-17. This panel enables you to flip one or more selected objects around a numerically angled axis.

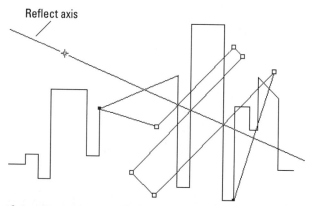

Figure 13-16: Drag with the reflect tool to flip the selected points across to the other side of the angled reflection axis.

Figure 13-17: Use the Reflect Axis option in the Reflect panel to specify the angle of the reflection axis with numerical accuracy.

The Reflect panel offers a Reflect Axis option box, which determines the angle of the reflection axis as measured from absolute horizontal. The Reflect Axis value works as follows:

✦ To flip an object upside down, enter 0 into the Reflect Axis option box and press Return/Enter. This setting reflects the object around a horizontal axis.

✦ To flip an object horizontally, enter a value of 90, which reflects the object around a vertical axis.

✦ To flip an object around an angled axis, enter some other value between 0 and 180 degrees (all other values are repetitious).

All the other options — Center, Contents, and Fill — work just as they do in the Scale panel. The coordinates in the Center option boxes represent a point on the line of the reflection axis, although this point may not be smack dab in the middle of the axis. Generally, you should click inside the illustration window to locate the transformation origin before entering a value into the Reflect Axis option box and pressing Return/Enter.

Rotating objects

You operate the rotate tool (it looks like a circle with an arrowhead) by dragging relative to one or more selected objects. The point at which you begin dragging determines the location of the transformation origin, which determines the center of the rotation, as illustrated by the enhanced rotation-in-action scene in Figure 13-18.

Rotate tool

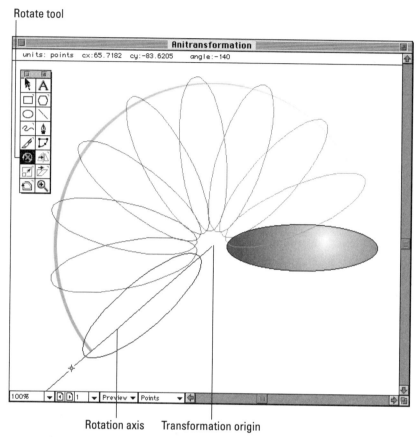

Figure 13-18: The transformation origin determines the center of the rotation.

Rotation axis   Transformation origin

Immediately after you begin dragging, FreeHand displays the *rotation axis*, which connects your cursor to the origin throughout your drag. Dragging directly to the right doesn't rotate the selection at all — regardless of the orientation or location of the object before you began dragging — because the axis is then resting at 0 degrees. Any other drag rotates the object with respect to this 0-degree position. For example, drag directly up to rotate the object 90 degrees, drag left to rotate it 180 degrees, and so on. Throughout your drag, you can monitor the angle of the rotation axis by peeking at the Angle item in the Info toolbar.

Tip

The rotate tool offers the most control when the distance between your cursor and the transformation origin is greater than or equal to the length of the selected object. The following steps demonstrate how this works.

1. Start with the selected receiver shown back in Figure 13-5. But this time, rather than beginning your drag in the middle of the shape, drag from the lower left corner of the shape, as illustrated by the location of the star cursor in Figure 13-19.

Figure 13-19: Begin dragging with the rotate tool at the lower left point in the selected shape to establish a transformation origin.

2. Drag rightward an inch or so from the origin, as shown in Figure 13-20, and experiment with moving the rotation axis up and down. When you drag close to the origin, FreeHand translates your movements into huge rotations. In the figure, for example, I've only dragged about a pica above the 0-degree position, but it's enough to make FreeHand rotate the shape 20 degrees.

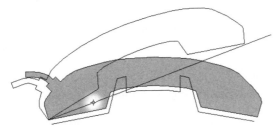

Figure 13-20: When you drag close to the transformation origin, small movements produce dramatic results.

3. Although dragging close to the origin lets you conserve mouse movements, it's generally a better idea to move away from the origin, where you have more control. To test this out, continue dragging rightward until your cursor is outside the path, as shown in Figure 13-21. Here I've dragged about four times the distance from the origin, as in the previous figure. My cursor is still only about a pica above the 0-degree position, but the rotation is about 5 degrees, roughly a quarter of what it was before. I'd have to drag nearly an inch above the 0-degree position to get the same rotation as shown in Figure 13-20.

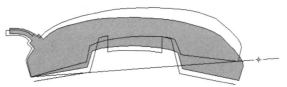

Figure 13-21: Drag far away from the transformation origin to make more refined adjustments.

4. Continue dragging farther and farther away from the origin. You can even drag far outside the illustration window along the perimeter of your screen if you want. In fact, the farther out you go, the more subtle and exact your rotations will be.

Of course, you can always constrain the performance of a transformation tool by pressing the Shift key. In the case of the rotate tool, Shift-dragging rotates a selected object by a multiple of 45 degrees from its original position.

Tip

For a quick and easy rotation method, double-click on a selected path to display the transformation handles. Drag outside the handles box to rotate the path around the center point that appears along with the transformation handles. Click on the center point and drag it to a new location to change the pivot of any rotations that you make via the transformation handles box. For more information, flip to the Transformation Handles section of this here chapter.

Rotating partial paths

Figure 13-22 shows the effect of rotating selected points independently of deselected points in a free-form path. As you drag, all selected points maintain their original distances from the transformation origin—a feature that makes rotating perhaps the most predictable transformation you can apply to a partial path.

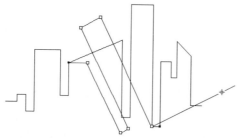

Figure 13-22: Drag with the rotate tool to spin the selected points around the transformation origin.

As is the case when you're reflecting selected elements, rotating has no effect on the length of segments between two selected points, only on their inclination. Segments between selected and deselected points stretch to keep up with the movements of the selected points, depending on their proximity to the origin. In Figure 13-22, the transformation origin is located right on top of a selected point that neighbors a deselected point. As a result, the selected point doesn't move, which means that the segment between it and the deselected neighbor is not affected.

Using the Rotate panel options

Figure 13-23 shows the Rotate panel, which you access by double-clicking on the rotate tool in the toolbox, Option/Alt-clicking with the tool in the illustration window, or clicking on the Rotate icon at the top of the Transform panel. Using this panel, you can rotate selected objects numerically.

Figure 13-23: The Rotate panel allows you to specify the number of degrees by which you want FreeHand to rotate a selected object.

Enter any value between negative and positive 180 (all other values are repetitious) in the Rotation Angle option box. The value is measured in degrees and is accurate to ¹⁄₁₀ degree. A negative value rotates an object clockwise; a positive value rotates it counterclockwise.

The Center, Contents, and Fills options work as usual. If you want the center of the transformation to be at some other spot other than the center of the selected objects, either click on that spot inside the illustration window or enter new coordinates into the option boxes.

Slanting objects

Slanting—also called *skewing*—is perhaps the most difficult transformation to conceptualize. To skew an object is to slant its vertical and horizontal proportions independently of each other. For example, a standard kite shape is a skewed version of a perfect square. As shown in Figure 13-24, I first skewed the shape vertically and then skewed it horizontally, in two separate operations. The result is a perfect diamond shape.

Skew tool

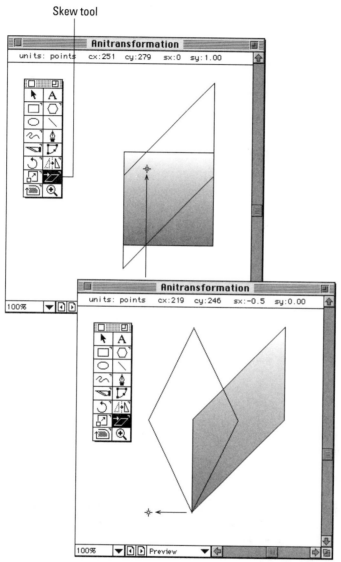

Figure 13-24: Transforming a square into a kite by skewing the shape in two steps, once vertically and once horizontally.

I transformed the kite in Figure 13-24 using the skew tool. As usual, the point at which you begin dragging determines the transformation origin. The direction in which a selected object slants depends on the direction in which you drag and the side of the origin on which the object appears. Portions of the selection on opposite sides of the origin slant in opposite directions, as illustrated in the first example of Figure 13-24. The left side of the square slants downward, while the right side slants up.

The skew tool works more predictably when you Shift-drag with it, which slants an object either exclusively horizontally or exclusively vertically, as demonstrated in the two examples in Figure 13-24. Predicting the outcome of a slant that you perform by simply dragging with the tool is very difficult. Even worse, dragging rarely produces the desired results. I couldn't have produced the kite shape in Figure 13-24 by dragging once with the skew tool. For best results, therefore, Shift-drag once to slant the selection horizontally to the desired degree; Shift-drag again to slant it vertically.

Here's how Shift-dragging with the skew tool works:

✦ Shift-drag up to slant selected elements located to the right of the transformation origin upward and slant any elements located to the left of the origin downward.

✦ Shift-drag down to slant the right elements downward and the left elements upward.

✦ Shift-drag to the right to slant elements in the selection above the transformation origin to the right and elements below to the left.

✦ Shift-drag to the left to slant the upper elements to the left and the lower elements to the right.

If you don't press the Shift key, all selected elements that are above and to the right of the transformation origin slant in the direction of the drag. Elements below and to the left of the origin slant in the opposite direction.

You can monitor the effects of your skewing by noting the XScale and YScale items in the Info toolbar. Both items represent ratios — the length of the skew over the width (XScale) or height (YScale) of the selected object. Take a look at the items in Figure 13-24, for example. In the first example, the XScale item is 0 because I'm Shift-dragging upward; there is no horizontal skew. But the YScale value is 1.00. This means that I've skewed the shape upward so that the bottom point in the right edge is even with the top point in the left edge.

I've skewed the object an amount equal to the full height of the object. In the second example, YScale is 0 because this is a horizontal skew. XScale, however, is 0.5, showing that I skewed it half of its width.

It may take some experimenting with the skew tool before you're able to accurately predict the results of your actions. If you need some practice, give the following steps a try. As usual, we'll be abusing the receiver path from long-past Figure 13-5.

1. Select the receiver with the arrow tool. Then Shift-drag upward with the skew tool from the center of the shape (the point indicated by the cursor in Figure 13-5). The right half of the phone shrugs upward with your drag because it is located on the right side of the transformation origin. The left half of the phone shrugs down, as shown in Figure 13-25. Release the mouse button once the YScale item in the Info toolbar reads 0.3.

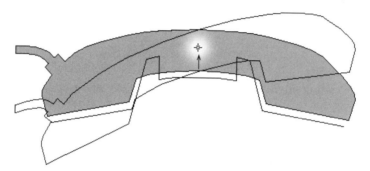

Figure 13-25: Shift-drag upward with the skew tool to slant the right half of the selected shape up and the left half down.

2. Shift-drag again with the skew tool, but this time drag to the left. The top of the shape slants backward, and the bottom portion slants forward, as shown in Figure 13-26. Release the mouse button and Shift key once the XScale value reads -1.8. FreeHand skews the shape backward by an amount equal to nearly twice its former width.

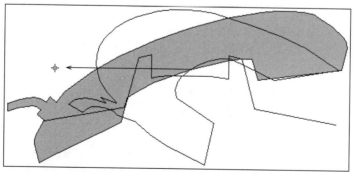

Figure 13-26: Shift-drag left to slant the top half of the receiver to the left and the bottom half to the right.

3. Press ⌘/Ctrl-Z twice in a row to undo both the vertical and horizontal skewing. Now try dragging up and to the right with the tool — without pressing the Shift key — to get the same results shown in Figure 13-26. The truth is, you can't. It just proves the old adage: Two Shift-drags are better than one without a Shift.

Slanting partial paths

What good would the skew tool be if you couldn't slant selected elements independently of their deselected neighbors? In Figure 13-27, I Shift-dragged to the left with the skew tool. The selected points move with the star cursor based on their proximity to the transformation origin. Points close to the origin move about the same distance as the cursor itself; points twice as far away move twice as far, points three times as far away move three times as far, and so on.

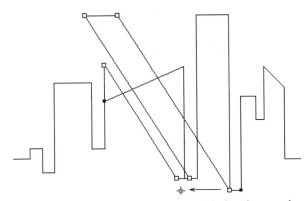

Figure 13-27: Shift-drag to the left with the skew tool to slant the selected segments so they lean backward.

The segments between selected points react differently depending on whether they are primarily vertical or horizontal. Figure 13-27 shows a horizontal skew, so all vertical segments between selected points slant backward; all selected horizontal segments don't slant at all. As usual, the segments between selected and deselected points just stretch or shrink to keep up.

Using the Skew panel

You access the Skew panel, shown in Figure 13-28, by double-clicking on the skew tool icon in the toolbox, Option/Alt-clicking with the tool in the illustration window, or clicking on the Skew icon at the top of the Transform panel.

Enter the degree to which you want to skew a selected object in the two Skew Angles option boxes. The H option determines the horizontal slant; the V value determines the vertical slant. Both negative and positive values are accepted. Here's how they work:

✦ A negative H value slants a selected object backward, as if you dragged to the left with the skew tool.

✦ A positive H value slants the object forward — and just in case you haven't seen FreeHand for awhile, this is the opposite of the way this option worked in Version 3.

✦ A positive V value slants the right side of the object upward and the left side downward, as if you dragged up with the skew tool.

✦ A negative V value slants the right side of the object downward and the left side upward.

Figure 13-28: In the Skew panel you specify the horizontal and vertical components of a skew in degrees.

With one exception, these items work the same way in the Info toolbar. Whereas FreeHand measures skews as ratios in the Info toolbar, it measures them in degrees inside the skew panel. One (ratios) is a relative system, the other (degrees) is absolute.

To understand how degrees work, imagine that you are slanting a rectangle. If you enter 30 in the H option box, FreeHand slants the vertical sides from their normal 90-degree posture to 60 degrees (90 - 30 = 60).

If you enter 30 in the V option box, the horizontal sides slant up from a 0-degree to a 30-degree incline. A value of 90 degrees in either the H or V option box flattens the selection to virtual nothingness, which is why FreeHand won't accept this value. The highest (or lowest) acceptable value is 89.9 (or -89.9). But values beyond negative or positive 45 degrees are rarely useful.

After you enter your values in the H and V option boxes, press Return/Enter to implement your changes. The Center option boxes and Contents and Fills check boxes work the same in the Skew panel as they do in the other transformation panels.

Transformation Handles

New to FreeHand 8 is the transformation handles feature. Transformation handles are the eight black boxes that surround a path (defining the transformation handles bounding box) when you double-click on it, as shown in Figure 13-29. These handles give you another method of moving, scaling, or rotating objects. You may drag inside the handles bounding box to move the selection, drag directly on a handle to scale the selection or drag outside the handles bounding box to rotate the selection. The cursor will change appropriately.

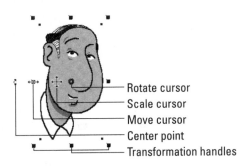

Rotate cursor
Scale cursor
Move cursor
Center point
Transformation handles

Figure 13-29: Double-click on a single path to display the transformation handles. With these handles you have another way of moving, scaling or rotation objects in FreeHand.

When the transformation handles display, the center point also shows up (labeled in Figure 13-29). When you scale or rotate with the appropriate tool in FreeHand, the center point (a point around which the transformations take place) is defined by where you first click. When you scale or rotate via the Transform panels, you specify the center point numerically. When you're working with the transformation handles, the center point is initially created at the spatial center of the selection. Thus, if you scale of rotate the selection while the transformation handles are first active, you transform around the center. The great thing about the transformation handles' center point is that you can move it independently of the selection. Simply drag it to a new location and any scalings and rotations that you then execute will happen in terms of the center point's new location.

To activate the transformation handles, you need to do one of the following:

✦ Double-click on a single path or group to display the transformation handles for that path or group.

✦ Select as many paths as you wish and then double-click on any of those paths to display the transformation handles that surround all selected paths.

Once you've surrounded a path with the transformation handles, you have a few of methods of modifying which paths are affected by the transformation handles. You can:

✦ ⌘/Ctrl-Shift-click on a new path to add that path to a group of paths that are currently surrounded by transformation handles.

✦ Press ⌘/Ctrl-A to add all other paths (on that same page) to the paths that are currently surrounded by the transformation handles.

✦ ⌘/Ctrl-click on a new path to deactivate the current transformation handles and activate the transformation handles around that new path. The new transformation handles will retain the same a center point of the old transformation handles instead of defining a new center point.

✦ If you activated the control handles around a path that is part of a larger grouped object, press the grave (`) key to enlarge the transformation handles to surround all paths that are part of that path's group.

✦ When the illustration is active (and not a panel) press the Tab key to deactivate the transformation handles.

Once you've chosen which paths to transform, you can:

✦ Press the Option/Alt key while you're moving, scaling or rotating paths via the transformation handles to transform a copy of the paths.

✦ ⌘/Ctrl-drag a path that is surrounded by transformation handles to move the path without moving the center point. This is just the opposite effect of dragging the center point independently of the selection.

✦ Shift-drag to constrain the transformation just as you can when you Shift-drag with of the transformation tools.

Whether you move, scale or rotate a selection with the transformation handles, it's possible that you will also transform the fill and stroke of the selection. You determine this with the settings of the same name in the Transform panels. In other words, if you want to rotate a selection via the transformation handles but you don't want to rotate its gradient fill, simply deactivate the Fills check box in the Rotate panel of the Transform panel.

Xtra Touches

Now, onward to the new group of methods for changing objects' appearances. Figure 13-30 shows the Xtra Tools panel and Operations panel with all the tools that allow you to change the appearance of objects labeled. You will learn, as you read on, that some of these stars shine far brighter than others.

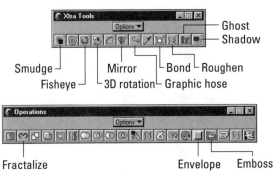

Figure 13-30: The Xtras that let you change the appearances of objects.

Smudging objects

The smudge tool is a strange one. It's billed as a means for giving object edges a soft, blended appearance — as if that were the one capability that you felt that FreeHand lacked. Here's what actually happens when you use the smudge tool. The procedure is illustrated in Figure 13-31. You select an object and choose the smudge tool from the Xtra Tools panel. The cursor becomes a cartoonish pointing finger. You drag to define the range of the smudge. A line appears while you drag. FreeHand then duplicates the selection a number of times and evenly distributes the duplicates along the line that you dragged. The longer the drag, the more space between the duplicates. The top portion of Figure 13-31 illustrates a short drag and the resulting smudge effect. The bottom portion of Figure 13-31 shows a much longer drag and the resulting effect.

By default, FreeHand blends both the fill and stroke of the selection to white. This accounts for the softening effect that smudging creates. However, you can assign different Smudge To colors for the fill and stroke. To do so, double-click on the smudge tool icon to display the Smudge dialog box, and then drag and drop the colors of your choice into the Fill and Stroke color wells. On shorter drags, the fill-color blend may not create any visual difference in your results. In Figure 13-31, I used identical color settings. In the top case, the blending of the fill color is not apparent. In the bottom case, the longer drag results in wider spaces between the duplicates, letting you see their fills. You can clearly see the fill blend from gray to white in the bottom case.

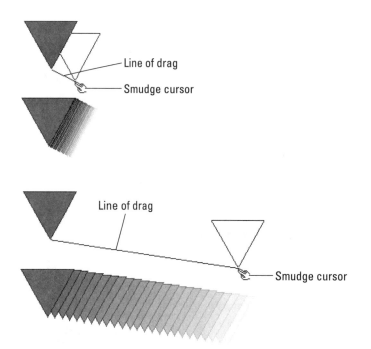

Figure 13-31: FreeHand evenly distributes duplicates of an object that you smudge along a line you drag with the smudge tool.

Tip

Just for fun, hold the Option/Alt key while you're dragging with the smudge tool. Instead of creating a line of duplicates, FreeHand will create a series of duplicates in which each is slightly larger than the last. The duplicates will, for the most part, retain the shape of the original and will all be centered around the original path.

Giving objects the fisheye

The fisheye lens tool lets you apply special photographic lens-type distortions to objects. Distorted objects can appear to have been stretched over a sphere or sucked into a vortex, depending on your Perspective setting in the Fisheye Lens dialog box. This dialog box is featured in Figure 13-32. The sample box shows how the Perspective setting would affect a grid. Use the slider or the adjacent option box to alter the perspective between Concave and Convex. The option box accepts values between -100 (concave) and 100 (convex), with 0 causing no distortion.

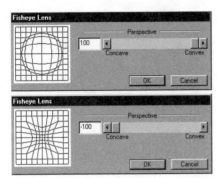

Figure 13-32: The Fisheye Lens dialog box lets you control the tool's distortion amount.

To use this tool, select the objects that you want to distort, and then, with the fisheye lens tool, drag a "lens" around the area you want to distort. Figure 13-33 shows the drag I performed with the fisheye lens tool. Figure 13-34 shows the results with Perspective set to maximum Convex. Figure 13-35 show the results with Perspective set to maximum Concave. Certainly you must wonder, as I do, why this tool is not called the fisheye/beady-eye lens tool. How is it that the fisheye functionality got not only top billing, but the only billing?

Figure 13-33: A lens appears when you drag the fisheye lens tool.

Figure 13-34: The fisheye effect set to maximum convexity results in this guy giving you the fisheye.

Figure 13-35: The fisheye effect set to maximum concavity results in this guy giving you the beady eye.

You can modify your lens using the following modifier key combinations:

✦ Option/Alt-drag the fisheye lens tool to drag a lens from the center outward.

✦ Shift-drag the fisheye lens tool to drag a circular lens.

✦ Shift-Option/Alt-drag the fisheye lens tool to drag a circular lens from the center outward.

Note

You should be aware of two limitations to the fisheye lens effect. First, to apply the fisheye lens to text, you must first convert the text to paths by choosing Text ➪ Convert To Paths. Second, the fisheye lens effect doesn't stretch tile fills and contents.

Rotating objects in 3D

To rotate objects in 3D, simply put on the green and red glasses that came with FreeHand and use the 3D rotation tool. No, no, no, I'm just kidding. The glasses don't come with FreeHand; you have to send away for them.

The 3D rotation tool is one of the most powerful features in FreeHand. Unfortunately, it's also one of the most obscure. This tool lets you rotate a two-dimensional object through three-dimensional space. To visualize this, picture a postage stamp centered inside of an acrylic sphere. If you rotate the sphere, the stamp's appearance can change from a square, to a diamond, and to a line, depending on the degree of rotation, the height of the sphere, and whether the sphere is to your left, right, or centered. I'm telling you, it gets complicated.

So much so that the 3D rotation tool even rates its own panel, which appears when you double-click on the 3D rotation tool in the Xtra Tools panel. The panel has two modes, Easy and Expert, as pictured in Figure 13-36. Whenever you perform a 3D rotation, FreeHand uses the settings in this panel. If you're in Easy mode, the first decision is to set your center of rotation, or pivot point.

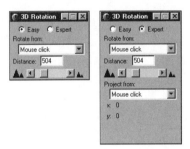

Figure 13-36: The 3D Rotation panel shown in Easy and Expert modes.

Rotate From sets the center point of the rotation. Referring back to our acrylic sphere, consider now that it has a stick protruding from it so that it resembles a round lollipop. You could swing it around by the end of the stick. In this case, the end of the stick would be the center of rotation. Several options are available from the Rotate From pop-up menu. These options work as follows:

✦ **Mouse Click:** FreeHand rotates the selection around the point where you begin your rotation drag.

✦ **Center of Selection:** FreeHand calculates the exact center of your selection and uses it as the center of rotation. See the top portion of Figure 13-37 for an example of this option.

✦ **Center of Gravity:** FreeHand takes into account the positioning of the objects and the empty space in a selection when determining the selection's center. The bottom portion of Figure 13-37 shows the center of gravity of the selection that encompasses unevenly distributed objects.

✦ **Origin:** FreeHand uses the bottom left corner of the selection as the center of rotation.

When you begin your rotation, FreeHand indicates the center of rotation with a small triangle, as illustrated in Figure 13-37.

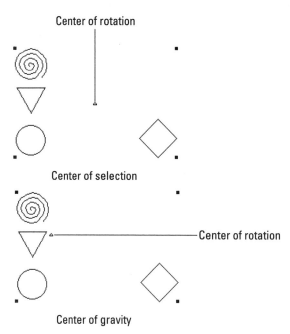

Figure 13-37: FreeHand calculates different rotation centers for the same selection, depending on your Rotate From choice.

Next, you need to set the distance at which to perform the rotation. Going back to our acrylic sphere, imagine holding it right up to your nose and tilting it away from you. The perspective effect for the stamp within the sphere would be far more severe than if you held the sphere at arm's length and tilted it. The same is true with your Distance setting. Greater distances create less extreme perspective-like distortions, while smaller distances create more dramatic distortions. The minimal distance you can assign is 100 points. The default setting is 504 points. Figure 13-38 demonstrates the difference your Distance setting can make.

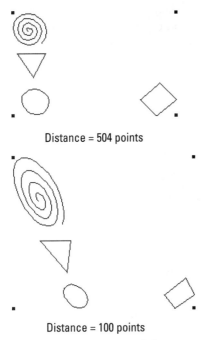

Distance = 504 points

Distance = 100 points

Figure 13-38: I performed the same 3D rotation on these two selections, varying only the Distance setting.

Well, if you're a brave soul, you may be willing to take a cautious stroll with me on the Expert side of the street. Your first decision is to choose a Project From option. This is actually a two-dimensional decision, so think flat. You want to set your XY coordinates for the rotation. Going back to our good friend, Mr. Acrylic Sphere, are you looking down or up on the sphere? Are you seeing the sphere from its right side or its left side? These questions are answered by your Project From setting. The first four options in the Project From pop-up menu are the same as in the Rotate From pop-up menu. Additionally, you can choose X/Y Coordinates. Doing so produces two option boxes at the bottom of the 3D Rotation panel for entering exact x and y coordinates. These work the same as the X and Y option boxes in the Transform panels.

Expert mode also tracks your mouse movements when you perform a rotation, constantly updating you with your current YZ angle and XZ angle. (These values are only visible in the 3D Rotation dialog box when you are dragging with the 3D rotation tool in the expert mode.) The YZ angle displays the number of degrees you've rotated the selection from true vertical; the XZ displays the number of degrees that you've rotated the selection from true horizontal.

Now you're ready to perform a rotation. After making your object selection, choose the 3D rotation tool from the Xtra Tools panel and begin to drag. A line appears from the point where you click. This line is the Z-axis. It's now time for you to establish the one remaining factor, and that's how many degrees to rotate the selection. The length of the Z-axis determines this. A shorter drag results in less rotation than a long drag.

Through the looking glass

The mirror tool, a new Xtra tool, lets you create a reflected copy of a selection. This reflection is the same one you would see if you held a plane mirror up to the screen. The mirror tool gives you control over what angle the imaginary mirror is positioned at and whether the mirror consists of single plane mirror or two plane mirrors used in conjunction as one. The result that the mirror tool delivers is not unique, but is simply one that you could produce if you Option/Alt-dragged with the standard reflect tool.

Double-click on the mirror icon in the Xtra Tool panel to display the Mirror dialog box, shown in Figure 13-39. The first pop-up menu gives you access to four choices of how to position the axis of reflection. The first two settings, Vertical or Horizontal, limits the mirror tool to reflection across a single plane. This reflection appears either above or below or to the side of the original as the setting's name would indicate. As you drag with the mirror tool, you locate the reflection axis. The next setting, Horizontal & Vertical, reflects the selected paths across two axis simultaneously. Imagine forming a specialized mirror by taking two plane mirrors — that is, two standard, flat mirrors — and gluing them together such that they are at right angles to one another. If you were to hold this contraption up to your screen, you would see your original path and three reflections of it. This is the same result of using the mirror tool with the Horizontal & Vertical option selected. It duplicates the selection three times: one reflected across the vertical axis, one reflected across the horizontal axis, and one reflected across both the vertical and horizontal axis. The final setting and the one featured in Figure 13-39, Multiple, also lets you duplicate selected paths a number of times. Continuing with the above thought experiment, further imagine, that instead of gluing the two mirrors to one another, you glue them both to a special hinge. This hinge, unlike its standard counterpart which would open to any angle, only opens to 50 preset angles. If you held this hinged mirror up to your screen, you would see a number of reflections based on the hinge's angle. With the mirror tool, you choose the number of reflections by changing the value in the option box to the left of the slider bar. Drag with the mirror tool to set the hinge point of the two imaginary mirrors that create the reflections. You can choose a value from 1 to 50.

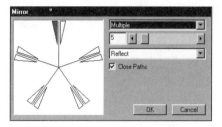

Figure 13-39: Double-click on the mirror icon in the Xtra Tool panel to display the Mirror dialog box where you decide the position and number of reflection axis through which the tool will reflect the selected paths.

If you are reflecting open paths with the mirror tool, you can opt to automatically join, at least part, of the reflection with the original path. With the Closed Paths check box selected in the Mirror dialog box, simply drag with the mirror tool to a location within a few pixels — specify this distance in the Pick Distance option box of the General panel of the Preference dialog box — of one of the original path's endpoints. Upon completion of the drag, one of the reflections will be seamlessly joined to the original path. Unfortunately, FreeHand will not further join the other reflections to mimic the composite path that's formed from the original and one of its reflections. If you desire this, you will have to join the other paths manually with the Modify ⇨ Join command.

Picture dumping

Another of FreeHand 8's new Xtra tools is the graphic hose. When you drag with the graphic hose tool you spray copies of predefined objects throughout you document. The source for the objects splattered on by the graphic hose tool is either one of the four object sets shipped with FreeHand or one that you create. Double-click on the graphic hose icon in the Xtra Tools panel to display the Hose dialog box (shown on the left of Figure 13-40) to choose the object set you wish to spray.

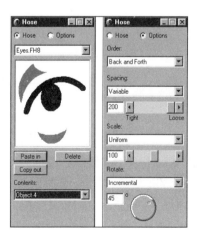

Figure 13-40: The Hose dialog box has two faces. In the one on the left, you choose and define object sets. In the one on the right, you specify how the graphic tool works.

In the first pop-up menu you can choose from any of the object sets that are currently defined. By default, FreeHand 8 includes four predefined object sets, each consisting of a few objects. (Well, actually, the Clover object set consist of one clover, especially designed for the non-discriminating leprechaun.) If you find that none of these rather prosaic object sets meet you needs, you can create your own. To do so, choose New from that first pop-up menu. After you have named you new object set, click on the Paste In button to add the last item that you copied from you illustration. Each time you paste in an object to the object set, FreeHand adds an object to the Contents pop-up menu, located at the bottom of the Hose dialog box. You may have up to ten objects in an object set. If you decide that one of the objects you have pasted in doesn't go with the rest of the set, choose that object from the Contents pop-up menu and click on the Delete button. If you wish to copy on the objects to the Clipboard, choose it from the Contents pop-up menu and click on the Copy Out button.

To access the Hose dialog box's alter ego, click on the Options radio button found at the top of the dialog box. The version of the Hose dialog box, shown on the right of Figure 13-40, lets you choose how the graphic hose will work.

✦ **Order:** You can opt have the graphic hose spew out the items of an object set in one of three manners. Choose Back and Forth to see the objects created in an ascending-to-descending order. In other words, if there are only three objects in the set, their creation would follow the first, second, third, second, first sequence. Choose loop to see the objects pile out in order with the sequence of their production repeating after each cycle. Choose random to create the objects in any old order.

✦ **Spacing:** As the objects drizzle out of the graphic hose, Freehand either distributes them regularly on a grid or in a freeform manner. If you choose Grid from the Spacing pop-up menu, you specify the distances between the grid's vertices in the resulting option box. For a freeform distribution, choose either the Random or Variable options. Random simply spews out the objects spacing them anywhere from 1 to 200 pixels away from one another. When you choose Variable, the objects' spacing is determined by how quickly you move the graphic hose tool around in your illustration.

✦ **Scale:** You can specify scale the objects you distribute with the graphic hose. Choose the Uniform option to have all your objects rescaled by the same percentage that you set in the option box. If you wish FreeHand to randomly rescale the objects as each one is created, choose the Random option and set the rescaleing limit in the option box.

✦ **Rotate:** Just as you can change the scaling of the objects as they're created with the graphic hose, you can choose to have them appear as rotated versions of the originals. Choose Uniform to have all the objects rotate the same amount. Choose Random to have each object randomly rotated from 0° to the amount you specify. To have each object rotate incrementally more than the last, choose the Incremental option from the pop-up menu.

A case of the bends

Next on the list of tools for which you may not readily find a use, is the bend tool. This tools allows you to curve paths inward or outward from the point where the mouse is clicked. To use the bend tool, select a path with the arrow tool, choose the bend tool from the Xtra Tools panel, and drag on the path with the bend tool. The distortion centers on the point where the mouse was clicked. Drag up to create a spiked effect, curving the path inward. Drag down to create a bloated effect, curving the path outward. Double-click on the bend tool to set the amount of distortion in the Bend dialog box. The higher the value the greater the distortion. Figure 13-41 shows the results of bending a rectangle.

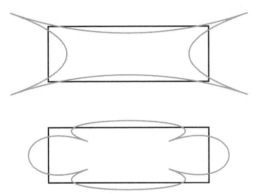

Figure 13-41: The top example shows the result of dragging upward with the bend tool. The bottom example shows the bloated effect of dragging down with the bend tool.

The rougher the better

Wandering down our list of Xtra tools, we next come to the roughen tool. Roughen adds points to a selected path and randomly distributes them away from the original path's location. Roughen gives an object a case of the frizzies resembling a bad hair day in a humid climate. The Roughen dialog box appears when you double click on the roughen icon in the Xtras Tools palette. Here you enter the number of points you wish to add per inch in the Amount option box. The higher the number the frizzier the effect. You can choose between a Rough edge and a Smooth edge using the respective radio boxes. Selecting Rough uses corner points to create a jagged edge. Smooth uses curve points to create a smooth, but distorted edge. Figure 13-42 shows the result of the Roughen tool.

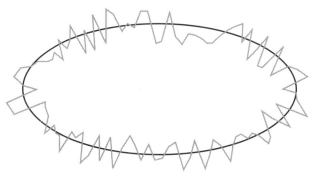

Figure 13-42: The result of dragging on an ellipse with the roughen tool.

Off the chart

It may shock you to learn this, but you use the chart tool to create and edit charts. Pretty straightforward, eh? To create a chart, click on the chart tool found in the Xtra Tools panel. Click and drag in the illustration window to determine the size of the chart. When you release the mouse the Chart dialog box will appear. The two main areas of the Chart dialog box are the Worksheet and the Chart Type.

In the worksheet area you enter and edit chart data. In the Chart Type area you select the chart type and add a variety of design elements such as column width, axis display, drop shadow, and legend. You can choose between the following chart types: Grouped column, Stacked column, Line, Pie, Area, and Scatter. You can add a number of effects by using the many options found in Chart dialog box but it takes a lot of work and planning. It will take some experimenting with the chart tool to see the various effects that can be achieved.

In any event, once a chart is plotted, you can treat it like any other graphic. The chart may be enlarged, scaled, rotated, moved, and edited. But be careful, once you ungroup a chart it permanently becomes a graphic and can no longer be edited using the Chart Xtra. Note that you can always go back in and change the chart under Xtras ⇨ Chart ⇨ Edit to change information or styles. You could also note that this charting feature is a good way to get a basic chart drawn, ungroup when data is accurate, then jazz it up with FreeHand's other great tools.

Shadow of FreeHand

A new feature to FreeHand is its capability to automatically add a drop shadow to a path. You have three different styles of drop shadows from which to choose. All three of these choices are shown in Figure 13-43. To use the shadow tool, simply select a path (or paths) with the arrow tool, click on the shadow tool icon in the Xtra Tools panel and drag the selected objects with the shadow tool. FreeHand displays an outline of the selected paths as you drag.

Hard edge   Soft edge   Zoom

Figure 13-43: With the shadow tool, you can add three different types of shadows to paths.

To choose between the styles of shadows and set their different options, double-click on the shadow tool icon in the Xtra Tools panel to display the Shadow dialog box. Two options (Scale and Offset) are common to all three styles of drop shadows and are discussed separately below. The three styles — Hard Edges, Soft Edges and Zoom — and their respective options are as follows:

✦ **Hard Edges:** Select the Hard Edges option to create a traditional drop shadow. You can choose from three types of fill for this drop shadow. Both the Tint — a lighter version of the original's fill color — and the Shade — a darker version of the original's — are set in terms of percentages. If you want the color of the shadow to completely differ from the originals color, choose the Color option from the Fill pop-up menu and drag a color swatch from the Color Mixer or the Color List. In the top example of Figure 13-43, the hard edge drop shadow uses a 50% Tint and it 90% of the original in size.

✦ **Soft Edges:** With the Soft Edges option you create a drop shadow with edges that blend between two colors. First, you choose a fill color. These choices (Color, Shade, and Tint) work the same as the Fill choices for the Hard Edges drop shadow. Second, you choose a Fade To color. The color you choose for this box — drag a color swatch from the Color Mixer or Color List — is the color that the fill color will blend into. Last, decide to how much of the shadow you want to fade to comprise. The higher the percentage, the further in the fade will begin. The middle example of Figure 13-43 shows a soft edge drop shadow with a 50% Tint that's 90% of the original in size. The Fade To color is white and the Soft Edge is set to 15%.

✦ **Zoom:** The Zoom option let's you create a shadow that's not really so much a shadow as it is a blend. FreeHand creates a blend that extends from the original path to where you drag the path with the shadow tool. You can choose both the fill and stroke color of the final step in the blend by dragging a color swatch on the appropriate color box in the Shadow dialog box.

Two options are common to all three styles of shadows.

✦ **Scale:** You can opt to scale the shadow up to two times greater than the original object. Either use the slider bar or enter a value between 0 and 200 into the option box.

✦ **Offset:** In the X and Y options boxes you enter the horizontal and vertical distances by which you wish to offset the shadow. The default settings of 0 and 0 positions the shadow directly behind the object.

Fractalizing objects

I was upfront with you in the beginning of this chapter when I said that these object-altering features have a novelty appeal. Well, the fractalize effect gets my vote for the Best-of-Show Novelty Award. To apply this effect to a selected object, choose the Fractalize icon in the Operations panel. Alternatively you can use the Xtras ➪ Distort ➪ Fractalize command. FreeHand then produces a geometric pattern from the object by generating additional segments from each of the object's vertices at regular intervals. The fun begins when you repeatedly apply the command to the same shape. If you remember, pressing ⌘-Shift-+ on Macs and Ctrl-Alt-Shift-X on PCs repeats the last Xtra performed. Figure 13-44 shows the results of applying the Fractalize effect to an object six times. The results are reminiscent of Tantric art.

If, for some reason, you want to apply this effect to text, first apply the Text ➪ Convert To Paths command to the text. You can only fractalize objects.

Emboss

With the new emboss operation, you can add an embossing effect to paths giving the illusion that the paths are raised. This will give the paths a textured appearance akin to the relief created when a notary public embosses an official document with her notary public tool. When FreeHand adds an embossing effect, it essentially clones the original path twice and offsets each of the clones in opposite directions. One clone serves as the highlight of the original path and the other serves as the shadow. The highlight traditionally gets a lighter shade of the original fill and the shadow receives a slightly darker.

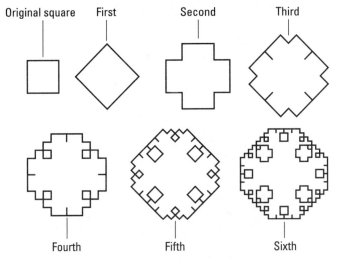

Figure 13-44: A square as it progresses through six fractalizations.

The five types of embossing that FreeHand offers include Emboss, Deboss, Chisel, Ridge and Quilt and are all shown in Figure 13-45. The Emboss option is gives the traditional embossing effect. The Deboss results in an emboss that is the same as the one created by the Emboss but with the highlight and shadow trading roles. The Chisel option creates a highlight that smoothly transforms into the shadow. The Ridge and Quilt options create specialized embossing effects in which both the highlight and the shadow are blends. The only difference between the two is that the role of the highlight and shadow are reversed in the Quilt option.

When you double-click on the emboss icon in the Operations panel, the Emboss dialog box displays. Each of the different embossing types are affected by the same three options. These options work as described below.

✦ **Vary:** Choose Contrast to use a highlight and shadow that are tints of the object's original fill color. The fill is lightened by the percent specified in the option box to form the highlight color. For the shadow, the original fill is darkened by the same amount. If you wish to specify specific colors for the highlight and shadow, choose the Color option and drag from the Color Mixer the colors you want into the Highlight and Shadow color boxes.

✦ **Depth:** Here you specify how much of an offset the emboss effect uses. In Figure 13-45, each of the embossing use a depth of 5 pixels. Although you can set the depth anywhere from 1 to 20 pixels, the 3 to 7 range is probably the most useful.

✦ **Angle:** The angle setting dictates the direction of the emboss. The highlight and shadow are offset in the direction that the angle specifies.

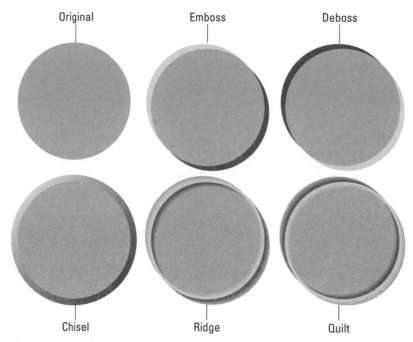

Figure 13-45: The original path and the result of applying each of the five emboss options to it.

Envelopes in the mail

The final tool in this discussion is the envelope tool, accessed through either the Xtras ⇨ Distort ⇨ Envelope command or from the Operations palette. Envelope distorts objects and groups of objects by altering their outer boundary. You can control the effect by editing the Envelope dialog box. Select the path to be altered and click on the envelope tool in the Operations menu. The dialog box appears as shown in Figure 13-46. A pop-up menu in the dialog box allows you to use 10 preset effects. These effects are Balloon, Bow Tie, Circle, Diamond, Fade Left, Fade Right, Octagon, Peak Right, Rainbow, and the ever popular Sag. Figure 13-46 shows the result of my favorite effect, the Circle.

Figure 13-46: The Envelope dialog box with the Circle option in effect.

You can also make your own special effects by dragging on the points and control handles in the preview window. When you distort the object to your liking, choose save from the pop-up window to name your very own effect for future use. The only other selection in the dialog box is Tighter Fit which makes the object follow the edges of the Envelope bounding box more closely. You can preview the result of your Envelope distortion by clicking on the Apply button. The selected object in the illustration conforms itself to look exactly like the preview window. To bring back the original shape, click the Reset to undo all of your moves. As in most of the Xtras, you must first convert the text to paths by choosing Text ➪ Convert to Paths before you can apply the Envelope effect to text. I had to convert the type shown in Figure 13-46 before I enveloped it.

Graphic Search and Replace

One of FreeHand's most useful convinces is the Edit ➪ Find And Replace ➪ Graphics. This new feature allows you to search for objects by name or characteristic and replace them with new attributes. Suppose you have just finished a complex drawing comprised of over 2,000 different objects. Among these objects are 750 one point lines that cross a variety of other objects.

You show the drawing to your boss and he says, "Fantastic! What a wonderful job! However, I'd like to see these little lines much fatter." (You know, bosses only talk that way because they really don't know any better.) You go back to your desk in despair because you have to use the magnification tool to enlarge the illustration and find each one point line, select it and make it fatter.

What a nightmare, right? Well, not with Graphic Search and Replace. In FreeHand you search for one point lines and replace them with whatever you wish. So to finish the story, after your boss gives you the mandate to fatten-up those lines you tell him that will take some time, you moan and groan a little and make him feel the pain of his decision. Then you go back to your computer and in two seconds search and replace. You then log onto the Internet and surf for the rest of the afternoon. The next morning you present the fattened illustration to your boss and hope he wants another massive change.

So how does this powerful feature work? First you need to access the Find And Replace Graphics dialog box by choosing the Edit ➪ Find And Replace ➪ Graphics command or ⌘/Ctrl-Option/Alt-E. Although the dialog box looks deceptively simple, it has an incredible depth. It is divided into two sections, Find and Replace and Select. First we'll deal with Select.

Building a selection

From the Select panel of the dialog box you have the power to search selected objects, a page, or the entire document. You also have the ability to build selections by searching for attributes and then adding the found objects to the selection. This lets you perform Boolean searches on graphic elements. No other drawing program gives you this capability.

The dialog box contains two main pop-up menus and one option box as shown in Figure 13-47. The Attribute pop-up menu is the search criteria. You have the option of choosing from the following list of attributes: Color, Style, Same as Selection, Fill Type, Stroke Type, Stroke Width, Font, Text Effect, Object Name, Object Type, Path Shape, Halftone, and Overprint. Each one of these selections prompts another set of options boxes and pop-up menus to further define the search.

The Search In pop-up menu defines the scope of the search either within the selected objects, within a page, or within the entire document. The Add to Selection option box lets you add to the found set building a search of any complexity. For example, you could search for every object with a red stroke, and then choose Add to Selection and search for every object with a black gradient fill. This will result in a selection of all objects with red strokes or black gradient fills. If you want to search for objects with red strokes and black gradient fills, you search for black gradient fills, change the Search In pop-up menu to Selection and then search for red strokes. By adding to and repeating this procedure, the search possibilities are almost limitless.

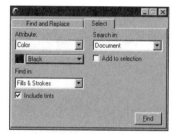

Figure 13-47: The Find and Replace Graphics dialog box with the Select panel selected.

Finding and replacing

From the Find and Replace panel of the dialog box, you have the ability to find and change attributes of objects. As with the Select panel, there are two main pop-up menus, Attribute and Change In which are the equivalent of the Search In pop-up menu.

The Attribute pop-up menu sports the following choices: Color, Stroke Width, Font, Remove, Path Shape, Simplify, Rotate, Scale, and Blend Steps. Choosing any of these prompts further pop-up menus and option boxes to define the attribute. The Change In pop-up menu gives you the choice of either searching within selected objects, within a page, or within the entire document.

Finding and replacing a color

Choose color from the Attribute pop-up menu and several new option boxes, swatch boxes, and pop-up menus appear in the Find and Replace dialog box. In the left swatch box, choose the color you wish to change from. In the right swatch box select the color you wish to change to. To select new colors either drag colors from the Color Mixer or use the pop-up menus to the right of each swatch box. From the Apply To pop-up menu choose whether you want the change to apply to just fills, just strokes, or both fills and strokes. If you wish to include tints, choose the Include Tints option box. Once you select the appropriate options, click on Change and the From color will be replaced by the To color. In the lower left-hand corner the dialog box will inform you how many items were changed.

The other options

The Color attribute is just one of the many new options in Find and Replace. You can also find and change the following:

✦ **Stroke Width:** Strokes within a given range of widths can be replaced with a new stroke width or the width can be modified using a mathematical equation.

✦ **Font:** Any font, style, or type size can be found and replaced with a font of a given style and size or the size can be modified using a mathematical equation.

✦ **Remove:** Invisible objects, overprinting, custom halftones, or contents can be found and removed.

✦ **Path Shape:** Path shapes pasted into the panel can be found and replaced with any object except TIFF and EPS images.

✦ **Simplify:** Paths with a given number of points can be found and replaced with simplified paths determined by a mathematical equation.

✦ **Rotate:** Found objects can be rotated according to the specified rotation angle.

✦ **Scale:** Found objects can be scaled according to the Scale specified.

✦ **Blend Steps:** Found blends with a given number of steps can be replaced with a blend of another number of steps or resampled at a given printer dpi.

✦   ✦   ✦

Duplicating Objects and Effects

Clones to the Rescue

The older you get, the more precious your time becomes. It's not just that you sense you'll eventually run out of time or that the rate at which time disappears increases exponentially with each passing year. You also have more to do. Make a living, clean the house, balance the checkbook, invest your savings, resolve conflicts, take care of family members, hobnob with associates — even getting together with friends can seem like a chore. These are the responsibilities that accompany the personal and financial freedoms of adulthood.

Now imagine for a moment that you can buy more time by cloning yourself, you know, like the movie *Multiplicity*. Certainly, there are some nagging details to consider before you jump into such a purchase. I mean, would your clones expect you to pitch in and work just as much as you do now? Would you have to manage them like other employees? Would they consume as much as you do, thereby nullifying the benefits of cloning? Would they all want their own bedrooms? Would you have to clone your spouse to keep your clones happy, so that they didn't tear around the countryside like demented Frankenstein's monsters? This is beginning to sound terrible!

Well, obviously it wouldn't be like that. Those kinds of clones would never sell. The clones that I'm asking you to imagine are the result of meticulous engineering and first-rate design. They can do what you do without supervision and have no ego to get in the way. You can go on one vacation after another as your clones slave away for the greater good of you. And for a limited time only, you can purchase a special adapter that allows you to eat all the Häagen-Dazs you want and have a clone exercise it off.

Send $100,000 now for your introductory starter kit. In the meantime, while I book my getaway to Brazil, I'll tell you about a means of cloning that is already at your disposal. FreeHand enables you to clone any object or text block as many times as you want. This feature is an amazing time-saver. No longer do you have to draw and redraw similar objects. Nor do you have to trace duplicates, as when drawing conventionally, or work from photocopies that take nearly as long to clean up as it takes to create an illustration from scratch.

Every clone in FreeHand is absolutely identical to the original; you don't lose any quality or functionality. Clones are fully editable, so you can modify them to fit special requirements. You can even repeat transformations or automatically reapply a transformation as you clone an object.

You have enough demands on your time without spending an inordinate amount of it inside FreeHand. If you draw something once, don't draw it again. This way, you can spend less time working on the computer and more time with other time-saving appliances, such as your dishwasher, your food processor, your fax machine, your washer and dryer, your VCR, your car, your vacuum cleaner, your cellular phone, your lawn mower. . . .

Heck, by time you get done with those things, you'll be grateful to take a break and get back to FreeHand.

Duplicating Objects and Type

FreeHand provides several sets of commands for replicating objects. All are located under the Edit menu.

The foremost commands included with all Macintosh programs are Cut, Copy, and Paste. Although these commands aren't the most efficient means for duplicating objects inside a document — a job better suited to the Clone and Duplicate commands — they do serve a variety of purposes in FreeHand:

✦ **Swapping objects between illustrations:** Cut or copy an object and paste it into another document. This method is also useful for transferring attribute styles and other settings to another document.

✦ **Transferring objects to different applications:** After you cut or copy objects, you can paste them into other applications. You can even cut or copy items from other applications and paste them in FreeHand. The program's support for foreign Clipboard objects is excellent.

✦ **Transferring attributes to different objects:** After you use the Copy Attribute command, you can paste the attributes of objects or text.

✦ **Duplicating or moving some typing inside a text block:** Select some characters with the text tool, choose the Copy command, and then paste the copied text into another position or into another text block. Use Cut and Paste to remove selected characters from one location and move them to another.

✦ **Stacking objects:** If you want to move an object several objects forward or backward within a layer, you can cut the object, select the object that's immediately in front of where you want to position the cut object, and choose Edit ➪ Paste Behind or Edit ➪ Paste In Front.

✦ **Creating special effects:** Choosing Cut or Copy is the first step in creating tile patterns and masks, as discussed in Chapters 11 and 15, respectively.

✦ **Saving one object from reversion:** If you hate the changes you've made to an illustration — except those applied to one object — cut or copy that one object to the Clipboard. Then use the Revert command to get rid of all the other changes. When the illustration is back to its previous form, press ⌘/Ctrl-V to place the object from the Clipboard back into the illustration.

Cloning objects

Cloning functions is much like the Copy command, with two important exceptions. First, cloning bypasses the Clipboard. It doesn't displace the current occupant of the Clipboard, and it doesn't replace that object with the cloned object. Second, cloning acts like a combined Copy-and-Paste command. The cloned object appears immediately in your illustration, in front of all other objects in the current layer. If the originals are spread about onto more than one layer, each clone appears at the front of the layer that contains its original.

You can clone objects by using either of two commands, Edit ➪ Clone (⌘- = on Macs and Ctrl-Shift-C on PCs) or Edit ➪ Duplicate (⌘ on Macs or Ctrl-D on PCs). The Clone command creates a clone of the selected object directly in front of the original — which means that your document appears to be no different after you choose Clone than it did before, a fact that invariably confuses new users. To see the clone, you have to drag it away from the original. (Only the cloned objects are selected immediately after you choose Clone, so dragging the selection moves only the clones.)

Like Clone, the Duplicate command creates a clone in front of all other objects in the layer. But it also offsets the clone 10 points down and 10 to the right from the original. The Duplicate command has the added capability to replicate a series of transformations, as described later in this chapter.

Some experienced users rely exclusively on the Clone command to create clones and reserve the Duplicate command for use with transformations. But my suggestion is this: If you want to create an effect that relies on a clone being positioned directly in front of an original or offset only slightly — as in the case of the stroking effects covered in Chapter 12 — use the Clone command. If you want to use the clone elsewhere in the illustration or reshape it to serve an entirely different function in your artwork, use the Duplicate command. Then you'll know that the clone is there in case you decide to go off and do something else for a moment.

Tip

Sometimes, I find myself creating several clones directly on top of each other. If you ever need to check how many clones occupy the same space, marquee them with the arrow tool to select them all and take a look at the Object Inspector. FreeHand tells you the number of selected objects just below the title bar.

Cloning partial objects

You can clone text objects separately from the type inside or bound to them. (The exception is a text block created with the text tool, which cannot be separated from its type.) Simply Option/Alt-click on the path with the arrow tool to select it independently of its type and then choose the Clone or Duplicate command. You can then use the object to hold more type, stroke or fill it to add an effect to the text, or use it for any of a thousand other purposes.

The same goes for cloning objects inside groups or composite paths. Option/Alt-click on the path and choose Edit ⇨ Clone or Edit ⇨ Duplicate. When you clone such an object, the original object remains part of the group or composite path, but FreeHand makes the clone entirely independent. If you want to bring the clone into the group or composite path, you have to ungroup (⌘/Ctrl-U) or split (⌘/Ctrl-Shift-J) the original objects, Shift-click on the clone with the arrow tool to add it to the selection, and regroup (⌘/Ctrl-G) or join (⌘/Ctrl-J) the objects back together.

The only chink in FreeHand's replicating capabilities is that you can't clone a partial path. Even if only a few points in a path are selected, FreeHand clones the entire thing. Compare this with Illustrator, which can copy and clone individual segments for integration into other objects. If you want to reuse just a segment or two in an existing path in FreeHand, you have to clone the whole path and use the knife tool to split off the portion of the path you want to retain.

Repeating Transformations

You can duplicate the effects of a recent transformation by choosing Modify ⇨ Transform ⇨ Transform Again (⌘-, on Macs and Ctrl-Shift-G on PCs). This command applies the most recently used transformation to the selected object. It doesn't matter how long ago the transformation effect was applied, as long as it was during the current session.

I'll use Figure 14-1 as an example. After drawing the fish and ellipse at the top of the figure, I skewed the ellipse as shown in the second example to offset it at a different angle from the fish. Later, I decided I wanted the fish to be skewed, too. I'd drawn a few paths but hadn't applied any transformations — including moving — since I skewed the ellipse. I selected the fish and pressed ⌘-, on Macs and Ctrl-Shift-G on PCs to apply the same skew percentages to the fish that I applied to the ellipse. The result appears at the bottom of Figure 14-1.

Tip

The Transform Again command only remembers the last transformation performed. But you can make it remember even older transformations by using the Undo command. Simply undo the results of any transformations performed since the transformation you want to repeat, select the object you want to transform, and press -, on Macs and Ctrl-Shift-G on PCs.

The problem with this technique, of course, is that you have to undo a lot of operations with which you may be perfectly happy. So before you go to all that trouble, check the Transform panel. The panels in the panel record the last transformations performed in each of the five transformation categories (Move, Rotate, Scale, Skew, and Reflect). If you're lucky, the transformation you want to repeat will be one of the five. If so, just click on the Apply button.

Another use for the Transform Again command is to apply a slight transformation several times to the same object. By using this technique, you can experiment with a transformation until you get it just right. If you go one step too far with a transformation, just press ⌘/Ctrl-Z to return the object to its previous position, size, or angle.

Suppose you've created a complicated object that's too small to match the size of another object in your illustration. Rather than going back and forth, scaling the object by guess and by golly, you can perform a slight enlargement — about a quarter of what you think is needed — and repeat the transformation several times by pressing ⌘-, on Macs and Ctrl-Shift-G on PCs. With each application of the command, the selected object grows by the specified percentage. When it gets too big, just press ⌘/Ctrl-Z to take it down a notch.

Figure 14-1: Starting with two shapes (top), I skewed the ellipse (middle) and then used the Transform Again command to skew the fish (bottom).

Series Duplication

Using the Duplicate command simply to create offset clones is fine, but it doesn't take full advantage of the command's capabilities. When used on the heels of a transformation operation, Duplicate functions much like Transform Again. But Duplicate clones an object before transforming it and can repeat a series of transformations instead of just one. These features come in handy when you want to create a string of objects and place them in a consistent pattern.

To use the Duplicate command to repeat a series of transformations, follow these steps:

1. Select the object that you want to clone and transform.

2. Choose Edit ➪ Clone or press ⌘-= on Macs and Ctrl-Shift-C on PCs to clone the object. You can also clone the object using the Duplicate command, but the Clone command is usually the better choice because it doesn't include an automatic offset, which can interfere with aligning objects in a series.

3. Transform the clone to your heart's content. You can move it twice, scale it once, rotate it once, whatever you want. However, if you're going to apply a certain kind of transformation twice — two moves, for example — be sure to apply them one right after the other, without some other transformation in between. Also, be sure not to deselect the clone or perform any operation other than a transformation.

4. Choose Edit ➪ Duplicate or press ⌘/Ctrl-D. FreeHand not only creates a new clone of the object, it also repeats every one of the transformations applied to it.

To create Figure 14-2, I started with the single fish shape at the top of the figure. I then selected the fish, cloned it, dragged it down to the location of the second fish, and used the Scale panel to enlarge the clone proportionally to 120 percent of its former size. To create the third and fourth fish, I merely pressed ⌘/Ctrl-D twice. FreeHand repeated the cloning, moving, and scaling operations automatically.

Figure 14-2: After selecting the fish (top), I cloned it, moved it, and scaled it (second). I then pressed ⌘/Ctrl-D twice in a row to clone the fish twice more and repeat the transformations (third and bottom).

By duplicating both transformation and object, you can achieve perspective effects. The following steps demonstrate how to use Clone, Duplicate, and a few transformations to create a gridwork of objects. These steps make use of the three paths shown in Figure 14-3. The bottom segment of the outermost path is longer than the top segment, giving it an illusion of depth. The inner ellipses are positioned slightly closer to the top segment of the outer shape, enhancing the illusion.

Figure 14-3: By using Clone, Duplicate, and a few transformations, you can turn these paths into the illustration shown in Figure 14-9.

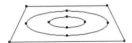

1. Select the paths and press ⌘-= on Macs and Ctrl-Shift-C on PCs to clone them. FreeHand positions the three cloned paths directly in front of the originals.

2. Select the skew tool. Begin dragging above the paths at the location indicated by the star cursor at the top of Figure 14-3. This establishes the transformation origin.

3. Continue dragging to the right. Press the Shift key while dragging to slant the cloned paths horizontally. After they reach the location of the selected paths in Figure 14-4, release the mouse button and Shift key. Notice that the cloned tile appears to lean into the original, extending back into the same visual horizon. This effect is a result of setting the transformation origin high above the paths.

Figure 14-4: Shift-drag to the right with the skew tool to slant the cloned paths to the left.

4. Press ⌘/Ctrl-D to create another clone and repeat the horizontal skew operation. Figure 14-5 shows the result, which further enhances the illusion of perspective.

Figure 14-5: Choose the Duplicate command to repeat the skew and clone operations.

5. Use the arrow tool to marquee the six paths that make up the two leftmost tiles. Press the grave (`) key to deselect the points and leave only the paths themselves selected. Then press ⌘-= on Macs and Ctrl-Shift-C on PCs to clone them.

6. In this step, you flip the clones about the center of the original tile to make the series symmetrical. Double-click on the reflect tool icon in the toolbox to switch to the Reflect panel in the Transform panel. Click with the reflect tool in the center of the right tile to transfer the coordinates of the desired transformation origin to the Center option boxes in the Reflect panel. Then enter a value of 90 into the Reflect Axis option box and press Return/Enter. The result is shown in Figure 14-6: five symmetrical tiles emerging from the surface of the page.

Figure 14-6: The result of selecting the six leftmost paths, cloning them, and flipping the clones about the center of the deselected set of paths.

7. You have now managed to impart a sense of perspective through the use of cloning, skewing, and flipping. But the illustration lacks . . . gee whiz, I don't know, call it "drama." What's needed are additional rows of slanting tiles, which are most easily created by scaling clones of the existing row over and over. To begin, press ⌘/Ctrl-A to select all the tiles. Then press ⌘-= on Macs and Ctrl-Shift-C on PCs to clone again.

8. Double-click on the scale tool icon in the toolbox to switch to the Scale panel in the Transform panel. Click with the scale tool above the tiles at the location indicated by the star cursor at the top of Figure 14-7. This establishes a transformation origin at the same location as the origin used to skew the first clone back in step 2.

Figure 14-7: Clone the entire row of tiles and click with the scale tool to set the transformation origin in the Scale panel.

9. Select the Uniform check box in the Scale panel, enter 150 into the Scale % option box, and press Return/Enter. Figure 14-8 shows how a second, larger row of tiles is created. Again, because of the placement of the transformation origin, the second row lines up perfectly with the first. By scaling the cloned shapes to 150 percent of their original size, you enlarge both the size of the shapes and the distance between the shapes and the transformation origin, thus pushing the shapes downward.

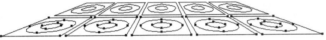

Figure 14-8: Scale clones of the top row of tiles to 150 percent to create two perfectly aligned rows.

10. Press ⌘/Ctrl-D to create a third row of larger clones directly beneath the second row.

11. To create the illustration shown in Figure 14-9, press ⌘/Ctrl-D several more times. Each series of paths increases in size and distance from the paths above it, thereby creating an even and continuous sense of perspective. Figure 14-9 is shown as it appears when printed. All shapes are filled and stroked. Foreground tiles are filled with darker shades of gray than background tiles, heightening the sense of depth. I also added a layer of shadows just for the sake of general coolness.

Figure 14-9: The result of choosing Duplicate several times and filling and stroking the resulting paths.

✦   ✦   ✦

Blends, Masks, and Composite Paths

The Most Special of Special Effects

This chapter is Chapter 11's older and more sophisticated
brother. In Chapter 11, you learned how to apply automated
fills, including gradations, tile patterns, and predefined
PostScript routines. You also learned to create multicolored
fills. You have to love the fact that the fill patterns are fully
automated, but they can be equally limiting. Although
repeating patterns are great for backgrounds and stylized
drawings, both can appear simplistic and overly geometric
when used inside more true-to-life illustrations.

This chapter offers another method to create a custom
gradation. It explains, for example, how you can create two or
more paths, fill them with different colors, and then blend them
to create a host of incremental color bands. Were you to blend
two colors using a gradient fill or a multicolor fill, the resulting
fill would contain only a dithering of the two colors. (Dithering
is a visual effect that arranges two colors in a pattern to give
the appearance of a broader range of colors.) Only the blending
of two colors gives you incremental color bands.

To apply the blend to the interior of a shape, you can cut the
blend and paste it inside the shape to create a mask. Blends
aren't the only objects you can mask; in fact, any graphic object
or text block you create in FreeHand can be pasted inside a
path, allowing you to create organic fill patterns that never
repeat. To top it all off, you can cut holes in a path to make
portions of the path transparent or apply a single fill across
multiple separate objects, both functions of composite paths.

FreeHand gives you the ability to blend multiple objects or paths, joining blends to a path, and creating spot-to-spot blends. Version 1 was the first drawing program to offer masking; blends were lifted from Illustrator in Version 2, and composite paths made a splash in Version 3. But all are as fresh, exciting, and teeming with untapped applications as they were the day they debuted. If you've just recently started using FreeHand, this chapter should make your eyes pop. But regardless of your experience level, this chapter is mandatory reading if you're at all interested in creating professional-quality illustrations.

Blending Paths

Blending is part duplication, part distribution, and part transformation. It creates a series of intermediate paths — called steps — between two selected freeform paths. I say that it's part duplication because the Blend command creates as many clones of a path as you like. It's part distribution because the steps are evenly distributed between the two original objects. And it's part transformation because Freeand automatically adjusts the shape of each step depending on where it lies. Steps near the first of the two original paths resemble the first path; steps near the second path more closely resemble the second path.

If blending had been introduced in the last year or so, it probably would have been called morphing because it creates a metamorphic transition between one shape and another. For example, suppose you create two paths — one that represents a caterpillar and one that represents a butterfly. By blending these two paths, you create several steps that represent metamorphic stages between the two life forms, as shown in Figure 15-1. The first intermediate path is shaped much like the caterpillar. Each intermediate path after that becomes less like the caterpillar and more like the butterfly.

FreeHand also blends the colors or the fills and strokes between two paths. If one path is white and the other is black, the steps between the paths are filled with a fountain of transitional gray values. Although each step is filled with a solid color (assuming you're blending objects with flat fills), the effect is that of a gradation. To create the steps shown in Figure 15-1, for example, I originally filled the caterpillar with black. That is why the steps get darker as they progress from the butterfly to the caterpillar. After creating the blend, I filled the caterpillar with white and applied heavier strokes to both the caterpillar and butterfly.

Figure 15-1: Blending a caterpillar and a butterfly creates a series of transformed and distributed duplicates between the two objects.

Applying the Blend command

To create a blend, you must first select two or more free-form paths. You can't blend paths that are part of groups, composite paths, or text objects without first separating them. (Option/Alt-clicking on the paths to select them independently doesn't work.) But, oddly enough, you can blend rectangles or ellipses without having to first ungroup them. Also, you can't blend an open path to a closed path. Both paths must be either open or closed. It's also a good idea to correct your paths' directions before blending them. To do so, select your paths and choose the Correct Direction icon from the Operations panel or choose Xtras ➪ Cleanup ➪ Correct Direction, or Modify ➪ Alter Path ➪ Correct Direction. And finally, both paths must be filled and stroked similarly. For example, if one path is stroked with a 6-point line weight, you can't blend it with a path that has a transparent stroke.

Tip

You can, however, blend between a path stroked with a 6-point line weight and one stroked with a 0-point line weight. Because a 0-point line weight results in the thinnest line your printer can create, the stroke is practically transparent when printed to a high resolution imagesetter. (When you proof the stroke to a laser printer or preview it on-screen, you'll be able to see the 0-point stroke clearly.)

To blend two paths, select the paths and choose Modify ⇨ Combine ⇨ Blend or Xtras ⇨ Create ⇨ Blend to create a series of steps. You can also blend the paths by pressing ⌘/Ctrl-Shift-B or by choosing the Blend icon in the Operations panel. FreeHand treats the frontmost path of the two originals as the first path in the blend and the rear path as the last path. For this reason, these paths are sometimes called the source and the windup, respectively. The steps are layered between the source and windup paths, descending in stacking order — one in back of another — as they approach the windup. FreeHand automatically combines original paths and steps into a grouped object that has special properties that are discussed in later sections. This object is called a blend. Alternatively, you can select one (and only one) point in each path, as illustrated in the first example in Figure 15-2.

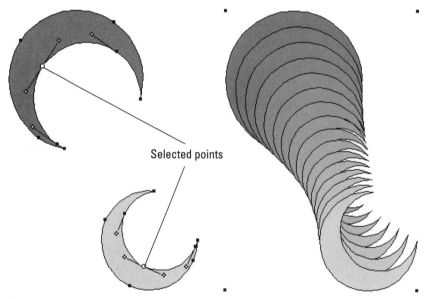

Selected points

Figure 15-2: Select one point in each of two paths (left) and then choose the Blend command to create a series of intermediary steps (right).

Selecting points allows you more control over the blend. If the paths are open, you must select an endpoint in each path. See "Selecting points in a blend" later in this chapter.

Adjusting values in the Blend panel

When you choose the Blend command, FreeHand automatically creates a default quantity of steps depending on the colors applied to the source and windup paths. The maximum number of default steps is 25, which FreeHand applies to a blend between a white path and a black path. If one or both of the selected paths are filled with a tint or gray value, FreeHand creates fewer steps.

After FreeHand applies its default number of steps, you can edit the steps by using the options in the Blend panel, a specialized Object Inspector (⌘/Ctrl-I). This panel, shown in Figure 15-3, contains three options that enable you to control the number of steps in a blend and the manner in which the steps are positioned and colored with respect to the originals.

Figure 15-3: The Blend panel allows you to control the number of steps in a gradation.

The three option boxes in the Blend panel work as follows:

✦ **Number of Steps:** In this option box, enter the number of intermediate paths that you want FreeHand to create. Any value is acceptable, provided you have sufficient memory allotted to FreeHand. The First and Last values update automatically.

✦ **First:** The two Range % values allow you to adjust the color and placement of the first and last steps in the blend. The value in the First option box affects how the first step is colored as a percentage of the difference between the fills and strokes of the source and windup paths. This value also determines the location of the first step as a percentage of the total distance between the source and windup paths.

✦ **Last:** This option works just like the First option, but it controls the color and location of the last step. The location is measured from the source path, not the windup.

Press Return/Enter to apply changes made to the values in the Blend panel. By the way, if you don't quite understand how each of these options works — especially the Range % values, which are pretty cryptic — don't keep reading the preceding paragraphs over and over; your brain will just turn to mush. Instead, read the following section, which explains the Blend panel options in more detail.

Specifying steps and range

Suppose you specify nine steps between your source and windup paths. FreeHand determines the positioning of each step as a percentage of the distance between both paths. The source — which is the front path — occupies the 0 percent position and the windup — the rear path — occupies the 100 percent position. To space the steps evenly, FreeHand automatically spaces the steps in 10 percent intervals. Therefore, the First option box contains the value 10 percent, and the Last option box contains 90 percent.

The two Range % values control the colors and placement of the steps. To understand how to modify these values, you need to understand how FreeHand assigns colors to blends. By way of an example, suppose that the source path is filled with white and stroked with a 50 percent black, 1-point line weight, as in the case of the lower crescent on the left side of Figure 15-4. Meanwhile, the windup path is filled with 50 percent black and stroked with a 100 percent black, 6-point line weight, as in the top crescent in the figure.

By default, the fill and stroke attributes of the steps are averaged incrementally as a function of the number of steps you specify. To calculate this average, FreeHand divides the difference for each attribute by the number of steps. In this case, the differences between source and windup paths are as follows:

> ✦ The difference in fill color = 50% black × 0% black (white) = 50%.

> ✦ The difference in stroke color = 100% black × 50% black = 50%.

> ✦ The difference in line weight = 6 points × 1 point = 5 points.

Note

The Blend command ignores other stroke attributes, such as line caps, joins, and dash patterns. It also ignores tile patterns and PostScript fill routines. However, FreeHand *can* blend shapes filled with gradations, as explained in the "Creating custom gradations" section later in this chapter.

With nine steps, a First value of 10 percent, and a Last value of 90 percent, the blend appears as shown on the right side of Figure 15-4. Table 15-1 lists the fill and stroke of the source and windup paths as well as those FreeHand assigns to each and every step.

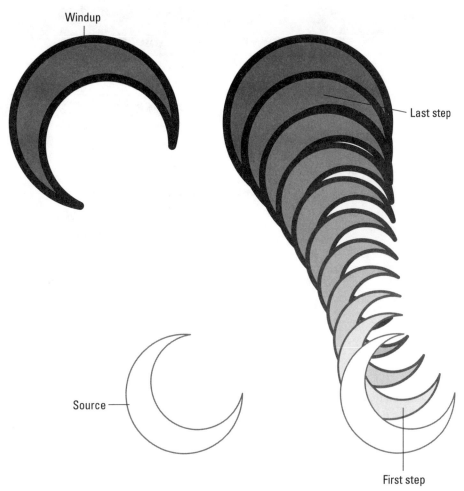

Figure 15-4: After filling and stroking two paths (left), I created a nine-step blend between them (right).

Table 15-1
A Sample Nine-Step Blend

Step	Percent Change	Fill Color	Stroke Color	Line Weight
Source		0% black	50% black	1 point
First	10%	5% black	55% black	1.5 point
Second	20%	10% black	60% black	2 point
Third	30%	15% black	65% black	2.5 point
Fourth	40%	20% black	70% black	3 point
Fifth	50%	25% black	75% black	3.5 point
Sixth	60%	30% black	80% black	4 point
Seventh	70%	35% black	85% black	4.5 point
Eighth	80%	40% black	90% black	5 point
Ninth (last)	90%	45% black	95% black	5.5 point
Windup		50% black	100% black	6 point

You can change the two Range % values to alter both the color and placement of the first and last steps. In the case of Figure 15-4, FreeHand would then automatically space the second through eighth steps evenly between the first and last steps. If you change the First value to 30 percent and the Last value to 70 percent, for example, you compress the steps closer together while leaving some breathing room between the steps and the source and windup paths.

Figure 15-5 shows an example of changing the Range % values. The eye at the top of the figure is filled with black and stroked with a white hairline outline. The eye at the bottom of the page is filled with white and stroked with a 2-point black outline. (The eyebrow and lower eyelid shapes are not involved in the blend.) Insofar as stacking order is concerned, the top eye is in back of the bottom eye.

After blending the two shapes and displaying the Blend panel, I specified five steps and changed the First option to 20 percent. The distance between the two eye paths is roughly 24 picas, so a First value of 20 percent changed the distance between the source path and the first step to 20 percent of 24 picas, which is about 5 picas. This slightly exaggerated the gap between the source path and the first step. It also affected the color of the fill and stroke. The fill is slightly lighter than it would have been if I hadn't raised the First value; the stroke is slightly darker.

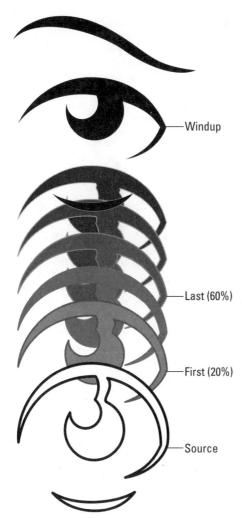

Figure 15-5: The result of changing the First value to 20 percent and the Last value to 60 percent.

To create the gap between the windup path and the last step, I lowered the Last value to 60 percent. This changes the distance from the last step to the source path to 60 percent of 24 picas, or about 14½ picas. It also lightens the fill of the last step and darkens the stroke.

Selecting points in a blend

Selecting points in a blend plays a crucial role in the appearance of blended paths, as it controls the placement of points inside the steps. The quantity and location of points in the steps, as well as the form of the segments between points, is based on two criteria:

✦ The number of points in the source and windup paths

✦ The specific point selected in each path when you choose the Blend command

The Blend command relies on points as guidelines. FreeHand tries to match each point in the source path with a point in the windup path. It then draws segments between each consecutive pair of points.

For the most predictable results, your source and windup paths should contain an identical number of points. This is extremely important. If the two paths contain different numbers of points, FreeHand has to periodically insert or remove points inside steps, which can result in some pretty strange looking transitions. When both paths contain an identical number of points, the Blend command produces a consistent series of steps that looks more or less like you thought it would.

The points that you select before choosing Blend also influence the appearance of the steps. FreeHand uses the selected points as origin points. It then progresses around the paths in the direction that each path was created, coupling a point from the source path with a point from the windup.

Try to select a similarly positioned point in each path. If possible, select a point that occupies a central position in its path (unless the paths are open, in which case FreeHand requires you to select an endpoint in each path).

If you select points that occupy different positions in the source and windup paths, FreeHand creates distorted steps. Figure 15-6 shows three examples. In each, I selected different pairs of points in the two source and windup triangles. Each point in one triangle blends toward a point in the other triangle based on its proximity to the selected point, as illustrated by the gray lines. The points are labeled according to the order in which FreeHand blends them, starting with the selected points.

Both the source and windup paths in the examples in Figure 15-6 proceed in a clockwise direction. Had one path proceeded in a counterclockwise direction, the steps would look different. For example, the blend at the top of the figure would look like the last blend, because FreeHand would have paired points 2 and 3 in the left triangle with points 3 and 2, respectively, in the right triangle.

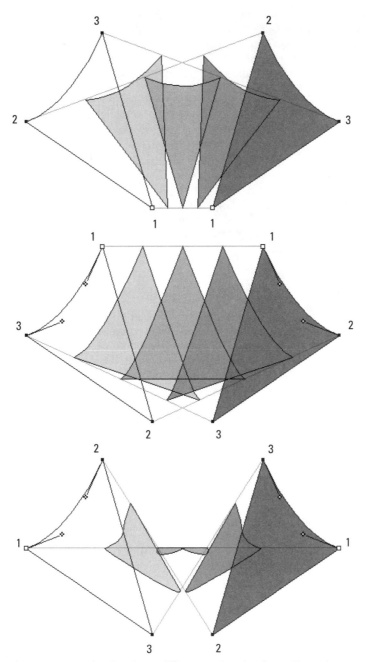

Figure 15-6: Selecting three different pairs of points affects the appearance of the steps, even though the source and windup paths are identical.

To confirm that your source and windup paths proceed in the same direction, select both of them by Option/Alt-clicking on one and Shift-Option/Alt-clicking on the other with the arrow tool. Then choose the Correct Direction icon in the Operations panel. Alternatively, you can choose Correct Direction from the Alter Path submenu in the Modify menu and the Path Operations in the Xtras menu.

Tip

Blending is also a good way to create and distribute multiple clones between two sets of paths. For example, if you want to create a line of five soldiers, you can create a soldier, clone it, and move it away from the original. Then you can select and blend between each pair of identical paths in your two soldiers, specifying three steps in the blend. The advantage to this method is that you only have to create one clone rather than four. And if you select the cloned soldier (by Option/Alt-marqueeing it) and move it, all the steps adjust automatically between the clone and the stationary original. The disadvantage is that you have to blend between each pair of paths. So if the soldier you want to duplicate comprises many paths, it may be easier to group the paths, clone them four times, and then use a Distribute option in the Align panel.

Creating custom gradations

In addition to the amazing morphing effects that you can produce using the techniques just described, you can also use the Blend command to create custom gradations. The top example in Figure 15-7 shows two paths viewed in the keyline mode. The central path is filled with white and the V-shaped path is filled with 70 percent black. Neither path is stroked, because a repeating stroke would interrupt a continuous gradation. Also, the central path is in front, making it the source path.

If you look at the paths, you'll notice that even though they're shaped differently, they contain the same number of points. Each offers a cusp point at the bottom of the shape and two points along each side. The outside path contains three extra points that form the top of the V. Although I didn't need these points to create the central shape, I added them to the top of the path to even things out — which is why the top of the path sports a total of five points.

After selecting the two paths, I selected the upper right point in each path and pressed ⌘/Ctrl-Shift-B to blend them. Inside the Blend panel, I bumped up the Number of Steps value to 68. With this value, FreeHand made each step 1 percent darker than the step in front of it. The second example of Figure 15-7 shows the resulting blend, as seen in the preview mode.

After creating a gradation, you'll probably want to incorporate it into a mask. Although I discuss masks in detail a few pages from now (in the "All about Clipping Paths" section), I'll briefly show you how this technique works here. To mask the gradation from Figure 15-7, I selected it and chose Edit ➪ Cut (⌘/Ctrl-X) to transfer it to the Clipboard. I then selected the path shown in Figure 15-8 and chose Edit ➪ Paste Inside (⌘/Ctrl-Shift-V) to create a glistening charm.

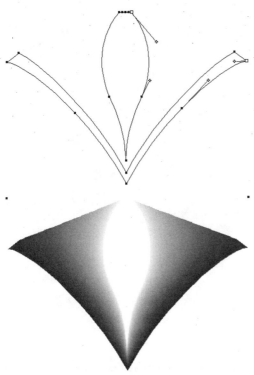

Figure 15-7: After selecting a white path (top,
center) and a black path (top, V-shaped),
I blended the paths to create a gradation
containing 68 steps (bottom).

Caution

You can blend between two paths filled or stroked with different spot colors.
FreeHand is smart enough to mix the colors to spot-color separations. For example,
if you blend between a path filled with Pantone red on the left and a path filled with
Pantone blue on the right, you ideally want FreeHand to print a black to white
gradation (reading left to right) on the red separation and a white to black
gradation on the blue separation. This would produce the effect of one blending
into the other without paying for extra inks. With FreeHand, you can do this without
having process colors put in for the steps. Finally, you can get the true spot-to-spot
color blends you always wanted.

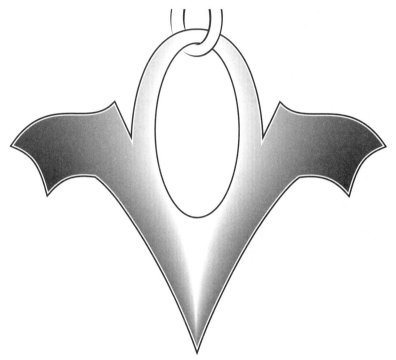

Figure 15-8: The result of cutting the gradation from the previous figure and pasting it into a clipping path.

Blending between gradations

Have I mentioned that FreeHand's blending capability is the best around? No? Well, it is. If you don't believe me, here's proof: In FreeHand, you can blend between two paths filled with directional and radial gradations. That's right, the program can actually create gradations between gradations. I should warn you, though, that doing so can be time-consuming.

The top example in Figure 15-9 features two slim paths filled with logarithmic gradations. (I've outlined the paths so that you can see them.) Both gradations flow in the same direction, but one flows from 80 percent black to white, and the other flows from white to 80 percent black. Blending between them creates a four-point gradation that flows from 80 percent black in the upper left and lower right corners and from white in the lower left and upper right corners. The second example in the figure shows the blend masked inside a letter converted to paths.

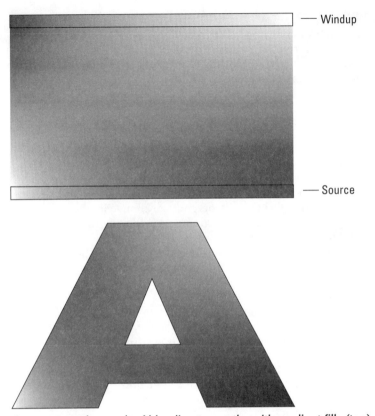

Figure 15-9: The result of blending two paths with gradient fills (top) and masking the blend inside a converted character outline (bottom).

Blending gradations is a great way to create even more stupendous gradations — try it out in color! — but it can be a little tricky. For the best results, use directional gradations. Although radial gradations do blend, they don't work nearly as well. Also, you can't blend between a graduated and a radial gradation. For graduated gradient blends, make sure that the gradations in both paths flow in the same direction. In other words, don't assign different Angle values in the Gradient panel of the Fill Inspector. Assign different colors to both of the To and both of the From swatches for the two gradations. FreeHand blends these colors, so you get the most mileage out of the effect if all the colors are different. And, finally, you must have the same number of color chips on both of the two gradient's color ramps — refer back to Chapter 11's "Multicolor fills" section for color chip and color ramp info.

Avoiding banding

If you'll be printing your final illustration to a 60 line-per-inch, 300 dot-per-inch laser printer, you won't need more than 24 steps, because such a device can print only 26 gray values. However, if you'll be outputting to a printer with a higher resolution, such a small number of steps may result in banding, which means that each step in a gradation appears clearly distinguishable from its neighbor.

If you're not bothered by a little math, you can determine the optimal number of steps required to create a smooth gradation. Use the following formula:

$$[(\text{dpi} \circ \text{lpi})^{\#2} + 1] \times \%\text{C} - 2$$

In this formula, dpi is the resolution of the printer in dots per inch; lpi is the screen frequency in lines per inch; and %C is the percentage change in color. For example, the percentage change in color between a source path filled with 20 percent black and a windup path filled with 90 percent black is 70 percent. If you intend to print this gradation to a Linotronic 300 with a resolution of 2,540 dots per inch and a default frequency of 120 lines per inch, the optimal blend contains 312 steps: $[(2,540 \circ 120)^{\#2} + 1] \times 0.7 - 2 = 312$.

The ringer is that Level 1 PostScript can't generate more than 256 distinct gray values — not to mention that having 312 steps will make your document huge and unwieldy, and the thing will take forever to print. Some folks will tell you just to knock down the number of steps to 256 and let PostScript render its maximum. But there are two problems with this approach. First, it still results in an incredibly complicated document. Second, the older PostScript can print 256 gray values between black and white, so it can handle only 70 percent as many values between 20 percent and 90 percent black.

I prefer to divide the solution yielded by the formula by 2, 3, or 4 — or any of the solution's integer factors. For example, dividing 312 by 4 results in 78. That's a much more manageable number of blends and is unlikely to produce bands if your printer's equipment is properly calibrated.

But this is just a rule of thumb. I've read ten or so solutions to banding — including one from Adobe, the inventors of PostScript — and I've seen banded gradations created using every one of them. None of the solutions is perfect. My personal solution usually works for me — that's why I stick with it.

Editing a blend

Here's another reason why FreeHand's blend feature is so great: You can edit it. FreeHand treats a blend as a unique kind of grouped object — just like a rectangle or ellipse, except better. You can change the number of steps, assign different colors, or reshape the source and windup paths. FreeHand adjusts the steps to your new specifications automatically.

To change the number or location of steps in a blend, select the blend with the arrow tool and enter new values into the option boxes in the Blend panel. When you press the Return/Enter key, FreeHand implements your changes.

Tip

To reshape or recolor a blend, Option/Alt-click with the arrow tool on the source or windup path to select that path separately from the rest of the blend. (You can't select an individual step in a blend; Option/Alt-clicking on a step selects the entire blend.) You can even select both the source and windup paths by Option/Alt-clicking on one and Shift-Option/Alt-clicking on the other.

After selecting the source or windup path, you can reshape it by dragging one or more points, adding or deleting points, dragging Bézier control handles, and so on. You can also apply a different fill, stroke, or attribute style to the path. FreeHand continuously updates the steps as you work, so you may find it easier to work in the keyline mode, which offers faster screen redraw.

Blending multiple paths

Up to this point, I've only mentioned blends that use two paths, but this is not all FreeHand can do. In fact, you can include as many paths as you desire within a single illustration. Simply click and Shift-click with the arrow tool on each path that you want included in you blend and press ⌘/Ctrl-Shift-B FreeHand creates a blend that passes through each of the selected paths in the order that they appear in the stacking order. If you find that the paths did not blend as expected, undo the blend and correct the stacking order of the paths and blend again.

Joining a blend to a path

After creating a blend, you have the option to join that blend to a path. To do so, select the blend and Shift-click on the path to select both pieces and then choose Modify ⇨ Combine ⇨ Join Blend To Path (⌘/Ctrl-Option/Alt-Shift-B). In Figure 15-10, a blend made from three paths — where the stacking order is the top path is on the bottom of the stack and the bottom path is on the top of the stack — is joined to a spiral. Once joined, you can Option/Alt-click on either the source or windup path to change color, edit the lines, or move the whole shape and, just as with any other blend, the joined blend will update to reflect your changes. By Option/Alt-clicking on the path, you can edit the path to your heart's content and the blend will reshape to your path. Here's a helpful hint: If you wish to edit the original path that's joined to a blend, but you can't see it because the blend is obstructing your view, go into keyline mode where you will easily be able to select it. If you want to break the blend from the path you can undo or ungroup. Ungrouping a blend from a path will not return the blend to its original shape. To do this, you have to use the Modify ⇨ Split command (⌘/Ctrl-Shift-J).

Figure 15-10: A blend made from three closed paths is joined to the wavy path.

Ungrouping a blend

If you want to adjust one or more of the steps manually or if you simply want to eliminate a blend, select the blend and press ⌘/Ctrl-U to ungroup it. Ungrouping frees the source and windup paths from the grouped steps. To separate the steps, press ⌘/Ctrl-U again.

After you ungroup a blend, you cannot access the Blend panel again except by undoing the Ungroup command or reblending the paths. Also, editing the source and windup paths no longer has an effect on the steps. However, you can now edit the steps independently, which can sometimes prove extremely useful. If you ungroup a spot color blend, a message will come up telling you the blend will become process colors. Don't let this scare you — your spot colors are really spot colors; check your separations.

All About Clipping Paths

Clipping path is the PostScript term for a path filled with other objects. A clipping path is also called a *masking object* or simply a *mask*, after the airbrushing technique in which masking tape (or some other masking tool, such as a frisket) is laid down to define the perimeter of a spray-painted illustration.

The basic concept behind the clipping path is simple: Instead of filling an object with a color, gradation, or repeating pattern, you fill it with other objects. The other objects inside the object, or mask, are called *masked elements* or just *contents*.

You can use absolutely any graphic object created in FreeHand as a clipping path. You can even use text objects (including text blocks drawn with the text tool), paths inside groups, and composite paths. Any number of lines, shapes, and other objects — grouped or ungrouped — can appear inside a clipping path. You can even mask another clipping path.

Creating a clipping path

Since Version 1, creating clipping paths in FreeHand has been a straightforward process. After filling and stroking all objects, assemble the mask and contents in their desired locations relative to the clipping object. Then select all the prospective contents and choose Edit ⇨ Cut (⌘/Ctrl-X) to transfer the selection to the Clipboard. Next, select the path you want to use as a mask and choose Edit ⇨ Paste Inside (⌘/Ctrl-Shift-V). FreeHand pastes the contents of the Clipboard into the interior of the mask. The contents fill the clipping object where they overlapped it. Any portions of the contents that are too big to fit within the boundaries of the masking object are hidden.

Figure 15-11 shows a popsicle inside some stripes. The following exercise demonstrates how to set the stripes inside the body of the popsicle to create a bomb-pop — you know, one of those three-color frozen treats kids like to rub all over their faces. You set the stripes inside the bomb-pop body without affecting the drip, the stick, or the little shiny mark on the right side of the popsicle.

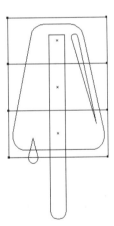

Figure 15-11: Mask and contents assembled, as viewed in the keyline mode.

1. Draw the shapes shown in Figure 15-11. Just rough them out. Feel free to come up with your own personal interpretations. The drip is filled with a radial gradation. The stripes are three rectangles filled with logarithmic gradations; the strokes are transparent. The other shapes get flat fills.

2. To create the clipping path, first move the stripes into position relative to the popsicle. Figure 15-11 shows the proper location of masked elements and mask as viewed in the keyline mode. (If I were to show them in the preview mode, you couldn't see the popsicle beneath the stripes or vice versa.) If necessary, enlarge the stripes so that they completely cover the popsicle

shape, as in the figure. This positioning determines the exact manner in which the contents fit inside the clipping path.

3. Select the three stripes — if they aren't already selected — and press ⌘/Ctrl-X to send them to the Clipboard.

4. Select the popsicle shape and choose Edit ➪ Paste Inside or just press ⌘/Ctrl-Shift-V. That's all there is to it. Figure 15-12 shows the resulting illustration as it appears when previewed or printed.

Figure 15-12: The finished bomb-pop as it appears with stripes inset.

5. For extra credit, add a shadow to the stick, also included in Figure 15-12. Draw a small rectangle around the stick at the point where it meets with the popsicle shape. The rectangle should cover the entire width of the stick, but it should only cover half of its height; leave the lower half of the stick uncovered.

6. Fill the rectangle with a logarithmic gradation progressing from 20 percent gray to white at a 270-degree angle (straight down). Make the stroke transparent (using the None option in the Stroke Inspector).

7. Cut the rectangle by pressing ⌘/Ctrl-X. Then select the stick shape and press ⌘/Ctrl-Shift-V to paste the rectangle inside the stick.

Why paste a gradation inside the stick rather than simply filling it with a gradation? Because we didn't want the gradation to fill the entire stick, just the upper portion of it. Masking is a great way to specify the exact locations of the beginning and ending colors of a gradation inside a path, something that FreeHand doesn't allow you to do from the Fill Inspector.

Provided the stick was behind the popsicle shape and the drip and reflection were in front of it, you get the result shown in Figure 15-11, regardless of the stacking order of the stripes. The Paste Inside command leaves the stacking order of the mask unchanged.

Note The contents of a clipping path display only when you preview or print the illustration. Masked elements are not visible in the keyline mode.

Adjusting masked elements

If you decide you don't like the appearance of a clipping path, you can make adjustments in the following ways:

✦ **Transforming masked elements:** To transform all masked elements inside a clipping path en masse, display the Transform panel and deselect the Contents check box inside any one of the panels. You can then transform the path independently of its contents. Transform the path opposite to the way you want to transform the masked elements. For example, if you want to rotate the contents of the path 40 degrees, rotate the clipping path -40 degrees. The mask will rotate; the contents won't.

Tip Be sure to keep track of your transformations exactly. If you perform more than a few, write them down. When you're finished, select the Contents check box in the Transform panel and reapply all your transformations opposite to the way you applied them before. In the rotation example, you would now rotate the clipping path 40 degrees. This moves the contents along with the mask, achieving the effect you wanted in the first place.

✦ **Selectively editing masked elements:** To alter a few masked elements inside a clipping path without affecting others, select the clipping path and choose Edit ➪ Cut Contents (⌘/Ctrl-Shift-X). FreeHand removes the contents of the path from the mask and places them at the front of the current layer. (Despite the word Cut in the command name, the contents are not sent to the Clipboard. The Clipboard's previous contents remain undisturbed.)

After reshaping, transforming, deleting, and otherwise editing the masked elements, select them, press ⌘/Ctrl-X (*now* they're in the Clipboard), select the clipping path, and press ⌘/Ctrl-Shift-V to restore the mask.

✦ **Adding more masking elements:** To add elements to an existing clipping path, position the objects relative to the path, press ⌘/Ctrl-X, select the clipping path, and press ⌘/Ctrl-Shift-V, just as if you were creating a new mask. Both new and original masked elements appear inside the clipping path, with the new elements appearing in front of the original elements.

If you want to mix the stacking order of the new masking elements with that of the old ones or you want the new elements to appear in back of the old ones, you have to use the Cut Contents command to remove the old contents. Then stack all the objects as desired and re-create the mask using the Cut and Paste Inside commands.

Creating and Using Composite Paths

Another way to display objects inside objects is to create one or more holes in the middle of a path by using the Join command in the Modify menu. For example, consider our friend Mr. Smudden in Figure 15-13. The first version shows Mr. Smudden's gorgeous face. But suppose you need to add a ski mask to the illustration. A real-life ski mask has eye holes that let you see where you're going while you hold up convenience stores. Therefore, your ski mask must also have holes for the eyes, as shown in the second example in the figure. The holes in the ski mask are actually paths that have been combined with the ski mask path using the Join command.

Eye holes and ski mask together are known as a composite path because, in a few key respects, FreeHand treats the object as a single path. All objects included in the composite path must be filled and stroked identically. And, as it does with a group, selecting any part of a composite path with the arrow tool selects all objects in the composite path. To select and manipulate individual paths, you have to Option/Alt-click on the path with the arrow tool, just as you do with a group.

Figure 15-13: Mr. Smudden on his day off (left) and Mr. Smudden dressed to apply for a nonqualifying, interest-free loan (right).

Poking holes

Like a clipping path, a composite path is easy to create in FreeHand:

1. First, assemble the objects that you want to combine in their desired relative positions. One path will act as the background path and one or more other paths will act as the holes. All holes should overlap some portion of the larger background path.

2. Select the background path and choose Modify ⇨ Arrange ⇨ Send to Back or press ⌘/Ctrl-B to send the path to the back of the layer.

3. Select all paths — background path and holes — and choose Modify ⇨ Join or press ⌘/Ctrl-J. Background and holes are now combined into a single composite path.

Figure 15-14 shows a doughnut on a checkered napkin. Unfortunately, it doesn't look much like a doughnut because the hole hasn't been removed. You can save this doughnut from a heartbreaking exile to the Island of Misfit Pastry — where neither Rudolf nor Julia Child dare venture — by completing the following steps. You will also create a shadow beneath the doughnut that is itself a composite path.

Figure 15-14: This doughnut would look more like a doughnut if you could see through its center.

1. Draw the objects in Figure 15-14. The doughnut is merely two circles. The stylized shadows on the doughnut are both stroked lines. The napkin is a square rotated 60 degrees and filled with a tile pattern.

   To create the tile pattern, just draw two squares and fill both with black. Position them so that the bottom right corner of one square is even with the upper left corner of the other. Then cut the two squares and paste them into the Fill Inspector as described in the "Object-oriented tile patterns" section of Chapter 11.

2. To ensure that the larger circle in the doughnut acts as the background, select the shape and press ⌘/Ctrl-B to send it to the back of its layer. In this case, this step is not essential — smaller shapes automatically poke holes in larger shapes — but it's a good precaution and it may help you to better see the results of the next operation.

3. The large circle now appears in back of the napkin, as shown in Figure 15-15. That's a little too far back, but the problem will take care of itself. Shift-click on the front circle with the arrow tool to select both circles and then choose Modify ➪ Join or press ⌘/Ctrl-J to combine them.

Figure 15-15: Send the large circle to the back of the illustration.

4. The doughnut now has a hole in it, but it covers the stylized shadow lines, because the Join command always moves all selected objects to the front of the layer. To nudge the doughnut to behind the shadow lines, choose Modify ➪ Arrange ➪ Move Backward or press ⌘/Ctrl-Option/Alt-Shift-K two or three times. The result appears in Figure 15-16.

5. To create the shadow, clone the doughnut by pressing ⌘/Ctrl-D. This has the added effect of offsetting the clone 10 points down and another 10 points to the right, which will do for our purposes.

6. Fill the clone with 50 percent black (by dragging the corresponding color swatch in the Tint panel and dropping it onto the clone). Set the stroke of the clone to None.

7. Press ⌘/Ctrl-B to send the clone to the back of the layer, as shown in Figure 15-17.

Figure 15-16: Joining the circles makes a hole and moves the large circle in front of the napkin.

Figure 15-17: The completed doughnut with shadow.

Note

In case you're wondering, the shadow appears to shade the napkin because the napkin is filled with a partially transparent tile pattern. As I instructed in step 1, the pattern contains only black squares. The appearance of white squares is created by an absence of black squares. Therefore, you can see through the transparent squares to the shadow at the back of the illustration.

Tip

You can also poke holes in objects by choosing the Punch icon from the Operations panel. Alternatively, you can choose Punch from the Path Operations submenu in the Xtras menu. In fact, if you were to substitute choosing the Join command in step 3 with the Punch command, the result would be exactly the same. (Punch has no keyboard equivalent, so Join is generally more convenient.)

Why does FreeHand have two commands that do the same thing? Actually, they perform different functions; their capabilities just happen to overlap in this one respect. If the selected paths do not entirely overlap — if they merely intersect slightly, for example — the Join command makes a hole out of the intersection, but the Punch command clips away the intersection and deletes the forward shape. If the selected paths don't overlap at all, Join combines the paths into a single continuous path (see the upcoming "Filling across multiple shapes" section), while Punch deletes the frontmost path.

If, after creating a composite path, you decide that you don't like it and want to break it back up into its separate objects, select the composite path and choose Modify ⇨ Split (⌘/Ctrl-Shift-J). FreeHand restores all paths to their previous independence. If the Remember Layer Info check box in the General panel of the Preferences dialog box is selected, FreeHand restores the independent shapes back to their previous layers.

Composite masking

A composite path can double as a clipping path, enabling you to create a path that is filled with objects and has holes punched out of it. After creating a composite path, position the masked elements in front of the path, cut all masked elements to the Clipboard, select the composite path, and choose the Paste Inside command.

In Figure 15-18, I added several stripes of icing in front of the doughnut. The following steps describe how to use the doughnut as a clipping path for the icing.

Figure 15-18: Several stripes of icing created by drawing a single line and cloning it many times.

1. Draw the icing stripes using the freehand tool. Actually, you only need to draw one line. Stroke the line with a white, 3-point outline. Clone it by pressing ⌘-= on Macs and Ctrl-Shift-C on PCs, and press the ← and ↓ keys to offset it slightly. Change the color of this line to 70 percent black. Then select both lines, clone them, drag the clones down and to the left a pica or so, and press ⌘/Ctrl-D four times in a row to replicate the stripes.

2. Select all the icing stripes and the two curved reflection lines with the arrow tool. These lines are packed so closely together that you may find it easier to select the lines in the keyline mode.

3. Press ⌘/Ctrl-X to transfer the paths to the Clipboard.

4. Select the doughnut and press ⌘/Ctrl-Shift-V to paste the stripes inside the larger of the two circles. The small circle continues to form a hole in the path; the stripes are invisible inside the hole. The completed illustration appears in Figure 15-19.

Figure 15-19: The finished doughnut with icing.

Filling across multiple shapes

Shapes joined into a composite path don't have to overlap. When they do, FreeHand creates holes where the paths intersect. But if they don't, FreeHand simply treats all the shapes as if they were parts of a single continuous path. It's sort of like a country composed of multiple islands.

The first example in Figure 15-20 may give you a clearer idea of what I'm talking about. The example shows four shapes combined into a composite path. Because I joined them together, FreeHand fills them as a single unit. As a result, the radial gradation inside the composite path begins as white in the center of the third shape and proceeds outward to deep gray in the first and last shapes. In other words, all shapes share the same continuous gradation.

Shapes in a composite path also share masked elements. In the middle example of Figure 15-20, I drew a series of lines and shapes that I wanted to mask with the composite path. After cutting them to the Clipboard and pasting them inside the composite path, I achieved the effect shown in the last example in the figure. The masked elements start in the first shape, continue into the second, then into the third, and so on.

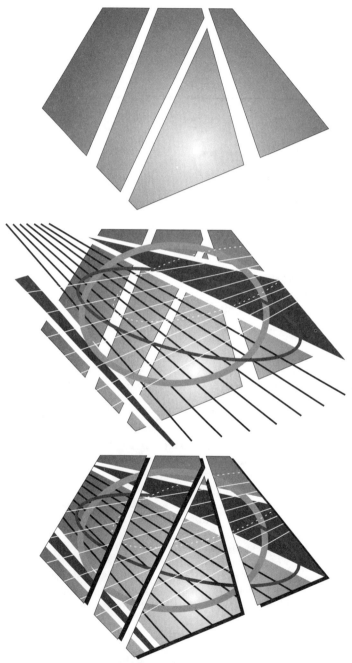

Figure 15-20: After filling a composite path with a radial gradation (top),
I drew a bunch of lines and shapes (middle), cut them, and pasted them
inside the composite path (bottom).

Composite paths and text

Many characters of type are automatically converted to composite paths when you choose Text ⇨ Convert To Paths. Characters with holes — *A, B, D, O,* and others — are actually defined as composite paths in the PostScript printer font definitions.

Each character, however, is its own independent composite path. The converted characters are automatically grouped, but grouping does not force them to share the same fill. Therefore, if you fill converted characters with a gradation, each character receives a separate gradient fill, as shown in the first example of Figure 15-21.

Figure 15-21: Converted text filled with directional gradations (top) and the same text after choosing Modify ⇨ Join (bottom).

If you select the converted text and choose Modify ⇨ Join, FreeHand changes all outlines to a single composite path. The gradation now flows across the entire length of the converted type, as shown in the second example in the figure.

✦   ✦   ✦

Desktop Publishing

Importing and Exporting Graphics

FreeHand Publishes

Since PageMaker invented the category of desktop publishing in 1985 — which I like to call "The Year Nothing Worked" and which was followed by 1986, "The Second Year Nothing Worked" — desktop publishing programs have been brokers for type and graphics. They enable you to bring together elements that were created in different applications and mix them inside a single document. Desktop publishing programs, such as PageMaker and QuarkXPress, are the middlemen of computer graphics. They aren't so hot in the creation department, but they sure can sell information.

That's why programs such as FreeHand resent them. FreeHand is very hot in the creation department — it's one of the best creators around — and it's tired of being dependent on overstuffed kingpins like PageMaker and XPress to get the page to the printer. Granted, FreeHand isn't as adept at creating and editing text as a word processor, and it lacks the image-editing capabilities of Photoshop, but it's otherwise able to create any page element you might desire.

It's capable of swapping artwork with Illustrator, Photoshop, Canvas, and half a dozen other popular programs. It can even edit imported object-oriented graphics. (Heck, about the only thing it can't do is open old FreeHand 1 files.)

FreeHand is also realistic. It knows that you aren't likely to throw away PageMaker or XPress just because some fly-by-night author keeps telling you how great FreeHand is at producing small documents. So it's fully capable of preparing illustrations for use in any program that supports the EPS format. It can even export drawings in the PICT and Illustrator formats and export text in Microsoft's RTF format. FreeHand is a can-do program that knows its way around the complex world of file-format diplomacy.

Cross-Reference

In case you haven't guessed from the title, this chapter covers importing and exporting of graphics only. If you want to know how to import text, read the "Importing Stories" section of Chapter 7.

Importing Graphics

FreeHand can import bitmapped images stored in the MacPaint, PICT, TIFF, EPS, GIF, JPEG, and PNG formats. It can also import object-oriented graphics stored as Illustrator 1.1 through 7.0, CorelDRAW 3 through 7, PICT, and AutoCAD DXF files. (MacPaint and TIFF formats can't accommodate objects.)

Because of how FreeHand works with different formats, and because of the limitations of the formats themselves, I recommend you save graphics that you intend to import into FreeHand according to the following rules:

✦ **Nix on MacPaint:** Don't save *anything* in the MacPaint format. If you have some old MacPaint images lying around, don't worry; FreeHand handles them just fine. But there's no point in using this format for future artwork.

✦ **Save grayscale images to TIFF:** Save your grayscale bitmapped images, including those you create in Photoshop, in the TIFF format. This is also an acceptable format for storing 8-bit (so-called "indexed") color images. PICT is acceptable, but FreeHand doesn't support PICT as well as it does TIFF. First of all, it takes longer to import a PICT image than a TIFF image. Second, FreeHand supports JPEG image compression, but the quality is still not as good as the TIFF.

Tip

When saving images in the TIFF format in Photoshop or some other painting program, be sure to select the LZW compression option if one is available. Using this option will save space on your hard disk without diminishing the image quality one iota. (In computer jargon, LZW is a *lossless* compression format — which means that it doesn't lose any image details.) LZW is fully supported by FreeHand.

✦ **Save color images to EPS:** If you use a PostScript printer, you may want to consider saving 24-bit color images in the EPS format before importing them into FreeHand. Though the EPS format handles images less efficiently than TIFF does, and takes up three to ten times as much disk space, FreeHand can print EPS files faster. This is because the pixel-to-PostScript conversion has already been done in an EPS file; FreeHand has to do it on the fly when printing a TIFF image.

I don't save images to the EPS format very often because I'm a selfish jerk. Think about it: Who are you helping by speeding up the printing process? Not yourself. Printing a black-and-white proof of an imported image on a laser printer isn't measurably faster for EPS images than for TIFF images. The real savings occur when printing color separations to a high-resolution device such as an imagesetter. But then you're saving the service bureau's time, not your own. So you may just want to stick with TIFF and save disk space. And please, don't tell your service bureau that I gave you this recommendation.

✦ **Save objects to EPS:** Most object-oriented drawing programs on both the Mac and Windows platforms now support the EPS format. Assuming that you'll eventually be printing your artwork to a PostScript printer, this is the format of choice for objects. If you want the ability to edit the graphic in FreeHand, save the drawing in the Adobe Illustrator format (AI on Windows), an editable and widely supported variation of EPS. Otherwise, FreeHand can import the file, and you'll be able to transform the entire graphic by scaling it, rotating it, and so on, but you won't be able to reshape or transform individual paths inside the graphic.

You can import artwork saved in any of these file formats and integrate it into your FreeHand document. You can transform, layer, duplicate, mask, and print any imported artwork, whether it's bitmapped or object-oriented. However, you can edit the contents of an imported graphic only if it's object-oriented and saved in the Illustrator-type EPS format.

Placing a graphic file

You can access a graphic created in another application and stored on disk in two ways. You can either try to open the graphic directly using File ➪ Open (⌘/Ctrl-O), or you can import the graphic into an open FreeHand document by choosing File ➪ Import (⌘/Ctrl-R).

✦ **Open:** When using Open command, FreeHand creates a new window for the document. If the graphic is an object-oriented, FreeHand tries to convert the objects so that you can edit them. If it can't, the graphic appears in the lower left corner of the page.

✦ **Import:** The Import command lets you import the graphic into the foreground document. You'll generally want to use this command when you've already created an illustration and you want to enhance it with imported artwork. After you choose File ➪ Import, select the desired file in the Import Document dialog box, and press Return/Enter, FreeHand presents you with a place cursor. Click with the cursor to import the graphic without scaling it. Drag with the cursor to scale the graphic as you import it. FreeHand sizes the image to your marquee.

To cancel the Import command after exiting the Import Document dialog box, just click on a tool in the toolbox. This selects the tool and gets rid of the place cursor.

If you enable the Convert Editable EPS When Imported option in the Importing/Exporting (Macs) or Import (Windows) panel of your Preferences dialog box, FreeHand tries to convert the objects when using the Import command just as it always does when you use the Open command. If this option is turned off, you can't edit the objects in the imported graphic.

Pasting a graphic file

You can also import a graphic via the Clipboard using the Cut, Copy, and Paste commands common to the Edit menus of all Macintosh and Windows applications. While inside a painting, drawing, or graphing program — such as Photoshop, Illustrator, or Microsoft Excel — select the portion of the picture that you want to import into FreeHand and press ⌘/Ctrl-C to copy it. Then switch to FreeHand and press ⌘/Ctrl-V to paste the graphic. That's all there is to it.

Although FreeHand is tops at converting graphics copied to the Clipboard — it always tries to convert copied objects so that you can edit them — it doesn't always get it right. If you encounter an out-of-memory error when pasting a color bitmap, or if bits and pieces of the graphic disappear, as sometimes happens when pasting objects, return to the originating program, save the graphic to disk in one of the formats listed earlier, and import the file into FreeHand using the Open or Import command.

Manipulating Imported Graphics

If FreeHand is able to convert the objects in an imported drawing into editable paths and text blocks, you'll know immediately because the objects will be riddled with points and handles. If FreeHand can't convert the graphic, it will be surrounded by four corner handles. Every once in a while, however, FreeHand imports the drawing as a grouped object, which also shows four corner handles. If you think that this might be the case with your graphic, select it and display the Modify menu. If the Ungroup command is available, choose it and see whether FreeHand separates the objects. If Modify ➪ Ungroup is dimmed, the graphic is not editable inside FreeHand.

Scaling the graphic

Even though a graphic is not editable, you can still transform it and duplicate it, as discussed in Chapters 13 and 14. You can also cut it and then paste it inside a clipping path, as discussed in Chapter 15.

Another way to manipulate an imported graphic is to drag one of its corner handles with the arrow tool. FreeHand scales the graphic just as it does when you drag the corner handle of a group. Shift-drag the corner handle to scale the graphic proportionally. Press the ⌘/Ctrl key while Shift-dragging to scale the graphic horizontally or vertically only.

All uneditable graphics, however, are not created equally. Because bitmapped images have a fixed resolution, FreeHand provides special means for scaling images to make them compatible with high-resolution output devices.

Note

Suppose that you're printing a 72-pixel per inch bitmapped image to a 300-dot per inch laser printer. Each pixel in your image is a $\frac{1}{72}$-inch square, while each pixel (or *dot*) in the laser printer is a $\frac{1}{300}$-inch square. Therefore, each pixel in the image wants to take up $4\frac{1}{6}$ printer dots ($\frac{1}{72} \div \frac{1}{300} = 300 \div 72 = 4\frac{1}{6}$). But because pixels can't be divided into pieces, each image pixel must be represented by a whole number of printer dots. Unfortunately, your laser printer can't just round down each image pixel to four dots square; if it did, it would shrink the size of the image. To maintain the size of the graphic, five image pixels in a row are assigned four printer dots, while every sixth pixel is assigned five dots. These occasional larger pixels give your bit-mapped image a throbbing appearance, known generically as a *moiré* pattern.

Phew, that was a tough one, eh? Don't sweat it too much; you can use the tip that I'm leading up to whether or not you understand exactly how this works.

To eliminate moiré patterns, scale the imported image so that the resolution of the image divides evenly into the resolution of the printer. For example, if you scale the image so that its resolution is 75 dots per inch, it divides evenly into the resolution of your printer — $300 \div 75 = 4$ printer dots per pixel.

But you don't want to whip out your calculator every time you print an imported image. So make FreeHand do the calculations for you. Switch to the Document Inspector and select the resolution of your final output device from the Printer Resolution pop-up menu, as shown in Figure 16-1. (If the desired resolution isn't listed, just enter the exact value into the Printer Resolution option box.)

Figure 16-1: Use the Printer Resolution pop-up menu in the Document Inspector to specify the resolution of the final output device.

I say final output device because you should be concerned with the appearance of your completed artwork, not some proof along the way. For example, if you print proofs to a 300-dpi laser printer but you'll eventually have your commercial printer output the illustration to a 2540-dpi Linotronic, select the 2540 option. Who cares if some moirés show up in your laser printed proofs? The final printed piece is all that matters.

Now for the tip: After you specify a target resolution, Option/Alt-drag a corner handle of the imported image with the arrow tool. You'll notice that FreeHand scales the image in increments; each increment represents a size that is exactly compatible with the resolution of your printer. To proportionally scale a bitmap to a compatible size, Shift-Option/Alt-drag a corner handle.

Editing a grayscale image

Scaling isn't the only special feature devoted to imported images. You can also adjust the brightness values of grayscale and monochrome images. (The techniques covered in this section are not applicable to color images.)

When the image is selected, switch to the Object Inspector (⌘/Ctrl-I) to see the options shown in Figure 16-2. Here you can control the location and scale of the image, colorize the image, and change the contrast and brightness of the image.

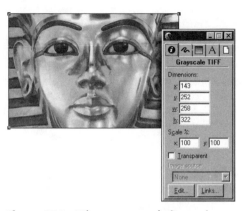

Figure 16-2: When a grayscale image is selected, the Object Inspector contains special image-editing options.

As always, the Dimension option boxes show the location of the lower left corner of the selected image in relation to the ruler origin, as well as the horizontal and vertical dimensions of the graphic. The two Scale % option boxes indicate any reduction or enlargement that you make to the image (by Option/Alt-dragging a corner handle, for example). Any value below 100 percent reduces the width or height; a value greater than 100 percent enlarges the image. These options are especially useful if you decide that you don't want to scale the image after all, in which case you just select the image and enter 100 percent for both options.

You can colorize a grayscale image by dragging a color from the Color List onto the color swatch below the Scale % option boxes. Both process colors and spot colors are accepted. (You can also drag the color directly onto the image in the illustration window.)

Select the Transparent check box to convert the image to black and white and make all white pixels transparent. This option can be useful for establishing textural effects. For example, you can create a monochrome "noise" pattern in Photoshop, which is an image composed entirely of random grayscale pixels. You can then save it to the TIFF format and import it into FreeHand. By selecting the image and activating the Transparent option, you make the white pixels transparent. You can then drag a color onto the color swatch in the Object panel and, voilà, you have a color fill pattern. Just position it over a path, cut it, and paste it into the path to mask it. You can even mix the pattern with another fill by applying a flat fill, gradation, or tile pattern to the clipping path. Or leave the clipping path transparent and use it to partially cover other paths. It's a great way to create your own custom textures similar to the PostScript texture fills built into FreeHand.

Image mapping

To change the brightness and contrast of an imported grayscale image, click on the Edit button at the bottom of the Object Inspector to display the Image dialog box shown in Figure 16-3. The options in this dialog box allow you to convert — or *map* — the original gray values in the selected image to new gray values. The *brightness graph* in the center of the dialog box contains 16 bars, each of which represents a brightness value in the image. (Most grayscale images actually contain 256 gray values, but FreeHand simplifies things by only showing you 16 in the graph.)

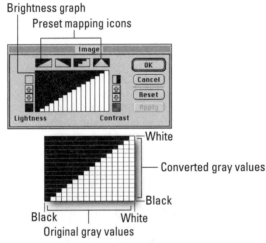

Figure 16-3: Using the bars inside the brightness graph (detailed at bottom) you can convert each of 16 gray values in a selected image to any level of brightness from black to white.

The horizontal position of each bar represents the original gray value, black being the leftmost bar and white being the rightmost bar, as illustrated in the second example in Figure 16-3. The height of each bar represents the converted appearance of the gray value, black being at the bottom and white being at the top. When an image is first selected, a *linear mapping* is in force, so that the height of each bar increases in even increments relative to the bar's position in the chart. A black pixel is mapped to black, a dark gray pixel is mapped to dark gray, and so on.

There are four different ways to control gray-value mapping in the Image dialog box. You can use any one or all of them:

✦ **Lightness:** Click on the Lightness scroll arrows to uniformly lighten or darken pixels in the selected image. Clicking on the ↑ lightens all values (except those already white); clicking on the ↓ darkens all values (except those already black). As these changes occur, they are reflected by the bars in the brightness graph.

✦ **Contrast:** Click on the Contrast scroll arrows to adjust the amount of contrast between pixels in the image. For example, clicking on the ↑ darkens values darker than medium gray and lightens lighter gray values, thus increasing the contrast toward a black-and-white image. Clicking on the ↓ lightens values darker than medium gray and darkens lighter values, which decreases the contrast toward flat gray. The bars in the brightness graph constantly reflect your changes.

Tip

When adjusting a scanned image that you intend to print to paper (rather than film), you may want to slightly decrease the contrast and increase the lightness. (For example, click twice on the Contrast ↓ and twice on the Lightness ↑.) This gives the halftone dots room to spread when the image is commercially reproduced without making the image appear overly dark or muddy. (For more information on halftones, read the "Halftone screens" section of Chapter 18.) Here's another tip: To clear the background of light gray shades, move some of the right bars to the top. Moving three bars should be sufficient.

✦ **Preset mapping icons:** Select one of the *mapping icons* above the gray-value bars to perform one of four special graphic effects, explained in the next section.

✦ **Move a bar:** Drag an individual bar up or down to lighten or darken a single gray value. You can also click at a point inside the brightness graph to raise or lower the corresponding bar to that location. If you drag in a roughly horizontal direction inside the chart, several bars adjust to follow the path of your drag.

To preview your changes in the illustration window, click the Apply button.

You can use options in the Image dialog box to make slight changes or to create special effects. Figure 16-4 shows the results of dragging selective bars up and down in the brightness graph. In the first example of the figure, I dragged the first four bars all the way to the top of the graph, making the very darkest pixels in the image white. As a result, Tut gets white eyes. I also dragged the next four bars all the way to the bottom, making the corresponding pixels black. This creates exaggerated shadows along the eyebrows, nose, and lips.

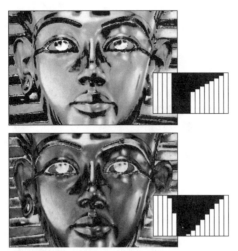

Figure 16-4: Two examples of special effects created by playing with the bars in the brightness graph.

In the second example in Figure 16-4, I lessened the severity of the exaggerated shadows by tapering the colors lighter than medium gray. I made medium gray black, the next-lighter gray dark gray, and so on, all the way up to white. This mapping helped restore some of the details I lost in the first image in the figure.

Keep in mind that there are no rights or wrongs when you're raising and lowering bars in the brightness graph. The beauty of this dialog box is that it can't do any permanent damage to an image. In fact, that's the only reason to use it. These options have been around for years, more than long enough for a dedicated image editor such as Photoshop to trounce all over them. But whereas Photoshop makes permanent changes to an image, FreeHand makes temporary ones. If you ever want to return to your original, untainted image, just display the Image dialog box and click on the Reset button. Everything goes back to normal.

Preset mapping icons

If you want to try out some preset effects, click on one of the icons at the top of the Image dialog box and then click on the Apply button to see what they look like applied to your image. Each effect is shown in Figure 16-5. The effects work as follows:

✦ **Normal:** Normal isn't actually an effect; choosing it produces the same results as clicking on the Reset button. Click on the Normal icon to return the gray-value bars to their original linear configuration. This is the icon you click on when you're done fooling around with the other ones.

✦ **Invert:** Click on this icon to invert the light and dark gray values in a selected image. White pixels become black, black pixels become white, and so on. The effect is like a photographic negative.

✦ **Posterize:** Click on this icon to establish a stair-stepped map that groups a range of gray values into one of four clusters. Converted values jump from black to 66 percent black to 33 percent black to white. Transitions between gray values are abrupt rather than smooth, which is ideal for artwork that you intend to photocopy or submit to some other low-quality printing process.

✦ **Solarize:** Click on this icon to double the brightness of all gray values between black and medium gray and both invert and double the brightness of all values lighter than medium gray. Both white and black pixels become black; light and dark gray pixels become medium gray, and medium gray pixels become white. The result is a unique glowing effect, as shown at the bottom of Figure 16-5.

Cropping imported graphics

Normally, when an application lets you import graphics, you expect some kind of cropping feature for deleting unwanted portions of the graphic. FreeHand provides no specific cropping feature. However, you can give an imported image a simulated cropping by creating a mask. Draw a rectangle or other path to represent the outline of the cropped image. Then position the imported image relative to the path, transfer it to the Clipboard using the Cut command (⌘/Ctrl-X), select the path, and choose Edit ➪ Paste Inside (⌘/Ctrl-Shift-V). The stroke of the path acts as the outline of the cropped graphic.

Linking graphic files

An illustration that contains a TIFF image or an EPS drawing must always be able to reference its original TIFF or EPS file in order for FreeHand to preview or to print the placed image successfully. Therefore, when you save an illustration, FreeHand remembers where the original imported graphic file was located on disk. If you try to open an existing illustration after moving its imported TIFF or EPS graphic to a different disk or folder, FreeHand displays a standard Open dialog box requesting that you locate the original graphic file on disk. Select the original TIFF or EPS file in the scrolling list and press Return/Enter. If you click the Cancel button, the illustration will not preview properly. If FreeHand can't reference the graphic file on disk during the printing process, neither an imported TIFF image nor an imported EPS drawing will print at all.

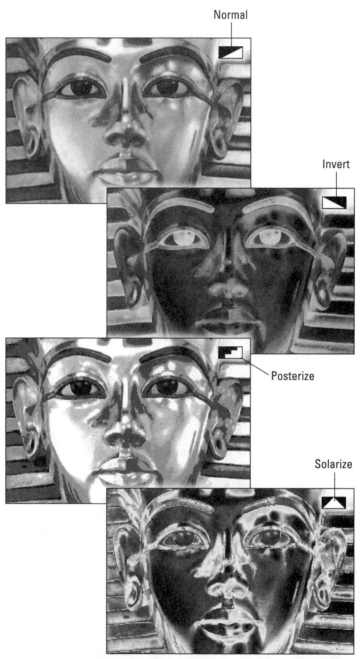

Figure 16-5: Tut subject to each of the preset mapping settings.

You can change a link's reference using the Links button in the bottom right corner of the Object Inspector, pictured in Figure 16-2. Pressing this button displays a directory dialog box. Locate the new link and you're set. This method presents a quick and easy way to bypass the Place command while switching linked images.

Exporting an Illustration

Illustrations created in FreeHand can be used in any Macintosh or Windows application that supports the EPS format. Your illustration can become part of a larger document such as a book or catalog, or part of a video or on-screen presentation.

Exporting an EPS or PICT file

To store an illustration in the EPS or PICT format, choose File ⇨ Export or press ⌘/Ctrl-Shift-R. The Export Document dialog box appears. In this dialog box (which is almost exactly the same as the Save dialog box in both function and form), you can name the file and select the file format in which you want FreeHand to store the file.

FreeHand can *export* (save your file) to a variety of file formats, including variations on the EPS, Illustrator, and bitmap formats. The options in the Format pop-up menu include the notable following:

✦ **Adobe Illustrator:** FreeHand can save to five Adobe Illustrator file formats. These formats are entirely editable and are widely supported by drawing programs on the Mac and Windows platforms. However, each format sacrifices some data from a FreeHand document. Illustrator 6.0, and now Illustrator 7.0, supports TIFF images. The Illustrator 5.5 format doesn't support imported TIFF images, custom PostScript strokes and fills, QuickDraw fills, custom halftone information, and stylistic text effects. The Illustrator 3 format ignores all of those items. It also doesn't support layers, tabs, columns and rows, the orientation of text bound to a path, and a few other text-formatting options. The Illustrator 88 format ignores all of those items as well as composite paths and text on a path. The Illustrator 1.1 format is the least capable, lacking support for masks, tile patterns, and color. Regardless of the format you select, FreeHand converts gradations to blends inside masks. FreeHand now supports the Illustrator for Windows format since Illustrator 7.0 is cross-platform.

♦ **ASCII and RTF:** These options export all text in the current document, whether or not it is selected. (Graphics are ignored.) The ASCII option exports plain text with no formatting; the RTF option exports most character-level and paragraph-level formatting attributes along with the text.

♦ **EPS:** The EPS options save the illustration to the EPS format. These options are by far the most capable, because no information whatsoever is lost. Select the Macintosh EPS option to save a PICT screen preview with the file. Select MS-DOS EPS to include a TIFF preview, suitable for importing into most Windows programs. Because the Generic EPS option creates no screen preview, it's equally applicable to both platforms, but you won't be able to see what the illustration looks like on-screen. Preview or no preview, all EPS formats print accurately and print exclusively to PostScript printers.

Note

All EPS documents created by FreeHand contain *Open Press Interface* (OPI) comments. Developed for outputting to ultra-high-end prepress systems such as Crosfield and Scitex, OPI specifications communicate the size, placement, and cropping of illustrations and imported graphics. You can then manipulate the illustration using a prepress system to create four-color, professional-quality output.

When you select one of the EPS formats, the Export Document dialog box provides access to a few additional options via the Setup button. These options includes the Include FreeHand Document in EPS check box. If your document includes multiple pages — the subject of the next chapter — you may want to export all of them or just one of them to the EPS format. Each page is exported to a separate file, cropped according to the page boundary. (To crop a very large illustration in one piece, you have to create a large custom page, as described in the next chapter.)

When the Include FreeHand Document in EPS check box is selected, the EPS file contains all the information necessary to edit the document. For example, if you pass the EPS file along to an associate or client, another artist could open the file and edit it. Some artists aren't too keen on this idea. If you want to prevent people from monkeying around with your documents, turn this option off.

The downside to turning off the check box is that you have to save two versions of every file, one that you can edit — which you save normally using File ⇨ Save — and one that you can pass along to clients or import into other applications yourself. I need the disk space, so I generally leave the option selected and save only one copy of my illustration via File ⇨ Export. Of course, I don't mind it when people mess with my artwork. Really, go ahead. Draw mustaches on every face in this book. You paid for it, you can mess it up. Just don't expect a refund.

Importing and exporting as PDF, GIF, JPEG, and PNG

FreeHand can export PDF (Adobe Acrobat's Portable Document Format). FreeHand can also open multiple page PDF files. PDF format retains document formatting, regardless of the application used to create the original file.

When exporting as a GIF (Graphic Interchange Format) file, FreeHand rasterizes your image to the resolution and anti-aliasing that you set in Bitmap Export Default dialog box—reached via the Setup button—in the Export dialog box. If you click on the More button in the Bitmap Export Defaults dialog, you can select the Interlaced GIF which gives you a quick display. You can check the Transparent GIF to create a transparent background based on the outline of the shapes in your document.

Imported JPEG (Joint Photographic Experts Group) files convert to TIFF images. When exporting a document as a JPEG, you have options like Image Quality and Progressive when rasterizing your image.

Finally the PNG (Portable Network Graphic) offers a lossless compressed bitmap for web paging. PNG files can be imported or exported from FreeHand. Export options include:

- ✦ **8, 16, and 24 bit:** Choose 256, thousands, and millions of colors.
- ✦ **32-bit with alpha channel:** 16 million colors including an alpha channel.
- ✦ **48 or 64-bit:** An extremely high number of colors.
- ✦ **Interlaced PNG:** Interlaced PNGs redraw progressively for a quicker display.

Drawing an export boundary

When FreeHand creates an EPS file, it automatically crops the document to the exact boundaries of the objects in the illustration. For example, suppose that you create a 3×4-inch illustration on a letter-size page. When you save the illustration, FreeHand saves the page size information. But when you export the illustration for use in another application, FreeHand is interested only in the graphic itself. After all, you don't want to import an $8\frac{1}{2} \times 11$-inch drawing into PageMaker when the graphic consumes only one-quarter of the drawing area. Therefore, the exported document measures 3×4 inches, exactly matching the size of the objects inside the document.

More often than not, FreeHand determines the size of an EPS file correctly. Every once in a while, however, FreeHand may crop a graphic a bit too drastically. The casualties are usually strokes. The edges of heavy outlines may be sliced off or a mitered join may disappear.

To prevent the loss of strokes around the edges of an exported illustration, or simply to create a margin around an illustration, draw a rectangle that completely surrounds your artwork. While the rectangle remains selected, drag the None color swatch onto both the Fill and Stroke icons in the Color List palette, making both fill and stroke transparent. The rectangle doesn't preview or print, but it does affect the size of the exported EPS file.

Generating a Document Report

Sometimes you don't need to export a document; you just need an inventory of its contents. Possibly you will be generating the output at a service bureau and need to know which fonts or colors the document uses. In such cases, you'll find FreeHand's report-generating capabilities to be invaluable.

Report generation was introduced into FreeHand with Version 5. Even if you think this feature is not something you need, I recommend that you review the information anyway. In the future, a situation may occur where creating a report is exactly what you require. Suddenly a little light will flash, and you'll remember me coercing you to read this portion anyway. Then you'll thank me for making you go through this now.

These reports can contain a wealth of information, far more than you may need. Luckily, you can pick and choose what information to include. You can also choose whether to review the information on-screen only, print it, or save it to a file.

Generating a report is extremely simple. Choose File ⇨ Report to open the Document Report dialog box. This dialog box lists the different categories on the left side. Each category has its own set of associated options. These options are displayed on the right side of the dialog box. Choosing a different category changes the options displayed in the panel on the right side of the dialog box.

After you select the information you want included with your report, you just need to decide how you want your information. Clicking the Report/OK button displays the information on your screen. At the bottom of this display are three buttons: Cancel, Print, and Save. If you just want to view the report, then you're all set: Choose Cancel and continue working. To print a report, choose Print. To save the report, choose Save. FreeHand presents a directory dialog box for you to save the file. The report is saved as a text file. You can then open it in a word processor.

✦   ✦   ✦

Setting Up Documents

FreeHand Does Small Documents

I think that I've mentioned FreeHand's prowess in the small-document department 10 or 12 times now, and no doubt this news was received with skepticism by longtime users who are heavily invested in the status quo. "FreeHand is a drawing program, dag-gum it," you might protest. "If I want to create documents, I'll use QuarkXPress, just like I've been doing for the last four years," or however long it's been. "Why do you keep making FreeHand out to be some kind of gift from the gods that's going to take care of all my publishing needs?"

Well, because it is. Okay, not *all* of your publishing needs. I'm not suggesting that you lay out magazines and other text-intensive documents with FreeHand. And the program isn't particularly suited to documents that contain more than, say, eight pages. But for design-intensive documents, it just can't be beat. Honestly, it mops the floor with XPress, and the things that it does to PageMaker are too gruesome for words.

"What about my service bureau?" you might counter. "They darn near refuse to print anything that's not in XPress. A guy there even told me that XPress is the only program that prints the least bit reliably. I doubt they'll be very interested in printing my FreeHand documents." It's true — you may get hassled a little bit. And I've heard accounts of some legitimate printing limitations when using FreeHand with highly sophisticated Scitex and Crosfield systems. But these aren't small-document printing problems; I'm talking about special effects-laden graphics with half a dozen imported images inside complex masks and layered all over each other.

Having worked at a service bureau, I can assure you that print operators can be as lazy as folks in any other industry. It's easier to use a single program for printing, and say that all the others have this problem or that, than it is to keep up with five or six different applications, every one of which has its own little quirks. Commercial printers may seem like high-tech wizards — and many are — but there's always the chance that they're more interested in getting home to the family than learning a new piece of software, especially if a four-page job is the only incentive that you're offering.

It's always difficult to buck the system. And although it's hard to believe that using one of the most solid graphics programs on the market falls into this category, some service bureaus look down their noses at printing from any program but QuarkXPress. It's up to you to be a maverick and force them to print some FreeHand documents. Really, it's for their own good.

Having shared my two cents on that topic — just enough to infuriate a few print operators — let me encourage you not to accept my word or anyone else's on this subject. Instead, do your own test. Use FreeHand to put together the next small-document job you have, whether it's a newsletter, report, flier, whatever. Write the text in a word processor so that you have access to a grammar-checker and thesaurus, and use Photoshop or the equivalent to prepare the images, but otherwise rely entirely on FreeHand. You'll have to create the document from scratch; FreeHand can't open XPress or PageMaker templates. So do this project on a day that you have time to experiment a little.

I know — you don't have any time. No one does. But make some time. If you aren't convinced after a few hours that FreeHand provides an environment more conducive to professional-level small-document production than any other software you've worked with, so be it. Write me off as a screwball rabble-rouser, swear off my books for good, and go back to XPress or PageMaker.

But if you're like me, you'll discover a side to FreeHand that you hadn't considered before. No more switching back and forth between graphics program and layout program trying to decide how to reshape a drawing so that it better fits with your design. After all, every tool that you need to put together outrageously complex layouts is available in FreeHand. You can reshape paths and rewrap text on the fly, bind text to paths, apply text styles, automate the creation of columns and rows, copyfit text, spell check, access a nearly infinite range of fill and stroke options, and — as described in this chapter — create custom page layouts. Only in FreeHand can you assign every single page in your document a different size and orientation.

All right, that's enough. You're probably beginning to think that I get a cut of the software sales or something. I doubt that a FreeHand sales rep could be as long-winded on this subject. Millions of dollars worth of FreeHand sold last year, and I'm making the program out to be some neglected little underdog. So I'll drop the subject now.

Really, I think if you'll just try it, though, you'll agree . . . no, no, I'm done. I said I'm done, so I'm done.

So far, I've spent hundreds of pages explaining how to create and manipulate type and graphics, but I've barely mentioned the page on which the objects sit. If you export most of your artwork to the EPS format and import it into a layout program — the standard desktop publishing route — you generally have no reason to even notice the page. As long as your artwork fits entirely inside the page boundary, FreeHand dutifully exports every detail and automatically crops the EPS file to fit.

But when you're printing final documents from FreeHand, the page becomes a primary concern. The page boundary in the illustration window represents the final page printed from the output device. Generally speaking, all objects print exactly as they appear relative to the page boundary in the illustration window.

If this is the first object-oriented drawing program you've ever used, you may need some background information on how pages in FreeHand work. When you create a new FreeHand document, you're presented with an empty page smack in the middle of the illustration window (assuming that you haven't changed the FreeHand Defaults file). So when you draw an object, it's automatically sitting on a page. You can then take that object and drag it off the page or drag it onto another page. Each page is free-floating and independent of other elements.

The Pasteboard

The area outside the page boundary is called the *pasteboard*. Labeled in Figure 17-1, the pasteboard is the electronic equivalent of a giant tabletop.

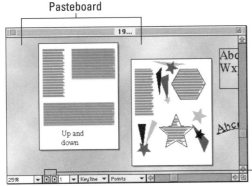

Figure 17-1: The pasteboard is an undefined work space that contains the pages in your document.

Note

Yup! The pasteboard can now officially be classified as gigantic. It's much, much bigger than way-back Version 4's pasteboard, which was only 54 × 54 inches big (and I also thought that was huge). The difference in sizes can cause problems if you find yourself needing to open Version 8 documents in Version 4. If you have plans to do this, make sure you enable the FreeHand 4 Page Placement in the Document panel of your Preferences dialog box when creating the document in FreeHand 8. You won't see eerie clouds darkening your pasteboard as you do in Figure 17-1. I added them to this figure in an attempt to clearly distinguish the page and the pasteboard. Besides, it looks so very cool.

The pasteboard is a convenient holding area for items that you don't want to print or that you think you may integrate into the artwork later. Suppose that you want to make a change to a set of objects, but you're not sure what your client will think of the revision. Before making your changes, clone the objects and drag them off onto the pasteboard. You can easily retrieve them from the pasteboard if the client gets grumpy over your alterations.

You can move around the pasteboard using the scroll bars and grabber hand. To view more of the pasteboard, zoom out with the zoom tool. If you zoom all the way out, you may see a gray area around the pasteboard. This nether area is outer space as far as FreeHand is concerned. If you move something to this area, you will loose it and will only be able to retrieve it by using the Undo command.

Creating Multipage Documents

By default, FreeHand creates single-page illustrations. However, you can add pages any time you want. Press ⌘/Ctrl-Option/Alt-D to access the Document Inspector, shown in Figure 17-2.

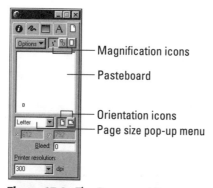

Figure 17-2: The Document Pages panel showing the entire pasteboard.

The central portion of the panel is a miniature representation of your document. You can display this representation at three different magnification views, depending on your magnification icon selection. Figure 17-3 shows each magnification icon selection and the associated view presented by the palette. The left icon enables you to see the entire pasteboard along with all pages. Personally, I feel this makes the page icons way too small for comfortable manipulation. The middle icon (and the default setting) presents the document as it appeared in FreeHand 8, which is about 2½ percent of its actual size. If this view encompasses your entire document, I recommend you stick with it. The right icon shows your pages at about 10 percent of actual size. This view works best for single-page documents. With the latter two views, the page displays its number on it so that you don't get confused as to which page is which.

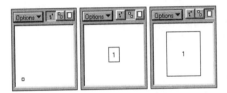

Figure 17-3: The three different document views offered from the Document Pages panel.

To create one or more new pages, select the Add Pages option from the Options pop-up menu in the panel, as illustrated in Figure 17-4. FreeHand displays the Add Pages dialog box. Enter the number of pages you want to add into the Number of Pages option box. You can also select a page size and orientation and enter a Bleed value, as described later in this chapter. If you're not sure what kind of page you need, just click the OK button or press Return/Enter. You can always change the size, orientation, and bleed size later.

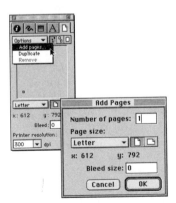

Figure 17-4: Select the Add Pages option to insert new pages into a document.

FreeHand adds the new pages to the right of the existing page. If there's not enough room, FreeHand adds the pages to the next available space, working to the right and downward. If the pasteboard is filled all the way to the bottom, FreeHand will try to add the new pages to the upper left corner of the pasteboard. If you try to add too many pages an alert box appears, explaining that FreeHand can't fulfill your excessive request.

Moving pages in the pasteboard

After creating your new pages, you can move them to different locations in the pasteboard by dragging them inside the Document Inspector. This is best done at the center magnification view. Dragging pages may have the added effect of changing the page order. For example, the left panel in Figure 17-5 shows the result of adding a single page to an illustration. The page is numbered 2 because it is to the right of the previous page. (FreeHand numbers pages from left to right and top to bottom, in the same way that you and I read type.)

Figure 17-5: The result of dragging the new page to a different location in the pasteboard.

However, when you drag the new page above and to the left of the previous page — as indicated by the arrow in the figure — FreeHand renumbers the new page 1, as in the second panel in Figure 17-5. The previous page becomes page 2. FreeHand updates the pages in the real pasteboard to keep up with your changes.

This feature brings up an interesting point: What happens to objects in your illustration when you drag a page? If the page already has objects on it, the objects move with the page, regardless of whether they reside entirely inside the page or barely overlap the page boundary. Objects that extend over two pages move with either page.

Caution

If you move a page to a location on the pasteboard that contains objects, the objects remain in their previous positions, but they automatically jump onto the page. If you move the page a second time, the objects move with the page. You can run into some real messes if you drag a page that already contains objects under a bunch of objects that previously resided on the pasteboard. The objects pile up quickly if you don't pay attention. That's why I recommend that you reduce the view size in the illustration window to 6 percent — the minimum standard zoom — to monitor the results of moving pages inside complicated illustrations. This way, if you accidentally disturb some objects, you can see the damage immediately and undo the move by pressing ⌘/Ctrl-Z.

Navigating between pages

To see all pages in an illustration, select the Fit All option from the view size pop-up menu in the lower left corner of the illustration window. (Alternatively, you can press ⌘/Ctrl-Option/Alt-0 (zero) or choose View ➪ Fit All.) As shown in Figure 17-1, this command reduces the view size to show all the pages but it does not necessarily show all the objects in your illustration. Objects in remote portions of the pasteboard — such as the partially visible text bound to paths on the far right side of Figure 17-1 — may remain outside the illustration window.

If you have more pages or your pages are spread further out than FreeHand can show at it's smallest view size (6%), then FreeHand shows you a view of the center of the pasteboard at 6%. In this case, this view is of limited value — actually, in most cases, it's probably of no value, but I did want to bring it to your attention. The first time this happens to you, you may find yourself a bit confused as to why FreeHand has chosen to show you something other that what you asked for.

To view the active page at the fit-in-window view size, press ⌘/Ctrl-Shift-W. The active page is the one that appears outlined in black in the miniature pasteboard in the Document Pages panel. All the other pages appear outlined in gray.

You can activate a different page by clicking on its icon in the Document Inspector. If you double-click on the page icon, FreeHand displays that page at the fit-in-window view size in the illustration window.

If you want to switch to a page and display it at some other view size, click on the page icon and press the corresponding view size keyboard equivalent. For example, if you're presently looking at page 1 and want to switch to page 2 at actual size, click on the page 2 icon and press ⌘/Ctrl-1.

When working in documents with three or more pages, you may find it helpful to scroll between the pages by clicking on the page-advance icons. These icons are located at the bottom of the illustration window, just to the right of the view size pop-up menu, as labeled in Figure 17-1. The left page-advance icon takes you to the previous page; the right icon takes you to the next page. If you click on the left icon when viewing the first page in a document, FreeHand takes you to the last page; clicking on the right icon takes you from the last page to the first. But regardless of which icon you click on, the page appears in the illustration window at the fit-in-window view size.

Editing Pages

You can change the size and orientation of any page in a document long after you create it. You can also clone whole pages and delete them. These options are fairly obvious, so I'll burn through the most essential facts first:

✦ **Page size:** To change the size of a page, click on its icon in the miniature pasteboard in the Document Inspector. Then select a different option from the page size pop-up menu, as shown on the left side of Figure 17-6. Table 17-1 lists the measurements of the various size options. (The letter options, like A3 and B5, are standard European sizes for paper [A] and envelopes [B].)

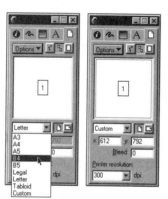

Figure 17-6: Select an option from the page size pop-up menu to change the size of the active page (left). Select Custom to create your own page size (right).

Table 17-1
FreeHand's Page Sizes

Page Name	Size in Inches	In Millimeters	In Points
A5	5.83 × 8.27	148 × 210	420 × 595
B5	6.93 × 9.84	176 × 250	499 × 708
Letter	8.50 × 11.00	216 × 279	612 × 792
A4	8.27 × 11.69	210 × 297	595 × 842
Legal	8.50 × 14.00	216 × 356	612 × 1,008
B4	9.84 × 13.89	250 × 353	708 × 1,000
Tabloid	11.00 × 17.00	279 × 432	792 × 1,224
A3	11.69 × 16.53	297 × 420	842 × 1,190
Custom	you enter size	you enter size	you enter size

✦ **Orientation:** To the right of the page size pop-up menu are two orientation icons. Select the left one to position the page upright (known as *portrait* orientation); select the right one to lay it on its side (known as *landscape* orientation).

✦ **Custom page size:** Below the page size pop-up menu is static text displaying the height and width of the current page size. If you select the Custom option from the page size pop-up menu, FreeHand activates two option boxes (see the second example in Figure 17-6). By entering values into these options, you can define your own custom page size. Enter the width of the page in the X option box; enter the height in the Y option box; press Return/Enter to implement your changes. FreeHand interprets the values in the current unit of measure.

Generally, you should only use the Custom option when printing to an imagesetter. After all, just because you can define a 20-square-foot page doesn't mean that you can feed it through your laser printer. To get large artwork to print from a consumer printer, you have to chop the artwork into pieces using a technique called *tiling*, as described in the next chapter.

✦ **Delete a page:** To delete the active page, select the Remove option from the Options pop-up menu at the top of the Document Inspector. If the page has any objects on it, FreeHand displays an alert box warning that you're about to delete the objects. Press Return/Enter if that's okay by you. FreeHand annihilates objects that are fully within the page boundary; it spares objects that extend out onto the pasteboard.

✦ **Clone a page:** To clone the active page as well as all objects that so much as touch that page, select Duplicate from the Options pop-up menu. If FreeHand balks, possibly an object extends beyond the edge of the pasteboard. In that case, you have to bring the objects into the page boundary to prevent them from flying off into outer space.

Printing different-size pages

Sounds easy enough, right? Unfortunately, there's one problem: When you combine pages with different sizes and orientations within a single document, you confuse the computer. Your system software is set up to handle no more than one page size per print job. So it's up to you to print the pages correctly.

Say you've created a two-page document. Both pages are letter size (8½ × 11 inches), but page 1 is oriented upright and page 2 is on its side. If you just print the pages normally, page 1 will print fine, but part of page 2 will be cut off because neither FreeHand nor the system software is capable of accounting for the horizontal page. As a small consolation, FreeHand warns you of this fact in advance by displaying another of its series of alert boxes.

When printing to a laser printer, you can solve the problem in only one way: You have to print each page independently. First print page 1 as a vertical page. Then tell FreeHand that you want to print a horizontal page (using options in the Print Setup dialog box, as discussed in the next chapter), and print page 2.

This solution isn't too realistic when you're submitting a document to be printed at a service bureau. If you think that the folks at the service bureau might complain over a simple FreeHand document, wait till you tell them that they have to print each page independently and make special changes in between. It won't go over too well.

What you need to do is set up a printed page size that's big enough to accommodate both pages. Because typesetters print to long rolls of film — not individual pieces of paper, as laser printers do — you have a lot more latitude when setting up custom pages. For example, you can ask your service bureau operator to select an 11 × 11-inch printed page size inside the Print Setup dialog box. Such a printed page size can handle both your upright page and the one on its side.

Actually, it's a little early to be talking about printing, but I just wanted to prepare you for what you're up against, particularly if you're an experienced FreeHand user. For more information on all printing issues, read the following chapter.

Bleed size

The last option in the Document Inspector is the Bleed option box, which enables you to print objects beyond the boundary of a page. Normally, objects that extend out into the pasteboard are cut off abruptly at the page boundary. Everything inside the page boundary prints; everything outside the boundary does not.

The *bleed* is an area outside the perimeter of a page that can be printed. It basically extends the page boundary by the amount that you enter in the Bleed option box.

If you're not familiar with bleeds, you're probably wondering why in the world you would want to extend the printable area. Why not just create a larger page if you want to print more stuff? The answer lies in the printing process. The pages of this book provide a case in point. This page, for example, has a nice, healthy margin around it. No word or graphic comes within two picas of the physical edge of the page. This boundary ensures even and consistent printing.

Now check out the first page of the next chapter. The first page of every chapter features a gray bar that touches the right edge of the page. Any time a page element extends off the edge of the paper, it's called a bleed.

To create an effective bleed, you have to print more of the bleeding element than actually reproduces in the printing process. The gray bar at the front of the chapters, for example, extends ½ inch or so beyond the page cut. This gives the printer room to maneuver. If the page is slightly crooked during the printing process, as many pages are, the bleed ensures that no gap appears between the gray bar and the edge of the page.

Okay, now back to FreeHand. Setting the bleed size enables you to print elements that extend off the page. For example, if you want to print an extra ½ inch of a graphic, enter 0.5i into the Bleed option box. (The i makes FreeHand interpret the value in inches.)

But this still doesn't answer the original question — why not just make the page size larger? As you learn in the next chapter, printers need *crop marks* to guide them. Crop marks tell the printer how to align the printed page with your artwork. The crop marks align to the page boundary, so the bleed extends beyond the crop marks. If you just made the page size larger, you would nudge the crop marks outward farther as well. As a result, the printer wouldn't be able to distinguish the elements you wanted to bleed from those that you wanted to appear fully inside the page.

Keep in mind that this information generally applies only to printing from professional-quality imagesetters. You can't create a bleed for a letter-size page on a laser printer because laser printers can't print all the way to the edge of the page. However, you can create bleeds for smaller-size items, such as mailers and business cards, on laser printers.

✦   ✦   ✦

Printing from FreeHand

Getting Your Work on Paper

Who says the printed page is dead? I wish it were, frankly; it's a horrible waste of natural resources, and we would all benefit if someone put a tourniquet on the steady flow of paper products through our mail slots. But we still communicate heavily via the printed page. Whatever advantages CD-ROM and multimedia may offer, they don't have the immediacy of paper. You don't need a computer, a player, a television, or any other special equipment to read a page. Heck, you don't need electricity—if it's dark, light a candle. The only platform incompatibility you encounter is the one inside your head. And even if you don't read the language, you can look at the pictures.

At any rate, until the human race masters the art of communicating telepathically, you'll need to print your FreeHand creations, either on your own printer or on a disk that you give to someone else to print. Unfortunately, printing can be a real pain (in addition to wasting a lot of good lumber that could otherwise be turned into butcher-block sofas and end tables). Either you press ⌘/Ctrl-P and it works, or you spend half your life trying to uncover some immeasurably minute problem that only a machine would have difficulty handling.

Could be, of course, that you're not taking the proper approach to solving your printer problems. Instead of searching for whatever's causing the machine to hang up, perhaps you need to supplicate the powerful and capricious printer gods. Recommended items for sacrifice include old modems, power cables, ribbons, empty cartridges, and ugly mouse pads that you were embarrassed to use anyway. Assemble these items in front of your printer, set them on fire, and pray, "Print my page right now or I'm going to torch you, too." That should get the printer's attention.

If this approach doesn't work, I'm afraid that you'll have to resort to reading this chapter. I can't promise that it will solve every one of your printing problems, but it will help you take advantage of FreeHand's huge and sometimes overwhelming supply of printing options. You learn how to print black-and-white proofs, create color separations, define custom halftone patterns, and solve a few problems along the way.

But, you know, I bet you're not giving it 100 percent. Maybe if you threw some old printouts into the fire and shouted, "Look at what I'm doing to your children!" Make sure to have a maniacal glint in your eye and laugh broadly. I really think it's worth a shot.

Outputting Pages

FreeHand can print to just about any output device you hook up to your computer. Assuming that your printer is turned on — "Oh, great, I burned down my office for nothing!" — properly attached, and in working order, printing from FreeHand is a four-step process, as outlined below.

1. If you're on a Mac, use the Chooser desk accessory to select the output device to which you want to print. On a PC, you use the Taskbar ➪ Settings ➪ Printer command to specify your output device. Or, you can also select your output device from within FreeHand via the Print Setup command despite what machine you're using. Unless your computer is part of a network that includes multiple printers, you probably rely on a single output device, in which case you can skip this step.

2. Mac users will need to choose File ➪ Page Setup to specify the size and orientation of the printed page. On a PC, right-click on the printer icon inside the printers dialog box and select Properties from the pop-up menu. Click the Paper tab and specify the page size and orientation of the printed page. You can also do this from within FreeHand. Choose File ➪ Print and click the Properties button.

3. Choose File ➪ Print (⌘/Ctrl-P) to adjust printing options and print the illustration to the selected output device.

4. Return/Enter to the print dialog box and click on the OK button to initiate the printing operation.

The following sections describe each of these steps in detail.

Choosing the printer and its driver

Because FreeHand is designed primarily as a PostScript-language drawing application, it provides the most reliable results when printing to a PostScript-compatible output device. Although you can print an illustration to a non-PostScript printer, many elements — most notably halftone screens, text effects, and imported EPS graphics — print as low-resolution bitmaps, exactly as they appear on-screen. Custom PostScript fill and stroke routines do not output at all to a non-PostScript device.

To select a printer, Mac people need to select the Chooser desk accessory from the list of desk accessories under the Apple menu, while PC folk need to choose Settings ➪ Printers from the Taskbar. On a Mac, the Chooser dialog box appears. The dialog box is split into two parts, with the left half devoted to a scrolling list of printer driver icons and the right half to specific printer options. In the Windows environment, you see a plain old window showing the contents of the Printers folder.

Select the printer driver icon that matches your model of printer. *Printer drivers* help your computer, system software, and FreeHand itself translate the contents of an illustration to the printer hardware and the page-description language it uses.

If the printer you choose is a PostScript compatible printer, you may then select the *PostScript printer definition* (PPD) file that matches your specific brand of printer. The PPD includes special information about your model of printer that tells FreeHand how to print tints and gray values and ensures a smoother printing process in general. On a Windows machine, you can select a PPD by clicking on the Use PPD check box in the Print dialog box. You will have to locate the proper PPD from the list that appears.

For Mac users, you can either choose a PPD via the Print dialog box from within FreeHand or use the Setup button in the Chooser dialog box to access PPD controls. The later method gives you an additional control, the Auto Setup button. Click on the Auto Setup button to instruct the system software to automatically select the correct PPD for your printer. If this fails, click on the Select PPD button and try to locate the proper PPD.

Note

You can get more PPD files from on-line services.

These services are also good places to find updated versions of your PostScript printer's driver itself.

Printing pages

To initiate the printing process, press ⌘/Ctrl-P or choose File ➪ Print. The specific dialog box that appears depends on the machine you are using and the kind of printer you selected.

No matter what kind of printer you're using, you'll find the following options:

✦ **Copies:** In the Copies option box, enter the number of copies of each page of your illustration that you want to print. To avoid wear and tear on your printer, just print one copy and reproduce it using a photocopier. For large print runs, have the pages commercially reproduced.

✦ **Pages:** Select the All radio button to print all pages in your illustration. If you only want to print a few of them — perhaps some pages are sized or oriented differently from others — enter the range of pages in the From option boxes. To print a single page, enter the same page number in both option boxes.

✦ **Tile:** To proof large artwork to a laser printer, you can *tile* it. Tiling means to divide the artwork onto different pieces of paper that you later reassemble by hand using traditional paste-up techniques. If you deactivate the Tile checkbox, FreeHand prints only one page for each page in your document. It aligns the lower left corner of the printed page with the lower left corner of the on-screen page.

If you want to tile your artwork, you can select either the Manual or Auto options from the pop-up menu. If you select Manual, FreeHand aligns the lower left corner of the printed page with the ruler origin. As with the case of not selecting tiling, it only prints one page. But you can reposition the ruler origin between printouts to create additional tiles.

Select the Auto option button to instruct FreeHand to automatically tile the illustration. FreeHand prints as many pieces of paper as are required to output each page of the document. The first tile begins at the lower left corner of the page; other tiles overlap the right and top edges of the first tile by the amount you specify in the Overlap option box.

✦ **Scale:** Enter a value into the Scale option box to enlarge or reduce the size at which the illustration prints. Reductions can be as small as 10 percent, and enlargements can be as large as 1,000 percent. If you specify a percentage that expands the illustration beyond the current paper size, you have to tile the illustration, as described previously.

If your illustration is larger than the current paper size, select the Fit on Paper option from the pop-up menu to create a reduced version of your artwork. FreeHand automatically calculates the exact reduction necessary to fit the entire illustration on a single sheet of paper. However, don't expect to be able to blow up your printed illustration to a larger size — for example, by using a photocopier or stat camera; doing so would increase the size of the printed pixels, which decreases resolution. Therefore, use this option only when creating proofs or thumbnails.

✦ **Destination/Print to File:** This option lets you generate a PostScript-language definition of the file on disk rather than printing it directly to your printer. Use the Destination/Print to File option when preparing an illustration to be printed on a remote PostScript printer. For more information on this option, read the "Printing to Disk" section later in this chapter.

✦ **Use PPD:** As I mentioned before, you can specify the PPD you want to use from within FreeHand. Simply click on the Use PPD check box and FreeHand allows you to choose from a list of PPDs that are available on your system. If you have already chosen a PPD or you wish to use the default that FreeHand assigns, just leave this checkbox alone.

The final feature of interest is the Setup/Preview button. If you are using a non-PostScript printer, click the Preview button to see what your artwork will look like when it's printed. If your selected printer is a PostScript-compatible printer, you are offered the Setup button. Clicking it will whisk you away to the Print Setup dialog box — the subject of the next section. Here you will also see a preview of the final print, but, because you're using a PostScript printer, you'll have access to a number of settings that only PostScript printers can handle.

Adjusting print options

In the Print dialog box, click on the Setup button to display the dialog box shown in Figure 18-1. This dialog box appears the same regardless of what computer you are using and of which PostScript printer driver you've selected. In the dialog box, you specify the paper size, the orientation of the page, the separations that you want to print, crop marks, and all kinds of other stuff. It's pretty amazing, you can even change the dot angles of the colors you are printing. Be warned: If you change the screen angles of your document to prevent a moiré pattern, you must tell your printer because their imagesetter *will* override your settings.

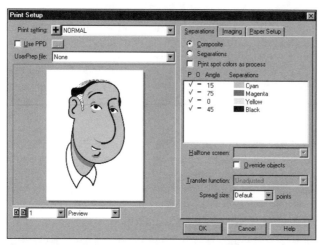

Figure 18-1: Click the Setup button in the Print dialog box to display the Print Setup dialog box, in which you adjust various options that are unique to PostScript printing in FreeHand.

To permanently alter the default settings inside the Print dialog box, adjust the options as desired inside the Print Setup dialog, click OK to return to the previous Print dialog box, and then click the Cancel button in the Print dialog box to return to the illustration window. Save the illustration over the existing FreeHand Defaults file, as described in "The FreeHand Defaults file" in Chapter 2.

The Print Setup dialog box consists of a few options on the left and three panels—Separations, Imaging, and Paper Setup—on the right. These panels are discussed in the following section.

The general options on the left are reflections of selections you made in the Print dialog box. You can stay the course with the decisions that you made previously, or you can choose anew if you wish. To quickly recap these options:

✦ **Print setting:** In this pop-up menu you can choose from default settings or set up your own settings and save for future use. If you make changes to the settings in the Print Setup dialog box when a default setting active, FreeHand reflects these changes by adding a small plus sign to the beginning of the setting's name. If you wish to save your changes as a new setting that will then appear in this pop-up menu, click on the large plus sign to the left of the pop-up menu and save the print settings by typing in a new name.

✦ **Use PPD:** If you've already selected a PPD in the Print dialog box, FreeHand simply reiterates that it's aware of your choice. If you've changed your mind, you can choose another PPD from within the Print Setup dialog box just as you can in the Print dialog box.

Also on the left side of the Print Setup dialog box you have a print preview box that gives you an idea of what the final print will look like. The preview comes equipped with the same page-advance icons and display mode pop-up menu that you're used in the normal FreeHand environment. This preview window is sensitive to some of the options in the Print Setup dialog box and will update to reflect your changes.

Separations panel

The separation panel, the first panel on the right of the Print Setup dialog box, gives you control over how the different colors in you document will print. They work as follows:

✦ **Color options:** You can either choose to have your work printed as a single composite image or a four-color separated document. There is a check mark next to each of the four printing colors to specify whether a plate prints. You can also change the screen angles of each color plate to avoid moiré patterns. If you do change the screen angles, be sure to let your service bureau know what you changed them to so they can adjust their imagesetter to match your specified angles. See the "Printing color separations" section (later in this chapter) for more information on these settings.

✦ **Halftone Screen:** The options in this Separations panel control the screen frequency and the resolution used by your printer. The screen frequency represents the number of halftone cells per linear inch and is measured in lines per inch, or *lpi*. *Halftone cells* are the dots used to represent gray values, process colors, and tints. Both are described in more detail in the "Halftone screens" section later in this chapter.

The *resolution* of the printer is the number of pixels printed per linear inch. Resolution is measured in dots per inch, or *dpi*, with *dots* being the common name for the printer's tiny pixels. When printing to a laser printer, you may not be able to change the resolution.

However, when printing to an imagesetter, you can speed up printing by reducing the resolution, or increase the quality of the printout by increasing the value.

✦ **Transfer Function:** Found in the Separations panel, this pop-up menu provides access to three options — Unadjusted, Normalize, and Posterize — each of which controls the lightness and darkness of gray values and tints printed from FreeHand. Select the Unadjusted option to bypass special instructions included in the current PPD file and rely on the default screen settings used by your printer.

Unfortunately, different printers render screens differently. A light tint printed from a typical laser printer, for example, is darker than the same tint printed from an imagesetter. To help eliminate this inconsistency, select the Normalize option, which uses special instructions from the PPD file to make screens printed from a low-resolution laser printer more accurately match those printed from a high-end imagesetter.

Choose Posterize to remap tints to one of four screen values — 100 percent, 67 percent, 33 percent, or 0 percent (white). Transitions between tints are abrupt rather than smooth. (An example of a posterized image appears back in Figure 16-5.) Select this option when printing speed is more important than quality. It dramatically speeds up the printing of gradations, for example, because FreeHand only has to render four steps instead of the 26 steps that a laser printer outputs by default.

✦ **Spread Size:** Use this option to trap all objects in your document. Trapping is a professional printing process whereby you extend the size of objects to compensate for inaccuracies in plate alignment. When colors from two different plates abut each other in your illustration and their plates are not perfectly aligned, a gap may result between the two colors. Trapping avoids such gaps.

The Spread Size option applies trapping to all applicable objects in your document. You can also trap on an object-by-object basis using the trap tool, as described in the upcoming section, "Trapping objects." Truth be told, it's best to only resort to trapping under the guidance of your professional printer. After you and your printer have decided that trapping is the way to go, it's best to use the trap tool to apply trapping on an object-by-object basis. Also, the trap tool offers two trapping methods, choke and spread, whereas this option only lets you spread an object. All of this is covered under the trap tool discussion. See "Trapping objects" later in this chapter for more information. You should not use both the Spread Size option and the trap tool. So, when should you use the Spread Size option? "Never" sounds good to me. But at least now you know what it does.

Imaging panel

The next panel on the right side of the Print Setup dialog box is the Imaging panel. Here you decide what additional features will print along with your artwork. The options include:

✦ **Labels & Marks:** The printer's marks are found in the Imaging panel Select the Crop Marks check box to print eight hairline *crop marks*, which mark the four corners of an illustration. When you print to an imagesetter, for example, all illustrations are printed on paper one or two feet wide, regardless of their actual size. When you have the illustration commercially reproduced, the printer will want to know the dimensions of the final paper size and how the illustration should be positioned on the final page. Crop marks specify the boundaries of the reproduced page and the position of your artwork relative to these boundaries.

Select the Registration Marks check box to print five *registration marks*, one centered along the top of the illustration, one centered along the bottom, one centered along each side, and a fifth in the lower right corner of the page.

Registration marks are used to align color separations. When you're printing a black-and-white or color composite, registration marks are not necessary. However, if you are printing separations, they're absolutely imperative because they provide the only reliable means for ensuring exact registration of different process and spot colors during the commercial printing process.

You have the choice to have Separation names listed when you print color separations: It prints Cyan, Magenta, or whatever is the name of the separation color. Again, be sure to select this option when printing color separations. Otherwise, your commercial printer won't know which separation is which.

Select the File Name and Date check box to print the filename and the date on which you last saved the current illustration in the upper left corner, just outside the crop marks. Use this option to avoid the which-version-is-which confusion that often accompanies the creation of electronic documents.

All margin notes — crop marks, registration marks, and page labels — print outside the area consumed by the page and bleed size, as specified in the Document Inspector. Therefore, be sure to select a size option from the Paper Setup panel (discussed in the next section) that's larger than the page size and bleed added together; otherwise, your margin notes will not print. If available for your PPD, the Extra paper sizes are especially useful for this purpose.

The commercial printer reproducing your illustration will use all margin notes, so be sure they are not removed when excess paper or film is trimmed from your printed separation.

✦ **Imaging Options:** Select the Emulsion Down radio button to print a flipped version of the illustration. The resulting illustration is a mirror image of its former self. The option name refers to the orientation of an illustration relative to the emulsion side of a piece of film. When printing film negatives, you will probably want to select Emulsion Down; when printing on paper, select the Emulsion Up radio button. If you're unsure which option to use, consult with your commercial printer.

Select Negative Image to change all blacks to white and whites to black. For example, 100 percent black becomes white, 40 percent black becomes 60 percent black, and so on. As a general rule, select the Positive Image option when printing to paper; select Negative Image only when printing to film. Again, be sure to confirm your selection with your commercial printer.

✦ **Output Options:** Select the Include Invisible Layers if you want hidden layers to print along with all the other layers in your document. Activate Split Complex Paths if you want FreeHand to breakup long paths as described in the upcoming section, "Splitting long paths." You can also decide which encode method you want FreeHand to use and whether your OPI (Open Prepress Interface) comments will print along with your separations. If you want your RGB colors to convert to process (CMYK) colors click the Convert RGB To Process check box.

Paper Setup panel

The final panel in the Print Setup dialog box, the Paper Setup panel, lets you take advantage of the paper options that are unique to the PPD that you've selected. You can choose an orientation of tall or wide. You can choose automatic so the printer reads the orientation of the page.

Paper: Based on information contained in the selected PPD file, the Paper Setup panel lists the page sizes that can be printed by your output device. If the selected printer allows you to set custom page sizes — as in the case of a professional-quality imagesetter — you can select a Custom option to change the Width and Height values to the right of the pop-up menu to editable option boxes. You can enter values as high as 19,008 points — or 22 feet — the size of the FreeHand pasteboard. But just because you can enter a value doesn't mean your printer can handle it. The actual maximum size is determined by the width of the paper used by the imagesetter. Some PPDs provide a MaxMeasure option in the Paper pop-up menu that selects the maximum permissible page size.

If a Transverse suffix follows an option in the Paper pop-up menu (as in Letter.Transverse), FreeHand rotates the page size relative to the roll of paper or film on which it is printed. By default, FreeHand places the long edge of the page parallel to the long edge of the paper. In most cases this is correct; but when printing to an imagesetter, you can usually reduce paper or film waste by setting pages transverse — that is, with the short edges of the page parallel to the long edges of the paper.

An Extra suffix adds an inch to both the horizontal and vertical dimensions of the page size, allowing room for margin notes, such as crop marks and page labels (discussed later in this immense list). For example, Letter.Extra measures $9\frac{1}{2} \times 12$ inches.

The Tall and Wide radio buttons below the Paper pop-up menu control the orientation of the page inside the specified paper size. Unless you specified a custom paper size large enough to accommodate both horizontal and vertical pages, as described in the "Printing different-size pages" section of Chapter 19, you should select the option that matches the orientation of pages that you want to print.

Printing color separations

I only briefly touched upon the options contained in the Separations panel of the Print Setup dialog box, and now I'd like to go into a bit more detail. But before I can fully explain these options, I need to introduce a little color-separation theory.

A specific color can be professionally reproduced on a sheet of paper in two ways. In the first method, called *spot-color printing*, inks are premixed to create the desired color and then applied to the paper. One separation is printed for each spot color used in the illustration. Spot-color printing is usually used when the illustration includes only one or two colors (in addition to black). This printing method is neither exceedingly expensive nor technically demanding. Spot-color printing allows for precise colors to be selected and applied with perfect color consistency.

In the other printing method, *four-color process printing*, cyan, magenta, yellow, and black ink are blended in specific percentages to create a visual effect approximating a whole rainbow of colors. Four-color process printing is technically demanding and tends to be more expensive than spot-color printing, but it also results in more colors.

When printing a process-color illustration, FreeHand generates a separation for each of the four component inks. Every colored object in an illustration is broken down into its component colors according to their original definitions in the Color Mixer panel.

It's possible to combine four-color process printing with spot-color printing. This option is more expensive than process printing alone and is subject to the capabilities of your commercial printer. But it combines the benefits of the four-color process — which permits many colors with few inks — and spot-color printing — which ensures precise color matching — in one printed piece. Many magazines, for example, use four-color process printing for photos and artwork and spot-color printing for advertisements and logos.

Now, on to the options offered by FreeHand, as shown in Figure 18-2. The scrolling list in the Separations panel of the Print Setup dialog box contains the name of every spot color defined in the current illustration, including black. If any process color has been defined, the three non-black process colors — cyan, magenta, and yellow — are also displayed. No tints are shown in the scrolling list. Instead, each tint is printed to the same separation as its parent color: 10 percent black prints to the black separation, 40 percent Pantone 123 prints to the Pantone 123 separation, and so on.

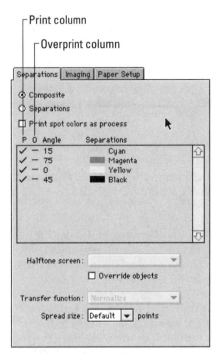

Figure 18-2: The scrolling Separations panel from the Print Setup dialog box.

The left side of the scrolling list is divided into three columns. The print column, headed by a *P*, determines whether the corresponding color prints. A check mark means that the separation in that row will print when the Separations option in the print dialog box is selected. No check mark means that the color won't print. To hide or display a check mark, click inside the print column. For example, to proof only the cyan separation, click in front of the magenta, yellow, and black rows to hide their check marks and prevent these colors from printing. (The check marks stay hidden until the next time you visit the Print Setup dialog box.)

The second column, headed by an *O*, is the overprint column. When no check mark appears in this column, the corresponding color knocks out any colors behind it, as described in the "Overprinting colors" section of Chapter 13. If a check mark precedes a color name, that color overprints colors that it overlaps. To change the overprint setting, click in the overprint column to display or hide a check mark. Because this option applies to *all* objects filled or stroked with a color, it's generally a bit drastic unless you're trying to create a specific effect. The only color that you may want to overprint on a regular basis is black. In fact, black traditionally overprints other colors because it's so dark that you don't see the colors behind it. So by overprinting, you avoid gaps between other process colors and black.

The number in the third column controls the *screen angle*, which is the angle at which halftone screens in the corresponding separation print. For example, say that one of the 300 dpi LaserWriter PPDs is selected (as is the case in Figure 18-2), FreeHand rotates each of the process-color screens. The following items explain how these angles work in the example:

✦ Cyan screens are rotated 15 degrees counterclockwise from the mean horizontal.

✦ Magenta screens are rotated 75 degrees, which produces the same effect as if they were rotated ×15 degrees from the mean horizontal. So the magenta rotation is exactly the opposite of the cyan rotation.

✦ Yellow screens aren't rotated at all.

✦ Black screens are rotated 45 degrees, smack dab in the middle of the others.

Other PPDs may rotate the screens to different angles. Typically, the yellow and black screens remain at 0 and 45 degrees respectively, while the cyan and magenta screens are rotated slightly differently. For example, if you select the Agfa ProSet 9800, the cyan screen rotates to 18.43 and the magenta rotates to 71.57 degrees. Again, these values produce exactly opposite effects ($90 \times 18.43 = 71.57$). This opposite relationship between cyan and magenta is one of the factors that ensures even printing of process colors.

Unless you know what you're doing, don't change the values associated with process colors. Spot colors, however, are a different matter. FreeHand rotates all spot colors to the same angle as black because they are not intended to overlap other colors. But if you overprint an object filled or stroked with a spot color, or you overprint the entire spot color separation by displaying a check mark in the overprint column, change this angle. To do so, double-click on the value in the screen angle column and enter a new value in the tiny dialog box that appears. Then press Return/Enter.

Tip

Generally speaking, set the screen angle of an overprinting spot color 45 degrees different from the process color that it overlaps most often. For example, if you combine the spot color and black—probably the most popular combination— change the screen angle to 0 degrees.

Initiating printing

When you've finished setting the options in the Print Setup dialog box, click the OK button or press Return/Enter to close the dialog box and return to the print dialog box. Press Return/Enter again to initiate the printing process. The standard dialog boxes that are presented during any PostScript printing process appear.

Printing to Disk

When you print a FreeHand illustration to a PostScript printer, FreeHand *downloads* a PostScript-language text file to the printer. The printer reads the file and creates your illustration according to its instructions. FreeHand also lets you print an illustration to disk; that is, write the PostScript-language text file to your hard drive. If you're familiar with the PostScript language, you can edit the file using a word processor. Or you can copy the file to a floppy disk or other removable media to transfer to your service bureau.

Printing to disk is easy. Prepare your artwork for printing as discussed in the previous sections of this chapter, defining all settings in the print and Print Setup dialog boxes as desired. Then, before pressing Return/Enter to initiate the Print command, either select File from the Destination pop-up (Macs) or select the Print to File Checkbox (Windows) in the print dialog box.

After you click on the OK button, the system software produces a specialized Save dialog. You can name the file and specify its destination, just as in any save dialog box. If you're using a Mac, you can also select from a few other options:

✦ **Format:** This option lets you select the format that you want to use to save the illustration. The pop-up menu offers three EPS options, but don't select them. You can create an editable EPS file from inside FreeHand. To create a file that you can download to a printer, select the PostScript option, which is the default setting.

✦ **ASCII or Binary:** If you'll be downloading the file from a Mac, select the Binary option. Binary encoding is much faster and much more efficient, and it results in smaller files. Only select the ASCII option if you'll be doing something weird with the file, like giving it to a Windows user.

✦ **Level 1 or 2:** You'll have to consult with your service bureau on this one. If the service bureau uses an imagesetter equipped with Level 2 PostScript, select the Level 2 Only option. If their imagesetter is equipped with Level 1 PostScript, select Level 1 Compatible.

✦ **Font Inclusion:** If you used any special fonts in your illustration — anything besides Times, Helvetica, Courier, and Symbol — select the All But Standard 13 option. This tells FreeHand to include printer font definitions for every font that you use except Times and the others. Including fonts greatly increases the size of the file on disk but it also prevents your text from printing incorrectly. If you know that your service bureau is already equipped with the fonts you're using, select the None option to keep the size of the file down.

Click on the Save button or press Return/Enter to save the file on disk.

Special Printing Considerations

All print jobs are not the same. Your illustration may require special treatment that the Print command options can't provide, or you may encounter complications that prevent your document from printing properly even though the illustration itself seems fine. In either of these scenarios, the information in the following sections may be of help. It explains how to trap objects, alter settings for halftone screens, avoid limitcheck errors, and solve out-of-memory errors.

Trapping objects

You may recall from the overprinting discussion that if you do not choose overprinting, FreeHand automatically knocks out underlying objects when printing separations. Therefore, when colors from two different plates abut each other and their plates are not perfectly aligned, a gap may result between the two colors. Trapping is a professional printing process to compensate for such inaccuracies in plate alignment. Although you could have manually created traps in earlier versions of FreeHand, Version 5 introduced automated trapping.

Trapping is not something for you to apply frivolously. It should not be your first plan of attack. Go for overprinting first. If that's not a viable solution, discuss the matter with your print house. Generally, trapping is best left to your professional printer. Also, either manually apply traps to objects with a demonstrated trapping need or, as a very last resort, use the Spread Size option in the Separations panel of the Print Setup dialog box, but don't apply both. Now that you have been thoroughly warned of the potential dangers, I'll tell you how to trap.

The control central for trapping is the Trap dialog box, pictured in Figure 18-3. To display this dialog box, select the object you want to trap and choose Xtras ⇨ Create ⇨ Trap or choose the Trap icon from the Operations palette. First, let's discuss the Reverse Traps check box.

Figure 18-3: When the Trap Color Method is set to Use Tint Reduction, a Tint Reduction option box appears in the Trap dialog box.

It's always best to trap your lighter color. The lighter color can be either the foreground object or the background object. These two different cases require two different types of traps, known as spreads and chokes, respectively. Figure 18-4 illustrates the difference between these two methods. On the left side, a light star sits over a dark field of gray.

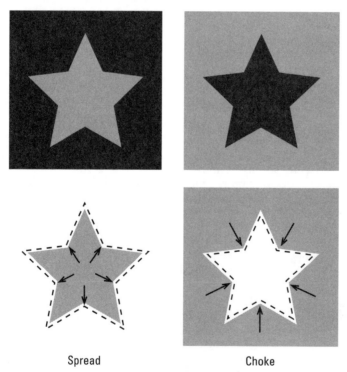

Spread   Choke

Figure 18-4: A spread trap (left) and a choke trap (right).

In this case, you would want the trap to expand the size of the star. The dashed line around the star in the bottom left of Figure 18-4 shows this method, which is called a spread. The trap object would encompass the area between the star and the dashed line. To create a spread, you do not enable the Reverse Traps check box. When the darker color sits over a light field, such as on the right side of Figure 18-4, you would resort to a choke trap. In this case, you want to decrease the size of the area knocked out by the star. In the bottom right of Figure 18-4, the choke object would be the area between the dashed line and the gray field. To create a choke, you must enable the Reverse Traps check box. In either case, you control the size of the trap using the Trap Width option box or the slider bar in the Trap dialog box.

Next, you need to set the shade of your trap. Selecting Use Maximum Value creates a trap the same color as the selected object. Selecting Use Tint Reduction adds the Tint Reduction option pictured in Figure 18-3. Reducing the shade of the trap object better blends the trap object into your illustration.

Halftones screens

In addition to altering halftone screen frequencies for an entire illustration from the Print Setup dialog box, you can control halftones on an object-by-object basis. However, if you want to adjust the halftone settings for an object, it must be filled or stroked with a gray value, tint, or process color (all directional and radial gradations fall into this camp). Any 100 percent color — black, white, a solid spot color, or a mix of 100 percent process colors — is not affected because such colors print as solid ink; no halftoning is required.

To alter the halftone screen for a specific text block or graphic object, select the object that you want to change and then press ⌘/Ctrl-H to display the Halftones panel shown in Figure 18-5. You can use the options in this palette to create special effects or to manipulate a document in preparation for some specific commercial printing process. Both the fill and stroke of the selected object are affected by your settings.

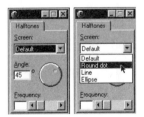

Figure 18-5: The Halftones palette as it appears when the default halftone setting is selected (left) and when the Screen pop-up menu is displayed (right).

Manipulations performed in the Halftones palette affect only the printing of selected objects; they do not in any way affect the manner in which objects display in the preview or keyline mode. Also, these options are applicable only for printing to PostScript printers.

Note

Before I go any further, let me explain how halftones work. The whole idea behind printing is to use as few inks as possible to create the appearance of a wide variety of colors. For example, if you wanted to print a picture of pink flamingos wearing red bow ties, your printer could print the flamingos in one pass using pink ink, let that color dry, and then load the red ink and print all the bow ties. But why go to all that trouble? After all, pink is just a lighter shade of red. Why not imitate the pink by lightening the red ink? Unfortunately, offset printing presses don't do lighter shades of colors. They recognize only solid color and the absence of color.

So how do you print the 30 percent shade of red necessary to represent pink? The answer is *halftoning*. Hundreds of tiny dots of ink are laid down on a page. Because the dots are so small, your eyes cannot quite focus on them. Instead, the dots appear to blend with the white background of the page to create a lighter shade of a color. Figure 18-6 shows a detail of the flamingo enlarged to display the individual dots. He isn't wearing a bow tie — the one he ordered from Neiman Marcus didn't come in.

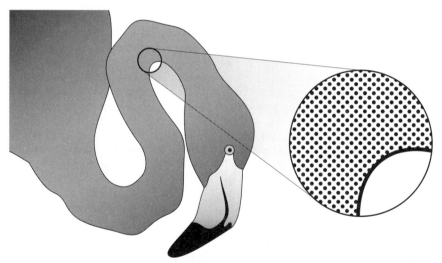

Figure 18-6: A tint or gray value is made up of hundreds of tiny dots called *halftone cells*, as illustrated by the enlarged detail on the right.

The dots in a tint are arranged into a grid of *halftone* cells, much like a checkerboard. The dots grow and shrink inside their cells to emulate different shades of color. Large dots create dark tints; small dots create light tints. Each pixel in your PostScript printer belongs to one of the halftone cells, and each halftone cell comprises some number of pixels.

As an example, consider the LaserWriter: By default, it prints 60 halftone cells per linear inch. Because the resolution of the LaserWriter is 300 pixels per linear inch, each halftone cell must measure 5 pixels wide by 5 pixels tall (300 ÷ 60 = 5), for a total of 25 pixels per cell. If all 25 pixels in a cell are turned off, the cell appears white. All pixels turned on produces solid ink; any number from 1 to 24 pixels turned on produces a particular gray value or tint. By turning on different numbers of pixels — from 0 up to 25 — the printer can create a total of 26 unique tints or gray values, as illustrated in Figure 18-7.

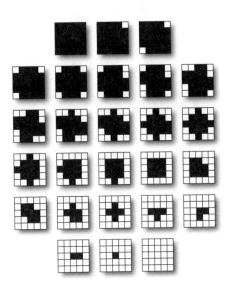

Figure 18-7: A 5 × 5-pixel halftone cell with different numbers of pixels activated, ranging from 25 (top left) to 0 (bottom right). Each cell represents a unique gray value or tint from 100 to 0 percent.

The options in the Halftone palette enable you to alter the shape, angle, and size of every halftone cell used to represent gray values, tints, and process colors in the fill and stroke of the selected object. The Screen pop-up menu determines the screen function, which is the pattern FreeHand uses to simulate gray values and tints. You can select from four options, each of which is shown applied to objects in Figure 18-8.

Figure 18-8: The default screen function (top), Round Dot function second), Line function (third), and Ellipse function (bottom) applied to the fill and stroke of two objects. The frequency is 12 lpi.

✦ **Default:** This option accepts the default screen function produced by the current output device. Some PostScript devices rely on round black dots against a white background inside light tints, white dots against a black background inside dark tints, and a squarish checkerboard pattern when simulating medium tints. On other printers, the Default option produces the same effect as the Round Dot option.

✦ **Round Dot:** This option represents gray values and tints using a pattern of perfectly circular black dots against a white background, even when representing light and medium tints.

✦ **Line:** The Line option represents gray values and tints using a series of parallel straight lines. When applied to a gradation, the lines gradually increase and decrease in thickness, resulting in spikes.

✦ **Ellipse:** This option creates a series of black ovals against a white background.

The value in the Angle option box determines the *screen angle*, which is the orientation of the halftone cells. By default, this grid is rotated 45 degrees with respect to the printed page. To rotate the halftone grid to some other angle, enter a value between 0 and 90 degrees (all other values create repeat effects) into the Angle option box. Examples are shown in Figure 18-9.

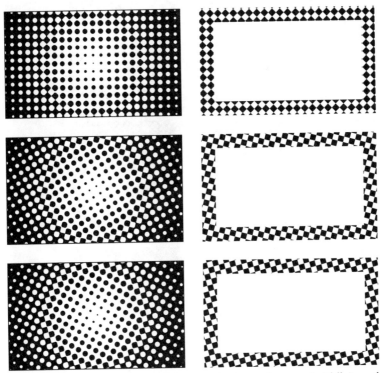

Figure 18-9: Angle values of 0 degrees (top), 30 degrees (middle), and 60 degrees (bottom) applied to the fill and stroke of two objects.

The value in the Frequency option box determines the *screen frequency*, which is the number of halftone cells that print per linear inch. Frequency is measured in lines per inch, or lpi. If no value appears in this option box, FreeHand accepts the default screen frequency for the current output device. Examples include 60 lpi for the LaserWriter and 120 lpi for the Linotronic 300. FreeHand accepts any value from 4 to 300 lpi.

As shown in Figure 18-10, higher Frequency values result in smoother-looking gray values and tints. However, raising the frequency also decreases the number of gray values a printer can render, because it decreases the size of each halftone cell, thus decreasing the number of pixels per cell. Therefore, when raising the Frequency value above the default setting, consider how your change affects the number of gray values printable by the current output device (as explained back in the "Avoiding banding" section of Chapter 17).

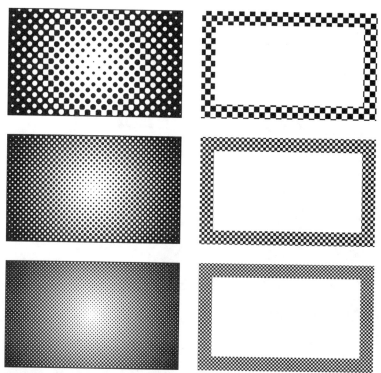

Figure 18-10: Screen frequencies of 12 lpi (top), 24 lpi (middle), and 36 lpi (bottom).

Be aware that changes made to halftone settings alter the default settings applied to new objects if the Changing Objects Changes Defaults check box in the Object panel of the Preferences dialog box is selected. Because you can't see halftone screens on-screen, you can easily start applying them to every new object that you create if you aren't careful.

Splitting long paths

You may encounter several errors when printing an illustration. One of the most common is the *limitcheck error*, which results from a limitation in your printer's PostScript interpreter. If the number of points in the mathematical representation of a path exceeds this limitation, the illustration will not print successfully.

Unfortunately, the points used in this mathematical representation are not the corner, curve, and connector points you used to define the objects. Instead, they are calculated by the PostScript interpreter during the printing process. When presented with a curve, the PostScript interpreter has to plot hundreds of tiny straight lines to create the most accurate rendering possible. So instead of drawing a perfect curve, your printer creates a many-sided polygon whose exact number of sides is determined by a device-dependent variable known as flatness. The default flatness for the LaserWriter is one pixel, or $\frac{1}{300}$ inch. The center of any tiny side of the polygon rendering may be at most $\frac{1}{300}$ inch from the farthest X,Y-coordinate of the actual mathematical curve, as demonstrated by Figure 18-11.

Each tiny line in the polygon rendering meets at a point. If the number of points exceeds your printer's built-in path limit, an alert box appears to inform you that the printer has encountered a limitcheck error, and the print job will be canceled. The path limit for the original LaserWriter was 1,500, seemingly enough straight lines to imitate any curve. But in practice, you can easily create a curve that proves too much for that limit. For example, a typical signature contains several complex loops that might tax the limitations of the most advanced output device.

There are two ways to avoid limitcheck errors. The most preferred method is to enter the resolution for the final output device in the Printer Resolution option box in the Document Setup panel of the Inspector palette. The next time you print or export the current illustration, FreeHand automatically breaks up every path that it considers to be at risk into several smaller paths. This doesn't affect the actual paths in your FreeHand document, just those in the EPS file and the PostScript description sent to the printer.

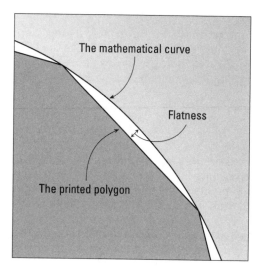

Figure 18-11: The flatness of a curve is the greatest distance between any tiny straight line used to represent the curve and its true mathematical description.

Note

If you don't want FreeHand to break up your paths, choose File ➪ Output Options to display the Output Options dialog box, shown in Figure 18-12. Then deselect the Split Complex Paths check box. I can't imagine any reason why you'd want to do this — as far as I know, this option is utterly without negative side effects — but I figured that if I go and slap a name like *Bible* on this book, I have to tell you everything.

Figure 18-12: The Output Options dialog box.

Unfortunately, FreeHand's automated path-splitting feature accounts only for the complexity of the path. It doesn't account for whether a path is filled with a complex tile pattern, which is a common cause of the limitcheck error.

If the automatic splitting technique doesn't solve your printing problem, you can use the Flatness value, also found in the Output Options dialog box. Enter a value between 0 and 100 in the Flatness option box. This value increases the distance that a straight line can vary from the mathematical curve, thus reducing the risk of limitcheck errors. However, the affected path also appears less smooth.

Tip

Another great use for the Flatness value — and for the Maximum Color Steps value that appears right above it — is to speed up the printing of proofs. If you lower the Maximum Color Steps value, which controls the number of steps used to print gradations (this value has no effect on steps in blends), and raise the Flatness value, FreeHand prints very quickly, as well as very roughly. When it comes time to print the final output, be sure to delete both values so that FreeHand relies on the printer's default settings.

Printing pattern tiles

As I mentioned a moment ago, tile patterns can cause limitcheck errors. But more often, they cause *out-of-memory* errors, especially if several patterns are used in a single illustration. To accelerate the printing process, FreeHand downloads tiles to your printer's memory, much as if they were nonresident fonts. The printer can then access tile definitions repeatedly throughout the printing of an illustration. However, if the illustration contains too many tile patterns, or if a single tile is too complex, the printer's memory may become full, in which case the print operation is canceled and an alert box informs you that an out-of-memory error has occurred.

It's been my experience that out-of-memory errors are about equally common when printing from new, high-resolution output devices as from old, low-memory printers. Imagesetters tend to include updated PostScript interpreters and have increased memory capacity, but they also need this additional memory to render the complex tile patterns at a higher resolution. But regardless of which kind of device you use, you can try any one of these techniques to remedy the problem:

✦ Change all typefaces in the current illustration to Times, Helvetica, or some other printer-resident font so that FreeHand doesn't have to download both patterns and printer fonts.

✦ Print objects painted with different tile patterns in separate illustrations. Then use traditional paste-up techniques to combine the pages into a composite proof.

✦ Send all objects filled with pattern tiles to a separate layer, hide the layer by clicking on its check mark in the Layers palette, and then deselect the Include Invisible Layers radio button in the Output Options dialog box before printing. This technique allows you to proof all portions of your illustration except objects filled with tile patterns. If the illustration prints successfully, you know that the tile patterns are the culprit and can set about getting rid of some.

Some service bureaus charge extra for printing a complex document that ties up an imagesetter for a long period of time. Tile patterns almost always complicate an illustration and increase printing time. Therefore, use masks and composite paths instead of patterns whenever possible.

✦   ✦   ✦

Shock Treatment on the World Wide Web

Strutting Your Stuff on the World Wide Web

Well, you've mastered FreeHand by now. Come on, no need to be modest. You've created all sorts of amazing images, but somehow your life doesn't seem quite complete. Something is still missing. Your beautiful images are languishing within your lonely little computer. You are just dying to show them off to the world so that they can earn the recognition they deserve. Well, what are you waiting for? Release them! Using The Flash file format graphics you can publish your amazing FreeHand images instantly on the World Wide Web.

What in the World Is the World Wide Web?

Unless you've been living in a cave for the past few years you have probably heard references to the following terms: information superhighway, cyberspace, Internet, World Wide Web, WWW, and the Web. Believe it or not, these terms have nothing to do with fast cars, space ships, fishnets, or insects. Some of these terms have subtle technical differences, but most people simply toss them around interchangeably. Most uses of these terms are really referring to the World Wide Web.

The World Wide Web is a magical place. As the name suggests, it is a world spanning an interconnected web of information. Nobody knows just how large it is or exactly how much information is available on the Web. It's growing at a phenomenal rate. The Web is made up of innumerable information units called Web pages. Each of these Web pages can contain information in various forms such as text, graphics, audio, multimedia, and so on. Web pages are viewed through software called a Web browser. The most common Web browsers are Netscape Navigator and Microsoft Explorer. While viewing a Web page, you may click on a hot link within that page to go to another Web page. That page may have more hot links that take you to yet more pages, which is why it's called a web. These interconnections crisscross all over the globe with no specific organization. There are no borders or boundaries on the Web. You can access a page like the one in Figure 19-1 from across the world just as easily as one that is on your own computer.

Figure 19-1: The DreamLight Web site is located at the following URL (Uniform Resource Locator): *http://www.dreamlight.com.*

Browsing Web pages is typically referred to as "surfing the net" because the pages themselves are located on the Internet. The Internet is the global network that ties all the computers together that make the World Wide Web possible. Each Web page is simply a text file that is stored on a computer within the Internet. If the Web page contains graphical information, the graphic files are also stored on the Internet and are linked into the text file. Other types of files can also be linked into the text files, including those that make nifty sounds and video.

The language that makes all this possible through simple text files is the *HyperText Markup Language* (HTML). We will cover enough HTML to enable you to add your FreeHand images to your Web pages. If you are interested in learning more about HTML, there are many good HTML references available. I suggest reading *HTML Manual of Style* by Larry Aronson to help you design better Web pages and avoid many of the common pitfalls. Figure 19-2 shows an HTML text file and Figure 19-3 shows a logo drawn in FreeHand used to create the Web page shown in Figure 19-1.

Figure 19-2: The DreamLight home page shown in HTML.

Figure 19-3: Web logo created in FreeHand.

Getting "Connected"

Creating your own Web site is easier than you may think. You don't even need to be "connected" (to the Internet, not the mob) to design and build your own Web site. You can build your entire site offline on your own computer. You only need to get connected when you are ready to upload your site to the Web for others to view. After your pages are uploaded to the Web, you will want to test the pages online to adjust and fine-tune them.

To create and view your own Web pages offline all you need are the following items:

✦ Some graphics software, such as FreeHand.

✦ A Web browser such as Netscape Navigator or Microsoft Explorer.

✦ A text editor such as SimpleText or an HTML editor.

In order to access the Internet and the World Wide Web to publish your own Web pages online you'll need the following additional items:

✦ A 14.4 or faster modem.

✦ An *Internet service provider* (ISP) account that includes space on their Web server.

✦ Software to connect you to the Internet, such as FreePPP.

✦ FTP software to upload your pages to the Internet such as Fetch.

Most ISPs include a software collection that has the PPP and FTP software that you'll need to connect to the Internet and upload your pages. ISPs can also provide detailed instructions on how to set up and access your own private Web space on their Web servers. If you know someone who is "connected," and I'll bet you do, just ask them which local ISP they use. If you'd like to learn more about the Internet, a good place to start is with the *Internet Starter Kit* by Adam C. Engst.

Becoming a Web Star

So you tried to become a rock 'n' roll star in the '80s but it didn't work out? Don't worry, this is the '90s — now you can become a Web star by creating amazing Web pages full of wonderful images. You already have one of the most powerful tools to create graphically rich Web pages, FreeHand.

You may have some existing illustrations that you have created in FreeHand that you wish to publish on the World Wide Web. Maybe you are considering creating new custom graphics to enhance your new Web page. Well, either way, the first thing you need to do is to define the objective or purpose of each image you wish to publish on the Web.

Defining the purpose of your image

An image without a purpose is a waste of space, and, more important, a waste of download time. Every bit of information displayed on a Web page must first be downloaded through the user's modem. Typically, a full page of text takes less time to download than a single small image. Don't fall prey to cluttering up your pages with endless wasteful images. Carefully define the purpose and objective of each image before adding it to your Web page. Any images that you add to a Web page should help contribute to the text and clarify the purpose of the page rather than distract from the text and confuse the purpose of the page.

Here are some typical uses of graphic images on a Web page:

✦ An identifying corporate or product logo or visual identity

✦ A graphical page header

✦ Buttons used to navigate through a number of Web pages

✦ Icons used to attract attention to important elements

✦ Maps and diagrams

✦ Info-graphics

✦ Small picture previews of items in a catalog or portfolio

✦ Full size images presented in a portfolio

Tip

Any images that are placed directly on a page are automatically downloaded to the user when they access that page. Therefore, you should keep any images that are placed directly on a page very small. If you are putting together a portfolio of images where the actual purpose of the image is to show the image itself, then you may include larger images through an optional link. This way, the user can view a small preview image on the page and then decide if they wish to download and view the larger version of the image or not. If you put many large images directly on your pages, you will quickly lose your audience as they become bored waiting for images to download.

Take a look at the following example pages from the DreamLight Virtual Gallery shown in Figures 19-4 and 19-5. The button strips along the top of the page are small icons because these are used on every page. When using buttons like these you should use the exact image files on multiple Web pages. This way the image files are actually only downloaded once and they are read from your hard disk on each subsequent page you view. This speeds up access to additional pages.

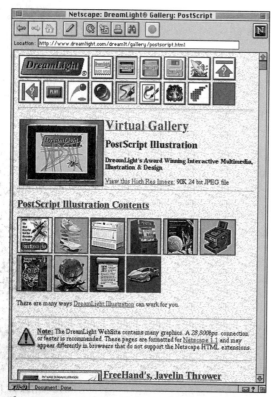

Figure 19-4: WebSite Gallery with thumbnail versions of the artwork.

Notice how different size versions of each image in the gallery are used. In the contents section, there are very small thumbnails of all the images in this section. When the users click on one of these thumbnails they are brought to an area of the page where there is a medium-sized version of the illustration, as shown in Figure 19-5.

At this point if the users wish to view a high resolution version of the image they can click on the medium-sized image to load the full size image. If the user doesn't specifically choose to view the high resolution version of the image it is never downloaded. This way the users only have to wait for large images to download that they actually choose to view.

Figure 19-5: WebSite PS Gallery Images with the medium-sized image previews.

FreeHand: The two-faced graphics program

Yes, FreeHand has a bit of a split personality. Most computer graphics boil down to two image types: vector graphics and raster graphics. FreeHand is capable of working with and exporting both types of graphics. Drawing objects directly in FreeHand is an example of creating vector graphics. FreeHand can also import, filter, and export various raster graphics formats. You can even convert between the two image types in FreeHand. You can auto trace a raster graphic which will create a vector graphic or you can rasterize a vector graphic. If this juggling has made you dizzy, let's take a closer look at each type of graphics.

Vector graphics

No, *vector* is not some high priced sports car. Well, come to think of it, vector may have been used as the name of one. Anyway, that's not what it's used for here. The term *vector* graphics dates back to the '60s when vector computer displays were first developed. These displays were capable of drawing images of mathematical formulas as a collection of plotted line segments. Vector graphics are sometimes called object-oriented drawings or, more recently, PostScript illustrations.

The individual objects are represented as mathematical formulas to the computer. Each object drawn is stored with the image and usually very easy to edit. The objects are usually drawn by plotting points or drawing curves. Unless a vector image is extremely complicated, it will usually take up very little disk space since all that is stored is the mathematical formula for each object. Vector graphics can be scaled to any magnification and the file size will not change — as shown in Figure 19-6. The file size is directly related to the image complexity. Native FreeHand and Illustrator files are examples of vector graphics. FreeHand is primarily a vector based illustration program. FreeHand can also auto trace a raster graphic to create a new vector graphic from it.

Figure 19-6 shows how a vector graphic looks in FreeHand at normal screen resolution. This is also how it would look on the Web as a vector format. Notice how the graphic looks a little jagged at normal magnification, but that when you zoom into the 400% close-up the apparent resolution increases resulting in a sharper image. All the shapes are redrawn by the computer using the screen resolution again. So now that the shapes are redrawn in a larger area, they can use more screen pixels to render. This is what's called resolution independent. The computer can compute the final output resolution based on the output device used, in this case, the computer monitor. When vector images are printed on high resolution devices they produce the sharpest results. Therefore, vector illustrations are often used in print media.

Figure 19-6: A vector image as seen on screen at normal magnification and then zoomed in to 400%.

Raster graphics

Raster graphics first evolved in the '70s when raster displays were developed based on existing television technology. Raster graphics are sometimes referred to as bitmapped graphics or bitmapped paintings. Raster graphics are represented as a large rectangular grid of tiny picture elements or pixels. Each horizontal row of these pixels is called a raster line. After an object is drawn in a raster image, the object is no longer stored. All that is stored are the pixels of the overall image bitmap this can make editing the original objects very difficult. Raster graphics are usually created in a manner similar to painting, where you stroke colors onto the canvas. These strokes change the colors of the pixels that are under the brush. Scanned images or native Adobe Photoshop or Macromedia xRes files are examples of raster graphics. Raster graphics tend to take up much more space than similar vector graphics, because each pixel must be stored. Large, high-resolution images can result in very large file sizes. Even though FreeHand is primarily a vector-based illustration program, it comes packed with a wide variety of raster features. FreeHand can import and embed raster images into an illustration. FreeHand can apply filters to raster images. FreeHand can even rasterize vector objects and export them in many raster formats.

Figure 19-7 shows how a raster graphic looks in FreeHand at normal screen resolution. This is also how it would look on the Web as a raster format. Notice that the image looks best at normal magnification, but when you zoom into the 400% close-up, the resolution seems to decrease. Because all that is stored in the image are the pixels in the grid, all the computer can do when you zoom in is to magnify the pixels. This is called resolution dependent. Whatever resolution the image was created at will be the only resolution at which it will render. Raster formats are typically used for scanned photographs and computer paintings.

Figure 19-7: A rasterized version of the same image viewed at normal magnification and then zoomed in to 400%.

To be (vector) or not to be (raster)

When putting images onto the Web, you will need to first determine which type of graphic is most appropriate for each image's specific purpose. You can put either or both types of graphics on a single Web page. As you can see from Table 19-1, each type of graphic has its own strengths and weaknesses. The vector type also has the added benefit of allowing you to embed raster images within a vector graphic. This can give you the best of both worlds when used appropriately.

Vector graphics are best used when a large area of the screen needs to be covered with an image composed of large flat graphic shapes. This type of an image would result in a large file size if stored as a raster image. Because it is to be viewed relatively large on screen, some slightly jagged edges shouldn't present much of a problem — especially if many of the shapes have horizontal or vertical edges which will render perfectly smooth anyway.

Large navigational graphics with buttons and menu choices are candidates for vector images because you can embed hot links into the image.

Vector graphics are perfect for items that the user needs to explore such as the charts, maps, or diagrams. Because it is resolution independent, the user can zoom in and pan around the image. You could make a map of your location that the user can zoom in to and pan around. You can put up images of high detail where the user can zoom in to check them out. You can put up FreeHand graphics to allow the user to see how they were created, because they draw layer by layer. You can even embed hot links into different shapes within the map or diagram that will take the user to other places on the Web.

Table 19-1 Top 10 Image Type Benefits for the Web		
	Vector	*Raster*
Highest Quality Screen View		X
Zooming and Panning Ability	X	
Most Photographic		X
Embedded Hot Links	X	
Smallest File Size*	X	
Most Common Direct Browser Support		X
Indexed Color Palette Control**		X
Highest Quality Printing	X	
Scaling Flexibility	X	
Highest Degree of Editing Flexibility	X	

*Generally vector files are smaller than raster files. This is true unless the raster images are very small on-screen or the vector files are extremely complicated.

**You may need to use a raster graphics program such as Adobe Photoshop or Macromedia xRes to access and control the indexed color palette being used in a raster graphic.

Raster graphics are best used for items that are photographic in nature. Scanned images or computer paintings are good examples. Also, for the best possible screen view of an illustration, you may wish to create a rasterized version of the illustration. This image will appear clearer on the page. If the image needs to have an irregular shape (other than rectangular) you will need to use a raster format capable of transparency.

Raster Based Image File Formats for the Web

FreeHand is capable of creating all the standard raster image formats that are used on the World Wide Web including GIF, JPEG, and the new PNG format. As new formats are enabled on the Web, Xtras can be added to FreeHand to enable direct export to new formats. Figure 19-8 shows a beach girl as originally created in FreeHand. In the following sections, this image will be exported in various formats for comparison.

Figure 19-8: Original FreeHand Illustration as it appears on-screen.

Graphics Interchange Format: GIF

This is the venerable standby on the Web. Good old GIF. The GIF format, pronounced "jiff" or "giff" was developed by CompuServe specifically for use with online BBS systems. This was the first image format available for the Web, and it is still widely used today. The appearance of GIF images on the Web was one of the single most significant factors in the Web's explosive popularity. Because this is the oldest image format available on the Web, it is directly supported by most of the Web browsers available today. If it is important for you to reach the widest possible audience with your images, then the GIF format should serve well. The GIF format is capable of handling indexed raster images with color depths from 1 to 8 bits which allows from 2 to 256 colors. Figure 19-9 shows a GIF image.

Figure 19-9: Beach Girl saved in the GIF format.

LZW compression

The GIF format uses an *Lempel-Ziv & Welch* (LZW) compression scheme that is capable of moderate compression ratios. LZW compression is a fully reversible algorithm. This simply means that compressing and decompressing an image will result in an exact duplicate of the original image with no loss of information. Therefore, this type of compression is referred to as "lossless."

Interlacing: GIF87a

The GIF87a version of the format enabled the use of interlacing. Interlacing helps convey information to the viewer faster. Before interlacing was available, a GIF image would display from the top-down one raster line at a time. If there were necessary details (such as buttons) near the bottom of the image, you had to wait until the entire image was loaded before you could see the bottom. An interlaced image is broken down into four passes, the first of which displays the entire image at low resolution very quickly. Each successive pass increases the resolution as the image is being downloaded as shown in Figure 19-10. This gives the user a better idea about what is loading so they can make decisions about the information without waiting for the entire image to load. I suggest interlacing all GIFs to take advantage of this apparent speed.

Figure 19-10: This is how an interlaced GIF file loads. The image appears to increase in resolution with each of four passes of the download. This way the image appears to fade in over time. The final image is shown in Figure 19-9.

Transparency: GIF89a

The latest version of the GIF format, GIF89a, allows transparency. This is useful when adding spot illustrations of irregular shapes to a Web page that has a background pattern or color. This way, the background shows through all transparent sections rather than having all the illustrations in solid rectangles, as shown in Figure 19-11. The transparency is achieved by specifying certain color slots from the image's color palette as being transparent. Anywhere that the "transparent" color is used the image will "drop-out" revealing the background of the page beneath. Each pixel is treated as 100 percent opaque or 100 percent transparent. There is no in-between.

Figure 19-11: Transparent GIF. Notice how the white rectangle around the image has been removed letting the background show through.

GIF licensing:

The GIF format is copyrighted by CompuServe, Incorporated, and the LZW compression used in the format is patented by Unisys Corporation. There has been recent talk that CompuServe and Unisys may decide to charge royalties for the use of the GIF/LZW formats. For this reason, many users are beginning to switch to the royalty free JPEG and newer PNG formats outlined below.

For more information about the GIF format you may download the full specification from the following ftp site:

`ftp://ftp.ncsa.uiuc.edu:/misc/file.formats/graphics.formats/gif89a.doc`

Exporting GIF files from FreeHand

To export a GIF file from FreeHand, follow these steps:

1. Hide any unused layers.
2. Choose File ⇨ Export (⌘/Ctrl-Shift-R) and the export window appears.
3. Select GIF from the format pop-up menu.
4. Name the file. If you're on a Mac, be sure to include the .gif at the end of the filename so the Web server can properly identify the file format. Then click on Options/Setup button. The Bitmap Export Defaults window will display, as shown in Figure 19-12.

Figure 19-12: GIF Bitmap Options.

5. I suggest that you select 72 dpi which is the normal screen resolution and Anti-aliasing 4. You can experiment with other values, but I've found 4 to produce the smoothest output.

6. Select both the Include Alpha Channel and Alpha Includes Background Options if you want the image to be transparent. This is a little misleading because it won't really add an alpha channel to the GIF. (GIFs don't support alpha channels.) What it really does is create a solid color where the background would show through the image.

7. Click More and the GIF Options box appears as shown in Figure 19-13.

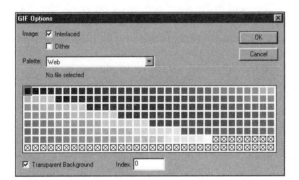

Figure 19-13: GIF Options.

8. Check Interlaced if you want to have the image fade in gradually rather than draw from top to bottom. Check Transparent Background if you wish to have the background show through portions of the image.

9. To finish the export click OK in both the GIF Options and the Bitmap Export Defaults dialog boxes and then click Export/Save in the Export Document dialog box. Your FreeHand file is now exported as a GIF file and stored on your hard drive.

Including GIF files in your Web pages

To add a GIF file to your Web page is as easy as adding the following line to the HTML page. This is a version of the *IMG* (image) tag. SRC stands for source file. Substitute the name of your actual file where it says *filename.gif* and substitute your actual width and height as well. You can tell the width and height of the image by importing the GIF file back into FreeHand, setting the page units to points, and reading the height and width in the Object inspector.

```
<IMG SRC="filename.gif" WIDTH=160 HEIGHT=160>
```

Joint Photographic Experts Group: JPEG

If 256 colors are too limiting for you, then you may be interested in meeting GIF's big brother—JPEG. The JPEG format, pronounced "J-peg," was developed by the Joint Photographic Experts Group as a variable compression scheme for photographic images. During the compression process, you may adjust the settings in favor of better image quality or higher compression. The JPEG format is capable of handling true color raster images with color depths above 8 bits. This enables you to use thousands or millions of colors with 16 or 24 bit color depths.

24 bit JPEG files can often compress smaller than 8 bit GIF files, thereby allowing the page designer to include higher quality images without any performance penalty. There is a "progressive" JPEG feature that works very similar to GIF's interlacing feature. The only feature not offered by the JPEG format is transparency. Most Web browsers support the use of JPEG images. Browsers such as Netscape Navigator permit JPEG files to be used directly on the pages just like GIF files. Other browsers that don't directly support the JPEG format can usually pass the images off to a helper application for viewing. Figure 19-14 shows an example of two JPEG images. The first has the compression image quality set to 50% and the second has it set to 90%. Notice how the second image appears cleaner than the first.

JPEG compression

JPEG compression uses complex mathematical algorithms to attain compression ratios of up to 20:1. Typical images achieve compression ratios from 5:1 to 15:1 using a "lossy" compression scheme. This means that some information is lost as the file is compressed. The higher the compression ratio, the more image detail that is lost. The lower the compression ratio, the higher the image quality that is retained. So, you should avoid recompressing JPEG images multiple times. You should save and always return to the master image for subsequent changes.

For more information on the JPEG format you may download the specifications from the following ftp site: `ftp://ftp.uu.net/graphics/jpeg/jpeg.documents.gz`

Figure 19-14: Beach Girl saved in the JPEG format. The one on the left sacrifices quality for a smaller file size. The one on the right looks better but takes up more room on disk.

Exporting JPEG files from FreeHand

To export a JPEG file from FreeHand, follow these steps:

1. Hide any unused layers.

2. Choose File ➪ Export (⌘/Ctrl-Shift-R) and the export window appears.

3. Select JPEG from the format pop-up menu.

4. Name the file. If you're on a Mac, be sure to include the .jpg or .jpeg filename extension so that the Web server can properly identify the file format. Click on Options/Setup. The Bitmap Export Defaults window will display.

5. I suggest that you select 72 dpi which is the normal screen resolution and Anti-aliasing 4. You can experiment with other values but I've found 4 to produce the smoothest output.

6. JPEG can't use an alpha channel or transparency so there is no need to check. Alpha includes background.

7. Click on More and the JPEG Options box appears as shown in Figure 19-15.

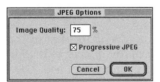

Figure 19-15: JPEG Options.

8. Enter the image quality percentage you want. The higher the percent, the better the image quality and the larger the file size. The lower the number, the worse the image quality and the smaller the file size. You can experiment with this setting until you achieve a good balance between quality and file size. This value is dependent on the image itself. Some images may need higher values to look good while others may get away with lower values. Check Progressive JPEG if you wish to have the image appear to fade in gradually rather than draw from top to bottom.

9. To finish the export click OK in both the JPEG Options and the Bitmap Export Defaults dialog boxes and then Click Export/Save in the Export Document dialog box. Your FreeHand file is now exported as a JPEG file and stored on your hard drive.

Including JPEG files in your Web pages

Adding a JPEG file to your Web page is as easy as adding the following line to the HTML page. This is a version of the IMG (image) tag. SRC stands for source file. Substitute the name of your actual file where it says *filename.jpg* and substitute your actual width and height as well. You can tell the width and height of the image by importing the JPEG file back into FreeHand, setting the page units to points and reading the height and width in the Object Inspector.

```
<IMG SRC="filename.jpg" WIDTH=160 HEIGHT=160>
```

Portable Network Graphics: PNG

And now, ladies and gentlemen, allow me to introduce the new kid on the block — "PNG." The PNG format, pronounced "Ping," is being recommended as a patent-free replacement for the GIF format. The PNG format was developed by the World Wide Web Consortium and CompuServe to provide a royalty-free GIF replacement. This format was specifically designed to transmit graphics over a network such as the Internet. As soon as the format is in widespread use it should quickly take over as the dominant raster image file format on the Web. PNG produces the best looking image of all the raster formats and is pictured in Figure 19-16. It should soon become the standard format on the Web.

The PNG format is capable of compressing both indexed color (8 bit or less) and true color (above 8 bit) images. The PNG format uses a lossless compression scheme that is capable of compressing files about 30 percent smaller than the GIF format. The progressive feature enables browsers to load the first pass much quicker than the first pass of an interlaced GIF file. Not only does the PNG format support transparency, it also supports full alpha channel blending. The PNG format also enables built-in gamma correction. Images typically appear darker on a PC than they do on a Macintosh. Gamma correction is a way to compensate for this difference.

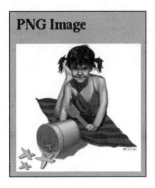

Figure 19-16: PNG image file format.

For more information about the PNG format visit the following Web site:

`http://www.w3.org/Graphics/PNG`

Exporting PNG files from FreeHand

To export a PNG file from FreeHand, follow these steps:

1. Hide any unused layers.

2. Choose File ➪ Export (⌘/Ctrl-Shift-R) and the export window appears.

3. Select PNG from the format pop-up.

4. Name the file. If you are using a Mac, be sure to include the .png filename extension so that the Web server can properly identify the file format. Click on Options/Setup button. The Bitmap Export Defaults window displays.

5. Select 72 dpi, which is the normal screen resolution, and Anti-aliasing 4. You can experiment with other values but I've found 4 to produce the smoothest output.

6. Select both the Include Alpha Channel and Alpha Includes Background Options if you wish the image to be transparent.

7. Click on More and the PNG Options box appears as shown in Figure 19-17.

Figure 19-17: PNG Options.

8. Select the bit depth of the resulting image that you want. 24-bit or 32-bit with Alpha will usually produce the highest quality results that you'd ever need, but the file size will be relatively large. 8-bit or 16-bit is usually sufficient. Check Interlaced PNG if you wish to have the image appear to fade in gradually rather than draw from top to bottom.

9. To finish the export, click on OK in both the PNG Options and the Bitmap Export Defaults dialog boxes and then Click Export/Save in the Export Document dialog box. Your FreeHand file is now exported as a PNG file and stored on your hard drive.

Including PNG files in your Web pages

Adding a PNG file to your Web page is as easy as adding the following line to the HTML page. Note that the PNG format does not use the IMG tag like a GIF or JPEG does; instead, it uses the EMBED tag. This is because PNG is not yet one of the internal Netscape image types. In the future, when Netscape is capable of directly supporting the PNG type, you may be able to use the IMG tag instead. Until then, you must use the EMBED tag which tells Netscape that the image is to be displayed by a plug-in.

SRC stands for source file. Substitute the name of your actual file where it says filename.png and substitute your actual width and height as well. You can tell the width and height of the image by importing the PNG file back into FreeHand, setting the page units to points and reading the height and width in the Object Inspector.

```
<EMBED SRC="filename.png" WIDTH=160 HEIGHT=160>
```

Vector Based Flash Graphics for the Web

Well, you thought all those raster image formats were exciting? Well, you haven't seen anything yet. It is now my infinite pleasure to introduce to you the star of our show. Without further ado, I present to you, the "vector" format—Shockwave Flash or, more succinctly, Flash. Until recently, the Web could only handle raster graphics. Macromedia's Flash package brings all the benefits of vector graphics to the Web. These benefits include zooming and panning, embedded hot links, small file size, high quality printing, scaling flexibility, and easy editing. Flash graphics are viewable on the Web through a Netscape or Explorer plug-in that is available from Macromedia's Web site.

The Flash format can handle both the traditional still-life graphics and the new animation graphics. The still-life variety covers all the usual artwork that one creates in FreeHand. The animation graphics are series of paths and objects that your create in FreeHand. These objects are then strung together to create the illusion of movement much like the images in a flip book.

The Flash format gives you the power of adding a vector graphic to your Web designs, but there is one sizable drawback: Although you can export your artwork to the Flash format in FreeHand, you can't open those same Flash file in FreeHand. You must install the Flash 2 player (included on the Flash 2 CD-ROM that come as part of the FreeHand package) or embed the images in a HTML file to view an image saved in the Flash format.

The three amigos of Flash

The Flash package is a group of three friendly companions. These three amigos are the URL Editor Xtra, Release To Layers Xtra, and Flash 2 player. The two Xtras are used in FreeHand to create and prepare Flash graphics and the player is used to view them as they would appear in a Web browser.

URL Editor Xtra

The URL Editor Xtra allows you to embed *Uniform Resource Locators* (URLs) into your graphics to act as hot links. This is useful for creating maps or diagrams that link to other Web pages or other images. If users click on these hot links they will be brought to the linked pages. The URL Editor Xtra is automatically installed when you install FreeHand.

Release To Layers Xtra

The Release To Layers Xtra allows FreeHand to separate all objects in a document to individual layers. When you export your document to a Flash format, each layer comprises a frame in your animation sequence. Once you've exported your file, you can view the animation in a browser (provided you've downloaded the appropriate plug-in) or in the Flash 2 player.

Flash 2 player

The Flash 2 player is a separate application that allows you to view and edit Flash files. It is not automatically installed when you install FreeHand. To install the Flash 2, simply run the installer located on the Flash 2 CD-ROM.

Creating Flash graphics

Okay, you've seen the light. You're ready to begin creating fantastic Flash graphics to amaze and astound the world. Creating Flash graphics is pretty much the same as creating normal FreeHand graphics. There are only a few differences to keep in mind as you explore your new found Web creativity.

Setting up FreeHand to create a Flash graphic

When designing graphics for use on a computer's display whether it's for multimedia or the World Wide Web you should use points as your units. A PostScript point, which is what FreeHand uses as points, is exactly $\frac{1}{72}$ of an inch. (The PostScript point was defined as $\frac{1}{72}$ of an inch to approximate the traditional Typesetter's point which is $\frac{1}{72.27}$ of an inch.) Therefore, the point unit of measurement exactly coincides with screen pixels which are also 72 pixels per inch. Use the Units pop-up menu in the Status toolbar.

Flash 2 player can display the entire page that the image was created on. Therefore, it is important to set the page size to the size you want the final graphic to be. Set your page size to custom and enter the dimensions you want the final graphic to be in points. For example, if you want to create a 400×400 pixel Flash graphic, you would set FreeHand's page size to custom: 400×400 points in the Document Inspector. Because the final resolution of the image will be 72 pixels per inch, you should also set the Printer resolution to 72 dpi.

Create your Flash graphics

After your page and units are properly set up, you can go ahead and create your graphic on this custom page. You can create your Flash graphic much as you would create any other graphic in FreeHand with only a few differences.

The following items are not supported in Flash graphics, so you should avoid them:

✦ Custom and PostScript strokes are not supported.

✦ Custom, textured, and PostScript fills are also not supported.

Placed EPS elements are not supported. However, if the original EPS is editable you can turn on the Convert Editable EPS When Imported option in the Import panel (Mac) or the Import/Export panel (Windows) of the Preferences dialog box before you import the EPS. This will convert the EPS to a native FreeHand format as long as the EPS was saved as editable. If the EPS is not editable, you'll have to go back to the original file that was used to create the EPS and simply copy and paste the editable elements directly into the Flash graphic.

You can create animation files with the Flash format. These animations will consist of a number of different objects shown in series, one after the other. Blends readily lend themselves to a Flash animation sequence and are an easy way to get started experimenting with animation. For example, if you create an animation from the blend between a red circle and a blue square, you'll see a colorful sequence of events that jump through each blend step transforming the circle into a square.

To create a animated Flash file, do the following.

1. Choose Edit ➪ Select ➪ All (⌘/Ctrl-A). This assumes that all the paths in your document are intended to be part of you animation sequence. If there are any objects that you don't want as part of your Flash file, either delete them or move them off the page.

2. Choose Xtras ➪ Animate ➪ Release To Layers or click on the Release To Layers icon in the Operations panel.

3. FreeHand creates as many new layers as needed and places each object on its own layer. For example, if you blend from a circle and a square and the Object Inspector reports that there are 25 steps in the blend, FreeHand will add 26 new layers. Twenty-five of these new layers are for the objects that make up the blend. The twenty-sixth layer is for the original square. The original circle remains on the Foreground layer.

4. Choose File ➪ Export (⌘/Ctrl-Shift-R).

Now that you've saved your Flash file, you can open it inside the Flash 2 player or as part of a HTML page.

Using text in Flash graphics

Text may be used within your Flash images. Viewing a Flash graphic is similar to opening the original graphic in FreeHand. This means that if the user's system does not have the proper fonts installed for a document, fonts will be substituted resulting in improper viewing.

Or, you can convert all your text to paths inside FreeHand (via the Text ➪ Convert To Paths command) or automatically when you export your file to the Flash format. For the latter, click the Setup button when you export your Flash file and choose the Convert To Paths option from the Text pop-up menu inside the Flash Export dialog box.

Using the URL Editor

Well, by now you have created an amazing Flash graphic. It's slick, it's happenin'; and yet, it's pretty isolated. Now it's time to learn how to link it to other items on the Web. You can use the URL Editor to embed hot links into your graphic that can take the user to other Web pages. URL stands for Universal Resource Locator and is sometimes referred to as an Internet address. Let's take a closer look at a URL:

```
http://www.dreamlight.com/dreamlt/welcome.html
```

The URL consists of three parts:

1. The method used to access the resource: http
2. The server name: www.dreamlight.com
3. The path to the file: dreamlt/welcome.html

This URL is called an absolute URL because it lists the exact method, server, and file path. A relative URL only lists the file path and assumes the method and server are the same as the current location of the Shockwave graphic currently being viewed. Note that this may be different than the location of the HTML page where the Flash graphic is embedded.

Let's assume we have a set of HTML documents in a folder called "world" and within the world folder we have another folder called "images." Now let's say we have a document called "globe.htm" which has a Flash graphic embedded on the page. The Flash graphic is named "globe.fh8." If we want to put a link to a document called "usa.htm" within the "globe.fh8" graphic we would use the following relative URL:

```
../usa.htm
```

This relative URL first uses the "../" to move up one level in the hierarchy. Since the graphic where this URL is used is within the "images" folder, moving up one level puts us in the "world" folder. Then the "usa.htm" brings us to the file we wish to link to. Note the "usa.fh8" graphic would be embedded in the "usa.htm" document. Figure 19-18 shows the hierarchy.

Figure 19-18: World folder containing our HTML documents and a sub folder with the Flash graphics.

Now let's add this relative URL to the globe graphic. First open the URL Editor by selecting Window ➪ Xtras ➪ URL Editor. The editor is shown in Figure 19-19.

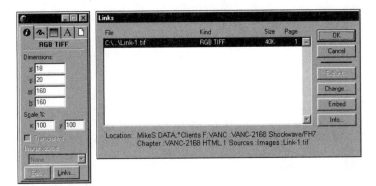

Figure 19-19: The URL Editor.

Now Choose New from the Options pop-up menu in the URL Editor to add a new URL to the list. Type in the URL into the New URL dialog box as shown in Figure 19-20 then click on OK. Immediately after entering the text of the URL, you must apply it to some object in the image or the URL will be deleted if you close the URL Xtra or switch to another application. Unused URLs are not kept in the document.

Figure 19-20: Type in the URL you'd like to add to your graphic.

To apply the new URL to an object simply select an object and then select the URL in the list that you wish to apply as shown in Figure 19-21. You can also drag the URL from the list and drop it right on the object. Do not apply URLs to groups. Only apply URLs to actual objects. You may Option/Alt-click on a path within a group to apply the URL to an object that belongs to a group.

Figure 19-21: Select the object in the graphic and then select the URL in the list to apply the URL to the object.

The URL Xtra is a bit finicky. Undo does not work properly with it so any changes you need to do to your URLs should be done manually through editing them or deleting them. Also don't leave any unused URLs in the list. Doing so will lose them when the URL Xtra is closed or the document is closed and may also confuse the URL Find command. Since selecting an object and then selecting a URL in the list applies that URL to the object just like applying colors or styles to objects, make use of the Tab key to deselect all objects before clicking on URLs in the list to edit or find.

Embedding your Flash graphics into HTML

After you have your Flash graphics created it's a simple matter to add them to your Web pages. You just embed the Flash graphic into your HTML page using what else but the EMBED tag.

```
<EMBED SRC="filename.fhc" HEIGHT=270 WIDTH=200>
```

As long as you keep the proportions of the sizes used in the embed tag the same as the proportion you used for your page size in FreeHand the image will scale appropriately. This is one of the benefits of a vector format. So to double the dimensions of the above embed tag simply edit the numbers.

```
<EMBED SRC="filename.fhc" HEIGHT=540 WIDTH=400>
```

There is no need to touch the original graphic, it will scale correctly.

Going on-line with Flash

Before you can actually upload your FreeHand Flash files to the server you must make sure the server is properly configured to handle the file types. Simply contact your Internet Server Provider and supply the systems administrator with the following information:

✦ MIME TYPE is image/x-FreeHand

✦ Files will be in Binary format

Once the administrator configures the server you may upload files.

Casting your images onto the Web

Once your images are ready to go on-line you may use any FTP software to send the images to the server. You must be sure that the files are being transferred as binary files in order for them to work properly. If you are not sure how to verify this, please check the documentation that came with your FTP software. Also be sure that you have the proper extensions at the end of the file names. Even though the Macintosh does not require file extensions, the Web server does require these extensions to properly recognize the file types.

✦   ✦   ✦

Index

J

K

L

(continued)

(continued)

(continued)

Illustrator 7
Studio Secrets™
0-7645-4026-2
$49.99

Official Kai's Power Tools®
Studio Secrets™
0-7645-4002-5
$44.99

Please send this order form to:

**IDG Books Worldwide, Inc.
Attn: Order Entry Dept.
7260 Shadeland Station,
Suite 100
Indianapolis, IN 46256
(800) 762-2974**

ORDER FORM

Qty	ISBN	Title	Price	Total
	0-7645-4038-6	Painter 5 Studio Secrets™	$49.99	
	0-7645-3134-4	Photoshop® and Illustrator Synergy Studio Secrets™	$49.99	
	0-7645-4028-9	Photoshop® 4 Studio Secrets™	$49.99	
	0-7645-4026-2	Illustrator 7 Studio Secrets™	$49.99	
	0-7645-4002-5	Official Kai's Power Tools® Studio Secrets™	$44.99	

Shipping & Handling Charges

	Description	First book	Each add'l. book	Total
Domestic	Normal	$4.50	$1.50	$
	Two Day Air	$8.50	$2.50	$
	Overnight	$18.00	$3.00	$
International	Surface	$8.00	$8.00	$
	Airmail	$16.00	$16.00	$
	DHL Air	$17.00	$17.00	$

*For large quantities call for shipping & handling charges.
**Prices are subject to change without notice.

Ship to:

Name _____

Company _____

Address _____

City/State/Zip _____ Daytime Phone _____

Payment: ☐ Check to IDG Books (US Funds Only)
☐ Visa ☐ Mastercard ☐ American Express

Card # _____ Expires _____ Signature _____

Subtotal _____

*CA residents add
applicable sales tax* _____

*IN and MA
residents add 5%
sales tax* _____

*CT, FL and NJ
residents add 6%
sales tax* _____

*IL residents add
6.25% sales tax* _____

*PA residents add
7% sales tax* _____

*WA residents add
8.2% sales tax* _____

*NY, TN and TX
residents add 8.25%
sales tax* _____

Shipping _____

Total _____

**IDG
BOOKS**
WORLDWIDE

my2cents.idgbooks.com